Professional Examinations

# Managerial Level

# Paper P8

# Financial Analysis

# CIMA Study Text

KAPLAN PUBLISHING
FOULKS LYNCH

***British Library Cataloguing-in-Publication Data***

A catalogue record for this book is available from the British Library.

Published by Kaplan Publishing Foulks Lynch
Unit 2 Foulks Lynch
Molly Millars Lane
Wokingham
Berkshire
RG41 2QZ

ISBN 1 84390 912 X

978 1 84390 912 5



Printed and bound in Great Britain.

***Acknowledgements***

We are grateful to the Chartered Institute of Management Accountants, the Association of Chartered Certified Accountants and the Institute of Chartered Accountants in England and Wales for permission to reproduce past examination questions. The answers have been prepared by Kaplan Publishing Foulks Lynch.

# INTRODUCTION

This is the third edition of this Study Text. Our aim was to produce an even better, more syllabus-tailored, exam-focused and student-friendly range of publications. To achieve this we have worked closely with numerous CIMA tutors and experts, and we are confident that this Study Text forms the best resource for your exam preparation.

It covers all syllabus topics to the required depth, and contains a wealth of exam-style and practice questions. Throughout the text you will find plenty of relevant examples, activities, diagrams and charts. These will put the subject matter in context and help you absorb the material easily.

The following points explain some of the concepts we had in mind when developing the layout of this book.

DEFINITION

- **Definitions**. The text defines key words and concepts, placing them in the margin with a clear heading, as on the left. The purpose of including these definitions is to focus your attention on the point being covered.

KEY POINT

- **Key points**. Also in the margin, you will see key points at regular intervals. The purpose of these is to summarise concisely the key material being covered.
- **Activities**. The text involves you in the learning process with a series of activities designed to catch your attention and make you concentrate and respond. The feedback to activities is at the end of each chapter.
- **Self-test questions**. At the end of each chapter there is a series of self-test questions. The purpose of these is to help you revise some of the key elements of the chapter. All the answers to these questions can be found in the text.
- **End of chapter questions**. At the end of each chapter we include examination-type questions. These will give you a very good idea of the sort of thing the examiner will ask and will test your understanding of what has been covered.

Good luck with your studies!

# CONTENTS

# SYLLABUS AND LEARNING OUTCOMES

## Syllabus outline

The syllabus comprises:

*Topic and study weighting*

| | | |
|---|---|---|
| A | Group Financial Statements | 35% |
| B | The Measurement of Income and Capital | 20% |
| C | Analysis and Interpretation of Financial Accounts | 35% |
| D | Developments in External Reporting | 10% |

## Learning aims

Students should be able to:

- prepare consolidated accounts and explain the accounting principles associated with this area, such as changes part way through an accounting period and in the merger method,
- appropriately employ relevant accounting standards,
- evaluate a business entity's financial statements and provide analysis of performance,
- explain the problems of profit measurement and alternative approaches to asset valuations,
- discuss and evaluate current developments in external reporting.

Below we reproduce the learning outcomes and syllabus content. The numbers in brackets denote the chapters in which each topic is covered.

## Learning outcomes and syllabus content

*A – Group Financial Statements – 35%*

### Learning outcomes

On completion of their studies students should be able to:

(i) explain the conditions required for an undertaking to be a subsidiary or an associate of another company; (4, 5)

(ii) explain and apply the rules for the exclusion of subsidiaries from consolidation; (4)

(iii) prepare a consolidated income statement, balance sheet and cash flow statement for a group of companies; (2, 4, 7, 10)

(iv) explain and apply the concepts of fair value at the point of acquisition and impairment of goodwill; (3)

(v) identify the impact on group financial statements when a subsidiary is acquired or disposed of part way through an accounting period (to include the effective date of acquisition and dividends out of pre-acquisition profits) and where shareholdings, or control, are acquired in stages; (4, 6)

(vi) explain the concept of an associate and a joint venture, and the principles of how they are accounted for; (5)

(vii) explain the pooling of interests method of consolidation; (no longer examinable)

(viii) compare and contrast pooling of interests, acquisition and equity methods of accounting; (5)

(ix) explain the principles of accounting for a capital reconstruction scheme or a demerger; (8)

(x) explain foreign currency translation principles, including the difference between the closing rate/net investment method and the historical rate method; (9)

(xi) explain the correct treatment for foreign loans financing foreign equity investments. (9)

### Syllabus content

- Relationships between investors and investees, and the exclusion of subsidiaries from consolidation with reference to dominant influence, participating interest, management on a unified basis and significant influence. (4)
- The preparation of consolidated financial statements (including the group cash flow statement) involving one or more subsidiaries, sub-subsidiaries and associates, under the acquisition and pooling of interests methods (IAS 7 & 27 and IFRS 3). (2, 3, 4, 7, 10)
- The treatment in consolidated financial statements of minority interests, pre- and post-acquisition reserves, goodwill (including its impairment), fair value adjustments, intra-group transactions and dividends, piece-meal and mid-year acquisitions, and disposals to include sub-subsidiaries and mixed groups. (2, 3, 4, 5, 6, 7, 9)
- The accounting treatment of associates and joint ventures (IAS 28 & 31) using the equity method and proportional consolidation method. (5)
- The accounting entries for mergers, demergers and capital reconstruction schemes. (8)

- Foreign currency translation (IAS 21) to include overseas transactions and investments in overseas subsidiaries.(9)

## *B – The Measurement of Income and Capital – 20%*

**Learning outcomes**

On completion of their studies students should be able to:

(i) explain the problems of profit measurement and alternative approaches to asset valuations; (11)

(ii) explain measures to reduce distortion in financial statements when price levels change; (11)

(iii) discuss the principle of substance over form applied to a range of transactions; (13)

(iv) discuss the possible treatments of financial instruments in the issuer's accounts (i.e. liabilities versus equity, and the implications for finance costs); (14)

(v) identify circumstances in which amortised cost, fair value and hedge accounting are appropriate for financial instruments, and explain the principles of these accounting methods; (14)

(vi) discuss the recognition and valuation issues concerned with pension schemes and the treatment of actuarial deficits and surpluses. (12)

**Syllabus content**

- The problems of profit measurement and the effect of alternative approaches to asset valuation; current cost and current purchasing power bases and the real terms system; accounting for changing prices (IAS 15) and hyper-inflation (IAS 29). (11)
- The principle of substance over form (IAS 1) and its influence in dealing with transactions such as sale and repurchase agreements, consignment stock, debt factoring, securitised assets, loan transfers and public and private sector financial collaboration. (13)
- Financial instruments classified as liabilities or shareholders' funds and the allocation of finance costs over the term of the borrowing (IAS 32 & 39). (14)
- The measurement and disclosure of financial instruments (IAS 39). (14)
- Retirement benefits, including pension schemes – defined benefit schemes and defined contribution schemes, actuarial deficits and surpluses (IAS 19). (12)

## *C – Analysis and Interpretation of Financial Accounts – 35%*

**Learning outcomes**

On completion of their studies students should be able to:

(i) calculate and interpret a full range of accounting ratios; (15)

(ii) analyse financial statements (in the context of information provided in the accounts and corporate report) to comment on performance and position; (15, 16)

(iii) prepare a concise report on the results of an analysis of financial statements; (15)

(iv) explain the limitations of accounting ratio analysis and analysis based on financial statements; (15)

(v) prepare and interpret segmental analysis, inter-firm and international comparisons. (15, 16)

**Syllabus content**

- Ratios in the areas of performance, profitability, financial adaptability, liquidity, activity, shareholder investment and financing, and their interpretation. (15)
- Calculation of earnings per share under IAS 33, to include the effect of bonus issues, rights issues and convertible stock. (16)
- Interpretation of financial statements via the analysis of the accounts and corporate reports. (15)
- Reporting the results of analysis. (15)
- Limitations of ratio analysis (e.g. comparability of businesses and accounting policies). (15)
- The identification of information required to assess financial performance and the extent to which financial statements fail to provide such information. (15)
- Segment analysis: inter-firm and international comparison (IAS 14). (16)
- Interpretation of financial obligations included in financial accounts (e.g. redeemable debt, earn-out arrangements, contingent liabilities). (15)
- The effect of short-term debt on the measurement of gearing. (15)
- The need to be aware of aggressive or unusual accounting policies ('creative accounting') (e.g. in the areas of cost capitalisation and revenue recognition). (15)

## *D – Developments in External Reporting – 10%*

**Learning outcomes**

On completion of their studies students should be able to:

(i) discuss pressures for extending the scope and quality of external reports; (17)

(ii) explain how financial information concerning the interaction of a business with the natural environment can be communicated in the published accounts; (17)

(iii) identify those environmental issues which should be disclosed; (17)

(iv) explain the process of measuring, recording and disclosing the effect of exchanges between a business and society – human resource accounting; (17)

(v) identify the influences on financial reporting of cultural differences across the world; (18)

(vi) identify major differences between IASs and US GAAP. (18)

**Syllabus content**

- Increasing stakeholder demands for information that goes beyond historical financial information and the model for an expanded Operating and Financial Review (OFR) proposed by the UK government. (17)
- Environmental and social accounting issues, differentiating between environmental measures and environmental losses, capitalisation of environmental expenditure, and the recognition of future environmental costs by means of provisions. (17)
- The Global Reporting Initiative: non-financial measures of environmental impact. (17)
- Human resource accounting. (17)
- The influence of different cultures on financial reporting. (18)
- Pressures for improved quality of financial reporting following large scale corporate collapses in the US and UK, and implications for corporate governance and external audit. (17)
- Major differences between IASs and US GAAP. (18)

# HELPING YOU WITH YOUR STUDIES

## Take control

*Create favourable conditions and a positive attitude*

- Plan to study at specific times each week. Devise a schedule and set goals.
- Choose a location where you can concentrate.
- Ask questions to be an active learner and to generate interest.
- Continually challenge yourself.

## Study

*Develop good learning techniques*

- Use the **SQR3** method – it works with reading accountancy and management subjects. **Survey** (get an overall picture before studying in detail), **Question** (important things to learn are usually answers to questions), **Read** actively (to answer your questions), **Recite** (recall what you have read and connect topics) and **Review** (what you have covered and accomplished).
- Use the **MURDER** method – **Mood** (set the right mood), **Understand** (issues covered and make note of any uncertain bits), **Recall** (stop and put what you have learned into your own words), **Digest** (go back and reconsider the information), **Expand** (read relevant articles and newspapers), **Review** (go over the material you covered to consolidate the knowledge).
- Create **associations** and analogies to relate new ideas to what you already know and to improve understanding.

## Practise

*Practise under exam conditions*

- **Practise** as much as possible – go through exam-style and standard questions under exam conditions.

## Prepare for the exam

*Develop exam technique*

- Be familiar with the structure of your exam and know how to approach and answer the questions.

# THE EXAMINATION

## Format of the examination:

There will be a written examination paper of three hours, plus 20 minutes' reading time, with the following sections:

| | *Marks* |
|---|---|
| **Section A:** A variety of compulsory objective test questions, each worth between 2 and 4 marks. Mini-scenarios may be given, to which a group of questions relate. | 20 |
| **Section B:** Three compulsory medium answer questions, each worth 10 marks. Short scenarios may be given, to which some or all questions relate. | 30 |
| **Section C:** Two questions, from a choice of three, each worth 25 marks. Short scenarios may be given, to which questions relate. | 50 |
| TOTAL | 100 |

***Note:*** The first 20 minutes of your exam is reading time. During reading time you can read, annotate and highlight the question paper, but you are not allowed to open the answer book, write in the answer book, add any loose sheets/supplements to your answer book or use a calculator. This change to the duration of the exams has been introduced by CIMA after we published our Exam Kits. Therefore you will notice that the exam length stated in this section will differ from the one stated in the Exam Kit. The length of the exam stated here is the correct one.

Before sitting the exam make sure that you are familiar with CIMA's *Exam Rules & Regulations*. You can find this document on the CIMA website (www.cimaglobal.com).

## Examination tips

- Spend the first few minutes of the examination **reading the paper** and where you have a **choice of questions**, decide which ones you will do.
- **Divide the time** you spend on questions in proportion to the marks on offer. One suggestion is to allocate 1½ minutes to each mark available, so a 10-mark question should be completed in 15 minutes.
- Unless you know exactly how to answer the question, spend some time **planning** your answer. Stick to the question and **tailor your answer** to what you are asked.
- **Fully explain** all your points but **be concise**. Set out all workings **clearly and neatly**, and state briefly what you are doing. Don't write out the question.
- If you do not understand what a question is asking, **state your assumptions**.
- If you **get completely stuck** with a question, leave space in your answer book and **return to it later.**
- Towards the end of the examination spend the last **five minutes** reading through your answers and **making any additions or corrections**.

## Answering the questions

- **Multiple-choice questions**: Read the questions carefully and work through any calculations required. If you don't know the answer, eliminate those options you know are incorrect and see if the answer becomes more obvious. Remember that only one answer to a multiple-choice question can be right!
- **Objective test questions**: These might ask for numerical answers, but could also involve paragraphs of text which require you to fill in a number of missing blanks, or for you to write a definition of a word or phrase, or to enter a formula. Others may give a definition followed by a list of possible key words relating to that description.
- **Essay questions**: Make a quick plan in your answer book and under each main point list all the relevant facts you can think of. Then write out your answer developing each point fully. Your essay should have a clear structure; it should contain a brief introduction, a main section and a conclusion. Be concise. It is better to write a little about a lot of different points than a great deal about one or two points.
- **Computations**: It is essential to include all your workings in your answers. Many computational questions require the use of a standard format: company income statement, balance sheet and cash flow statement for example. Be sure you know these formats thoroughly before the examination and use the layouts that you see in the answers given in this book. If you are asked to comment or make recommendations on a computation, you must do so. There are important marks to be gained here. Even if your computation contains mistakes, you may still gain marks if your reasoning is correct.
- **Reports, memos and other documents**: Some questions ask you to present your answer in the form of a report or a memo or other document. Use the correct format – there could be easy marks to gain here.

# MATHS TABLES AND FORMULAE

Present value of £1 i.e. $(1 + r)^{-n}$ where r = interest rate, n = number of periods until payment or receipt.

| Periods (n) | Interest rates (r) 1% | 2% | 3% | 4% | 5% | 6% | 7% | 8% | 9% | 10% |
|---|---|---|---|---|---|---|---|---|---|---|
| 1 | .990 | .980 | .971 | .962 | .962 | .943 | .935 | .926 | .917 | .909 |
| 2 | .980 | .961 | .943 | .925 | .907 | .890 | .873 | .857 | .842 | .826 |
| 3 | .971 | .942 | .915 | .889 | .864 | .840 | .816 | .794 | .772 | .751 |
| 4 | .961 | .924 | .888 | .855 | .823 | .792 | .763 | .735 | .708 | .683 |
| 5 | .951 | .906 | .863 | .822 | .784 | .747 | .713 | .681 | .650 | .621 |
| 6 | .942 | .888 | .837 | .790 | .746 | .705 | .666 | .630 | .596 | .564 |
| 7 | .933 | .871 | .813 | .760 | .711 | .665 | .623 | .583 | .547 | .513 |
| 8 | .923 | .853 | .789 | .731 | .677 | .627 | .582 | .540 | .502 | .467 |
| 9 | .914 | .837 | .766 | .703 | .645 | .592 | .544 | .500 | .460 | .424 |
| 10 | .905 | .820 | .744 | .676 | .614 | .558 | .508 | .463 | .422 | .386 |
| 11 | .896 | .804 | .722 | .650 | .585 | .527 | .475 | .429 | .388 | .350 |
| 12 | .887 | .788 | .701 | .625 | .557 | .497 | .444 | .397 | .356 | .319 |
| 13 | .879 | .773 | .681 | .601 | .530 | .469 | .415 | .368 | .326 | .290 |
| 14 | .870 | .758 | .661 | .577 | .505 | .442 | .388 | .340 | .299 | .263 |
| 15 | .861 | .743 | .642 | .555 | .481 | .417 | .362 | .315 | .275 | .239 |
| 16 | .853 | .728 | .623 | .534 | .458 | .394 | .339 | .292 | .252 | .218 |
| 17 | .844 | .714 | .605 | .513 | .436 | .371 | .317 | .270 | .231 | .198 |
| 18 | .836 | .700 | .587 | .494 | .416 | .350 | .296 | .250 | .212 | .180 |
| 19 | .828 | .686 | .570 | .475 | .396 | .331 | .277 | .232 | .194 | .164 |
| 20 | .820 | .673 | .554 | .456 | .377 | .312 | .258 | .215 | .178 | .149 |

| Periods (n) | Interest rates (r) 11% | 12% | 13% | 14% | 15% | 16% | 17% | 18% | 19% | 20% |
|---|---|---|---|---|---|---|---|---|---|---|
| 1 | .901 | .893 | .885 | .877 | .870 | .862 | .855 | .847 | .840 | .833 |
| 2 | .812 | .797 | .783 | .769 | .756 | .743 | .731 | .718 | .706 | .694 |
| 3 | .731 | .712 | .693 | .675 | .658 | .641 | .624 | .609 | .593 | .579 |
| 4 | .659 | .636 | .613 | .592 | .572 | .552 | .534 | .516 | .499 | .482 |
| 5 | .593 | .567 | .543 | .519 | .497 | .476 | .456 | .437 | .419 | .402 |
| 6 | .535 | .507 | .480 | .456 | .432 | .410 | .390 | .370 | .352 | .335 |
| 7 | .482 | .452 | .425 | .400 | .376 | .354 | .333 | .314 | .296 | .279 |
| 8 | .434 | .404 | .376 | .351 | .327 | .305 | .285 | .266 | .249 | .233 |
| 9 | .391 | .361 | .333 | .308 | .284 | .263 | .243 | .225 | .209 | .194 |
| 10 | .352 | .322 | .295 | .270 | .247 | .227 | .208 | .191 | .176 | .162 |
| 11 | .317 | .287 | .261 | .237 | .215 | .195 | .178 | .162 | .148 | .135 |
| 12 | .286 | .257 | .231 | .208 | .187 | .168 | .152 | .137 | .124 | .112 |
| 13 | .258 | .229 | .204 | .182 | .163 | .145 | .130 | .116 | .104 | .093 |
| 14 | .232 | .205 | .181 | .160 | .141 | .125 | .111 | .099 | .088 | .078 |
| 15 | .209 | .183 | .160 | .140 | .123 | .108 | .095 | .084 | .074 | .065 |
| 16 | .188 | .163 | .141 | .123 | .107 | .093 | .081 | .071 | .062 | .054 |
| 17 | .170 | .146 | .125 | .108 | .093 | .080 | .069 | .060 | .052 | .045 |
| 18 | .153 | .130 | .111 | .095 | .081 | .069 | .059 | .051 | .044 | .038 |
| 19 | .138 | .116 | .098 | .083 | .070 | .060 | .051 | .043 | .037 | .031 |
| 20 | .124 | .104 | .087 | .073 | .061 | .051 | .043 | .037 | .031 | .026 |

## Cumulative present value of £1

This table shows the Present Value of £1 per annum, Receivable or Payable at the end of each year for n years $\frac{1-(1+r)^{-n}}{r}$.

| Periods (n) | Interest rates (r) 1% | 2% | 3% | 4% | 5% | 6% | 7% | 8% | 9% | 10% |
|---|---|---|---|---|---|---|---|---|---|---|
| 1 | 0.990 | 0.980 | 0.971 | 0.962 | 0.952 | 0.943 | 0.935 | 0.926 | 0.917 | 0.909 |
| 2 | 1.970 | 1.942 | 1.913 | 1.886 | 1.859 | 1.833 | 1.808 | 1.783 | 1.759 | 1.736 |
| 3 | 2.941 | 2.884 | 2.829 | 2.775 | 2.723 | 2.673 | 2.624 | 2.577 | 2.531 | 2.487 |
| 4 | 3.902 | 3.808 | 3.717 | 3.630 | 3.546 | 3.465 | 3.387 | 3.312 | 3.240 | 3.170 |
| 5 | 4.853 | 4.713 | 4.580 | 4.452 | 4.329 | 4.212 | 4.100 | 3.993 | 3.890 | 3.791 |
| 6 | 5.795 | 5.601 | 5.417 | 5.242 | 5.076 | 4.917 | 4.767 | 4.623 | 4.486 | 4.355 |
| 7 | 6.728 | 6.472 | 6.230 | 6.002 | 5.786 | 5.582 | 5.389 | 5.206 | 5.033 | 4.868 |
| 8 | 7.652 | 7.325 | 7.020 | 6.733 | 6.463 | 6.210 | 5.971 | 5.747 | 5.535 | 5.335 |
| 9 | 8.566 | 8.162 | 7.786 | 7.435 | 7.108 | 6.802 | 6.515 | 6.247 | 5.995 | 5.759 |
| 10 | 9.471 | 8.983 | 8.530 | 8.111 | 7.722 | 7.360 | 7.024 | 6.710 | 6.418 | 6.145 |
| 11 | 10.368 | 9.787 | 9.253 | 8.760 | 8.306 | 7.887 | 7.499 | 7.139 | 6.805 | 8.495 |
| 12 | 11.255 | 10.575 | 9.954 | 9.385 | 8.863 | 8.384 | 7.943 | 7.536 | 7.161 | 6.814 |
| 13 | 12.134 | 11.348 | 10.635 | 9.986 | 9.394 | 8.853 | 8.358 | 7.904 | 7.487 | 7.103 |
| 14 | 13.004 | 12.106 | 11.296 | 10.563 | 9.899 | 9.295 | 8.745 | 8.244 | 7.786 | 7.367 |
| 15 | 13.865 | 12.849 | 11.938 | 11.118 | 10.380 | 9.712 | 9.108 | 8.559 | 8.061 | 7.606 |
| 16 | 14.718 | 13.578 | 12.561 | 11.652 | 10.838 | 10.106 | 9.447 | 8.851 | 8.313 | 7.824 |
| 17 | 15.562 | 14.292 | 13.166 | 12.166 | 11.274 | 10.477 | 9.763 | 9.122 | 8.544 | 8.022 |
| 18 | 16.398 | 14.992 | 13.754 | 12.659 | 11.690 | 10.828 | 10.059 | 9.372 | 8.756 | 8.201 |
| 19 | 17.226 | 15.679 | 14.324 | 13.134 | 12.085 | 11.158 | 10.336 | 9.604 | 8.950 | 8.365 |
| 20 | 18.046 | 16.351 | 14.878 | 13.590 | 12.462 | 11.470 | 10.594 | 9.818 | 9.129 | 8.514 |

| Periods (n) | Interest rates (r) 11% | 12% | 13% | 14% | 15% | 16% | 17% | 18% | 19% | 20% |
|---|---|---|---|---|---|---|---|---|---|---|
| 1 | 0.901 | 0.893 | 0.885 | 0.877 | 0.870 | 0.862 | 0685 | 0.847 | 0.840 | 0.833 |
| 2 | 1.713 | 1.690 | 1.668 | 1.647 | 1.626 | 1.605 | 1.585 | 1.566 | 1.547 | 1.528 |
| 3 | 2.444 | 2.402 | 2.361 | 2.322 | 2.283 | 2.246 | 2.210 | 2.174 | 2.140 | 2.106 |
| 4 | 3.102 | 3.037 | 2.974 | 2.914 | 2.855 | 2.798 | 2.743 | 2.690 | 2.639 | 2.589 |
| 5 | 3.696 | 3.605 | 3.517 | 3.433 | 3.352 | 3.274 | 3.199 | 3.127 | 3.058 | 2.991 |
| 6 | 4.231 | 4.111 | 3.998 | 3.889 | 3.784 | 3.685 | 3.589 | 3.498 | 3.410 | 3.326 |
| 7 | 4.712 | 4.564 | 4.423 | 4.288 | 4.160 | 4.039 | 3.922 | 3.812 | 3.706 | 3.605 |
| 8 | 5.146 | 4.968 | 4.799 | 4.639 | 4.487 | 4.344 | 4.207 | 4.078 | 3.954 | 3.837 |
| 9 | 5.537 | 5.328 | 5.132 | 4.946 | 4.772 | 4.607 | 4.451 | 4.303 | 4.163 | 4.031 |
| 10 | 5.889 | 5.650 | 5.426 | 5.216 | 5.019 | 4.833 | 4.659 | 4.494 | 4.339 | 4.192 |
| 11 | 6.207 | 5.938 | 5.687 | 5.453 | 5.234 | 5.029 | 4.836 | 4.656 | 4.486 | 4.327 |
| 12 | 6.492 | 6.194 | 5.918 | 5.660 | 5.421 | 5.197 | 4.968 | 4.793 | 4.611 | 4.439 |
| 13 | 6.750 | 6.424 | 6.122 | 5.842 | 5.583 | 5.342 | 5.118 | 4.910 | 4.715 | 4.533 |
| 14 | 6.982 | 6.628 | 6.302 | 6.002 | 5.724 | 5.468 | 5.229 | 5.008 | 4.802 | 4.611 |
| 15 | 7.191 | 6.811 | 6.462 | 6.142 | 5.847 | 5.575 | 5.324 | 5.092 | 4.876 | 4.675 |
| 16 | 7.379 | 6.974 | 6.604 | 6.265 | 5.954 | 5.668 | 5.405 | 5.162 | 4.938 | 4.730 |
| 17 | 7.549 | 7.120 | 6.729 | 6.373 | 6.047 | 5.749 | 5.475 | 5.222 | 4.990 | 4.775 |
| 18 | 7.702 | 7.250 | 6.840 | 6.467 | 6.128 | 5.818 | 5.534 | 5.273 | 5.033 | 4.812 |
| 19 | 7.839 | 7.366 | 6.938 | 6.550 | 6.198 | 5.877 | 5.584 | 5.316 | 5.070 | 4.843 |
| 20 | 7.963 | 7.469 | 7.025 | 6.623 | 6.259 | 5.929 | 5.628 | 5.353 | 5.101 | 4.870 |

# Formulae

## Annuity

Present value of an annuity of £1 per annum, receivable or payable for n years, commencing in one year, discounted at r% per annum:

$$PV = \frac{1}{r}\left[1 - \frac{1}{[1+r]^n}\right]$$

## Perpetuity

Present value of £1 per annum, payable or receivable in perpetuity, commencing in one year, discounted at r% per annum:

$$PV = \frac{1}{r}$$

## Growing perpetuity

Present value of £1 per annum, receivable or payable, commencing in one year, growing in perpetuity at a constant rate of g% per annum, discounted at r% per annum:

$$PV = \frac{1}{r-g}$$

Chapter 1

# THE *FRAMEWORK*

## Contents

# Introduction

This chapter sets your studies for this paper in context by describing the frameworks within which financial statements are prepared and presented.

KEY POINT

The IASB's *Framework for the Preparation and Presentation of Financial Statements* (the *Framework*) sets out and explains the principles that underpin financial reporting.

The IASB's *Framework for the Preparation and Presentation of Financial Statements* (the *Framework*) sets out and explains the principles that underpin financial reporting. The ideas in the *Framework* have influenced recent international standards (IASs and IFRSs) and may influence the development of standards in future. The *Framework* is also intended to provide guidance where a transaction is not covered by an existing accounting standard.

This chapter covers the main requirements of two important standards. IAS 1 *Presentation of Financial Statements* sets out overall requirements for the presentation of financial statements, guidelines for their structure and minimum requirements for their content.

If you have already studied for Paper P7 *Financial Accounting and Tax Principles* you should already have covered this material in depth and it is unlikely to be examined in detail in this paper. For example, you will not be asked to prepare a set of financial statements and notes for publication (as in Paper P7). However, you will almost certainly need to draw upon this knowledge when answering questions on other topics, particularly when analysing and interpreting financial statements.

## 1 The IASB *Framework for the Preparation and Presentation of Financial Statements*

### 1.1 Introduction

KEY POINT

The purpose of the *Framework* is to:

- assist the IASB in the development of future accounting standards and in its review of existing International Accounting Standards
- assist the IASB by providing a basis for reducing the number of alternative accounting treatments permitted by International Accounting Standards.

The purpose of the *Framework* is to:

- assist the IASB in the development of future accounting standards and in its review of existing International Accounting Standards
- assist the IASB by providing a basis for reducing the number of alternative accounting treatments permitted by International accounting standards
- assist national standard-setting bodies in developing national standards
- assist preparers of financial statements in applying International accounting standards and in dealing with topics that do not form the subject of an International accounting standard
- assist auditors in forming an opinion whether financial statements conform with International accounting standards
- assist users of financial statements in interpreting the information contained in financial statements prepared in conformity with International Accounting Standards
- provide those who are interested in the work of the IASB with information about its approach to the formulation of International Accounting Standards.

The *Framework* is not an accounting standard. Nothing in the *Framework* overrides a specific International Accounting Standard.

## 1.2 The objective of financial statements

The objective of financial statements is to provide information about the financial position, performance and changes in financial position of an entity that is useful to a wide range of users in making economic decisions.

Financial statements also show the results of the stewardship of management, that is the accountability of management for the resources entrusted to it. Those users who wish to assess the stewardship of management do so in order that they may make economic decisions, for example, whether to hold or sell their investment in the entity or whether to re-appoint or replace the management.

Users of the financial statements need information that focuses on the financial position, performance and cash flow of an entity. The balance sheet is the primary source of information about financial position. The income statement and the statement of changes in equity are the primary sources of information about performance. Information on cash flows is provided by a cash flow statement.

The component parts of the financial statements interrelate. They each reflect different aspects of the same transactions or other events. None of the statements is likely to serve only a single purpose. None of the statements, on their own, provide all the information necessary for particular needs of users.

The financial statements also contain notes and supplementary schedules and other information.

KEY POINT

The objective of financial statements is to provide information about the financial position, performance and changes in financial position of an entity that is useful to a wide range of users in making economic decisions.

## 1.3 Underlying assumptions

The *Framework* identifies the underlying assumptions governing financial statements – the accrual basis and going concern.

- The accrual basis of accounting means that the effects of transactions and other events are recognised as they occur and not as cash or its equivalent is received or paid.
- The going concern basis assumes that the entity has neither the need nor the intention to liquidate or curtail materially the scale of its operations.

DEFINITION

The accrual basis of accounting means that the effects of transactions and other events are recognised as they occur and not as cash or its equivalent is received or paid.

The going concern basis assumes that the entity has neither the need nor the intention to liquidate or curtail materially the scale of its operations.

## 1.4 The qualitative characteristics of financial statements.

Qualitative characteristics are the attributes that make the information provided in financial statements useful to others.

The four principal qualitative characteristics are understandability, relevance, reliability and comparability.

***Understandability***

Information provided in financial statements should be readily understandable by users. For this purpose, users are assumed to have abilities, i.e. reasonable knowledge of business and economic activities and accounting and a willingness to study the information with reasonable diligence. Information about complex matters should not be excluded simply because it may be too difficult for certain users to understand.

KEY POINT

Qualitative characteristics are the attributes that make the information provided in financial statements useful to others.

The four principal qualitative characteristics are understandability, relevance, reliability and comparability.

***Relevance***

KEY POINT

Information has the quality of relevance when it influences the economic decisions of users by helping them evaluate past, present or future events or by confirming, or correcting, their past evaluations.

To be useful, information must be relevant to the decision-making needs of users.

Information has the quality of relevance when it influences the economic decisions of users by helping them evaluate past, present or future events or by confirming, or correcting, their past evaluations.

Information about financial position and past performance helps users to predict future financial position and performance and other matters in which users are directly interested, such as dividend and wage payments. Information need not be in the form of an explicit forecast for it to be useful in this way. However, the usefulness of the financial statements can be enhanced by the way in which information about past transactions and events is displayed. For example, the income statement becomes more useful for predicting future performance if unusual, abnormal and infrequent items of income or expense are separately disclosed.

***Reliability***

KEY POINT

Information is reliable when it is free from material error and bias and can be depended upon by users to represent faithfully in terms of valid description that which it either purports to represent or could reasonably be expected to represent.

To be useful, information must also be reliable.

Information is reliable when it is free from material error and bias and can be depended upon by users to represent faithfully in terms of valid description that which it either purports to represent or could reasonably be expected to represent.

This means that transactions and other events must be accounted for and presented in accordance with their substance and economic reality and not merely their legal form (the concept of 'substance over form').

Reliable information is neutral. Financial statements are not neutral if information is selected or presented in such a way as to influence the making of a decision or judgement in order to achieve a predetermined outcome.

Although information must be neutral, preparers of financial statements have to exercise prudence. They must be cautious when making judgements where there is uncertainty (for example, when estimating the collectability of doubtful receivables). Assets and income should not be overstated and liabilities and expense should not be understated. However, the exercise of prudence does not allow the creation of excessive provisions, the deliberate understatement of assets or income or the deliberate overstatement of liabilities or expenses, because the financial statements would not be neutral and therefore would not be reliable.

To be reliable, the information in financial statements must be complete. An omission can cause information to be false or misleading.

***Comparability***

Users must be able to compare the financial statements of an entity over time to identify trends in its financial position and performance. Users must also be able to compare the financial statements of different entities to evaluate their relative financial position, performance and financial adaptability.

Users should be informed of the accounting policies employed in preparation of the financial statements, any changes in those policies and the effects of such changes. Compliance with accounting standards, including the disclosure of the accounting policies used by the entity, helps to achieve comparability.

Because users wish to compare the financial position, performance and changes in financial position of an entity over time, it is important that the financial statements show corresponding information for the preceding periods.

***Materiality***

KEY POINT

Information is material if its omission or mis-statement could influence the economic decisions of users taken on the basis of the financial statements.

Information is material if its omission or mis-statement could influence the economic decisions of users taken on the basis of the financial statements.

Materiality depends on the size of the item or error judged in the particular circumstances of its omission or mis-statement. Thus, materiality provides a threshold or cut-off point rather than being a primary qualitative characteristic that information must have if it is to be useful.

KEY POINT

In practice a balancing, or trade-off, between qualitative characteristics is often necessary.

***Constraints in relation to qualitative characteristics***

- Balance between qualitative characteristics – in practice a balancing, or trade-off, between qualitative characteristics is often necessary. Generally the aim is to achieve an appropriate balance among the characteristics in order to meet the objective of financial statements.
- Timeliness – if there is undue delay in the reporting of information it may lose its relevance.
- Benefit and cost – the balance between benefit and cost is a pervasive constraint rather than a qualitative characteristic. The benefits derived from information should exceed the cost of providing it.

## 1.5 The elements of financial statements

KEY POINT

The *Framework* identifies five elements of financial statements: assets; liabilities; equity; income; and expenses.

The *Framework* identifies five elements of financial statements: assets; liabilities; equity; income; and expenses. Notice that income and expenses are defined in terms of increases and decreases in assets and liabilities.

***Assets***

An asset is a resource controlled by the entity as a result of past events and from which future economic benefits are expected to flow to the entity.

***Liabilities***

A liability is a present obligation of the entity arising from past events, the settlement of which is expected to result in an outflow from the entity of resources embodying economic benefits.

***Equity interest***

Equity interest is the residual interest in the assets of the entity after deducting all its liabilities.

***Income***

Income is increases in economic benefits during the accounting period in the form of inflows or enhancements of assets or decreases in liabilities that result in increases in equity, other than those relating to contributions from equity participants.

***Expenses***

Expenses are decreases in economic benefits during the accounting period in the form of outflows or depletions of assets or incurrences of liabilities that result in decreases in equity, other than those relating to distributions to equity participants.

## 1.6 Recognition of the elements of financial statements

KEY POINT

An item that meets the definition of an element should be recognised in the financial statements if:

(a) it is probable that any future economic benefit associated with the item will flow to the entity; and

(b) the item has a cost or value that can be measured with reliability.

Recognition involves depiction of an item in words and by a monetary amount and the inclusion of that amount in the financial statement totals.

An item that meets the definition of an element should be recognised in the financial statements if:

(a) it is probable that any future economic benefit associated with the item will flow to the entity; and

(b) the item has a cost or value that can be measured with reliability.

## 1.7 Measurement of the elements of financial statements

The *Framework* identifies four possible measurement bases: historical cost; current cost; realisable value; and present value.

(a) **Historical cost** – Assets are recorded at the amount of cash or cash equivalents paid or the fair value of the consideration given to acquire them at the time of acquisition. Liabilities are recorded at the amount of proceeds received in exchange for the obligation.

(b) **Current cost** – Assets are carried at the amount of cash or cash equivalents required to acquire them currently. Liabilities are carried at the undiscounted amount currently required to repay them.

(c) **Realisable value** – Assets are carried at the amount which could currently be obtained by an orderly disposal. Liabilities are carried at their settlement values – the amount to be paid to satisfy them in the normal course of business.

(d) **Present value** – Assets are carried at the present discounted value of the future net cash inflows that the item is expected to generate in the normal course of business, and liabilities at the present discounted value of the expected outflows necessary to settle them.

Although historical cost is the commonest basis, the others are often used to modify historical cost. For example, inventories are usually carried at the lower of cost and net realisable value, investments may be carried at market value and long-term liabilities may be carried at their present value.

## 1.8 Concepts of capital and capital maintenance

KEY POINT

There are two main concepts of capital maintenance – financial and physical.

Definitions of profit may refer to the need to maintain the capital of the entity. In fact there are two main concepts of capital maintenance.

- **Financial capital maintenance** – Under this concept a profit is earned only if the financial or money amount of the net assets at the end of a period exceeds the financial or money amount of net assets at the beginning of the period.
- **Physical capital maintenance** – Under this concept a profit is earned only if the physical productive capacity of the business at the end of the period exceeds the physical productive capacity at the beginning of the period. The physical capital maintenance concept requires the adoption of the current cost basis of measurement.

  The selection of the measurement bases and concept of capital maintenance together determine the accounting model used in preparing the financial statements. For example normal historical cost accounting combines the historical cost basis with financial capital maintenance.

  IASs and IFRSs do not currently require the exclusive use of any particular measurement basis or concept of capital maintenance.

***Activity 1***

There are two possible methods of standard setting:

(a) identify a particular problem as it arises and set a standard for reporting that has the support of a majority of interested parties, or

(b) establish a broad set of principles and objectives which will underpin the setting of accounting standards, and make plans for setting standards for a series of problem areas in financial reporting based on these principles and objectives.

Which of these is the better method and why?

*Feedback to this activity is at the end of the chapter.*

## 2 International accounting standards

### 2.1 Introduction

International accounting standards set out recognition, measurement, presentation and disclosure requirements dealing with transactions and events. They apply to general purpose financial statements.

There are two types of standard currently in force:

- **International Accounting Standards (IASs)** issued by the International Accounting Standards Committee (IASC). The IASC was the international standard setting body that operated before 2001.
- **International Financial Reporting Standards (IFRSs)** issued by the International Accounting Standards Board (IASB) which has been operational since 2001.

The IASB has adopted all the existing IASs issued by the IASC, so that they all remain in force until amended or withdrawn in the future. In this book the generic term 'international accounting standards' is used to refer to both IASs and IFRSs.

KEY POINT

There has been a steady movement towards adoption of IASs.

The IASB does not have the power to enforce compliance with IASs. The authorities in individual countries decide whether to adopt IASs or to require the use of domestic accounting standards. However, in recent years there has been a steady movement towards adoption of IASs:

- The International Organisation of Securities Commissions (IOSCO) has endorsed a 'core' set of IASs. IOSCO is an influential organisation of the world's stock market regulators, in which the US Securities and Exchange Commission (SEC) is a key member. This endorsement means that, in theory, when companies seek a listing on a foreign stock exchange, they can present financial statements prepared in accordance with IASs, rather than the generally accepted accounting principles (GAAP) of the country in which the stock exchange operates.
- The European Union (EU) has adopted a Regulation which requires all EU listed companies to prepare their consolidated financial statements in compliance with IAS.
- Non-listed companies in the UK are able to choose to adopt IASs rather than UK accounting standards.

- The Financial Reporting Council of Australia has announced that it intends to require Australian reporting entities to adopt IASs.

### 2.2 Objectives of the IASB

The objectives of the IASB are:

- to develop, in the public interest, a single set of high quality, understandable and enforceable global accounting standards that require high quality, transparent and comparable information in financial statements and other financial reporting to help participants in the world's capital markets and other users make economic decisions
- to promote the use and rigorous application of those standards
- to take account of, as appropriate, the special needs of small and medium-sized entities and emerging economies
- to bring about convergence of national accounting standards and International Accounting Standards to high quality solutions.

### 2.3 The operating structure

The current operating structure has been in place since 2001 and consists of several bodies:

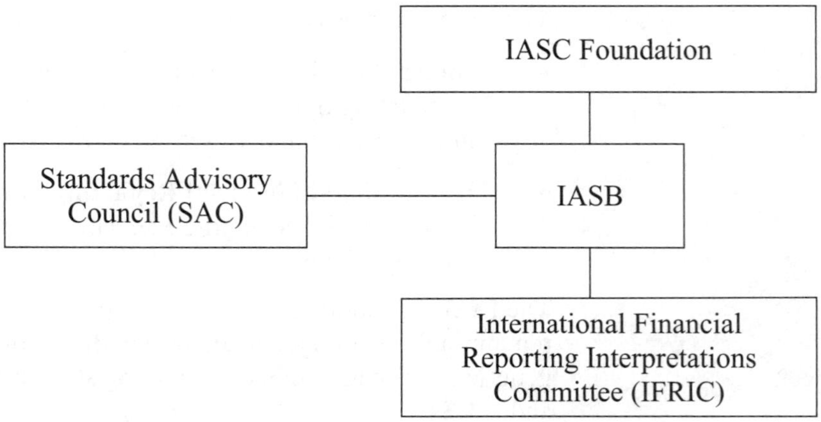


- **The IASC Foundation** appoints the members of the IASB, IFRIC and the Standards Advisory Council. It also monitors the IASB's effectiveness, raises funds, approves IASB's budget and has responsibility for constitutional changes.
- **The International Accounting Standards Board (IASB)** develops and issues accounting standards. IASB members are chosen on the basis of technical expertise rather than nationality.
- **The Standards Advisory Council (SAC)** provides a formal vehicle for groups and individuals of diverse geographical and functional backgrounds to give advice to the Board.
- **The International Financial Reporting Interpretations Committee (IFRIC)** ensures proper compliance with accounting standards by considering points of contention where divergent interpretations have emerged. It issues authoritative Interpretations.

KEY POINT

The IASB is the body responsible for issuing international accounting standards.

### 2.4 The development of an international standard

The procedure for the development of an IAS is as follows.

- The IASB identifies a subject and appoints an advisory committee to advise the board on the issues arising.
- The IASB may publish a discussion paper seeking public feedback on possible accounting solutions.
- Following review of comments received, the IASB publishes an Exposure Draft for public comment.
- Following review of further comments received, and after the voting approval of at least 9 of the IASB's 14 members, the IASB publishes the final text of a new standard.

### 2.5 Benchmark treatment and allowed alternative treatment

Some IASs permit two alternative accounting treatments for the same type of transaction or event. These are sometimes known as the benchmark treatment and the allowed alternative treatment. In practice, both the benchmark and the allowed alternative treatment have equal status. However, the treatment adopted must be applied consistently.

## 3 IAS 1 *Presentation of Financial Statements*

### 3.1 Introduction

KEY POINT

IAS 1 sets out overall requirements for the presentation of financial statements, guidelines for their structure and minimum requirements for their content.

IAS 1 sets out overall requirements for the presentation of financial statements, guidelines for their structure and minimum requirements for their content. This ensures that an entity's financial statements can be compared with those for the previous period and with the financial statements of other entities.

### 3.2 Components of financial statements

A complete set of financial statements comprises:

(a) a balance sheet

(b) an income statement

(c) a statement of changes in equity showing either:

  (i) all changes in equity, or

  (ii) changes in equity other than those arising from transactions with equity holders (owners) in their capacity as equity holders

(d) a cash flow statement; and

(e) notes, consisting of a summary of significant accounting policies and other explanatory notes.

### 3.3 Fair presentation and compliance with IFRSs

KEY POINT

Financial statements shall present fairly the financial position, financial performance and cash flows of an entity.

IAS 1 states that the financial statements shall present fairly the financial position, financial performance and cash flows of an entity.

An entity whose financial statements comply with IFRSs shall make an explicit and unreserved statement of such compliance in the notes. Financial statements shall not be described as complying with IFRSs unless they comply with all the requirements of IFRSs.

KEY POINT

Fair presentation is normally achieved by applying IFRSs.

IAS 1 allows an entity to depart from the requirements of an IAS or IFRS if compliance would make the financial statements so misleading that they would no longer meet the objectives set out in the *Framework*. In these **extremely rare** circumstances an entity should disclose:

(a) that management has concluded that the financial statements present fairly the entity's financial position, financial performance and cash flows

(b) that it has complied with applicable IASs, except that it has departed from a particular requirement in order to achieve a fair presentation

(c) the title of the IAS or IFRS from which the entity has departed, the nature of the departure, including the treatment that would normally be required, the reason why that treatment would be misleading, and the treatment adopted, and

(d) the financial impact of the departure on each item in the financial statements that would have been reported in complying with the requirement.

## 3.4 Other overall considerations

KEY POINT

Financial statements should be prepared on a going concern basis unless management either intends to liquidate the entity or to cease trading, or has no realistic alternative but to do so.

An entity should prepare its financial statements, except for cash flow information, using the accrual basis of accounting.

***Going concern***

Financial statements should be prepared on a going concern basis unless management either intends to liquidate the entity or to cease trading, or has no realistic alternative but to do so.

***Accrual basis of accounting***

An entity should prepare its financial statements, except for cash flow information, using the accrual basis of accounting.

***Consistency***

The presentation and classification of items in the financial statements should be retained from one period to the next unless:

(a) there has been a significant change in the nature of the entity's operations or a review of its financial statements, so that another presentation or classification would be more appropriate; or

(b) an IAS requires a change in presentation.

***Materiality and aggregation***

Each material class of similar items should be presented separately in the financial statements. Items of a dissimilar nature or function should be presented separately unless they are immaterial.

***Offsetting***

Items should not be offset unless this is required or permitted by an IAS.

***Comparative information***

Comparative information should be disclosed for the previous period for all amounts reported in the financial statements unless an IAS permits or requires otherwise.

## 3.5 Identification of the financial statements

(a) Financial statements should be clearly identified and distinguished from other information in the same published document.

(b) Each component of the financial statements should be clearly identified. In addition, the following information should be prominently displayed, and repeated when it is necessary for a proper understanding of the information presented:

   (i) the name of the reporting entity or other means of identification

   (ii) whether the financial statements cover the individual entity or a group of entities

   (iii) the balance sheet date or the period covered by the financial statements, whichever is appropriate to the related component of the financial statements

   (iv) the reporting currency (the currency in which the financial statements are presented)

   (v) the level of rounding used in presenting amounts in the financial statements.

## 3.6 Reporting period

Financial statements should be presented at least annually. When an entity's balance sheet date changes and annual financial statements are presented for a period longer or shorter than one year, an entity should disclose, in addition to the period covered by the financial statements:

(a) the reason for using a longer or shorter period

(b) the fact that comparative amounts for the income statement, statement of changes in equity, cash flows and related notes are not comparable.

## 3.7 Classifying assets and liabilities

KEY POINT

All assets and liabilities should be presented broadly in order of liquidity.

An entity should present current and non-current assets, and current and non-current liabilities, as separate classifications on the face of its balance sheet except when a presentation based on liquidity provides information that is reliable and is more relevant. When that exception applies, all assets and liabilities should be presented broadly in order of liquidity.

Whichever method of presentation is adopted, for each asset and liability line item that combines amounts expected to be recovered or settled within (a) no more than 12 months after the balance sheet date and (b) more than 12 months after the balance sheet date, an entity should disclose the amount expected to be recovered or settled after more than 12 months.

***Current assets***

An asset should be classified as current when it satisfies any of the following criteria:

(a) it is expected to be realised in, or is intended for sale or consumption in, the entity's normal operating cycle

(b) it is held primarily for the purpose of being traded

(c) it is expected to be realised within 12 months after the balance sheet date, or

(d) it is cash or a cash equivalent (as defined in IAS 7 *Cash Flow Statements*) unless it is restricted from being exchanged or used to settle a liability for at least 12 months after the balance sheet date.

All other assets should be classified as non-current.

***Current liabilities***

A liability should be classified as current when it satisfies any of the following criteria:

(a) it is expected to be settled in the entity's normal operating cycle

(b) it is held primarily for the purpose of being traded

(c) it is due to be settled within 12 months after the balance sheet date; or

(d) the entity does not have an unconditional right to defer settlement of the liability for at least 12 months after the balance sheet date.

All other liabilities shall be classified as non-current.

## 3.8 Information to be presented on the face of the balance sheet

As a minimum, the face of the balance sheet should include line items which present the following amounts:

(a) property, plant and equipment

(b) investment property

(c) intangible assets

(d) financial assets (excluding amounts shown under (e), (h) and (i))

(e) investments accounted for using the equity method

(f) biological assets

(g) inventories

(h) trade and other receivables

(i) cash and cash equivalents

(j) trade and other payables

(k) provisions

(l) financial liabilities (excluding amounts shown under (j) and (k)

(m) liabilities and assets for current tax as defined in IAS 12 *Income Taxes*

(n) deferred tax liabilities and deferred tax assets as defined in IAS 12 *Income Taxes*

(o) minority interest, presented within equity

(p) issued capital and reserves attributable to equity holders of the parent.

The total of assets classified as held for sale in accordance with IFRS 5 *Non-current Assets Held for Sale and Discontinued Operations* should also be disclosed as a line item on the face of the balance sheet.

Additional line items, headings and sub-totals should be presented on the face of the balance sheet when such presentation is relevant to an understanding of the entity's financial position.

## 3.9 Information to be presented either on the face of the balance sheet or in the notes

An entity should disclose, either on the face of the balance sheet or in the notes to the balance sheet, further sub-classifications of the line items presented, classified in a manner appropriate to its operations.

Examples of items which could require further analysis are:

(a) tangible assets, analysed by class as described in IAS 16 *Property, Plant and Equipment*

(b) receivables, analysed between amounts receivable from trade customers, other members of the group, receivables from related parties, prepayments and other amounts

(c) equity capital and reserves, analysed to show separately the various classes of paid in capital, share premium and reserves.

IAS 1 also requires a number of detailed disclosures relating to each class of share capital together with a description of the nature and purpose of each reserve within equity.

### 3.10 Information to be presented on the face of the income statement

As a minimum, the face of the income statement should include line items which present the following amounts for the period:

(a) revenue

(b) finance costs

(c) share of profits and losses of associates and joint ventures accounted for using the equity method

(d) tax expense

(e) the post-tax profit or loss of discontinued operations

(f) profit or loss.

Additional line items, headings and sub-totals should be presented on the face of the income statement when such presentation is relevant to an understanding of the entity's financial performance.

### 3.11 Information to be presented either on the face of the income statement or in the notes

***Material items***

KEY POINT

When items of income and expense are material, their nature and amount should be disclosed separately.

When items of income and expense are material, their nature and amount should be disclosed separately. These items are sometimes known as 'exceptional items'.

IAS 1 gives these examples of such items:

(a) write-down of inventories to net realisable value

(b) write-down of the value of property, plant and equipment to recoverable amount

(c) restructuring of the activities of an entity

(d) disposals of items of property, plant and equipment

(e) disposals of investments

(f) discontinuing operations

(g) litigation settlements

(h) other reversals of provisions.

KEY POINT

Material items are normally disclosed by including them in one of the standard income statement headings with a note giving full details. In some cases it may be more appropriate to include the item separately on the face of the income statement.

***Extraordinary items***

Material items are normally disclosed by including them in one of the standard income statement headings with a note giving full details. In some cases it may be more appropriate to include the item separately on the face of the income statement.

No items of income and expense should be presented as extraordinary items, either on the face of the income statement or in the notes. Extraordinary items are items that arise from events or transactions that are clearly distinct from the ordinary activities of an entity and therefore not expected to recur frequently or regularly.

This is a recent change to IAS 1. Before this change extraordinary items were shown separately on the face of the income statement, below profit after tax. Profit after tax is used to calculate several key measures of financial performance used by investment analysts and other groups interested in the financial statements. Although extraordinary items were supposed to be extremely rare, preparers of financial statements often classified material losses as extraordinary in order to improve profit after tax and to give the impression that the entity's overall performance was better than in fact it was.

***Analysis of expenses***

An entity should present an analysis of expenses using a classification based on either the nature of expenses or their function within the entity.

IAS 1 encourages the inclusion of this analysis on the face of the income statement, and goes on to explain and illustrate the meaning of the terms used. Illustrations of income statements using both formats are given later in the chapter.

(a) **The nature of expense method**

Expenses are aggregated in the income statement according to their nature (for example depreciation, purchases of materials, transport costs, wages and salaries, advertising costs), and are not reallocated amongst various functions within the entity.

Such an approach might be appropriate for a manufacturing concern.

(b) **The function of expense or cost of sales method**

This method classifies expenses according to their function as part of cost of sales, distribution or administrative activities. This presentation often provides more relevant information to users than the classification of expenses by nature, but the allocation of costs to functions can be arbitrary and involves considerable judgement.

If this method is adopted, entities must disclose additional information in the notes:

(a) depreciation and amortisation expense

(b) employee benefits expense.

***Dividends***

The amount of dividends recognised as distributions to equity holders during the period and the dividend per share should also be disclosed on the face of the income statement or the statement of changes in equity or in notes.

## 3.12 Statement of changes in equity

KEY POINT

A statement of changes in equity shows the movements during the period in all the capital and reserve headings which in total make up the equity of the entity.

This statement is usually presented in columnar form and shows the movements during the period in all the capital and reserve headings which in total make up the equity of the entity.

The statement should show:

(a) profit or loss for the period

(b) each item of income and expense for the period that, as required by other Standards, is recognised directly in equity, and the total of these items

(c) the effects of changes in accounting policies and the correction of errors recognised in accordance with IAS 8.

In addition, an entity should present, either within this statement or in the notes:

(d) transactions with equity owners (e.g. increases in share capital), showing separately distributions to owners (e.g. dividends)

(e) the balance of retained earnings at the beginning of the period and at the balance sheet date, and the movements for the period

(f) a reconciliation between the carrying amount of each class of equity capital, share premium and each reserve at the beginning and the end of the period, separately disclosing each movement.

An illustrative example of the statement of changes in equity is given in IAS 1 and this appears later in the chapter.

## 3.13 Statement of recognised income and expense

As an alternative to the statement of changes in equity which shows items (a) to (f) described in the previous paragraph, a company may present a statement of recognised income and expense.

This statement shows all gains and losses, whether they appear in the income statement or not, i.e. it shows only items (a) to (c) described above. The statement is confined to the current year's gains and losses.

If this statement is presented it remains necessary to disclose by note the movements on share capital and reserves required in the statement of changes in equity (items (d) to (f) described above).

The statement of recognised income and expense is helpful to users because it focuses on the overall performance of the period, regardless of whether the gains and losses appear in the income statement.

An illustrative example appears later in this chapter.

## 3.14 Notes to the financial statements

***General***

The notes should:

(a) present information about the basis of preparation of the financial statements and the specific accounting policies used

(b) disclose the information required by IFRSs that is not presented on the face of the balance sheet, income statement, statement of changes in equity or cash flow statement; and

(c) provide additional information that is not presented on the face of the balance sheet, income statement, statement of changes in equity or cash flow statement, but is relevant to an understanding of any of them.

The notes to the financial statements should be presented systematically, with cross-references between the notes and the balance sheet, income statement and cash flow statement.

KEY POINT

The notes to the financial statements should be presented systematically, with cross-references between the notes and the balance sheet, income statement and cash flow statement.

***Accounting policies***

An entity should disclose:

(a) the measurement basis (or bases) used in preparing the financial statements; and

(b) the other accounting policies used that are relevant to an understanding of the financial statements.

KEY POINT

An entity should disclose:

(a) the measurement basis (or bases) used in preparing the financial statements; and

(b) the other accounting policies used that are relevant to an understanding of the financial statements.

In addition, an entity should disclose the judgements, apart from those involving estimations, management has made that have the most significant effect on the amounts recognised in the financial statements. For example, management makes judgements in order to determine:

(a) whether financial assets are held-to-maturity investments (see Chapter 14)

(b) whether, in substance, particular sales of goods are financing arrangements and therefore do not give rise to revenue (see Chapter 13); and

(c) whether the substance of the relationship between the entity and a special purpose entity indicates that the special purpose entity is controlled by the entity (see Chapter 13).

***Key sources of estimation uncertainty***

Management often has to make estimates about the effects of uncertain future events on assets and liabilities at the balance sheet date. For example, the value of inventories may be affected by the development of new products and the amount at which a provision is measured may be affected by the outcome of a court case.

KEY POINT

Management often has to make estimates about the effects of uncertain future events on assets and liabilities at the balance sheet date.

An entity should disclose information about:

(a) key assumptions concerning the future

(b) other key sources of estimation uncertainty at the balance sheet date, if these have a significant risk of causing a material adjustment to the carrying amounts of assets and liabilities within the next financial year.

KEY POINT

An entity should disclose information about:

(a) key assumptions concerning the future

(b) other key sources of estimation uncertainty at the balance sheet date.

***Other disclosures***

An entity should disclose:

(a) information that enables users of its financial statements to evaluate the entity's objectives, policies and processes for managing capital

(b) the amount of dividends proposed or declared before the financial statements were authorised for issue but not recognised as a distribution to equity holders during the period, and the related amount per share; and

(c) the amount of any cumulative preference dividends not recognised.

An entity shall disclose the following, if not disclosed elsewhere in information published with the financial statements:

(a) the domicile and legal form of the entity, its country of incorporation and the address of its registered office (or principal place of business, if different from the registered office)

(b) a description of the nature of the entity's operations and its principal activities; and

(c) the name of the parent and the ultimate parent of the group.

## 4 Illustrative financial statements

IAS 1 includes examples of income statements, a balance sheet and statements of changes in equity. These meet the requirements of the IAS. However, the formats are not mandatory and may be adapted if this is necessary to achieve a fair presentation in each entity's particular circumstances.

Some of the items in the financial statements (for example, 'available-for-sale investments' in the balance sheet and 'cash flow hedges' in the statement of changes in equity) will probably be unfamiliar to you. These items will be covered in later chapters.

**XYZ Group**
**Balance sheet as at 31 December 20X2**

| | *20X2* | *20X1* |
|---|---|---|
| | $000 | $000 |
| **ASSETS** | | |
| **Non current assets** | | |
| Property, plant and equipment | X | X |
| Goodwill | X | X |
| Other intangible assets | X | X |
| Investments in associates | X | X |
| Available-for-sale investments | X | X |
| | | |
| **Current assets** | | |
| Inventories | X | X |
| Trade receivables | X | X |
| Other current assets | X | X |
| Cash and cash equivalents | X | X |
| | X | X |
| **Total assets** | X | X |

| | | |
|---|---|---|
| **EQUITY AND LIABILITIES** | | |
| **Equity attributable to equity holders of the parent** | | |
| Share capital | X | X |
| Other reserves | X | X |
| Retained earnings | X | X |
| | X | X |
| **Minority interest** | X | X |
| **Total equity** | X | X |
| **Non-current liabilities** | | |
| Long-term borrowings | X | X |
| Deferred tax | X | X |
| Long-term provisions | X | X |
| **Total non-current liabilities** | X | X |
| **Current liabilities** | | |
| Trade and other payables | X | X |
| Short-term borrowings | X | X |
| Current portion of long-term borrowings | X | X |
| Current tax payable | X | X |
| Short-term provisions | X | X |
| **Total current liabilities** | X | X |
| **Total liabilities** | X | X |
| **Total equity and liabilities** | X | X |

**XYZ Group**
**Income statement for the year ended 31 December 20X2**
**(illustrating the classification of expenses by function)**

| | *20X2* | *20X1* |
|---|---|---|
| | $000 | $000 |
| **Revenue** | X | X |
| Cost of sales | (X) | (X) |
| Gross profit | X | X |
| Other income | X | X |
| Distribution costs | (X) | (X) |
| Administrative expenses | (X) | (X) |
| Other expenses | (X) | (X) |
| Finance costs | (X) | (X) |
| Share of profit of associates | X | X |
| **Profit before tax** | X | X |
| Income tax expense | (X) | (X) |
| **Profit for the period** | X | X |
| Attributable to: | | |
| Equity holders of the parent | X | X |
| Minority interest | X | X |
| | X | X |

**XYZ Group**
**Income statement for the year ended 31 December 20X2**
**(illustrating the classification of expenses by nature)**

| | *20X2* | *20X1* |
|---|---|---|
| | $000 | $000 |
| **Revenue** | X | X |
| Other income | X | X |
| Changes in inventories of finished goods and work in progress | (X) | X |
| Work performed by the entity and capitalised | X | X |
| Raw material and consumables used | (X) | (X) |
| Employee benefits expense | (X) | (X) |
| Depreciation and amortisation expense | (X) | (X) |
| Impairment of property, plant and equipment | (X) | (X) |
| Other expenses | (X) | (X) |
| Finance costs | (X) | (X) |
| Share of profit of associates | X | X |
| **Profit before tax** | X | X |
| Income tax expense | (X) | (X) |
| **Profit for the period** | X | X |
| | | |
| Attributable to: | | |
| Equity holders of the parent | X | X |
| Minority interest | X | X |
| | X | X |

**XYZ Group**
**Statement of changes in equity for the year ended 31 December 20X2**

| | *Attributable to equity holders of the parent* | | | | | *Minority* | *Total* |
|---|---|---|---|---|---|---|---|
| | *Share capital* | *Other reserves* | *Translation-reserve* | *Retained earnings* | *Total* | *interest* | *equity* |
| | $000 | SC00 | $000 | $000 | $000 | $000 | $000 |
| **Balance at 31 December 20X1** | X | X | (X) | X | X | X | X |
| Changes in accounting policy | | | | (X) | (X) | (X) | (X) |
| Restated balance | X | X | (X) | X | X | X | X |
| **Changes in equity for 20X2** | | | | | | | |
| Gain on properly revaluation | | X | | | X | X | X |
| Available-for-sale investments: | | | | | | | |
| Valuation gains/(losses) taken to equity | | (X) | | | (X) | | (X) |
| Transferred to profit or loss on sale | | (X) | | | (X) | | (X) |
| Cash flow hedges: | | | | | | | |
| Gains/(losses) taken to equity | | X | | | X | X | X |
| Transferred to profit or loss for the period | | X | | | X | X | X |
| Transferred to initial carrying amount of hedged items | | (X) | | | (X) | | (X |
| Exchange differences on translating foreign operations | | | (X) | | (X) | (X) | (X) |

| | | | | | | | |
|---|---|---|---|---|---|---|---|
| Tax on items taken directly to or transferred from equity | | (X) | X | | (X) | (X) | (X) |
| Net income recognised directly in equity | | X | (X) | | X | X | X |
| Profit in the period | | | | X | X | X | X |
| Total recognised income and expense for the period | | X | (X) | X | X | X | X |
| Dividends | | | | (X) | (X) | (X) | (X) |
| Issue of share capital | X | | | | X | | X |
| Equity share options issued | | X | | | X | | X |
| **Balance at 31 December 20X2** | X | X | (X) | X | X | X | X |

**XYZ Group**
**Statement of recognised income and expense**
**for the year ended 31 December 20X2**

| | *20X2* | *20X1* |
|---|---|---|
| | $000 | $000 |
| Gain/(loss) on revaluation of properties | (X) | X |
| Available-for-sale investments: | | |
| Valuation gains/(losses) taken to equity | (X) | (X) |
| Transferred to profit or loss on sale | X | (X) |
| Cash flow hedges: | | |
| Gains/(losses) taken to equity | X | X |
| Transferred to profit or loss for the period | (X) | X |
| Transferred to the initial carrying amount of hedged items | (X) | (X) |
| Exchange differences on translation of foreign operations | (X) | (X) |
| Tax on items taken directly to or transferred from equity | X | (X) |
| **Net income recognised directly in equity** | (X) | X |
| **Profit for the period** | X | X |
| **Total recognised income and expense for the period** | X | X |
| Attributable to: | | |
| Equity holders of the parent | X | X |
| Minority interest | X | X |
| | | |
| Effect of changes in accounting policy: | | |
| Equity holders of the parent | | (X) |
| Minority interest | | (X) |
| | | (X) |

## Summary

- The IASB has adopted an important conceptual document, the *Framework for the Preparation and Presentation of Financial Statements.* This *Framework* deals with the objective, qualitative characteristics and elements of financial statements; and the recognition of the elements of financial statements.
- IAS 1 covers the presentation of financial statements. It contains guidelines for their structure and sets out minimum requirements for their content, including items which must be disclosed on the face of the balance sheet and the income statement and items which must be disclosed either on the face of the primary financial statements or in the notes. IAS 1 also states that financial statements must be presented fairly.

## Self-test questions

**1** What are the purposes of the IASB's *Framework*? (1.1)

**2** Define the five elements of financial statements. (1.5)

**3** What four measurement bases may be used in financial statements? (1.7)

**4** Distinguish between financial capital maintenance and physical capital maintenance. (1.8)

**5** What are the objectives of the IASB? (2.2)

**6** What are the stages in the development of an IAS? (2.4)

**7** What are the components of a complete set of financial statements? (3.2)

**8** What criteria determine whether assets should be classified as current? (3.7)

**9** What minimum information should be presented on the face of the income statement? (3.10)

**10** Distinguish between the nature of expense method and the function of expense method of classifying expenses in the income statement. (3.11)

**11** What information is disclosed in the statement of changes in equity? (3.12)

## Objective test questions

### Question 1

The IASB's *Framework for the Preparation and Presentation of Financial Statements* recognises materiality as the threshold quality of financial information. In addition, financial information should show four other desirable qualitative characteristics. These are:

**A** relevance, reliability, consistency and clarity

**B** relevance, reliability, comparability and understandability

**C** acceptability, reliability, comparability and understandability

**D** acceptability, reliability, consistency and understandability.

### Question 2

The IASB's *Framework* recognises four possible measurement bases for use in financial reporting, one of these is historical cost, the other three are:

**A** current cost, recoverable amount, present value

**B** entry value, exit value, replacement cost

**C** current cost, realisable value and present value

**D** recoverable amount, realisable value, deprival value.

---

*For the answers to these questions, see the 'Answers' section at the end of the book.*

## Practice question

### Conceptual framework

List and explain the advantages which result from the development of a 'conceptual framework for accounting'. **(10 marks)**

---

*For the answer to this question, see the 'Answers' section at the end of the book.*

## Feedback to activity

### Activity 1

The answer is (b). Those parties who feel they have the most to lose will be first to comment on a new proposed standard. Therefore if a dubious accounting practice is in danger of being outlawed a majority of respondents to an exposure draft may favour the dubious method. Standard setting by consensus view or by democratic majority opinion in these circumstances appears to be unsatisfactory. On the other hand, there seem to be a lot of advantages to a well considered strategy as portrayed in method (b). For example, standards would be more likely to be consistent with each other. New standards would be issued at staged regular intervals rather than spasmodically. The danger of duplication of effort would be reduced. And the justification for the standards set would be based on a predetermined set of principles.

Chapter 2

# GROUP ACCOUNTS: THE BALANCE SHEET

## Syllabus content

- The preparation of consolidated financial statements (including the group cash flow statement) involving one or more subsidiaries, sub-subsidiaries and associates, under the acquisition and pooling of interests methods (IAS 7 & 27 and IFRS 3).
- The treatment in consolidated financial statements of minority interests, pre- and post-acquisition reserves, goodwill (including its impairment), fair value adjustments, intra-group transactions and dividends, piece-meal and mid-year acquisitions, and disposals to include sub-subsidiaries and mixed groups.

## Chapter contents

# Introduction

So far in your studies you have only prepared accounts for individual companies. One of the most important parts of the syllabus for this paper concerns the preparation of accounts for groups of companies. In this chapter we begin to consider what happens when an entity conducts its activities through a number of companies, rather than a single company. Although each company remains a separate entity in law, the economic reality is that they operate as if they were one single entity. Therefore we need to prepare group accounts (sometimes called consolidated accounts) in order to show the results and the assets and liabilities of the group as a whole.

In this chapter you will learn how to prepare a simple balance sheet for a group. The group income statement is covered in Chapter 4.

## 1 Introduction to consolidated accounts

### 1.1 What is a 'group'?

Although every company is a separate entity from the legal point of view, from the economic point of view several companies may not be separate at all. When one company owns enough shares in another company to have a majority of votes at that company's annual general meeting, the first company may appoint all the directors of, and decide what dividends should be paid by, the second company. This degree of control enables the first company to manage the trading activities and future plans of the second company as if it were merely a department of the first company.

The first company referred to above is called the parent, and the second is called a subsidiary. The essential feature of a group is that one company controls all the others.

KEY POINT

The essential feature of a group is that one company controls all the others.
International accounting standards require a parent company to produce consolidated financial statements which show the position and results of the whole group as if it were a single company.

International accounting standards require a parent company to produce consolidated financial statements which show the position and results of the whole group as if it were a single company.

There are four International Accounting Standards relevant to the preparation of consolidated financial statements:

IFRS 3 *Business Combinations*

IAS 27 *Consolidated and Separate Financial Statements*

IAS 28 *Investments in Associates*

IAS 31 *Interests in Joint Ventures.*

The detailed requirements of these standards are covered later in this text.

### 1.2 General procedure

Each company in a group prepares its accounting records and annual financial statements in the usual way. From the individual companies' balance sheets, the parent prepares a consolidated balance sheet for the group, and likewise a consolidated income statement from the individual companies' income statements.

## 2 The basic balance sheet consolidation

### 2.1 Example

**Balance sheets at 31 December 20X4**

| | *P* | *S* |
|---|---|---|
| | $000 | $000 |
| Non-current assets | 60 | 40 |
| Investment in S at cost | 50 | |
| Current assets | 40 | 40 |
| | 150 | 80 |
| Ordinary share capital ($1 shares) | 100 | 50 |
| Retained earnings | 30 | – |
| Current liabilities | 20 | 30 |
| | 150 | 80 |

P acquired all the shares in S on 31 December 20X4 for a cost of $50,000.

The consolidated balance sheet differs from the parent's balance sheet. The investment in the subsidiary is replaced by the underlying net assets which the investment represents.

KEY POINT

The cost of the investment in the subsidiary and the ordinary share capital and reserves of the subsidiary reflect a relationship that exists only *within* the group and so they are cancelled against one another.

The cost of the investment in the subsidiary and the ordinary share capital and reserves of the subsidiary reflect a relationship that exists only *within* the group and so they are cancelled against one another.

This leaves a balance sheet showing:

- the net assets of the whole group (P + S)
- the share capital of the group which is always solely the share capital of the parent (P only)
- the retained earnings, comprising profits made by the group: in this case we have profits made by the parent but none made by the subsidiary to bring into the calculations.

So, by cross adding the net assets of each company, and cancelling the investment in S and the share capital of S we arrive at the consolidated balance sheet given in the solution below.

***Solution***

**P**

**Consolidated balance sheet at 31 December 20X4**

| | $000 |
|---|---|
| Non-current assets (60 + 40) | 100 |
| Current assets (40 + 40) | 80 |
| | 180 |
| Share capital ($1 ordinary shares) | 100 |
| Retained earnings | 30 |
| Current liabilities (20 + 30) | 50 |
| | 180 |

KEY POINT

Under no circumstances will any share capital of any subsidiary company ever be included in the figure of share capital on the consolidated balance sheet.

***Note***: Under no circumstances will any share capital of any subsidiary company ever be included in the figure of share capital on the consolidated balance sheet.

## 2.2 Goodwill on consolidation

When the investment in the subsidiary costs more or less than the net assets acquired in the subsidiary, there will be a difference between the cost of the investment in the subsidiary and the share capital of the subsidiary.

By modifying the previous example we can tackle this problem:

**Balance sheets at 31 December 20X4**

| | *P* | *S* |
|---|---|---|
| | $000 | $000 |
| Non-current assets | 60 | 40 |
| Investment in S at cost | 60 | |
| Current assets | 30 | 40 |
| | 150 | 80 |
| Ordinary share capital ($1 shares) | 100 | 50 |
| Retained earnings | 30 | – |
| Current liabilities | 20 | 30 |
| | 150 | 80 |

DEFINITION

**Goodwill on consolidation** represents the excess of the purchase consideration over the fair value of the net assets acquired.

KEY POINT

Goodwill is included in the consolidated balance sheet as a non-current asset.

P acquired all the shares in S on 31 December 20X4 for a cost of $60,000.

In this case the cost of the shares in S exceeds S's share capital by $10,000. This is the goodwill on consolidation (sometimes known as the premium on acquisition). It represents the excess of the purchase consideration over the fair value of the net assets acquired. Goodwill is included in the consolidated balance sheet as a non-current asset. The calculation may be set out as a consolidation schedule as follows:

| | $000 | $000 | *Notes* |
|---|---|---|---|
| Cost of investment | | 60 | 1 |
| Less: Share of net assets acquired (at fair value) | | | |
| Ordinary share capital | 50 | | 2 |
| Retained earnings | – | | 3 |
| | 50 | | |
| Group share | × 100% | (50) | 4 |
| Goodwill on consolidation | | 10 | 5 |

**Notes to the calculation**

1 The cost of the investment will appear in the balance sheet of P.

2 We are actually comparing the cost of the investment with the net assets of the subsidiary acquired, as represented by the share capital and reserves of the subsidiary at the date of acquisition. Remember: Net assets = Capital + Reserves.

3 In this case there are no reserves of the subsidiary to consider. However, it is important to note here that the reserves which are taken into consideration in the calculation of goodwill are those at the date of acquisition of the subsidiary. Whilst the share capital of the subsidiary is unlikely to have altered since that date, the retained earnings will have changed.

4 As 100% of the shares in S were acquired, we compare the cost of the shares with 100% of the net assets of S. If only a proportion of the shares are acquired, say 90%, we compare the cost of those shares with the appropriate share (90%) of the net assets acquired. This is illustrated later on in the chapter.

Having first calculated goodwill, the net assets of the parent and the subsidiary can be cross-cast and the consolidated balance sheet completed.

**P**

**Consolidated balance sheet at 31 December 20X4**

| | $000 |
|---|---|
| Non-current assets (60 + 40) | 100 |
| Goodwill | 10 |
| Current assets (30 + 40) | 70 |
| | 180 |
| Share capital ($1 ordinary shares) | 100 |
| Retained earnings | 30 |
| Current liabilities (20 + 30) | 50 |
| | 180 |

KEY POINT

Negative goodwill is recognised immediately as a gain in the income statement.

Where the cost of the investment is less than the net assets purchased, a credit balance arises on the consolidation, i.e. a profit. This is known as negative goodwill. Negative goodwill is recognised immediately as a gain in the income statement.

We will be covering goodwill in more detail in a later chapter.

## 2.3 Fair value

Where an exam question gives the fair values of net assets at the date of acquisition which differ from book values, the calculation of goodwill and the consolidation must be carried out by reference to the fair values given rather than the book values.

In addition, the subsidiary's assets must be revalued before they are added to the parent's assets in the consolidated balance sheet.

Again, we will be covering the concept of fair value and how to determine the fair value of a subsidiary's assets in a later chapter.

## 2.4 Reserves

KEY POINT

A distinction must be made between pre-acquisition reserves and post-acquisition reserves.

In the examples above, the shareholders' interest consisted solely of ordinary share capital. Usually, of course, shareholders' interest includes also retained earnings. An additional point is that P may have acquired the controlling interest in S part way through the year. When looking at the revenue reserves of S at the year end, a distinction must be made between:

(a) those reserves of S which existed at the date of acquisition by P (pre-acquisition reserves); and

(b) the increase in the reserves of S which arose after acquisition by P (post-acquisition reserves).

This is because the investment in S at cost includes a payment for S's reserves at the date of acquisition.

***Example***

**Balance sheets at 31 December 20X4**

| | *P* | *S* |
|---|---|---|
| | $000 | $000 |
| Non-current assets | 50 | 40 |
| Investment in S at cost | 70 | – |
| Current assets | 30 | 40 |
| | 150 | 80 |
| Ordinary share capital ($1 shares) | 100 | 50 |
| Retained earnings | 30 | 20 |
| Current liabilities | 20 | 10 |
| | 150 | 80 |

You are further informed that P acquired all the shares in S at 30 June 20X4 when the retained earnings of S amounted to $15,000.

Prepare the consolidated balance sheet at 31 December 20X4.

**Step 1**

First, deal with the goodwill which is computed at the date of take-over. The cost of the investment ($70,000) is compared with the net assets of S at 30 June 20X4 as represented by ordinary share capital ($50,000) and retained earnings ($15,000). Note that here we are concerned are the reserves at the date of acquisition ($15,000) as opposed to reserves at the date of consolidation ($20,000). The calculation becomes:

**Goodwill on consolidation**

| | $000 | $000 |
|---|---|---|
| Cost of investment | | 70 |
| Less: Share of net assets acquired: | | |
| Ordinary share capital | 50 | |
| Retained earnings | 15 | |
| | 65 × 100% | 65 |
| Goodwill on consolidation | | 5 |

**Step 2**

KEY POINT

Profits made by S prior to acquisition by P (pre-acquisition profits) are not regarded as those of the group whereas profits of S arising after acquisition (post-acquisition profits) are regarded as group profits.

In addition, a new consolidation schedule, a consolidated retained earnings schedule, is required. The object of this is to show the distributable profit of the group at the balance sheet date. Profits made by S prior to acquisition by P (pre-acquisition profits) are not regarded as those of the group whereas profits of S arising after acquisition (post-acquisition profits) are regarded as group profits. Allocate the reserves of S at the balance sheet date (31 December 20X4) between pre-acquisition and post-acquisition. Pre-acquisition reserves are effectively capitalised, being dealt with in the goodwill consolidation schedule (shown above), whereas post-acquisition reserves, together with the present balance on P's reserves, are transferred to consolidated retained earnings.

The consolidated retained earnings schedule is set out as follows:

| | | $000 |
|---|---|---|
| P: | (all) | 30 |
| S: | (only post-acquisition, i.e. balance sheet date less date of acquisition) (20 – 15) | 5 |
| | | 35 |

**Step 3**

The consolidated balance sheet now appears as follows:

**P**
**Group balance sheet at 31 December 20X4**

| | $000 | $000 |
|---|---|---|
| Non-current assets | | |
| Tangible assets (50 + 40) | 90 | |
| Intangible assets | | |
| Goodwill | 5 | 95 |
| Current assets (30 + 40) | | 70 |
| | | 165 |
| Share capital – $1 ordinary shares | | 100 |
| Retained earnings | | 35 |
| | | 135 |
| Current liabilities (20 + 10) | | 30 |
| | | 165 |

## 2.5 Minority interests

What happens if P owns only 80% of the ordinary shares of S? In this case there is said to be a minority interest of 20%. What problems does this present?

The main decision to make on accounting principles is whether to consolidate all the net assets of S, or merely to consolidate the proportion of the net assets represented by the shares held and the proportion of the reserves which apply to those shares, i.e. consolidate only 80% of the net assets of S.

KEY POINT

The directors are preparing accounts which show their stewardship of all the assets under their control, even though there are owners other than the parent company.

KEY POINT

The **minority interest** is presented quite separately in the consolidated balance sheet. It is not part of the shareholders' funds.

The directors are preparing accounts which show their stewardship of all the assets under their control, even though there are owners other than the parent company.

Therefore, the generally accepted solution is to consolidate all the subsidiary's net assets and then bring in a counterbalancing liability on the consolidated balance sheet to represent that part of the assets controlled but not owned. This is the **minority interest**.

This liability is presented quite separately in the consolidated balance sheet. It is not part of the shareholders' funds.

The balance sheet format in IAS 1 (not obligatory but obviously recommended for examination use) includes the minority interest immediately after the subtotal of capital and reserves.

***Example***

**Balance sheets at 31 December 20X4**

| | *P* | *S* |
|---|---|---|
| | $000 | $000 |
| Non-current assets | 50 | 40 |
| Investment in S at cost | 70 | – |
| Current assets | 30 | 40 |
| | 150 | 80 |
| Ordinary share capital ($1 shares) | 100 | 50 |
| Retained earnings | 30 | 20 |
| Current liabilities | 20 | 10 |
| | 150 | 80 |

P acquired 40,000 $1 shares in S on 30 June 20X4 for $70,000, when the retained earnings of S amounted to $15,000. Prepare the consolidated balance sheet at 31 December 20X4.

***Solution***

A third consolidation schedule is required to calculate the minority interest in the net assets of the subsidiary.

**Minority interest**

Net assets of S at the balance sheet date

| | |
|---|---|
| | $000 |
| Share capital | 50 |
| Retained earnings | 20 |
| | 70 |
| Minority % | × 20% |
| | 14 |

The other two consolidation schedules will appear as shown below. Each is affected by the fact that the parent company now owns only 80% of the shares in the subsidiary.

**Goodwill**

| | | $000 | $000 |
|---|---|---|---|
| Cost of investment | | | 70 |
| Less: | Share of net assets acquired: | | |
| | Share capital | 50 | |
| | Retained earnings | 15 | |
| | | 65 | |
| Group share | | × 80% | |
| | | | (52) |
| | | | 18 |

**Retained earnings**

| | $000 |
|---|---|
| P Limited: all | 30 |
| S Limited: P Limited's share of S Limited's post-acquisition profits 80% (20 – 15) | 4 |
| | 34 |

Note how the reserves of S are allocated during the consolidation process:

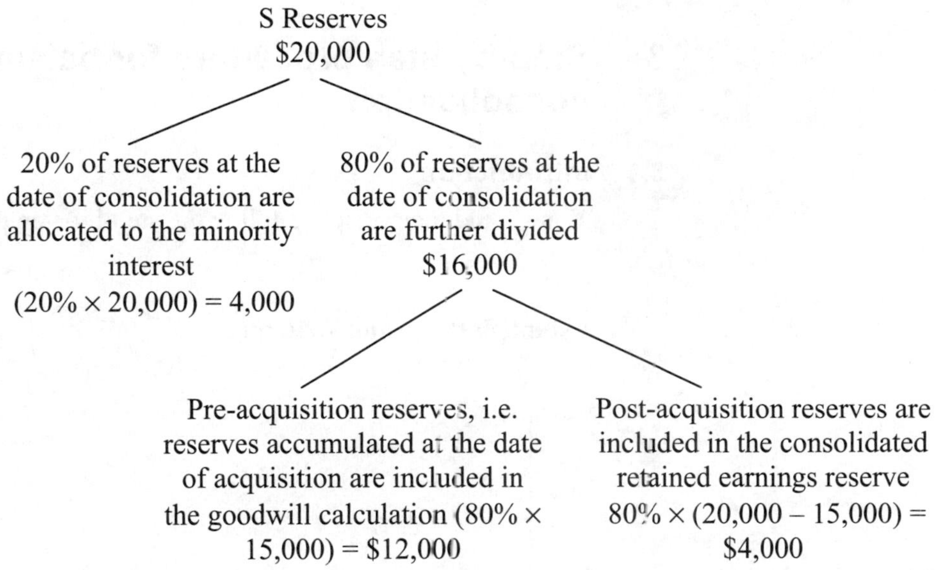


Similarly, the share capital of S is allocated to the goodwill calculation (the group's share, 80%) and to the minority interest calculation (the minority's share, 20%).

Taking the balances from the consolidation schedules and then adding the other balance sheet items together, the consolidated balance sheet at 31 December 20X4 can be constructed:

| | $000 | $000 |
|---|---|---|
| Non-current assets | | |
| Tangible assets (50 + 40) | 90 | |
| Intangible assets | | |
| Goodwill | 18 | 108 |
| Current assets (30 + 40) | | 70 |
| | | 178 |
| Share capital | 100 | |
| Retained earnings | 34 | 134 |
| Minority interest | | 14 |
| Current liabilities (20 + 10) | | 30 |
| | | 178 |

This last example includes all the three basic elements of a balance sheet consolidation:

(a) reserves in subsidiary company

(b) acquisition of less than 100% of S's shares

(c) acquisition earlier than balance sheet date.

You should rework this example.

## 3 Step-by-step procedure for balance sheet consolidation

### 3.1 Introduction

You should memorise the following step-by-step procedure.

**Step 1**

**Establish the group structure**

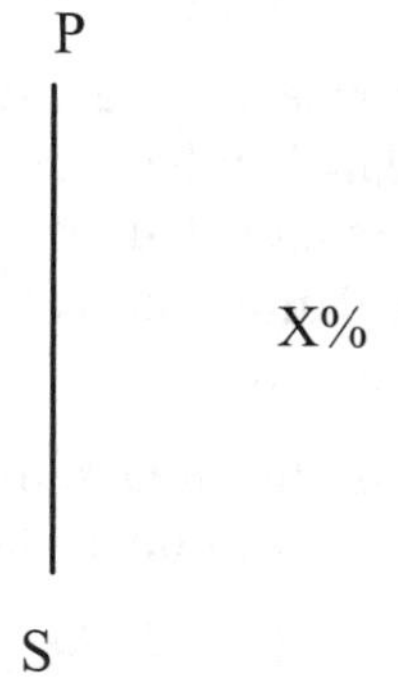

**Step 2**

**Net assets of subsidiary**

| | *At acquisition* | *At balance sheet date* |
|---|---|---|
| | $ | $ |
| Share capital | X | X |
| Reserves | X | X |
| Fair value adjustments | X | X |
| | X | X |

**Step 3**

**Goodwill**

| | $ |
|---|---|
| Cost of investment | X |
| Less: group share of net assets of S at acquisition date (Step 2) | (X) |
| | X |

**Step 4**

**Minority interest**

| | $ |
|---|---|
| Minority interest share of net assets of S at balance sheet date (Step 2) | X |

**Step 5**

**Reserves**

| | $ |
|---|---|
| P | X |
| S: Group share of post-acquisition reserves (Group % × (net assets at balance sheet date – net assets at acquisition)) (Step 2) | X |
| | X |

**Step 6**

**Prepare the consolidated balance sheet**

### *Activity 1*

The summarised draft balance sheets of a group at 31 December 20X4 were:

| | *P* | *S* | | *P* | *S* |
|---|---|---|---|---|---|
| | $ | $ | | $ | $ |
| Sundry assets | 106,000 | 34,500 | Share capital ($1 ord.) | 100,000 | 20,000 |
| Investment in S Ltd | | | Retained earnings | 22,000 | 6,500 |
| (shares at cost) | 27,000 | – | Payables | 11,000 | 8,000 |
| | 133,000 | 34,500 | | 133,000 | 34,500 |

Prepare the consolidated balance sheet at 31 December 20X4 for each of the following alternatives.

(a) P acquired all the shares in S on 1 January 20X4, when S had retained earnings of $6,000.

(b) Facts as in (a) above, except that only 16,000 ordinary shares in S were purchased for $27,000.

(c) Facts as in (a) above, except that only 16,000 ordinary shares in S were purchased for $27,000 on 1 January 20X4. Property which was not depreciated was estimated by the directors of P to be under-valued by $5,000 on 1 January 20X4. No adjustment has been made in the books of S.

*Feedback to this activity is at the end of the chapter.*

## 4 Inter-company items

KEY POINT

Inter-company items must be eliminated when the consolidated balance sheet is prepared, in order to show the proper position of the economic unit, the group.

### 4.1 Introduction

The individual balance sheets of the parent and subsidiary companies are likely to include inter-company items, i.e. amounts owing between the group companies. These inter-company items must be eliminated when the consolidated balance sheet is prepared, in order to show the proper position of the economic unit, the group.

### 4.2 Current accounts

At the year end current accounts may not agree, owing to the existence of in-transit items such as goods or cash. The usual rules are:

(a) If the goods or cash are in transit between the parent and the subsidiary, make the adjusting entry to the balance sheet of the parent, irrespective of the direction of transfer, i.e.

Dr Cash in transit

Cr Current account with subsidiary

Note that this is for the purpose of consolidation only.

(b) If the goods or cash are in transit between subsidiaries, then adjust in the books of the ultimate recipient.

(c) Once in agreement, the current accounts may be contra'd and cancelled as part of the process of cross casting the assets and liabilities of the balance sheet. This can be achieved, along with any other adjustments, as a working paper which would show:

   (i) the net assets in the balance sheets of each company

   (ii) all adjustments to these figures along with cancelled inter-company items

   (iii) the final figures which will appear in the consolidated balance sheet, resulting from the cross casting of items in (i) and (ii) above.

However, as this working paper would take time to generate in an exam, it is useful to use the balance sheets given in the exam paper itself to form this working paper.

### *Example*

**Balance sheets at 31 December 20X4**

| | *P* | *S* |
|---|---|---|
| | $ | $ |
| Investment in S (at cost) | 19,000 | |
| S current account | 10,000 | |
| Cash at bank | 10,000 | 23,000 |
| Sundry net assets | 41,000 | 16,000 |
| | 80,000 | 39,000 |
| Share capital ($1 ord) | 50,000 | 10,000 |
| Retained earnings | 30,000 | 20,000 |
| P current account | | 9,000 |
| | 80,000 | 39,000 |

P bought 7,500 shares in S on 1 January 20X4 when the balance on the accumulated profits of S was $12,000. The current account difference has arisen as a cheque sent by S to P on 30 December 20X4 was not received by P until 3 January 20X5. Prepare the consolidated balance sheet at 31 December 20X4.

### *Solution*

An adjustment for cash in transit has to be made before the consolidation can be completed. An extra step is therefore required in the consolidation procedure; it is a good idea to make this sort of adjustment early on so that it is not forgotten.

**Step 1**

Shareholdings in S Limited

P
| 75%
S

**Step 2**

Adjustments

Cash in transit

| | | | |
|---|---|---|---|
| Dr | Cash in transit | $1,000 | |
| | Cr S current account (P's balance sheet) | | $1,000 |

Cancel the current accounts which are now in agreement. (Note that at this stage most of the top half of the consolidated balance sheet can be prepared – a useful tip for the exam room when time is of the essence.)

| | | *P* | *S* | *Group* |
|---|---|---|---|---|
| | | $ | $ | $ |
| Investment in S (at cost) | | 19,000 | | |
| S current account | ~~(1,000)~~ | ~~10,000~~ | | |
| Cash at bank | | 10,000 | 23,000 | **33,000** |
| **Cash in transit** | **1,000** | – | | **1,000** |
| Sundry net assets | | 41,000 | 16,000 | **57,000** |
| P current account | | | ~~(9,000)~~ | |
| | | 80,000 | 30,000 | |

**Step 3**

Net assets

| | *At acquisition* | *At balance sheet date* |
|---|---|---|
| | $ | $ |
| Share capital | 10,000 | 10,000 |
| Retained earnings | 12,000 | 20,000 |
| | 22,000 | 30,000 |

**Step 4**

Goodwill

| | $ |
|---|---|
| Cost of investment | 19,000 |
| Less: Share of net assets of S at the acquisition date (75% × 22,000) | (16,500) |
| Goodwill | 2,500 |

**Step 5**

Minority interest

| | $ |
|---|---|
| Minority share of net assets of S at balance sheet date: (25% × 30,000) | 7,500 |

**Step 6**

Reserves

Consolidated retained earnings

| | $ |
|---|---|
| P: | 30,000 |
| S: 75% (30,000 – 22,000) | 6,000 |
| | 36,000 |

**Step 7**

**P**

**Consolidated balance sheet at 31 December 20X4**

| | $ |
|---|---|
| Goodwill | 2,500 |
| Sundry net assets | 57,000 |
| Cash at bank (10,000 + 23,000 + 1,000) | 34,000 |
| | 93,500 |
| Share capital | 50,000 |
| Retained earnings | 36,000 |
| Minority interest | 7,500 |
| | 93,500 |

### 4.3 Unrealised profits

KEY POINT

Where goods have been sold by one group company to another at a profit and some of these goods are still in the purchaser's inventory at the year end, then the profit on the sale of these goods is unrealised from the viewpoint of the group as a whole. Unrealised profit must be eliminated from the group accounts.

Where goods have been sold by one group company to another at a profit and some of these goods are still in the purchaser's inventory at the year end, then the profit on the sale of these goods is unrealised from the viewpoint of the group as a whole.

This is because we are treating the group as if it is a single entity. No-one can make a profit by trading with themselves.

(a) **Parent sells to subsidiary** – Where goods are sold by P to S, and some of the goods are in inventory at the year end, there are two steps:

(i) calculate the unrealised profit in closing inventory

(ii) make the consolidation adjustment for the unrealised profit

Dr Consolidated retained earnings

Cr Consolidated inventory

(in P's balance sheet)

This reduces inventory to cost to the group and removes unrealised profit from the group reserves.

(b) **Subsidiary sells to parent** – Suppose P owns 90% of S. During the year S sells goods to P at cost plus 25%. At the year end the closing inventory of P includes $8,000 of goods, at invoice value, acquired originally from S. What adjustments are required in the consolidation working papers?

IAS 27 is not completely clear on the treatment of the unrealised profit in this case. It merely states that the unrealised profit should be eliminated 'in full', but does not make it clear whether a portion of it should be charged against the minority interest. Normal practice is to charge the minority interest with its proportion, so this is the treatment adopted here.

The elimination should be set against the interests held by the group and the minority interest in proportion to their holdings in the company whose individual financial statements recorded the eliminated profits or losses.

Thus, sales from the parent to the subsidiary produce profits in the parent. Any unrealised profits should be charged against the group. Sales from the subsidiary to the parent produce profits in the subsidiary company. The unrealised profits should be split between the group and the minority.

Returning to the example, the total unrealised profit is:

$$\frac{25}{125} \times \$8,000 = \$1,600$$

***Note:*** The denominator in the fraction. The $8,000 is at selling price to S, i.e. 100 + 25.

Consolidated inventory must be reduced (credited) by $1,600, the minority interest will be reduced by its share of this (10% × 1,600), $160, and the remaining 90%, $1,440, will be borne by the group as a reduction in retained earnings.

Again, this may be achieved by means of a consolidation adjustment:

| | | $ | $ |
|---|---|---|---|
| Dr | Consolidated retained earnings | | |
| | 90% × 1,600 | 1,440 | |
| Dr | Minority interests | | |
| | 10% × 1,600 | 160 | |
| | Cr Consolidated inventory | | 1,600 |

***Example***

**Balance sheets at 31 December 20X4**

| | *P* | *S* |
|---|---|---|
| | $ | $ |
| Investment in S (at cost) | 75,000 | |
| Inventory | 12,000 | 5,000 |
| Other net assets | 83,000 | 95,000 |
| | 170,000 | 100,000 |
| Share capital ($1 ord) | 50,000 | 40,000 |
| Retained earnings | 120,000 | 60,000 |
| | 170,000 | 100,000 |

P acquired 32,000 shares in S on 1 January 20X4 when the balance on the retained earnings reserve of S was $50,000. During the year S sold goods to P for $80,000 making a standard mark up of 25%. At 31 December 20X4, P included in its inventory value $5,000, being the price paid for goods purchased from S. Prepare the consolidated balance sheet as at 31 December 20X4.

***Solution***

**Step 1**

Group structure

P
|  80%
S

**Step 2**

Adjustment

Unrealised profit on inventory

$$5{,}000 \times \frac{25}{125} = \$1{,}000$$

S sold the goods and made the profit. Therefore the adjustment is made to the balance sheet of S, so that both the group and the minority will bear their share of the unrealised profit.

This is done by reducing the net assets of S at the balance sheet date (Step 3 below).

**Step 3**

Net assets

| | *At acquisition* | *At balance sheet date* |
|---|---|---|
| | $ | $ |
| Share capital | 40,000 | 40,000 |
| Retained earnings | 50,000 | 60,000 |
| Provision for unrealised profit (PUP) | | (1,000) |
| | 90,000 | 99,000 |

**Step 4**

Goodwill

| | $ |
|---|---|
| Cost of investment | 75,000 |
| Less: Share of net assets of S at the acquisition date (80% × 90,000) | (72,000) |
| Goodwill | 3,000 |

***Note***: This calculation is unaffected by the unrealised profit as the net assets of S at the date of acquisition are sold.

**Step 5**

Minority interest

| | $ |
|---|---|
| Minority share of net assets of S at balance sheet date: | |
| (20% × 99,000) | 19,800 |

**Step 6**

Reserves

Consolidated retained earnings

| | $ |
|---|---|
| P: | 120,000 |
| S: 80% (99,000 – 90,000) | 7,200 |
| | 127,200 |

**Step 7**

**P**

**Consolidated balance sheet at 31 December 20X4**

| | $ |
|---|---|
| Goodwill | 3,000 |
| Inventory (12 + 5 – 1) | 16,000 |
| Other net assets (83 + 95) | 178,000 |
| | 197,000 |
| Share capital | 50,000 |
| Retained earnings | 127,200 |
| Minority interest | 19,800 |
| | 197,000 |

## 4.4 Transfers of non-current assets

The problems involved are similar to those considered under inventory, but there is the added complication of depreciation on the non-current assets.

***Example***

At the beginning of the year S (60% owned by P) transfers an item of plant costing $20,000 to P. P pays $25,000 for the plant, depreciating over five years with a nil scrap value at the end of the period using the straight line basis.

***Solution***

There are two points here:

(a) There is an unrealised profit of $5,000 in the transfer price of the non-current asset.

(b) During the first year in which the plant is used P incurs a depreciation charge of 20% of $25,000. Had the goods been transferred at cost, the depreciation charge would have been only $4,000. This, of course, works in the opposite direction to (a) from the group's viewpoint.

**Step 1**

Calculate the cost and accumulated depreciation on the transferred asset as it stands in the balance sheet.

| | *Per balance sheet* |
|---|---|
| | $ |
| Cost | 25,000 |
| Accumulated depreciation | 5,000 |
| NBV | 20,000 |

**Step 2**

Compare these figures with how the non-current asset would appear had there been no transfer (i.e. how the asset should appear).

| | *Per balance sheet* | *Should be* |
|---|---|---|
| | $ | $ |
| Cost | 25,000 | 20,000 |
| Accumulated depreciation | 5,000 | 4,000 |
| | 20,000 | 16,000 |

**Step 3**

Calculate the adjustments required.

| | *Per balance sheet* | *Should be* | *Adjustment* | | |
|---|---|---|---|---|---|
| | $ | $ | $ | | |
| Cost profit | 25,000 | 20,000 | 5,000 | (a) | Unrealised |
| Accumulated depreciation | 5,000 | 4,000 | 1,000 | (b) | Depreciation overcharge |
| | 20,000 | 16,000 | | | |

**Step 4**

Deal with the adjustments.

(a) Unrealised profit on transfer

An allowance for unrealised profit will be made, which reduces the cost of the non-current asset from its transfer value to the original cost to the group. The debit will either be wholly to consolidated reserves or shared between the group and minority interest depending upon where the original profit was recorded. In this case:

| | | $ | $ |
|---|---|---|---|
| Dr | Consolidated retained earnings (60% × 5,000) | 3,000 | |
| Dr | Minority interest (40% × 5,000) | 2,000 | |
| | Cr Non-current asset cost (allowance for unrealised profit) | | 5,000 |

(b) Each year the allowance for unrealised profit will be reduced by $1,000 to adjust for the excess depreciation charged. The consolidated reserves, and minority interest when appropriate, will be credited. After five years, at the end of the useful life of the asset, the allowance for unrealised profit will be fully written back. In this particular case, the depreciation is charged in P, and therefore the profit adjustment is wholly attributable to the group:

| | | $ | $ |
|---|---|---|---|
| Dr | Accumulated depreciation (allowance for unrealised profit) | 1,000 | |
| | Cr Consolidated retained earnings | | 1,000 |

**Step 5**

The non-current assets section of the balance sheet will show:

| | *Cost* | *Dep'n* | |
|---|---|---|---|
| | $ | $ | $ |
| Non-current assets | | | |
| Plant (25,000 – 5,000) | 20,000 | | |
| (5,000 – 1,000) | | 4,000 | 16,000 |

## 5 Preference shares and loan notes in subsidiaries

### 5.1 Preference shares in a subsidiary company

Preference shares held by one company in another are normally irrelevant in determining whether the parent/subsidiary company relationship exists. This is because preference shares do not normally carry votes and therefore do not normally give control.

KEY POINT

Preference shares held by one company in another are normally irrelevant in determining whether the parent/subsidiary company relationship exists.

Preference shares (sometimes called preferred shares) are either treated as part of equity or as liabilities depending on their characteristics. In this section, we assume that preference shares are part of equity.

This affects the calculations and the consolidation schedules as detailed below.

(a) **Shareholdings in S**

| | *Ordinary shares* | *Preference shares* |
|---|---|---|
| | % | % |
| Group | A | C |
| Minority | B | D |
| | 100 | 100 |

The % holdings of each type of share are calculated.

(b) **Goodwill on consolidation**

| | $ | $ |
|---|---|---|
| Cost of investment (ordinary + preference shares) | | X |
| Less: Share of net assets acquired | | |
| Ordinary share capital | X | |
| Retained earnings | X | |
| | X | |
| Group share | × A% | |
| | | (X) |

| | | |
|---|---|---|
| Preference share capital | X | |
| Group share | × C% | |
| | | (X) |
| Goodwill | | X |

The group shareholding percentage in ordinary shares is applied to the ordinary share capital and reserves, whilst the group shareholding percentage in preference shares is applied to the preference share capital.

(c) **Reserves**

The calculation is performed as usual, taking the ordinary shareholding percentage (A%) of the subsidiary's post-acquisition profits.

(d) **Minority interest**

| | $ | $ |
|---|---|---|
| Net assets of S at the balance sheet date: | | |
| Attributable to ordinary shareholdings: | | |
| Ordinary share capital | X | |
| Retained earnings | X | |
| | X | |
| Minority share | × B% | |
| | | X |
| Attributable to preference shareholdings: | | |
| Preference share capital | X | |
| Minority share | × D% | |
| | | X |
| Total minority interest | | X |

Again, share capital and reserves are split between those attributable to ordinary shareholdings and those attributable to preference shareholdings. The minority interest in each is then found separately.

***Example***

The draft balance sheet of S at 31 January 20X5 is as follows:

| | $ | | $ |
|---|---|---|---|
| Net assets | 180,000 | Ordinary share capital | 100,000 |
| | | Retained earnings | 30,000 |
| | | Preference share capital | 50,000 |
| | 180,000 | | 180,000 |

At 31 January 20X5 P has retained earnings of $150,000. On 31 January 20X2 P acquired 70% of the ordinary share capital of S at a cost of $90,000 and 40% of the preference share capital of S for $22,000. The retained earnings of S at acquisition were $10,000.

Show the consolidation schedules and shareholdings in S.

***Solution***

***Shareholdings in S***

| | *Ordinary shares* | *Preference shares* |
|---|---|---|
| | % | % |
| Group | 70 | 40 |
| Minority | 30 | 60 |
| | 100 | 100 |

***Net assets of S***

| | *At acquisition* | *At balance sheet date* |
|---|---|---|
| | *$* | *$* |
| Attributable to ordinary shareholders: | | |
| Ordinary share capital | 100,000 | 100,000 |
| Retained earnings | 10,000 | 30,000 |
| | 110,000 | 130,000 |
| Attributable to preference shareholders: | | |
| Preference share capital | 50,000 | 50,000 |

***Goodwill***

| | $ |
|---|---|
| Cost of investment (90 + 22) | 112,000 |
| Less: Share of net assets of S at the acquisition date | |
| Ordinary shareholders: (70% × 110,000) | (77,000) |
| Preference shareholders: (40% × 50,000) | (20,000) |
| Goodwill | 15,000 |

*Reserves – consolidated retained earnings*

| | | $ |
|---|---|---|
| P: | | 150,000 |
| S: | 70% (130,000 – 110,000) | 14,000 |
| | | 155,000 |

*Minority interest*

| | $ |
|---|---|
| Net assets of S Limited at balance sheet date: | |
| Attributable to ordinary shareholdings (30% × 130,000) | 39,000 |
| Attributable to preference shareholdings (60% × 50,000) | 30,000 |
| | 69,000 |

***Tutorial note:*** What would happen if P owned 70% of the ordinary share capital of S, but none of the preference share capital? In this case all the nominal value of the preference capital would be dealt with in the minority interest account.

## 5.2 Loan notes in a subsidiary company

Loan notes are irrelevant for the purpose of determining the parent/subsidiary relationship.

***Procedure***

(a) The nominal value of loan notes held by the parent is cancelled with that same value of loan notes of the subsidiary as the balance sheets are cross cast. This leaves the loan notes of the subsidiary, held by outsiders, in the balance sheet.

(b) Loan notes held by outsiders are shown separately on the consolidated balance sheet – they are not part of the minority interest.

***Activity 2***

Maximus acquired 90,000 $1 ordinary shares, and $10,000 loan notes in Minimus on 30 June 20X1.

The balances in the books of Maximus and Minimus as at 31 December 20X4 were as follows:

| | *Maximus* | *Minimus* |
|---|---|---|
| | $ | $ |
| Non-current assets, at cost less depreciation | 380,000 | 225,000 |
| 150,000 ordinary shares in Minimus, at cost | 240,000 | – |
| $10,000 loan notes in Minimus | 10,000 | – |
| Current assets | 200,000 | 143,500 |
| | 830,000 | 368,500 |
| Ordinary shares of $1 | 500,000 | 200,000 |
| 7% loan notes | – | 40,000 |
| Revaluation reserve | 50,000 | 30,000 |
| Retained earnings | 150,000 | 66,000 |
| Payables | 130,000 | 32,500 |
| | 830,000 | 368,500 |

You are also given the following information:

(a) The revaluation reserve and retained earnings of Minimus as at 30 June 20X1 were $12,000 and $30,500 respectively.

(b) The inventory of Minimus at 31 December 20X4 includes $22,800 in respect of goods purchased from Maximus Limited. Maximus invoices Minimus at cost plus 20%.

**You are required** to prepare the consolidated balance sheet of Maximus and its subsidiary Minimus as at 31 December 20X4. Workings should be shown. Follow the step-by-step procedure outlined earlier to tackle this question.

*Feedback to this activity is at the end of the chapter.*

# 6 Dividends and loan interest of subsidiaries

## 6.1 Introduction

Group companies often pay dividends or interest to other group companies. For each dividend or interest payment we need to determine:

- what entries should have been made by each company involved
- what entries have actually been made
- the entries to correct or complete the treatment

and then continue with the consolidation.

## 6.2 Dividends – the correct treatment

Only dividends actually paid in the period are recognised in the financial statements. They are a distribution to the owners of equity shares and are debited against (deducted from) the retained earnings reserve.

IAS 10 (Revised) *Events after the Balance Sheet Date*, states that proposed dividends declared after the balance sheet date (the usual situation) are not recognised as liabilities. This is because they were not an obligation at the balance sheet date. Proposed dividends are disclosed in the notes to the financial statements.

**Dividend paid**

| | | |
|---|---|---|
| Paying company: | Dr | Retained earnings ('Dividend paid') |
| | | Cr Cash |
| Receiving company: | Dr | Cash |
| | | Cr Retained earnings ('Dividend received') |

On consolidating a balance sheet, an adjustment may be required to ensure that both the paying company and the receiving company have accounted for dividends in this way.

### 6.3 Loan interest payable by a subsidiary

Unlike proposed dividends, loan interest is a liability and therefore interest payable is accrued in current liabilities in the paying company's balance sheet.

The receiving company should therefore include its share of the interest receivable at the balance sheet date as a receivable in current assets. On consolidation, only the net amount of interest payable outside the group should be shown as a current liability.

## Summary

- Group financial statements are prepared when the activities of a business are conducted through a number of different companies.
- The usual form of group financial statements is 'consolidated financial statements'. Under this method, the activities of all the group companies are represented as being, in effect, those of a single entity (the group).
- The basic procedure for preparing a consolidated balance sheet is to add together the assets and liabilities shown in the financial statements of each individual company. However, adjustments are necessary to deal with:
  - cancelling items
  - goodwill on acquisition
  - minority interest
  - inter-company transactions.

Having completed your study of this chapter, you should have achieved the following learning outcome:

- prepare a consolidated balance sheet for a group of companies.

## Self-test questions

1. What is the essential feature of a group? (1.1)
2. What is represented by the excess of the price paid over the fair value of the separable net assets acquired? (2.2)
3. What is goodwill? (2.2)
4. What is the accounting treatment for negative goodwill? (2.2)
5. Why must a distinction be drawn between a subsidiary's pre-acquisition and post-acquisition reserves? (2.4)

**6** How are current account balances between the parent and the subsidiary accounted for in drawing up a consolidated balance sheet? (4.2)

**7** If P holds 100% of S's ordinary shares but only 10% of S's loan notes, is S still a subsidiary of P? (5.2)

**8** What is the correct accounting treatment for intra-group dividends paid during an accounting period? (6.2)

## Objective test questions

### Question 1

Vaynor acquired 100,000 ordinary shares in Weeton and 40,000 ordinary shares in Yarlet some years ago. No goodwill arose on the acquisitions.

Extracts from the balance sheets of the three companies as on 30 September 20X7 were:

| | *Vaynor* | *Weeton* | *Yarlet* |
|---|---|---|---|
| | $000 | $000 | $000 |
| Ordinary shares of $1 each | 500 | 100 | 50 |
| Reserves | 90 | 40 | 70 |

At acquisition the reserves of Weeton showed a deficit of $10,000 and of Yarlet a credit balance of $30,000.

What were the consolidated reserves of Vaynor on 30 September 20X7?

### Question 2

Holder acquired 150,000 $1 ordinary shares in Sub on 1 July 20X6 at a cost of $300,000. Sub's retained earnings at 1 July 20X6 were $36,000 and its issued ordinary share capital was $200,000.

The amount of goodwill arising on consolidation is:

**A** $64,000

**B** $84,000

**C** $123,000

**D** $138,000

### Question 3

Castor acquires 75% of the share capital of Pollux on 1 December 20X1. The consideration given is $1 million in cash and 300,000 $1 ordinary shares of Castor. The market value of each of Castor's shares on 1 December is $3.00. On 1 December the fair value of Pollux's net assets is $1 million.

What is the amount of goodwill on acquisition to be dealt with in Castor's consolidated accounts?

*For the answers to these questions, see the 'Answers' section at the end of the book.*

# Practice question

## Oak and Chestnut

The draft balance sheets of Oak and its subsidiary Chestnut at 30 September 20X8 are as follows:

| | Oak | | Chestnut | |
|---|---|---|---|---|
| | $ | $ | $ | $ |
| **ASSETS** | | | | |
| **Non-current assets** | | | | |
| Tangible assets, net book value | | | | |
| Land and buildings | | 225,000 | | 270,000 |
| Plant | | 202,500 | | 157,500 |
| | | 427,500 | | 427,500 |
| Investment | | | | |
| Shares in Chestnut at cost | | 562,500 | | |
| **Current assets** | | | | |
| Inventory | 255,000 | | 180,000 | |
| Receivables | 375,000 | | 90,000 | |
| Bank | 112,500 | | 22,500 | |
| | | 742,500 | | 292,500 |
| **Total assets** | | 1,732,500 | | 720,000 |
| **EQUITY AND LIABILITIES** | | | | |
| **Equity** | | | | |
| $1 ordinary shares fully paid | | 1,125,000 | | 450,000 |
| Reserves | | 450,000 | | 202,500 |
| | | 1,575,000 | | 652,500 |
| **Current liabilities** | | 157,500 | | 67,500 |
| Total equity and liabilities | | 1,732,500 | | 720,000 |

The following information is also available.

(i) Oak purchased 360,000 shares in Chestnut some years ago when that company had a credit balance of $105,000 in reserves. The goodwill had been fully written down through the income statement by 30 September 20X7.

(ii) For the purpose of the takeover, the land of Chestnut was revalued at $120,000 in excess of its book value. This was not reflected in the accounts of Chestnut. Land is not depreciated.

(iii) At 30 September 20X8 Chestnut owed Oak $15,000 for goods purchased.

(iv) The inventory of Chestnut includes goods purchased from Oak at a price which includes a profit to Oak of $10,500.

**Required:**

(a) Prepare the consolidated balance sheet for Oak as at 30 September 20X8. **(20 marks)**

(b) Explain the accounting treatment of inter-company trading transactions and balances when consolidating accounts. Use the data for the companies in this question to illustrate your answer. **(5 marks)**

**(Total: 25 marks)**

*For the answer to this question, see the 'Answers' section at the end of the book.*

## Feedback to activities

### Activity 1

***Note:*** Your balance sheets should be prepared in vertical format. The examiner will occasionally give you 'draft' horizontal balance sheets as in the question, but your solution should always accord with best practice.

(a) **Step 1**

Group structure

P
|     100%
S

**Step 2**

Net assets

| | *At acquisition* | *At balance sheet date* |
|---|---|---|
| | $ | $ |
| Share capital | 20,000 | 20,000 |
| Retained earnings | 6,000 | 6,500 |
| | 26,000 | 26,500 |

**Step 3**

Goodwill

| | $ |
|---|---|
| Cost of investment | 27,000 |
| Less: Share of net assets of S at the acquisition date (100% × 26,000) | (26,000) |
| Goodwill | 1,000 |

**Step 4**

Minority interest

There is no minority interest at the balance sheet date as P owns 100% of the shares of S.

**Step 5**

Reserves

Consolidated retained earnings

| | $ |
|---|---|
| P: | 22,000 |
| S: 100% (26,500 – 26,000) | 500 |
| | 22,500 |

**Step 6**

**P Group: Consolidated balance sheet at 31 December 20X4**

| | $ |
|---|---|
| Goodwill | 1,000 |
| Sundry assets | 140,500 |
| | 141,500 |
| Share capital | 100,000 |
| Retained earnings | 22,500 |
| Current liabilities | 19,000 |
| | 141,500 |

(b) **Step 1**

Group structure

P
|    80%
S

**Step 2**

Net assets

| | *At acquisition* $ | *At balance sheet date* $ |
|---|---|---|
| Share capital | 20,000 | 20,000 |
| Retained earnings | 6,000 | 6,500 |
| | 26,000 | 26,500 |

**Step 3**

Goodwill

| | $ |
|---|---|
| Cost of investment | 27,000 |
| Less: Share of net assets of S at the acquisition date (80% × 26,000) | (20,800) |
| Goodwill | 6,200 |

**Step 4**

Minority interest

| | $ |
|---|---|
| Minority share of net assets of S at balance sheet date: | |
| (20% × 26,500) | 5,300 |

**Step 5**

Reserves

Consolidated retained earnings

| | $ |
|---|---|
| P: | 22,000 |
| S: 80% (26,500 – 26,000) | 400 |
| | 22,400 |

**Step 6**

**P Group: Consolidated balance sheet at 31 December 20X4**

| | $ |
|---|---|
| Goodwill | 6,200 |
| Sundry assets | 140,500 |
| | 146,700 |
| Share capital | 100,000 |
| Retained earnings | 22,400 |
| Minority interest | 5,300 |
| Current liabilities | 19,000 |
| | 146,700 |

(c) **Step 1**

Group structure

P
|  80%
S

**Step 2**

Net assets

| | *At acquisition* | *At balance sheet date* |
|---|---|---|
| | $ | $ |
| Share capital | 20,000 | 20,000 |
| Retained earnings | 6,000 | 6,500 |
| Fair value adjustment | 5,000 | 5,000 |
| | 31,000 | 31,500 |

**Step 3**

Goodwill

| | $ |
|---|---|
| Cost of investment | 27,000 |
| Less: Share of net assets of S at the acquisition date (80% × 31,000) | (24,800) |
| Goodwill | 2,200 |

**Step 4**

Minority interest

| | $ |
|---|---|
| Minority share of net assets of S at balance sheet date: (20% × 31,500) | 6,300 |

**Step 5**

Reserves

Revaluation reserve

This is an entirely pre-acquisition reserve and therefore none will be included in group reserves.

Consolidated retained earnings

| | $ |
|---|---|
| P: | 22,000 |
| S: 80% (31,500 – 31,000) | 400 |
| | 22,400 |

**Step 6**

**P Group: Consolidated balance sheet at 31 December 20X4**

| | $ |
|---|---|
| Goodwill | 2,200 |
| Sundry assets (106,000 + 34,500 + 5,000) | 145,500 |
| | 147,700 |
| Share capital | 100,000 |
| Retained earnings | 22,400 |
| Minority interest | 6,300 |
| Current liabilities (11,000 + 8,000) | 19,000 |
| | 147,700 |

## Activity 2

**Step 1**

**Establish the group structure**

Maximus

| 75%

Minimus

**Step 2**

Adjustments

Unrealised profit on inventory $= \frac{20}{120} \times \$22{,}800 = \$3{,}800$

The profit was made by Maximus, therefore the retained earnings of Maximus are reduced.

**Step 3**

Net assets

| | *At acquisition* | *At balance sheet date* |
|---|---|---|
| | $ | $ |
| Share capital | 200,000 | 200,000 |
| Revaluation reserve | 12,000 | 30,000 |
| Retained earnings | 30,500 | 66,000 |
| | 242,500 | 296,000 |

**Step 4**

Goodwill

| | $ |
|---|---|
| Cost of investment | 240,000 |
| Less: Share of net assets of S at the acquisition date (75% × 242,500) | (181,875) |
| Goodwill | 58,125 |

**Step 5**

Minority interest

| | $ |
|---|---|
| Minority share of net assets of S at balance sheet date: (25% × 296,000) | 74,000 |

**Step 6**

Reserves

Revaluation reserve

| | $ |
|---|---|
| P: | 50,000 |
| S: 75% (30,000 – 12,000) | 13,500 |
| | 63,500 |

Consolidated retained earnings

| | $ |
|---|---|
| P: (150,000 – 3,800) | 146,200 |
| S: 75% (66,000 – 30,500) | 26,625 |
| | 172,825 |

**Note:** because the revaluation reserve of Minimus has increased since acquisition consolidated retained earnings and the consolidated revaluation reserve must be calculated separately.

**Step 7**

Prepare the consolidated balance sheet.

**Consolidated balance sheet of Maximus and its subsidiary, Minimus at 31 December 20X4**

| | $ | $ |
|---|---|---|
| Non-current assets: | | |
| Tangible assets: | | |
| Cost, less depreciation | 605,000 | |
| Intangible assets | | |
| Goodwill | 58,125 | |
| | | 663,125 |
| Current assets (200,000 + 143,500 – 3,800) | | 339,700 |
| | | 1,002,825 |
| Equity: | | |
| Ordinary share capital | | 500,000 |
| Revaluation surplus | | 63,500 |
| Retained earnings | | 172,825 |
| | | 736,325 |
| Minority interest | | 74,000 |
| Non-current liabilities | | |
| 7% loan notes (40,000 – 10,000) | | 30,000 |
| Current liabilities | | 162,500 |
| | | 1,002,825 |

Chapter 3

# FAIR VALUE AND GOODWILL

## Syllabus content

- The preparation of consolidated financial statements (including the group cash flow statement) involving one or more subsidiaries, sub-subsidiaries and associates, under the acquisition and pooling of interests methods (IAS 7 & 27 and IFRS 3).
- The treatment in consolidated financial statements of minority interests, pre and post- acquisition reserves, goodwill (including its impairment), fair value adjustments, intra-group transactions and dividends, piece-meal and mid-year acquisitions, and disposals to include sub-subsidiaries and mixed groups.

## Contents

## Introduction

This chapter looks in more detail at two very important aspects of preparing a balance sheet for a group.

When one company acquires a subsidiary, the assets and liabilities of the subsidiary must be included in the consolidated financial statements at their fair values. As you have already learned, goodwill arises on consolidation, and this is measured as the difference between the fair value of the purchase consideration (normally cash, equity shares, or a combination of these) and the fair value of the assets and liabilities acquired.

This chapter considers the requirements of IFRS 3 *Business Combinations*. It also briefly covers a further standard that is relevant in dealing with goodwill: IAS 36 *Impairment of Assets*.

# 1 IFRS 3 *Business Combinations*

## 1.1 Objectives

DEFINITION

A **business combination** is the bringing together of separate entities or businesses into one reporting entity. Business combinations arise when one or more companies become subsidiaries of another company.

A **business combination** is the bringing together of separate entities or businesses into one reporting entity. Business combinations arise when one or more companies become subsidiaries of another company.

IFRS 3 was issued early in 2004. It sets out the way in which business combinations should be reported in the financial statements. It states that:

- all business combinations should be accounted for by applying the **purchase method**
- the acquirer recognises the acquiree's identifiable assets, liabilities and contingent liabilities at their fair values at the acquisition date, and
- the acquirer also recognises **goodwill**, which is capitalised (recognised in the balance sheet) and subsequently tested for impairment rather than amortised.

The purchase method is the method of preparing consolidated financial statements that was covered in the previous chapter. In theory there are other methods that could be used, but IFRS 3 does not allow them.

The topics of fair value and goodwill are covered in detail later in this chapter.

## 1.2 Identifying the acquirer

KEY POINT

An acquirer must be identified for all business combinations. The acquirer is the combining entity that obtains control of the other combining entities.

In order to apply the purchase method, an acquirer must be identified for all business combinations. The acquirer is the combining entity that obtains control of the other combining entities or businesses. **Control** is the power to govern the financial and operating policies of an entity or business so as to obtain benefits from its activities.

In most cases it is fairly obvious which entity is the acquirer. However, sometimes it may be difficult to identify an acquirer. IFRS 3 provides guidance in this situation:

(a) if the fair value of one of the combining entities is significantly greater than that of the other combining entity, the entity with the greater fair value is likely to be the acquirer

(b) if the business combination is effected through an exchange of voting ordinary equity instruments for cash or other assets, the entity giving up cash or other assets is likely to be the acquirer, and

(c) if the business combination results in the management of one of the combining entities being able to dominate the selection of the management team of the resulting combined entity, the entity whose management can dominate is likely to be the acquirer.

KEY POINT

It can be particularly difficult to identify an acquirer in a business combination effected through an exchange of equity shares. In this situation, the entity that issues the equity shares is normally the acquirer.

Sometimes a business combination is carried out through an exchange of equity shares. For example, X can acquire equity shares in Y by issuing equity shares to the shareholders of Y instead of paying for the shares in cash. It can be particularly difficult to identify an acquirer in this situation.

IFRS 3 provides guidance:

(a) The entity that issues the equity shares is normally the acquirer.

(b) Where the identity of the acquirer is not clear, it is necessary to consider all pertinent facts and circumstances so as to determine which of the combining entities has the power to govern the financial and operating policies of the other entity (or entities) so as to obtain benefits from its (or their) activities.

### 1.3 Disclosure

IFRS 3 contains extensive disclosure requirements. It requires an acquirer to disclose information that enables users of its financial statements to evaluate:

(a) the nature and financial effect of business combinations that were effected:

(i) during the period

(ii) after the balance sheet date but before the financial statements were authorised for issue

(b) the financial effects of gains, losses, error corrections and other adjustments recognised in the current period that relate to business combinations that were effected in the current or in previous periods

(c) changes in the carrying amount of goodwill during the period.

## 2 Fair value adjustments

### 2.1 Introduction

DEFINITION

**Fair value** is the amount at which an asset could be exchanged or a liability settled, between knowledgeable, willing parties in an arm's length transaction

**Fair value** is the amount at which an asset could be exchanged or a liability settled, between knowledgeable, willing parties in an arm's length transaction.

In order to account for an acquisition, the acquiring company must measure the cost of what it is accounting for, which will normally represent:

- the cost of the investment in its own balance sheet; and
- the amount to be allocated between the identifiable net assets of the subsidiary and goodwill in the consolidated financial statements.

The subsidiary's identifiable assets and liabilities are included in the consolidated accounts at their fair values for the following reasons.

- Consolidated accounts are prepared from the perspective of the group, rather than from the perspectives of the individual companies. The book values of the subsidiary's assets and liabilities are largely irrelevant, because the consolidated accounts must reflect their cost to the group (i.e. to the parent), not their original cost to the subsidiary. The cost to the group is their fair value.
- Purchased goodwill is the difference between the cost of an acquired entity and the aggregate of the fair values of that entity's identifiable assets and liabilities. If fair values are not used, the value of goodwill will be meaningless.

KEY POINT

Applying the purchase method involves the following steps:
(a) identifying an acquirer
(b) measuring the cost of the business combination, and
(c) allocating the cost of the business combination to the assets acquired and liabilities assumed.

Therefore applying the purchase method involves the following steps:

(a) identifying an acquirer (see previous chapter)

(b) measuring the cost of the business combination, and

(c) allocating, at the acquisition date, the cost of the business combination to the assets acquired and liabilities assumed.

### 2.2 Cost of a business combination

DEFINITION

The **acquisition date** is the date on which the acquirer effectively obtains control of the acquiree.

The cost of a business combination consists of:

(a) the fair values, at the date of exchange (normally the acquisition date), of assets given, liabilities incurred or assumed, and equity instruments issued by the acquirer, in exchange for control of the acquiree; plus

(b) any costs directly attributable to the business combination.

The **acquisition date** is the date on which the acquirer effectively obtains control of the acquiree.

KEY POINT

In practice, the cost of a business combination usually consists of cash, equity shares or a combination of the two.

In practice, the cost of a business combination usually consists of cash, equity shares or a combination of the two. IFRS 3 sets out the following rules.

***Deferred consideration***

Sometimes all or part of the consideration (usually the cash element) does not become payable until a later date.

When settlement of any part of the cost of a business combination is deferred, the fair value of the deferred consideration is determined by discounting the amounts payable to their present value at the date of exchange.

***Equity instruments***

The fair value of quoted equity instruments is taken as the published price at the date of exchange, except in rare circumstances.

***Future losses and other costs incurred as a result of a combination***

Future losses or other costs expected to be incurred as a result of a combination are not liabilities incurred or assumed by the acquirer in exchange for control of the acquiree (see the IASB *Framework*). Therefore they are not included in the cost of the combination.

***Costs of the combination***

The cost of a business combination includes any costs directly attributable to the combination, for example professional fees paid to accountants, legal advisers, valuers and other consultants. Costs that cannot be directly attributed to the combination (for example, general administrative costs) should not be included in the cost of the combination. Instead they are recognised as an expense when incurred.

Issue costs of financial liabilities and equity shares are not included in the cost of acquisition. These are included in the initial measurement of the liability or deducted from the proceeds of the share issue, as required by IAS 32 and IAS 39 (see Chapter 14).

***Adjustments to the cost of a business combination contingent on future events***

A business combination agreement may allow for adjustments to the cost of the combination that are contingent on (that depend on) one or more future events. For example, the final amount to be paid might depend on a specified level of profit being maintained or achieved in future periods.

In this situation, the adjustment should be included in the cost of the combination at the acquisition date if the adjustment is probable and can be measured reliably. **Probable** means more likely than not.

## 2.3 Recognition of identifiable assets and liabilities

The acquirer should recognise the identifiable assets, liabilities and contingent liabilities that it has acquired at their fair values at the acquisition date if they satisfy the following criteria:

(a) in the case of an asset other than an intangible asset, it is probable that any associated future economic benefits will flow to the acquirer, and its fair value can be measured reliably

(b) in the case of a liability other than a contingent liability, it is probable that an outflow of resources embodying economic benefits will be required to settle the obligation, and its fair value can be measured reliably

(c) in the case of an intangible asset or a contingent liability, its fair value can be measured reliably.

Net assets which meet these recognition criteria are described as **identifiable** assets and liabilities. Where net assets are acquired which do not meet these criteria, they are treated as part of purchased goodwill, since goodwill is determined as the difference between the fair value of the price paid and the fair value of the identifiable net assets acquired.

## 2.4 The determination of fair values

General guidelines in IFRS 3 are as follows.

(a) Marketable securities should be valued at current market value.

(b) Non-marketable securities should be valued at estimated value. Estimates should take into account price-earnings ratios, dividend yields and expected growth rates of comparable securities.

(c) Receivables should be valued at the present value of amounts expected to be received. Discounting is unlikely to be necessary for short-term receivables.

(d) Inventories:

  (i) finished goods should be valued at selling prices less the sum of disposal costs and a reasonable profit allowance

  (ii) work in progress should be valued at ultimate selling prices less the sum of completion costs, disposal costs and a reasonable profit allowance

  (iii) raw materials should be valued at current replacement costs.

(e) Property, plant and equipment should be valued at market value. If there is no market value because of the specialised nature of the item and the item is rarely sold, fair value may need to be estimated using depreciated replacement cost or similar.

(f) Intangible assets should be valued at market value, or if no active market exists, on a basis that reflects the amounts the acquirer would have paid for the assets in arm's length transactions between knowledgeable willing parties, based on the best information available.

(g) Employee benefit plans should be valued at the present value of the defined benefit obligation less the fair value of any plan assets. Assets should only be recognised if it is probable they will be available to the acquirer in the form of refunds or a reduction in future contributions.

(h) Tax assets and liabilities should be valued at the amount of the tax benefit arising from tax losses or the taxes payable in respect of profit or loss in accordance with IAS 12 *Income Taxes*, assessed from the perspective of the combined entity.

(i) Payables should be valued at the present value of amounts expected to be paid. As with receivables, discounting will not be necessary for short-term payables.

(j) Onerous contracts and other identifiable liabilities should be valued at the present values of amounts expected to be paid.

(k) Contingent liabilities should be valued at the amount that a third party would charge to assume those contingent liabilities. Such an amount should reflect all expectations about possible cash flows and not the single most likely or the expected maximum or minimum cash flow.

### 2.5 Problem areas

KEY POINT

The broad principle is that only assets and liabilities that existed **at the date of acquisition** can be recognised.

The broad principle is that only assets and liabilities that existed **at the date of acquisition** can be recognised.

Therefore, for example, a provision for future operating losses or for the costs of restructuring the group after the acquisition cannot be recognised, because this is not a liability of the group or the acquirer at the acquisition date.

KEY POINT

IFRS 3 ensures that the cost of reorganising or restructuring a group is recognised as a post-acquisition expense.

This rule prevents 'creative accounting'. If an acquirer recognises a provision for restructuring costs, the provision reduces goodwill, but does not affect the income statement in the period in which the acquisition takes place. The provision is then released to the income statement in future periods and is used to smooth profits or disguise losses arising after the acquisition. IFRS 3 ensures that the cost of reorganising or restructuring a group is recognised as a post-acquisition expense.

Two other potential problem areas are considered below.

***Intangible assets***

Intangible assets may only be recognised if they are identifiable. An intangible asset is identifiable only if it:

(a) is separable, i.e. capable of being separated or divided from the entity and sold, transferred, licensed, rented or exchanged, either individually or together with a related contract, asset or liability; or

(b) arises from contractual or other legal rights, regardless of whether those rights are transferable or separable from the entity or from other rights and obligations.

***Contingent liabilities***

Contingent liabilities of the acquirer are recognised if their fair value can be measured reliably.

Note that this is an exception to the usual rule in IAS 37 *Provisions, Contingent Liabilities and Contingent Assets*, whereby contingent liabilities are not recognised, but only disclosed.

After their initial recognition, the acquirer should measure contingent liabilities that are recognised separately at the higher of:

(a) the amount that would be recognised in accordance with IAS 37; and

(b) the amount initially recognised.

If fair value cannot be measured reliably the acquirer must disclose the information required by IAS 37.

## 2.6 Example

Joynt acquired 85% of Goulding.

- At acquisition the balance sheet of Goulding showed net assets with a book value of £1,305,000. Included in this total are freehold land with a book value of £300,000 (market value £720,000), patents with a book value of £175,000 (market value £200,000) and goodwill (arising on the acquisition of an unincorporated business some years ago) with a book value of £350,000. The fair value of all other assets and liabilities is approximately equal to book value.
- The directors of Joynt intend to close down one of the divisions of Goulding and wish to provide for operating losses up to the date of closure which are forecast as £29,000.
- An investment in plant and machinery will be required to bring the remaining production line of Goulding up to date. This will amount to £220,000 in the next 12 months.
- In addition, the costs of reorganising Goulding to reflect the corporate image of Joynt are estimated at £70,000.
- The consideration comprised cash of £90,000 and 900,000 shares with a nominal value of 25p and fair value of 130p each.
- The costs of the share issue were £37,000, and professional fees to bankers and solicitors in respect of the acquisition amounted to £75,000. In addition, the finance director of Joynt has estimated that the time and expenses incurred by the directors of Joynt in negotiating and completing the deal amounted to £16,000.

**Required:**

Calculate goodwill arising on consolidation.

## 2.7 Solution

Net assets acquired at fair value:

| | £ |
|---|---|
| Net assets at book value | 1,305,000 |
| Fair value adjustments: | |
| Freehold land (720-300) | 420,000 |
| Patents (200-175) | 25,000 |
| Goodwill | (350,000) |
| Net assets at fair value | 1,400,000 |

The fair value adjustments derive from IFRS 3 requirements.

- Freehold land is valued at market value.
- Intangibles (patents) are valued at estimated market value.
- Goodwill is not an identifiable asset and must therefore be written off.
- The closure of the division, the investment in plant, and the reorganisation costs are quite clearly post-acquisition and will therefore be specifically excluded.

Goodwill:

| Purchase consideration | £ |
|---|---|
| Cash | 90,000 |
| Shares (900,000 × £1.30) | 1,170,000 |
| Professional fees | 75,000 |
| | 1,335,000 |
| Net assets acquired (85% × 1,400,000) | (1,190,000) |
| Goodwill | 145,000 |

**Explanation**

- Cash is always at fair value!
- Shares are valued at market value.
- Direct fees only are allowed.
- The costs of issuing shares are excluded.

### *Activity 1*

X acquired 80% of the ordinary share capital of Y on 30 September 20X4 for $320,000.

The net assets in the draft accounts of Y at that date were $350,000.

The following information is relevant.

(a) Y owns its factory which is included in the accounts at $100,000 and no adjustment has been made to recognise the valuation of $120,000 put on the property when it was professionally revalued on 15 September 20X4.

(b) The fair value of Y's inventory at 30 September 20X4 is estimated to be $4,000 less than its book value at that date.

(c) In August 20X4 Y announced its decision to close down a small workshop with the loss of some jobs. The net costs of closure are estimated at $10,000. No provision has been made at 30 September 20X4.

What is the goodwill arising on the acquisition of Y?

*Feedback to this activity is at the end of the chapter.*

## 2.8 Where fair values are provisional

**KEY POINT**

It may be necessary to use provisional amounts when accounting for the acquisition for the first time and to adjust them subsequently, when more information is available.

Determining fair values for the purchase consideration and the net assets acquired can be a complex exercise. It may be necessary to use provisional amounts when accounting for the acquisition for the first time and to adjust them subsequently, when more information is available.

IFRS 3 allows the use of provisional values and states that the acquirer shall recognise any adjustments to those provisional values as a result of completing the initial accounting:

(a) within 12 months of the acquisition date; and

(b) from the acquisition date. Therefore:

  (i) the carrying amount of an identifiable asset, liability or contingent liability that is recognised or adjusted as a result of completing the initial accounting should be calculated as if its fair value at the acquisition date had been recognised from that date

  (ii) goodwill should be adjusted from the acquisition date by an amount equal to the adjustment to the fair value at the acquisition date of the identifiable asset, liability or contingent liability being recognised or adjusted

  (iii) comparative information presented for the periods before the initial accounting for the combination is complete should be presented as if the initial accounting had been completed from the acquisition date, including any additional depreciation, or other profit or loss effect recognised as a result of completing the initial accounting.

No further adjustments can be recognised after the 12-month period has elapsed, unless they are necessary to correct an error.

## 2.9 Dealing with fair value adjustments in the consolidated balance sheet

**KEY POINT**

In order to deal correctly with fair value adjustments, we need to calculate the net assets of the subsidiary:

(a) at acquisiton; and

(b) at the balance sheet date.

As we have seen, fair value adjustments affect the goodwill calculation. They also affect the consolidated balance sheet, for the period of the acquisition and in subsequent periods.

In order to deal correctly with fair value adjustments, we need to calculate the net assets of the subsidiary:

(a) at acquisition; and

(b) at the balance sheet date.

The amounts to be included as fair value adjustments may well have changed between these two dates. For example:

(a) inventory is normally sold within 12 months

(b) non-current assets are depreciated

(c) where long-term loans are discounted to net present value, the discount unwinds and net present value increases in subsequent periods.

### *Example*

Hazlenut acquired 80% of the share capital of Peppermint two years ago, when the reserves of Peppermint stood at $125,000.

Hazlenut paid an initial cash consideration of $1 million. Additionally, Hazlenut issued 200,000 shares with a nominal value of $1 and a current market value of $1.80. It was also agreed that Hazlenut would pay a further $500,000 in three years' time. Current interest rates are 10% per annum.

Below are the balance sheets of Hazlenut and Peppermint as at 31 December 20X4:

| | *Hazlenut* | *Peppermint* |
|---|---|---|
| | $000 | $000 |
| Non-current assets | 5,500 | 1,500 |
| Investment in Caramel at cost | 1,000 | |
| | 6,500 | 1,500 |
| Current assets | | |
| Inventory | 550 | 100 |
| Receivables | 400 | 200 |
| Cash | 200 | 50 |
| | 1,150 | 350 |
| | 7,650 | 1,850 |
| Equity | | |
| Share capital | 2,000 | 500 |
| Retained earnings | 1,400 | 300 |
| | 3,400 | 800 |
| Non-current liabilities | 3,000 | 400 |
| Current liabilities | 1,250 | 650 |
| | 7,650 | 1,850 |

At acquisition the fair values of Peppermint's non-current assets exceeded their book value by $200,000. They had a remaining useful life of five years at this date.

Goodwill has suffered an impairment of $215,000 since the acquisition.

**Requirement:**

Prepare the consolidated balance sheet as at 31 December 20X4.

***Solution***

**Step 1 Group structure**

Hazlenut

| 80%
| 2 years ago

Peppermint

**Step 2 Calculate net assets at acquisition and at the balance sheet date**

Non-current assets have been revalued upwards at the acquisition date. This means that there will be additional depreciation on the fair value adjustment. This reduces the carrying amount of non-current assets and also consolidated retained earnings (the depreciation is charged post-acquisition).

| | *Acquisition* | *B/S date* |
|---|---|---|
| | $000 | $000 |
| Share capital | 500 | 500 |
| Retained earnings | 125 | 300 |
| Fair value adjustment | 200 | 200 |
| Depreciation adjustment (200 × 2/5) | | (80) |
| | 825 | 920 |

**Step 3 Calculate goodwill**

The cost of the investment in Hazlenut's balance sheet is $1 million i.e. the cash consideration paid. Hazlenut has not yet recorded the other consideration of shares and deferred consideration. The following adjustments are needed:

| | | | |
|---|---|---|---|
| Dr | Investment | $360,000 | |
| | Cr Share Capital | | $200,000 |
| | Cr Share Premium | | $160,000 |

To record the share issue

| | | | |
|---|---|---|---|
| Dr | Investment | $376,000 | |
| | Cr Deferred consideration | | $376,000 |

To record the deferred consideration.

Note that the deferred consideration is discounted to its present value.

| | $000 |
|---|---|
| Cost of investment | |
| Cash | 1,000 |
| Shares (200 × 1.80) | 360 |
| Deferred consideration ($500 \times 1/1.1^3$) | 376 |
| | 1,736 |
| FV of net assets acquired (80% × 825) | (660) |
| Goodwill | 1,076 |
| Impairment loss | (215) |
| Goodwill | 861 |

**Step 4 Calculate minority interests**

| | $000 |
|---|---|
| Net assets at balance sheet date | 920 |
| MI share (20%) | 184 |

**Step 5 Deal with the unwinding of the discount**

At acquisition, Hazlenut should recognise a liability of $376,000 – being the present value of the future cash flow at that date.

At the balance sheet date there is only one year to go until the deferred consideration will be paid. Therefore the liability in Hazlenut's balance sheet at this date is $500 \times 1/1.1^1 = 455$.

The following adjustment is needed:

| | |
|---|---|
| Dr Consolidated retained earnings | $79,000 |
| Cr Deferred consideration liability | $79,000 |

To record the unwinding of the discount (455 – 376)

**Step 6 Calculate the retained earnings reserve**

| | $000 |
|---|---|
| Hazlenut (1,400 – 79) | 1,321 |
| Peppermint (80% × (920 – 825)) | 76 |
| Impairment | (215) |
| | 1,182 |

We can now draw up the consolidated balance sheet.

**Consolidated balance sheet at 31 December 20X4**

| | $000 |
|---|---|
| Non-current assets: | |
| Tangible assets (5,500 + 1,500 + 200 – 80) | 7,120 |
| Goodwill | 861 |
| | 7,981 |
| Current assets | |
| Inventory (550 + 100) | 650 |
| Receivables (400 + 200) | 600 |
| Cash (200 + 50) | 250 |
| | 1,500 |
| Total assets | 9,481 |
| Equity: | |
| Share capital (2,000 + 200) | 2,200 |
| Share premium | 160 |
| Retained earnings | 1,182 |
| | 3,542 |
| Minority interests | 184 |

| | |
|---|---|
| Total equity | 3,726 |
| Non-current liabilities | 3,400 |
| Current liabilities: | |
| Trade and other payables (1,250 + 650) | 1,900 |
| Deferred consideration (376 + 79) | 455 |
| | 2,355 |
| Total liabilities | 5,755 |
| | 9,481 |

# 3 Goodwill

## 3.1 Initial recognition

DEFINITION

IFRS 3 defines **goodwill** as future economic benefits arising from assets that are not capable of being individually identified and separately recognised.

IFRS 3 defines **goodwill** as future economic benefits arising from assets that are not capable of being individually identified and separately recognised.

In the context of an acquisition, goodwill is the difference between the cost of an acquired entity and the total of the fair values of that entity's identifiable assets and liabilities.

IFRS 3 states that an acquirer should recognise goodwill acquired in a business combination as an asset. Goodwill is included in the balance sheet and reported as an intangible non-current asset.

Goodwill is measured at its cost, which is the excess of the cost of the business combination over the acquirer's interest in the net fair value of the identifiable assets, liabilities and contingent liabilities of the acquired entity.

An acquired entity may have identifiable assets and liabilities that cannot be recognised, for example because their fair value cannot be measured reliably. These are included within purchased goodwill. Examples of assets which may need to be included within purchased goodwill include a subsidiary's own internally generated goodwill and internally generated brand names if these exist.

## 3.2 Subsequent accounting treatment

KEY POINT

IFRS 3 states that after initial recognition, the acquirer should measure goodwill acquired in a business combination at cost less any accumulated impairment losses.

KEY POINT

Goodwill is not amortised (depreciated). Instead, it is tested for impairment annually.

IFRS 3 states that after initial recognition, the acquirer should measure goodwill acquired in a business combination at cost less any accumulated impairment losses.

This means that, unlike most other non-current assets, goodwill is not amortised (depreciated). Instead, it is tested for impairment annually, or more frequently if events or changes in circumstances indicate that it might be impaired, in accordance with IAS 36 *Impairment of Assets*. The procedure for doing this is covered later in the chapter.

If goodwill is not impaired, it continues to be carried in the balance sheet at cost. If goodwill is found to be impaired (to have lost value) it is written down to its recoverable amount. The impairment is recognised in the income statement as an expense.

IFRS 3 replaced IAS 22, which required straight line amortisation of goodwill arising on a business combination. Under IAS 22 goodwill was assumed to have a useful economic life of 20 years or less, but in exceptional circumstances a longer period could be used provided that this treatment could be justified and that annual impairment tests were carried out.

Arguments for amortisation of goodwill include:

(a) Amortisation reflects what happens to goodwill after it is acquired. It is consumed and replaced with internally generated goodwill. As internally generated goodwill cannot be recognised, amortisation ensures that the acquired goodwill is recognised in profit or loss and no internally generated goodwill is recognised as an asset in its place.

(b) It allocates the cost of acquired goodwill over the periods it is consumed. Therefore it is consistent with the treatment of other intangible and tangible fixed assets that do not have indefinite useful lives.

(c) The useful life of acquired goodwill cannot be predicted with a satisfactory level of reliability, nor can the pattern in which that goodwill diminishes be known. However, systematic amortisation over an arbitrary period provides the only practical solution to an intractable problem.

In spite of these arguments, IFRS 3 prohibits amortisation of goodwill. The reasoning behind this was that it is impossible to predict the useful economic life of goodwill or the pattern in which it is consumed. Therefore amortisation does not provide useful information to users of the financial statements. There are other arguments against amortisation:

(a) The amortisation charge reflects the consumption of acquired goodwill, whilst the internally generated goodwill replacing it is not recognised. Again, this treatment is inconsistent and fails to provide useful information.

(b) The useful life of a tangible non-current asset can only be finite, because the asset will eventually physically wear out. Therefore amortisation of tangible assets makes sense. In contrast, goodwill does not physically wear out and therefore there may be no upper limit on its useful life. Therefore it is not appropriate to amortise goodwill.

KEY POINT

The IASB concluded that carrying goodwill in the balance sheet subject to impairment testing would provide more useful information to users and would be more conceptually sound than amortisation.

The IASB concluded that carrying goodwill in the balance sheet subject to impairment testing would provide more useful information to users and would be more conceptually sound than amortisation. The disadvantage of this approach is that testing for impairment can be difficult and impractical, especially for smaller entities. However, the IASB believes that the benefits of this approach outweigh the disadvantages.

### 3.3 Excess of acquirer's interest in the net fair value of acquiree's identifiable assets, liabilities and contingent liabilities over cost

Sometimes the group's share of the fair values of an acquiree's net assets is greater than the cost of the investment. This may happen because:

(a) there have been errors in measuring the fair value of either the cost of the combination or the acquiree's identifiable assets; or

(b) the group has made a bargain purchase (for example, because the acquired entity has been making losses).

KEY POINT

Negative goodwill is included in the income statement as a gain.

The excess of the acquirer's share in the acquired net assets over cost is sometimes called **negative goodwill**.

IFRS 3 states that in this situation, the acquirer should first reassess the identification and measurement of the acquiree's identifiable assets, liabilities and contingent liabilities and the measurement of the cost of the combination. This will identify any errors.

Any excess remaining is then recognised immediately in profit or loss. In other words, negative goodwill is included in the income statement as a gain.

### 3.4 Disclosure

IFRS 3 requires an entity to disclose information that enables users of its financial statements to evaluate changes in the carrying amount of goodwill during the period.

This includes a reconciliation of the carrying amount of goodwill at the beginning and end of the period, showing separately:

(a) the gross amount and accumulated impairment losses at the beginning of the period

(b) additional goodwill recognised during the period

(c) goodwill included in a disposal group classified as held for sale in accordance with IFRS 5 and goodwill derecognised during the period

(d) impairment losses recognised during the period in accordance with IAS 36

(e) net exchange differences arising during the period in accordance with IAS 21 *The Effects of Changes in Foreign Exchange Rates*

(f) any other changes in the carrying amount during the period, and

(g) the gross amount and accumulated impairment losses at the end of the period.

## 4 IAS 36 *Impairment of Assets*

### 4.1 Introduction

DEFINITION

**Impairment** is a reduction in the recoverable amount of a non-current asset or goodwill below its carrying amount.

**Impairment** is a reduction in the recoverable amount of a non-current asset or goodwill below its carrying amount.

An asset is carried at more than its recoverable amount if its carrying amount is greater than the amount that could be recovered from using it or selling it.

### 4.2 Identifying impairments

KEY POINT

An entity is normally only required to carry out detailed impairment reviews if there is evidence that an impairment may have occurred.

An entity is normally only required to carry out detailed impairment reviews if there is evidence that an impairment may have occurred. Indications that an impairment might have happened can come from external or internal sources:

(a) external sources of information:

  (i) unexpected decreases in an asset's market value

  (ii) significant adverse changes have taken place, or are about to take place, in the technological, market, economic or legal environment

  (iii) increased interest rates have decreased an asset's 'recoverable amount'

  (iv) the entity's net assets are more than its market capitalisation

(b) internal sources of information:

(i) evidence of obsolescence or damage

(ii) there is, or is about to be, a material reduction in usage of an asset

(iii) evidence that the economic performance of an asset has been, or will be, worse than expected.

### 4.3 Assets that must be tested annually

There are two types of asset which **must** be tested for impairment annually, even if there is no indication of impairment. These are:

(a) intangible assets with an indefinite useful life or intangible assets not yet available for use. The test must be performed at the same time every year

(b) goodwill acquired in a business combination.

### 4.4 Calculating an impairment loss

KEY POINT

An impairment occurs if the carrying amount of an asset is greater than its recoverable amount.

DEFINITIONS

The **carrying amount** is the amount at which an asset is recognised after deducting any accumulated depreciation (amortisation) and accumulated impairment losses thereon.

The **recoverable amount** is the higher of fair value less costs to sell and value in use.

**Fair value less costs to sell** is the amount obtainable from the sale of an asset in an arm's length transaction between knowledgeable, willing parties, less the costs of disposal.

**Value in use** is the present value of future cash flows expected from using an asset.

An impairment occurs if the carrying amount of an asset is greater than its recoverable amount.

The **carrying amount** is the amount at which an asset is recognised after deducting any accumulated depreciation (amortisation) and accumulated impairment losses.

The **recoverable amount** is the higher of fair value less costs to sell and value in use.

**Fair value less costs to sell** is the amount obtainable from the sale of an asset in an arm's length transaction between knowledgeable, willing parties, less the costs of disposal.

**Value in use** is the present value of future cash flows expected from using an asset.

The reasoning behind these definitions is that, when an asset becomes impaired, the decision must be made whether to continue to use it or to sell it. This decision is based on the cash flows that can be generated by following each course of action, so that an entity will not continue to use the asset if it can realise more cash by selling it and vice versa. This means that when an asset is stated at the higher of fair value less costs to sell or value in use it is recorded at its maximum potential value to the entity.

***Activity 2***

The following information relates to three assets:

| | *A* | *B* | *C* |
|---|---|---|---|
| | $000 | $000 | $000 |
| Carrying amount | 100 | 150 | 120 |
| Fair value less costs to sell | 110 | 125 | 100 |
| Value in use | 120 | 130 | 90 |

(a) What is the recoverable amount of each asset?

(b) Calculate the impairment loss for each of the three assets.

*Feedback to this activity is at the end of the chapter.*

### 4.5 Measurement of recoverable amount

***Measuring net selling price***

Possible indicators of net selling price are:

(i) a binding sale agreement

(ii) if an active market exists, the current market price less costs of disposal.

Failing either of these indicators, the best information available must be relied upon.

***Measuring value in use***

Value in use is determined by estimating future cash inflows and outflows to be derived from the use of the asset and its ultimate disposal, and applying a suitable discount rate to these cash flows.

### 4.6 Recognition and measurement of an impairment loss

If the recoverable amount of an asset is less than its carrying amount, the carrying amount of the asset is reduced to its recoverable amount. That reduction is an impairment loss.

KEY POINT

An impairment loss should be recognised immediately as an expense in the income statement, except that an impairment loss on a revalued asset may first be offset against any revaluation surplus for that asset.

An impairment loss should be recognised immediately as an expense in the income statement, except that an impairment loss on a revalued asset may first be offset against any revaluation surplus for that asset.

The depreciation charge for the asset should be adjusted in future periods to allocate the asset's revised carrying amount, less its residual value (if any), on a systematic basis over its remaining useful life.

### 4.7 Cash-generating units

KEY POINT

In practice, cash flows belong to groups of assets rather than to individual assets.

In practice, cash flows often belong to groups of assets rather than to individual assets. For example, a factory production line will be made up of many individual machines and robots, but the revenues will be earned by the production line as a whole.

These groups of assets are called cash generating units. Impairment should be calculated for the unit as a whole, not for the individual assets within it.

Two problems arise:

(1) how to deal with goodwill

(2) how to allocate the impairment for the unit as a whole to the individual assets within that unit.

### 4.8 Cash-generating units and goodwill

Goodwill does not generate cash flows independently of other assets or groups of assets. Therefore goodwill acquired in a business combination must be allocated to each of the acquirer's cash-generating units that are expected to benefit from the synergies of the combination.

KEY POINT

A cash-generating unit to which goodwill has been allocated should be tested for impairment annually by comparing the carrying amount of the unit, including the goodwill, with the recoverable amount of the unit.

A cash-generating unit to which goodwill has been allocated should be tested for impairment annually by comparing the carrying amount of the unit, including the goodwill, with the recoverable amount of the unit. If the carrying amount of the unit exceeds the recoverable amount, the unit is impaired and a loss must be recognised.

The impairment test is then carried out in two stages:

1 Each unit is tested for impairment individually by comparing its carrying amount (excluding goodwill) with its recoverable amount. If the recoverable amount exceeds the carrying amount, the unit is impaired and an impairment loss is recognised.

2 The group of units is then tested for impairment as a whole. The carrying amount of the group (including the related goodwill) is compared with its recoverable amount. If the recoverable amount is greater than the carrying amount, the goodwill is impaired.

### *Example*

On 1 January 20X5 Toadstool acquired all the equity shares of Mushroom. Goodwill of $60 million arose on the acquisition.

The net assets of Mushroom have been allocated into three cash-generating units. On 31 December 20X5, Toadstool carried out an impairment review of the goodwill. The carrying values and value in use of each of the three cash-generating units were as follows:

| | *Unit 1* | *Unit 2* | *Unit 3* |
|---|---|---|---|
| | $million | $million | $million |
| Carrying value of unit | 40 | 65 | 45 |
| Value in use of unit | 45 | 50 | 50 |

It was not possible to allocate the goodwill on consolidation to the individual cash-generating units. The value in use of Mushroom as a single cash generating unit is $150 million.

How is the impairment review of the goodwill carried out?

### *Solution*

**Step 1** Review each of the three cash generating units for impairment. This shows that Unit 2 is impaired (its carrying value is greater than its value in use).

**Step 2** Recognise an impairment loss of $15 million for Unit 2. The total carrying value of Mushroom is now as follows:

| | $ million |
|---|---|
| Unit 1 | 40 |
| Unit 2 (65 – 15) | 50 |
| Unit 3 | 45 |
| Goodwill | 60 |
| | 195 |

**Step 3** Review Mushroom as a whole. The carrying value of $195 million is greater than the value in use of $150 million and therefore there is an impairment loss of $45 million. This must relate to the goodwill, which is written down to its recoverable amount of $15 million ($60 million – $45 million).

## 4.9 Allocation of an impairment loss to the unit's assets

KEY POINT

If an impairment loss arises on a cash-generating unit, then it is allocated among the assets in the unit in the following order:

(1) goodwill

(2) other assets pro rata to their carrying amount.

If an impairment loss arises on a cash-generating unit then, in the absence of obvious impairment to individual assets, it is allocated among the assets in the unit in the following order:

(1) goodwill

(2) other assets pro rata to their carrying amount.

However, the carrying amount of an asset cannot be reduced below the highest of:

(a) its fair value less costs to sell (if determinable)

(b) its value in use (if determinable), and

(c) zero.

The amount of the impairment loss that would otherwise have been allocated to the asset is allocated pro rata to the other assets of the unit.

### *Example*

Tinud has identified an impairment of $41m for one of its cash generating units. The carrying value of the unit's net assets was $150m, whereas the unit's recoverable amount was only $109m.

The net selling price of the unit's assets were insignificant except for the property, which had a market value of $35m. The net monetary assets will be realised in full.

The table below shows how the impairment will be allocated.

| | *Draft values* $m | *Impairment* $m | *Impaired values* $m | *Comments* |
|---|---|---|---|---|
| Goodwill | 13 | (13) | – | a |
| Property | 20 | – | 20 | b |
| Machinery | 49 | (14) | 35 | d |
| Vehicles | 35 | (10) | 25 | d |
| Patents | 14 | (4) | 10 | d |
| Net monetary assets | 19 | – | 19 | c |
| | 150 | (41) | 109 | |

**Comments**

(a) Firstly, the goodwill is reduced.

(b) No impairment can be made against the property because its net selling price is greater then its carrying value.

(c) Likewise, no impairment can be made against the net monetary assets (receivables, cash, etc) because they will be realised in full.

(d) The balance of $28m ($41m – $13m) is apportioned between the remaining assets on a pro rata basis as follows:

| | *Draft NBV* $m | *Proportion of $28m loss* | *Impairment* | *Revised NBV* |
|---|---|---|---|---|
| Machinery | 49 | 49 / 98 | (14) | 35 |
| Vehicles | 35 | 35 / 98 | (10) | 25 |
| Patents | 14 | 14 / 98 | (4) | 10 |
| | 98 | | (28) | 70 |

Note that where there has been a notional adjustment to goodwill to include goodwill attributable to the minority interest, this is ignored in allocating the impairment loss.

***Activity 3***

An impairment loss of $60,000 arises in connection with a cash-generating unit. The carrying amount of the assets in the cash generating unit, before the impairment, is as follows:

| | $000 |
|---|---|
| Goodwill | 20 |
| Patent (with no market value) | 10 |
| Tangible non-current assets | 40 |
| | 70 |

How should the impairment loss be allocated?

*Feedback to this activity is at the end of the chapter.*

### 4.10 Disclosure requirements

KEY POINT

There are extensive disclosure requirements in IAS 36.

There are extensive disclosure requirements in IAS 36, the most important of which are:

(a) the amount of any impairment losses recognised in the income statement, and the headings under which they appear

(b) the amount of any reversals of impairment losses recognised in the income statement, and the headings under which they appear

(c) the amount of impairment losses or reversals recognised directly in equity (i.e. in revaluation surplus)

(d) segmental analysis of items (a) to (c) above

(e) notes giving details of the events and circumstances leading to impairment losses or reversals

(f) details of estimates used to measure recoverable amounts of cash-generating units containing goodwill or intangible assets with indefinite useful lives.

## Summary

- In order to account for an acquisition, the acquiring company must measure the cost of the investment in its own balance sheet and the amount to be allocated between the identifiable net assets of the subsidiary. IFRS 3 explains how to determine the fair values of both.
- Goodwill arising on a business combination is recognised as an asset and measured at cost less accumulated impairment losses. Goodwill is not amortised.
- Any excess of an acquirer's interest in the net fair value of the acquiree's identifiable net assets over cost (negative goodwill) is recognised immediately in profit or loss.
- An asset is impaired if its carrying amount is greater than its recoverable amount. Recoverable amount is the higher of fair value less costs to sell and value in use.

- Two types of asset must be tested for impairment annually, even if there is no indication of impairment: intangible assets with an indefinite useful life; and goodwill acquired in a business combination. Other assets need only be tested if there is some indication that an impairment has occurred.

Having completed your study of this chapter, you should have achieved the following learning outcome:

- explain and apply the concepts of fair value at the point of acquisition and impairment of goodwill.

## Self-test questions

**1** What is fair value? (2.1)

**2** How are equity instruments (shares) normally valued when they form part of the cost of a business combination? (2.2)

**3** What is meant by identifiable assets? (2.3)

**4** Can a provision for restructuring the group after an acquisition ever be recognised? (2.5)

**5** How should goodwill arising on a business combination be treated in the consolidated financial statements? (3.1, 3.2)

**6** What is negative goodwill? (3.3)

**7** What is impairment? (4.1)

**8** How is an impairment loss calculated? (4.4)

**9** What is a cash-generating unit? (4.7)

**10** How is an impairment loss allocated to the assets in a cash-generating unit? (4.9)

## Objective test questions

### Question 1

Which of the following is/are acceptable when assessing fair values on acquisition in accordance with IFRS 3 *Business Combinations*?

(1) Valuation of property, plant and equipment at market value where this is higher than book value.

(2) Discounting receivables to present values where the debt is not due to be recovered for two years.

(3) Inclusion of contingencies where the probability of the outcome would lead to the acquired company only disclosing the contingency, not including amounts in the accounts.

**A** (1) only

**B** (2) only

**C** (1) and (2) only

**D** (1), (2) and (3)

### Question 2

Give three examples of circumstances which indicate that an impairment loss relating to an asset may have occurred.

*For the answers to these questions, see the 'Answers' section at the end of the book.*

## Exam-type question

### Chrysanthemum

The draft balance sheets of Chrysanthemum and its subsidiary, Daisy at 31 December 20X5 are given below:

| | *Chrysanthemum* | | *Daisy* | |
|---|---|---|---|---|
| | $000 | $000 | $000 | $000 |
| Non-current assets: | | | | |
| Property, plant and equipment | 7,280 | | 6,400 | |
| Investments | 4,560 | | - | |
| | | 11,840 | | 6,400 |
| Current assets: | | | | |
| Inventories | 3,200 | | 2,000 | |
| Receivables | 2,400 | | 1,600 | |
| Cash in hand | 640 | | 480 | |
| | | 6,240 | | 4,080 |
| | | 18,080 | | 10,480 |
| Equity: | | | | |
| Share capital | | | | |
| ($1 shares) | | 4,000 | | 3,000 |
| Retained earnings | | 2,640 | | 2,200 |
| | | 6,640 | | 5,200 |
| Long-term loans | | 6,400 | | 1,600 |
| Current liabilities: | | | | |
| Trade payables | 2,000 | | 1,360 | |
| Taxation | 480 | | 360 | |
| Bank overdraft | 2,560 | | 1,960 | |
| | | 5,040 | | 3,680 |
| | | 18,080 | | 10,480 |

You are provided with the following additional information:

(a) On 1 October 20X5 Chrysanthemum purchased 2.4 million shares in Daisy at an agreed value of $1.90 per share. The purchase was financed by an additional issue of loan notes, carrying an interest rate of 10%.

(b) Daisy produced interim financial statements, drawn up as at 1 October 20X5, in connection with the acquisition by Chrysanthemum. The balance sheet of Daisy at that date showed the following:

| | $000 | | $000 |
|---|---|---|---|
| Property, plant and equipment (c) | 6,300 | Trade payables | 1,280 |
| Inventories (d) | 1,600 | Taxation | 240 |
| Receivables | 1,160 | Bank overdraft | 1,460 |
| Cash in hand | 480 | Long-term loans (e) | 1,600 |
| | | Share capital ($1 shares) | 3,000 |
| | | Retained earnings | 1,960 |
| | 9,540 | | 9,540 |

(c) At 1 October 20X5 the property, plant and equipment of Daisy had a total market value of $6.7 million. It was being depreciated at 25% per annum pro rata on that cost. This policy is also appropriate for the consolidated financial statements of Chrysanthemum. None of the items included in the interim financial statements drawn up as at 1 October 20X5 were disposed of prior to 31 December 20X5. No item was fully depreciated by 30 September 20X5.

(d) The inventories of Daisy which were shown in the interim financial statements at cost of $1.6 million had an estimated fair value of $1.7 million at 1 June 20X5. All items of inventory in hand at 1 October 20X5 had been sold by 31 December 20X5.

(e) The long-term loan carries a rate of interest of 10% per annum, payable on 30 September annually in arrears. The loan is redeemable at par on 30 September 20X8. The interest cost is representative of current market rates. The accrued interest payable by Daisy at 31 December 20X5 is included in trade payables at that date.

**Required:**

(a) Compute the goodwill on consolidation of Daisy that will be included in the consolidated financial statements of the Chrysanthemum group for the year ended 31 December 20X5, explaining your treatment of the items mentioned in the notes above. You should refer to the provisions of relevant Accounting Standards. **(10 marks)**

(b) Prepare the consolidated balance sheet of the Chrysanthemum group at 31 December 20X5. **(15 marks)**

***Note:*** ALL your numerical workings can be rounded to the nearest $000.

**(Total: 25 marks)**

*For the answer to this question see the 'Answers' section at the end of the book.*

## Feedback to activities

### Activity 1

**Step 1**

Adjust the value of Y's net assets at 30 September 20X4 to fair value.

| | $ |
|---|---|
| Net assets per question | 350,000 |
| Revaluation of property | 20,000 |
| Write-off of inventory | (4,000) |
| Provision for reorganisation costs* | (10,000) |
| | 356,000 |

* Note that it is Y which has decided to close the workshop, and that this decision was made prior to the year-end, so a provision can be established correctly for this item.

**Step 2**

Calculate goodwill

| | $ |
|---|---|
| Fair value of consideration | 320,000 |
| Net assets acquired 80% × $356,000 | 284,800 |
| Goodwill arising | 35,200 |

## Activity 2

(a) A: $120,000, B: $130,000, C: $100,000

(b) A: Nil, B: $20,000, C: $20,000

## Activity 3

The impairment loss is allocated as follows:

| | *Before impairment* | *Loss* | *After impairment* |
|---|---|---|---|
| | $000 | $000 | $000 |
| Goodwill | 20 | (20) | – |
| Patent (with no market value) | 10 | (8) | 2 |
| Tangible assets | 40 | (32) | 8 |
| | 70 | (60) | 10 |

Chapter 4

# GROUP ACCOUNTS: THE INCOME STATEMENT

## Syllabus content

- Relationships between investors and investees, and the exclusion of subsidiaries from consolidation with reference to dominant influence, participating interest, management on a unified basis and significant influence.
- The preparation of consolidated financial statements (including the group cash flow statement) involving one or more subsidiaries, sub-subsidiaries and associates, under the acquisition and pooling of interests methods (IAS 7 & 27 and IFRS 3).
- The treatment in consolidated financial statements of minority interests, pre- and post- acquisition reserves, goodwill (including its impairment), fair value adjustments, intra-group transactions and dividends, piece-meal and mid-year acquisitions, and disposals to include sub-subsidiaries and mixed groups.

## Contents

# Introduction

In this chapter you will learn how to prepare an income statement for a group. As well as the preparation of the basic income statement, you will also learn how to deal with intra-group transactions and the situation where a subsidiary is acquired part-way through the year (a mid year acquisition). Exam questions on the group income statement almost invariably feature one or both of these.

Lastly, you will look at the definition of a subsidiary and learn how to apply it in practice. You will also cover the (rare) circumstances under which subsidiaries can be excluded from the group accounts.

When you have finished this chapter, you will have covered all the basic principles of consolidation. The next few chapters cover the preparation of group accounts in more complicated situations and so it is very important that you take the time to master the material you have learned so far before you move on.

## 1 Consolidated income statement

### 1.1 Introduction

Just as the income statement of a single company shows the results of the year's trading of that company, so does the consolidated income statement show the results of trading in the year by the parent together with its subsidiaries.

KEY POINT

Consolidated income statements are prepared by combining the information given in the income statements of the individual companies, after making any adjustments that may be necessary to eliminate inter-company items.

Consolidated income statements are prepared by combining the information given in the income statements of the individual companies, after making any adjustments that may be necessary to eliminate inter-company items, unrealised profits and so on.

### 1.2 Composition of group unchanged in current year

In this section it is assumed that no new subsidiaries are acquired during the year, nor are any existing subsidiaries disposed of.

Consider the following simple example:

***Example***

P acquired, several years ago, the entire ordinary share capital of S. Their results for the year ended 30 November 20X4 were as follows:

| | *P* | *S* |
|---|---|---|
| | $ | $ |
| Sales revenue | 8,500,000 | 2,200,000 |
| Cost of sales and expenses | 7,650,000 | 1,980,000 |
| Trading profit before tax | 850,000 | 220,000 |
| Income taxes | 400,000 | 100,000 |
| | 450,000 | 120,000 |

***Solution***

The consolidated income statement is arrived at by a simple 'combining exercise'.

**Consolidated income statement for year ended 30 November 20X4**

| | $ |
|---|---|
| Sales revenue | 10,700,000 |
| Cost of sales and expenses | 9,630,000 |
| Group profit before tax | 1,070,000 |
| Tax | 500,000 |
| Net profit for the period | 570,000 |

### 1.3 The effect of a minority interest

What happens if, in the previous example, P acquired only 75% of the share capital of S?

This does not affect sales revenue and cost of sales. They remain the same, as we wish to show total income under the control of the parent company.

KEY POINT

Profit for the period must be analysed between the profit attributable to the minority interest and the profit attributable to equity holders.

In this situation, not all the profit for the period is 'owned' by the parent. IAS 1 *Presentation of Financial Statements* states that profit for the period must be analysed between the profit attributable to the minority interest and the profit attributable to equity holders (ordinary shareholders) of the parent'. The analysis must be shown on the face of the income statement. The illustrative income statement in Chapter 1 shows a suggested presentation.

The minority interest in the income statement is not an expense and it must never be presented as an expense.

In this example, the minority shareholders' interest in the profit is calculated as 25% × $120,000 = $30,000.

***Activity 1***

Now prepare the consolidated income statement assuming a 25% minority interest.

*Feedback to this activity is at the end of the chapter.*

### 1.4 Retained earnings brought forward

It is sometimes necessary to calculate the amount of retained earnings brought forward from the previous year. As far as the consolidated financial statements are concerned, the balance brought forward consists of:

- P's own retained earnings balance brought forward, plus
- P's share of the post-acquisition retained profits of S.

***Activity 2***

Facts as in the previous activity, but you are provided with additional information.

(a) Retained earnings brought forward at the beginning of the year amounted to $2,300,000 for P and $400,000 for S.

(b) P acquired the shares in S when the revenue reserves of S amounted to $100,000.

Calculate the brought forward and carried forward figure for retained earnings in the consolidated financial statements.

*Feedback to this activity is at the end of the chapter.*

## 1.5 Inter-company dividends

Some complications in preparing consolidated income statements arise because of dividends paid from one company to another.

Investment income of the parent may, for example, include:

(a) ordinary dividends received from subsidiaries

(b) income from other investments.

Only (b) is shown separately as income in a consolidated income statement, inter-company dividends being eliminated on consolidation.

The subsidiaries in a group often pay dividends in order to transfer surplus cash to the parent company. No net profit or loss accrues to the group in the process. For example, if Leg owns 80% of the ordinary shares of Foot, and Foot pays an ordinary dividend of $10,000, then $2,000 will be paid to the outside shareholders in Foot and $8,000 will be paid to Leg. Suppose the balance sheets of Foot before and after the dividend were:

| | *Before* | *After* |
|---|---|---|
| | $ | $ |
| Sundry net assets | 13,000 | 3,000 |
| Share capital | 1,000 | 1,000 |
| Reserves | 12,000 | 2,000 |
| | 13,000 | 3,000 |

and that the reserves of Foot at acquisition were $2,000. We can then summarise the effects of the dividend on the group as follows.

(a) **Goodwill on acquisition**

The amount to be deducted from the cost of investment is 80% of the net assets acquired, 80% × $(1,000 + 2,000) = $2,400, which is obviously unaffected by dividends paid some years later.

(b) **Minority interests**

| | | |
|---|---|---|
| | | $ |
| Before | 20% × $13,000 | 2,600 |
| After | 20% × $3,000 | 600 |
| Reduction in group liability | | 2,000 |
| Compare: Reduction in group cash | | 2,000 |

We see that the group neither gains nor loses overall on account of the minority's portion of the dividend.

(c) **Consolidated retained earnings**

| | | |
|---|---|---|
| | | $ |
| Before | 80% × $(12,000 – 2,000) | 8,000 |
| After | 80% × $(2,000 – 2,000) | Nil |
| Reduction in consolidated reserves arising from Foot Limited | | 8,000 |

There is, however, a compensating effect, in that the reserves of Leg increased by $8,000 on receipt of the dividend from Foot. Since all of Leg's reserves are incorporated into the consolidated reserves, there will be no net effect on consolidated reserves.

## 1.6 Mid year acquisitions

The main problem here is how to deal with the pre-acquisition profits of the new subsidiary. The approach is to exclude the pre-acquisition items of the subsidiary from the relevant group figures.

KEY POINT

Each line item in the subsidiary's income statement must be apportioned on a time basis.

This means that each line item in the subsidiary's income statement must be apportioned on a time basis. For example, if the group's year-end is 31 December and the subsidiary was acquired on 1 July, the consolidated income statement includes only six months' revenue, cost of sales, expenses and so on, for the subsidiary.

Because only the subsidiary's post-acquisition profit is included in the consolidated income statement, the amount attributable to the minority interest is its share of the post-acquisition profit, not its share of the profit for the whole year.

### *Activity 3*

The trading results of P and S for the year ended 31 July 20X4 were as follows:

| | *P* | *S* |
|---|---|---|
| | $ | $ |
| Sales revenue | 1,430,000 | 600,000 |
| Cost of sales and expenses | 1,160,000 | 504,000 |
| Trading profit | 270,000 | 96,000 |
| Less: Tax | 135,000 | 48,000 |
| Retained profit | 135,000 | 48,000 |
| Retained earnings brought forward at 1 August 20X3 were: | 900,000 | 200,000 |

P acquired 75% of the ordinary share capital of S on 28 February 20X4. Assume that profits are earned evenly over the year. Prepare the consolidated income statement for the year and show the movements in retained earnings for the year.

*Feedback to this activity is at the end of the chapter.*

## 1.7 Pre-acquisition dividends

KEY POINT

A pre-acquisition dividend is a dividend paid to a parent company by a subsidiary out of pre-acquisition profits.

A pre-acquisition dividend is a dividend paid to a parent company by a subsidiary out of pre-acquisition profits. There are two possible ways of accounting for pre-acquisition dividends in the accounts of the parent and in the consolidated financial statements.

- Treat the dividend as a return to the parent company of part of the cost of its investment (i.e. a reduction in the carrying value of the parent's investment in the subsidiary). This is the traditional view of pre-acquisition dividends. The reasoning for it is that only post-acquisition profits can be treated as profits of the group and therefore only dividends paid out of post-acquisition profits can be treated as income. A further argument for this treatment is that a dividend paid out of pre-acquisition profits reduces the value of the parent's investment in the subsidiary to less than cost.
- Treat the dividend as a realised profit in the hands of the parent (i.e. as investment income). The rationale for this treatment is that the payment of a pre-acquisition dividend does not cause a permanent diminution in the value of the parent's investment in the subsidiary. Therefore no write-down is necessary.

Accounting standards do not provide a definitive answer to the problem. The cost of an investment should be reduced by dividends receivable only if they clearly represent a recovery of part of cost, but this is unlikely to be obvious in practice.

Both methods are illustrated in the example below.

### Example

The facts are the same as in Activity 3 above, except that on 1 March 20X4 S pays a dividend of $12,000. Show the journal entry for recording the dividend received in the books of P and calculate consolidated reserves at 31 July 20X4 assuming that:

(a) the dividend is treated as investment income; and

(b) the dividend is treated as a return of the cost of the investment.

### Solution

***Tutorial note:*** In the consolidated income statement, investment income received by P is cancelled against the dividend paid by S.

(a) **Investment income**

*Journal entry*

Dr Cash (75% × 12,000) $9,000

Cr Investment income $9,000

*Analysis of subsidiary's retained earnings*

| | *Total* | *Pre-acquistion* | *Post-acquisition* |
|---|---|---|---|
| | | (7/12) | (5/12) |
| | $ | $ | $ |
| B/f | 200,000 | 200,000 | - |
| Profit after tax | 48,000 | 28,000 | 20,000 |
| Dividend | (12,000) | - | (12,000) |
| | 236,000 | 228,000 | 8,000 |

*Consolidated retained earnings*

| | $ | $ |
|---|---|---|
| P (1,035,000 + 9,000) | | 1,044,000 |
| S: (75% × 8,000) | | 6,000 |
| | | 1,050,000 |

The dividend is treated as occurring post-acquisition, although it is paid out of pre-acquisition profits.

(b) **Return of cost of investment**

*Journal entry*

Dr Cash (75% × 12,000) $9,000

Cr Cost of investment $9,000

*Analysis of subsidiary's retained earnings*

| | *Total* | *Pre-acquistion* (7/12) | *Post-acquisition* (5/12) |
|---|---|---|---|
| | $ | $ | $ |
| B/f | 200,000 | 200,000 | - |
| Profit after tax | 48,000 | 28,000 | 20,000 |
| Dividend | (12,000) | (12,000) | - |
| | 236,000 | 216,000 | 20,000 |

*Consolidated retained earnings*

| | $ | $ |
|---|---|---|
| P | | 1,035,000 |
| S; (75% × 20,000) | | 15,000 |
| | | 1,050,000 |

The cost of the investment is reduced by the amount of the dividend, therefore goodwill is reduced.

# 2 Consolidation working papers

## 2.1 Introduction

The following examples bring together the principles explained in the previous sections and illustrate an approach that can be taken to show sufficient detail to support the figures computed for the published consolidated income statement. For many of the required figures the consolidated figure is no more than the addition of the parent and subsidiary companies' figures, and thus a 'master' schedule is used to show the additions made.

### *Example of approach*

The draft income statements and summarised statements of changes in equity for the year ended 31 March 20X7 of the companies in a group are as follows:

| **Income statements** | *Tyndale* | *Wycliffe* | *Luther* |
|---|---|---|---|
| | $ | $ | $ |
| Sales revenue | 216,300 | 24,400 | 126,000 |
| Cost of sales | 136,269 | 15,372 | 79,380 |
| Gross profit | 80,031 | 9,028 | 46,620 |
| Administrative expenses | (21,630) | (2,440) | (12,600) |
| Income from shares in group companies | 7,512 | – | – |
| Profit before tax | 65,913 | 6,588 | 34,020 |
| Tax | 28,119 | 3,172 | 16,380 |
| Profit for the year | 37,794 | 3,416 | 17,640 |

| Statements of changes in equity | | | |
|---|---|---|---|
| At 1 April 20X6 | 236,728 | 107,076 | 123,940 |
| Profit for the year | 37,794 | 3,416 | 17,640 |
| Dividends paid | (20,000) | (1,952) | (10,080) |
| At 31 March 20X7 | 254,522 | 108,540 | 131,500 |

The history of the group is as follows:

- Tyndale bought 75% of the ordinary shares (the only type) in Wycliffe seven years ago when that company's total equity amounted to $105,124 (share capital of $100,000 and reserves of $5,124).
- Luther has an issued share capital of 100,000 ordinary shares of $1 each. Tyndale purchased 60,000 of these two years ago when the balance on Luther's reserves was $16,380.

Prepare the consolidated income statement and the consolidated statement of changes in equity for the year ended 31 March 20X7.

***Solution***

**Step 1**

Reconcile the intra-group dividends.

**Reconciliation of intra-group dividends**

| | $ |
|---|---|
| Per Tyndale, received | 7,512 |
| Should agree with: | |
| Wycliffe, paid $1,952 × 75% | 1,464 |
| Luther, paid $10,080 × 60% | 6,048 |
| | 7,512 |

Therefore, no adjustments are required.

**Step 2**

Set out the master schedule.

**Master schedule**

| *Group details* | *Tyndale Parent* | *Wycliffe 75% 12 months* | *Luther 60% 12 months* | *Adjustments* | *Consolidated* |
|---|---|---|---|---|---|
| | $ | $ | $ | $ | $ |
| Sales revenue | 216,300 | 24,400 | 126,000 | | 366,700 |
| Cost of sales | (136,269) | (15,372) | (79,380) | | (231,021) |
| Administrative expenses | (21,630) | (2,440) | (12,600) | | (36,670) |
| Investment income | – | – | – | | – |
| Tax | (28,119) | (3,172) | (16,380) | | (47,671) |
| Net profit after tax | 30,282 | 3,416 | 17,640 | | 51,338 |
| Minority interests (25%; 40%) | – | (854) | (7,056) | | (7,910) |

**Step 3**

Calculate equity brought forward.

| | $ |
|---|---|
| Tyndale | 236,728 |
| Wycliffe 75% × $(107,076 – 105,124) | 1,464 |
| Luther 60% × $(123,940 – 116,380) | 4,536 |
| | 242,728 |

**Step 4**

The consolidated income statement and consolidated statement of changes in equity can now be prepared:

**Tyndale and its subsidiaries**
**Consolidated income statement for the year ended 31 March 20X7**

| | $ |
|---|---|
| Revenue | 366,700 |
| Cost of sales | 231,021 |
| Gross profit | 135,679 |
| Administrative expenses | 36,670 |
| Profit before tax | 99,009 |
| Tax | 47,671 |
| Profit for the year | 51,338 |
| Attributable to: | |
| Equity holders of the parent | 43,428 |
| Minority interests | 7,910 |
| | 51,338 |

**Consolidated statement of changes in equity for the year ended 31 March 20X7**

| | $ |
|---|---|
| At 31 March 20X6 | 242,728 |
| Profit for the year attributable to equity holders of the parent | 43,428 |
| Dividends paid | (20,000) |
| At 31 March 20X7 | 266,156 |

***Explanatory notes***

1 The master schedule is drafted with a column for each company and a 'consolidated' column. The group structure is summarised at the head of each column.

The meaning of the notes is that Tyndale is the parent; Wycliffe is a 75% owned subsidiary and has been for the present year; Luther is 60% owned for the present year.

2 In any example with intra-group dividends, begin by reconciling the amounts receivable by the parent with the amounts payable by the subsidiaries. This may reveal errors or omissions in accounting for the

dividends and, if so, they should be corrected before beginning the consolidation.

3 For items from 'sales revenue' to 'profit for the year', we enter:

| | |
|---|---|
| For parent | the full amount |
| For subsidiary owned throughout the year | the full amount |
| For subsidiaries acquired during the year | the amount representing post-acquisition transactions |

4 The figure of $51,338 profit for the year completes the consolidated income statement, and it represents the total profit that the directors have obtained by using the assets that they control.

However, not all of this will accrue to the shareholders of Tyndale. Profit for the period must be allocated between the amount belonging to the minority interest and the amount belonging to the shareholders of the parent.

In this case, because all the companies have only ordinary shares, it is easy to calculate the minority share. It is simply the minority shareholders' fraction of the ordinary shares, multiplied by the last figure, profit for the period, in the column for the relevant subsidiary.

5 Equity brought forward consist of:

(a) all the parent's equity (share capital and reserves)

(b) the group share of the subsidiaries' post-acquisition profits.

6 Once the master schedule has been filled in, the actual consolidated income statement can be written out, using the figures from the 'consolidated' column.

7 It is possible to prove equity carried forward:

| | $ |
|---|---|
| Tyndale (236,728 + 30,282) | 67,010 |
| Wycliffe 75% × $(107,076 + 3,416 – 105,124) | 4,026 |
| Luther 60% × $(123,940 + 17,640 – 116,380) | 15,120 |
| Dividend paid | (20,000) |
| | 266,156 |

# 3 Cancellation of intra-group transactions

## 3.1 Introduction

**KEY POINT**

Intra-group trading and any unrealised profits on inventory must be eliminated from the consolidated income statement.

Intra-group trading and any unrealised profits on inventory must be eliminated from the consolidated income statement.

If in a certain year:

- A buys an inventory item for $60
- A sells it to B for $80, B being a member of the same group as A
- B still holds the item at the balance sheet date, then

the income statements of the two companies will include, in respect of these events:

| | *A* | *B* |
|---|---|---|
| | $ | $ |
| Sales revenue | 80 | – |
| Cost of sales | 60 | – |
| Gross profit, and hence every other income statement sub-total | 20 | – |

This $20 is the unrealised profit whose cancellation in the balance sheet was discussed before. In the income statement, we must also eliminate the $80 and $60 as the income statement of a single company that had carried out the same transactions as A and B would contain no entries at all in respect of it.

What if B had sold the item for $95 by the balance sheet date? The income statements of the two companies would then have shown:

| | *A* | *B* |
|---|---|---|
| | $ | $ |
| Sales revenue | 80 | 95 |
| Cost of sales | 60 | 80 |
| Gross profit (and other sub-totals) | 20 | 15 |

Both companies have realised their profits and so these should not be adjusted. However, a single equivalent company would show in its income statement:

| | $ |
|---|---|
| Sales revenue | 95 |
| Cost of sales | 60 |
| Gross profit (and other sub-totals) | 35 |

In this case we need eliminate only the $80 from sales revenue and the $80 from cost of sales in order to establish the correct revenue and cost of sales figures.

In either case the adjustment is conveniently carried out by means of the adjustments column in the master schedule.

**Effect on minority interests**

If the unrealised profit originally arose in the subsidiary, the minority interest must be adjusted for its share in the unrealised profit. However this is an adjustment made in calculating the minority's share of post tax profits; in the first instance all the unrealised profit must be eliminated to determine the correct amount of gross profit earned by the group trading as if it were a single entity.

***Example***

The income statements of Entry and Exit for the year ended 31 July 20X7 are as follows:

| | *Entry* | *Exit* |
|---|---|---|
| | $ | $ |
| Sales revenue | 6,956 | 3,290 |
| Cost of sales | 3,108 | 1,470 |
| Gross profit | 3,848 | 1,820 |
| Administrative expenses | (1,044) | (560) |
| Net profit before tax | 2,804 | 1,260 |
| Tax | 1,258 | 595 |
| Net profit after tax | 1,546 | 665 |

**Further information**

(a) In the year ended 31 July 20X7 Entry sold to Exit goods costing $500 for $625 (20% profit margin).

(b) At 31 July 20X7 Exit had sold 40% of these goods for $300.

Prepare the consolidated income statement of Entry and its subsidiary for the year ended 31 July 20X7.

***Solution***

**Step 1**

**Rules for dealing with inter-company trading**

(a) Eliminate from sales and cost of sales all inter-company sales at the selling price.

Therefore deduct $625 from both sales revenue and cost of sales.

(b) Compute unrealised profit in goods not sold, i.e. the same calculation as for the consolidated balance sheet.

Closing inventory re goods sold from Entry to Exit

60% × $625 = $375

Unrealised profit

20% × $375 = $75

The $75 is added to cost of sales and deducted from the inventory value in the balance sheet.

These two adjustments can now be transferred to the consolidation schedule.

As the sale was made by the parent company there is no adjustment to minority interests required (see tutorial note below).

**Step 2**

**Master schedule**

| *Group details* | *Entry* | *Exit 60% 12 months* | *Adjustments* | *Consolidated* |
|---|---|---|---|---|
| | $ | $ | $ | $ |
| Sales revenue | 6,956 | 3,290 | (625) | 9,621 |
| Cost of sales | (3,108) | (1,470) | 550 | (4,028) |
| Gross profit | 3,848 | 1,820 | (75) | 5,593 |
| Administrative expenses | (1,044) | (560) | | (1,604) |
| Tax | (1,258) | (595) | – | (1,853) |
| Profit for the year | 1,546 | 665 | – | 2,136 |
| Minority interest (40% × 665) | | 266 | | 266 |

***Tutorial note:*** If the unrealised profit on inter-company trading originally arose in the subsidiary the minority interests' share in profits would be reduced by:

40% × $75 = $30

$236 would thus be shown in the consolidated income statement. Note in particular that the unrealised profit of $75 would still have to be deducted to arrive at consolidated gross profit.

**Step 3**

**Entry and its subsidiary**
**Consolidated income statement for year ended 31 July 20X7**

| | $ |
|---|---|
| Revenue | 9,621 |
| Cost of sales | 4,028 |
| Gross profit | 5,593 |
| Administrative expenses | 1,604 |
| Profit before tax | 3,989 |
| Tax | 1,853 |
| Profit for the year | 2,136 |
| Profit attributable to shareholders in Entry | 1,870 |
| Profit attributable to minority interest | 266 |
| | 2,136 |

### 3.2 Intra-group interest

Where a parent company makes a loan to a subsidiary company, the resulting interest represents an expense in the subsidiary shown under the heading of interest payable. The parent will include the interest under the heading 'interest receivable'.

On consolidation both these amounts must be eliminated by making an appropriate entry in the adjustments column in the consolidation schedule.

## 4 Further adjustments to the consolidated income statement

### 4.1 Impairment of goodwill

Under IFRS 3 *Business Combinations,* goodwill arising on an acquisition must be reviewed for impairment annually. If goodwill is found to be impaired, an impairment loss is recognised in the consolidated income statement.

Impairment losses are normally included in administrative expenses.

### 4.2 Fair value adjustments

Fair value adjustments to the subsidiary's assets may affect the consolidated income statement.

***Example***

On 1 January 20X4 P acquires a subsidiary, S. At that date, the fair values of most of S's assets and liabilities are roughly equivalent to their book values, with two exceptions:

(a) Non-current assets with a book value of $150,000 have a fair value of $200,000.

(b) The fair value of inventory exceeds its book value by $20,000.

The non-current assets are depreciated over a useful life of five years. The inventory is sold during the year ended 31 December 20X4.

What is the effect on the consolidated income statement for the year ended 31 December 20X4?

***Solution***

The depreciation charge for the year increases by $10,000 (the depreciation on the fair value adjustment of $50,000).

The second fair value adjustment increases opening inventory by $20,000 and as the items were sold during the year, cost of sales also increases by $20,000.

# 5 IAS 27 *Consolidated and Separate Financial Statements*

KEY POINT

IAS 27 lays down some principles to be applied in consolidation and also defines the circumstances in which subsidiaries may be excluded from consolidation.

IAS 27 lays down some principles to be applied in consolidation and also defines the circumstances in which subsidiaries may be excluded from consolidation.

## 5.1 Control

DEFINITIONS

A **parent** is an entity that has one or more subsidiaries.

A **subsidiary** is an entity, including an unincorporated entity, such as a partnership, that is **controlled** by another entity (known as the parent).

**Control** is the power to govern the financial and operating policies of an entity so as to obtain benefits from its activities.

IAS 27 provides several important definitions:

A **parent** is an entity that has one or more subsidiaries.

A **subsidiary** is an entity, including an unincorporated entity, such as a partnership, that is **controlled** by another entity (known as the parent).

**Control** is the power to govern the financial and operating policies of an entity so as to obtain benefits from its activities.

Control is usually based on ownership of more than 50% of voting power, but other forms of control are possible. IAS 27 gives four other situations in which control exists – when the parent has:

(a) power over more than half the voting rights by virtue of an agreement with other investors

(b) power to govern the financial and operating policies of the entity under a statute or an agreement

(c) power to appoint or remove the majority of the members of the board of directors

(d) power to cast the majority of votes at a meeting of the board of directors.

## 5.2 Exemptions from the requirement to prepare consolidated financial statements

IAS 27 states that a parent must prepare **consolidated financial statements**, ie, the financial statements of a group presented as a single economic entity.

However, there are exemptions from this requirement.

KEY POINT

The main exemption from preparing consolidated financial statements is for parent companies which are themselves subsidiaries.

The main exemption from preparing consolidated financial statements is for parent companies which are themselves subsidiaries.

The following diagram illustrates the point.

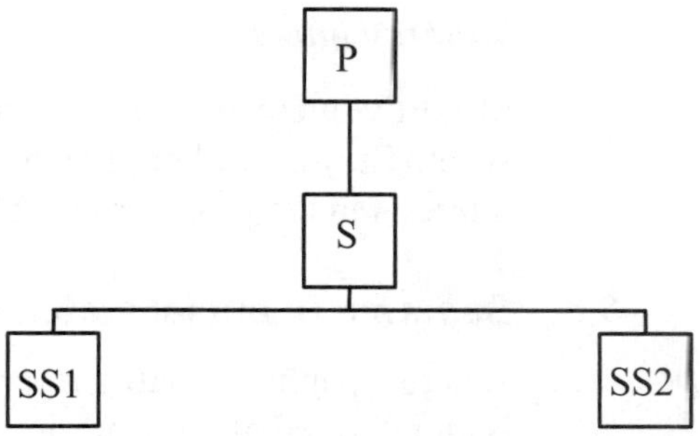


P must prepare consolidated financial statements combining all four companies.

S is also a parent company with two subsidiaries. S does not have to prepare consolidated financial statements if:

(a) it is 100% owned by P; or

(b) it is less than 100% owned, but the minority interest (including those not otherwise entitled to vote) do not object; or

(c) P (or the ultimate parent of P, if P is itself a subsidiary) produces consolidated financial statements available for public use that comply with IFRSs.

A parent is also exempt from preparing consolidated financial statements if it is not a public company and is not in the process of becoming a public company.

Where a parent chooses to take advantage of one of these exemptions it must comply with the IAS 27 requirements for **separate financial statements** (see below).

### 5.3 Subsidiaries held for sale

All subsidiaries must be included in the consolidated financial statements.

If a subsidiary is held exclusively with a view to disposal within 12 months from acquisition, it may be classified as 'held for sale' if it meets certain criteria. A subsidiary that is classified as held for sale is accounted for under IFRS 5 *Non-current Assets and Discontinued Operations*. This means that it is included in the balance sheet as a non-current asset and measured at the lower of its carrying amount and fair value less costs to sell.

### 5.4 Consolidation procedures

***General***

Intragroup balances, transactions, income and expenses should be eliminated in full.

***Differing accounting dates***

Some companies in the group may have differing accounting dates. In many cases such companies will prepare financial statements up to the group accounting date for consolidation purposes. IAS 27 allows financial statements made up to a date not more than three months different to be used, with due adjustment for significant transactions or other events between the dates.

***Accounting policies***

All group companies should have uniform accounting policies for the purpose of preparing the consolidated financial statements. This means that the individual financial statements of some subsidiaries may have to be adjusted before consolidation.

***Minority interests***

Minority interests should be presented within equity in the consolidated balance sheet. They should be shown separately from the parent's equity. Minority interests in the profit or loss of the group should also be separately disclosed.

## 5.5 Separate financial statements

Where a parent prepares separate financial statements (for example, because it is an intermediate parent), investments in subsidiaries are accounted for either:

(a) at cost; or

(b) in accordance with IAS 39 (see Chapter 14); this means that they are measured at fair value.

The same accounting must be applied for each category of investments. Subsidiaries classified as held for sale are accounted for in accordance with IFRS 5.

Where separate financial statements are prepared because a parent has elected not to prepare consolidated financial statements it must disclose:

(a) the fact that the financial statements are separate financial statements and the exemption from consolidation has been used

(b) the name and details of its parent that publishes consolidated financial statements that comply with IFRSs

(c) a list of significant subsidiaries, including:

- name
- country of incorporation or residence
- proportion of ownership interest and, if different, proportion of voting power held

(d) a description of the method used to account for the subsidiaries listed under (c).

## 5.6 Other disclosures

Notes to the consolidated financial statements should disclose:

(a) the nature of the relationship between the parent and a subsidiary which is consolidated even though the parent owns less than 50% of the voting power

(b) the reasons why any investee in which the parent owns more than 50% of the equity has not been consolidated because of the absence of control

(c) where the consolidated financial statements have been based on financial statements of a subsidiary made up to a different reporting date from the parent, this fact and the reason

(d) the nature and extent of any significant restrictions on the ability of subsidiaries to transfer funds to the parent as dividends or to repay borrowings.

## Summary

- As with a consolidated balance sheet, the basic procedure for preparing a consolidated income statement is simply to add together the income statements for the individual companies within the group. A convenient way to do this is by means of the master schedule illustrated in this chapter. On this schedule you can enter adjustments for:
  - inter-company transactions, including trading transactions, payment of dividends and interest by subsidiaries to the parent company
  - minority interests.
- IAS 27 contains rules for when group accounts need not be prepared.

Having completed your study of this chapter, you should have achieved the following learning outcomes:

- explain the conditions required for an undertaking to be a subsidiary or an associate of another company
- explain and apply the rules for the exclusion of subsidiaries from consolidation
- prepare a consolidated income statement for a group of companies
- identify the impact on group financial statements when a subsidiary is acquired part way through an accounting period.

## Self-test questions

**1** If a parent and a 75% subsidiary both have sales revenue of $10,000 for a year, will consolidated revenue be $20,000 or S17,500? (1.3)

**2** What comprises a group's consolidated retained earnings balance brought forward at the start of a year? (1.4)

**3** How is intra-group interest on loans dealt with in the consolidated income statement? (3.2)

**4** How does IAS 27 define a subsidiary? (5.1)

**5** When is a parent company exempted from preparing consolidated accounts? (5.2)

**6** When may a subsidiary be excluded from the consolidation? (5.3)

## Objective test question

### Question 1

Ufton is the sole subsidiary of Walcot. The cost of sales figures for 20X1 for Walcot and Ufton were $11 million and $10 million respectively. During 20X1 Walcot sold goods which had cost $2 million to Ufton for $3 million. Ufton has not yet sold any of these goods.

What is the consolidated cost of sales figure for 20X1?

**A** $16 million

**B** $18 million

**C** $19 million

**D** $20 million

*For the answers to this question, see the 'Answers' section at the end of the book.*

## Practice questions

### Question 1: N and S

N acquired 60% of the ordinary shares of S several years ago when the reserves of S were $80,000.

The summarised income statements of the two companies for the year ended 30 September 20X7 are as follows:

| | *N* | | *S* | |
|---|---|---|---|---|
| | $000 | $000 | $000 | $000 |
| Sales revenue | | 4,500 | | 1,100 |
| Cost of sales | | 2,320 | | 620 |
| Gross profit | | 2,180 | | 480 |
| Expenses | | 1,400 | | 220 |
| Trading profit | | 780 | | 260 |
| Investment income | | 48 | | |
| Profit before tax | | 828 | | |
| Income tax expense | | 200 | | 80 |
| Profit after tax | | 628 | | 180 |

N sold goods to S during the year at an invoice price of $250,000. The goods were invoiced at cost + 25%. Of these goods, one half were still in inventory at the end of the year.

Dividends paid were as shown below:

| | | | | |
|---|---|---|---|---|
| Dividends paid: | | | | |
| Ordinary | 420 | | 80 | |

**You are required** to prepare the consolidated income statement for the year ended 30 September 20X7. **(20 marks)**

## Question 2: R

The finance director of R has asked you to prepare the consolidated income statement of the R group. He has provided you with the following summarised income statements and information.

**Summarised income statements for the year ended 31 March 20X4**

| | *R* | *S* | *J* |
|---|---|---|---|
| | $ | $ | $ |
| Gross profit | 728,000 | 149,000 | 510,000 |
| Net operating expenses | 182,000 | 37,250 | 127,500 |
| Profit from operations | 546,000 | 111,750 | 382,500 |
| Investment income | 49,500 | - | - |
| Profit before tax | 595,500 | 111,750 | 382,500 |
| Income tax expense | 162,250 | 29,000 | 89,000 |
| Net profit for the year | 433,250 | 82,750 | 293,500 |
| **Statement of changes in equity** | | | |
| Balance b/f | 624,000 | 244,000 | 220,000 |
| Net profit for the year | 433,250 | 82,750 | 293,500 |
| Dividends paid 31 March 20X4 | (200,000) | (10,000) | (60,000) |
| Retained profits c/f | 857,250 | 316,750 | 453,500 |

Additional information:

(a) The issued share capital of S consists of 200,000 ordinary shares of $1 each. R acquired 150,000 ordinary shares for $210,000 on 1 October 20X3.

(b) The issued share capital of J consists of 120,000 shares of $1 each. R acquired 84,000 ordinary shares of J for $120,000 on 1 April 20X0 when the reserves of J were $30,000.

(c) The profits of S are deemed to accrue evenly throughout the year.

(d) During the year, R made sales of $50,000 to J. The inventories of J contain $10,000 of purchases from R. R has a profit margin of 20% on sales.

**You are required** to prepare the consolidated income statement and consolidated statement of changes in equity of the R group for the year ended 31 March 20X4.

*Show all your workings.* **(20 marks)**

*For the answers to these questions, see the 'Answers' section at the end of the book.*

# Feedback to activities

## Activity 1

**Consolidated income statement for year ended 30 November 20X4**

| | $ |
|---|---|
| Sales revenue | 10,700,000 |
| Cost of sales and expenses | 9,630,000 |
| Group profit before taxation | 1,070,000 |
| Tax | 500,000 |
| Profit for the year | 570,000 |
| Attributable to: | |
| Equity holders of the parent | 540,000 |
| Minority interests | 30,000 |
| Profit for the year | 570,000 |

***Tutorial note:*** The profit attributable to the parent consists of:

| | $ |
|---|---|
| Profit of P | 450,000 |
| P share of profit of S 75% × $120,000 | 90,000 |
| | 540,000 |

## Activity 2

**Retained earnings**

| | $ |
|---|---|
| Brought forward | |
| P | 2,300,000 |
| S 75% × $(400,000 – 100,000) | 225,000 |
| | 2,525,000 |
| Retained for the year | 540,000 |
| Carried forward | 3,065,000 |

It is important to note that the calculation of retained earnings brought forward is of the same form as the calculation of group retained earnings for the consolidated balance sheet. To demonstrate that this is so, here are extracts from the working papers for the balance sheet consolidations at 30 November 20X3 and 30 November 20X4:

**Consolidated retained earnings at 30 November 20X3:**

| | $000 |
|---|---|
| P | 2,300 |
| S 75% (400 – 100) | 225 |
| Retained earnings at 30 November 20X3 as above | 2,525 |

**Consolidated retained earnings at 30 November 20X4:**

| | $000 |
|---|---|
| P** | 2,750 |
| S 75% (520 – 100)* | 315 |
| Retained earnings at 30 November 20X4 as above | 3,065 |

* Reserves of the two companies at the end of the year are:

| | *P* | *S* |
|---|---|---|
| | $ | $ |
| Retained earnings brought forward | 2,300,000 | 400,000 |
| Retained earnings for the year | 450,000 | 120,000 |
| Retained earnings carried forward | 2,750,000 | 520,000 |

## Activity 3

**Consolidated income statement for year ended 31 July 20X4**

| | $ |
|---|---|
| Revenue $(1,430,000 + 5/12 × 600,000) | 1,680,000 |
| Cost of sales and expenses $(1,160,000 + 5/12 × 504,000) | 1,370,000 |
| Profit before tax $(270,000 + 5/12 × 96,000) | 310,000 |
| Tax $(135,000 + 5/12 × 48,000) | 155,000 |
| Profit for the period | 155,000 |
| Attributable to: | |
| Equity holders of the parent | 150,000 |
| Minority interest $(25% × 5/12 × (96,000 – 48,000)) | 5,000 |
| | 155,000 |

**Movement on retained earningss**

| | $ |
|---|---|
| Retained earnings at 1 August 20X3 | 900,000 |
| Group retained earnings for the year | 150,000 |
| | 1,050,000 |

***Note:*** The reserves brought forward can only consist of P's reserves, as S was not a subsidiary at that date.

Chapter 5

# ASSOCIATES AND JOINT VENTURES

## Syllabus content

- The treatment in consolidated financial statements of minority interests, pre- and post-acquisition reserves, goodwill (including its impairment), fair value adjustments, intra-group transactions and dividends, piece-meal and mid-year acquisitions, and disposals to include sub-subsidiaries and mixed groups.
- The accounting treatment of associates and joint ventures (IAS 28 & 31) using the equity method and proportional consolidation method.

## Contents

# Introduction

In this chapter we look at situations where a company may not be able to exercise **control** over an investee, but can **influence** its operating and financial policies. An entity over which an investor can exercise significant influence is called an associate. An arrangement whereby two or more venturers undertake an activity subject to joint control is called a joint venture.

This chapter covers the preparation of the income statement and balance sheet where a company has an associate or a joint venture and also looks at the requirements of the two relevant accounting standards: IAS 28 *Investments in Associates* and IAS 31 *Interests in Joint Ventures*.

## 1 Associates

### 1.1 Introduction

As we have seen, if an entity holds more than 50% of the equity shares in another entity it normally controls that other entity and a parent/subsidiary relationship exists. Control is the power to govern the financial and operating policies of an entity so as to gain benefits from its activities.

DEFINITION

**Significant influence** is the power to participate in the financial and operating policy decisions of an entity in which an investment is held, but is not control or joint control over these policies.

An **associate** is an entity, including an unincorporated entity such as a partnership, over which the investor has significant influence and which is neither a subsidiary nor an interest in a joint venture.

At the other extreme are investments too small to give any influence, and where the purpose of the investment is to generate income and capital gains.

However, there is a size of holding between these two, not large enough to result in control, but large enough to give significant influence.

**Significant influence** is the power to participate in the financial and operating policy decisions of an entity in which an investment is held, but is not control or joint control over these policies.

An **associate** is an entity, including an unincorporated entity such as a partnership, over which the investor has significant influence and which is neither a subsidiary nor an interest in a joint venture.

IAS 28 *Investments in Associates* explains the conditions under which an entity has significant influence over another and sets out the accounting treatment for those investments giving influence but not control.

KEY POINT

A holding of 20% or more of the voting power is presumed to give significant influence, unless it can be clearly demonstrated that this is not the case.

A holding of 20% or more of the voting power is presumed to give significant influence, unless it can be clearly demonstrated that this is not the case. Conversely, it is presumed that a holding of less than 20% does not give significant influence, unless such influence can be clearly demonstrated.

KEY POINT

You must look beyond the simple percentage stake held in each situation. The test, to be an associate, is whether the investor has significant influence over the investee in the circumstances of the case.

For example, if company X owns 15% of company Y, it would normally be assumed that X does not have significant influence over Y, and Y would be treated in X's financial statements as a simple investment. However, if X has the right to nominate a director to serve on Y's board of directors and no other shareholder owns more than 1% of Y's shares, then X probably does have significant influence. You must look beyond the simple percentage stake held in each situation. The test, to be an associate, is whether the investor has significant influence over the investee in the circumstances of the case.

IAS 28 explains that an investor probably has significant influence if:

(a) it is represented on the board of directors

(b) it participates in policy-making processes, including decisions about dividends or other distributions

(c) there are material transactions between the investor and the investee

(d) there is interchange of managerial personnel, or

(e) there is provision of essential technical information.

***Activity 1***

Which of the following investments of Gamma Trust should be treated as associates? Assume that all shares carry equal voting rights.

1 19% of the equity shares in Goose Limited. Gamma Trust is the largest shareholder, has a director on the board, and provides management expertise to this rapidly growing company.

2 22% of the equity share capital of Delta Traders, a company in the same line of business as most of Gamma Trust. In the past there has been an unsuccessful bid for Delta Traders by Gamma Trust. Gamma Trust has no director on Delta Traders' board, and its views on the management of Delta Traders are neither sought nor accepted. The majority shareholders use their combined voting rights to keep any nominee of Gamma Trust off the board, and to prevent any motion proposed by Gamma Trust from being passed at general meetings.

3 21% of the equity share capital of Nova Manufacturers Limited. This shareholding was recently increased from 10%, as the young company is expanding rapidly. The company's business is not within Gamma Trust's core business range, and Gamma Trust hopes to sell its investment within the year.

4 47% of the equity share capital of Alpha Wholesale Limited. The other shareholders are split between various small investors. Gamma Trust nominates seven of the 10 directors on the board of Alpha Wholesale, under a written agreement between the two companies.

*Feedback to this activity is at the end of the chapter.*

## 1.2 The equity method of accounting

KEY POINT

The **equity method** is a method of accounting whereby the investment is initially recorded at cost and adjusted thereafter for the post-acquisition change in the investor's share of net assets of the associate.

To understand the accounting treatment of associates in the consolidated accounts we first need to understand the equity basis of accounting. The **equity method** is a method of accounting whereby the investment is initially recorded at cost and adjusted thereafter for the post-acquisition change in the investor's share of net assets of the associate. The profit or loss of the investor includes the investor's share of the profit or loss of the investee.

Treating the associate as a simple investment would be misleading to users of the financial statements. The income statement would only record dividends received and this would not reflect the fact that the investor has significant influence and therefore an interest in the entity's performance. Therefore the income statement includes the group share of the profits and losses of such an associate.

***Consolidated balance sheet***

The initial cost of the investment is increased each year by the investor's share of the associate's post tax profit (or reduced if there is a loss). The retained profit (i.e. after deducting dividends) is used.

Any difference between cost and the fair value of the group's share of the associate's net assets is treated as goodwill.

KEY POINT

The value of the investment at each balance sheet date is cost plus the group's share of the associate's post tax profit.

KEY POINT

In the income statement the investor's share of the associate's profit for the year is included as a separate line item.

These two adjustments mean that the value of the investment at each balance sheet date is cost plus the group's share of the associate's post tax profit.

Investments in associates should be classified as non-current assets and shown separately in the balance sheet.

***Consolidated income statement***

In the income statement the investor's share of the associate's profit for the year is included as a separate line item instead of the dividends receivable.

## 1.3 Consolidated balance sheet: example

P acquired 25% of the ordinary share capital of A for $640,000 on 31 December 20X2 when the retained earnings of A stood at $720,000. P appointed two directors to the board of A and the investment is regarded as long term. Both companies prepare their financial statements to 31 December each year. The summarised balance sheet of A on 31 December 20X4 is as follows.

| | $000 |
|---|---|
| Sundry net assets | 2,390 |
| **Equity** | |
| Share capital | 800 |
| Share premium | 450 |
| Retained earnings | 1,140 |
| | 2,390 |

A has made no new issues of shares nor has there been any movement in the share premium account since P acquired its holding.

Show the amount at which the investment in A will be shown in the consolidated balance sheet of P as on 31 December 20X4.

***Solution***

*Investment in associate*

| | $ |
|---|---|
| 25% × $2,390,000 | 597,500 |
| Goodwill (W1) | 147,500 |
| | 745,000 |

This figure could also be calculated as:

| | $ |
|---|---|
| Cost | 640,000 |
| Share of post-acquisition profits (25% × (1,140 – 720)) | 105,000 |
| | 745,000 |

***Working***

(W1) Goodwill

| | | $ | $ |
|---|---|---|---|
| Cost | | | 640,000 |
| Less: Share of net assets at acquisition | | | |
| Share capital | | 800,000 | |
| Share premium | | 450,000 | |
| Reserves | | 720,000 | |
| | 25% × | 1,970,000 | (492,500) |
| Goodwill | | | 147,500 |

### 1.4 Effect on total reserves

KEY POINT

Total reserves in the published financial statements are increased by the group share of post acquisition reserves of the associate.

Total reserves in the published financial statements are increased by the group share of post acquisition reserves of the associate.

The consolidation schedule for group reserves will include this item in respect of associated undertakings as shown below:

Consolidated retained earnings

| | $000 |
|---|---|
| P: | X |
| S: S% (now – acquisition) | X |
| A: 25% (now – acquisition (1,140 – 720)) | 105 |
| | X |

### 1.5 Consolidated income statement: example

Following on from the facts above, the consolidated income statement of the P group (before including any amounts for A) and the income statement of A for the year ended 31 December 20X4 are as follows.

| | *P* | *A* |
|---|---|---|
| | $000 | $000 |
| Sales revenue | 11,000 | 4,000 |
| Cost of sales | (6,500) | (3,000) |
| Gross profit | 4,500 | 1,000 |
| Distribution costs | (1,000) | (500) |
| Administrative expenses | (700) | (300) |
| Profit before tax | 2,800 | 200 |
| Income tax expense | (1,200) | (60) |
| Profit for the period | 1,600 | 140 |
| Minority interest | (300) | – |
| Profit attributable to the parent | 1,300 | 140 |

Show the amounts to be included in the consolidated income statement of the P group for the year ended 31 December 20X4.

***Solution***

| | $000 |
|---|---|
| Revenue | 11,000 |
| Cost of sales | (6,500) |
| Gross profit | 4,500 |
| Distribution costs | (1,000) |
| Administrative expenses | (700) |
| Share of profit of associate (25% × 140) | 35 |
| Profit before tax | 2,835 |
| Income tax expense | (1,200) |
| Profit for the period | 1,635 |
| Attributable to: | |
| Equity holders of the parent | 1,335 |
| Minority interests | 300 |
| | 1,635 |

KEY POINT

Trading transactions between member companies of the group and the associate are not cancelled out.

## 1.6 Transactions between the group and the associate

Trading transactions and/or loans may be made between member companies of the group (i.e. parent and subsidiaries) and the associate. As the associate is not consolidated it follows that these transactions are not cancelled out. For example, a loan made by the parent to an associate will remain as a loan on the consolidated balance sheet (as an asset). The liability recorded in the associate's balance sheet will merely reduce the net assets (which are recorded as one figure – share of net assets – on the consolidated balance sheet).

***Trading between group and associate***

An adjustment will only be required if there is unrealised profit at the balance sheet date, i.e. inventories exist as a result of the trading. The elimination should be taken in the consolidated income statement against either the group or the associate according to which of them recorded the profit on the transaction. The adjustment in the balance sheet should be made against:

(a) consolidated inventory (if the unrealised profit is in respect of part of this inventory), or

(b) investment in associate (if the inventory is in the associate).

***Example – parent sells to associate***

Garamond has several subsidiaries and a 30% associate, Arial. Extracts from the income statements of Garamond plus its subsidiaries and Arial are shown below:

| | *Garamond and subsidiaries* | *Arial* |
|---|---|---|
| | $000 | $000 |
| Revenue | 55,000 | 24,000 |
| Cost of sales | (30,000) | (13,000) |
| Gross profit | 25,000 | 11,000 |

During the year ended 31 December 20X3, Garamond made sales of $3,000,000 to Arial. The goods were sold at cost plus a 25% mark-up. At 31 December 20X3, Arial had one third of these goods still in inventory.

**Required:**

Calculate the consolidated revenue, cost of sales and gross profit for the Garamond Group for the year ended 31 December 20X3 and explain the effect of the intra-group sale on the consolidated balance sheet at 31 December 20X3.

***Solution***

The parent has made sales to the associate and has recorded the unrealised profit at the year end. This means that the group's share of the unrealised profit is eliminated against the **parent's** gross profit:

| | $000 | $000 |
|---|---|---|
| Dr Revenue | 300 | |
| Cr Cost of sales | | 300 |

To eliminate the group's share of the revenue that relates to the unrealised profit (30% × 3,000 × 1/3).

| | $000 | $000 |
|---|---|---|
| Dr Cost of sales | 60 | |
| Cr Investment in associate | | 60 |

To eliminate the group's share of the unrealised profit (30% × 3,000 × 1/3 × 25/125).

**Extract from the consolidated income statement for the year ended 31 December 20X3**

| | $000 |
|---|---|
| Revenue (55,000 – 300) | 54,700 |
| Cost of sales (30,000 – 300 + 60) | (29,760) |
| Gross profit | 24,940 |

**Effect on the consolidated balance sheet:**

Because the **associate** is holding the unsold inventory at the year end, the group's share of the unrealised profit is eliminated against the investment in associate (the group's share of the net assets of the associate, including inventories).

Therefore the investment in the associate and consolidated reserves are both reduced by $60,000.

***Example – associate sells to parent***

The facts are as in the example above, except that it is Arial which made sales of $3,000,000 to Garamond. The goods were sold at cost plus a 25% mark-up. At 31 December 20X3, Arial had one third of these goods still in inventory.

***Solution***

The associate has sold the goods to the parent; therefore the group share of unrealised profit is eliminated against the **associate's** gross profit. Only one adjustment is necessary:

| | $000 | $000 |
|---|---|---|
| Dr Share of profit of associate | 60 | |
| Cr Consolidated inventory | | 60 |

To eliminate the group's share of the unrealised profit (30% × 3,000 × 1/3 × 25/125).

**Effect on the consolidated income statement:**

The share of the associate's profit is reduced by $60,000. Revenue and cost of sales are not adjusted.

**Effect on the consolidated balance sheet:**

Because the **parent** is holding the unsold inventory at the year end, the group's share of the unrealised profit is eliminated against consolidated inventory.

Therefore consolidated inventory and consolidated reserves are both reduced by $60,000.

### *Activity 2*

On 1 January 20X5 Kennedy, which has a 100% subsidiary, acquired 25% of the equity shares of Campbell for $400,000. At that date, the retained earnings of Campbell were $220,000. The income statements and the summarised balance sheets of the Kennedy Group and Campbell are shown below.

**Income statements for the year ended 31 December 20X5**

| | *Kennedy Group* | *Campbell* |
|---|---|---|
| | $000 | $000 |
| Revenue | 2,600 | 1,420 |
| Cost of sales | (1,600) | (800) |
| Gross profit | 1,000 | 620 |
| Operating expenses | (460) | (360) |
| Profit before tax | 540 | 260 |
| Income tax expense | (120) | (60) |
| Profit for the year | 420 | 200 |

**Balance sheets at 31 December 20X5**

| | *Kennedy Group* | *Campbell* |
|---|---|---|
| | $000 | $000 |
| Non-current assets | 2,000 | 600 |
| Investment in Campbell | 400 | |
| Current assets | 800 | 520 |
| | 3,200 | 1,120 |
| Share capital | 1,500 | 500 |
| Retained earnings | 1,350 | 420 |
| Current liabilities | 350 | 200 |
| | 3,200 | 1,120 |

At 1 January 20X5 the fair values of the properties of Campbell were $100,000 greater than their book values. The effect on the depreciation charge for the year is immaterial.

At 31 December 20X5 goodwill is not considered to be impaired.

During the year Campbell sold goods that originally cost $250,000 to Kennedy, making a profit of $40,000. Half these goods remained in inventory at 31 December 20X5.

Prepare the consolidated financial statements of the Kennedy Group for the year ended 31 December 20X5.

*Feedback to this activity is at the end of the chapter.*

# 2 IAS 28: further requirements

## 2.1 Applying the equity method

The rules in IAS 28 are similar to the rules for exemptions and exclusions in IAS 27 *Consolidated and Separate Financial Statements*. An investment in an associate must be accounted for using the equity method except when:

(a) IAS 27 allows a parent that also has an investment in an associate not to present consolidated financial statements; or

(b) all of the following apply:

  (i) the investor is a wholly-owned subsidiary; or a partially-owned subsidiary of another entity and its other owners do not object to the investor not applying the equity method

  (ii) the investor is not a public company and is not in the process of becoming a public company

  (iii) the ultimate or any intermediate parent of the investor produces consolidated financial statements available for public use that comply with IFRSs.

IAS 28 also states that an associate should not be equity accounted if it is classified as 'held for sale' in accordance with IFRS 5 *Non-current Assets Held for Sale and Discontinued Operations*. Instead it should be accounted for in accordance with IFRS 5.

The use of the equity method must be discontinued from the date that the investor ceases to have significant influence over an associate. The investment is then accounted for in accordance with IAS 39.

## 2.2 Differing accounting dates

The investor should use the most recent available financial statements of the associate when applying the equity method. If the accounting dates of the group and the associate differ, the associate should prepare statements as at the same date as the financial statements of the investor. If this is not practicable, financial statements of the associate prepared to a different date may be used, with disclosure of the effects of any significant events or transactions between the dates. The difference between the reporting date of the associate and the reporting date of the investor must be no more than three months.

## 2.3 Differing accounting policies

The investor's financial statements should be prepared using uniform accounting policies.

If an associate uses different accounting policies from those of the investor, its financial statements must be adjusted when the associate's financial statements are used by the investor in applying the equity method.

## 2.4 Separate financial statements

An investment in an associate shall be accounted for in the investor's separate financial statements in accordance with the requirements of IAS 27:

(a) at cost; or

(b) in accordance with IAS 39 (see Chapter 14); this means that it is measured at fair value.

The same accounting must be applied for each category of investments.

### 2.5 Contingencies

The investor should disclose:

(a) its share of the contingent liabilities of an associate incurred jointly with other investors; and

(b) those contingent liabilities that arise because the investor is severally liable for all or part of the liabilities of the associate.

### 2.6 Other disclosure requirements

KEY POINT

Investments in associates accounted for using the equity method should be classified as non-current assets.

Investments in associates accounted for using the equity method should be classified as non-current assets. The following should be separately disclosed:

(a) the investor's share of the profit or loss

(b) the carrying amount of the investments

(c) the investor's share of any discontinued operations of associates.

The investor's share of changes recognised directly in the associate's equity should be recognised directly in equity by the investor and should be disclosed in the statement of changes in equity as required by IAS 1 *Presentation of Financial Statements*.

Other required disclosures include:

(a) summarised financial information of associates

(b) the reasons why the presumption that an investor does not have significant influence is overcome if the investor holds less than 20% of the voting power of the investee but concludes that it has significant influence

(c) the reasons why the presumption that an investor has significant influence is overcome if the investor holds 20% or more of the voting power of the investee but concludes that it does not have significant influence

(d) where financial statements of an associate made up to a different reporting date from the investor have been used for the purpose of equity accounting, this fact and the reason

(e) the nature and extent of any significant restrictions on the ability of associates to transfer funds to the parent as dividends or to repay borrowings

(f) if an associate has not been accounted for using the equity method

(g) summarised financial information of associates that are not accounted for using the equity method.

# 3 Interests in joint ventures

## 3.1 Types of joint venture

A **joint venture** is a contractual arrangement whereby two or more parties undertake an economic activity that is subject to joint control.

**Joint control** is the contractually agreed sharing of control over an economic activity.

In practice, joint control means that none of the parties alone can control the activity, but all together can do so. Important decisions on financial and operating policy require each venturer's consent.

The following characteristics are common to all joint ventures:

(a) two or more venturers are bound by a contractual arrangement; and

(b) the contractual arrangement establishes joint control.

Joint ventures can take many different forms, but IAS 31 *Interests in Joint Ventures* identifies three main types: jointly controlled operations, jointly controlled assets, and jointly controlled entities.

DEFINITION

A **joint venture** is a contractual arrangement whereby two or more parties undertake an economic activity that is subject to joint control.

**Joint control** is the contractually agreed sharing of control over an economic activity.

***Jointly controlled operations***

A jointly controlled operation is a joint venture which involves the use of the assets and other resources of the venturers rather than the establishment of an entity which is separate from the venturers themselves. Each venturer uses its own assets and incurs its own expenses and liabilities. Profits are shared among the venturers in accordance with the contractual agreement.

For example, A and B decide to enter into a joint venture agreement to produce a new product. A undertakes one manufacturing process and B undertakes the other. A and B each bear their own expenses and take an agreed share of the sales revenue from the product.

IAS 31 states that a venturer should account for its interests in jointly controlled operations by recognising:

(a) the assets that it controls and the liabilities that it incurs; and

(b) the expenses that it incurs and its share of the income that it earns from the sale of goods or services by the joint venture in its financial statements.

KEY POINT

IAS 31 states that a venturer should account for its interests in jointly controlled operations by recognising:

(a) the assets that it controls and the liabilities that it incurs; and

(b) the expenses that it incurs and its share of the income that it earns from the sale of goods or services by the joint venture in its financial statements.

***Jointly controlled assets***

A jointly controlled asset is a joint venture in which the venturers control jointly (and often own jointly) an asset contributing to or acquired for the purpose of the joint venture.

The venturers each take a share of the profit or income from the asset and each bears a share of the expenses involved.

For example, C and D together buy a house which they let to tenants. C is responsible for the initial refurbishment and maintenance of the house and D finds the tenants and collects the rents. C and D each take an agreed share of the rental income from the house.

KEY POINT

A jointly controlled asset is a joint venture in which the venturers control jointly (and often own jointly) an asset contributing to or acquired for the purpose of the joint venture.

Where a venturer has an interest in a jointly controlled asset, IAS 31 requires it to recognise the following in its financial statements:

(a) its share of the jointly controlled assets, classified according to the nature of the assets

(b) any liabilities that it has incurred

(c) its share of any liabilities incurred jointly with the other venturers in relation to the joint venture

(d) any income from the sale or use of its share of the output of the joint venture, together with its share of any expenses incurred by the joint venture, and

(e) any expenses that it has incurred in respect of its interest in the joint venture.

***Jointly controlled entities***

KEY POINT

A jointly controlled entity is a joint venture which involves the establishment of a company, partnership or other entity in which each venturer has an interest.

A jointly controlled entity is a joint venture which involves the establishment of a company, partnership or other entity in which each venturer has an interest. The contractual agreement between the venturers provides for their joint control over the entity. Otherwise, a jointly controlled entity operates in the same way as any other entity. Each venturer is entitled to a share of the entity's results.

For example, E and F enter into a joint venture agreement to manufacture and sell a new product. They set up a company which carries out these activities. E and F each own 50% of the equity share capital of the company and are its only directors. They share equally in major policy decisions and are each entitled to 50% of the profits of the company.

A jointly controlled entity maintains its own accounting records and prepares and presents financial statements in the same way as other entities.

Each venturer usually contributes cash or other resources to the jointly controlled entity. These contributions are included in the accounting records of the venturer and recognised in its financial statements as an investment in the jointly controlled entity.

KEY POINT

If you are required to deal with a joint venture in the exam it will almost certainly be a jointly controlled entity.

If you are required to deal with a joint venture in the exam it will almost certainly be a jointly controlled entity.

## 3.2 Accounting for jointly controlled entities in the financial statements of the venturer

KEY POINT

A venturer must account for its interest in a jointly controlled entity in its financial statements.

KEY POINT

IAS 31 allows two methods: proportionate consolidation or the equity method.

A venturer must account for its interest in a jointly controlled entity in its financial statements. This applies whether or not it also has investments in subsidiaries or whether or not it prepares consolidated financial statements.

IAS 31 allows two methods: proportionate consolidation or the equity method.

***Proportionate consolidation***

**Proportionate consolidation** is a method of accounting whereby a venturer's share of each of the assets, liabilities, income and expenses of a jointly controlled entity is combined line by line with similar items in the venturer's financial statements or reported as separate line items in the venturer's financial statements.

DEFINITION

**Proportionate consolidation** is a method of accounting whereby a venturer's share of each of the assets, liabilities, income and expenses of a jointly controlled entity is combined line by line with similar items in the venturer's financial statements or reported as separate line items in the venturer's financial statements.

The reasoning behind this treatment is that when a venturer has an interest in a jointly controlled entity it has control over its share of future economic benefits through its share of the assets and liabilities of the venture. Proportionate consolidation means that the balance sheet of the venturer includes its share of the assets that it controls jointly and its share of the liabilities for which it is jointly responsible. The income statement of the venturer includes its share of the income and expenses of the jointly controlled entity.

There are two main ways in which the information can be presented. The two methods are equally acceptable, although method (a) may be easier in the exam.

(a) The venturer **combines its share** of each of the assets, liabilities, income and expenses of the jointly controlled entity **with the similar items, line by line**, in its financial statements.

(b) The venturer includes **separate line items** for its share of the assets, liabilities, income and expenses of the jointly controlled entity in its financial statements.

Whichever format is used, it is inappropriate to offset items unless a legal right of set-off exists.

***Example***

ABC joins with other business partners to establish a new joint venture company, XYZ. ABC pays $50,000 for a 30% share in XYZ, on that company's incorporation.

At 31 December 20X6 the balance sheets are as follows:

| | *ABC and subsidiaries* | *XYZ* |
|---|---|---|
| | $000 | $000 |
| Non-current assets | 2,000 | 400 |
| Investment in XYZ | 50 | |
| Current assets | 500 | 200 |
| | 2,550 | 600 |
| Share capital | 1,000 | 100 |
| Retained earnings | 1,200 | 300 |
| Current liabilities | 350 | 200 |
| | 2,550 | 600 |

Prepare the consolidated balance sheet for the ABC group at 31 December 20X6, incorporating the joint venture using proportional consolidation.

***Solution***

Method (a)

**ABC Group**
**Consolidated balance sheet as at 31 December 20X6**

| | $000 |
|---|---|
| Non-current assets (2,000 + 30% × 400) | 2,120 |
| Goodwill arising (50 – 30% × 100) | 20 |
| Current assets (500 + 30% × 200) | 560 |
| | 2,700 |

| | |
|---|---|
| Share capital (parent company only) | 1,000 |
| Retained earnings (1,200 + 30% × 300) | 1,290 |
| Current liabilities (350 + 30% × 200) | 410 |
| | 2,700 |

The stake was acquired on XYZ's incorporation, when there were no retained earnings, so the pre-acquisition reserves are zero. The net assets of XYZ on acquisition would be the share capital only, totalling $100,000.

Method (b)

**ABC Group**
**Consolidated balance sheet as at 31 December 20X6**

| | $000 | $000 |
|---|---|---|
| Non-current assets: group | 2,000 | |
| joint venture | 120 | |
| | | 2,120 |
| Goodwill arising (50 – 30% × 100) | | 20 |
| Current assets: group | 500 | |
| joint venture | 60 | |
| | | 560 |
| | | 2,700 |
| Share capital (parent company only) | | 1,000 |
| Retained earnings: group | 1,200 | |
| joint venture | 90 | |
| | | 1,290 |
| Current liabilities: group | 350 | |
| joint venture | 60 | |
| | | 410 |
| | | 2,700 |

Note that the amount of assets and liabilities is the same under both methods, as is total retained earnings. The difference is in the way that the information is presented.

***Equity method***

KEY POINT

The IASB believes that proportionate consolidation is the best way of reflecting the economic reality of the relationship between the venture and the jointly controlled entity.

The equity method was covered earlier in this chapter. An interest in a jointly controlled entity is accounted for exactly as if it were an associate.

The IASB believes that proportionate consolidation is the best way of reflecting the economic reality of the relationship between the venture and the jointly controlled entity. However, it recognises that there are arguments against proportionate consolidation and therefore it permits the use of the equity method as an alternative.

## 3.3 Exemptions and exceptions

IAS 31 contains similar rules to those in IAS 27 and IAS 28.

An interest in a jointly controlled entity must be accounted for using either proportionate consolidation or the equity method except when:

(a) IAS 27 allows a parent that also has an interest in a jointly controlled entity not to present consolidated financial statements; or

(b) all of the following apply:

  (i) the venturer is a wholly-owned subsidiary; or a partially-owned subsidiary of another entity and its other owners do not object to the investor not applying proportionate consolidation or the equity method

  (ii) the venturer is not a public company and is not in the process of becoming a public company

  (iii) the ultimate or any intermediate parent of the venturer produces consolidated financial statements available for public use that comply with IFRSs.

IAS 31 also states that an interest in a jointly controlled entity should not be proportionately consolidated or equity accounted if it is classified as held for sale in accordance with IFRS 5 *Non-current Assets Held for Sale on Discontinued Operations* (see Chapter 18).

The use of proportionate consolidation/the equity method must be discontinued from the date that the investor ceases to have joint control or significant influence over the jointly controlled entity. IAS 39 then applies.

### 3.4 Separate financial statements

An interest in a jointly controlled entity should be accounted for in the venturer's separate financial statements in accordance with the requirements of IAS 27:

(a) at cost; or

(b) in accordance with IAS 39 (see Chapter 14); this means that it is measured at fair value.

The same accounting must be applied for each category of investments.

### 3.5 Transactions between a venturer and a joint venture

KEY POINT

When a venturer contributes or sells assets to a joint venture, recognition of any portion of a gain or loss from the transaction must reflect the substance of the transaction.

When a venturer contributes or sells assets to a joint venture, recognition of any portion of a gain or loss from the transaction must reflect the substance of the transaction. Provided the substance of the transaction is a sale, the venturer should recognise only that portion of the gain or loss that is attributable to the interests of the other venturers.

When a venturer purchases assets from a joint venture, the venturer shall not recognise its share of the profits of the joint venture from the transaction until it resells the assets to an independent party.

### 3.6 Disclosure requirements

***Contingent liabilities and capital commitments***

Unless the probability of loss is remote, a venturer should separately disclose:

(a) any contingent liabilities that the venturer has incurred in relation to its interests in joint ventures and its share in each of the contingent liabilities that have been incurred jointly with other venturers;

(b) its share of the contingent liabilities of the joint ventures themselves for which it is liable; and

(c) those contingent liabilities that arise because the venturer is liable for the liabilities of the other venturers.

A venturer should disclose the following:

(a) any capital commitments of the venturer in relation to its interests in joint ventures and its share in the capital commitments that have been incurred jointly with other venturers; and

(b) its share of the capital commitments of the joint ventures themselves.

***Other***

A venturer should disclose:

(a) a listing and description of interests in significant joint ventures and the proportion of ownership interest held in jointly controlled entities

(b) if the line-by-line reporting format for proportionate consolidation or the equity method has been used, the aggregate amounts of each of current assets, long-term assets, current liabilities, long-term liabilities, income and expenses related to its interests in joint ventures

(c) the method it uses to recognise its interests in jointly controlled entities.

***Activity 3***

Three oil exploration companies enter into a joint venture agreement with each other to drill for oil in a Central Asian country and form a new company, Drilldeep, for this purpose, owned one third each by the three venturers. Similarly each venturer appoints two directors to the company's board, the financial and operating policies to be agreed mutually after discussion.

How should each oil company account for Drilldeep in their consolidated financial statements?

*Feedback to this activity is at the end of the chapter.*

## 4 Comparison of consolidation, equity method and proportionate consolidation

### 4.1 Example

The separate summarised financial statements for the year to 31 December 20X2 of P and S are:

**Balance sheets as at 31 December 20X2**

| | *P* | *S* |
|---|---|---|
| | $ | $ |
| Non-current assets | 2,200 | 10,000 |
| Cost of investment | 1,800 | – |
| Net current assets | 1,000 | 1,000 |
| | 5,000 | 11,000 |
| Share capital | 2,000 | 1,000 |
| Reserves | 3,000 | 2,000 |
| Loans | – | 8,000 |
| | 5,000 | 11,000 |

**Income statements for year ended 31 December 20X2**

| | *P* | *S* |
|---|---|---|
| | $ | $ |
| Sales revenue | 4,000 | 20,000 |
| Cost of sales | 3,500 | 18,900 |
| Profit from operations | 500 | 1,100 |
| Interest payable | – | 800 |
| | 500 | 300 |
| Tax | 270 | 160 |
| Profit for year | 230 | 140 |

P acquired an 80% interest in S four years ago when the reserves of S were $500.

Show the group balance sheets and income statements under the consolidation method, the equity method, and the proportionate consolidation methods.

**Step 1**

**Goodwill** – This will be the same under each method.

| | $ |
|---|---|
| Share capital and reserves of S at acquisition | 1,500 |
| P share 80% × $1,500 | 1,200 |
| Cost of investment | 1,800 |
| Goodwill | 600 |

**Step 2**

**Minority interest at 31 December 20X2** – only included under the consolidation method.

| | $ |
|---|---|
| Net assets of S at 31 December 20X2 | 3,000 |
| Minority share | 20% |
| | 600 |

**Step 3**

**Group reserves** – The same amount of profit is dealt with under any of the methods.

| | $ |
|---|---|
| P | 3,000 |
| S 80% $(3,000 – 1,500) | 1,200 |
| | 4,200 |

**Group balance sheet of P and subsidiary as at 31 December 20X2**

| | *Consolidation* | *Equity method* | *Proportionate consolidation* |
|---|---|---|---|
| | $ | $ | $ |
| **Net assets** | | | |
| Non-current assets | 12,200 | 2,200 | 10,200 |
| Goodwill arising on acquisition of investment in subsidiary | 600 | 600 | 600 |
| Share of net assets in subsidiary (80% × $3,000) | – | 2,400 | – |
| Net current assets | 2,000 | 1,000 | 1,800 |
| | 14,800 | 6,200 | 12,600 |

| | | | |
|---|---|---|---|
| **Equity** | | | |
| Share capital | 2,000 | 2,000 | 2,000 |
| Reserves | 4,200 | 4,200 | 4,200 |
| | 6,200 | 6,200 | 6,200 |
| Minority interests | 600 | – | – |
| Loans | 8,000 | – | 6,400 |
| | 14,800 | 6,200 | 12,600 |

**Group income statements of P for the year ended 31 December 20X2**

| | *Consolidation* | *Equity method* | *Proportionate consolidation* |
|---|---|---|---|
| | $ | $ | $ |
| Sales revenue | 24,000 | 4,000 | 20,000 |
| Cost of sales | 22,400 | 3,500 | 18,620 |
| Profit from operations | 1,600 | 500 | 1,380 |
| Share of profit of subsidiary (80% × $140) | | 112 | |
| Interest payable | (800) | | (640) |
| | 800 | 612 | 740 |
| Tax $(270 + 160) | 430 | | |
| | | 270 | 398 |
| | 370 | 342 | 342 |
| Minority interest 20% × $140 | 28 | | |
| Profit attributable to P Group | 342 | 342 | 342 |

## 4.2 Evaluating the alternative group accounting methods

The group balance sheets are completely different in form, and give contrasting images of the financial stability of the group. The equity method group balance sheet appears to show a safe state of affairs. The consolidated balance sheets, however, reveal the considerable long-term loans incurred by the subsidiary.

It is because the equity method fails to reveal the underlying assets and liabilities that its use is not regarded as a valid method of showing group accounts in the majority of situations. The equity method is, however, used in situations where there is significant influence, rather than control or joint control.

One view of proportionate consolidation is that it is a good compromise. It shows the proportion of the assets and liabilities that the parent actually owns. Another view of proportionate consolidation is that the amounts in the balance sheet are meaningless (for example, is it valid to include 50% of a building?).

Similar comments can be made in relation to the three income statements.

There are two further things to note:

(a) The shareholders' funds (share capital and reserves) and profit for the period attributable to the group are the same under all three methods.

(b) However, some key performance measures, particularly those based on balance sheet figures (such as return on capital employed, the current ratio and the gearing ratios) would be very different under each of the three methods. This means that financial statements prepared under different methods are not comparable and therefore do not meet the objective of financial statements: to provide users with information that is useful for making economic decisions.

KEY POINT

The shareholders' funds (share capital and reserves) and profit for the period attributable to the group are the same under all three methods.

Some key performance measures, particularly those based on balance sheet figures (such as return on capital employed, the current ratio and the gearing ratios) would be very different under each of the three methods.

## Summary

- An associate is an entity in which the investor has significant influence but not control. Associates are included in the consolidated financial statements using the equity method of accounting.
- A joint venture is an arrangement whereby two or more venturers undertake an activity subject to joint control. The recommended treatment is for jointly controlled entities to be included in the consolidated financial statements using proportionate consolidation.

Having completed your study of this chapter, you should have achieved the following learning outcomes:

- explain the conditions required for an undertaking to be a subsidiary or associate of another company
- explain the concept of an associate and a joint venture, and the principles of how they are accounted for.

## Self-test questions

**1** What is an associate? (1.1)

**2** What are the implications when 20% of another company is owned? (1.1)

**3** What is the meaning of significant influence? (1.1)

**4** How is the investment in an associated company treated in the consolidated balance sheet? (1.3)

**5** How are transactions between the group and the associate dealt with in the consolidated financial statements? (1.6)

**6** What is joint control? (3.1)

**7** What are the two methods of accounting for interests in jointly controlled entities allowed by IAS 31? (3.2)

**8** When should a jointly controlled entity not be proportionately consolidated or equity accounted? (3.3)

## Objective test questions

### Question 1

Pear Inc acquired 30% of the equity capital of Apple Inc on 1 January 2002 at a cost of $240,000. At this date the retained profits of Apple Inc were $200,000.

The equity capital of Apple has remained unchanged at $ 400,000.

The net assets of Apple Inc as at 31 December 2003 amount to $720,000

What is the equity value of the investment in Apple Inc in the consolidated balance sheet of Pear Inc as at 31 December 2003?

### Question 2

Which of the following statements are in accordance with the requirements of IAS 31 *Financial Reporting of Interests in Joint Ventures?*

I A joint venture is a contracted arrangement whereby two or more parties undertake an economic activity which is subject to joint control

II The benchmark treatment is for jointly controlled entities to be included in the consolidated financial statements on a normal consolidation basis, as used for subsidiaries

III The equity method of accounting is the allowed alternative treatment

**A** I, and III only

**B** I, and II only

**C** II and III only

**D** All three statements

*For the answers to these questions, see the 'Answers' section at the end of the book.*

## Exam-type question

### Bacup

The summarised balance sheets of Bacup, Townley and Rishworth as at 31 March 20X7 are as follows:

| | *Bacup* $000 | *Townley* $000 | *Rishworth* $000 |
|---|---|---|---|
| Non-current assets: | | | |
| Tangible assets | 3,820 | 4,425 | 500 |
| Development expenditure | - | 200 | - |
| Investments | 1,600 | - | - |
| | 5,420 | 4,625 | 500 |
| Current assets: | | | |
| Inventory | 2,740 | 1,280 | 250 |
| Receivables | 1,960 | 980 | 164 |
| Cash at bank | 1,260 | - | 86 |
| | 5,960 | 2,260 | 500 |
| Total assets | 11,380 | 6,885 | 1,000 |
| Equity: | | | |
| Ordinary shares of 25 cents each | 4,000 | 500 | 200 |
| Reserves: | | | |
| Share premium | 800 | 125 | |
| Retained earnings at 31 March 20X6 | 2,300 | 380 | 450 |
| Retained for year | 1,760 | 400 | 150 |
| | 8,860 | 1,405 | 800 |

| | | | |
|---|---|---|---|
| Current liabilities: | | | |
| Trade payables | 2,120 | 3,070 | 142 |
| Bank overdraft | - | 2,260 | - |
| Taxation | 400 | 150 | 58 |
| | 2,520 | 5,480 | 200 |
| Total equity and liabilities | 11,380 | 6,885 | 1,000 |

**The following information is relevant:**

(i) **Investments**

Bacup acquired 1.6 million shares in Townley on 1 April 20X6 paying 75 cents per share. On 1 October 20X6 Bacup acquired 40% of the share capital of Rishworth for $400,000.

(ii) **Group accounting policies**

*Development expenditure*

Development expenditure is to be written off as incurred. The development expenditure in the balance sheet of Townley relates to a project that was commenced on 1 April 20X5. At the date of acquisition the value of the capitalised expenditure was $80,000. No development expenditure of Townley has yet been depreciated.

(iii) **Intra-group trading**

The inventory of Bacup includes goods at a transfer price of $200,000 purchased from Townley after the acquisition. The inventory of Rishworth includes goods at a transfer price of $125,000 purchased from Bacup. All transfers were at cost plus 25%.

The receivables of Bacup include an amount owing from Townley of $250,000. This does not agree with the corresponding amount in the books of Townley due to a cash payment of $50,000 made on 29 March 20X7, which had not been received by Bacup at the year end.

(iv) **Share premium**

The share premium account of Townley arose prior to the acquisition by Bacup.

**Required:**

A consolidated balance sheet of the Bacup group as at 31 March 20X7.

**(20 marks)**

*For the answer to this question, see the 'Answers' section at the end of the book.*

## Feedback to activities

### Activity 1

1 Goose is an associate, despite Gamma Trust holding less than 20% of the shares, because of the significant influence Gamma Trust has over the management.

2 Delta Traders is not an associate, since, unusually for such a large shareholding, Gamma Trust has no real effective influence over Delta Traders. Gamma Trust has to explain the special circumstances clearly in a note to the accounts.

3 The 21% shareholding probably means that Gamma Trust has significant influence over Nova Manufacturing, so this is an associate. The fact that Gamma Trust intends to sell its investment is irrelevant to determining whether it is an associate or not.

4 Alpha Wholesale is a subsidiary, not an associate, of Gamma Trust, since Gamma Trust's control over the board of directors and the written agreement give it effective control.

## Activity 2

**Consolidated income statement for the year ended 31 December 20X5**

| | $000 |
|---|---|
| Revenue | 2,600 |
| Cost of sales | (1,600) |
| Gross profit | 1,000 |
| Operating expenses | (460) |
| Share of profit of associate (25% × 200 – 20) | 45 |
| Profit before tax | 585 |
| Income tax expense | (120) |
| Profit for the year | 465 |

**Consolidated balance sheet at 31 December 20X5**

| | $000 |
|---|---|
| Non-current assets | 2,000 |
| Investment in associate (W2) | 450 |
| Current assets (800 – 25% × 20) | 795 |
| | 3,245 |
| Share capital | 1,500 |
| Retained earnings (1,350 + 45) | 1,395 |
| Current liabilities | 350 |
| | 3,245 |

***Workings***

(W1) **Goodwill**

| | $000 | $000 |
|---|---|---|
| Cost of investment | | 400 |
| Net assets acquired: | | |
| Share capital | 500 | |
| Retained earnings | 220 | |
| Fair value adjustment | 100 | |
| | 820 | (205) |
| | | 195 |

(W2) **Investment in associate**

| | $000 |
|---|---|
| Share of net assets (25% × 920 + 100) | 255 |
| Plus goodwill | 195 |
| | 450 |

### Activity 3

Since this is the usual form of joint venture, a jointly controlled entity with each venturer sharing the benefits and risks in common but without overall control, Drilldeep should be accounted for using proportional consolidation in the consolidated financial statements. However, IAS 31 also permits the use of the equity method.

Chapter 6

# CHANGES IN A GROUP

## Syllabus content

- The treatment in consolidated financial statements of minority interests, pre- and post-acquisition reserves, goodwill (including its impairment), fair value adjustments, intra-group transactions and dividends, piece-meal and mid-year acquisitions, and disposals to include sub-subsidiaries and mixed groups.

## Contents

## Introduction

This is the first of four chapters that deal with the more complicated aspects of the group balance sheet and the group income statement. These are the situations that you are likely to meet in the exam.

This chapter focuses on changes to a group. These arise because the investing company (the parent) buys or sells shares in another company. There are several possibilities. An investing company could:

- acquire shares in another company for the first time (acquisition of a subsidiary or an associate), or
- increase an existing shareholding (e.g. an associate may become a subsidiary), or
- sell its entire shareholding (disposal of a subsidiary or an associate), or
- sell part of its shareholding (e.g. a subsidiary may become an associate).

# 1 Changes of parent company interest

### 1.1 The problems caused by piecemeal acquisitions

KEY POINT

A step-by-step or piecemeal acquisition arises when shares in the subsidiary are acquired in stages over a period of time. In this situation, the main problem is the calculation of goodwill.

A step-by-step or piecemeal acquisition arises when shares in the subsidiary are acquired in stages over a period of time. In this situation, the main problem is the calculation of goodwill.

There are two possible approaches:

(a) calculate goodwill at the date on which the investment becomes a subsidiary (ie, the date on which the parent acquires control)

(b) calculate goodwill separately on each 'slice' of share capital acquired.

The two approaches can give very different results.

KEY POINT

Where there is a piecemeal acquisition, IFRS 3 requires each transaction to be treated separately.

Where there is a piecemeal acquisition, IFRS 3 requires each transaction to be treated separately. The cost of the transaction and the fair values of the assets and liabilities acquired at the date of each transaction are used to determine the amount of any goodwill associated with that transaction.

This results in a step-by-step comparison of the cost of the individual investments with the acquirer's interest in the fair values of the identifiable assets and liabilities acquired at each step.

### 1.2 Example

Company X acquires an 80% holding in Company Y over a number of years as shown below.

| *Holding acquired* | *Fair value of net assets of Y* | *Price paid* |
|---|---|---|
| % | $m | $m |
| 30 | 10 | 3.50 |
| 25 | 12 | 3.10 |
| 25 | 16 | 5.95 |
| 80 | | 12.55 |

The investee's balance sheet at the consolidation date shows:

| | $m |
|---|---|
| Net assets | 20 |
| Share capital | 4 |
| Reserves | 16 |
| | 20 |

The amount of issued share capital has remained unchanged.

What amounts will be included in the consolidated balance sheet?

***Solution***

**Step 1**

Determine whether the company is a subsidiary at the date of consolidation and, if so consolidate assets and liabilities with minority being allocated their share of share capital and reserves at that date.

MI 20% × \$20m = \$4m

**Step 2**

Perform separate calculations of goodwill as at each transaction date.

*Goodwill computations*

| | *Transaction* | | | *Total* |
|---|---|---|---|---|
| | *1* | *2* | *3* | |
| | $m | $m | $m | $m |
| Cost of investment | 3.5 | 3.1 | 5.95 | |
| Share of net assets acquired at each relevant date: | | | | |
| 30% × \$10m | 3.0 | | | |
| 25% × \$12m | | 3.0 | | |
| 25% × \$16m | | | 4.00 | |
| Goodwill | 0.5 | 0.1 | 1.95 | 2.55 |
| Post-acquisition reserves | | | | |
| 30% × (16 – (10 – 4)) | 3.0 | | | |
| 25% × (16 – (12 – 4)) | | 2.0 | | |
| 25% × (16 – (16 – 4)) | | | 1.0 | 6.00 |

**Step 3**

Effect on group balance sheet

| | $m |
|---|---|
| Consolidated net assets | 20.00 |
| Goodwill | 2.55 |
| MI | (4.00) |
| | 18.55 |
| Addition to group reserves | (6.00) |
| Elimination of cost of investment | 12.55 |

## 1.3 Where the investee has previously been treated as an associate or as a simple investment

In the example above, the parent initially acquires a 30% stake in the subsidiary. If Company X can exercise significant influence over Company Y, Company Y is an associate and it is equity accounted from that date until the purchase of the second, 25% stake, at which point it becomes a subsidiary.

Suppose that the initial stake in Company Y had only been 15%. Company Y would then have been a simple investment. No goodwill would have been calculated at that point. Instead the investment in Company Y would have been carried in the balance sheet at either cost or fair value, as required by IAS 39 (see Chapter 13).

The point to grasp here is that the method is **exactly the same**, regardless of the size of the initial acquisition or the way in which it is accounted for before control is gained.

# 2 Disposals of subsidiaries

## 2.1 Disposal of subsidiaries

During the year, a parent company may decide to sell all or part of its shareholding in an individual company. Possible situations may include:

- the disposal of all the shares held in the subsidiary
- the disposal of part of the shareholding, still leaving a controlling interest after the sale
- the disposal of part of the shareholding, leaving a residual holding after the sale which is regarded either as an associated company investment or a trade investment.

Each of the situations will be examined in this chapter.

## 2.2 The basic principle

KEY POINT

Where there is a material disposal, the consolidated income statement should include:

(a) the appropriate proportion of the results of the subsidiary up to the date of sale

(b) the gain or loss on the sale of the investment. The calculation of the gain or loss is the difference between:

(i) the proceeds of sale, and

(ii) the parent company share of the net assets of the subsidiary, at the date of sale, **plus** goodwill on consolidation to the extent that it has not been written down as a result of impairment.

Where there is a material disposal (i.e. sale of a substantial shareholding), the consolidated income statement should include:

(a) the appropriate proportion of the results (i.e. revenue and profit) of the subsidiary up to the date of sale

(b) the gain or loss on the sale of the investment. The calculation of the gain or loss is the difference between:

(i) the proceeds of sale, and

(ii) the parent company share of the net assets of the subsidiary, at the date of sale, **plus** goodwill on consolidation to the extent that it has not been written down as a result of impairment.

## 2.3 Preparing group accounts following a disposal of shares

First we shall examine the situation where a parent company disposes of its entire shareholding in a subsidiary (a 'total disposal'). Consider the following balance sheets.

### *Example*

**Balance sheet at 31 December 20X8**

| | *H* | *S* |
|---|---|---|
| | $000 | $000 |
| Shares in S at cost (75%) | 82.5 | – |
| Other sundry assets | 257.5 | 100 |
| | 340.0 | 100 |
| Issued share capital – $1 ordinary | 200.0 | 60 |
| Reserves | 140.0 | 40 |
| | 340.0 | 100 |

H acquired the shares in 20X3 when S's reserves stood at $10,000. The whole holding was sold for $115,000 on 31 December 20X8.

Ignore taxation.

Prepare the consolidated balance sheet before the disposal and analyse the gain which will be reported on the sale.

### *Solution*

**Consolidated balance sheet before disposal**

| | $000 | $000 |
|---|---|---|
| Goodwill on consolidation (82.5 – 75% × (60 + 10)) | | 30.0 |
| Other sundry net assets | | 357.5 |
| | | 387.5 |
| Issued share capital – $1 ordinary | | 200.0 |
| Consolidated reserves | | |
| H | 140.0 | |
| S (75% × (40 – 10)) | 22.5 | 162.5 |
| | | 362.5 |
| Minority interest (25% × 100) | | 25.0 |
| | | 387.5 |

The gain on sale would be computed.

(a) Separate accounts of H

| | $000 |
|---|---|
| Proceeds | 115.0 |
| Carrying amount – cost | (82.5) |
| | 32.5 |

(b) Consolidation

| | $000 |
|---|---|
| Proceeds | 115.0 |
| Less: Share of net assets (75% × 100) | (75.0) |
| Goodwill not yet written off | (30.0) |
| | 10.0 |

The difference between the gains represents the profits relating to the shares sold retained in the subsidiary, i.e. $22,500 which are already included in consolidated reserves.

Thus the gains may be computed using an alternative method:

| | | $000 |
|---|---|---|
| (a) | Separate accounts of H (as above) | 32.5 |
| | Less: Post-acquisition profits to date of disposal | (22.5) |
| (b) | Gain to group | 10.0 |

***Example – income statement***

Balance sheets as in the example above. The income statements for the year ended 31 December 20X8 are as follows.

| | *H and other subsidiaries* | *S* |
|---|---|---|
| | $000 | $000 |
| Revenue | 300 | 200 |
| Cost of sales | (190) | (120) |
| Gross profit | 110 | 80 |
| Administrative expenses | (30) | (25) |
| Distribution costs | (20) | (15) |
| Profit before tax | 60 | 40 |
| Tax | (21) | (14) |
| Profit for the year | 39 | 26 |

The entire holding in S is sold on 30 September 20X8 for $135,000. Taxation on any gain is to be ignored. H has not yet accounted for the disposal. H has other, 100%, subsidiaries.

Prepare the consolidated income statement for the year incorporating the gain on the disposal.

Work to the nearest $.

***Solution***

**Step 1**

The gain on sale would be computed as follows

**H's accounts**

| | $ | $ |
|---|---|---|
| Proceeds | | 135,000 |
| Cost | | (82,500) |
| **Gain to H** | | 52,500 |
| **Consolidated accounts** | | |
| Proceeds | | 135,000 |
| Less: Share of net assets at disposal | | |
| B/d (60 + 14 [40 – 26]) | 74,000 | |
| In year up to disposal (26 × 9/12) | 19,500 | |
| Group share (75%) | 93,500 | (70,125) |
| | | 64,875 |
| Less: Goodwill not yet written off | | (30,000) |
| Gain to group | | 34,875 |

**Step 2**

The consolidated income statement would be as follows

**H Consolidated income statement for the year ended 31 December 20X8**

| | *Total* |
|---|---|
| | $ |
| Revenue (300,000 + 200,000 × 9/12) | 450,000 |
| Cost of sales (190,000 + 120,000 × 9/12) | (280,000) |
| Gross profit | 170,000 |
| Distribution costs (20,000 + 15,000 × 9/12) | (31,250) |
| Administrative expenses (30,000 + 25,000 × 9/12) | (48,750) |
| Profit on disposal of subsidiary | 34,875 |
| Profit before tax | 124,875 |
| Tax | |
| (21,000 + 9/12 × 14,000) | (31,500) |
| Profit for the period | 93,375 |
| Attributable to: | |
| Equity holders of the parent | 88,500 |
| Minority interest (25% × $26,000 × 9/12) | 4,875 |
| | 93,375 |

***Discontinued operations***

It is possible that the disposal of S qualifies as a discontinued operation. If this is the case, IFRS 5 *Non-current Assets Held for Sale and Discontinued Operations* requires separate disclosure of the profit on disposal and the results of the discontinued operation on the face of the income statement.

IFRS 5 is not directly examinable in this paper and therefore it is unlikely that you will be required to make the disclosures for discontinued operations in the exam.

## 2.4 Partial disposal – subsidiary to associate

In this situation the disposal will reduce the shareholding below 50%. The entity will be consolidated up to the date of disposal and equity accounted from the date of disposal. Any gain or loss is computed as previously.

***Example***

**Income statements for the year ended 31 December 20X9**

| | *H* | *S* | *A* |
|---|---|---|---|
| | $ | $ | $ |
| Profit before tax | 100,000 | 80,000 | 30,000 |
| Tax | 35,000 | 28,000 | 10,500 |
| Profit for the period | 65,000 | 52,000 | 19,500 |

H acquired its investments as follows:

| *Company* | *%* | *Date* | *Cost* | *Share capital* | *Reserves at acquisition* | *Goodwill on consolidation* |
|---|---|---|---|---|---|---|
| | | | $ | $ | $ | $ |
| S | 80 | 20X0 | 110,000 | 100,000 | 12,000 | 20,400 |
| A | 60 | 20X5 | 60,000 | 70,000 | 10,000 | 12,000 |

One third of H's shares in A were sold on 31 March 20X9 for $35,000. Goodwill on consolidation has been written off. A's reserves at 1 January 20X9 amounted to $25,000.

***Solution***

**Step 1**

The gain on sale would be computed as follows:

| | | $ | $ |
|---|---|---|---|
| **H** | | | |
| Proceeds | | | 35,000 |
| Cost 20/60 × $60,000 | | | (20,000) |
| | | | 15,000 |
| **Group** | | | |
| Proceeds | | | 35,000 |
| Share of net assets at date of disposal | | | |
| Brought forward – share capital | | 70,000 | |
| – reserves | | 25,000 | |
| In year up to disposal 3/12 × $19,500 | | 4,875 | |
| | 20% × | 99,875 | (19,975) |
| Group gain | | | 15,025 |

**Step 2**

A consolidation schedule could be prepared as follows:

| | *H* | | *S* | | *A Subsidiary (3/12)* | *A As associate (9/12 × 40%)* | *Consolidated* |
|---|---|---|---|---|---|---|---|
| | $ | | $ | | $ | $ | $ |
| Profit before tax | 100,000 | | 80,000 | | 7,500 | | 187,500 |
| Share of associate | | | | | | 5,850 | 5,850 |
| | | | | | | | 193,350 |
| Tax | (35,000) | | (28,000) | | (2,625) | | (65,625) |
| | 65,000 | | 52,000 | | 4,875 | 5,850 | 127,725 |
| Minority | | (20%) | (10,400) | (40%) | (1,950) | | (12,350) |
| | | | 41,600 | | 2,925 | | 115,375 |

**Step 3**

The consolidated income statement would be as follows:

**H Consolidated income statement for the year ended 31 December 20X9**

| | $ |
|---|---|
| Profit from operations | 187,500 |
| Share of profit of associate | 5,850 |
| Profit on disposal of continuing operations | 15,025 |
| Profit before tax | 208,375 |
| Tax | (65,625) |
| Profit for the period | 142,750 |
| Attributable to: | |
| Equity holders of the parent | 130,400 |
| Minority interest | 12,350 |
| | 142,750 |

## 2.5 Accounting for a partial disposal of shares in a remaining subsidiary

Although there will be a gain on sale, the subsidiary will be consolidated for the whole year, only the % holding will change, not the entity's status as a subsidiary.

### *Example*

Facts as in example above except that only 5% of A's issued shares were sold on 31 March 20X9 for $12,000.

### *Solution*

**Step 1**

The gain on sale would be computed as follows:

| | | $ | $ |
|---|---|---|---|
| **H** | | | |
| Proceeds | | | 12,000 |
| Cost 5/60 × $60,000 | | | (5,000) |
| | | | 7,000 |
| **Group** | | | |
| Proceeds | | | 12,000 |
| Share of net assets at date of disposal | | | |
| Brought forward – share capital | | 70,000 | |
| – reserves | | 25,000 | |
| In year up to disposal 3/12 × $19,500 | | 4,875 | |
| | 5% × | 99,875 | (4,994) |
| Group gain | | | 7,006 |

**Step 2**

A consolidation schedule could be prepared as follows:

| | *H* | *S* | *A* | *Consolidated* |
|---|---|---|---|---|
| | $ | $ | $ | $ |
| Profit before tax | 100,000 | 80,000 | 30,000 | 210,000 |
| Tax | (35,000) | (28,000) | (10,500) | (73,500) |
| PAT | 65,000 | 52,000 | 19,500 | |

Minority interest

| | | $ |
|---|---|---|
| In S | 20% × 52,000 | 10,400 |
| In A | 40% × 3/12 × $19,500 | 1,950 |
| | 45% × 9/12 × $19,500 | 6,581 |
| | | 18,931 |

**Step 3**

The consolidated income statement would be as follows:

**H Consolidated income statement for 20X9**

| | $ |
|---|---|
| Profit from operations | 210,000 |
| Profit on disposal of continuing operations | 7,006 |
| Profit before tax | 217,006 |
| Tax | (73,500) |
| Profit for the year | 143,506 |
| Attributable to: | |
| Equity holders of the parent | 124,575 |
| Minority interest | 18,931 |
| | 143,506 |

## 2.6 Partial disposal – subsidiary to simple investment

A subsidiary would normally become a simple investment if the parent's interest fell below 20%. The subsidiary's results are included in the income statement until the date of disposal.

A simple investment is normally included in the balance sheet at cost or fair value under IAS 39. However, the group has included its share of the subsidiary's post-acquisition results in consolidated reserves. Arguably, it still owns a small share of these profits, even after the disposal. There are two possible ways of dealing with this situation:

- include the investment in the balance sheet at cost and eliminate all the post-acquisition profits from consolidated reserves, or
- include the investment in the balance sheet at a valuation based on the remaining share of the net assets at the date of disposal (that is, value it under the equity method).

IAS 27 states that the carrying amount of the investment at the date that the entity ceases to be a subsidiary should be regarded as its cost on initial measurement under IAS 39. This will be the same as the carrying amount under the equity method.

## 2.7 Taxation

The tax payable on the gain is based on the gain in the parent's books, not the gain in the group accounts.

| | $ |
|---|---|
| Sale proceeds | X |
| Less: Cost | X |
| Gross gain | X |
| Tax computed as tax rate × gross gain | X |

This tax is then included in the tax charge relating to the discontinued operation.

***Activity 1***

H purchased 80% of the ordinary share capital of S on 31 December 20X4 for $15,000. S's share capital and reserves at that date were as follows:

| | $ |
|---|---|
| Share capital | 10,000 |
| Reserves | 5,000 |
| | 15,000 |

On 31 December 20X8, H sold 25% of its holding in S for $10,000. S's profit after tax for the year ended 31 December 20X8 is $6,000, its opening reserves for 20X8 being $24,000.

What is the profit or loss arising on the disposal of S to be included in the consolidated accounts for the year ended 31 December 20X8?

*Feedback to this activity is at the end of the chapter.*

# Summary

- Piecemeal (step-by-step) acquisitions are dealt with by treating each significant acquisition as a separate transaction and performing a fair value exercise at each acquisition date.
- Disposals require the calculation of a gain on disposal by reference to the book value of the net assets of the subsidiary at the date of disposal and goodwill originally purchased to the extent that it has not been written off.
- Where there has been a disposal during an accounting period, the balance sheet reflects the group structure at the period end and the income statement includes the results of the subsidiary up to the date of disposal.

Having completed your study of this chapter, you should have achieved the following learning outcome:

- identify the impact on group financial statements when a subsidiary is disposed of partway through an accounting period and where shareholdings, or control, are acquired in stages.

## Self-test questions

1 How is a piecemeal acquisition dealt with? (1.2)

2 How is the gain or loss on the sale of the subsidiary calculated? (2.2)

3 How may IFRS 5 affect the disposal of subsidiaries? (2.3)

4 How is taxation dealt with on disposal of a subsidiary? (2.7)

## Objective test questions

### Question 1

Hartlepool acquired the following shareholdings in Southend:

31 December 20W7 10% for $50,000 when Southend's reserves totalled $300,000

31 December 20X0 60% for $350,000 when Southend's reserves totalled $400,000

Southend has a total share capital of 100,000 $1 ordinary shares.

Calculate the amount of goodwill arising on consolidation.

### Question 2

Pringle Inc bought 80% of the issued ordinary shares of Skips Inc twenty five years ago at a cost of $330,000 when the net assets of the company amounted to $280,000.

Goodwill arising on the consolidation has been completely written off as a result of impairment losses.

On the final day of the current accounting period Pringle Inc sold its entire shareholding in Skips for proceeds of $460,000. At this date the net assets of Skips Inc amounted to $400,000.

*Taxation is to be ignored.*

Calculate the profit or loss on disposal reported in the consolidated income statement for the current period.

*For the answers to these questions, see the 'Answers' section at the end of the book.*

## Exam-type questions

### Harrods

The summarised balance sheets as at 30 June 20X5 of Harrods and Selfridges are given below:

| | *Harrods* | *Selfridges* |
|---|---|---|
| | $000 | $000 |
| Assets | | |
| Non-current assets | | |
| Property, plant and equipment | 25,500 | 22,200 |
| Investment in Selfridges | 15,450 | |
| | 40,950 | 22,200 |

| | $000 | $000 |
|---|---|---|
| Current assets: | | |
| Inventories | 11,150 | 4,300 |
| Receivables | 5,200 | 1,100 |
| Cash | 1,000 | 500 |
| | 17,350 | 5,900 |
| | 58,300 | 28,100 |
| Equity and liabilities: | | |
| Equity | | |
| Share capital | 20,000 | 10,000 |
| Retained earnings | 36,200 | 9,400 |
| | 56,200 | 19,400 |
| Non-current liabilities | - | 4,000 |
| Current liabilities | | |
| Trade and other payables | 2,100 | 2,200 |
| Bank overdraft | – | 2,500 |
| | 2,100 | 4,700 |
| Total liabilities | 2,100 | 8,700 |
| | 58,300 | 28,100 |

The following additional information is given:

(1) Harrods acquired 60% of the ordinary share capital of Selfridges on 30 June 20X1 when the retained earnings reserve of Selfridges stood at $2,500,000. Harrods acquired an additional 30% of the ordinary share capital on 1 November 20X4 when the retained earnings reserve stood at $7,400,000.

(2) The inventories of Selfridges include an item purchased from Harrods for $1,200,000 which had not been paid for at that date. Harrods had accounted for it as a sale in the normal way at its standard mark-up of 25% on cost.

(3) All goodwill arising on consolidation should be written down to 80% of its original cost, due to impairment.

**Required:**

Prepare the consolidated balance sheet of Harrods at 30 June 20X5. **(10 marks)**

## Apricot

The summarised balance sheets of A and its two subsidiaries, B and C, at 31 December 20X2 are shown below:

**Summarised balance sheets at 31 December 20X2**

| | *A* | *B* | *C* |
|---|---|---|---|
| | $000 | $000 | $000 |
| Investment in subsidiaries: | | | |
| A in B | 1,164 | | |
| A in C | 1,120 | | |
| Other net assets | 2,516 | 1,260 | 1,400 |
| | 4,800 | 1,260 | 1,400 |
| Equity share capital | | | |
| ($1 shares) | 1,500 | 500 | 400 |
| Revenue reserves | 3,300 | 760 | 1,000 |
| | 4,800 | 1,260 | 1,400 |

The summarised income statements for A and B for the year ended 31 December 20X3 are as follows:

| | *A* | *B* |
|---|---|---|
| | $000 | $000 |
| Profit before tax | 1,200 | 250 |
| Taxation | 360 | 60 |
| Profit for the year | 840 | 190 |

Additional information:

(i) A acquired 80% of the ordinary share capital of B on 1 January 20W4 when the reserves of B were $420,000.

(ii) A acquired 90% of the ordinary share capital of C on 1 January 20W5 when the reserves of C were $320,000.

(iii) Goodwill has been completely written off as a result of impairment losses.

(iv) On 1 January 20X3, A disposed of 350,000 shares in C for $1,925,000. The relevant profit on sale has NOT been included in the income statement of A.

(v) Assume a rate of income tax of 25%.

(vi) There were no changes in the issued share capital of the subsidiaries since acquisition by A.

**Required**:

(a) Prepare the consolidated income statement and balance sheet of the A group at 31 December 20X3. **(20 marks)**

(b) Prepare a reconciliation of opening and closing consolidated reserves. **(5 marks)**

*(Show all your workings.)* **(Total: 25 marks)**

*For the answer to these questions, see the 'Answers' section at the end of the book.*

## Feedback to activity

### Activity 1

**Step 1**

Calculate consolidated goodwill.

| | $ |
|---|---|
| Cost | 15,000 |
| 80% net assets acquired | 12,000 |
| Goodwill | 3,000 |

**Step 2**

Calculate the gain/loss.

| | $ | $ |
|---|---|---|
| Proceeds | | 10,000 |
| Less: Share of net assets at 1.1.X8 (10 + 24) × 20% | 6,800 | |
| Share of profit for year to disposal 20% × 6,000 | 1,200 | |
| | | (8,000) |
| | | 2,000 |
| Less: Goodwill (3,000 × 25%) | | (750) |
| | | 1,250 |

Gain to be included in the consolidated accounts is $1,250.

# Chapter 7

# COMPLEX GROUPS

## Syllabus content

- The preparation of consolidated financial statements (including the group cash flow statement) involving one or more subsidiaries, sub-subsidiaries and associates, under the acquisition and pooling of interests methods (IAS 7 & 27 and IFRS 3).
- The treatment in consolidated financial statements of minority interests, pre- and post-acquisition reserves, goodwill (including its impairment), fair value adjustments, intra-group transactions and dividends, piece-meal and mid-year acquisitions, and disposals to include sub-subsidiaries and mixed groups.

## Contents

# Introduction

Until now, you have only dealt with simple group structures in which a parent owns one or more subsidiaries or associates. However, it is possible for a subsidiary itself to have a subsidiary company. This chapter covers the preparation of the group balance sheet and group income statement in this situation.

## 1 Vertical and mixed groups

### 1.1 The different possible structures of a group

**KEY POINT**

More complex group structures exist where a subsidiary of a parent company owns all or part of a shareholding which makes another company also a subsidiary of the parent company.

More complex group structures exist where a subsidiary of a parent company owns all or part of a shareholding which makes another company also a subsidiary of the parent company. There are two sorts of complex group:

- a vertical group where a subsidiary of a parent also has a subsidiary of its own, and
- a mixed group. where the parent also owns shares directly in a sub-subsidiary.

Examples of both are illustrated below.

### 1.2 Vertical groups

(a) Suppose H owns 70% of A. A is thus a subsidiary of H.

(b) If, in addition, A owns 60% of B, then B is a subsidiary of A. Furthermore, B is said to be a sub-subsidiary of H.

(c) H has a direct interest in A and an indirect interest in B (exercised via A's holding in B). H has an effective interest of only 42% (70% × 60%) in B. Nevertheless, B is a sub-subsidiary of H because H has a controlling interest in A and A has a controlling interest in B. There is now a 'vertical group' consisting of H, A and B.

H's interest in B:

70% × 60% = 42%

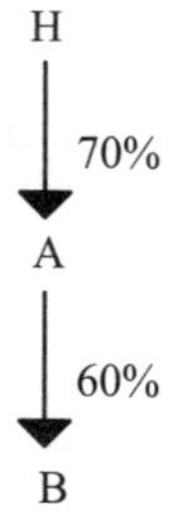


Where a parent company owns a controlling interest in a subsidiary which in turn owns a controlling interest in a sub-subsidiary, then the group accounts of the ultimate parent company must include the underlying net assets and earnings of both the subsidiary and the sub-subsidiary companies.

### 1.3 Mixed groups

In a mixed group situation the parent company has a direct controlling interest in at least one subsidiary. In addition, the parent company and the subsidiary together hold a controlling interest in a further company.

***Example 1***

For example, H owns 80% of S, H owns 40% of W, S owns 30% of W.

This is a mixed group situation.

- S is a subsidiary of H
- H and S between them own more than 50% of W (the fact that S is not a wholly-owned subsidiary of H is irrelevant).

W is thus a member of the H group and must, therefore, be included in the consolidated balance sheet.

Diagrammatically, the situation is as follows:

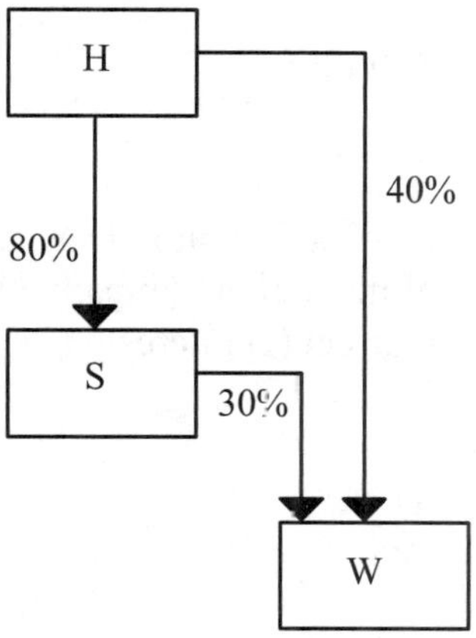


H's interest in W = (80% × 30%) + 40% = 64%

***Example 2***

H owns 35% of S, S owns 40% of W and H owns 40% of W. This is not a mixed group situation. Neither S nor W is a member of the H group, although S and W may both be 'associates' of H.

H's interest in W might be calculated as before as (35% × 40%) + 40% = 54%. Although H has an arithmetic interest in W which is more than 50%, it does not have parent company control of W, as it does not control S's 40% stake in W.

***Activity 1***

H owns 60% of S, S owns 25% of W, H owns 30% of W.

Is W a subsidiary company of H?

*Feedback to this activity is at the end of the chapter.*

## 2 Vertical groups – consolidation procedure

### 2.1 Methods of consolidation

Calculations of the goodwill on consolidation, the minority shareholders' interest and so on become more complicated. Nevertheless, the normal approach is used, subject to certain modifications.

Two situations will be considered in turn:

- Situation 1 – where the subsidiary is acquired first and then the sub-subsidiary
- Situation 2 – where the subsidiary acquires the sub-subsidiary first and is subsequently taken over by the parent company.

### *Example 1 – Subsidiary acquired first*

The draft balance sheets of H, S and T, as at 31 December 20X4, are as follows:

| | *H* | *S* | *T* | | *H* | *S* | *T* |
|---|---|---|---|---|---|---|---|
| | $000 | $000 | $000 | | $000 | $000 | $000 |
| Net assets | 180 | 80 | 80 | Share capital | 200 | 100 | 50 |
| Shares in subsidiary | 120 | 80 | | Retained earnings | 100 | 60 | 30 |
| | 300 | 160 | 80 | | 300 | 160 | 80 |

You ascertain that H acquired 75,000 $1 shares in S on 1 January 20X4 when the revenue reserves of S amounted to $40,000. S acquired 40,000 $1 shares in T on 30 June 20X4 when the revenue reserves of T amounted to $25,000; they had been $20,000 on the date of H's acquisition of S.

***Solution 1***

**Step 1**

Draw a diagram of the group structure and then set out the respective interests of the parent company and the minority, distinguishing between direct (D) and indirect (I) interests:

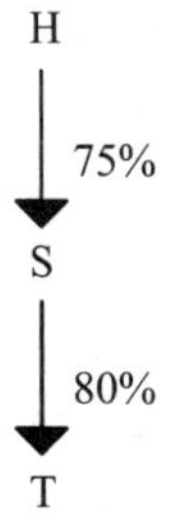


| | *S* | | | *T* |
|---|---|---|---|---|
| Interest of: | | | | |
| H shareholders | 75% (D) | 75% × 80% = | | 60% (I) |
| Minority shareholders | 25% (D) | | 20% (D) | |
| | | 25% × 80% = | 20% (I) | |
| | | | | 40% |
| | 100% | | | 100% |

KEY POINT

The effective minority interest consists of two distinct elements:

- the direct minority
- the indirect minority.

Make sure that you understand the above calculations. The main difficulty lies in the calculation of the minority interest in T. The effective minority interest of 40% consists of two distinct elements:

- the direct minority of 20% , i.e. the 20% of the share capital of T not owned by S
- 25% of S is not owned by H. This 25% minority of S thus have a stake in T via their company's holding in T, equivalent to 25% of 80%, i.e. 20%. This is the indirect minority in T.

### Step 2

Draw a diagram setting out the relationship between the various companies, and show the revenue reserves at key dates:

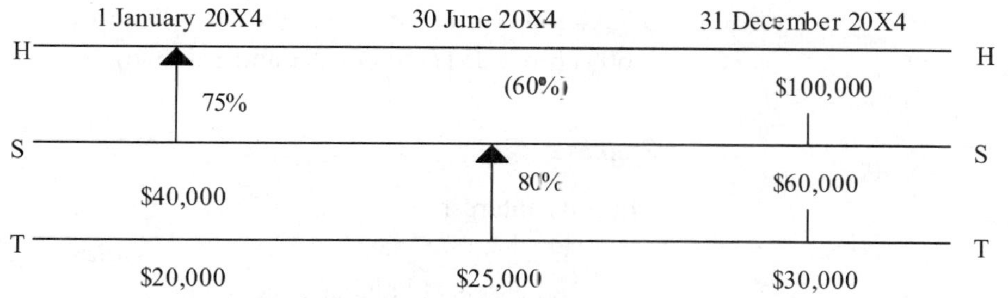


### Step 3

KEY POINT

Goodwill is determined separately for each subsidiary.

Goodwill

Two calculations are required, one for each subsidiary. They are performed separately as goodwill is determined for each subsidiary.

| | *Notes* | *S* | | *T* | |
|---|---|---|---|---|---|
| | | $000 | $000 | $000 | $000 |
| Cost of investment | | | | | |
| (75% × 80) | 1 | | 120 | | 60 |
| Less: Share of net assets at acquisition date | | | | | |
| Share capital | | 100 | | 50 | |
| Retained earnings | 2 | 40 | | 25 | |
| | 3 | 140 (75%) | (105) | 75 (60%) | (45) |
| | | | 15 | | 15 |

***Notes***

1 The cost of H's investment in S is $120,000, and this figure is used in the calculation. The cost of S's investment in T is $80,000. However, H owns only 75% of S, so the 'effective' cost to H of its indirect holding is T is $60,000 (75% × $80,000).

KEY POINT

Care must be taken in determining the date for the split between post-acquisition and pre-acquisition reserves.

The split is considered from the viewpont of the ultimate parent company.

2 Care must be taken in determining the date for the split between post-acquisition and pre-acquisition reserves. The parent company acquired control of S on 1 January 20X4, so this is the relevant date: but what about S's acquisition of shares in T? When talking about the pre-acquisition/post-acquisition split, the problem is considered from the viewpoint of the ultimate parent company, H. The test is to ask the question 'When did T become a member of the H group?'

The answer is 30 June 20X4. Profits of T arising after this date are post-acquisition as regards the H group. The information given regarding T's reserves at 1 January 20X4 is irrelevant in this context.

3 The interest of H in S and the effective interest of H in T are taken from the table in Step 1. Whilst S owns 80% of T's share capital and reserves, H only owns 75% of S. Thus, the effective interest of 60% (75% × 80%) is used.

**Step 4**

Consolidated retained earnings

| | $000 |
|---|---|
| H | 100 |
| S 75% (60 – 40) (see note 3 above) | 15 |
| T 60% (30 – 25) (see notes 2 and 3 above) | 3 |
| | 118 |

**Step 5**

Minority interest

| | | Notes | $000 | $000 |
|---|---|---|---|---|
| S: | Net assets at balance sheet date | | | |
| | Share capital | | 100 | |
| | Retained earnings | | 60 | |
| | | | 160 | |
| | Less: Cost of investment in T | 4 | (80) | |
| | | 5 | 80 (25%) | 20 |
| T: | Net assets at balance sheet date | | | |
| | Share capital | | 50 | |
| | Retained earnings | | 30 | |
| | | 5 | 80 (40%) | 32 |
| | | | | 52 |

***Notes***

4 The minority shareholders in S are entitled to their share of the net assets of S. However, one of the assets of S is the cost of the investment in T which, in the consolidation process, is replaced with the net assets of T. The minority shareholders in S are entitled to their share of these also. They receive their share of T's net assets as the minority interest in S form the indirect minority interest in T. So, the minority in S receive their share of the net assets of S after having deducted the cost of the investment in T, and their share of the net assets of T as they form the indirect part of the minority interest in T.

5 The percentage interests are taken from the table in Step 1.

**Step 6**

The consolidated balance sheet can now be prepared:

**Summarised consolidated balance sheet of H and its subsidiary companies as at 31 December 20X4**

| | $ |
|---|---|
| Goodwill | 30,000 |
| Net assets | 340,000 |
| | 370,000 |
| Equity: | |
| Share capital | 200,000 |
| Retained earnings | 118,000 |
| | 318,000 |
| Minority interest | 52,000 |
| | 370,000 |

***Activity 2***

The balance sheets of H, S and M as at 31 December 20X5 were as follows:

| | *H* | *S* | *M* |
|---|---|---|---|
| | $ | $ | $ |
| 45,000 shares in S | 72,000 | | |
| 16,000 shares in M | 25,000 | | |
| 12,000 shares in M | | 20,000 | |
| Sundry net assets | 118,000 | 115,000 | 75,000 |
| | 215,000 | 135,000 | 75,000 |
| Ordinary share capital ($1 shares) | 120,000 | 60,000 | 40,000 |
| Reserves | 95,000 | 75,000 | 35,000 |
| | 215,000 | 135,000 | 75,000 |

All shares were acquired on 31 December 20X2 when S reserves amounted to $30,000 and M reserves amounted to $10,000.

**You are required** to calculate the goodwill arising on the consolidation of S and M.

*Feedback to this activity is at the end of the chapter.*

***Example 2 – Subsidiary acquires sub-subsidiary first***

The draft balance sheets of H, S and T as at 31 December 20X4 are as follows:

| | *H* | *S* | *T* | | *H* | *S* | *T* |
|---|---|---|---|---|---|---|---|
| | $000 | $000 | $000 | | $000 | $000 | $000 |
| Net assets | 180 | 80 | 80 | Share capital | 200 | 100 | 50 |
| Shares in subsidiary | 120 | 80 | | Revenue reserves | 100 | 60 | 30 |
| | 300 | 160 | 80 | | 300 | 160 | 80 |

S acquired 40,000 $1 shares in T on 1 January 20X4 when the revenue reserves of T amounted to $25,000. H acquired 75,000 $1 shares in S on 30 June 20X4 when the revenue reserves of S amounted to $40,000 and those of T amounted to $30,000.

***Solution 2***

The main area of difficulty lies in the allocation of the reserves of the subsidiary companies between pre-acquisition and post-acquisition. (Remember that the object of the exercise is to prepare a consolidated balance sheet of the H group.)

- **Revenue reserves of S** – When did S become a member of the H group? Answer: 30 June 20X4 – so only revenue reserves of S arising after 30 June 20X4 can be regarded as post-acquisition from the viewpoint of the H group.
- **Revenue reserves of T** – Care must be taken here! When did T become a member of the H group? Certainly not on 1 January 20X4, because S was not a subsidiary of H at that time. The answer is 30 June 20X4, because only from that time was T a subsidiary of S and a member of the H group. Hence, only revenue reserves of T arising after 30 June 20X4 can be viewed as post-acquisition as regards the H group.

The same procedures as outlined above can now be performed for the consolidation, dealing with the two acquisitions separately. The detailed workings are left for the student to do.

The only difference from the earlier example is that the revenue reserves of T were \$5,000 more at the date when H became T's ultimate parent company. Hence, 'goodwill on consolidation' will be reduced by \$3,000 (H's interest in T × \$5,000 = \$3,000).

| | |
|---|---|
| Goodwill (at cost) | \$27,000 |
| Consolidated reserves | \$115,000 |

# 3 Mixed groups – consolidation procedure

## 3.1 Approach

The approach is similar to the method of dealing with sub-subsidiaries, i.e. an effective interest is computed and used to allocate share capital and reserves. The approach will be illustrated by the following example.

### *Example*

The following are the summarised balance sheets of T, P and A as at 31 December 20X4:

| | *T* | *P* | *A* |
|---|---|---|---|
| | \$ | \$ | \$ |
| Non-current assets | 140,000 | 61,000 | 170,000 |
| Investments (see notes) | 200,000 | 65,000 | – |
| Net current assets | 10,000 | 14,000 | 10,000 |
| | 350,000 | 140,000 | 180,000 |
| Ordinary shares of \$1 each | 200,000 | 80,000 | 100,000 |
| Retained earnings | 150,000 | 60,000 | 80,000 |
| | 350,000 | 140,000 | 180,000 |

You ascertain that:

(a) On 1 January 20X3 P acquired 35,000 ordinary shares in A at a cost of \$65,000 when the revenue reserves of A amounted to \$40,000.

(b) On 1 January 20X4 T acquired 64,000 ordinary shares in P at a cost of \$120,000 and 40,000 shares in A at a cost of \$80,000. The revenue reserves of P and A amounted to \$50,000 and \$60,000 respectively on 1 January 20X4.

**You are required** to prepare the consolidated balance sheet of the T group as at 31 December 20X4.

### *Solution*

**Step 1**

The basic approach is similar to that used in vertical groups.

Group structure

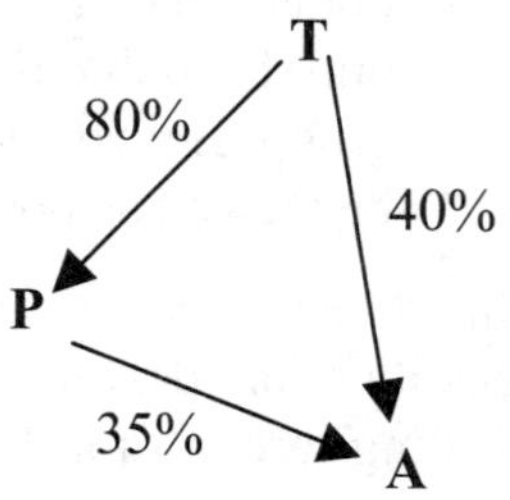

Respective interest in P and A:

| | *P* | | | | *A* | |
|---|---|---|---|---|---|---|
| T shareholders | 80% | (D) | Direct | = | 40% | |
| | | | Indirect 80% × 35% | = | 28% | 68% |
| Minority shareholders | 20% | (D) | Direct | = | 25% | |
| | | | Indirect 20% × 35% | = | 7% | 32% |
| | 100% | | | | | 100% |

***Notes:***

1 T effectively owns 68% of A. This comprises a direct holding of 40% and an indirect holding (exercised through T's controlling interest in P) of 28%.

2 A is a member of the T group because T and P (a subsidiary of T) together own more than 50% of the share capital of A (in fact, together they hold 75%).

Diagrammatic representation of shareholdings and revenue reserves:

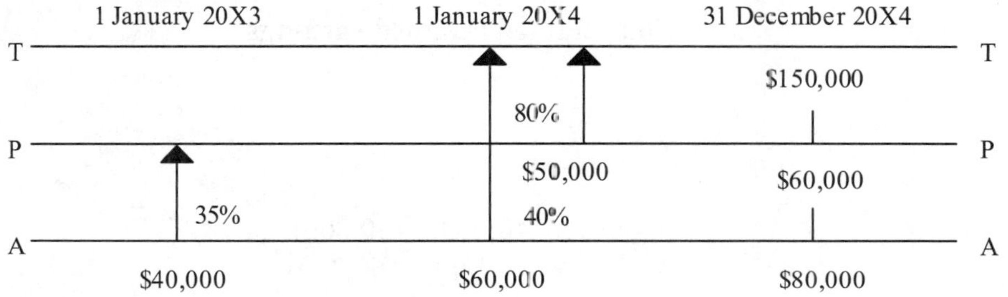


**Step 2**

Prepare consolidation schedules:

**Net assets of subsidiaries**

| | *P* | | *A* | |
|---|---|---|---|---|
| | *Acquisition* | *Balance sheet date* | *Acquisition* | *Balance sheet date* |
| | $ | $ | $ | $ |
| Share capital | 80,000 | 80,000 | 100,000 | 100,000 |
| Retained earnings | 50,000 | 60,000 | 60,000 | 80,000 |
| | 130,000 | 140,000 | 160,000 | 180,000 |

**Goodwill**

| | *P* | *A* |
|---|---|---|
| | $ | $ |
| Cost of investment: | | |
| T | 120,000 | 80,000 |
| P (indirect) (80% × 65,000) | | 52,000 |
| | | 132,000 |

| | | |
|---|---|---|
| Less: share of net assets acquired: | | |
| 80% × 130,000 | (104,000) | |
| 68% × 160,000 | | (108,800) |
| | 16,000 | 23,200 |

**Minority interests**

| | $ | $ |
|---|---|---|
| Net assets of P at balance sheet date | 140,000 | |
| Less cost of investment in A | (65,000) | |
| | 75,000 | |
| Minority share (20%) | | 15,000 |
| Minority share of net assets of A at balance sheet date: | | |
| (32% × 180,000) | | 57,600 |
| | | 72,600 |

**Consolidated retained earnings**

| | $ |
|---|---|
| T | |
| | 150,000 |
| P (80% × 140,000 – 130,000) | 8,000 |
| A (68% × 180,000 – 160,000) | 13,600 |
| | 171,600 |

**Step 3**

**Consolidated balance sheet of T and its subsidiary companies as at 31 December 20X4**

| | $ | $ |
|---|---|---|
| Non-current assets: | | |
| Tangible assets | | 371,000 |
| Goodwill | | 39,200 |
| Net current assets | | 34,000 |
| Total assets less current liabilities | | 444,200 |
| Equity: | | |
| Share capital | 200,000 | |
| Retained earnings | 171,600 | |
| | | 371,600 |
| Minority interest | | 72,600 |
| | | 444,200 |

Having worked through the solution to this question, try working it on your own.

***Activity 3***

Using the information in Activity 2, show the minority interest to be included in the consolidated balance sheet at 31 December 20X5.

*Feedback to this activity is at the end of the chapter.*

# 4 The income statement of a complex group

## 4.1 Method of consolidation

The consolidation of income statements in these situations is similar to the consolidation of balance sheets in that the usual procedure is employed following two preliminary steps:

- finding the ultimate parent company's effective percentage interest for each subsidiary
- finding the date of acquisition by the ultimate parent company.

***Example***

The income statements for the year ended 30 April 20X8 of three companies in a group are:

| | *H* | *N* | *S* |
|---|---|---|---|
| | $ | $ | $ |
| Sales revenue | 74,000 | 50,000 | 37,500 |
| Cost of sales | 44,400 | 30,000 | 22,500 |
| Gross profit | 29,600 | 20,000 | 15,000 |
| Income from shares in group companies | 8,000 | 3,600 | – |
| Net profit before tax | 37,600 | 23,600 | 15,000 |
| Income tax expense | 16,280 | 11,000 | 8,250 |
| Net profit after tax | 21,320 | 12,600 | 6,750 |

**Statement of changes in equity**

| | *H* | *N* | *S* |
|---|---|---|---|
| | $ | $ | $ |
| As at 30 April 20X7 | 114,272 | 58,000 | 28,000 |
| Profit for the period | 21,320 | 12,600 | 6,750 |
| Dividends paid | (15,000) | (10,000) | (6,000) |
| As at 30 April 20X8 | 120,592 | 60,600 | 28,750 |

**Additional information**

- H acquired 80% of the ordinary shares of N several years ago when the reserves of N were $4,000 and those of S $2,500. N has 50,000 $1 ordinary shares.
- N acquired 60% of the ordinary shares in S even longer ago when the reserves of S were $1,800. S has 25,000 $1 ordinary shares.

Prepare the consolidated income statement of H and its subsidiaries for the year ended 30 April 20X8 together with a consolidated statement of changes in equity for the year.

***Solution***

**Master schedule**

| | *H* | *N* | *S* | *Consolidated* |
|---|---|---|---|---|
| Group details | | *80%* | *48% (W1)* | |
| | | *12 months* | *12 months* | |
| | $ | $ | $ | |
| Sales revenue | 74,000 | 50,000 | 37,500 | 161,500 |
| Cost of sales | (44,400) | (30,000) | (22,500) | (96,900) |
| Income tax | (16,280) | (11,000) | (8,250) | (35,530) |

| | H | N | S | Consolidated |
|---|---|---|---|---|
| Group details | | *80%* | *48% (W1)* | |
| | | *12 months* | *12 months* | |
| | $ | $ | $ | |
| Profit after tax | 13,320 | 9,000 | 6,750 | 29,070 |
| Minority interest | – | (1,800) (W3) | (3,510) (W4) | (5,310) |
| Dividends – Internal: | | | | |
| N | 8,000 (W5) | (8,000) | | |
| S | – | 2,880 (W6) | (2,880) | |
| Profit for the period | 21,320 | | | |
| Dividend – H | (15,000) | | | (15,000) |
| Brought forward | 114,272 | 3,200 (W7) | 240 (W8) | 117,712 |
| Carried forward | 120,592 | 5,280 | 600 | 126,472 |

***Workings***

(W1) 80% × 60% = 48%

(W2) Reconciliation of dividends:

| | | | |
|---|---|---|---|
| N from S | 60% × $6,000 | = | $3,600 |
| H from N | 80% × $10,000 | = | $8,000 |

Therefore, no adjustment needed.

(W3) 20% × $9,000 = $1,800

(W4) 52% × $6,750 = $3,510

(W5) 80% × $10,000 = $8,000

(W6) 48% × $6,000 = $2,880

(W7) 80% × $(8,000 – 4,000) = $3,200

(W8) 48% × $(3,000 – 2,500) = $240

***Notes:*** For the purposes of reconciling the dividends receivable and payable in W2, which is a preliminary check on the accuracy of the original income statements, we need to take the direct holding percentages. Thus, N will receive 60% of S's dividend and should, therefore, have accounted for this amount. Alternatively, the master schedule is concerned, as regards that dividend, only with its effect on the composition of the consolidated revenue reserves account. Therefore, since 48% only of the post-acquisition reserves of S is incorporated in the consolidated reserves, only 48% of the dividend needs be deducted from the S column.

Likewise, although 60% of the dividend will be received by N, only 80% of that 60%, i.e. 48%, will become part of H's share of N's reserves, and so it is appropriate to add only 48% to the N column (see W6).

**H and its subsidiaries**
**Consolidated income statement for year ended 30 April 20X8**

| | $ |
|---|---|
| Sales revenue | 161,500 |
| Cost of sales | 96,900 |
| Profit before tax | 64,600 |
| Income tax expense | 35,530 |
| Profit for the period | 29,070 |
| Profit attributable to the minority interest | 5,310 |
| Profit attributable to shareholders of H | 23,760 |

**Statement of changes in equity**

| | $ |
|---|---|
| As at 30 April 20X7 | 117,712 |
| Retained profit | 23,760 |
| Dividends paid | (15,000) |
| As at 30 April 20X8 | 126,472 |

## Summary

- There are two main types of complex group structure: vertical groups and mixed groups.
- To prepare group accounts for a complex group it is necessary to calculate the parent's effective interest in each subsidiary and sub-subsidiary. This is used to calculate goodwill and to allocate reserves between pre- and post-acquisition. Otherwise, the group balance sheet and group income statement are prepared using the method covered in earlier chapters.

Having completed your study of this chapter, you should have achieved the following learning outcome:

- prepare a consolidated income statement and balance sheet for a group of companies.

## Self-test questions

**1** What is a vertical group? (1.2)

**2** What is a mixed group? (1.3)

**3** If a subsidiary acquires a sub-subsidiary before the parent acquires the subsidiary, how are pre- and post-acquisition reserves allocated? (2.1)

## Objective test question

### Question 1

The information below is to be used in answering both questions which follow.

Plant Inc acquired 80% of the 400,000 $1 issued ordinary shares of Shrub Inc at a cost of $480,000 on 1 January 2002 when the reserves of Shrub Inc amounted to $160,000.

Shrub Inc acquired 180,000 of the 200,000 $1 shares in Twig Inc at a cost of $320,000 on 30 June 2002 when the reserves of Twig Inc amounted to $100,000. The company's reserves were $80,000 on the date of Plant Inc's acquisition of Shrub Inc.

The reserves of the three companies as at 31 December 2003 were as follows: Plant Inc $400,000, Shrub Inc $240,000 and Twig Inc $120,000.

1 What figure will appear for goodwill in the consolidated balance sheet of Plant Inc as at 31 December 2003?

2 What figure will appear for minority interest in the consolidated balance sheet of Plant Inc as at 31 December 2003?

*For the answer to this question, see the 'Answers' section at the end of the book.*

## Practice question

### H Ltd

The balance sheets of H, S and T, as at 31 December 20X8 were as follows:

| | *H* | *S* | *T* |
|---|---|---|---|
| | $ | $ | $ |
| 60,000 shares in S | 95,000 | | |
| 30,000 shares in T | | 48,000 | |
| Sundry net assets | 125,000 | 87,000 | 90,000 |
| | 220,000 | 135,000 | 90,000 |
| Ordinary share capital ($1 shares ) | 100,000 | 75,000 | 50,000 |
| Reserves | 120,000 | 60,000 | 40,000 |
| | 220,000 | 135,000 | 90,000 |

Consider three scenarios for how the investments were acquired:

| | | *Balances on* | |
|---|---|---|---|
| | | *S* | *T* |
| | | *Reserves* | *Reserves* |
| | | $ | $ |
| (a) | Both investments acquired 31 December 20X1 | 10,000 | 8,000 |
| (b) | H in S on 31 December 20X2 | 12,000 | 15,000 |
| | S in T on 31 December 20X4 | 20,000 | 18,000 |
| (c) | S in T on 31 December 20X5 | 30,000 | 25,000 |
| | H in S on 31 December 20X7 | 40,000 | 29,000 |

**You are required** to prepare the consolidated balance sheet of H and its subsidiary companies, as at 31 December 20X8 for each of the three possible situations.

**(25 marks)**

*For the answer to this question, see the 'Answers' section at the end of the book.*

## Exam-type question

### Exotic Group

The Exotic Group carries on business as a distributor of warehouse equipment and importer of fruit. It diversified its activities during the 1980s to include the import and distribution of fruit, and expanded its operations by the acquisition of shares in Melon in 1989 and in Kiwi in 1991.

Accounts for all companies are made up to 31 December.

The draft income statements for Exotic, Melon and Kiwi for the year ended 31 December 1994 are as follows:

| | *Exotic* | *Melon* | *Kiwi* |
|---|---|---|---|
| | $000 | $000 | $000 |
| Revenue | 45,600 | 24,700 | 22,800 |
| Cost of sales | (18,050) | (5,463) | (5,320) |
| Gross profit | 27,550 | 19,237 | 17,480 |
| Distribution costs | (3,325) | (2,137) | (1,900) |
| Administrative expenses | (3,475) | (950) | (1,900) |

| | | | |
|---|---|---|---|
| Operating profit | 20,750 | 16,150 | 13,680 |
| Interest paid | (325) | | |
| Profit before tax | 20,425 | 16,150 | 13,680 |
| Tax | (8,300) | (5,390) | (4,241) |
| Retained profit for the year | 12,125 | 10,760 | 9,439 |
| Retained profit at 31 December 1993 was | 20,013 | 13,315 | 10,459 |

The draft balance sheets as at 31 December 1994 are as follows:

| | *Exotic* | *Melon* | *Kiwi* |
|---|---|---|---|
| | $000 | $000 | $000 |
| Non-current tangible assets (NBV) | 35,483 | 24,273 | 13,063 |
| Investments | | | |
| Shares in Melon | 6,650 | | |
| Shares in Kiwi | | 3,800 | |
| Current assets | 1,568 | 9,025 | 8,883 |
| | 43,701 | 37,098 | 21,946 |
| Share capital and reserves | | | |
| Ordinary $1 shares | 8,000 | 3,000 | 2,000 |
| Retained earnings | 22,638 | 24,075 | 19,898 |
| | 30,638 | 27,075 | 21,898 |
| Current liabilities | 13,063 | 10,023 | 48 |
| | 43,701 | 37,098 | 21,946 |

The following information is available relating to Exotic, Melon and Kiwi:

(1) On 1 January 1989 Exotic acquired 2,700,000 $1 ordinary shares in Melon for $6,650,000 at which date there was a credit balance on the retained earnings reserve of Melon of $1,425,000. No shares have been issued by Melon since Exotic acquired its interest.

(2) On 1 January 1991 Melon acquired 1,600,000 $1 ordinary shares in Kiwi for $3,800,000 at which date there was a credit balance on the retained earnings reserve of Kiwi of $950,000. No shares have been issued by Kiwi since Melon acquired its interest.

(3) During 1994, Kiwi had made inter-company sales to Melon of $480,000 making a profit of 25% on cost and $75,000 of these goods were in inventory at 31 December 1994.

(4) During 1994, Melon had made inter-company sales to Exotic of $260,000 making a profit of 331/3% on cost and $60,000 of these goods were in inventory at 31 December 1994.

(5) On 1 November 1994 Exotic sold warehouse equipment to Melon for $240,000 from inventory. Melon has included this equipment in its non-current assets. The equipment had been purchased on credit by Exotic for $200,000 in October 1994 and this amount is included in its current liabilities as at 31 December 1994.

(6) Melon charges depreciation on its warehouse equipment at 20% on cost. It is company policy to charge a full year's depreciation in the year of acquisition to be included in the cost of sales.

(7) Exotic paid a dividend of $9,500,000 during the year ended 31 December 1994.

**Required:**

(a) Prepare a consolidated income statement for the Exotic Group for the year ended 31 December 1994. **(15 marks)**

(b) Prepare a consolidated balance sheet as at that date. **(10 marks)**

**(Total: 25 marks)**

*For the answer to this question, see the 'Answers' section at the end of the book.*

## Feedback to activities

### Activity 1

Diagrammatically, the situation is as follows:

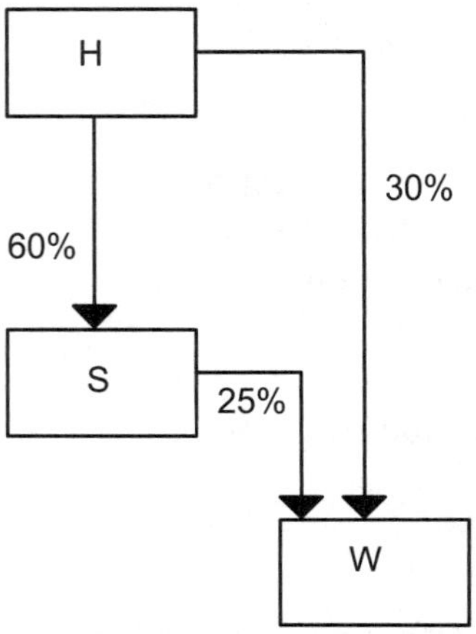


H's arithmetic interest in W = (60% × 25%) + 30% = 45%.

W is a subsidiary of H. H effectively controls S, and thus S's use of all its shares in W. Added to its own shares, H is then able to control the voting of 25% (through S) plus 30% of W's shares, i.e. 55%. For computational purposes, however, the group interest must be taken as 45% with a minority interest, as always the difference between 100% and the group interest, of 55%.

### Activity 2

**Step 1**

Calculate group shareholdings.

In S

$\frac{45,000}{60,000} \times 100\% =$ 75%

In M

| | |
|---|---|
| Direct 16,000/40,000 × 100% = | 40% |
| Indirect 75% × 12,000/40,000 × 100% = | 22.5% |
| | 62.5% |

**Step 2**

Calculate goodwill arising on S.

| | | $ | $ |
|---|---|---|---|
| Cost of investment | | | 72,000 |
| Less: | Share of net assets acquired: | | |
| | Share capital | 60,000 | |
| | Reserves | 30,000 | |
| | | 90,000 (75%) | 67,500 |
| Goodwill | | | 4,500 |

**Step 3**

Calculate goodwill arising on M.

| | | $ | $ |
|---|---|---|---|
| Cost of investment | | | |
| In H's books | | | 25,000 |
| In S's books | | | |
| | 75% × $20,000 | | 15,000 |
| | | | 40,000 |
| Less: | Share of net assets acquired: | | |
| | Share capital | 40,000 | |
| | Reserves | 10,000 | |
| | | 50,000 (62.5%) | 31,250 |
| | | | 8,750 |

## Activity 3

**Step 1**

Calculate minority interest percentages.

In S 25.0%

In M 37.5%

**Step 2**

Calculate minority interest.

| | $ |
|---|---|
| S 25% × 135,000 | 33,750 |
| M 37.5% × 75,000 | 28,125 |
| Less adjustment (25% × 20,000) | (5,000) |
| | 56,875 |

Chapter 8

# RECONSTRUCTIONS AND DEMERGERS

## Syllabus content

- The accounting entries for mergers, demergers and capital reconstruction schemes.

## Contents

## Introduction

This chapter covers the various ways in which a single company or a group can change its organisation and structure. A single company normally does this by means of changes in its capital and long-term liabilities. A group may reorganise by merging or demerging one or more of its subsidiaries or by changing its group structure. In most cases dealing with these situations is basically a matter of double entry bookkeeping.

# 1 Reduction of share capital

### 1.1 Introduction

Limited liability companies may decide to reduce their share capital subject to compliance with local legal requirements.

Reduction of capital may involve:

(a) removing or reducing the liability on any of a company's shares in respect of share capital not paid up

(b) cancelling paid up share capital which is lost or unrepresented by assets

(c) paying off any paid up share capital which is in excess of the company's needs: capital reduction may reduce the funds available for the payment of creditors and, therefore, local legal requirements may require the safeguarding of creditors' interests.

### 1.2 Accounting for a capital reduction

KEY POINT

Removal or reduction of liability on capital not paid up involves no book entry. It is only necessary to change the description of the issued capital on the balance sheet.

The accounting for situations (a) and (c) above is very simple. Removal or reduction of liability on capital not paid up involves no book entry. It is only necessary to change the description of the issued capital on the balance sheet.

X has $1 shares in issue which have only 80c paid. These can be redesignated 80c shares fully paid. This would also require the authorised capital to be altered.

If actual repayment of capital takes place, then the accounting entry would be:

Dr Share capital
Cr Bank

However, the most common form of reduction is the cancellation of paid up share capital which is lost or unrepresented by assets. This can be followed by consolidation of shares into a smaller number of the same denomination. One example is where a company has consistently made losses and has a debit balance on the accumulated profits reserve. This may be removed by writing it off against the cancelled share capital.

***Example – capital unrepresented by assets***

Failure Limited has the following balance sheet:

| | $ |
|---|---|
| Net assets | 52,500 |
| Share capital – 70,000 $1 ordinary shares | 70,000 |
| Retained losses | (17,500) |
| | 52,500 |

The share capital is only represented by $52,500 of net assets. The accumulated losses account is a fictitious asset which can be written off by reducing the share capital through a capital reduction account. The ordinary shares can be redesignated as 75c shares.

### *Solution*

The entries required are:

| | | | | |
|---|---|---|---|---|
| Dr | Ordinary share capital | | $17,500 | |
| | Cr | Capital reduction account | | $17,500 |
| Dr | Capital reduction account | | $17,500 | |
| | Cr | Retained losses | | $17,500 |

Assets may also be revalued at the time of a capital reduction which would require the following entries:

**Amounts written off assets**

Dr Capital reduction account
Cr Asset account

**Increases in asset values**

Dr Asset account
Cr Capital reduction account

If any credit balance remains on capital reduction account it would be transferred to a capital reserve.

### *Activity 1*

X has the following summarised balance sheet at 31 December 20X1:

| | $ |
|---|---|
| Property | 30,000 |
| Other assets | 20,000 |
| | 50,000 |
| 40,000 $1 ordinary shares | 40,000 |
| Retained loss | (20,000) |
| Trade payables | 30,000 |
| | 50,000 |

The following scheme of capital reduction is proposed to eliminate the accumulated loss:

(a) 25c per share is to be written off each ordinary share – the shares will then be consolidated into new $1 shares

(b) the property is to be revalued to $40,000.

Show the capital reduction account and the summarised balance sheet after completion.

*Feedback to this activity is at the end of the chapter.*

# 2 Capital reduction by purchase of own shares

## 2.1 Introduction

KEY POINT

Companies can effectively reduce their capital by making use of the right to redeem/purchase some of their own shares.

KEY POINT

For unquoted companies the redemption/purchase provisions could be particularly useful to companies with a small number of shareholders where one of them dies, retires or leaves the service of the company.

KEY POINT

In many countries, purchased own shares must be cancelled. In some countries, they may be retained and are then called 'treasury shares'.

Companies can effectively reduce their capital by making use of the right to redeem/purchase some of their own shares. This is particularly useful to quoted companies as they can go onto the stock market and purchase their own shares. When these shares are subsequently cancelled by the company, it has reduced its capital in a cost effective way.

For unquoted companies the redemption/purchase provisions could be particularly useful to companies with a small number of shareholders where one of them dies, retires or leaves the service of the company. The other shareholders may be unable or unwilling to purchase the shares themselves, but can arrange for the company to do so.

In many countries, purchased own shares must be cancelled. In some countries, they may be retained and are then called 'treasury shares'. IAS 32 *Financial Instruments: Presentation* requires that treasury shares should be presented in the balance sheet as a deduction from equity rather than as an asset. Additionally, no gain or loss should be recognised in the income statement on the subsequent reissue of treasury shares; any consideration received should be shown as a change in equity.

### *Example*

A purchases 5,000 of its shares on the stock market for $30,000 and cancels them, as it does not have suitable opportunities for investment of surplus funds and it regards its share price as being relatively low at the present time.

The shares were originally issued at a premium of 50c per share.

The summarised balance sheet of A before the purchase is:

| | *A* |
|---|---|
| | $ |
| Net assets | 100,000 |
| Ordinary shares of $1 | 20,000 |
| Share premium | 10,000 |
| Revaluation reserve | 15,000 |
| Retained earnings | 55,000 |
| | 100,000 |

What is the balance sheet of A after the purchase?

### *Solution*

The balance sheet becomes

| | $ | |
|---|---|---|
| Net assets $(100 – 30(cash)) | 70,000 | |
| Ordinary shares $(20 – 5) | 15,000 | |
| Share premium | 10,000 | |
| Revaluation reserve | 15,000 | |
| Capital reserve | 5,000 | (W1) |
| Retained earnings | 25,000 | (W2) |
| | 70,000 | |

***Workings***

(W1) **Transfer to capital reserve**

| | $ |
|---|---|
| NV of shares redeemed | 5,000 |
| Less: Proceeds of fresh issue of shares | Nil |
| | 5,000 |

(W2) **Retained earnings**

| | |
|---|---|
| Original balance | 55,000 |
| Less: Premium on redemption | (25,000) |
| To capital reserve | (5,000) |
| | 25,000 |

***Tutorial note:*** The premium on redemption must come from distributable profits as there is no fresh issue of shares.

KEY POINT

The reason for the transfer to capital reserve is to protect the rights of creditors. Capital can be returned to shareholders provided that the fund of assets available to pay creditors (the creditors' buffer) is not reduced as a result of the redemption/purchase of shares.

The reason for the transfer to capital reserve is to protect the rights of creditors. Capital can be returned to shareholders provided that the fund of assets available to pay creditors (the creditors' buffer) is not reduced as a result of the redemption/purchase of shares.

**Proof**

| | *Before purchase of shares* $ | *After purchase of shares* $ |
|---|---|---|
| Net assets | 100,000 | 70,000 |
| Less: Reduction of assets if maximum dividend paid to shareholders (balance on retained earnings account) | 55,000 | 25,000 |
| Creditors' buffer | 45,000 | 45,000 |

Despite the return of capital the creditors' buffer remains the same amount because the above provisions reduce the amount of distributable profits.

***Activity 2***

Company A in the example above redeems 25% of its ordinary shares for $30,000. It finances the redemption by issuing $30,000 10% Preference shares.

The ordinary shares were originally issued at a premium of 50c per share.

What is the balance sheet of A after the purchase?

*Feedback to this activity is at the end of the chapter.*

# 3 Reconstruction schemes

## 3.1 Introduction

DEFINITION

A **reconstruction** is the transfer of a company's undertaking and assets to a new company in consideration of the issue of the new company's shares to the first company's members.

A **reconstruction** is the transfer of a company's undertaking and assets to a new company in consideration of the issue of the new company's shares to the first company's members. This can be done for a variety of reasons including:

- for the purpose of an acquisition or merger
- for rearranging the capital and the rights of members as between themselves
- for arranging a compromise with creditors.

If the reconstruction scheme is not for a simple acquisition or merger then it is normally required because the company is in a poor financial position. The company is making a 'fresh start' and a reconstruction scheme permits compromises with creditors and more complex reorganisation of the company structure than allowed under a simple capital reduction scheme.

KEY POINT

The term reconstruction is also used to denote an internal scheme of reduction and reorganisation.

However, the term reconstruction is also used to denote an internal scheme of reduction and reorganisation. The idea of the a reconstruction scheme is to write off all fictitious assets and over-valuations and to spread the loss arising over the shareholders and creditors. This enables the company to pay dividends as soon as it makes profits.

### *Example*

The Shires Property Construction Company found itself in financial difficulty. The following is a trial balance at 31 December 20X6 extracted from the books of the company:

| | $ |
|---|---|
| Land | 156,000 |
| Building (net) | 27,246 |
| Equipment (net) | 10,754 |
| Goodwill | 60,000 |
| Inventory and work-in-progress | 120,247 |
| Receivables | 70,692 |
| Retained losses | 39,821 |
| | 484,760 |
| Ordinary shares of $1 each | 200,000 |
| 8% Loan 20X9 | 150,000 |
| Interest payable on loan | 12,800 |
| Trade payables | 96,247 |
| Bank overdraft | 25,713 |
| | 484,760 |

The authorised share capital is 200,000 ordinary shares of $1 each.

During a meeting of shareholders and directors, it was decided to carry out a scheme of internal reconstruction. The following scheme has been agreed:

1. Each ordinary share is to be redesignated as a share of 25c.
2. The ordinary shareholders are to accept a reduction in the nominal value of their shares from $1 to 25c, and subscribe for a new issue on the basis of 1 for 1 at a price of 30c per share.
3. The loan holders are to accept 20,000 ordinary shares of 25c each in lieu of the interest payable. It is agreed that the value of the interest liability is equivalent to the nominal value of the shares issued. The interest rate is to be increased to 9.5%. A further $9,000 of this 9.5% loan is to be issued and taken up by the existing holders at $90 per $100.
4. Goodwill and the accumulated losses balance are to be written off.
5. The bank overdraft is to be repaid.
6. $40,000 is to be paid of trade payables now and the balance at quarterly intervals.
7. The remaining assets were professionally valued and should be included in the books and accounts as follows:

| | $ |
|---|---|
| Land | 120,000 |
| Building | 80,000 |
| Equipment | 10,000 |
| Inventory and work-in-progress | 50,000 |

8 It is expected that, due to changed conditions and new management, operating profits will be earned at the rate of $50,000 per year after depreciation but before interest and tax. Due to losses brought forward it is unlikely that any tax liability will arise until 20X9.

**You are required to:**

(a) show the necessary journal entries including cash, to effect the reconstruction scheme

(b) prepare the balance sheet of the company immediately after the reconstruction.

***Solution***

(a) **Journal entries**

| | | | *Dr* $ | *Cr* $ |
|---|---|---|---|---|
| 1 | | Ordinary shares of $1 each | 200,000 | |
| | | Ordinary shares of 25c each | | 50,000 |
| | | Reconstruction account | | 150,000 |
| | | Redesignation of issued ordinary share capital as 25c shares (formerly $1 shares) and transferring excess nominal value to reconstruction account. | | |
| 2 | | Cash | 60,000 | |
| | | Ordinary shares of 25c each – 200,000 | | 50,000 |
| | | Share premium account 5c – 200,000 | | 10,000 |
| | | Issue of 200,000 25c ordinary shares at a premium of 5c to present ordinary shareholders. | | |
| 3 | (a) | Interest payable on loan | 12,800 | |
| | | Ordinary shares of 25c each – 20,000 | | 5,000 |
| | | Reconstruction account – difference | | 7,800 |
| | | Capitalisation of unpaid loan interest. | | |
| | (b) | 8% Loan 20X9 | 150,000 | |
| | | 9.5% Loan 20X9 | | 150,000 |
| | | Increase in interest rate on 20X9 Loan to 9.5%. | | |
| | (c) | Cash | 8,100 | |
| | | Reconstruction account | 900 | |
| | | 9.5% Loan 20X9 | | 9,000 |
| | | Issue of $9,000 loan at a discount of 10% | | |
| | | ***Note:*** the $900 could have been debited to share premium account. | | |
| 4 | | Reconstruction account | 99,821 | |
| | | Goodwill | | 60,000 |
| | | Retained losses | | 39,821 |
| | | Writing off of goodwill and debit balance on accumulated profits/losses. | | |

| | | | |
|---|---|---|---|
| 5 | No journal entry required. | | |
| 6 | Trade payables | 40,000 | |
| | Cash | | 40,000 |
| | Payment to trade payables. | | |
| 7 | Land | | 36,000 |
| | Building | 52,754 | |
| | Equipment | | 754 |
| | Inventory and work-in-progress | | 70,247 |
| | Reconstruction account | 54,247 | |
| | | 107,001 | 107,001 |
| | Revaluation of assets. | | |

(b)

**The Shires Property Construction Company**
**Balance sheet at 1 January 20X7 (after reconstruction)**

| | $ | $ |
|---|---|---|
| Non-current assets | | |
| Land at valuation | | 120,000 |
| Building at valuation | | 80,000 |
| Equipment at valuation | | 10,000 |
| | | 210,000 |
| Current assets | | |
| Inventories | 50,000 | |
| Receivables | 70,692 | |
| Cash | 2,387 | |
| | | 123,079 |
| | | 333,079 |
| Share capital | | |
| Ordinary shares of 25c each | | 105,000 |
| Share premium account | | 10,000 |
| Capital reconstruction account | | 2,832 |
| | | 117,832 |
| Non-current liabilities | | |
| 9.5% Loan 20X9 | | 159,000 |
| Current liabilities | | |
| Trade payables | | 56,247 |
| | | 333,079 |

***Workings***

**Reconstruction account**

| | $000 | | $000 |
|---|---|---|---|
| 9.5% Loan | 900 | Ordinary shares | 150,000 |
| Goodwill & retained losses | 99,821 | Loan interest | 7,800 |
| Revaluation | 54,247 | | |
| Balance c/d | 2,832 | | |
| | 157,800 | | 157,800 |

**Cash**

| | $000 | | $000 |
|---|---|---|---|
| Ordinary shares of 25c each | 60,000 | Balance b/d | 25,713 |
| 9.5% loan | 8,100 | Trade payables | 40,000 |
| | | Balance c/d | 2,387 |
| | 68,100 | | 68,100 |

### 3.2 Evaluating a reconstruction scheme

**KEY POINT**

You will not be asked to devise a reconstruction scheme in the exam. However, you may be asked to comment on a proposed scheme.

You will not be asked to devise a reconstruction scheme in the exam. However, you may be asked to comment on a proposed scheme.

In order to do this, you will need to look at the scheme from the point of view of each of the groups of people affected. These could include:

- equity shareholders
- loan creditors (debenture holders or the bank)
- potential suppliers of additional finance (e.g. venture capitalists).

**KEY POINT**

You should ask yourself whether (and what) each group gains or loses as a result of the scheme.

You should ask yourself whether (and what) each group gains or loses as a result of the scheme. This means considering the alternative to the scheme (often liquidation).

***Example***

Consider the ways in which the reconstruction scheme for the Shires Property Construction Company affects the loan holders.

On the face of it, the loan holders have done very well. If the scheme had not been implemented it is unlikely that they would have received any interest in the near future. As a result of the scheme they receive ordinary shares immediately. Their interest has been increased by 1% but the redemption date has not been changed. The 10% capital gain (on the new loans issued) over a period of less than three years is another advantage.

However, given the estimated level of profits it is unlikely that enough cash will be available to repay the loan in three years time. Alternatively, holders of the loan might agree to exchange the loan for ordinary shares.

## 4 Group restructuring

A group restructuring could consist of any of the following:

(a) the transfer of shares in a subsidiary from one group company to another

(b) the addition of a new parent company to a group

(c) the transfer of shares in one or more subsidiaries of a group to a new entity that is not a group entity but whose shareholders are the same as those of the group's parent

(d) the combination into a group of two or more companies that before the combination had the same shareholders.

The next sections consider the possible commercial reasons and accounting for possible restructuring arrangements.

### 4.1 Creating a new holding entity

A group might set up a new holding entity for an existing group in order to improve co-ordination within the group or as a vehicle for flotation.

A typical situation would be as shown below.

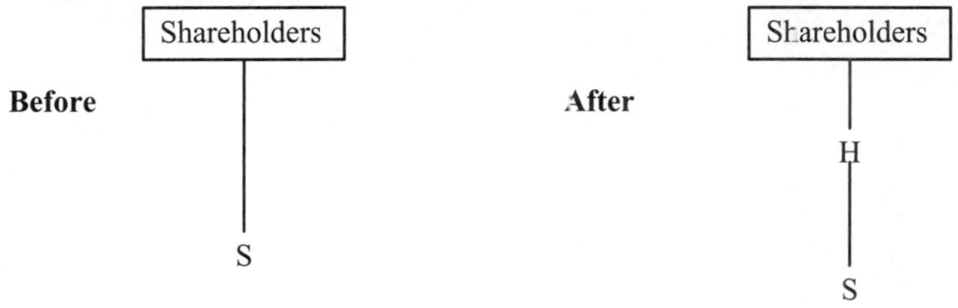

H becomes the new holding entity of S. Usually H issues shares to the shareholders of S in exchange for shares of S, but occasionally the shareholders of S may subscribe for shares in H and H may pay cash for S.

A new holding entity can also be set up as a means of returning capital to the shareholders. In this situation, H issues shareholders in S with cash or debentures in exchange for their existing shares.

### 4.2 Accounting treatment

IFRS 3 excludes from its scope any business combinations involving entities or businesses under common control. It states that:

- 'standard' business combinations must be accounted for using the purchase method
- goodwill arising on consolidation is capitalised, not amortised, but subject to an annual impairment review.

At present, there is no mandatory guidance for the accounting for these items however the purchase method should certainly be used in examination questions.

## 5 Changing direct ownership of an entity within a group

### 5.1 The effects of changes in the direct ownership of subsidiaries

The reorganisation of the group should not result in any changes to the group financial statements. The reorganisations are achieved by transferring the shareholdings from one group company to another. No assets leave or are added to the group as a result.

However, accounting problems may arise in the individual entity(ies) which originally held the investment(s). The transferor entity has disposed of an asset.

### 5.2 Types of re-organisation

(a) **Subsidiary moved up**

**Before**

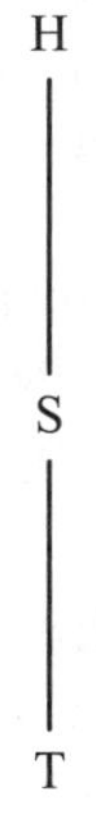


**After**

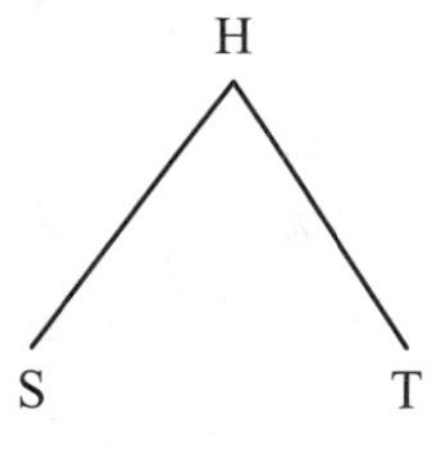

(b) **Subsidiary moved down**

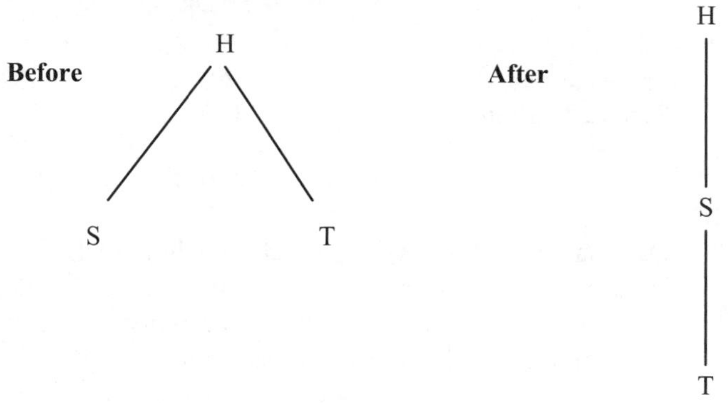


(c) **Subsidiary moved along**

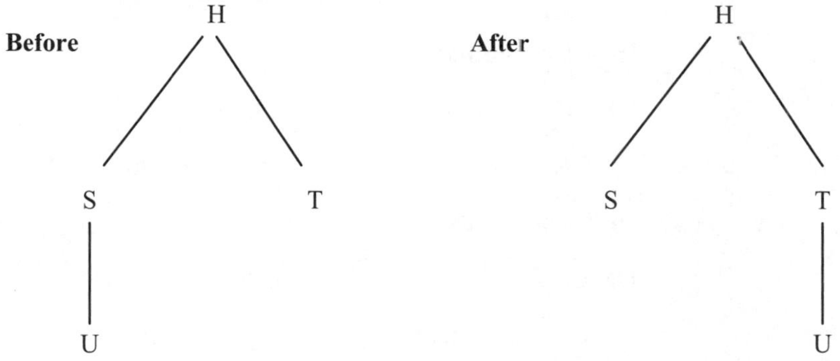


### *Activity 3*

X owns 100% of Y and Y owns 100% of Z. Y's investment in Z is transferred to X, so that Z becomes a direct subsidiary of X. Suggest reasons why the group might have carried out this reorganisation.

*Feedback to this activity is at the end of the chapter.*

## 5.3 Subsidiary moved up

This can be achieved in one of two ways:

(a) S transfers its investment in T to H as a dividend *in specie*. If this is done then S must have sufficient distributable profits to pay the dividend.

(b) H purchases the investment in T from S for cash. In practice the purchase price often equals the fair value of the net assets acquired, so that no gain or loss arises on the transaction.

In some jurisdictions, a parent cannot issue shares to a subsidiary and so this type of reorganisation cannot be carried out by means of a share-for-share exchange.

### *Example*

A has owned 100% of B since its incorporation. B acquired 100% of C many years ago when the balance on C's reserves was $5 million. Goodwill arising on the acquisition has been fully written off.

The balance sheets of the three companies at 31 December 20X2 are as follows:

| | *A* | *B* | *C* |
|---|---|---|---|
| | $m | $m | $m |
| Non-current assets | 300 | 100 | 25 |
| Investment in B | 30 | | |
| Investment in C | | 35 | |
| Net current assets | 80 | 50 | 10 |

| | | | |
|---|---|---|---|
| | 410 | 185 | 35 |
| Share capital | 60 | 30 | 20 |
| Retained earnings | 350 | 155 | 15 |
| | 410 | 185 | 35 |

On 1 January 20X3 A purchased the whole of B's investment in C for $35 million in cash. The fair value of the assets of C was $35 million at that date.
Show how the accounts of the three individual companies and the group would appear immediately after this transaction.

### *Solution*

**In A's accounts:**

| | | |
|---|---|---|
| DR Investment in C | £35m | |
| CR Cash | | £35m |

**In B's accounts:**

| | | |
|---|---|---|
| DR Cash | £35m | |
| CR Investment in C | | £35m |

| | *A* | *B* | *C* | *Group* |
|---|---|---|---|---|
| | $m | $m | $m | $m |
| Non-current assets | 300 | 100 | 25 | 425 |
| Investment in B | 30 | – | – | |
| Investment in C | 35 | – | – | |
| Net current assets | 45 | 85 | 10 | 140 |
| | 410 | 185 | 35 | 565 |
| Share capital | 60 | 30 | 20 | 60 |
| Retained earnings (W) | 350 | 155 | 15 | 505 |
| | 410 | 185 | 35 | 565 |

***Working***

| Group retained earnings: | $m |
|---|---|
| A | 350 |
| B | 155 |
| C (post-acquisition) (15 – 5) | 10 |
| | 515 |
| Less: Goodwill on acquisition of C (35 – 25) | (10) |
| | 505 |

Notice that the group accounts are exactly the same after the reorganisation as they were before. From the perspective *of the group* nothing has changed. The group has not made an acquisition or a disposal and the fact that C is now a subsidiary of A rather than a subsidiary of B does not affect the amount of pre-acquisition reserves. These are 'frozen' at the date that C first became a member of the group.

### 5.4 Subsidiary moved down

This reorganisation may be carried out where there are tax advantages in establishing a 'sub-group', or where two or more subsidiaries are linked geographically. This can be carried out either by:

(a) a share-for-share exchange (S issues shares to H in return for the shares in T); or

(b) a cash transaction (S pays cash to H).

### 5.5 Subsidiary moved along

This is carried out by T paying cash (or other assets) to S. The consideration would not normally be in the form of shares because a typical reason for such a reconstruction would be to allow S to be managed as a separate part of the group or even disposed of completely. This could not be achieved effectively were S to have a shareholding in T. If the purpose of the reorganisation is to allow S to leave the group, the purchase price paid by T should not be less than the fair value of the investment in U, otherwise S may be deemed to be receiving financial assistance for the purchase of its own shares, which is illegal in many jurisdictions.

***Example***

| | *A* | *B* | *C* |
|---|---|---|---|
| | $m | $m | $m |
| Investment in B | 50 | | |
| Investment in C | 45 | | |
| Property, plant and equipment | 60 | 65 | 70 |
| Net current assets | 30 | 32 | 25 |
| | 185 | 97 | 95 |
| Share capital ($1 shares) | 100 | 50 | 45 |
| Reserves | 85 | 47 | 50 |
| | 185 | 97 | 95 |

- On 31 December 20X0 A transfers its shares in C to a new company, D. D issues 60 million $1 shares to the **shareholders** of A.
- The net assets of the A group will be reduced by $95 million as a result of this disposal. This will be reflected in the **consolidated** accounts as a distribution (a dividend in specie) of $95 million. The individual accounts of A will show a dividend in specie of $45 million (the cost of the investment). The consolidated balance sheet of the A group will no longer include any net assets of C and the individual balance sheets will be as follows:

| | *A* | *B* | *Consolidated* |
|---|---|---|---|
| | $m | $m | $m |
| Investment in B | 50 | | |
| Investment in C | – | | |
| Property, plant and equipment | 60 | 65 | 125 |
| Net current assets | 30 | 32 | 62 |
| | 140 | 97 | 187 |

| | | | |
|---|---|---|---|
| Share capital ($1 shares) | 100 | 50 | 100 |
| Reserves (reserves of A reduced by $45m) | 40 | 47 | 87 |
| | 140 | 97 | 187 |

### 5.6 The combination into a group of two or more companies that before the combination had the same shareholders

This is essentially the reverse of the scenario in the previous example, perhaps where controlling shareholders wish to manage their interests within a single structure. It might be achieved by one of the companies becoming a subsidiary of the other and the new parent issuing further equity shares to the former shareholders of its new subsidiary.

***Example***

Two groups, C and D, have the same shareholders. The two groups combine so that D becomes a subsidiary of C. C issues more equity shares to the shareholders of D and the structure changes as follows:

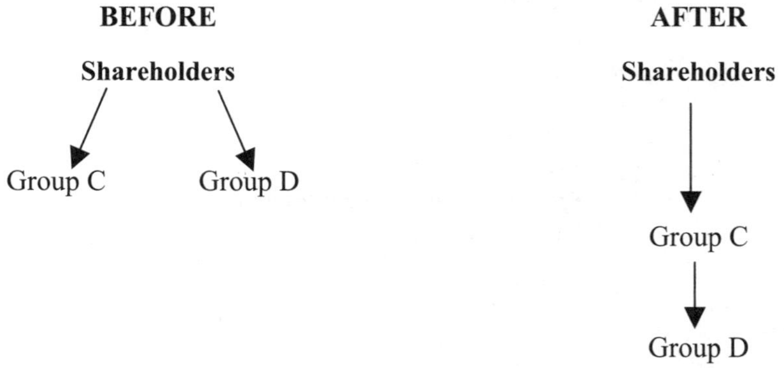


## 6 Changes in the internal structure of a group

### 6.1 The reasons why groups change their internal structures

KEY POINT

The internal structure of a group is the number of companies and/or divisions that exist and the legal, accounting and reporting relationships between the companies/divisions.

The internal structure of a group is the number of companies and/or divisions that exist and the legal, accounting and reporting relationships between the companies/divisions.

The legal structure tends to reflect the way the group wants to manage the total operations and the way the individual sections report.

Thus a group may have a pyramid structure as below.

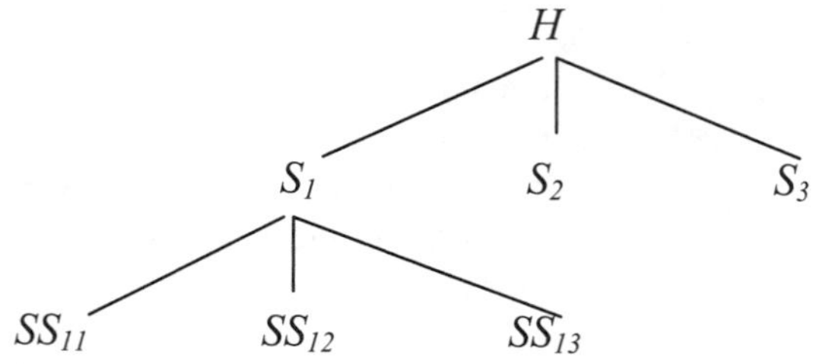


The bottom level companies (sub-subsidiaries) report to the next level (subsidiaries) which in turn report to the parent company. This structure supports a hierarchical style of management.

Other groups may prefer a flatter organisational structure with perhaps the number of subsidiaries being reduced and most subsidiaries being directly owned by the parent company.

Clearly with changes in management at the top of a group or changes in the operating environment for a group, changes may be thought necessary in the legal structure of a group. It is of course possible for the reporting and management structure to operate in a different way from the legal structure but, in the long run, it is easier if the two coincide.

Further reasons why a group may change its structure include taxation (the total taxation borne by the group can be affected by the legal structure of the group) and overseas operations (which may need to be operated as separate subsidiaries to comply with local laws).

### 6.2 The effects of changes in the direct ownership of subsidiaries

KEY POINT

In principle the reorganisation of the group should result in no changes in the group financial statements. The reorganisations are achieved by transferring the shareholdings from one group company to another. No assets leave or are added to the group as a result.

In principle the reorganisation of the group should result in no changes in the group financial statements. The reorganisations are achieved by transferring the shareholdings from one group company to another. No assets leave or are added to the group as a result.

### 6.3 Why a company may demerge some of its subsidiaries

DEFINITION

A **demerger** is the splitting of a group into two or more parts, each of which continues to be owned by the original shareholders but with no legal relationship with the former other parts of the group.

A **demerger** is the splitting of a group into two or more parts, each of which continues to be owned by the original shareholders but with no legal relationship with the former other parts of the group.

A demerger is an extreme form of internal restructuring. The group becomes two groups but from the shareholders' point of view it is a restructuring as they retain the same effective interest in the two groups as they had in the original group.

KEY POINT

The main reason for a demerger is to enhance shareholder value.

The main reason given for demergers is to 'enhance shareholder value'. In the view of the directors making the decision, the stock market has a history of placing a value on the old group which does not equal the true value of the group. Splitting the group results in two publicly quoted groups which may be valued by the stock market at more than the former combined entity. This seems to have been the case with the demergers that have been done in the past but it is not a common type of reorganisation.

The impetus for demerging may be an unwanted bid by another company and is thus a means of defending the group from take-over.

### 6.4 Preparing the financial statements after a demerger

The preparation of financial statements after a demerger is quite straightforward providing you understand the nature of the transactions. In accounting terms a group is giving some of its assets, i.e. investments in subsidiaries, to its shareholders by distributing the shareholdings to them. This may be done directly or through the medium of another company. The end effect to the shareholders is the same.

A direct distribution of the investment is a distribution *in specie* as in the illustration below.

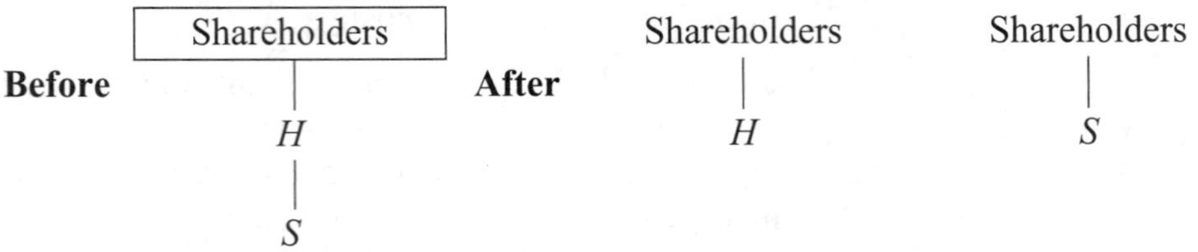


KEY POINT

In accounting terms, the company is paying a dividend in the form of shares rather than cash.

In accounting terms, the company is paying a dividend in the form of shares rather than cash. The entry in the parent company books is therefore:

Dr Retained earnings
Cr Cost of investments

with the (probably) book value of the investment.

Alternatively a new company may be formed and the shares issued to the shareholders in the existing group. The investment (or subsidiary) is transferred to the new company as below.

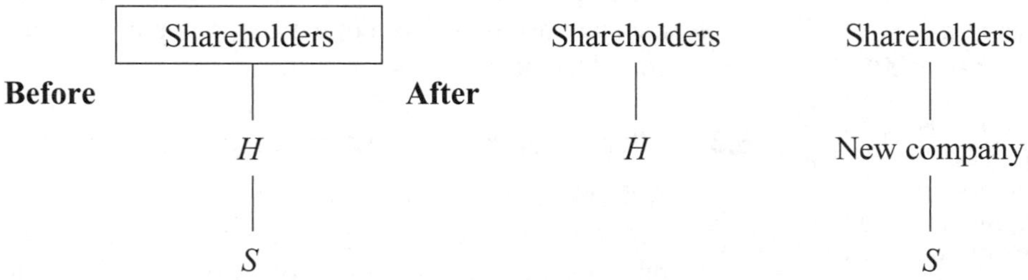


In the old parent company, the transaction is dealt with in the same way as for a direct distribution, i.e. a 'dividend' is being paid to the shareholders, the value of which is (probably) made to be equivalent to the book value of the net assets transferred to the new company or the cost of investment of the subsidiary being transferred.

### *Example*

The summarised consolidated balance sheet of the X Group is shown below, together with the individual summarised balance sheets of X and its wholly owned subsidiary Y at 31 December 20X6.

| | *X Group* | *X* | *Y* |
|---|---|---|---|
| | $000 | $000 | $000 |
| Investment in Y | – | 800 | – |
| Other net assets | 3,600 | 2,200 | 1,400 |
| | 3,600 | 3,000 | 1,400 |
| Share capital | 2,000 | 2,000 | 800 |
| Retained earnings | 1,600 | 1,000 | 600 |
| | 3,600 | 3,000 | 1,400 |

On 1 January 20X7, X forms a new company, Z. Z issues 800,000 $1 ordinary shares to the shareholders of X in exchange for X's investment in Y, so that Y is demerged.

Prepare the summarised financial statements of X and the X Group immediately after the demerger.

### *Solution*

***Tutorial note:*** X has effectively made a distribution of $800,000 to its shareholders. The group's net assets are reduced by $1,400,000 and X's net assets by $800,000. The reduction is disclosed as a movement on retained earnings.

| | *X Group* | *X* |
|---|---|---|
| | $000 | $000 |
| Net assets | 2,200 | 2,200 |
| Share capital | 2,000 | 2,000 |
| Retained earnings b/f | 1,600 | 1,000 |
| Demerger | (1,400) | (800) |
| | 2,200 | 2,200 |

## Summary

- A single company can reorganise its capital structure in several ways:
  - by reducing its share capital
  - by redeeming or purchasing its own shares
  - by devising and carrying out a reconstruction scheme.
- Groups may change their internal structures. A demerger is the splitting of a group into two or more parts, each of which continues to be owned by the original shareholders.

Having completed your study of this chapter, you should have achieved the following learning outcome:

- explain the principles of accounting for a capital reconstruction scheme or a demerger.

## Self-test questions

**1** What are the accounting entries for carrying out a capital reduction? (1.2)

**2** Why might a company wish to purchase its own shares? (2.1)

**3** Why are reconstructions carried out? (3.1)

**4** What are the two methods of achieving a re-organisation where a subsidiary is 'moved up'? (5.3)

**5** Why do groups have differing internal structures? (6.1)

**6** Why might a company demerge some of its subsidiaries? (6.3)

## Objective test questions

### Question 1

Which of the following is the main reason why groups may undertake a demerger?

**A** To reduce the audit fee

**B** To simplify the consolidation process

**C** To improve management efficiency

**D** To increase shareholder value

### Question 2

Disaster Inc's balance sheet as at 31 March 2004 is as follows:

| | $ |
|---|---|
| Book value of net assets | 1,100,000 |
| Ordinary share capital | 2,000,000 |
| Retained losses | (900,000) |
| | 1,100,000 |

The carrying value of net assets includes a freehold property at an amount of $400,000. This has been professionally valued at $ 600,000.

What is the most appropriate amount to be written off share capital as part of a capital reduction scheme?

*For the answers to these questions, see the 'Answers' section at the end of the book.*

## Exam-type question

### P Group

The following balance sheets relate to P, Q, R and S as at 31 May 20X7 immediately before the transaction mentioned below:

| | *P* | *Q* | *R* | *S* |
|---|---|---|---|---|
| | $m | $m | $m | $m |
| Property, plant and equipment | 3,500 | 550 | 60 | 90 |
| Investment in Q | 900 | | | |
| Investment in R | | 90 | | |
| Investment in S | 50 | | | |
| Net current assets | 1,830 | 400 | 70 | 60 |
| | 6,280 | 1,040 | 130 | 150 |
| Share capital ($1 shares) | 1,350 | 100 | 30 | 20 |
| Share premium account | 1,550 | 100 | 10 | 20 |
| Retained earnings | 3,250 | 810 | 80 | 105 |
| Non-current liabilities | 130 | 30 | 10 | 5 |
| | 6,280 | 1,040 | 130 | 150 |

The directors of P decided to reconstruct the group at 31 May 20X7. Under the scheme the existing group was split into two separate groups. This involved P disposing of its shareholding in Q to another entity E. In return E issued 300 million shares of $1 each to the shareholders of P.

The following information relates to the dates of acquisition of the investments in group companies:

| *Investor* | *Entity acquired* | *% acquired* | *Balance on share premium* | *Balance on reserves* |
|---|---|---|---|---|
| | | | $m | $m |
| P | Q | 100 | 100 | 250 |
| P | S | 60 | 20 | 90 |
| Q | R | 80 | 10 | 60 |

P's investment in Q was made before the other two investments. All goodwill on consolidation was fully written off at 31 May 20X6.

**Required:**

Prepare the consolidated balance sheet of the P and E groups as at 31 May 20X7 immediately after the group reconstruction has been put into effect.

**(25 marks)**

*For the answer to this question, see the 'Answers' section at the end of the book.*

# Feedback to activities

## Activity 1

**Step 1**

Open capital reduction account and insert amounts arising from the scheme.

**Capital reduction account**

| | $ | | $ |
|---|---|---|---|
| Retained loss | 20,000 | Ordinary share capital | 10,000 |
| | | Property | 10,000 |
| | 20,000 | | 20,000 |

**Step 2**

Prepare the balance sheet after capital reduction is complete.

**Balance sheet**

| | $ |
|---|---|
| Property | 40,000 |
| Other assets | 20,000 |
| | 60,000 |
| Ordinary share capital – 30,000 $1 shares | 30,000 |
| Trade payables | 30,000 |
| | 60,000 |

## Activity 2

The balance sheet becomes:

| | $ |
|---|---|
| Net assets $(100 + 30 – 30) | 100,000 |
| Ordinary shares $(20 – 5) | 15,000 |
| Share premium | 7,500 (W2) |
| Revaluation reserve | 15,000 |
| Retained earnings | 32,500 (W3) |
| Preference shares | 30,000 |
| | 100,000 |

***Workings***

(W1) **Transfer to capital reserve**

| | $ | $ |
|---|---|---|
| NV of shares redeemed | | 5,000 |
| Less: Proceeds of fresh issue of shares | | 30,000 |
| ∴ No need for transfer to capital reserve | | |

(W2) **Share premium account**

| | | |
|---|---|---|
| Original balance | | 10,000 |
| Less: Lowest of | | |
| Actual premium or redemption | 25,000 | |
| Original premium on shares now being redeemed 5,000 x 50c | 2,500 | |
| Current balance on share premium account | 10,000 | |
| | | (2,500) |
| | | 7,500 |

***Tutorial note:*** The premium offset against share premium is effectively the lowest of three figures:

(a) the actual premium on redemption, i.e. if there is no premium on redemption then there can be no offset!

(b) the original premium on issue

(c) the balance on share premium, i.e. a negative balance on share premium account is not allowed.

(W3) **Retained earnings**

| | $ |
|---|---|
| Original balance | 55,000 |
| Less: Premium on redemption to the extent not set off against share premium $(25,000 – 2,500) | (22,500) |
| | 32,500 |

As fresh capital of $30,000 has replaced old capital of $30,000 the creditors' buffer should be maintained without any transfers to capital reserve.

In this case the creditors' buffer actually increases as most of the premium on redemption reduces distributable profits even though new capital has come in to replace the old.

## Activity 3

If Y and Z are in different businesses this restructuring enables the different businesses to be carried out through directly owned subsidiaries.

**The change would also allow X to sell Y without disposing of Z.**

Chapter 9

# FOREIGN CURRENCY TRANSLATION

## Syllabus content

- The treatment in consolidated financial statements of minority interests, pre- and post-acquisition reserves, goodwill (including its impairment), fair value adjustments, intra-group transactions and dividends, piece-meal and mid-year acquisitions, and disposals to include sub-subsidiaries and mixed groups.
- Foreign currency translation (IAS 21) to include overseas transactions and investments in overseas subsidiaries.

## Contents

## Introduction

Many companies enter into transactions in foreign currencies. This chapter begins by covering the technique for dealing with individual foreign currency transactions in the accounts of a single company.

We then consider the situation which is most likely to feature in the exam: preparation of the group accounts where a parent has a foreign subsidiary. The subsidiary's accounts have to be translated from its own local currency into the currency in which the group accounts will be presented, so that they can then be consolidated.

# 1 Transactions in foreign currencies

### 1.1 Basic principles

KEY POINT

Foreign currency transactions should be recorded using the spot exchange rate at the date the transaction occurred.

DEFINITION

The **spot exchange rate** is the exchange rate for immediate delivery.

KEY POINT

Monetary balances denominated in a foreign currency should be retranslated at the balance sheet date rate, with the exchange difference taken to the income statement.

DEFINITION

The **closing rate** is the spot exchange rate at the balance sheet date.

It is quite likely that during an accounting period, a company will enter into transactions in a currency other than its own domestic (i.e. functional) currency. For example, it may buy or sell goods or services whose price is denominated in a foreign currency, or borrow or lend funds where the amounts payable or receivable are denominated in a foreign currency.

IAS 21 *The Effects of Changes in Foreign Exchange Rates* states that foreign currency transactions should be recorded using the spot exchange rate at the date the transaction occurred.

The **spot exchange rate** is the exchange rate for immediate delivery.

At each balance sheet date:

(a) monetary items (receivables, payables, bank balances and loans) are translated using the closing rate;

(b) non-monetary items (eg, non-current assets, inventory, investments) that are measured at historic cost are translated using the exchange rate at the date of the transaction; and

(c) non-monetary items that are measured at fair value are translated using the exchange rate at the date when the fair value was determined.

The **closing rate** is the spot exchange rate at the balance sheet date.

In practice this means that no further translation is required for non-monetary assets carried at historical cost. However, monetary items at the balance sheet date are retranslated at the closing rate of exchange. Exchange differences are taken to the income statement.

### 1.2 Non-current assets

Once these assets have been translated at the historical rate and recorded they are carried in terms of the currency of the individual company.

Thus where a UK company purchases plant and machinery, for its own use in the UK, from an American supplier on 30 June 20X7 for $90,000 when the rate of exchange was £1 = $1.80, it will record the asset at £50,000 ($90,000 @ 1.80). No further translation will occur. All depreciation charged on this asset will be based on £50,000.

## 1.3 Receivables

Where goods are sold to overseas customers and payment is to be received in a currency other than the functional currency, the following transactions must be recorded:

- the sale – at the rate of exchange applicable at the time of sale
- the receipt of cash – the actual proceeds.

Any exchange difference (the balance remaining on the customer's account) will be reported as part of the profit for the period from normal operations.

### *Example*

If on 7 May 20X6 a dollar-based company sells goods to a German company for €48,000 when the rate of exchange was $1 = €3.2, the sale will be recorded:

| | $ | $ |
|---|---|---|
| Dr Customer €48,000 @ 3.2 | 15,000 | |
| Cr Sales | | 15,000 |

Assuming on 20 July 20X6 the customer remits a draft for € 48,000 which realises $15,150:

| | $ | $ |
|---|---|---|
| Dr Bank | 15,150 | |
| Cr Customer | | 15,150 |

The credit balance of $150 on the customer's account will represent a profit on exchange to be taken to the income statement as part of the operating profit for the year.

### *Activity 1*

Facts are as above except that the company prepares accounts to 30 June annually. At the balance sheet date the rate of exchange was $1 = €3.15. What will be the movements on the customer's account?

*Feedback to this activity is at the end of the chapter.*

## 1.4 Payables

The same principles as those set out for receivables also apply to payables.

### *Activity 2*

A company preparing accounts in dollars buys goods from a Swiss supplier for Sw Fr 8,700 when the rate of exchange was $1 = Sw Fr 3. The company settled the amount due with a bankers draft for Sw Fr 8,700 when the rate of exchange was $1 = Sw Fr 2.8. Prepare the supplier's account.

*Feedback to this activity is at the end of the chapter.*

KEY POINT

Where a company raises a loan abroad, denominated in a currency other than its own currency, the amount outstanding must be retranslated at the closing rate at each year end. Again, this is because a loan is a monetary item. Any difference on exchange must form part of the profit from normal operations.

## 1.5 Loans

Where a company raises a loan abroad, denominated in a currency other than its own currency, the amount outstanding must be retranslated at the closing rate at each year end. Again, this is because a loan is a monetary item. Any difference on exchange must form part of the profit from normal operations.

***Example***

A dollar-based company takes out a five-year loan of £1m from a UK bank. The proceeds amounted to $2,000,000 (when rate of exchange was $1 = £0.50). At the balance sheet date the rate had moved to $1 = £0.45.

The loan must be translated at this rate to $2,222,222. The loss on exchange of $(2,222,222 – 2,000,000) = $222,222 will be reported as part of profit from normal operations. Retranslation will occur at each balance sheet date.

**Loan**

| | £ | $ | | £ | $ |
|---|---|---|---|---|---|
| Bal c/d @ £0.45 | 1,000,000 | 2,222,222 | Bank @ £0.50 | 1,000,000 | 2,000,000 |
| | | | Income statement (loss on exchange) | | 222,222 |
| | 1,000,000 | 2,222,222 | | 1,000,000 | 2,222,222 |

## 1.6 Non-monetary assets carried at fair value

Non-monetary assets such as properties are often carried at fair value. These assets are translated at the date at which the fair value was determined. Because IAS 16 requires gains and losses on revaluation to be recognised in equity (a revaluation reserve) exchange gains and losses are also taken to equity.

***Example***

A dollar-based company purchases land for 150,000 currency units (CU) when the rate of exchange is CU1.5 = $1. It revalues the land to CU180,000 when the rate of exchange is CU1.6 = $1.

On initial recognition the land is included in the balance sheet at $100,000 (150,000/1.5). On revaluation it is measured at $112,500 (180,000/1.6). There is a revaluation gain of $18,750 (30,000/1.6) and an exchange loss of $6,250 (100,000 – 150,000/1.6). Both these items are taken to reserves and reported in the statement of changes in equity.

## 1.7 Summary

- **Transactions during accounting period** – These should be translated and recorded at the rate of exchange ruling at the date of the transaction.
- **Monetary items at balance sheet date** – Where these items (receivables, payables, bank balances, loans) are denominated in a foreign currency they should be translated and recorded at the closing rate (or, if appropriate, at the rate at which the transaction is contracted to be settled).
- **Non-monetary items at balance sheet date** – Where these items are carried at cost less depreciation, they should be translated and recorded at the exchange rate at the date of acquisition. Where these items are carried at fair value less depreciation, they should be translated and recorded at the exchange rate at the date of revaluation.
- **Exchange differences** – All exchange differences should be reported in the income statement, unless they relate to a gain or loss on a non-monetary item that is recognised in equity (in which case the exchange difference is also taken to equity).

## 1.8 Equity investment financed by foreign currency loan – hedging

KEY POINT

Hedging loans are designed to hedge against foreign currency movements. This is because exchange rates for both the equity investment and the overseas currency loan will move in the same direction – either both up or both down.

It is not unusual for companies making overseas investments to raise the funds locally in an overseas currency. Such loans are known as hedging loans as they are designed to hedge against foreign currency movements. This is because exchange rates for both the equity investment and the overseas currency loan will move in the same direction – either both up or both down.

Special rules apply to hedging transactions. Without these special rules, the normal rules of IAS 21 have the following effect:

- the loan is a monetary item and is retranslated at the closing rate of exchange. Any resulting exchange gain or loss is taken to the income statement
- the investment is a non-monetary item and is therefore carried at the historic exchange rate with no subsequent exchange differences arising.

KEY POINT

Hedge accounting matches the gains and losses.

This treatment fails to reflect the true substance of the arrangement as the loan and investment are directly related. Any gain or loss on one is, in principle, cancelled out by an equivalent loss or gain on the other, and no 'true' exchange difference arises.

Hedge accounting matches the gains and losses.

***Conditions for hedge accounting***

Hedge accounting is covered by IAS 39 *Financial Instruments: Recognition and Measurement.* Under IAS 39 hedge accounting is **required** where a hedging relationship meets all the following conditions:

(a) The hedging relationship must be designated as a hedge at its inception. There must be formal documentation, identifying the hedged item, the hedge instrument, the nature of the risk that is to be hedged and how the entity will assess the hedging instrument's effectiveness.

(b) The hedge is expected to be highly effective. A hedge is highly effective if the changes in the value of the hedged item (the investment) are almost fully offset by the changes in the value of the hedging instrument (the loan).

(c) The effectiveness of the hedge can be measured reliably.

(d) The hedge is assessed on an ongoing basis (annually) and has been effective during the reporting period.

***The mechanics***

If hedge accounting is used:

(a) the effective portion of the gain or loss on the hedging instrument (the loan) is recognised directly in equity through the statement of changes in equity

(b) only the ineffective portion of the gain or loss is recognised in the income statement.

### Example

On 1 January 20X8 100% of a Swiss subsidiary was acquired by H at a cost of Fr960,000 when the rate was Fr6 = $1. The whole of the purchase price was borrowed from a German bank when the rate was €4 = $1.

Rates at 31 December 20X8:

$1 = 5 Fr = €3.2.

Show the carrying value of the investment and loan, and explain the necessary accounting entries at 31 December 20X8. Assume that the arrangement meets the conditions for hedge accounting.

### Solution

| | | Fr(000) | *Rate* | $000 |
|---|---|---|---|---|
| (a) | Investment carrying value | | | |
| | – purchase | 960 | 6.0 | 160 |
| (b) | Loan | *€(000)* | | |
| | – at borrowing date | 640 | 4.0 | 160 |
| | – at 31.12.X8 | 640 | 3.2 | 200 |
| | Loss on restating loan | | | (40) |

The effective portion of the gain or loss is the notional exchange gain that would arise if the investment were re-translated at the balance sheet date:

| | | €(000) | *Rate* | $000 |
|---|---|---|---|---|
| Investment carrying value | – purchase | 960 | Cost | 160 |
| | – 31.12.X8 | 960 | 5 | 192 |
| Gain on restating carrying value | | | | 32 |

Therefore only $32,000 is recognised in equity; the ineffective portion is recognised in the income statement, which reports a loss of $8,000.

## 2 Foreign operations

### 2.1 Functional currency and presentation currency

DEFINITION

A **foreign operation** is an entity that is a subsidiary, associate, joint venture or branch of a reporting entity, the activities of which are based or conducted in a country or currency other than those of the reporting entity.

A **foreign operation** is an entity that is a subsidiary, associate, joint venture or branch of a reporting entity, the activities of which are based or conducted in a country or currency other than those of the reporting entity.

Companies frequently establish local branches or subsidiaries in foreign countries. These often maintain full accounts in the local currency and these must clearly be translated into the currency of the parent before they can be consolidated.

There are two possible translation methods. The method to be used depends on whether the foreign operation has the same functional currency as the parent or a different functional currency from the parent.

IAS 21 has introduced the concept of functional currency and presentation currency.

DEFINITION

**Functional currency** is the currency of the primary economic environment in which the entity operates.

DEFINITION

**Presentation currency** is the currency in which the financial statements are presented.

**Functional currency** is the currency of the primary economic environment in which the entity operates.

**Presentation currency** is the currency in which the financial statements are presented.

Functional currency is a matter of fact, but an entity can present its financial statements in any currency it chooses.

For most individual companies, both functional currency and presentation currency are the currency of the country in which they are based and in which they carry out all or most of their operations. However, there may be reasons for choosing to present financial statements in a different currency from the functional currency. For example, a German company could have the Euro as its functional currency but could adopt the US dollar as a presentation currency if it were seeking a listing on a US Stock Exchange.

Determining the functional currency of an entity is more likely to be problematic when the entity is a foreign operation of a parent entity.

## 2.2 Determining the functional currency

IAS 21 states that an entity's functional currency is normally the currency:

(a) that mainly influences sales prices for goods and services and the cost of providing goods or services (often the currency in which items are denominated and settled); and

(b) of the country whose competitive forces and regulations mainly determine the sales prices of its goods and services.

The following factors may also provide evidence of an entity's functional currency:

(a) the currency in which funds from financing activities (ie issuing debt and equity instruments) are generated

(b) the currency in which receipts from operating activities are usually retained.

KEY POINT

To determine the functional currency of a foreign operation an entity should consider whether the activities of the foreign operation are carried out as an extension of the parent, rather than being carried out with a significant degree of autonomy.

To determine the functional currency of a foreign operation (and whether its functional currency is the same as that of the parent) an entity should consider:

(a) whether the activities of the foreign operation are carried out as an extension of the parent, rather than being carried out with a significant degree of autonomy. An example of the former is when the foreign operation only sells goods imported from the parent and remits the proceeds to it. An example of the latter is when the operation accumulates cash and other monetary items, incurs expenses, generates income and arranges borrowings, all substantially in its local currency

(b) whether transactions with the parent are a high or a low proportion of the foreign operation's activities

(c) whether cash flows from the activities of the foreign operation directly affect the cash flows of the parent and are readily available for remittance to it

(d) whether cash flows from the activities of the foreign operation are sufficient to service its debt obligations without funds being made available by the parent.

## 2.3 Change in functional currency

Once the functional currency is determined it does not change unless the entity's activities change. For example, a change in the currency that mainly influences the sales prices of goods and services may lead to a change in an entity's functional currency.

When there is a change in an entity's functional currency, the entity should apply the translation procedures applicable to the new functional currency **prospectively** from the date of the change. In other words, an entity translates all items into the new functional currency using the exchange rate at the date of the change.

## 2.4 Translation methods

In practice, whether a foreign operation has the same functional currency as its parent (and therefore the method of translation used) depends on the relationship between the two entities.

***Semi-autonomous entity***

KEY POINT

A quasi-autonomous foreign entity should be translated using the closing rate/presentation currency method, while a dependent foreign entity should be translated using the historical/functional currency method.

Where the foreign operation is relatively independent of its parent, its transactions do not impinge directly on cash flows and profits of the parent. The foreign operation almost certainly has a different functional currency from that of the parent. In order to prepare the consolidated financial statements, the individual accounts of the foreign operation are translated from its own functional currency to a presentation currency – the functional currency of the parent.

It is the net investment in the foreign entity which is of interest rather than the individual assets and liabilities. This net investment is translated using the **closing rate** and the resulting exchange difference dealt with in reserves.

This method is sometimes known as the **closing rate method** or **net investment method.** In this text it will be called the **presentation currency method**.

***An extension of the parent***

Where the foreign operation is, in reality, the parent company operating abroad, foreign transactions will impinge directly on cash flows and profits of the parent. The foreign operation has the same functional currency as the parent.

IAS 21 assumes that this type of foreign operation keeps its accounting records in the functional currency of the parent. This means that the individual accounts of the foreign operation do not have to be translated. Therefore IAS 21 only recognises one method of translating the financial statements of a foreign operation: the closing rate or presentation currency method described above.

In theory, the foreign operation may keep its accounting records and prepare individual financial statements in its local currency (rather than its functional currency). In this situation, the foreign operation's transactions should be accounted for as if they were those of the parent. This means that the accounts are translated using the same method as for transactions in individual companies.

This method is sometimes known as the **historical method** or the **temporal method**. In this text it will be called the **functional currency method**.

# 3 Consolidated financial statements incorporating a foreign subsidiary

## 3.1 Presentation currency method/closing rate method

KEY POINT

Under the presentation currency method, all assets and liabilities are translated into the presentation currency at the closing rate.

KEY POINT

All income and expense items should be translated at the exchange rates at the dates of the transactions.

KEY POINT

In the closing rate method, exchange differences arising are taken to reserves.

(a) **Balance sheet**

Under the presentation currency method, all assets and liabilities are translated into the presentation currency at the closing rate.

(b) **Income statement**

All income and expense items should be translated at the exchange rates at the dates of the transactions.

For practical reasons, an average rate for the period is normally used to approximate the actual exchange rates. However, if exchange rates fluctuate significantly, the use of the average rate is inappropriate.

Special rules exist where the foreign entity reports in the currency of a hyperinflationary economy – IAS 29 is covered in a later chapter.

(c) **Exchange differences**

All exchange differences arising on consolidation should be recognised as a separate component of equity (i.e. in a separate reserve).

These exchange differences are not taken to the income statement because they have little or no direct effect on the present and future cash flows from operations.

## 3.2 Sources of exchange differences

Exchange differences arise because items are translated at different points in time at different rates of exchange.

It must be remembered that

| | | | | |
|---|---|---|---|---|
| Opening equity | + | Profit | = | Closing equity |
| (Opening net assets) | + | (Increase in net assets) | = | (Closing net assets) |

(a) **Opening equity (= opening net assets)**

These will have been translated for the purpose of last year's accounts at last year's closing rate of exchange. For the purposes of the current year's accounts these items are translated at this year's closing rate of exchange since the opening net assets will be included within the closing net assets which are translated at the closing rate.

(b) **Profit for year**

The net assets generated by the profit must be translated at this year's closing rate (again within the closing net assets).

Thus the exchange difference will arise from the translation of:

(i) **opening equity** – from last year's closing rate to this year's closing rate

(ii) **profit** – from the average rate to the closing rate.

### 3.3 Example

Grofine bought 75% of S on 31 December 20X1 when the net assets of S were Z12,000,000 and the exchange rate was Z3 = $1.

At 31 December 20X3 the balance sheets were as follows.

| | *Grofine* | *S* |
|---|---|---|
| | $000 | Z000 |
| Non-current assets | – | 2,400 |
| Investment in S | 5,000 | – |
| Net current assets | 652 | 20,800 |
| | 5,652 | 23,200 |
| Share capital | 5,000 | 4,000 |
| Reserves | 652 | 19,200 |
| | 5,652 | 23,200 |

The rate of exchange at 31 December 20X3 was Z2.5 = $1.

The income statement of S for the year ended 31 December 20X3 was as follows.

| | *S* |
|---|---|
| | Z000 |
| Revenue | 22,000 |
| Cost of sales | (11,490) |
| Gross profit | 10,510 |
| Distribution and admin expenses | (3,910) |
| Profit for the year | 6,600 |

The statement of changes in equity of S for the year ended 31 December 20X3 was as follows.

| | *S* |
|---|---|
| | Z000 |
| Opening balance | 18,600 |
| Profit for the year | 6,600 |
| Dividends paid | (2,000) |
| Closing balance | 23,200 |

The average rate of exchange for the year was Z2.3 = $1.

The dividend was paid when the rate of exchange was Z2.3 = $1.

Grofine did not trade during the year.

The rate of exchange at 31 December 20X2 was Z2 = $1.

At 31 December 20X3 goodwill arising on the acquisition of S was impaired by 25% of its original value. The impairment arose during the year ended 31 December 20X3.

**Required:**

Using the presentation currency method prepare the consolidated balance sheet of Grofine as at 31 December 20X3, together with the consolidated income statement and statement of changes in equity for the year ended 31 December 20X3.

## 3.4 Translating the financial statements

***The balance sheet***

The net assets (assets and liabilities) are translated at the closing rate:

| | Z000 | *Rate* | $000 |
|---|---|---|---|
| Non-current assets | 2,400 | 2.5 | 960 |
| Net current assets | 20,800 | 2.5 | 8,320 |
| Net assets | 23,200 | | 9,280 |

This gives us the figure for closing equity (net assets at the balance sheet date).

To translate equity (share capital and reserves) we need to split out pre-acquisition reserves and post-acquisition reserves.

Share capital and pre-acquisition reserves are translated at historic rate (the rate ruling on the date of the acquisition). This gives us net assets at the date of the acquisition.

Post-acquisition reserves are the balancing figure, which is used to calculate consolidated reserves.

| | Z000 | *Rate* | $000 |
|---|---|---|---|
| Share capital | 4,000 | 3 | 1,333 |
| Pre-acquisition reserves | 8,000 | 3 | 2,667 |
| Post-acquisition reserves | 11,200 | Balance | 5,280 |
| Total equity | 23,200 | 2.5 | 9,280 |

Post acquisition reserves are made up of two amounts:

(a) post acquisition retained earnings (post-acquisition profits); and

(b) exchange differences.

***The income statement***

This is translated at the average rate for the year:

| | Z000 | *Rate* | $000 |
|---|---|---|---|
| Revenue | 22,000 | 2.3 | 9,565 |
| Cost of sales | (11,490) | | (4,995) |
| Gross profit | 10,510 | | 4,570 |
| Distribution and admin expenses | (3,910) | | (1,700) |
| Profit | 6,600 | | 2,870 |

***Statement of changes in equity***

We already have the figures for closing equity and for the profit for the year.

Opening equity is translated at the closing rate at 31 December 20X2 and the dividend paid is translated at the actual rate on the date it was paid. Exchange differences are the balancing figure.

| | Z000 | Rate | $000 |
|---|---|---|---|
| Opening balance | 18,600 | 2 | 9,300 |
| Profit for the year | 6,600 | 2.3 | 2,870 |
| Dividends paid | (2,000) | 2.3 | (870) |
| Exchange differences | | Balance | (2,020) |
| Total equity | 23,200 | 2.5 | 9,280 |

We can prove the figure for exchange differences:

| | $000 | $000 |
|---|---|---|
| Opening net assets at opening rate | (9,300) | |
| Opening net assets at closing rate (18,600 @ 2.5) | 7,440 | |
| | | 1,860 |
| Retained profit for year at average rate | (2,000) | |
| Retained profit for the year at closing rate (4,600 @ 2.5) | 1,840 | |
| | | 160 |
| Exchange loss | | 2,020 |

## 3.5 Consolidated financial statements: the principles

Once the financial statements have been translated, the basic consolidation principles are exactly the same as in any other group situation.

There are a few special points to bear in mind.

***Goodwill on consolidation***

KEY POINT

Goodwill arising on consolidation must be translated at **closing rate**.

This is calculated in the normal way, by comparing the fair value of the cost of investment with the fair value of net assets at acquisition.

IAS 21 states that goodwill arising on consolidation must be translated at **closing rate**.

***Minority interests***

Minority interests in the balance sheet are the minority's share of the net assets of the subsidiary translated at the closing rate at the balance sheet date.

***Exchange differences***

(a) **At the separate accounts stage**

Any monetary items denominated in a foreign currency (e.g. foreign loans) must be recorded in the separate accounts at the closing rate at each balance sheet date. Any difference arising is dealt with as part of the profit from normal operations.

(b) **Consolidation stage**

All exchange differences arising on consolidation must be dealt with as reserve movements.

IAS 21 states that these exchange differences must be taken to a separate component of equity (a separate translation reserve). This means that in theory, post acquisition reserves must be split between post-acquisition retained earnings and exchange differences.

In practice it is very unlikely that you will be asked to do this in the exam.

### 3.6 Consolidated financial statements: the mechanics

We continue with our example, Grofine, and carry out the normal consolidation workings.

**Group structure**

Grofine

75%

S

**Net assets of subsidiary**

***Note:*** We have already worked out net assets at acquisition and at the balance sheet date, but the working is given here for completeness.

| | *Acquisition* | *1/1/X3* | *31/1/X3* |
|---|---|---|---|
| | Z000 | Z000 | Z000 |
| Share capital | 4,000 | 4,000 | 4,000 |
| Retained earnings | 8,000 | 14,600 | 19,200 |
| | 12,000 | 18,600 | 23,200 |
| Translated: | $,000 | $,000 | $,000 |
| | @3 | @2 | @2.5 |
| | 4,000 | 9,300 | 9,280 |

**Goodwill**

Goodwill is calculated in the local currency and retranslated at the closing rate each year.

| | Z000 | Z000 |
|---|---|---|
| Cost of investment (5,000 × 3) | | 15,000 |
| Net assets acquired : (75% × 12,000) | | (9,000) |
| | | 6,000 |
| Less impairment (25%) | | (1,500) |
| | | 4,500 |

| | $000 |
|---|---|
| Translated at closing rate (2.5) | 1,800 |

Because goodwill has to be retranslated at each balance sheet date, there is a further exchange difference. This is calculated as follows:

| | $000 |
|---|---|
| Translated at closing rate (6,000 @ 2.5) | 2,400 |
| Translated at acquisition (6,000 @ 3) | (2,000) |
| Exchange gain | 400 |

This is included in consolidated reserves.

**Minority interests**

| | $000 |
|---|---|
| Net assets at balance sheet date (25% × 9,280) | 2,320 |

**Consolidated reserves at 31 December 20X3**

| | $000 |
|---|---|
| Grofine | 652 |
| S (75% × 5,280) or (75% × 9,280 – 4,000) | 3,960 |
| Impairment loss (1,500 @ 2.3) | (652) |
| Exchange difference on retranslation of goodwill | 400 |
| Exchange difference on retranslation of impairment loss (652 – 1,500 @ 2.5) | 52 |
| | 4,412 |

To complete the consolidated statement of changes in equity, we need to calculate the subsidiary's opening reserves. We can either do this using the normal net assets working above or by reconstructing the subsidiary's balance sheet and translating it.

**Consolidated reserves at 1 January 20X3**

| | Z000 | *Rate* | $000 |
|---|---|---|---|
| Share capital | 4,000 | 3 | 1,333 |
| Pre-acquisition reserves | 8,000 | 3 | 2,667 |
| Post-acquisition reserves | 6,600 | Balance | 5,300 |
| Total equity | 18,600 | 2 | 9,300 |

Then the consolidated reserves working can be completed.

| | $000 |
|---|---|
| S (75% × 5,300) or (75% × 9,300 – 4,000) | 3,975 |
| Exchange difference on retranslation of goodwill: (6,000 @ 2 – 2,000) | 1,000 |
| | 4,975 |

We can now prepare the consolidated financial statements.

**Consolidated balance sheet at 31 December 20X3**

| | $000 |
|---|---|
| Non-current assets | |
| Tangible assets | 960 |
| Goodwill (W) | 1,800 |
| Net current assets (652 + 8,320) | 8,972 |
| | 11,732 |
| Share capital | 5,000 |
| Reserves (W) | 4,412 |
| | 9,412 |
| Minority interest (W) | 2,320 |
| | 11,732 |

**Consolidated income statement for the year ended 31 December 20X3**

| | $000 |
|---|---|
| Revenue | 9,565 |
| Cost of sales | (4,995) |
| Gross profit | 4,570 |
| Distribution and admin expenses (1,700 + 652) | (2,352) |
| Profit for the year | 2,218 |
| Attributable to: | |
| Equity holders of the parent | 1,500 |
| Minority interest (25% × 2,870) | 718 |
| | 2,218 |

**Statement of changes in equity for the year ended 31 December 20X3**

| | $000 |
|---|---|
| At 1 January 20X3 (5,000 + 4,975) | 9,975 |
| Profit for the year attributable to the parent | 1,500 |
| Exchange differences (see below) | (2,063) |
| At 31 December 20X3 | 9,412 |

Again, we can prove the figure for exchange differences.

| | $000 | $000 |
|---|---|---|
| Exchange loss in the subsidiary (as before) | 2,020 | |
| Group share (75%) | | 1,515 |
| Goodwill at opening rate (6,000 @ 2) | 3,000 | |
| Goodwill at closing rate (6,000 @ 2.5) | (2,400) | |
| Exchange loss | | 600 |
| Impairment loss at average rate (1,500 @ 2.3) | 652 | |
| Impairment loss at closing rate (1,500 @ 2.5) | (600) | |
| Exchange gain | | (52) |
| | | 2,063 |

## 3.7 An alternative method of preparing the consolidated financial statements

Some exam questions only ask for the consolidated balance sheet and consolidated income statement. You may not have to prepare a consolidated statement of changes in equity or calculate or prove the exchange difference. If this is the case, there is an alternative method of translation that you may find slightly quicker and easier in an exam situation.

***The balance sheet***

As before, the net assets (assets and liabilities) are translated at the closing rate:

| | Z000 | *Rate* | $000 |
|---|---|---|---|
| Non-current assets | 2,400 | 2.5 | 960 |
| Net current assets | 20,800 | 2.5 | 8,320 |
| Net assets | 23,200 | | 9,280 |

Share capital and reserves are also translated at the closing rate.

| | Z000 | *Rate* | $000 |
|---|---|---|---|
| Share capital | 4,000 | 2.5 | 1,600 |
| Reserves | 19,200 | 2.5 | 7,680 |
| Total equity | 23,200 | 2.5 | 9,280 |

***The income statement***

This is translated at the average rate for the year, as before:

| | Z000 | *Rate* | $000 |
|---|---|---|---|
| Revenue | 22,000 | 2.3 | 9,565 |
| Cost of sales | (11,490) | | (4,995) |
| Gross profit | 10,510 | | 4,570 |
| Distribution and admin expenses | (3,910) | | (1,700) |
| Profit | 6,600 | | 2,870 |

***Consolidation workings***

**Group structure**

Grofine

75%

S

**Net assets of subsidiary**

| | *Acquisition* Z000 | *31/1/X3* Z000 |
|---|---|---|
| Share capital | 4,000 | 4,000 |
| Retained earnings | 8,000 | 19,200 |
| | 12,000 | 23,200 |

| Translated: | $,000 @2.5 | $,000 @2.5 |
|---|---|---|
| | 4,800 | 9,280 |

**Goodwill**

| | Z000 |
|---|---|
| Cost of investment (5,000 × 3) | 15,000 |
| Net assets acquired : (75% × 12,000) | (9,000) |
| | 6,000 |
| Less impairment (25%) | (1,500) |
| | 4,500 |
| | $000 |
| Translated at closing rate (2.5) | 1,800 |

**Minority interests**

| | $000 |
|---|---|
| Net assets at balance sheet date (25% × 9,280) | 2,320 |

**Consolidated reserves at 31 December 20X3**

Because goodwill must be translated at closing rate there will be an exchange difference, as before. However, using this method, the subsidiary's net assets at acquisition and post-acquisition reserves are all translated at closing rate. Goodwill is the difference between the cost of the investment and the net assets acquired. The net assets acquired have already been retranslated. This means that the only adjustment needed is for the exchange difference on the retranslation of the cost of the investment.

| | $000 |
|---|---|
| Grofine | 652 |
| S (75% × 9,280 – 4,800) | 3,360 |
| Impairment loss (1,500 @ 2.3) | (652) |
| Exchange difference on retranslation of cost of investment (15,000 @ 2.5 – 5,000) | 1,000 |
| Exchange difference on retranslation of impairment loss (652 – 1,500 @ 2.5) | 52 |
| | 4,412 |

We can now prepare the consolidated balance sheet and the consolidated income statement, which are exactly as before.

KEY POINT

If the subsidiary has the same functional currency as the parent, its financial statements are translated using the same method as for transactions in individual companies.

## 3.8 Functional currency method/temporal method

If the subsidiary has the same functional currency as the parent, its financial statements are translated using the same method as for transactions in individual companies:

- non-monetary assets (e.g. property, plant and equipment and inventory) are translated at actual (historic) rate (see below)
- monetary assets are translated at closing rate
- share capital and pre-acquisition reserves are translated at historic rate (the rate on the date the subsidiary was acquired)
- income statement items are translated at the average rate or at historic rate (if they relate to non-monetary assets).

***Non-monetary assets***

The subsidiary's non-monetary assets must be translated at the rate ruling when the asset was acquired. For consolidation purposes this is as follows:

- **Assets owned at acquisition of shares by parent company** – at the rate ruling at that date (not the rate when the assets were acquired), i.e. cost to the group will be the fair value attributed at acquisition
- **Assets acquired since acquisition** – at the rate when each asset was acquired.

Depreciation must be translated at the same rate as that applied to the relevant assets. Consequently the profit for the year will be translated:

- Profit before depreciation (strictly rate when each transaction occurs) – Average rate
- Depreciation – Asset rates

## 3.9 Example

Grofine bought 75% of S on 31 December 20X1 when the net assets of S were Z12,000,000 and the exchange rate was Z3 = $1.

At 31 December 20X3 the balance sheet of S was as follows.

| | *S* |
|---|---|
| | *Z000* |
| Non-current assets | 2,400 |
| Inventories | 1,710 |
| Other net current assets | 19,090 |
| | 23,200 |
| | |
| Share capital | 4,000 |
| Pre-acquisition reserves | 8,000 |
| Post-acquisition reserves | 11,200 |
| | 23,200 |

The rate of exchange at 31 December 20X3 was Z2.5 = $1 and the inventories were purchased when the rate was $2.4 = £1.

The income statement of S for the year ended 31 December 20X3 was as follows.

| | S |
|---|---|
| | Z000 |
| Revenue | 22,000 |
| Opening inventory | 2,200 |
| Purchases | 11,000 |
| | 13,200 |
| Closing inventory | (1,710) |
| Cost of sales | 11,490 |
| Gross profit | 10,510 |
| Distribution and admin expenses | (3,610) |
| Depreciation | (300) |
| Exchange differences | – |
| Profit for the year | 6,600 |

The statement of changes in equity of S for the year ended 31 December 20X3 was as follows.

| | S |
|---|---|
| | Z000 |
| Opening balance | 18,600 |
| Profit for the year | 6,600 |
| Dividends paid | (2,000) |
| Closing balance | 23,200 |

The average rate of exchange for the year was Z2.3 = $1.

The rate of exchange at 31 December 20X2 was Z2 = $1.

Inventory at 31 December 20X2 was Z2,200,000; this was purchased when the exchange rate was Z2.2 = $1. No non-current assets have been purchased since Grofine acquired S.

The dividend was paid when the rate of exchange was Z2.3 = $1

**Required:**

Using the functional currency method, translate the balance sheet of S as at 31 December 20X3 together with the income statement for the year ended 31 December 20X3.

## 3.10 Solution

**Balance sheet at 31 December 20X3**

All the non-current assets are translated at the rate ruling on the acquisition date (31 December 20X1), as this is the date on which they were acquired by the group.

Inventories are translated at the actual rate on the date they were acquired.

All other assets and liabilities are translated at closing rate.

This gives us a figure for total net assets/total equity. The components of equity are translated in exactly the same way as under the presentation currency method: share capital and pre-acquisition reserves are translated at the rate on the acquisition date and the balancing figure is post-acquisition reserves.

| | *S* | *Rate* | *S* |
|---|---|---|---|
| | Z000 | | $000 |
| Non-current assets | 2,400 | 3 | 800 |
| Inventories | 1,710 | 2.4 | 712 |
| Other net current assets | 19,090 | 2.5 | 7,636 |
| | 23,200 | | 9,148 |
| Share capital | 4,000 | 3 | 1,333 |
| Pre-acquisition reserves | 8,000 | 3 | 2,667 |
| Post-acquisition reserves | 11,200 | Balance | 5,148 |
| | 23,200 | | 9,148 |

**Income statement for the year ended 31 December 20X3**

The same principles apply here.

| | *S* | *Rate* | *S* |
|---|---|---|---|
| | Z000 | | $000 |
| Revenue | 22,000 | 2.3 | 9,565 |
| Opening inventory | 2,200 | 2.2 | 1,000 |
| Purchases | 11,000 | 2.3 | 4,783 |
| | 13,200 | | 5,783 |
| Closing inventory | (1,710) | 2.4 | (712) |
| | 11,490 | | 5,071 |
| Gross profit | 10,510 | | 4,494 |
| Distribution and admin expenses | (3,610) | 2.3 | (1,569) |
| Depreciation | (300) | 3 | (100) |
| Profit | 6,600 | | 2,825 |

Exchange differences arise from the subsidiary's operating activities and therefore they must be included in the income statement.

To calculate the exchange differences, we need to reconstruct the opening balance sheet, with 'other net current assets' as a balancing figure.

**Balance sheet at 31 December 20X2**

| | *Sc* | *Rate* | *S* |
|---|---|---|---|
| | Z000 | | $000 |
| Non-current assets (2,400 + 300) | 2,700 | 3 | 900 |
| Inventories | 2,200 | 2.2 | 1,000 |
| Other net current assets (balancing figure) | 13,700 | 2 | 6,850 |
| | 18,600 | | 8,750 |
| Share capital | 4,000 | 3 | 1,333 |
| Pre-acquisition reserves | 8,000 | 3 | 2,667 |
| Post-acquisition reserves (11,200 – 4,600) | 6,600 | Balance | 4,750 |
| | 18,600 | | 8,750 |

We can then attempt to derive the figure as follows:

| | $000 |
|---|---|
| Opening net assets | 8,750 |
| Profit for the year | 2,825 |
| Dividend paid (2,000 @ 2.3) | (870) |
| Exchange difference (balancing figure) | (1,557) |
| Closing net assets | 9,148 |

Another way of finding the figure for exchange differences is shown below:

| | Opening net monetary assets | + Retained 'money' 22,000 - 11,000 - 3,610 - 2,000 = | = Closing net monetary assets |
|---|---|---|---|
| Z000 | 13,700 | + 5,390 | = 19,090 |
| Rate of exchange | 2 | 2.3 | 2.5 |
| $000 | 6,850 | + 2,343 | ≠ 7,636 |

The balancing figure required is the exchange difference (a loss) of £1,557.

The income statement can now be completed:

**Income statement for the year ended 31 December 20X3**

| | *S* Z000 | *Rate* | *S* $000 |
|---|---|---|---|
| Revenue | 22,000 | 2.3 | 9,565 |
| Opening inventory | 2,200 | 2.2 | 1,000 |
| Purchases | 11,000 | 2.3 | 4,783 |
| | 13,200 | | 5,783 |
| Closing inventory | (1,710) | 2.4 | (712) |
| | 11,490 | | 5,071 |
| Gross profit | 10,510 | | 4,494 |
| Distribution and admin expenses | (3,610) | 2.3 | (1,569) |
| Depreciation | (300) | 3 | (100) |
| Exchange differences | | | (1,557) |
| Profit | 6,600 | | 1,268 |

## 3.11 Disposal of a foreign operation

On disposal of a foreign operation, the cumulative exchange differences which have been deferred in equity relating to that operation should be recognised in the income statement in the same period in which the gain or loss on disposal is recognised.

In the case of a partial disposal, only the relevant proportion of the related accumulated exchange differences should be taken to the income statement.

This is sometimes known as 'recycling' – the exchange differences are effectively recognised twice: once in the statement of changes in equity when they arise and again in the income statement on disposal of the foreign operation.

### 3.12 Disclosure requirements

An entity should disclose:

- the amount of exchange differences included in the net profit or loss for the period
- net exchange differences classified as equity as a separate component of equity, and a reconciliation of the amount of such exchange differences at the beginning and end of the period.

When the presentation currency is different from the functional currency, that fact should be stated, together with disclosure of the functional currency and the reason for using a different presentation currency.

When there is a change in the functional currency of either the reporting entity or a significant foreign operation, that fact and the reason for the change in functional currency should be disclosed.

## Summary

- An entity may enter into foreign currency transactions in two ways: it may have transactions in foreign currencies or it may have foreign operations.
- Individual transactions are translated and recorded at the rate of exchange ruling at the date of the transaction. At each balance sheet date, monetary items are retranslated at the closing rate. Non-monetary items are normally not retranslated but remain at their historic rate. Exchange differences are normally taken to the income statement.
- Where an entity has a foreign operation, the method of translation depends on whether the operation has the same functional currency as the parent or a different functional currency.
- A semi-autonomous operation normally has a different functional currency from the parent. Its individual financial statements are translated at the closing rate.
- An operation which is an extension of the parent has the same functional currency as the parent. Its individual financial statements are translated in the same way as individual foreign currency transactions.

Having completed your study of this chapter, you should have achieved the following learning outcomes:

- explain foreign currency translation principles, including the difference between the closing rate/net investment method and the historical rate method
- explain the correct treatment for foreign loans financing foreign equity investments.

## Self-test questions

1 How should monetary items denominated in a foreign currency at the balance sheet date be treated? (1.1)

2 How should loans denominated in a foreign currency be treated? (1.5)

3 What is a presentation currency? (2.1)

4 How should an entity determine its functional currency? (2.2)

**5** In group accounts, when should the temporal/functional currency method be used? (2.4)

**6** At what rate should income statement items be translated under the closing rate/presentation currency method? (3.1)

**7** How is goodwill arising on consolidation determined for a foreign subsidiary? (3.5)

**8** How are exchange differences arising on consolidation dealt with under the closing rate method? (3.5)

**9** Explain the accounting for exchange differences on disposal of a foreign entity. (3.11)

## Objective test questions

### Question 1

International Inc purchases a non current asset from an overseas supplier on 30 June 20X3for €180,000 when the rate of exchange is $1 = €1.50.

The company sells goods to an overseas customer for €112,000 in August 20X3 when the rate of exchange was $1 = €1.40.

International Inc prepares accounts to 31 December each year. At 31 December 20X3 the company has paid for the asset, but the amount receivable from the customer is still outstanding. The exchange rate at this date is $1 = €1.60.

What is the amount of the currency gain or loss to be reported in the financial statements for the year to 31 December 20X3?

**A** Profit $10,000

**B** Loss $10,000

**C** Loss $17,500

**D** Profit $17,500

### Question 2

Which of the following is not an example of a situation in which an overseas subsidiary is likely to have the same functional currency as its parent?

**A** The subsidiary, located in Africa, is a supplier of sub- assemblies to the parent company in Europe, which are then incorporated into the parent company's final products.

**B** The subsidiary is located in a tax haven.

**C** The subsidiary operates in a territory in which the national government appoints a majority of the Board of Directors of foreign controlled companies.

**D** The subsidiary acts as a North American distribution centre, receiving goods from its parent company in Europe, selling them locally and remitting the proceeds to the parent company.

*For the answers to these questions, see the 'Answers' section at the end of the book.*

## Exam-type question

### FG

The balance sheets of FG (a dollar-based company) and its subsidiary JK (whose functional currency is the Crown) at 31 December 20X8 and their income statements for the 12 months then ended are given below:

**Balance sheets at 31 December 20X8**

| | *FG* | | *JK* | |
|---|---|---|---|---|
| | $000 | $000 | C000 | C000 |
| Non-current assets: | | | | |
| Property, plant and equipment | 18,000 | | 27,000 | |
| Investments | 4,400 | | - | |
| | | 22,400 | | 27,000 |
| Current assets: | | | | |
| Inventories | 9,000 | | 16,200 | |
| Trade receivables | 7,650 | | 13,500 | |
| | | 16,650 | | 29,700 |
| | | 39,050 | | 56,700 |
| Equity: | | | | |
| Share capital | | | | |
| ($1/€1 shares) | | 10,000 | | 10,000 |
| Reserves | | 10,960 | | 16,500 |
| | | 20,960 | | 26,500 |
| Non-current liabilities | | 9,000 | | 18,000 |
| Current liabilities: | | | | |
| Trade payables | 3,600 | | 5,400 | |
| Bank overdraft | 5,490 | | 6,800 | |
| | | 9,090 | | 12,200 |
| | | 39,050 | | 56,700 |

**Income statements – year ended 31 December 20X8**

| | *FG* | *JK* |
|---|---|---|
| | $000 | C000 |
| Revenue | 45,000 | 54,000 |
| Cost of sales | (22,500) | (27,000) |
| Gross profit | 22,500 | 27,000 |
| Other operating expenses | (13,500) | (14,400) |
| Profit from operations | 9,000 | 12,600 |
| Investment income | 1,600 | - |
| Interest payable | (900) | (1,800) |
| Profit before tax | 9,700 | 10,800 |
| Income tax expense | (3,240) | (3,800) |
| Profit for the year | 6,460 | 7,000 |

**Statements of changes in equity – year ended 31 December 20X8**

| | *FG* | *JH* |
|---|---|---|
| | $000 | C000 |
| At 1 January 20X8 | 18,000 | 23,500 |
| Profit for the year | 6,460 | 7,000 |
| Dividends | (3,500) | (4,000) |
| At 31 December 20X8 | 20,960 | 26,500 |

***Notes to the financial statements***

(1) On 31 December 20X4, FG purchased 8 million shares in JH. The reserves of JK on this date stood at 4.5 million Crowns.

(2) Exchange rates at relevant dates have been as follows:

| *Date* | C *to the $* |
|---|---|
| 31 December 20X4 | 4.0 |
| 31 December 20X7 | 2.5 |
| 31 December 20X8 | 2.0 |
| Average rate for year ended 31 December 20X8 | 2.4 |

(3) The non-current liabilities represent long-term borrowings. The long-term borrowings of JK are denominated in Crowns.

**Required:**

(a) Translate the balance sheet of JK into dollars ($) and then prepare the consolidated balance sheet of the FG group at 31 December 20X6. **(12 marks)**

(b) Translate the income statement of JK into dollars ($) and then prepare the consolidated income statement of the FG group for the year ended 31 December 20X8. **(4 marks)**

(c) Prepare the consolidated statement of changes in equity for the year ended 31 December 20X8. Your workings should include a proof of the figure for exchange differences. **(9 marks)**

**(Total: 25 marks)**

*For the answer to this question, see the 'Answers' section at the end of the book.*

## Feedback to activities

### Activity 1

**Customer's account**

| 20X6 | € | $ | 20X6 | € | $ |
|---|---|---|---|---|---|
| May 7 | | | Jun 30 | | |
| Sales a/c | 48,000 | 15,000 | Balance c/d (at 3.15) | 48,000 | 15,238 |
| June 30 | | | | | |
| Income statement (profit on exchange) | | 238 | | | |
| | 48,000 | 15,238 | | 48,000 | 15,238 |
| Jul 1 | | | Jul 10 | | |
| Balance b/d | 48,000 | 15,238 | Bank a/c (proceeds) | 48,000 | 15,150 |
| | | | Jun 30 | | |
| | | | Income statement (loss on exchange) | | 88 |
| | 48,000 | 15,238 | | 48,000 | 15,238 |

*Note:*

(a) as a monetary item, receivables are retranslated at each balance sheet date with the exchange difference taken to the income statement

(b) average rates of exchange (say on a monthly basis) might be used in practice for translating the sales into the functional currency

(c) exchange differences would be transferred (as they were recognised) to a separate account, the balance on which would be transferred to the income statement at the end of the accounting period.

### Activity 2

The supplier's account would appear as follows:

**Supplier's account**

| | SwFr | $ | | SwFr | $ |
|---|---|---|---|---|---|
| Bank account (remittance (2.8)) | 8,700 | 3,107 | Purchases account (3) | 8,700 | 2,900 |
| | | | Income statement (loss on exchange) | | 207 |
| | 8,700 | 3,107 | | 8,700 | 3,107 |

# Chapter 10

# CASH FLOW STATEMENTS

## Syllabus content

- The preparation of consolidated financial statements (including the group cash flow statement) involving one or more subsidiaries, sub-subsidiaries and associates, under the acquisition and pooling of interests methods (IAS 7 & 27 and IFRS 3).

## Contents

## Introduction

This final chapter on group accounts deals with the group cash flow statement.

It begins by explaining how to prepare a cash flow statement for a single company. If you have already studied for Paper P7 the method should already be familiar to you.

We then cover the preparation of cash flow statements for a group of companies, including the treatment of associates, mid year acquisitions and disposals and foreign currency transactions. Exam questions in this paper will feature a group, rather than a single company, and will almost certainly include an acquisition or a disposal.

Lastly, we look at the advantages and limitations of the cash flow statement from the point of view of the user of the financial statements. Exam questions frequently ask for discussion or explanation of these.

# 1 IAS 7 *Cash Flow Statements*

### 1.1 Objective of cash flow statements

KEY POINT

The objective of IAS 7 is to ensure that entities provide information about the historical changes in cash and cash equivalents. Although IAS 7 does not prescribe a format for cash flow statements, it does require the cash flows to be classified into:

- operating activities
- investing activities
- financing activities.

The objective of IAS 7 is to ensure that entities provide information about the historical changes in cash and cash equivalents by means of a cash flow statement which classifies cash flows during the period between those arising from operating, investing and financing activities.

Users of financial statements need information on the liquidity, viability and financial adaptability of entities. Deriving this information involves the user in making assessments of the future cash flows of the entity. Future cash flows are regarded (in financial management theory and increasingly in practice in large companies) as the prime determinant of the worth of a business.

Although IAS 7 does not prescribe a format for cash flow statements, it does require the cash flows to be classified into:

- operating activities
- investing activities
- financing activities.

This classification may require a particular transaction to be shown partly under one heading and partly under another. For example, when the cash repayment of a loan includes both interest and capital, the interest might be shown as an operating activity and the capital element as a financing activity.

The combination of the three types of cash flow leads to the overall movement in cash and cash equivalents, terms which are defined below.

An appendix to IAS 7 gives illustrative layouts for the cash flow statement, and these are used in the remainder of this chapter.

The objective of the standard headings is to ensure that cash flows are reported in a form that highlights the significant components of cash flow and facilitates comparison of the cash flow performance of different businesses.

Each cash flow should be classified according to the substance of the transaction giving rise to it. The substance of a transaction determines the most appropriate standard heading under which to report cash flows that are not specified in the standard categories.

### 1.2 Definitions

DEFINITIONS

**Cash** consists of cash on hand and demand deposits.

**Cash equivalents** are short-term, highly liquid investments that are readily convertible into known amounts of cash and which are subject to an insignificant risk of changes in value.

**Cash** consists of cash on hand and demand deposits.

**Cash equivalents** are short-term, highly liquid investments that are readily convertible into known amounts of cash and which are subject to an insignificant risk of changes in value.

The definitions of cash and cash equivalents are central to the preparation and interpretation of cash flow statements.

Bank overdrafts may be counted as a negative element in cash and cash equivalents. Longer-term bank borrowings are generally considered to be part of financing activities.

The components of cash and cash equivalents should be disclosed in a note to the cash flow statement, with a reconciliation to the equivalent items in the balance sheet.

## 2 Classification of cash flows

### 2.1 Operating activities

DEFINITION

**Cash flows** are inflows and outflows of cash and cash equivalents.

Cash flows are inflows and outflows of cash and cash equivalents.

Cash flows from operating activities are in general the cash effects of transactions and other events relating to operating or trading activities. Net cash flow from operating activities represents the net increase or decrease in cash resulting from the operations shown in the income statement in arriving at operating profit.

There are two possible methods for reporting net cash flow from operating activities:

KEY POINT

The **direct method** shows operating cash receipts and payments (including, in particular, cash receipts from customers, cash payments to suppliers and cash payments to and on behalf of employees), aggregating to the net cash flow from operating activities.

The **indirect method** starts with profit before tax and adjusts it for non-cash charges and credits to reconcile it to the net cash flow from operating activities.

- The **direct method** shows operating cash receipts and payments (including, in particular, cash receipts from customers, cash payments to suppliers and cash payments to and on behalf of employees), aggregating to the net cash flow from operating activities.
- The **indirect method** starts with profit before tax and adjusts it for non-cash charges and credits to reconcile it to the net cash flow from operating activities.

A simplified comparison of the two methods is shown below. The methods differ only as regards the derivation of the item 'Net cash inflow from operating activities'. Subsequent inflows and outflows for investing and financing are the same.

| **Direct method** | | **Indirect method** | |
|---|---|---|---|
| | $000 | | $000 |
| Cash received from customers | 15,424 | Profit before tax | 6,022 |
| Cash payments to suppliers | (5,824) | Depreciation charges | 899 |
| Cash paid to and on behalf of employees | (2,200) | Increase in inventory | (194) |
| Other cash payments | (511) | Increase in receivables | (72) |
| | | Increase in payables | 234 |
| Net cash inflow from operating activities | 6,889 | | 6,889 |

The principal advantage of the direct method is that it shows operating cash receipts and payments. Knowledge of the specific sources of cash receipts and the purposes for which cash payments were made in past periods may be useful in assessing future cash flows. IAS 7 encourages, but does not require, the use of the direct method.

The principal advantage of the indirect method is that it highlights the differences between reported profit and net cash flow from operating activities. Many users of financial statements believe that such a reconciliation is essential to give an indication of the quality of the reporting entity's earnings. Some investors and creditors assess future cash flows by estimating future income and then allowing for accruals adjustments; thus information about past accruals adjustments may be useful to help estimate future adjustments.

## 2.2 Calculation of net cash flow from operating activities

Reported profit is computed using the accruals concept; net cash flow from operating activities only records the cash inflows and outflows arising out of trading.

The main categories of items in the income statement and on a balance sheet which form part of the reconciliation between profit before tax and net cash flow from operating activities are:

(a) **Depreciation** – Depreciation is a book write off of capital expenditure. Depreciation therefore represents an addition to profit in deriving cash inflow.

(b) **Profit/loss on disposal of non-current asset** – The cash inflow from a sale is recorded under 'investing activities'. If the profit or loss on the sale has been included in reported profits, an adjustment is necessary in computing operating cash flow. A loss on disposal is added to reported profit; a profit on disposal is deducted from reported profit.

(c) **Balance sheet change in receivables** – The change between opening and closing receivables represents the adjustment required to move from operating profit to net cash inflow.

    (i) An increase in receivables is a deduction from profit

    (ii) A decrease in receivables is an addition to profit.

(d) **Balance sheet change in inventories** – Again, the adjustment required is the change between opening and closing inventories:

    (i) An increase in inventories is a deduction from profit

    (ii) A decrease in inventories is an addition to profit.

(e) **Balance sheet change in payables** – To the extent that a purchase results in a charge to the income statement:

    (i) an increase in payables between two balance sheet dates is an addition to profit

    (ii) a decrease in payables is a deduction from profit.

If the purchase does not result in a charge to the income statement in the current year, the corresponding payable is not included in the reconciliation of profit to net cash inflow. For example, an amount payable in respect of a non-current asset is not included.

### *Activity 1*

A new business made operating profits of $300,000 in its first year. Extracts from the closing balance sheet are given below. Calculate the net cash inflow from operating activities.

| | $ |
|---|---|
| Receivables | 125,000 |
| Inventory | 118,000 |
| Payables | 135,000 |
| An analysis of payables showed: | |
| For raw materials | 102,700 |
| For non-current asset | 12,000 |
| For various expenses | 13,500 |
| Accruals | 6,800 |

*Feedback to this activity is at the end of the chapter.*

### 2.3 Calculation of gross cash flows from operating activities (the direct method)

KEY POINT

Reporting entities are encouraged to use the direct method for reporting net cash flow from operating activities.

As previously stated, reporting entities are encouraged to use the direct method for reporting net cash flow from operating activities. The relevant cash flows can be derived:

(a) from the accounting records of the entity by totalling the cash receipts and payments directly; or

(b) from the opening and closing balance sheets and income statement for the year by constructing summary control accounts for:

(i) sales (to derive cash received from customers)

(ii) purchases (to derive cash payments to suppliers)

(iii) wages (to derive cash paid to and on behalf of employees).

### 2.4 Interest and dividends

Interest paid is normally shown as part of operating activities.

Dividends paid are shown in the IAS 7 specimen format as part of financing activities, but may also be shown under operating activities.

### 2.5 Income taxes

Cash flows arising from taxes on income should be separately disclosed as part of operating activities unless they can be specifically identified with financing and investing activities. It is reasonable to include income taxes as part of operating activities unless a question gives a clear indication to the contrary.

If income tax payments are allocated over more than one class of activity, the total should be disclosed by note.

The computation of income taxes paid may present a practical problem.

It is often convenient to arrive at the figure by means of a single tax working account into which all balances relating to income taxes are entered.

***Activity 2***

Extracts from X's income statement for the year ended 31 December 20X8 show:

| | $ | $ |
|---|---|---|
| Sales revenue | | X |
| Costs | | X |
| Profit before tax | | X |
| Tax: | | |
| Income taxes | 300,000 | |
| Deferred tax | 50,000 | |
| | | 350,000 |
| Dividends paid: | | |
| Interim | 96,000 | |
| Final | 240,000 | |
| | | 336,000 |

Extracts from X's balance sheets are:

| | *31 December* | |
|---|---|---|
| | *20X7* | *20X8* |
| | $ | $ |
| Current liabilities | | |
| Income taxes | 140,000 | 271,000 |
| Non-current liabilities | | |
| Deferred tax | 140,000 | 190,000 |

Calculate the amount of tax paid by X in the year.

*Feedback to this activity is at the end of the chapter.*

## 2.6 Investing activities

Cash flows to appear under this heading include:

- cash paid for property, plant and equipment and other non-current assets
- cash received on the sale of property, plant and equipment and other non-current assets
- cash paid for investments in or loans to other entities (excluding movements on loans from financial institutions, which are shown under financing)
- cash received for the sale of investments or the repayment of loans to other enterprises (again excluding loans from financial institutions)
- interest received on investments or loans
- dividends received on investments.

## 2.7 Financing activities

Financing cash flows comprise receipts or repayments of principal from or to external providers of finance.

Financing cash inflows include:

- receipts from issuing shares or other equity instruments
- receipts from issuing debentures, loans, notes and bonds and from other long term and short term borrowings (other than overdrafts, which are normally included in cash and cash equivalents).

Financing cash outflows include:

- repayments of amounts borrowed (other than overdrafts)
- the capital element of finance lease rental payments
- payments to reacquire or redeem the entity's shares.

# 3 Non-cash transactions

## 3.1 Non-cash transactions

KEY POINT

Transactions not resulting in movements of cash or cash equivalents should not be included in the cash flow statement.

Transactions not resulting in movements of cash or cash equivalents should not be included in the cash flow statement.

These transactions should be disclosed in the notes to the cash flow statement if disclosure is necessary for an understanding of the underlying transactions.

Examples of non-cash transactions are:

- acquiring assets by finance leases
- conversion of debt to equity.

## 3.2 Finance leases

Finance leases are accounted for by the lessee capitalising the present value of the minimum lease payments. A liability and a corresponding asset are produced which do not reflect cash flows in the accounting period.

The cash flow statement records the cash flow, i.e. the rentals paid, with the reduction in liability shown under financing.

# 4 Group cash flow statements

## 4.1 IAS 7 as it relates to consolidated cash flows

KEY POINT

Where a company has subsidiaries, cash flow statements should be based on the group accounts, and the starting figure should therefore be the group operating net cash inflow.

Where a company has subsidiaries, cash flow statements should be based on the group accounts, and the starting figure should therefore be the group operating net cash inflow.

Cash flows that are internal to the group should be eliminated in the preparation of a consolidated cash flow statement.

There are specific points to note in relation to minority interests, associates and acquisitions and disposals of subsidiaries. These are examined in the following sections.

## 4.2 Minority interests

KEY POINT

Dividends paid to minority interests should be disclosed separately – probably under financing activities.

Dividends paid to minority interests should be disclosed separately – probably under financing activities.

***Example***

The following information has been extracted from the consolidated financial statements of WG for the years ended 31 December:

| | *20X6* | *20X5* |
|---|---|---|
| | $000 | $000 |
| Dividends payable to minority shareholders (declared before the year end) | 100 | 160 |
| Minority interest in group net assets | 780 | 690 |
| Minority interest in consolidated profit after tax | 120 | 230 |

What is the dividend paid to minority interests in the year?

***Solution***

**Minority interests**

| | $000 | | $000 |
|---|---|---|---|
| Dividends paid (bal fig) | 90 | Balance b/d dividends payable | 160 |
| Balance c/d dividends payable | 100 | Balance b/d minority interest | 690 |
| Balance c/d minority interest | 780 | Share of profits in year | 120 |
| | 970 | | 970 |

## 4.3 Associates

Associates reflect a cash flow in or out of the group to the extent that:

- dividends are received out of the profits of the associate
- trading occurs between the group and associate, or
- further investment is made in the associate.

Associates are dealt with under the equity method of accounting and this terminology is used below.

***General***

KEY POINT

The cash flows of any equity accounted entity should be included in the group cash flow statement only to the extent of the actual cash flows between the group and the entity concerned, for example dividends received in cash and loans made or repaid.

The cash flows of any equity accounted entity should be included in the group cash flow statement only to the extent of the actual cash flows between the group and the entity concerned, for example dividends received in cash and loans made or repaid.

***Dividends***

It is only dividends paid which represent a cash inflow. Proposed dividends declared before the balance sheet date represent an increase in group receivables (i.e. the share of the dividend payable which is received by the investing company will not form part of the asset 'Investment in associate' but will be included in group receivables).

Thus, in reconciling group net cash inflow to group profit before tax the balance sheet movement in receivables must exclude proposed dividends from the associate so that dividends received can be shown in the cash flow statement.

Dividends received from associates should be included as a separate item in the group cash flow statement, probably under investing activities.

### *Trading between group and associate*

Trading between the group and an associate will give rise to inter-company balances in the group balance sheet at the year end. The balances will be treated in the same way as any other trading receivables and payables, i.e. the balance sheet movement forms part of the reconciliation between group profit before tax and group net cash inflow from operating activities.

It follows that when cash is paid/received in respect of inter-company balances the cash is included in the 'cash received from customers/cash payments to suppliers' section of the cash flow statement. It may, however, be appropriate to show the cash outflow/inflow separately from the group customers and suppliers.

### *Change in investment in associate*

A change in investment in the associate can arise when:

- an additional shareholding is purchased or part of the shareholding is sold
- loans are made to/from the associate or amounts previously loaned are repaid.

Provided cash consideration is involved, any change will be shown under the investing activities section of the cash flow statement.

### Example

The following information has been extracted from the consolidated financial statements of H for the year ended 31 December 20X1:

**Group income statement**

| | $000 | $000 |
|---|---|---|
| Profit from operations | | 734 |
| Share of profit of associate | | 68 |
| Profit before tax | | 802 |
| Tax on profit | | (324) |
| Profit after tax | | 478 |

**Group balance sheet**

| | *20X1* | *20X0* |
|---|---|---|
| | $000 | $000 |
| Investments in associates | | |
| Share of net assets | 466 | 456 |
| Loan to associate | 380 | 300 |
| Current assets | | |
| Receivables | 260 | 190 |
| Included with group receivables are the following amounts: | | |
| Dividend receivable from associate | 48 | 29 |
| Current account with associate | 40 | 70 |

Show the relevant figures to be included in the group cash flow statement for the year ended 31 December 20X1 and the amount at which receivables will be shown in the reconciliation of profit to net cash inflow.

***Solution***

**Extracts from cash flow statement**

| | $000 |
|---|---|
| **Cash flows from operating activities** | |
| Profit before tax | 856 |
| Share of profit of associate | (68) |
| Increase in receivables (W2) | (51) |
| **Investing activities:** | |
| Dividend received from associate (W1) | 39 |
| Loan to associate | (80) |

***Workings***

(W1)

**Associate**

| | $000 | | $000 |
|---|---|---|---|
| Balance b/d | | Dividend received (bal fig) | 39 |
| Share of net assets | 456 | Balance c/d | |
| Dividend receivable | 29 | Share of net assets | 466 |
| Share of profits | 68 | Dividend receivable | 48 |
| | 553 | | 553 |

***Tutorial note:*** an alternative approach to the above working is to construct initially an income statement showing profit information relating to the associate:

| | $000 |
|---|---|
| Share of profits | 68 |
| Dividends from 20X1 profits (bal fig) | 58 |
| Increase in share of net assets (i.e. share of retained profits 466 – 456) | 10 |

Then adjust $58,000 by the opening and closing dividend receivable (29 + 58 – 48) $39,000.

(W2) **Increase in receivable**

| | *20X0* | | *20X1* |
|---|---|---|---|
| | $000 | | $000 |
| Receivables per balance sheet | 190 | | 260 |
| Less: Dividend receivable | (29) | | (48) |
| | 161 | | 212 |
| Increase | | $51,000 | |

## 4.4 Acquisitions and disposals of subsidiaries during the year

KEY POINT

Where a subsidiary joins or leaves a group during a financial year the cash flows of the group should include the cash flows of the subsidiary concerned for the same period as that for which the group's income statement includes the results of the subsidiary.

Where a subsidiary joins or leaves a group during a financial year the cash flows of the group should include the cash flows of the subsidiary concerned for the same period as that for which the group's income statement includes the results of the subsidiary.

KEY POINT

Payments to acquire subsidiaries and receipts from disposals of subsidiaries must be reported separately in the cash flow statement under investing activities.

Payments to acquire subsidiaries and receipts from disposals of subsidiaries must be reported separately in the cash flow statement under investing activities. They are reported in the cash flow statement net of cash and cash equivalents acquired or disposed of.

A note to the cash flow statement should show a summary of the effects of acquisitions and disposals of subsidiaries, disclosing:

(a) the total purchase or disposal consideration

(b) the amount of cash and cash equivalents included in the purchase or disposal consideration

(c) the amount of cash and cash equivalents in the subsidiary acquired or disposed of, and

(d) the amount of the assets and liabilities other than cash or cash equivalents in the subsidiary acquired or disposed of, summarised by each major category.

### 4.5 Computational aspects of dealing with acquisitions and disposals

The substance of an acquisition of a subsidiary is that the group has purchased the assets of the subsidiary. However, in the cash flow statement we only wish to record the actual cash flow. Thus, for example, the additional non-current assets under the control of the group as a result of the acquisition will not be separately stated under the heading 'investing activities'. Care needs to be taken when expenditure on non-current assets is derived as a balancing figure. Non-current assets of the subsidiary at acquisition must be included in the ledger account used to derive the balancing figure.

Similar care needs to be applied in relation to other assets and liabilities in the subsidiary at acquisition.

For example, the balance sheet movement in inventory may need to be computed and shown as a reconciling item between profit and net cash inflow. Where there has been an acquisition the movement in inventory can be analysed:

| *Beginning of year* | *Part-way through year* | *End of year* |
|---|---|---|
| Group inventory excluding subsidiary not yet acquired | Subsidiary acquired ($9,384 inventory included in net assets acquired) | Group inventory including subsidiary acquired in year |
| $53,019 | Increase in inventory | $74,666 |

Increase in inventory = $74,666 – (53,019 + 9,384) = $12,263.

***Activity 3***

X acquired Y in the current accounting period. Extracts from the group accounts of X show:

| | *Last year* | *This year* |
|---|---|---|
| | $000 | $000 |
| NBV of non-current assets | 10,000 | 16,000 |

Depreciation charged in the group income statement is $2,600,000, and the NBV of disposals is $600,000. The fair value of Y's non-current assets when Y was acquired by X is $4,800,000.

What was the group's expenditure on non-current assets during the current accounting period?

*Feedback to this activity is at the end of the chapter.*

## 4.6 Partly-owned subsidiary acquired in current year

This is not as complicated as it sounds. The note to the cash flow statement summarising the net assets acquired and for what consideration will include an item 'minority interest'. The amount will be the minority interests' share of net assets of the subsidiary at the date of acquisition. It will have no direct bearing on the figures shown in the cash flow statement except where dividends paid to minority interests have to be computed as a balancing figure. In such an event the minority interests' share of net assets at acquisition will be a credit in the minority interest account constructed to derive dividends paid.

## 4.7 Disposal of subsidiary

A disposal is treated using the same principles as for an addition. To the extent that cash is received as consideration, this will be shown as a receipt under investing activities.

If any group assets or liabilities are being analysed to determine a cash inflow or outflow the book value of the subsidiary's assets/liabilities will need to form part of the analysis. For example tax liabilities in the subsidiary at the date of disposal will represent a debit in a taxation account being written up to determine tax paid.

**Tax account**

| | $ | | $ |
|---|---|---|---|
| Cash paid (balancing figure) | X | Balance b/d: group (P + S) liability | X |
| Tax liability in subsidiary at date of disposal | X | Tax charge for year | X |
| Balance c/d: group (P) liability | X | | – |
| | X | | X |

The debit entry for the tax liability in the subsidiary is equivalent to the balance c/d at the end of the accounting period for the remaining part of the group liability.

## 4.8 Detailed example

Several years ago H acquired 80% of the ordinary share capital of S. It also acquired a 25% shareholding in A and the company is regarded as an associate. On 1 January 20X8 H acquired the entire share capital of J. You are provided with the following information regarding the group accounts:

**Consolidated income statement for the year ended 31 December 20X8**

| *Note* | | $ | $ |
|---|---|---|---|
| 1 | Profit from operations | | 3,961,300 |
| 2 | Sale of property | | 500,000 |
| | Interest received | | 9,800 |
| | Interest paid | | (12,100) |
| | Share of profit of associate | | 28,320 |

| | |
|---|---|
| Profit before tax | 4,487,320 |
| Tax | (2,216,480) |
| Profit for the year | 2,270,840 |
| Profit attributable to the minority interest | (41,664) |
| Profit attributable to the equity holders of the parent | 2,229,176 |

**Consolidated statement of changes in equity**

| | *Share capital* | *Retained earnings* | *Total* |
|---|---|---|---|
| | $ | $ | $ |
| At 1 January 20X8 | 3,000,000 | 6,206,850 | 9,206,850 |
| Retained profit | | 2,229,176 | 2,229,176 |
| Dividends paid | | (195,000) | (195,000) |
| Issue of ordinary shares | 1,200,000 | – | 1,200,000 |
| At 31 December 20X8 | 4,200,000 | 8,241,026 | 12,441,026 |

**Consolidated balance sheets (summarised)**

| *Note* | | *31 Dec 20X7* | *31 Dec 20X8* |
|---|---|---|---|
| | | $ | $ |
| 2 | Property | 8,276,718 | 9,744,658 |
| 3 | Plant and machinery | 2,673,400 | 3,955,400 |
| | Goodwill on consolidation | 66,500 | 192,500 |
| 4 | Associate | 80,750 | 98,570 |
| | Inventory | 2,065,000 | 3,400,100 |
| | Receivables | 854,200 | 1,250,000 |
| | Cash | 21,100 | 136,750 |
| | | 14,037,668 | 18,777,978 |
| | Ordinary share capital ($1 shares) | 3,000,000 | 4,200,000 |
| | Retained earnings | 6,206,850 | 8,241,026 |
| | Minority interest | 620,000 | 642,464 |
| | Long-term loan | – | 150,000 |
| | Payables | 984,500 | 1,640,640 |
| | Tax | 3,226,318 | 3,903,848 |
| | | 14,037,668 | 18,777,978 |

You are provided with the following additional information:

1 **Profit from operations** – Profit from operations is arrived at after charging depreciation amounting to $558,000. Interest paid is after adjusting for an opening accrual of $600 and a closing accrual of $4,600.

2 **Sale of property** – This represents the profit on sale of property. The property was in the books at $940,000.

3 **Plant and machinery**

| | *Cost* | *Agg. depn.* | *NBV* |
|---|---|---|---|
| | $ | $ | $ |
| At 1 January 20X8 | 3,500,000 | 826,600 | 2,673,400 |
| Additions: | | | |
| J | 1,100,000 | 240,000 | 860,000 |
| Others | 980,000 | – | 980,000 |
| Depreciation – charge for year | | 558,000 | (558,000) |
| | 5,580,000 | 1,624,600 | 3,955,400 |

4 **Associate**

| | *At 31 December 20X7* | *At 31 December 20X8* |
|---|---|---|
| | $ | $ |
| Cost | 72,000 | 72,000 |
| Retaomed earnings | 8,750 | 26,570 |
| | 80,750 | 98,570 |

Included within receivables are dividends receivable from associate: 31 December 20X7, $29,000; 31 December 20X8, Nil.

5 **Acquisition of J**

| | $ | $ |
|---|---|---|
| Consideration: | | |
| Equity shares | | 1,200,000 |
| Cash | | 600,000 |
| | | 1,800,000 |
| Assets acquired: | | |
| Plant and machinery | 860,000 | |
| Inventory | 836,500 | |
| Receivables | 449,300 | |
| Payables | (262,000) | |
| Cash | 532,400 | |
| Tax | (742,200) | |
| | | 1,674,000 |
| Goodwill | | 126,000 |

**You are required** to prepare a cash flow statement in a form suitable for publication. Ignore tax on dividends.

***Solution***

**Step 1**

**Working capital movements**

| | *Start of year* | *Subsidiary* | *End of year* | *Movement* |
|---|---|---|---|---|
| | $ | $ | $ | $ |
| Inventory | 2,065,000 | 836,500 | 3,400,100 | 498,600 |
| Receivables | 854,200 | 449,300 | 1,250,000 | (24,500) |
| Dividend from associate | (29,000) | | – | |
| Payables | 984,500 | 262,000 | 1,640,640 | 390,140 |
| Interest accrual | (600) | | (4,600) | |

**Step 2**

**Associate**

As the dividends received from the associate have not been given, reconstruct the group's share of profits from the associate from available information:

| | $ |
|---|---|
| Profit | 28,320 |
| Dividend (bal fig) | 10,500 |
| Retained profit | 17,820 |
| Dividend receivable b/d | 29,000 |
| Dividends out of current year's profit | 10,500 |
| Less: Dividend receivable c/d | – |
| Dividends paid | 39,500 |

**Step 3**

**Minority interests**

Profits earned by subsidiaries are retained within the group, except to the extent that a dividend is paid to the minority shareholders.

**Minority interest account**

| | $ | | $ |
|---|---|---|---|
| Cash (bal. fig.) | 19,200 | Balance b/d | 620,000 |
| Balance c/d | 642,464 | Income statement | 41,664 |
| | 661,664 | | 661,664 |

**Step 4**

**Taxation**

**Tax account**

| | $ | | $ |
|---|---|---|---|
| Cash (bal. fig.) | 2,281,150 | Balance b/d | 3,226,318 |
| Balance c/d | 3,903,848 | Income statement (note 3) | 2,216,480 |
| | | Tax – balance on J at acquisition | 742,200 |
| | 6,184,998 | | 6,184,998 |

The tax paid is normally arrived at as a balancing figure. As the subsidiary had tax payable at acquisition, the amount must be brought into the group tax account because when the liability is paid, it will form part of group tax paid.

**Step 5**

**Property**

**Property account – Cost**

| | $ | | $ |
|---|---|---|---|
| Balance b/d | 8,276,718 | Disposals account (NBV) | 940,000 |
| Additions (bal fig) | 2,407,940 | Balance c/d | 9,744,658 |
| | 10,684,658 | | 10,684,658 |

**Property disposals account**

| | $ | | $ |
|---|---|---|---|
| Property at NBV | 940,000 | Cash proceeds | 1,440,000 |
| Profit on sale | 500,000 | | |
| | 1,440,000 | | 1,440,000 |

As the profit item relates to a disposal of a non-current asset, the sale proceeds are shown under investing activities in the cash flow statement.

**Step 6**

**Purchase of subsidiary**

Only the net cash effect of the purchase should be shown. Non-cash consideration is thus excluded and any cash in the subsidiary at acquisition effectively reduces the cash price paid. The opposite would apply if there were an overdraft in the subsidiary at acquisition.

| | $ |
|---|---|
| Cash paid | 600,000 |
| Cash in subsidiary | 532,400 |
| | 67,600 |

Note that all the shares issued during the year were issued in consideration for the purchase of the subsidiary; therefore **no** shares were issued for cash.

**Step 7**

**Prepare cash flow statement**

**H – Consolidated cash flow statement for year ended 31 December 20X8**

| | $ | $ |
|---|---|---|
| **Cash flows from operating activities** | | |
| Group profit before tax | 4,487,320 | |
| Adjustments for: | | |
| Depreciation | 558,000 | |
| Share of associate's profit | (28,320) | |
| Profit on sale of property | (500,000) | |
| Interest receivable | (9,800) | |
| Interest payable | 12,100 | |
| Operating profit before working capital changes | 4,519,300 | |
| Increase in inventories | (498,600) | |
| Decrease in receivables | 24,500 | |
| Increase in payables | 390,140 | |
| Cash generated from operations | 4,435,340 | |
| Interest paid (600 + 12,100 – 4,600) | (8,100) | |
| Income tax paid | (2,281,150) | |
| Net cash from operating activities | | 2,146,090 |
| **Cash flows from investing activities** | | |
| Dividends received from associate | 39,500 | |
| Interest received | 9,800 | |
| Purchase of property, plant and equipment | (3,387,940) | |
| Proceeds from sale of property | 1,440,000 | |
| Acquisition of J, net of cash acquired (Note 2) | (67,600) | |
| Net cash used in investing activities | | (1,966,240) |

| | | |
|---|---|---|
| **Cash flows from financing activities** | | |
| Issue of loan | 150,000 | |
| Dividends paid to minority interest | (19,200) | |
| Dividends paid to H shareholders | (195,000) | |
| Net cash used in financing activities | | (64,200) |
| Net increase in cash and cash equivalents | | 115,650 |
| Cash and cash equivalents at the beginning of the year | | 21,100 |
| Cash and cash equivalents at the end of the year | | 136,750 |

**Notes to the cash flow statement**

1 **Cash and cash equivalents**

These consist of cash on hand and balances with banks.

| | *31 Dec 20X7* | *31 Dec 20X8* |
|---|---|---|
| | $ | $ |
| Cash | 21,100 | 136,750 |

2 **Acquisition of subsidiary**

Part of the consideration for the purchase of subsidiary J during the year comprised ordinary shares. The net assets acquired and form of consideration are shown below.

| | $ | | $ |
|---|---|---|---|
| Net assets acquired: | | Discharged by: | |
| Non-current assets | 860,000 | Shares issued | 1,200,000 |
| Goodwill | 126,000 | Cash | 600,000 |
| Inventory | 836,500 | | |
| Receivables | 449,300 | | |
| Payables | (262,000) | | |
| Tax | (742,200) | | |
| Cash | 532,400 | | |
| | 1,800,000 | | 1,800,000 |

The cash flow on acquisition, net of cash acquired, was therefore 600,000 – 532,400 = $67,600.

## 5 Foreign exchange gains and losses in cash flow statements

### 5.1 Individual company stage

KEY POINT

Exchange differences are not cash flows. Therefore they must be excluded from the cash flow statement.

The basic principle to grasp here is that exchange differences are not cash flows. Therefore they must be excluded from the cash flow statement.

In most instances exchange differences arising at the individual company stage are reported as part of profit before tax. If the foreign currency transaction has been settled in the year the cash flows will reflect the reporting currency cash receipt or payment and thus no problem arises.

KEY POINT

An unsettled foreign currency transaction gives rise to an exchange difference for which there is no cash flow effect in the current year. Such exchange differences need to be eliminated in computing net cash flows from operating activities.

However, an unsettled foreign currency transaction gives rise to an exchange difference for which there is no cash flow effect in the current year. Such exchange differences need to be eliminated in computing net cash flows from operating activities.

Fortunately this will not require much work if the unsettled foreign currency transaction is in working capital. Adjusting profit by balance sheet movements in working capital will automatically adjust correctly for the non-cash flow exchange gains and losses.

### 5.2 Preparation of consolidated cash flow statements involving a foreign subsidiary

KEY POINT

IAS 7 states that the cash flows of a foreign subsidiary should be translated at the exchange rates between the reporting currency and the foreign currency at the dates of the cash flows.

IAS 7 states that the cash flows of a foreign subsidiary should be translated at the exchange rates between the reporting currency and the foreign currency at the dates of the cash flows.

If cash balances are partly denominated in a foreign currency, the effect of exchange rate movements on cash is reported in the cash flow statement in order to reconcile the cash balances at the beginning and end of the period. This amount is presented separately from cash flows from operating, investing and financing activities.

### 5.3 Presentation currency method

KEY POINT

Using the presentation currency method, the exchange will relate to the opening net assets of that entity and also to the difference difference between the average and the closing rates of exchange on translation of the income statement.

The presentation currency method is normally used to translate the financial statement of a foreign subsidiary. The exchange difference will relate to the opening net assets of that entity (i.e. non-current assets, inventories, receivables, cash, payables and loans) and also to the difference between the average and the closing rates of exchange on translation of the income statement.

The group's share of the translation exchange differences go directly to reserves. If there are foreign currency loans in the books of the parent the exchange differences on the loan normally pass through the income statement.

Care needs to be taken in two areas.

- **Analysis of non-current assets** – Non-current assets may require analysis in order to determine cash expenditure. Part of the movement in non-current assets may reflect an exchange gain/loss.
- **Analysis of minority interests** – If minority interests require analysis to determine the dividend paid to them, it must be remembered that they have a share in the exchange gain/loss arising from the translation of the subsidiary's accounts.

***Example***

A gain of $160,000 was made on the translation of the financial statements of a 75% owned foreign subsidiary for the year ended 31 December 20X7. This gain is found to be made up as follows.

| | $ |
|---|---|
| Gain on opening net assets | |
| Non-current assets | 90,000 |
| Inventories | 30,000 |
| Receivables | 50,000 |
| Payables | (40,000) |
| Cash | 30,000 |
| | 160,000 |

A loss of $70,000 was made on the parent company's foreign currency loan. This loss has been charged to consolidated reserves in the draft financial statements below.

**Balance sheets as at 31 December**

| | *20X7* | *20X6* |
|---|---|---|
| | $000 | $000 |
| Non-current assets | 2,100 | 1,700 |
| Inventories | 650 | 480 |
| Receivables | 990 | 800 |
| Cash | 500 | 160 |
| | 4,240 | 3,140 |
| Share capital | 1,000 | 1,000 |
| Consolidated revenue reserves | 1,600 | 770 |
| | 2,600 | 1,770 |
| Minority interest | 520 | 370 |
| Long-term loan | 250 | 180 |
| Payables | 870 | 820 |
| | 4,240 | 3,140 |

There were no non-current asset disposals during the year.

**Income statement for the year ended 31 December 20X7**

| | $000 |
|---|---|
| Group profit before tax (after depreciation of $220,000) | 2,170 |
| Tax | (650) |
| Group profit after tax | 1,520 |
| Minority interest | (260) |
| Profit attributable to the parent | 1,260 |

Prepare a cash flow statement for the year ended 31 December 20X7.

### *Solution*

The first stage is to produce a statement of reserves so as to analyse the movements during the year.

**Statement of reserves**

| | $000 |
|---|---|
| Reserves brought forward | 770 |
| Profit for the year | 1,260 |
| Dividends paid (balancing figure) | (480) |
| Exchange gain ((160,000 × 75%) 120,000 – 70,000) | 50 |
| Reserves carried forward | 1,600 |

**Cash flow statement for the year ended 31 December 20X7**

**Cash flows from operating activities**

| | $000 |
|---|---|
| Profit before tax | 2,170 |
| Depreciation charges | 220 |
| Increase in inventory(170 – 30) | (140) |
| Increase in receivables (190 – 50) | (140) |
| Increase in payables (50 – 40) | 10 |
| Cash generated from operations | 2,120 |

***Tutorial note:*** since the group's share of all exchange differences goes straight to reserves, there are no foreign exchange adjustments.

| | $000 | $000 |
|---|---|---|
| **Cash flow statement (continued)** | | |
| Cash generated from operations | 2,120 | |
| Income taxes paid | (650) | |
| Net cash from operating activities | | 1,470 |
| **Cash flows from investing activities** | | |
| Purchase of non-current assets (W2) | (530) | |
| Net cash used in investing activities | | (530) |
| **Cash flows from financing activities** | | |
| Dividends paid to minority interests (W1) | (150) | |
| Dividends paid | (480) | |
| | | (630) |
| Exchange gain on cash | | 30 |
| Increase in cash | | 340 |
| Cash at 1 Jan 20X7 | | 160 |
| Cash at 31 Dec 20X7 | | 500 |

***Workings***

(W1)

**Minority interest**

| | $000 | | $000 |
|---|---|---|---|
| Dividend paid (bal fig) | 150 | Balance b/d | 370 |
| Balance c/d | 520 | Income statement | 260 |
| | | Exchange gain (160 × 25%) | 40 |
| | 670 | | 670 |

(W2)

**Non-current assets**

| | $000 | | $000 |
|---|---|---|---|
| Balance b/d | 1,700 | Depreciation | 220 |
| Exchange gain | 90 | Balance c/d | 2,100 |
| Additions (bal fig) | 530 | | |
| | 2,320 | | 2,320 |

# 6 Cash flow information

KEY POINT

In order to survive, a business depends on its ability to generate cash.

## 6.1 The benefits of producing a cash flow statement

In order to survive, a business depends on its ability to generate cash. There have been numerous examples of apparently highly profitable companies which have failed as a result of liquidity problems.

KEY POINT

A cash flow statement provides information that is not available from the balance sheet and the income statement.

Cash flow statements enable users of the financial statements to assess the liquidity, solvency and financial adaptability of a business. A cash flow statement provides information that is not available from the balance sheet and the income statement.

A cash flow statement is believed to provide useful information to users of the financial statements for the following reasons.

- Unlike profits, cash flows are not affected by an entity's choice of accounting policies or by the exercise of judgement. Cash flows can be verified objectively and therefore they allow little scope for 'creative accounting'.
- Cash flow information is thought to have predictive value. It may assist users of financial statements in making judgements on the amount, timing and degree of certainty of future cash flows.
- It gives an indication of the relationship between profitability and cash generating ability, and thus of the quality of the profit earned. The reconciliation of profit before tax to cash generated from operations is particularly useful as it highlights movements in working capital.
- Cash flow may be more easily understood than profit, particularly by users who are unfamiliar with the technical aspects of financial reporting.
- The cash flow statement provides information which may be useful in interpreting the income statement and balance sheet. For example, it shows cash flow from capital transactions as well as from revenue transactions. It may highlight a company's financial adaptability (for example, its ability to generate future profits and cash flows by selling assets or by issuing shares).

### 6.2 Are cash flows and balances difficult to manipulate?

It is often argued that cash flows and balances cannot be manipulated because cash flow is a matter of fact. It is not subject to estimates and it can only be treated in one way.

KEY POINT

It is possible to arrange receipts and payments of cash so that the cash balance is as high or low as possible.

However, cash balances are measured at a point in time. This means that it is possible to arrange receipts and payments of cash so that the cash balance is as high or low as possible. A business may make a special effort to collect receivables just before the year end; it may also delay paying suppliers until just after the year end.

A business may also structure transactions so that the cash balance is favourably affected. For example, if assets are acquired under leasing agreements cash outflows are spread over several accounting periods rather than one accounting period.

These practices are legitimate ways of managing cash. Cash management is an important aspect of stewardship and therefore desirable. However, more deliberate manipulation is possible. Loans may be raised and repaid immediately after the year-end. Assets may be sold and then immediately repurchased.

### 6.3 The dangers of concentrating on cash

KEY POINT

Cash flow is necessary for survival in the short term, but in order to survive in the long term a business must be profitable.

KEY POINT

Cash management may result in a healthy bank balance at the expense of profits.

Cash flow cannot be regarded as equivalent to earnings. Cash flow is necessary for survival in the short term, but in order to survive in the long term a business must be profitable. Profits generate cash flow.

Cash management may result in a healthy bank balance at the expense of profits. For example, if a company offers discounts as an incentive to pay promptly, profits are reduced. More significantly, it is often necessary to sacrifice cash flow in the short term in order to generate profits in the long term. Most businesses need to invest in property, plant and equipment in order to generate profits, but this normally results in a temporary cash outflow. A huge cash balance is not a sign of good management if the cash could be invested elsewhere to generate profit.

It has been stated that cash flow information is particularly useful because it has some predictive value. However, cash flow statements are based on historical information and therefore do not provide complete information for assessing future cash flows.

It should also be remembered that cash flows result from earlier activities. There are often significant timing differences (for example) between sales and the resulting cash inflow. Present cash flows may not be a reliable indicator of future cash flows. Neither cash flow nor profit provide a complete picture of a company's performance when looked at in isolation. The component parts of the financial statements interrelate because they reflect different aspects of the same transactions.

## Summary

- The group cash flow statement shows the cash flows making up the increase or decrease in cash for the group for the period. The central principle is that only cash flows that are external to the group should be reported in the group cash flow statement.
- Foreign exchange differences on the restatement of items denominated in a foreign currency do not represent cash flows in the accounting period and therefore need to be excluded from the cash flow statement.

Having completed your study of this chapter, you should have achieved the following learning outcome:

- prepare a consolidated cash flow statement for a group of companies.

## Self-test questions

1. What are the standard headings under which IAS 7 requires cash flows to be classified? (1.1)
2. How does IAS 7 define cash? (1.2)
3. What does the direct method of reporting net cash flows from operating activities show? (2.1)
4. What cash flows are shown under financing activities? (2.7)
5. How should minority interests be treated in a group cash flow statement? (4.2)

6 How does an associate lead to a cash flow into or out of a group? (4.3)

7 Where in the group cash flow statement should payments to acquire subsidiaries be reported? (4.4)

8 What are the cash flow effects of exchange differences dealt with at the individual company stage? (5.1)

9 What two areas of identifying group cash flow may be a problem if the presentation currency method has been used? (5.3)

10 State two benefits of producing a cash flow statement. (6.1)

## Objective test questions

### Question 1

The consolidated balance sheet of Bugs shows a minority interest of $640,000 at 31 March 20X1 and $700,000 at 31 March 20X2. The consolidated income statement shows a minority interest of $100,000.

What amount should appear in the group cash flow statement for minority interest?

**A** Receipt of $40,000

**B** Payment of $40,000

**C** Payment of $60,000

**D** Receipt of $100,000

***Using the following information, answer questions 2 and 3.***

Given below is an extract from the consolidated balance sheet of Fraser group.

| | *31 Dec 20X2* | *31 Dec 20X1* |
|---|---|---|
| | $000 | $000 |
| Investment in associate | 400 | 360 |
| Current liabilities | | |
| Income tax | 120 | 110 |

You are also given a summarised consolidated income statement for the year ending 31 December 20X2.

| | $000 | $000 |
|---|---|---|
| Profit from operations | | 240 |
| Share of profit of associates | | 60 |
| | | 300 |
| Income tax expense | | 60 |
| Profit after tax | | 240 |

### Question 2

What figure would appear in the group cash flow statement for the associate?

**A** Receipt of $20,000

**B** Payment of $20,000

**C** Receipt of $60,000

**D** Payment of $80,000

### Question 3

What figure would appear in the group cash flow statement for tax paid?

**A** $50,000

**B** $60,000

**C** $70,000

**D** $90,000

---

*For the answers to these questions, see the 'Answers' section at the end of the book.*

## Exam-type questions

### Abalone

Abalone prepares financial statements to 31 March each year. The consolidated income statement for the year ended 31 March 20X7, and the consolidated balance sheets at the beginning and end of that period, are given below:

**Consolidated income statement – year ended 31 March 20X7**

| | *Note* | $m |
|---|---|---|
| Revenue | | 6,450 |
| Cost of sales | (1) | (3,000) |
| Gross profit | | 3,450 |
| Other operating expenses | (1) | (1,530) |
| Profit from operations | | 1,920 |
| Finance costs | (2) | (375) |
| Profit before tax | | 1,545 |
| Income tax expense | (3) | (525) |
| Profit for the year | | 1,020 |
| | | |
| Attributable to: | | |
| Equity holders of the parent | | 870 |
| Minority interests | | 150 |
| | | 1,020 |

**Consolidated balance sheet at 31 March**

| | *20X7* | *20X6* | |
|---|---|---|---|
| | $m | $m | *Note* |
| Property, plant and equipment | 6,150 | 5,550 | (5) |
| Intangible assets | 150 | - | (6) |
| Current assets | 5,550 | 5,100 | (7) |
| | 11,850 | 10,650 | |

| | | | |
|---|---|---|---|
| Share capital | 1,800 | 1,800 | |
| Retained earnings | 3,300 | 2,850 | |
| | 5,100 | 4,650 | |
| Minority interests | 1,125 | 930 | |
| | 6,225 | 5,580 | |
| Non-current liabilities | 1,950 | 1,800 | (9) |
| Deferred taxation | 480 | 345 | |
| Current liabilities | 3,195 | 2,925 | (8) |
| | 11,850 | 10,650 | |

***Notes to financial statements***

(1) Depreciation charged in the consolidated income statement for the period totalled $1,455 million. There were no disposals of non-current assets in the period.

(2) There was no accrual of interest at the beginning or at the end of the year.

(3) *Taxation*

| | $m |
|---|---|
| Income tax on the profits for the period | 450 |
| Deferred taxation | 75 |
| | 525 |

(4) It is the policy of Abalone not to pay interim dividends.

(5) Abalone finances a number (but NOT all) of its non-current asset purchases using finance leases. In the period, non-current assets which would have cost $900 million to purchase outright were acquired under finance leases.

(6) On 1 October 20X6 Abalone acquired 75% of the ordinary share capital of Tench for a cash payment of $825 million. This acquisition made Tench a subsidiary of Abalone. The balance sheet of Tench at 1 October 20X6 showed the following balances:

| | $m |
|---|---|
| Property, plant and equipment | 750 |
| Inventories | 600 |
| Receivables | 450 |
| Trade payables | (300) |
| Taxation (including deferred taxation) | (120) |
| Bank overdraft | (480) |
| | 900 |

(7) Current assets at the beginning and end of the year were as follows:

| | *31/3/X7* | *31/3/X6* |
|---|---|---|
| | $m | $m |
| Inventories | 2,250 | 2,400 |
| Receivables | 3,300 | 2,700 |
| | 5,550 | 5,100 |

(8) Current liabilities at the beginning and end of the year were as follows:

| | *31/3/X7* | *31/3/X6* |
|---|---|---|
| | $m | $m |
| Trade payables | 1,875 | 1,635 |
| Taxation | 338 | 308 |
| Obligations under finance leases | 750 | 675 |
| Bank overdraft | 232 | 307 |
| | 3,195 | 2,925 |

(9) The non-current liabilities were all obligations under finance leases.

**Requirements:**

Prepare the consolidated cash flow statement for the Abalone group for the year ended 31 March 20X7.

Notes to the cash flow statement are NOT required. **(25 marks)**

## Wimborne

The draft income statement and statement of changes in equity for the year ended 30 September 20X3 and balance sheets of Wimborne for the years ended 30 September 20X2 and 30 September 20X3 are as follows:

**Consolidated income statement for the year ended 30 September 20X3**

| | $000 |
|---|---|
| Revenue | 112,430 |
| Cost of sales | (58,583) |
| Gross profit | 53,847 |
| Distribution costs and administrative expenses | (31,456) |
| Profit from operations | 22,391 |
| Finance costs | (1,350) |
| Investment income | 175 |
| Loss on disposal of non-current asset investment | (2,500) |
| Profit before tax | 18,716 |
| Income tax expense | (6,750) |
| Profit for the year | 11,966 |
| Attributable to: | |
| Equity holders of the parent | 10,421 |
| Minority interests | 1,545 |
| | 11,966 |

**Consolidated statement of changes in equity for the year ended 30 September 20X3**

| | $000 |
|---|---|
| At 1 October 20X2 | 15,725 |
| Profit for the year | 10,421 |
| Revaluation loss on property | (1,400) |
| Exchange gain on translation | 1,762 |
| Dividends paid | (1,675) |
| At 30 September 20X3 | 24,833 |

**Consolidated balance sheets at 30 September**

| | *20X3* | *20X2* |
|---|---|---|
| | $000 | $000 |
| Non-current assets: | | |
| Property, plant and equipment | 25,700 | 22,430 |
| Investments | 3,400 | 6,900 |
| | 29,100 | 29,330 |
| Current assets: | | |
| Inventories | 19,773 | 17,702 |
| Receivables | 12,470 | 12,358 |
| Cash | 10,125 | 5,100 |
| | 42,368 | 35,160 |
| | 71,468 | 64,490 |
| Equity: | | |
| Share capital | 3,000 | 3,000 |
| Reserves | 21,833 | 12,725 |
| | 24,833 | 15,725 |
| Minority interests | 5,100 | 3,400 |
| | 29,933 | 19,125 |
| Non-current liabilities: | | |
| Bank loans | 7,500 | 11,850 |
| Deferred tax | 4,300 | 3,094 |
| | 11,800 | 14,944 |
| Current liabilities: | | |
| Trade and other payables | 23,365 | 25,592 |
| Tax liabilities | 6,370 | 4,829 |
| | 29,735 | 30,421 |
| | 71,468 | 64,490 |

***Notes:***

1 During the year the group disposed of its interest in Ringwood, an entity over which it did not exercise significant influence. Ringwood had cost $4.5 million in 20W5 and was sold for $2 million.

2 The exchange gain is made up as follows:

| | $000 |
|---|---|
| Property, plant and equipment | 2,117 |
| Inventories | 205 |
| Receivables | 158 |
| Cash | 140 |
| Loans | (476) |
| Trade and other payables | (124) |
| Minority interests | (258) |
| | 1,762 |

3 The depreciation charge for the year ended 30 September 20X3 was $3,197,000. There were no disposals of property, plant and equipment during the year.

4 Cash comprises the following:

| | *20X3* | *20X2* |
|---|---|---|
| | $000 | $000 |
| Six month term deposits | 7,500 | 5,000 |
| 30-day money market deposits | 2,000 | – |
| Current account balances | 625 | 100 |
| | 10,125 | 5,100 |

**Required:**

Prepare the consolidated cash flow statement for the Wimborne group for the year ended 30 September 20X3, in accordance with IAS 7 Cash Flow Statements. Notes to the cash flow statement are not required.

**(25 marks)**

*For the answers to these questions, see the 'Answers' section at the end of the book.*

## Feedback to activities

### Activity 1

| | $ |
|---|---|
| Profit before tax | 300,000 |
| Increase in inventory | (118,000) |
| Increase in receivables | (125,000) |
| Increase in payables (135 – 12) | 123,000 |
| Net cash inflow from operating activities | 180,000 |

To show the real adjustments from profit before tax to net cash inflow relating to inventory and payables a calculation would be required of the amount of inventory which has not been paid for. If this information has been obtained in the above example, say $50,000, the reconciliation statement becomes:

| | $ |
|---|---|
| Profit before tax | 300,000 |
| Increase in inventory (118 – 50) | (68,000) |
| Increase in receivables | (125,000) |
| Increase in payables (135 – 12 – 50) | 73,000 |
| Net cash inflow from operating activities | 180,000 |

### Activity 2

**Income taxes – working account**

| | $ | | $ |
|---|---|---|---|
| Tax paid | | Balances brought down | |
| (balancing figure) | 169,000 | Income taxes | 140,000 |
| Balances carried down | | Deferred tax | 140,000 |
| Income taxes | 271,000 | Income statement | |
| Deferred tax | 190,000 | Income taxes | 300,000 |
| | | Deferred tax | 50,000 |
| | 630,000 | | 630,000 |

There is sufficient information to compute the tax paid in the year directly, but it is often easier to compute tax as a balancing figure rather than directly.

### Activity 3

**Non-current assets – NBV**

| | $000 | | $000 |
|---|---|---|---|
| Balance b/d | 10,000 | Depreciation charge | 2,600 |
| In subsidiary at acquisition | 4,800 | Disposals | 600 |
| Additions (bal fig) | 4,400 | Balance c/d | 16,000 |
| | 19,200 | | 19,200 |

Expenditure is $4,400,000

Chapter 11

# PROBLEMS OF PROFIT MEASUREMENT

## Syllabus content

- The problems of profit measurement and the effect of alternative approaches to asset valuation; current cost and current purchasing power bases and the real terms system; accounting for changing prices and hyperinflation (IAS 29).

## Contents

## Introduction

This is the first of four chapters that deal with various aspects of the measurement of income and capital. This chapter focuses on the general topic of asset valuation and profit measurement; the other chapters look at specific accounting issues.

It begins by considering the disadvantages of historic cost accounting and moves on to look at alternatives to this. It also covers the ways in which traditional historic cost accounts have been modified to deal with some of the effects of changing prices. IAS 29 *Financial Reporting in Hyperinflationary Economies* requires financial statements to be restated in terms of the measuring unit at the balance sheet date, where an entity operates under hyperinflation. This may be relevant where a group has foreign subsidiaries. In addition, a number of other standards either permit or require certain types of asset and liability to be measured at fair value, rather than historic cost.

# 1 Traditional historical cost accounting

## 1.1 The traditional approach

The traditional approach to accounting has the following features.

- Accounting transactions are recorded at their original historical monetary cost.
- Items and events for which no monetary transaction has occurred are usually ignored altogether.
- The income for each period is normally taken into account only when the revenue is realised in the form of cash or in some form which will soon be converted into cash.
- The profit for the period is found by matching the cost of items consumed in generating the revenue for the period (such items include non-current assets which depreciate through use, obsolescence or the passage of time).
- In every case, a prudent view is taken of the value of assets, income and expenses.

KEY POINT

In periods in which prices change significantly, historical cost financial statements have grave deficiencies.

These features of accounting have served users well over many years in accounting for the stewardship of the directors. However, in periods in which prices change significantly, historical cost financial statements have grave deficiencies.

## 1.2 The deficiencies of historical cost accounting

- The amounts at which non-monetary assets (such as property, plant and equipment and inventories) are stated bear no relation to their current value and therefore provide a poor guide to the resources available to the business.
- Holding gains are not shown in the financial statements until assets are sold, even though many believe that these make an important contribution to an entity's overall financial performance.
- In a company's income statement, out-of-date costs are matched against current revenues. This produces an overstated and misleading profit figure.

- The income statement fails to show gains or losses made by owing money or holding monetary assets such as trade receivables and trade payables. When prices are rising, holding a cash balance results in a loss of purchasing power while borrowing money may result in a gain in purchasing power.
- Because profits are overstated and assets are understated, return on capital employed and similar measures may be extremely misleading.
- Trend information, such as that provided by comparative figures or in a five-year summary, is distorted because it fails to take into account the changing value of money over time.

As a result of the above, users of financial statements find it extremely difficult to assess a company's progress from year to year or to compare the results of different operations.

***Example***

Company A acquires a new machine in 20X4. This machine costs $50,000 and has an estimated useful life of ten years.

Company B acquires an identical machine in 20X5, except that it buys a machine exactly one year old, with an estimated useful life of nine years. The cost of the machine is $48,000.

Depreciation charges (straight-line basis) in 20X5 are as follows:

| | | |
|---|---|---|
| Company A | $\frac{1}{10} \times \$50,000$ | = $5,000 |
| Company B | $\frac{1}{9} \times \$48,000$ | = $5,333 |

Net book values at the end of 20X5 are

| | | |
|---|---|---|
| Company A | $50,000 – (2 × $5,000) | = $40,000 |
| Company B | $48,000 – $5,333 | = $42,667 |

Both companies are using identical machines during 20X5, but the income statements will show quite different profit figures because of adherence to historical cost. Ask yourself the question whether the comparison of balance sheets and income statements for the two companies in 20X5 is meaningful.

### 1.3 Advantages of the historical cost approach

One of the principal advantages claimed for historic cost accounting is that it is objective. The accounts are based on verifiable facts, rather than on subjective opinion.

In spite of this, subjective opinions are extremely important in conventional accounting, for example:

- revaluation of non-current assets
- arriving at depreciation charges (this requires estimates of useful life and residual value)
- valuing inventory
- making allowances for doubtful debts and obsolete and slow-moving inventory.

The other advantage of historic cost accounting is that it is understandable and easy to apply. However, it is often argued that in fact historic cost accounting is not particularly easy to understand. Non-accountants may believe that the balance sheet represents the actual value of an entity's net assets, not their cost.

### 1.4 Possible alternatives to historical cost accounting

Despite its limitations, historical cost accounts are still used because it has been difficult to find and to agree on a suitable and workable alternative.

One reasonably practical answer is modified historic cost accounting. Many companies measure non-current assets at a valuation, rather than historic cost. Even this is not as simple as it first appears, because there are several possible ways in which an asset can be valued. We look at some of these later in the chapter.

However, revaluation is only a partial answer. We also need to look at the way in which profit is measured, or capital maintenance.

The IASB *Framework* identifies four possible ways of measuring assets: historic cost, current cost, realisable value and present value. It also identifies two concepts of capital maintenance: financial capital maintenance (used in historic cost accounting) and physical capital maintenance. The *Framework* does not require the use of any particular measurement basis or concept of capital maintenance.

## 2 Measuring assets

### 2.1 The case for current value accounting

The objective of financial statements is to provide information about the reporting entity's financial performance and position that is useful to a wide range of users for assessing the stewardship of management and for making economic decisions.

What is wrong with the traditional historical cost basis of measurement used by accountants? Whilst being both easy to ascertain and objective, it fails to relate directly to any of the three decisions that might reasonably be made about an asset:

- Another, similar asset might be purchased. Management need to know the **current replacement cost**, which might have changed substantially since the present asset was purchased at its historical cost.
- The asset might be sold. Management need to know the amount which would be realised from sale, less any costs involved in disposal, i.e. the **net realisable value**. Again, this bears no relationship to historical cost.
- The asset might be used in the business. Management need to estimate the future cash flows arising from the asset and discount these to their present value, i.e. their '**economic value**'. Clearly, there is no relationship with historical cost in this case.

***Valuing assets***

There are three ways of valuing assets:

- current entry value (replacement cost) – often referred to as replacement cost and widely considered as a possible basis of measurement to value assets and to determine the cost of items consumed
- current **exit value** (net realisable value) – based on the use of net realisable values
- **deprival value** (value to the business) – defined as the loss a business would suffer if deprived of an asset.

KEY POINT

The accounting profession is currently divided as to which measurement basis should be used. Until recently, deprival value was accepted as being the most relevant for accounting purposes.

At present, the accounting profession is divided as to which of these three alternatives should be adopted in financial statements. However, until recently, deprival value was accepted as providing the most relevant information to users.

## 2.2 Deprival value

KEY POINT

If the business were deprived of an asset, would it replace it?

If yes, deprival value = replacement cost.

If no, would the business have sold the asset? (Deprival value = NRV)

Or would it have used the asset? (Deprival value = EV).

To identify deprival value we need to identify all three of the measures of value discussed above: replacement cost, net realisable value and economic value. Then we can identify two important relationships between values:

- the higher of net realisable value (NRV) and economic value (EV) – if management own an asset, they have control over the choice between use and disposal, and if it is economically rational they will choose the option having the highest value
- the lower of replacement cost (RC) and recoverable amount.

This may be portrayed diagrammatically as follows:

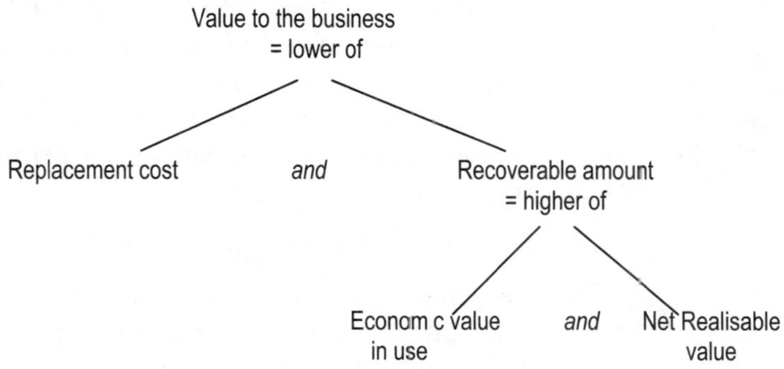


If they are deprived of an asset, management have a choice as to whether or not to replace it. If they are economically rational, they will replace the asset only if they can generate a surplus either by resale or by use. (This is the idea behind the definition of recoverable value in IAS 36 *Impairment of Assets*, which was covered in an earlier chapter.)

### *Activity 1*

(a) **Normal business**

A company owns a machine with a five-year useful life and no residual value.

At 1 December 20X2 the machine is two years old. The replacement cost at that date of a brand new machine of the same type is $100,000.

If the machine were sold it would fetch about $30,000 but there would be dismantling costs of about $5,000.

It is estimated that the machine could generate cash flows of $40,000 per annum if it were used in the business for the next three years. Assume that the cash flows arise at the end of the year and that a factor of 10% per annum is appropriate for discounting purposes.

Calculate the deprival value of the asset.

(b) **Company anticipating closure**

Assume that the facts are as in (a) above but that the business is in such a poor state that there are no positive cash flows to be obtained from continuing to use the asset.

Calculate the deprival value of the asset.

(c) **Company with low NPV**

Assume that the facts are as in (a) above but that the cash flows associated with the continued use of the asset are $22,000 per annum.

Calculate the deprival value of the asset.

*Feedback to this activity is at the end of the chapter.*

## 3 Asset valuation in financial statements

### 3.1 Introduction

KEY POINT

It is accepted that information based on current or fair values provides more relevant information to users of the financial statements than information based on historical cost.

It is extremely unlikely that the IASB will introduce any form of general inflation accounting in the foreseeable future.

However, it is accepted that information based on current or fair values provides more relevant information to users of the financial statements than information based on historical cost. For this reason, many entities adopt a modified form of historical cost accounting in which some assets are revalued at regular intervals. This is permitted under current accounting standards.

### 3.2 Standards permitting revaluation

Certain IASs allow a choice between a 'cost model', in which assets are carried at historical cost less accumulated depreciation and a 'revaluation model' in which assets are carried at fair value. Depending on the type of asset, changes in fair value may either be taken immediately to the income statement or may be recognised in equity until the asset is sold.

**IAS 16 *Property, Plant and Equipment***

Under the revaluation model, items of property, plant and equipment are measured at fair value less accumulated depreciation based on the revalued amount. Revaluations must be carried out regularly, but not necessarily every year or at prescribed intervals. Gains on revaluation are taken directly to equity.

**IAS 38 *Intangible Assets***

Under the revaluation model, intangible assets are carried at fair value, less accumulated amortisation based on the revalued amount. The required accounting is as for property, plant and equipment.

**IAS 40 *Investment Property***

Under the fair value model, investment property is measured at fair value. Annual revaluations are required. Changes in fair value are recognised immediately in the income statement; there is no depreciation.

### 3.3 Standards requiring fair value accounting

IAS 41 *Agriculture* requires biological assets and agricultural produce to be measured at fair value less selling costs. Gains and losses are recognised in the income statement.

IAS 39 *Financial Instruments: Recognition and Measurement* requires some financial assets and liabilities, including derivatives, to be measured at fair value. Gains and losses are recognised either in the income statement or in equity, depending on the type of asset.

IAS 39 is covered in detail later in the text.

### 3.4 Fair value and current value

As we saw in the previous section, there are several possible bases for valuing assets. All these bases are subjective. None of them is appropriate in all situations.

DEFINITION

**Fair value** is defined as the amount for which an asset could be exchanged between knowledgeable, willing parties in an arm's length transaction.

The IASB appears to be moving towards greater use of fair value. **Fair value** is defined as the amount for which an asset could be exchanged between knowledgeable, willing parties in an arm's length transaction. In practice this normally means open market value.

This is not the same as current value. Current value is not defined in IASs, but is normally understood to be equivalent to deprival value or value to the business. For example, under UK accounting standards **current value** is defined as the lower of replacement cost and recoverable amount (which is the higher of net realisable value and value in use).

Supporters of the value to the business model argue that it reflects the economic situation and the intentions of management. To some extent it avoids the problem of choosing a measurement base.

KEY POINT

Fair value is often less complex to apply than value to the business.

Fair value is often less complex to apply than value to the business (for example, there is no need to calculate the present value of future income streams relating to an asset). However, it has some important disadvantages.

- It is not appropriate where the entity has no immediate plans to sell the asset.
- Where market values fluctuate it can make the financial statements volatile, especially where gains and losses are taken directly to the income statement. This means that users may find it difficult to understand underlying trends and to predict future performance.
- There may not be an active market for some kinds of asset (for example, very specialised or unique assets).

### 3.5 Other disadvantages of revaluation

Neither IAS 16 nor IAS 38 requires annual revaluations. If assets are revalued but the valuations are not kept up to date, the balance sheet may become even less meaningful than one based on historical cost.

The modified historical cost basis often means that some non-current assets (usually properties) are revalued, while others remain at historical cost. Although some argue that this provides useful information to users, others argue that this simply produces confusing figures.

## 4 Capital maintenance concepts

### 4.1 The basic principle

Profit for a period is measured by comparing closing net assets with opening net assets. This is the basis of the accounting equation:

ASSETS less LIABILITIES = CAPITAL

OPENING NET ASSETS + PROFIT – DISTRIBUTIONS = CLOSING NET ASSETS

Under historic cost accounting, as long as closing shareholders' funds (equity capital and reserves) are equal to or greater than opening shareholders' funds in '$' terms the entity has maintained its capital.

As we have seen, this is not always a relevant way of measuring profit in times of inflation.

KEY POINT

The measurement of profit is determined by the capital maintenance concept which is adopted.

KEY POINT

Capital maintenance concepts can be classified as:

- physical capital maintenance (PCM)
- financial capital maintenance (FCM).

DEFINITION

**Financial capital maintenance** is the concept that profit is earned only if the financial (or money) amount of the net assets at the end of the period exceeds the financial (or money) amount of net assets at the beginning of the period.

DEFINITION

**Physical capital maintenance** is the concept that profit is earned only if the physical productive capacity (or operating capability) of the entity (or the resources or funds needed to achieve that capacity) at the end of the period exceeds the physical productive capacity at the beginning of the period.

### 4.2 Alternatives to traditional capital maintenance

The measurement of profit is determined by the capital maintenance concept which is adopted. There are two main concepts of capital maintenance:

- **financial capital maintenance (FCM)** – financial capital maintenance can be further divided into 'money' financial capital maintenance and real financial capital maintenance
- **physical capital maintenance (PCM)** alternatively known as operating capital maintenance (OCM).

**Financial capital maintenance**

CIMA *Official Terminology* defines this as:

The concept that profit is earned only if the financial (or money) amount of the net assets at the end of the period exceeds the financial (or money) amount of net assets at the beginning of the period, after excluding any distributions to, and contributions from, owners during the period.

Historic cost accounting reflects the concept of **money financial capital maintenance**.

**Real financial capital maintenance** measures capital as a fund of general purchasing power. In order to maintain purchasing power, the opening capital is uplifted by the general inflation rate.

Therefore profit is the difference between closing shareholders' funds and opening shareholders' funds at current prices.

**Physical capital maintenance**

CIMA *Official Terminology* defines this as:

The concept that profit is earned only if the physical productive capacity (or operating capability) of the entity (or the resources or funds needed to achieve that capacity) at the end of the period exceeds the physical productive capacity at the beginning of the period, after excluding any distributions to, and contributions from, owners during the period.

Physical capital maintenance measures capital as the productive capacity of a company's assets (the volume of goods and services that it is capable of producing). Profit can only be measured after providing for any increases needed to maintain the company's operating capital. Non-current assets and inventories are included in the balance sheet at their value to the business. The charges for cost of sales and depreciation are based on these values.

Therefore profit is the difference between closing productive capacity and opening productive capacity.

***Example of capital maintenance concepts***

A company begins with share capital of $100 and cash of $100. At the beginning of the year, one item of inventory is bought for $100. The item is sold at the end of the year for $150. Its replacement cost at that time is $120 and general inflation throughout the year is 10%. Any 'profit' is distributed to shareholders at the end of the year.

| | *Financial capital maintenance* 'Money' | *Financial capital maintenance* Real | *Physical capital maintenance* |
|---|---|---|---|
| | $ | $ | $ |
| Sales | 150 | 150 | 150 |
| Less: Cost of sales | 100 | 100 | 120 |
| Operating profit | 50 | 50 | 30 |
| Less: Inflation adjustment | – | 10 | – |
| Profit for year | 50 | 40 | 30 |
| Dividend | 50 | 40 | 30 |
| | – | – | – |
| Capital and non-distributable reserves (at year end) | 100 | 110 | 120 |

Under 'money' financial capital maintenance there is no attempt to adjust for inflation, i.e. the accounts are historical cost accounts.

Under real financial capital maintenance the emphasis is on maintaining the purchasing power of the opening capital. The shareholders require funds of $110 in order to maintain their purchasing power. ($110 buys the same quantity of goods at the year end as $100 at the beginning of the year.)

Under physical capital maintenance cost of sales is increased to reflect the specific $20 increase in the price of inventory. The physical capital maintenance balance sheet total figure is then sufficient to replace the inventory, which is the whole objective.

### 4.3 Accounting for the effects of inflation

We have seen that there are two main alternatives to money financial capital maintenance. These are reflected in the alternatives to historic cost accounting:

KEY POINT

The two alternative approaches to historical cost accounting are current purchasing power (CPP) and current cost accounting (CCA).

1 presenting accounts in the same real terms from one year to another (**current purchasing power** or **CPP**)

2 protecting the operating capabilities of companies (**current cost accounting** or **CCA**)

3 some combination of the two.

**Option 1** involves accounting for general price changes. The owners of the business are shareholders who may suffer from general inflation as the purchasing power of their investment in the business declines. Changes in general prices are thus used to record the effect.

**Option 2** involves the consideration of specific price changes. Here the perspective of the business as a separate entity is paramount. The effects of price changes on the specific assets owned by the business are therefore used.

Neither of these alternatives is ideal, but both can produce information that is relevant to users of financial statements.

## 4.4 Choice of capital maintenance concept

There are two main factors to consider when choosing a capital maintenance concept. These are the needs of the user and the nature of the company's business.

KEY POINT

Financial capital maintenance is normally more relevant to shareholders. Physical capital maintenance is normally more relevant to managers and employees.

***Users***

Shareholders will generally be interested in maximising the purchasing power of their investment and the return on their investment. Therefore financial capital maintenance and current purchasing power accounting are probably most relevant.

Managers and employees may be more concerned with an entity's ability to continue trading and therefore operating capital maintenance and current cost accounting are probably most relevant. If the company does not maintain its operating capacity, there will be a reduction in the scale of its activities which may mean that employees are made redundant.

KEY POINT

Financial capital maintenance is provides information which is particularly relevant to entities in which asset value increases generate profits. Physical capital maintenance is more relevant for manufacturing businesses.

***Nature of business***

Financial capital maintenance is provides information which is particularly relevant to entities in which asset value increases generate profits. The true measure of the performance of such entities is their ability to produce 'real' profits above the profits which arise from general inflation.

Physical capital maintenance is more relevant for manufacturing businesses as it demonstrates the ability of the business to continue to produce the same volume of goods and services.

# 5 Current purchasing power accounting

## 5.1 The concept

KEY POINT

CPP accounts are prepared by adjusting all the amounts in the accounts to reflect the value of money at one point in time.

CPP accounts are prepared by adjusting all the amounts in the accounts to reflect the value of money at one point in time. Thus, the unit of measurement is the 'CPP unit' rather than the monetary unit. In principle, the CPP unit can be based on the value of money at any point in time. In practice, the value of money at the balance sheet date is used.

CPP accounts are prepared by updating all items in the income statement, and all non-monetary items in the balance sheet, by the CPP factor:

$$\textbf{CPP factor} = \frac{\text{Index at the balance sheet date}}{\text{Index at date of entry in accounts}}$$

Depreciation is adjusted by reference to the date of acquisition of the related non-current asset item.

DEFINITION

**Monetary items** are those whose amounts are fixed by contract or otherwise in terms of numbers of currency units (e.g. dollars), regardless of changes in general price levels.

**Non-monetary items** include such assets as inventory, plant and buildings.

**Monetary items** are those whose amounts are fixed by contract or otherwise in terms of numbers of currency units (e.g. dollars), regardless of changes in general price levels. Examples of monetary items are cash, receivables, payables and loan capital.

Monetary items are not adjusted, because their value in CPP units is their monetary amount.

In the CPP accounts, it is necessary to compute a gain or loss from holding monetary items in times of inflation.. This is because holders of monetary assets lose general purchasing power during a period of inflation, while holders of monetary liabilities gain general purchasing power. This gain or loss is recognised in the income statement.

In this and the next section, examples of the methods used to prepare CPP and CCA accounts are shown. You will **not** be required to prepare accounts or to calculate any figures in the exam, but you could be asked to explain the way in which the accounts differ from historical cost accounts or what the various adjustments mean.

## 5.2 The preparation of CPP accounts

***Example***

W was formed on 1 January 20X8, with a fully-subscribed share capital of $200,000. On the same date a loan of $100,000 was raised.

On 31 March 20X8, storage facilities with a 20-year life and no residual value were purchased for $150,000. On the same date 1,000 widgets were purchased for $100,000. On 30 June 20X8, 600 widgets were sold for $90,000. Expenses of $10,000 were paid on 30 June 20X8. All transactions were for cash.

The company provides a full year's depreciation in the year of acquisition of an asset.

A general price index moved:

| | | |
|---|---|---|
| 1 January | 20X8 | 660 |
| 31 March | 20X8 | 715 |
| 30 June | 20X8 | 780 |
| 31 December | 20X8 | 858 |

Assuming straight-line depreciation, you are required to:

1 prepare historical cost accounts for the year to 31 December 20X8

2 prepare CPP accounts for the year to 31 December 20X8.

***Solution***

**The income statement**

All of the items in the income statement are uplifted by the CPP factor:

$$\frac{\text{Index at the balance sheet date}}{\text{Index at date of entry in accounts}}$$

The gain or loss on monetary items is calculated.

| | | | HC $ | CPP factor | CPP $ |
|---|---|---|---|---|---|
| (W1) | **Bank movements** | | | | |
| | 1 January 20X8 | Shares issued | 200,000 | $\frac{858}{660}$ | 260,000 |
| | 1 January 20X8 | Loan raised | 100,000 | $\frac{858}{660}$ | 130,000 |
| | 31 March 20X8 | Storage | (150,000) | $\frac{858}{715}$ | (180,000) |
| | 31 March 20X8 | Purchases | (100,000) | $\frac{858}{715}$ | (120,000) |
| | 30 June 20X8 | Sales | 90,000 | $\frac{858}{780}$ | 99,000 |
| | 30 June 20X8 | Expenses | (10,000) | $\frac{858}{780}$ | (11,000) |
| | Loss on monetary items (Bal fig) | | | | (48,000) |
| | 31 December 20X8 | Balance | 130,000 | | 130,000 |
| (W2) | **Loan movement** | | | | |
| | 1 January 20X8 | Loan raised | 100,000 | $\frac{858}{660}$ | 130,000 |
| | Gain on monetary item (Bal fig) | | | | (30,000) |
| | 31 December 20X8 | Balance | 100,000 | | 100,000 |

**W**

**Income statement for the year ended 31 December 20X8**

| | HC $ | HC $ | CPP factor | CPP $ | CPP $ |
|---|---|---|---|---|---|
| Sales | | 90,000 | $\frac{858}{780}$ | | 99,000 |
| Purchases | 100,000 | | $\frac{858}{715}$ | 120,000 | |
| Less: Closing inventory | 40,000 | | $\frac{858}{715}$ | 48,000 | |
| Cost of sales | | 60,000 | | | 72,000 |
| Gross profit | | 30,000 | | | 27,000 |
| Depreciation | 7,500 | | $\frac{858}{715}$ | 9,000 | |
| Expenses | 10,000 | | $\frac{858}{780}$ | 11,000 | |
| | | 17,500 | | | 20,000 |
| | | | | | 7,000 |
| Loss on monetary items (48,000(W1) – 30,000(W2)) | | | | | (18,000) |
| Net profit/(loss) | | 12,500 | | | (11,000) |

**The balance sheet**

In the balance sheet it is only the non-monetary items which are adjusted.

**Balance sheet as at 31 December 20X8**

| Non-current assets | $ | $ | | *CPP* $ | *CPP* $ |
|---|---|---|---|---|---|
| Plant: | | | | | |
| Cost | | 150,000 | $\frac{858}{715}$ | | 180,000 |
| Depreciation | | 7,500 | $\frac{858}{715}$ | | 9,000 |
| | | 142,500 | | | 171,000 |
| Current assets: | | | | | |
| Inventory | 40,000 | | $\frac{858}{715}$ | 48,000 | |
| Bank | 130,000 | | - | 130,000 | |
| | | 170,000 | | | 178,000 |
| | | 312,500 | | | 349,000 |
| Share capital | | 200,000 | $\frac{858}{660}$ | | 260,000 |
| Retained profit/(loss) | | 12,500 | | | (11,000) |
| | | 212,500 | | | 249,000 |
| Loan | | 100,000 | | | 100,000 |
| | | 312,500 | | | 349,000 |

## 5.3 The advantages and disadvantages of CPP accounting

***Advantages***

- CPP accounting is both simple to apply and **objective**, because it relies on a standard index.
- Because it adjusts for changes in the unit of measurement, it is a true system of **inflation accounting**.
- It measures the impact on the company in terms of shareholders' **purchasing power**.

***Disadvantages***

- CPP fails to capture economic substance when specific and general price movements diverge. This means that it may not provide relevant information when an entity is affected by specific price changes.

KEY POINT

CPP does not show the current values (value to the business) of assets and liabilities.

- Information stated in terms of constant purchasing power units can be **unfamiliar**.
- CPP **does not show the current values** (value to the business) of assets and liabilities. It values money, not assets.
- The physical capital of the business is not maintained.

# 6 Current cost accounting

## 6.1 The concept

KEY POINT

The current cost income statement is charged with the value to the business of assets consumed during the period.

The current cost balance sheet reflects the current value of inventory and non-current assets.

Current cost accounting can be complex. You only need to understand the general principles.

- The current cost income statement is charged with the value to the business of assets consumed during the period. In particular, the charges for consuming inventory (cost of sales) and non-current assets (depreciation) are based on current rather than historical values.

- The current cost balance sheet reflects the current value of inventory and non-current assets.

## 6.2 The current cost balance sheet

KEY POINT

In most cases, the value to the business of property is its market value on an existing use basis, while for plant and machinery it is net current replacement cost.

Non-current assets should be included in the balance sheet at their value to the business, i.e. the amount of compensation a company would require if it were deprived of the asset.

In most cases, the value to the business of property is its market value on an existing use basis, while for plant and machinery it is net current replacement cost.

The current cost of inventory is normally its replacement cost at the date of sale.

In practice, specific price indexes are often used.

Only non-current assets and inventories are adjusted. All the other assets and liabilities are monetary items and therefore they are already stated at their value to the business.

***Example***

**Historic cost balance sheets**

| | | *20X1* | | *20X0* |
|---|---|---|---|---|
| Non-current assets | $000 | $000 | $000 | $000 |
| Cost | | 1,000 | | 1,000 |
| Depreciation | | 300 | | 200 |
| | | 700 | | 800 |
| Current assets: | | | | |
| Inventory | 1,400 | | 1,350 | |
| Receivables | 620 | | 450 | |
| Cash | 50 | | – | |
| | | 2,070 | | 1,800 |
| | | 2,770 | | 2,600 |
| Share capital | | 800 | | 800 |
| Reserves | | 670 | | 535 |
| | | 1,470 | | 1,335 |
| Loan stock | | 550 | | 650 |
| Current liabilities | | 750 | | 615 |
| | | 2,770 | | 2,600 |

**Additional information:**

(1) The gross replacement cost of the non-current assets was $1,500,000 on 31 December 20X0 and $1,750,000 at 31 December 20X1.

(2) Inventories were bought on average two months before the year end. The indices for the input prices of goods and services used by the business are as follows:

| | |
|---|---|
| 31 October 20X0 | 116 |
| 31 December 20X0 | 118 |
| 31 October 20X1 | 130 |
| 31 December 20X1 | 131 |

**You are required** to prepare the current cost balance sheets.

***Solution***

**Current cost balance sheets**

| | *20X1* | | *20X0* | |
|---|---|---|---|---|
| | $000 | $000 | $000 | $000 |
| Non-current assets (NBV) (W1) | | 1,225 | | 1,200 |
| Current assets: | | | | |
| Inventory (W2) | 1,411 | | 1,373 | |
| Receivables | 620 | | 450 | |
| Cash | 50 | | – | |
| | | 2,081 | | 1,823 |
| | | 3,306 | | 3,023 |
| Share capital | | 800 | | 800 |
| Reserves (balancing figure) | | 1,206 | | 958 |
| | | 2,006 | | 1,758 |
| Loan stock | | 550 | | 650 |
| Current liabilities | | 750 | | 615 |
| | | 3,306 | | 3,023 |

***Workings***

(W1) Non-current assets at current cost

$$\text{Historic cost NBV} \times \frac{\text{Gross replacement cost at B/S date}}{\text{Historic cost}}$$

31 December 20X0 $$800 \times \frac{1,500}{1,000} = 1,200$$

31 December 20X1 $$700 \times \frac{1,750}{1,000} = 1,225$$

(W2) Inventories at current cost

$$\text{Historic cost} \times \frac{\text{Index at B/S date}}{\text{Index at purchase}}$$

31 December 20X0 $$1,350 \times \frac{118}{116} = 1,373$$

31 December 20X1 $$1,400 \times \frac{131}{130} = 1,411$$

### 6.3 The current cost income statement

The current cost income statement is effectively a reconciliation between historic cost profit and current cost profit. Four adjustments are made:

- The **depreciation adjustment.** This is the difference between depreciation based on historic cost and depreciation based on current cost.
- The **cost of sales adjustment**. This is the difference between the current cost of sales and the historic cost of sales. It uplifts the cost of the inventory sold to its value to the business at the date that it is sold. This adjustment eliminates that part of the profit that is not a 'real' profit, but a holding gain.
- The **monetary working capital adjustment** (MWCA) (sometimes called the loss on net monetary position). This is the increase in the real value of monetary working capital (trade receivables less trade payables) that has occurred during the year. When trade receivables are realised in cash the company makes a loss because the cash is based on the historic amount of the debt rather than the current amount. The adjustment recognises this loss in the income statement and ensures that enough earnings are retained in the business to maintain the current level of monetary working capital.
- The **gearing adjustment**. This applies where an entity is partially financed by debt. It adds back the proportion of the depreciation, cost of sales and monetary working capital adjustments which are financed by loans (debt), rather than by equity. The idea behind this is that the other current cost adjustments are borne partly by equity shareholders and partly by lenders. The gearing adjustment shows the current cost profit attributable to the shareholders.

The mechanics of calculating these adjustments are outside the scope of your syllabus.

#### *Example*

The following information relates to the company in 6.2 above.

**Historic cost income statement for the year ended 31 December 20X1**

| | $000 |
|---|---|
| Profit from operations | 267 |
| Interest | 33 |
| Profit before tax | 234 |
| Income tax expense | 40 |
| Profit for the year | 194 |

**Additional information:**

(1) The current cost operating adjustments have been calculated as follows:

| | |
|---|---|
| Cost of sales adjustment | $159,000 |
| Depreciation adjustment | $75,000 |
| Monetary working capital adjustment | $(7,000) |
| Gearing adjustment | $56,000 |

(2) Dividends of $59,000 were paid during the year.

**You are required** to prepare the current cost income statement for the year ended 31 December 20X1 and to show the analysis of reserves at that date.

***Solution***

**Current cost income statement for the year ended 31 December 20X1**

| | $000 | $000 |
|---|---|---|
| Historic cost profit from operations | | 267 |
| Less: current cost operating adjustments: | | |
| Cost of sales adjustment | 159 | |
| Monetary working capital adjustment | (7) | |
| Depreciation adjustment | 75 | |
| | | (227) |
| Current cost profit from operations | | 40 |
| Gearing adjustment | 56 | |
| Interest | (33) | |
| | | 23 |
| Current cost profit before tax | | 63 |
| Income tax expense | | (40) |
| Current cost profit for the year attributable to shareholders | | 23 |

In times of rising prices, the cost of sales adjustment and the depreciation adjustment reduce profit. The depreciation charge is based on the current cost of assets and cost of sales is based on the current value of inventory.

The monetary working capital adjustment can reduce or increase profit. In this case, it has increased profit, which suggests that trade payables are higher than receivables.

The gearing adjustment is added back to profit.

**Reserves at 31 December 20X1**

Reserves consist of retained earnings and a current cost reserve. Retained earnings is calculated below:

| | $000 |
|---|---|
| Historic cost retained earnings at 1 January 20X1 | 535 |
| Current cost profit for the year attributable to shareholders | 23 |
| Less dividends paid | (59) |
| Retained earnings at 31 December 20X1 | 499 |

The current cost reserve is the balancing figure.

| | $000 |
|---|---|
| Retained earnings | 499 |
| Current cost reserve | 707 |
| Reserves at 31 December 20X1 | 1,206 |

We can prove the current cost reserve:

| | $000 |
|---|---|
| Holding gains: | |
| Non-current assets (1,225 – 700) | 525 |
| Inventory (1,411 – 1,400) | 11 |
| Adjustments to current cost income statement (227 – 56) | 171 |
| | 707 |

### 6.4 The advantages and disadvantages of CCA

KEY POINT

Under CCA, physical capital is maintained, assets are stated at their value to the business and holding gains are eliminated from profit.

*Advantages*

The most important advantage of CCA is its relevance to users who wish to assess the **current state** or **recent performance** of the business.

Under CCA, physical capital is maintained, assets are stated at their value to the business and holding gains are eliminated from profit.

KEY POINT

The main disadvantages of current value are its possible greater **subjectivity** and lower reliability than historical cost.

*Disadvantages*

The main disadvantages of current value are its possible greater **subjectivity** and lower reliability than historical cost. A further disadvantage is its lack of familiarity. There may also be practical problems in using current cost accounting, such as the following.

- It is not always easy to obtain an index which is perfectly suitable for measuring the movement in the current cost of a particular type of asset.
- It is often difficult to obtain a suitable market value for specialist items.
- There may be no intention to replace an asset, possibly due to a change in the nature of the business.
- There may be no modern equivalent asset due to the advance of technology.

It has also been argued that CCA is not a system of inflation accounting as such, because it only adjusts for changes in the value of assets.

## 7 Real terms accounting

### 7.1 Introduction

As we have seen, neither current purchasing power nor current cost accounting are ideal as alternatives to historic cost accounting. Each system represents a particular view of an entity and implies particular objectives and priorities.

KEY POINT

**Real terms accounting** is a further system of inflation accounting that attempts to combine features of CPP and CCA accounting.

**Real terms accounting** is a further system of inflation accounting that attempts to combine features of CPP and CCA accounting.

An asset can be subject to two kinds of inflation:

- specific price inflation (unrealised holding gains)
- general inflation.

Real terms accounting attempts to show the effects of both.

***Example***

At the beginning of the year a company bought land costing $900. The land is worth $1,200 at the year end. General inflation throughout the year is 10%.

| | $ |
|---|---|
| Unrealised holding gain from property (1,200 – 900) | 300 |
| Less: Inflation adjustment ($900 at 10%) | (90) |
| 'Real' holding gain | 210 |

The 'real' holding gain represents the overall change in shareholders' wealth during the period.

## 7.2 The accounts

**The balance sheet**

This is almost exactly the same as under CCA accounting. Non-monetary assets are remeasured to their current cost.

The only difference is in the composition of the reserves. Instead of a current cost reserve there is a financial maintenance reserve.

**The income statement**

This is a reconciliation between historic cost profit and total 'real' gains. There are a number of different ways of presenting this, but essentially there are two adjustments:

- **Unrealised holding gains arising during the year**. This is the amount by which the current cost of the entity's assets (non-current assets and inventories) has increased during the year.
- **Inflation adjustment to shareholders' funds**. This is the amount by which general inflation has eroded the purchasing power of shareholders' funds during the year.

***Example***

The facts are as in the example of current cost accounting in the previous section.

**Historic cost income statement for the year ended 31 December 20X1**

| | $000 |
|---|---|
| Profit from operations | 267 |
| Interest | 33 |
| Profit before tax | 234 |
| Income tax expense | 40 |
| Profit for the year | 194 |

**Additional information:**

(1) The retail price index stood at 140 on 1 January 20X1 and 157 on 31 December 20X1.

(2) Dividends of $59,000 were paid during the year.

**You are required** to prepare the real terms current cost income statement for the year ended 31 December 20X1 and to show the analysis of reserves at that date.

### *Solution*

**Real terms current cost income statement for the year ended 31 December 20X1**

| | $000 | $000 |
|---|---|---|
| Historic cost profit for the financial year | | 194 |
| Add: unrealised holding gains arising during the year (W1) | 113 | |
| Less: inflation adjustment to shareholders' funds (W2) | (213) | |
| Real holding losses | | (100) |
| Total real gains | | 94 |

***Workings***

(W1) Unrealised holding gains arising during the year

| | $000 | $000 |
|---|---|---|
| Non-current assets: | | |
| Uplift from HC at end of year (1,225 – 700) | 525 | |
| Uplift from HC at beginning of year (1,200 – 800) | (400) | |
| | | 125 |
| Inventories: | | |
| Uplift from HC at end of year (1,411 – 1,400) | 11 | |
| Uplift from HC at beginning of year (1,373 – 1,350) | (23) | |
| | | (12) |
| | | 113 |

(W2) Inflation adjustment to shareholders' funds

$$\text{Opening CC shareholders' funds} \times \frac{\text{movement in RPI}}{\text{RPI at start of year}}$$

$$1{,}758 \times \frac{157 - 140}{140} = 213$$

**Reserves at 31 December 20X1**

Reserves consist of real gains and a financial capital maintenance reserve. The financial capital maintenance reserve is the inflation adjustment to shareholders' funds. Real gains is calculated below:

| | $000 |
|---|---|
| Current cost reserves at 1 January 20X1 | 958 |
| Real gains for the year | 94 |
| Less dividends paid | (59) |
| Retained earnings at 31 December 20X1 | 993 |

Reserves are analysed below:

| | $000 |
|---|---|
| Real gains | 993 |
| Financial capital maintenance reserve | 213 |
| Reserves at 31 December 20X1 | 1,206 |

## 8 IAS 29 *Financial Reporting in Hyperinflationary Economies*

### 8.1 Introduction

KEY POINT

Where an entity's financial statements are translated into another currency, hyper-inflation often gives rise to significant exchange differences which absorb reserves. In this situation, the financial statements may be so distorted that they no longer fairly present an entity's financial performance and financial position.

As we have seen, there are well known disadvantages of basing financial statements on historical cost.

- The amounts at which assets are measured in the balance sheet do not reflect their current values. Assets are likely to be significantly under-valued.
- Profits are likely to be overstated. Revenue is artificially inflated and often appears to rise rapidly, while depreciation is based on out of date costs.

Where an entity's financial statements are translated into another currency, hyper-inflation often gives rise to significant exchange differences which absorb reserves. In this situation, the financial statements may be so distorted that they no longer fairly present an entity's financial performance and financial position.

### 8.2 Hyperinflation

KEY POINT

IAS 29 requires adjustments to be made whenever an entity reports in the currency of a hyperinflationary economy.

IAS 29 requires adjustments to be made whenever an entity reports in the currency of a hyperinflationary economy, but no precise definition of hyperinflation is given. However, IAS 29 does give some indications of hyperinflation:

(a) the general population prefers to keep its wealth in non-monetary assets or in a relatively stable foreign currency. Amounts of local currency held are immediately invested to maintain purchasing power;

(b) the general population regards monetary amounts not in terms of the local currency but in terms of a relatively stable foreign currency. Prices may be quoted in that currency;

(c) sales and purchases on credit take place at prices that compensate for the expected loss of purchasing power during the credit period, even if the period is short;

(d) interest rates, wages and prices are linked to a price index; and

(e) the cumulative inflation rate over three years is approaching, or exceeds, 100%.

## 8.3 Restatement

KEY POINT

The basic requirement of IAS 29 is that the financial statements of an entity that reports in the currency of a hyperinflationary economy should be stated in terms of the measuring unit current at the balance sheet date.

It is very unlikely that you will be asked to restate a set of financial statements in the exam.

The basic requirement of IAS 29 is that the financial statements of an entity that reports in the currency of a hyperinflationary economy should be stated in terms of the measuring unit current at the balance sheet date.

It is very unlikely that you will be asked to restate a set of financial statements in the exam, but you should be aware of the general procedure for doing so, which is similar to the procedure for preparing CPP financial statements.

***Balance sheet***

(a) Non-monetary items in the balance sheet are restated by applying a general price index. For example, items of property, plant and equipment are restated from the date of acquisition (or the date of revaluation, if applicable) to the balance sheet date.

(b) Monetary items are not restated because they are already expressed in terms of the monetary unit current at the balance sheet date.

(c) At the date that IAS 29 is first applied, items in owner's equity (eg, equity shares) are restated by applying a general price index from the dates they were contributed or otherwise arose. Any revaluation surplus is eliminated. Restated retained earnings are derived as a balancing figure.

(d) At the end of subsequent periods, all components of owners' equity are restated by applying a general price index from the beginning of the period or the date of contribution, if later.

***Income statement***

All items in the income statement are restated by applying the change in the general price index from the dates when the items of income and expenses were initially recorded in the financial statements.

***Gain or loss on net monetary position***

The gain or loss on the net monetary position is the difference resulting from the restatement of non-monetary assets, owners' equity and income statement items. It should be included in net income and separately disclosed.

## 8.4 Dealing with hyperinflation in a foreign operation

KEY POINT

Where a group has a foreign subsidiary that operates in a country with a hyperinflationary economy, the financial statements of the foreign operation are adjusted to reflect current price levels (using indices) before the translation process is undertaken.

Where a group has a foreign subsidiary that operates in a country with a hyperinflationary economy, the financial statements of the foreign operation are adjusted to reflect current price levels (using indices) before the translation process is undertaken. This includes taking any gain or loss on the net monetary position through the income statement.

### *Example*

On 1 January 20X1 Cinnamon set up a subsidiary, Anise, in a country which suffered from high rates of inflation. The currency of this country is measured in Tambala (T). On the same date Anise acquired freehold land for T400,000.

Relevant exchange rates are as follows:

1 January 20X1 T5 = $1

31 December 20X4 T25 = $1

The relevant price index was 100 at 1 January 20X1 and 550 at 31 December 20X4.

Show the value at which the freehold land would be included in the consolidated financial statements of Cinnamon at 31 December 20X4:

(a) using normal translation rules (the closing rate/presentation currency method)

(b) adjusting to reflect current price levels.

***Solution***

| | *T* | *Rate* | *Inflation adjusted* | *Rate* | $ |
|---|---|---|---|---|---|
| At 1 January 20X1 | 400,000 | | | 5 | 80,000 |
| (a) Closing rate | 400,000 | | | 25 | 16,000 |
| (b) Current prices | 400,000 | 550/100 | 2,200,000 | 25 | 88,000 |

Use of the closing rate method without adjustments produces an amount based on the original cost. Because the exchange rate has increased from 5 to 25 over the three-year period, there is a cumulative exchange loss of $64,000 and the land appears to have fallen to only a quarter of its original value. The exchange loss may also significantly reduce reserves.

The adjustment for hyper-inflation is used to overcome the 'disappearing assets' problem. Method (b) adjusts the value of the land so that it reflects the effect of hyper-inflation over the three-year period. The land now appears to have increased in value since it was first acquired.

### 8.5 Economies that cease to be hyperinflationary

When an economy ceases to be hyperinflationary, and an entity discontinues preparing its accounts in accordance with IAS 29, it should treat the amounts expressed in the measuring unit at the previous balance sheet date as the basis for the carrying amounts in subsequent financial statements.

### 8.6 Disclosures

IAS 29 requires the following disclosures:

(a) the fact that the financial statements have been restated and, as a result, are stated in terms of the measuring unit current at the balance sheet date; and

(b) the identity and level of the price index at the balance sheet date and the movement in the index during the current and the previous reporting period.

## Summary

- The debate as to the measurement of income, assets and liabilities is made important by the deficiencies of HC accounting in an era of changing prices.
- Several current international standards permit or require the use of fair values for measuring certain assets. This can provide useful information to users of the financial statements, but may also cause practical problems.
- CPP and CCA are two possible solutions or partial solutions, with neither having gained universal support as a general replacement for HC accounting.
- IAS 29 requires entities that operate in hyperinflationary economies to restate their financial statements in terms of current values. Where a group has a

foreign subsidiary that operates under hyperinflation, the financial statements are restated before they are translated into the functional currency of the parent and included in the consolidation.

Having completed your study of this chapter, you should have achieved the following learning outcomes:

- explain the problems of profit measurement and alternative approaches to asset valuation
- explain measures to reduce distortion in financial statements when price levels change.

## Self-test questions

1 What are five deficiencies of HC accounting in a period of changing prices? (1.2)

2 What is another name for entry value accounting? (2.1)

3 In the definition of deprival value what is the recoverable amount? (2.2)

4 How is deprival value arrived at? (2.2)

5 Which basis of revaluing assets is favoured by the IASB? (3.4)

6 What is physical capital maintenance? (4.2)

7 What four adjustments are made in the current cost income statement? (6.2)

8 What is real terms accounting? (7.1)

9 What are the possible indications of hyperinflation? (8.2)

10 How does a parent account for a foreign subsidiary that operates in a hyperinflationary economy? (8.4)

## Objective test questions

### Question 1

Depro Inc, a property company, bought a five year lease on a large commercial property at a cost of $3,000,000 in a rapidly developing area. At 31 December 20X3 the lease has three years to run.

It is estimated that the cost of buying a five-year lease on similar premises in the same area is currently $4,000,000.

A local agent has advised that, if the company's lease were sold at 31 December 20X3 it would realise $2,000,000 but, because of the nature of the area in which the property is located, there would be restoration costs of approximately $100,000.

It is estimated that the property will generate rental income cash flows with a total net present value of $2,100,000 during the next three years.

Calculate the deprival value of the asset as at 31 December 20X3.

### Question 2

Which of the following statements, relating to systems which adjust financial statements for the impact of changing prices, are correct?

I The current purchasing power system is based on measuring the effect of changes in the purchasing power of currency

II The current cost accounting system attempts to reflect the value to the business of its operating assets

III The current purchasing power system is based on the "operating capability" concept of capital maintenance

IV Current cost accounts are prepared by adjusting all amounts in the accounts to reflect the value of money at one point in time.

**A** All four statements

**B** I, II and III only

**C** I, and II only

**D** III, and IV only

---

*For the answers to these questions, see the 'Answers' section at the end of the book.*

## Exam-type question

### Barty

'The recognition and correct treatment of holding gains in company financial statements are vital for a proper understanding of the position and performance of the business entity.'

**You are required:**

(a) to explain briefly the significance of the treatment of holding gains for the measurement of business profit **(5 marks)**

(b) to set out the arguments for and against the recognition of holding gains. **(10 marks)**

The following relates to the accounts of Barty, a property investment company.

The accounts contain:

**Balance sheet as at 31 December 20X7**

| | 20X7 | 20X6 |
|---|---|---|
| | $000 | $000 |
| Investment properties at market value | 14,125 | 12,579 |
| Other assets | 140 | 421 |
| | 14,265 | 13,000 |
| Share capital | 2,000 | 2,000 |
| Retained earnings | 4,720 | 4,597 |
| Investment property revaluation surplus | 7,545 | 6,403 |
| | 14,265 | 13,000 |

**Income statement for the year ended 31 December 20X7**

| | $000 |
|---|---|
| Rental income | 1,526 |
| Administrative expenses | (160) |
| Profit before tax | 1,366 |
| Income tax expense | (793) |
| Profit after tax | 573 |
| Dividends paid | (450) |
| Retained profit | 123 |

**Adjusted earnings statement for the year ended 31 December 20X7**

| | $000 | $000 |
|---|---|---|
| Net profit after tax for the year | | 573 |
| Unrealised gains for the year on revaluations of investment properties | 925 | |
| Less: Inflation adjustment to shareholders' funds | (520) | |
| Real holding gains | | 405 |
| Total real gains | | 978 |
| Dividends paid | | (450) |
| Amount retained | | 528 |

*Further information:*

- Investment properties are revalued annually at each year end.
- Investment properties were acquired for $621,000 during 20X7.
- A general price index has risen by 4% during 20X7.

(c) **You are required** to comment on the adjusted earnings statement prepared by the company. **(10 marks)**

**(Total: 25 marks)**

*For answer to this question, see the 'Answers' section at the end of the book.*

## Feedback to activity

### Activity 1

| | | | $ |
|---|---|---|---|
| (a) | NRC = | Gross replacement cost | 100,000 |
| | | Less: Accumulated depreciation ⅖ | 40,000 |
| | | | 60,000 |
| | NRV = | Sale proceeds | 30,000 |
| | | Less: Costs to sell | 5,000 |
| | | | 25,000 |
| | NPV = | discounted value of future cash flows | |

| | | |
|---|---|---|
| Year 1 | $\frac{40,000}{1.1}$ = | 36,363 |
| Year 2 | $\frac{40,000}{1.21}$ = | 33,057 |
| Year 3 | $\frac{40,000}{1.331}$ = | 30,052 |
| Total | | 99,472 |

DV = lower of $60,000 and (higher of $25,000 and $99,472)

Deprival value is the replacement cost of $60,000

(b) RC as before 60,000

NRV as before 25,000

NPV when there are no cash flows = Nil

DV = lower of $60,000 and (higher of $25,000 and nil)

Deprival value is the net realisable value of $25,000

(c) RC as before 60,000
NRV as before 25,000

NPV = discounted value of future cash flows

| | | |
|---|---|---|
| Year 1 | $\frac{22,000}{1.1}$ = | 20,000 |
| Year 2 | $\frac{22,000}{1.21}$ = | 18,181 |
| Year 3 | $\frac{22,000}{1.331}$ = | 16,529 |
| Total | | 54,710 |

DV = lower of $60,000 and (higher of $25,000 and $54,710)

Deprival value is the net present value of $54,710

Chapter 12

# ACCOUNTING FOR EMPLOYEE BENEFIT COSTS

## Syllabus content

- Retirement benefits, including pension schemes – defined benefit schemes and defined contribution schemes, actuarial deficits and surpluses (IAS 19).

## Contents

# Introduction

Many employers provide pension schemes for their employees. A pension scheme is normally a separate entity from the employer itself and therefore it prepares its own accounts. Pension scheme accounts are not included in your syllabus. However, the employer still has to account for the cost of providing pensions in its own financial statements and this can give rise to particular accounting problems.

The chapter begins by explaining the different types of pension schemes and some of the terminology involved. You are unlikely to be examined on the detail of this, but you need a general awareness of the way in which pension schemes operate in order to understand the problems of accounting for pension costs.

The most important part of the chapter concerns the requirements of IAS 19 *Employee Benefits*. IAS 19 is a complex standard. However, the Examiner will be testing your understanding of the main principles and the numbers involved are normally fairly simple.

It is becoming increasingly common for directors and other employees to receive share options as part of their remuneration. This chapter also looks at IFRS 2 *Share-Based Payment,* which explains how to account for the effects of transactions in which an entity receives goods or services in exchange for its equity instruments.

## 1 Short-term employee benefits

IAS 19 covers accounting for short-term employee benefits, which do not present the accounting problems of retirement benefit plans.

KEY POINT

Short-term employee benefits should be charged in the income statement for the period(s) benefiting from the services.

The provisions are designed to ensure that costs fall in the periods benefiting from them.

***Details:***

- **Wages, salaries and social security contributions** – Recognise as expenses as the services are rendered, with accruals at the balance sheet date.
- **Annual leave and sick leave** – Accrue for annual leave and sick leave entitlements at the balance sheet date if the employee may accumulate them for future periods.
- **Profit-sharing and bonuses** – Recognise in the period in which the related profit is recognised.
- **Death-in-service benefits** – If the benefits are insured, the cost is the premium paid. If not insured, payments made or due to be made for deaths up to the balance sheet date should be taken.

## 2 Retirement benefit plans

### 2.1 Types of plan

KEY POINT

There are two main types of pension plan: defined contribution plans; and defined benefit plans.

There are two main types of pension plan.

***Defined contribution plans***

In a defined contribution plan the employer and employee will pay a defined contribution into a pension scheme each period. The contribution may be a fixed percentage of salary or a fixed cash amount. When an employee retires, their pension will be limited to the funds available in the pension plan. If the plan has performed badly, then the pensioner loses out. The former employer has no obligation to make good any shortfalls in the scheme. Traditionally, defined contribution schemes tended to be for small employers or for personal pension plans. However, large employers are starting to convert from defined benefit schemes to defined contribution schemes.

The cost to the employer can be measured with reasonable certainty. The charge in the income statement will be the contributions accruing during the year. Normally, the only balance sheet entry is an accrual for contributions in respect of work done that have not yet been paid over to the pension plan

***Defined benefit plans***

In a defined benefit plan the benefits to be paid will usually depend upon either the average pay of the employee during their career, or more typically, their final pay. An actuary will calculate how much must be paid into the plan each year in order to provide the promised pension. This will normally be a steady percentage of payroll cost, but if the plan performs badly then the employer may have an obligation to make good any deficit. This obligation may be a specific legal requirement or a constructive obligation in the interest of good staff relations. Because the employer normally has to make good any deficits, then the employer can also benefit from any surplus in the fund. This is normally done by taking a pension holiday during which the employer will pay reduced contributions. Defined benefit plans are normally used by large employers only.

The cost to the employer is obviously going to fluctuate from year to year. This causes the main accounting problem addressed by IAS 19.

### 2.2 Actuarial considerations

KEY POINT

An actuary's advice is required to determine the calculations required with defined benefit plans.

In view of the very long-term nature of the retirement benefit commitment it is necessary to make use of actuarial calculations in determining the cost in respect of defined benefit plans. In the case of defined contribution plans there is no need for actuarial advice in order to establish the retirement benefit cost although such advice may be required for other purposes in connection with the operation of the plan.

In defined benefit plans the choice of assumptions can have a major effect on the contribution rate calculated at each valuation.

The assumptions which the actuary must make in carrying out their valuation will be about matters such as future rates of inflation and pay increases, increases to benefits in payment, earnings on investments, the number of employees joining the scheme, the age profile of employees and the probability that employees will die or leave the company's employment before they reach retiring age. The actuary will view the assumptions as a whole, they will make assumptions which are mutually compatible, in the knowledge that, if experience departs from the assumptions made, the effects of such departures may well be offsetting, notably in the case of investment yields and increases in prices and earnings.

DEFINITIONS

**Funding** is the transfer of assets to an entity (the fund) separate from the enterprise to meet future obligations for the payment of retirement benefits.

**Current service cost** is the increase in the present value of the defined benefit obligation resulting from employee service in the current period.

**Past service cost** is the increase in the present value of the defined benefit obligation for employee service in past periods, resulting in the current period from the introduction of, or changes to, post-employment benefits.

**Actuarial gains and losses** comprise experience adjustments (the effects of differences between the previous actuarial assumptions and what has actually occurred), and the effects of changes in actuarial assumptions.

### 2.3 Some further definitions

To understand the provisions of IAS 19, especially those relating to defined benefit plans, it is necessary to understand the meaning of some technical terms used:

(a) **Funding**

Funding is the transfer of assets to an entity (the fund) separate from the enterprise to meet future obligations for the payment of retirement benefits.

Funding needs to be distinguished from the rate at which costs are charged in the income statement.

(b) **Current service cost**

Current service cost is the increase in the present value of the defined benefit obligation resulting from employee service in the current period.

(c) **Past service cost**

Past service cost is the increase in the present value of the defined benefit obligation for employee service in past periods, resulting in the current period from the introduction of, or changes to, post-employment benefits.

Past service cost may be either positive (when benefits are introduced or improved) or negative (when existing benefits are reduced).

(d) **Actuarial gains and losses**

These comprise:

(i) experience adjustments (the effects of differences between the previous actuarial assumptions and what has actually occurred), and

(ii) the effects of changes in actuarial assumptions.

## 3 The requirements of IAS 19

KEY POINT

An entity should recognise:

- a **liability** when an employee has provided service in exchange for employee benefits to be paid in the future
- an **expense** when the entity consumes the economic benefit arising from service provided by the employee in exchange for employee benefits.

### 3.1 Objective of the standard

The objective of IAS 19 is to prescribe the accounting and disclosure requirements for employee benefits. An entity should recognise:

- a **liability** when an employee has provided service in exchange for employee benefits to be paid in the future
- an **expense** when the entity consumes the economic benefit arising from service provided by the employee in exchange for employee benefits.

The achievement of these objectives is routine for short-term employee benefits as explained above. It becomes more difficult when dealing with post-employment benefit plans (retirement benefit plans).

As outlined above, there are two main types of post-employment benefit plan, the defined contribution plan and the defined benefit plan.

KEY POINT

Accounting for defined contribution plans is reasonably simple, because the obligation of the employing entity is determined by the contributions to be made in each accounting period.

### 3.2 Defined contribution plans

Accounting for defined contribution plans is reasonably simple, because the obligation of the employing entity is determined by the contributions to be made in each accounting period. These contributions are usually based on employees' salary levels in the period.

IAS 19 requires disclosure of the amount recognised as an expense in the period.

### 3.3 Defined benefit plans

An entity should recognise a liability in its balance sheet. In simple terms this is the present value of the defined benefit obligation at the balance sheet date, less the fair value (normally the market value) of plan assets at the balance sheet date.

The expense recognised in the income statement is the net of: current service cost; interest cost; expected return on any plan assets; and actuarial gains and losses.

The starting point for calculating the amount of the liability and the expense is an actuarial valuation of the defined benefit obligation.

KEY POINT

A defined benefit plan is usually based on employees' terminal salary. Provision for the benefit has to be made many years in advance of its arising, and it is therefore necessary to use actuarial techniques to estimate annual expenses and the accrued liability.

A defined benefit plan is usually based on employees' terminal salary. Provision for the benefit has to be made many years in advance of its arising, and it is therefore necessary to use actuarial techniques to estimate annual expenses and the accrued liability. Estimates have to be made of factors such as:

- employee turnover
- employee mortality
- future increases in salary
- the expected rate of return on plan assets
- the discount rate to be used in computations.

KEY POINT

The discount rate used to determine the present value of the defined benefit plan liability should be the current market yield obtainable on high quality corporate bonds.

Estimates of future salary increases should take account of inflation, seniority, promotion and other relevant factors, such as supply and demand in the employment market.

The discount rate should be determined by reference to market yields at the balance sheet date on high quality corporate bonds or, if this is not practicable, by reference to yields on government bonds.

The illustration in the next section shows the operation of the projected unit credit method of determining the present value of obligations under a defined benefit plan, and hence determining the current period expense to be recognised.

### 3.4 The projected unit credit method

The allocation of benefit costs to accounting periods can be made in several ways. The method required in IAS 19 is the projected unit credit method, also known as the accrued benefit method pro-rated on service or as the benefit/years of service method.

### 3.5 Introducing a new plan or improving the benefits in an existing plan

When a new retirement benefit plan is introduced, employees are usually given benefit rights for years of service before the introduction of the plan. To cover the costs of these past service costs the employer will incur a considerable liability which has to be recognised.

The method of accounting for these costs depends on the status of the benefits. If employees have the right to receive benefits under the plan immediately, the benefits are said to be 'vested' and the cost must be recognised immediately. If employees become entitled to benefits only at some later date, the benefits become vested at that later date, and the costs may be spread on a straight-line basis over the average period until the vesting date.

The same principle applies when the benefits under an existing plan are improved.

***Illustration***

An entity operates a pension plan that provides a pension of 2% of final salary for each year of service. The benefits become vested after five years of service. On 1 January 20X5 the enterprise improves the pension to 2.5% of final salary for each year of service starting from 1 January 20X1. At the date of the improvement, the present value of the additional benefits for service from 1 January 20X1 to 1 January 20X5 is as follows:

| | $000 |
|---|---|
| Employees with more than five years' service at 1.1.X5 | 150 |
| Employees with less than five years' service at 1.1.X5 | |
| (average period until vesting: three years) | 120 |
| | 270 |

The entity will recognise $150,000 immediately because those benefits are already vested. The enterprise recognises $120,000 on a straight-line basis over three years from 1 January 20X5.

### 3.6 Actuarial gains and losses

KEY POINT

As time passes, differences will arise because the actual out-turn does not match the original estimates. The corrections for these differences are called experience adjustments.

The initial liability recognised for a defined benefit plan is based on a number of assumptions, as we have seen. As time passes, differences will arise because the actual out-turn does not match the original estimates. The corrections for these differences are called experience adjustments.

In addition, the actuarial assumptions may be changed in the light of events.

The combined effects of these changes to the position of the plan are referred to as actuarial gains and losses.

IAS 19 has detailed requirements as to the recognition as income or expense of these gains and losses; they are to be recognised if they exceed the greater of:

- 10% of the present value of the plan obligation
- 10% of the fair value of plan assets.

KEY POINT

Actuarial gains and losses must be recognised in the income statement if they exceed a 10% corridor.

In other words, the liability recognised in the balance sheet may deviate within a 10% 'corridor', but once it moves more than 10% from the current estimate of the plan obligations or assets a gain or loss must be recognised to adjust the liability back into the corridor. The whole of the gain or loss need not be recognised immediately, it may be spread over the expected average remaining working lives of the employees.

IAS 19 allows an entity to adopt other methods of adjusting for actuarial gains and losses provided the following conditions are satisfied:

- the alternative method results in a faster recognition of actuarial gains and losses
- the same basis is applied to both gains and losses
- the basis is applied consistently from period to period.

In addition, an entity may choose to recognise actuarial gains and losses immediately they occur, in the statement of changes in equity or the statement of recognised income and expense. This is an alternative to recognising actuarial gains and losses in the income statement using the '10% corridor' approach.

An entity adopting this accounting policy would be required to apply it consistently to all its actuarial gains and losses.

The IASB believes that this approach should be available because it would provide transparent information about defined benefit plans in the financial statements. In particular, this approach would make users aware of the full extent of actuarial gains and losses, which can be large and volatile.

## 3.7 A comprehensive example

This example is a slightly simplified version of one appearing in an Appendix to IAS 19.

Exam questions will almost certainly be considerably simpler than this. However, you do need to understand and to be able to explain the way in which the calculations work. Therefore you should study and work through this example carefully.

***Background information***

The following information is given about a funded defined benefit plan. To keep interest computations simple, all transactions are assumed to occur at the year end. The present value of the obligation and the fair value of the plan assets were both 1,000 at 1 January 20X1. Net cumulative unrecognised actuarial gains at that date were 140.

| | *20X1* | *20X2* | *20X3* |
|---|---|---|---|
| Discount rate at start of year | 10.0% | 9.0% | 8.0% |
| Expected rate of return on plan assets at start of year | 12.0% | 11.1% | 10.3% |
| Current service cost | 130 | 220 | 150 |
| Benefits paid | 150 | 180 | 190 |
| Contributions | 90 | 100 | 110 |
| Present value of obligation at 31 December | 1,141 | 1,197 | 1,295 |
| Fair value of plan assets at 31 December | 1,092 | 1,109 | 1,093 |
| Expected average remaining working lives of employees (years) | 10 | 10 | 10 |

**Step 1**

The first step is to summarise these figures to determine the amount of the actuarial gains or losses for the period.

The present values of the obligations at the end of each year are known, and so are the fair values of the plan assets.

It is therefore possible to find the actuarial gains or losses as balancing figures:

| | *20X1* | *20X2* | *20X3* |
|---|---|---|---|
| Present value of obligation, 1 January | 1,000 | 1,141 | 1,197 |
| Interest cost | 100 | 103 | 96 |
| Current service cost | 130 | 220 | 150 |
| Benefits paid | (150) | (180) | (190) |
| Actuarial (gain) loss on obligation (balancing figure) | 61 | (87) | 42 |
| Present value of obligation, 31 December | 1,141 | 1,197 | 1,295 |
| Fair value of plan assets, 1 January | 1,000 | 1,092 | 1,109 |
| Expected return on plan assets | 120 | 121 | 114 |
| Contributions | 90 | 100 | 110 |
| Benefits paid | (150) | (180) | (190) |
| Actuarial gain (loss) on plan assets (balancing figure) | 32 | (24) | (50) |
| Fair value of plan assets, 31 December | 1,092 | 1,109 | 1,093 |

***Notes:***

1 It is necessary to make the calculations year by year because the closing figures for 20X1 form the opening figures for the following year.

2 **Obligations**

(a) The interest cost figures are calculated by applying the given discount rate to the opening obligation values.

(b) The current service cost is the increase in the present value of the obligation resulting from employee service in the current year.

(c) Benefits paid reduce the obligation.

(d) The actuarial gains or losses emerge as balancing figures.

3 **Assets**

(a) The expected return on plan assets is obtained by applying the given percentages to the opening plan asset values.

(b) Contributions from the employer for the year are given and increase plan assets.

(c) Benefits paid are also given and they reduce plan assets.

(d) The actuarial gains or losses on plan assets emerge as balancing figures.

4 **General**

It may be difficult to understand which figures appear in the 'obligations' calculation and which in the 'assets' calculation. The point is that actual cash receipts and payments appear in the plan assets calculation, whereas the obligations calculation is concerned with movements in the future liability. Benefits paid appear in both calculations because the payment reduces assets but also reduces the liability.

**Step 2**

Calculate the limits of the 'corridor'. These are the greater of:

- 10% of the present value of the obligation before deducting plan assets
- 10% of the fair value of any plan assets.

| | *20X1* | *20X2* | *20X3* |
|---|---|---|---|
| 10% of opening obligations | 100 | 114 | 120 |
| 10% of opening plan assets | 100 | 109 | 111 |
| The corridor limits are therefore: | 100 | 114 | 120 |

**Step 3**

Work out whether any actuarial gains or losses need to be recognised. This means checking to see whether the net cumulative unrecognised gains and losses fall outside the corridor limits.

| | *20X1* | *20X2* | *20X3* |
|---|---|---|---|
| Net cumulative unrecognised actuarial gains (losses) at 1 January | 140 | 107 | 170 |
| Limits of 'corridor' at 1 January | 100 | 114 | 120 |
| Excess [A] | 40 | – | 50 |
| Average expected remaining working lives (years) [B] | 10 | 10 | 10 |
| Actuarial gain (loss) to be recognised [A/B] | 4 | – | 5 |
| Unrecognised actuarial gains (losses) at 1 January | 140 | 107 | 170 |
| Actuarial gain (loss) for year – obligation | (61) | 87 | (42) |
| Actuarial gain (loss) for year – plan assets | 32 | (24) | (50) |
| Subtotal | 111 | 170 | 78 |
| Actuarial (gain) loss recognised | (4) | – | (5) |
| Unrecognised actuarial gains (losses) at 31 December | 107 | 170 | 73 |

This table has to be prepared year by year because the closing figure for 20X1 is the opening figure for 20X2, and so on.

***Notes:***

**20X1**

- In 20X1 there is an opening 140 actuarial gain. This is 40 outside the corridor limit of 100, so a gain of 4 has to be recognised in the income statement. The gain is 4 because the 40 has to be spread over the 10 year future service life of the employees.
- The unrecognised actuarial gains at the end of 20X1 are calculated by picking up the loss on the plan obligation and the gain on the plan assets from Step 1. The opening balance is 140, so the closing balance becomes 111, reduced to 107 because 4 of the closing gain is recognised in the income statement.

**20X2**

- The opening figure for 20X2 is 107. This is inside the corridor limit, so no gain or loss needs to be recognised.
- The cumulative position at the end of 20X2 is calculated by bringing in the gain on the obligation and the loss on the plan assets from Step 1. The closing figure is 170.

**20X3**

- The opening figure of 170 is 50 outside the corridor limit, so a gain of 5 is to be recognised in the income statement.
- The cumulative unrecognised actuarial gain at the end of 20X3 is calculated by bringing in the loss on the obligation and the loss on the plan assets, leading to a closing figure of 73 after deducting the 5 recognised as a gain in the income statement.

**Step 4**

Calculate the amounts to appear in the balance sheet and income statement.

(a) **The balance sheet liability**

This is the difference between the plan obligations and the plan assets (net liability) plus the unrecognised gains calculated at Step 3:

| | *20X1* | *20X2* | *20X3* |
|---|---|---|---|
| Present value of the obligation | 1,141 | 1,197 | 1,295 |
| Fair value of plan assets | (1,092) | (1,109) | (1,093) |
| | 49 | 88 | 202 |
| Unrecognised actuarial gains (losses) | 107 | 170 | 73 |
| **Liability recognised in balance sheet** | 156 | 258 | 275 |

(b) **The income statement expense**

This is the current service cost plus interest cost, minus the return on plan assets, adjusted for the recognised actuarial gain in years 20X1 and 20X3:

| | *20X1* | *20X2* | *20X3* |
|---|---|---|---|
| Current service cost | 130 | 220 | 150 |
| Interest cost | 100 | 103 | 96 |
| Expected return on plan assets | (120) | (121) | (114) |
| Net actuarial (gain) loss recognised in year | (4) | – | (5) |
| **Expense recognised in the income statement** | 106 | 202 | 127 |

(c) **Further disclosures**

The entity is also required to disclose the movements in the net liability during the year and the actual return on plan assets (see Disclosure requirements below):

**Movements in the net liability recognised in the balance sheet**

| | *20X1* | *20X2* | *20X3* |
|---|---|---|---|
| Opening net liability | 140 | 156 | 258 |
| Expense as above | 106 | 202 | 127 |
| Contributions | (90) | (100) | (110) |
| Closing net liability | 156 | 258 | 275 |

This statement reconciles the figures in the balance sheet using the charges in the income statement.

**Actual return on plan assets**

| | *20X1* | *20X2* | *20X3* |
|---|---|---|---|
| Expected return on plan assets | 120 | 121 | 114 |
| Actuarial gain (loss) on plan assets | 32 | (24) | (50) |
| Actual return on plan assets | 152 | 97 | 64 |

## 3.8 Curtailments and settlements

KEY POINT

A **curtailment** occurs when an entity either: is demonstrably committed to make a material reduction in the number of employees covered by a plan; or amends the terms of a defined benefit plan such that a material element of future service by current employees will no longer qualify for benefits.

A **curtailment** occurs when an entity either:

- is demonstrably committed to make a material reduction in the number of employees covered by a plan; or
- amends the terms of a defined benefit plan such that a material element of future service by current employees will no longer qualify for benefits, or will qualify only for reduced benefits.

A curtailment often occurs when an entity carries out a restructuring. For example, the entity may close a factory and make all the employees redundant.

KEY POINT

A **settlement** occurs when an entity enters into a transaction that eliminates all further legal or constructive obligation for part or all of the benefits provided under a defined benefit plan. For example, employees may receive a lump sum in exchange for their rights to receive specified benefits.

A **settlement** occurs when an entity enters into a transaction that eliminates all further legal or constructive obligation for part or all of the benefits provided under a defined benefit plan. For example, employees may receive a lump sum in exchange for their rights to receive specified benefits.

Gains and losses on the curtailment or settlement of a defined benefit plan are recognised in the income statement when the curtailment or settlement occurs.The gain or loss on a curtailment or settlement should comprise:

- any resulting change in the present value of the defined benefit obligation
- any resulting change in the fair value of the plan assets
- any related actuarial gains and losses and past service cost that had not previously been recognised.

## 3.9 Disclosure requirements

KEY POINT

IAS 19 requires extensive disclosures in respect of defined benefit plans.

IAS 19 has extensive disclosure requirements.

An entity should disclose the following information about defined benefit plans:

(a) the entity's accounting policy for recognising actuarial gains and losses

(b) a general description of the type of plan

(c) a reconciliation of the assets and liabilities recognised in the balance sheet, showing at least:

(i) the present value at the balance sheet date of defined benefit obligations that are wholly unfunded

(ii) the present value (before deducting the fair value of plan assets) at the balance sheet date of defined benefit obligations that are wholly or partly funded

(iii) the fair value of any plan assets at the balance sheet date

(iv) the net actuarial gains or losses not recognised in the balance sheet

(v) the past service cost not yet recognised in the balance sheet on the introduction of a plan or improvements to an existing one

(vi) the amounts recognised in the balance sheet

(d) the amounts included in the fair value of plan assets for:

(i) each category of the reporting entity's own financial instruments

(ii) any property occupied by, or other assets used by, the reporting entity

(e) a reconciliation showing the movements during the period in the net liability (or asset) recognised in the balance sheet

(f) the total expense recognised in the income statement for each of the following, and the line item(s) of the income statement in which they are included:

(i) current service cost

(ii) interest cost

(iii) expected return on plan assets

(iv) actuarial gains and losses

(v) past service cost

(vi) the effect of any curtailment or settlement

(g) the actual return on plan assets

(h) the principal actuarial assumptions used as at the balance sheet date, including, where applicable:

(i) the discount rates

(ii) the expected rates of return on any plan assets for the periods presented in the financial statements

(iii) the expected rates of salary increases (and of changes in an index or other variable specified in the formal or constructive terms of a plan as the basis for future benefit increases)

(iv) medical cost trend rates

(v) any other material actuarial assumptions used.

An entity should disclose each actuarial assumption in absolute terms (for example as an absolute percentage) and not just as a margin between different percentages or other variables.

### *Activity 1*

Boar operates a defined benefit retirement benefits plan. For the year ended 31 December 20X4, the following information is relevant:

The expected return on the plan assets is $8 million.

The estimated current service cost is $10 million.

The unwinding of the discount on plan liabilities is $4 million.

Contributions paid to the plan total $12 million.

Actuarial gains less losses for the period give a net loss of $15 million.

Net cumulative unrecognised actuarial gains less losses from previous periods are immaterial.

What is the charge to the income statement in respect of retirement benefits for the year ended 31 December 20X4?

*Feedback to this activity is at the end of the chapter.*

### 3.10 Termination benefits

Termination benefits are payments made as a result of an employer's decision to terminate an employee's employment before normal retirement date or because of an employee's decision to accept voluntary redundancy.

The cost of these payments should be recognised when the employer is demonstrably committed to making them. If they are due to be paid more than twelve months after the balance sheet date they should be discounted at the rate based on the yield at the balance date on high quality corporate bonds.

## 4 IFRS 2 *Share-Based Payment*

### 4.1 The problem

The use of share-based payment has increased in recent years. For example, part of the remuneration of directors is often in the form of shares or options. An entity's employees may become entitled to shares or share options, provided they remain in the entity's employment for a specific period of time.

Until recently, there has been no accounting standard providing comprehensive guidance on accounting for share-based payment. If companies paid their employees in cash, an expense was recognised in the income statement. However, if companies paid their employees in share options, no expense was recognised. This was an accounting anomaly.

### 4.2 Should share-based payment be recognised in the financial statements?

There are a number of arguments for *not* recognising share-based payment. The IASB has rejected them all, arguing in favour of recognising share-based payment.

***No cost therefore no charge***

A charge for shares or options should not be recognised because the entity does not have to sacrifice cash or other assets. There is no cost to the entity.

This argument ignores the fact that a transaction has occurred. The employees have provided valuable services to the entity in return for valuable shares or options. If this argument were applied, the financial statements would fail to reflect the economic transactions that had occurred.

***Earnings per share would be hit twice***

The charge to the income statement for the employee services consumed reduced the entity's earnings. At the same time there is an increase in the number of shares issued (or to be issued).

However, the double impact on earnings per share simply reflects the two economic events that have occurred: the entity has issued shares, thus increasing the denominator of the EPS calculation, and it has also consumed the resources it received for those shares, thus reducing the numerator. Issuing shares to employees, instead of paying them in cash, requires a greater increase in the entity's earnings in order to maintain its earnings per share. Recognising the transaction ensures that its economic consequences are reported.

***Adverse economic consequences***

Recognition of employee share-based payment might discourage entities from introducing or continuing employee share plans.

If this were the case, this might be because the requirement for entities to account properly for employee share plans had revealed the economic consequences of such plans. This would correct the present economic distortion, whereby entities are able to obtain and consume resources by issuing valuable shares or options without having to account for such transactions.

The IASB has now issued IFRS 2 *Share-Based Payment.*

## 4.3 The basic principle

KEY POINT

IFRS 2 requires an entity to reflect the effects of share-based payment transactions in its financial statements.

IFRS 2 requires an entity to reflect the effects of share-based payment transactions in its financial statements.

There are two main types of transaction:

(a) **equity-settled share-based payment transactions**, in which the entity receives goods or services in exchange for equity instruments of the entity (including shares or share options)

(b) **cash-settled share-based payment transactions**, in which the entity acquires goods or services in exchange for amounts of cash that are based on the price (or value) of the entity's shares or other equity instruments of the entity.

When an entity receives goods or services as a result of a share-based payment transaction it recognises either an expense or an asset. Goods are normally recognised as assets, while services (such as those received from an employee) are normally recognised as an expense.

If the goods or services are received in exchange for equity (eg, for share options), the entity recognises an increase in equity.

KEY POINT

To recognise an equity-settled share-based payment transaction:

Dr Expense/Asset
Cr Equity

To recognise a cash-settled share-based payment transaction:

Dr Expense/Asset
Cr Liability

If the goods or services are received or acquired in a cash-settled share-based payment transaction the entity recognises a liability.

So, to recognise an equity settled share-based payment transaction, the double entry is:

Dr Expense/Asset
Cr Equity

and to recognise a cash settled share-based payment transaction:

Dr Expense/Asset
Cr Liability

There are two further issues in accounting for share-based payment: how to measure the value of the goods and services received; and how to allocate the effects of the transaction to accounting periods.

## 4.4 Measurement

KEY POINT

IFRS 2 states that the goods or services received and the corresponding increase in equity should be measured at **fair value**.

***Equity-settled share-based payment transactions***

IFRS 2 states that the goods or services received and the corresponding increase in equity should be measured at **fair value**. **Fair value** is the amount for which an asset could be exchanged, a liability settled, or an equity instrument granted could be exchanged, between knowledgeable, willing parties in an arm's length transaction.

The transaction is measured either at the fair value of the goods and services received or the fair value of the equity instruments granted:

- Where the transaction is with **parties other than employees**, the transaction is measured at the fair value of the goods and services received. (There is a rebuttable presumption that this can be estimated reliably.) Fair value should be measured at **the date the entity obtains the goods** or the other party to the transaction renders service.
- Where the fair value of the goods or services received cannot be measured reliably, their value should be measured by reference to the fair value of the equity instruments granted, measured at **grant date**.
- Where the transaction grants shares, share options or other equity instruments to employees as part of their remuneration package, the entity measures the transaction at the fair value of the equity instruments granted. (This is because it is difficult to value employee services reliably.) The fair value of the equity instruments should be measured at **grant date**.

DEFINITION

**Grant date** is the date at which the entity and another party (including an employee) agree to a share-based payment arrangement.

**Grant date** is the date at which the entity and another party (including an employee) agree to a share-based payment arrangement. At grant date the entity confers on the other party the right to cash, other assets, or equity instruments of the entity, provided the specified vesting conditions, if any, are met.

***Valuing equity instruments***

KEY POINT

Where a transaction is measured by reference to the fair value of the equity instruments granted, fair value should be based on **market prices**.

Where a transaction is measured by reference to the fair value of the equity instruments granted, fair value should be based on **market prices**. If market prices are not available, the entity should estimate the fair value of the equity instruments granted using a recognised valuation technique. (You will not be asked to apply a valuation technique in the exam.)

***Cash-settled share-based payment transactions***

The basic principle is that the entity measures the goods or services acquired and the liability incurred at the **fair value of the liability**.

Until the liability is settled, the entity should **remeasure** the fair value of the liability at each reporting date until the liability is settled and at the date of settlement. Changes in fair value are recognised in profit or loss (ie, in the income statement) for the period.

Examples of cash settled share-based payment transactions:

(a) share appreciation rights: employees become entitled to a future cash payment based on the increase in the entity's share price from a specified level over a specified period of time

(b) an entity might grant to its employees a right to receive a future cash payment by granting to them a right to shares that are redeemable.

## 4.5 Allocating the expense to accounting periods

When share options are granted to employees as part of their remuneration package, the employees usually have to meet specified conditions before actually becoming entitled to the shares. For example, they may have to complete a specified period of service or to achieve particular performance targets. For this reason, the transaction normally has to be recognised over more than one accounting period.

KEY POINT

IFRS 2 states that an entity should account for services as they are rendered by the counterparty (eg, the employee) during the vesting period.

DEFINITION

The **vesting period** is the period during which all the specified vesting conditions of a share-based payment arrangement are to be satisfied.

IFRS 2 states that an entity should account for services as they are rendered by the counterparty (e.g. the employee) during the vesting period.

To **vest** means to become an entitlement. Under a share-based payment arrangement, a counterparty's right to receive cash, other assets, or equity instruments of the entity **vests** upon satisfaction of any specified vesting conditions.

The **vesting period** is the period during which all the specified vesting conditions of a share-based payment arrangement are to be satisfied.

For example if an employee is granted share options on condition that he or she completes five years' service, then the services are rendered by the employee over that five-year vesting period.

The entity should recognise an amount for the goods or services received during the vesting period based on the best available estimate of the number of equity instruments expected to vest. It should revise that estimate if subsequent information indicates that the number of equity instruments expected to vest differs from previous estimates. On vesting date, the entity should revise the estimate to equal the number of equity instruments that actually vest.

### *Example*

On 1 January 20X1 an entity grants 100 share options to each of its 500 employees. Each grant is conditional upon the employee working for the entity until 31 December 20X3. The fair value of each share option is $15.

During 20X1 20 employees leave and the entity estimates that 20% of the employees will leave during the three year period.

During 20X2 a further 20 employees leave and the entity now estimates that 15% of its employees will leave during the three-year period.

During 20X3 a further 10 employees leave.

**Required:**

Calculate the remuneration expense that will be recognised in respect of the share-based payment transaction for each of the three years ended 31 December 20X3.

### *Solution*

The entity recognises the remuneration expense as the employees' services are received during the three-year vesting period. The amount recognised is based on the fair value of the share options granted at the grant date (1 January 20X1).

The entity estimates the number of options expected to vest by estimating the number of employees likely to leave. This estimate is revised at each year end. The expense recognised for the year is based on this estimate. On the vesting date (31 December 20X3) it recognises an amount based on the number of options that actually vest.

A total of 50 employees left during the three year period and therefore 45,000 options (500 – 50 × 100) vested.

The amount recognised as an expense for each of the three years is calculated as follows:

| | | *Expense for year* | *Cumulative expense at year-end* |
|---|---|---|---|
| | | $ | $ |
| 20X1 | 50,000 × 80% × 15 × 1/3 | 200,000 | 200,000 |
| 20X2 | 50,000 × 85% × 15 × 2/3 | 225,000 | 425,000 |
| 20X3 | 45,000 × 15 | 250,000 | 675,000 |

### 4.6 Disclosures

KEY POINT

Entities should disclose information that enables users of the financial statements to understand the nature and extent of share-based payment arrangements that existed during the period.

Entities should disclose information that enables users of the financial statements to understand the nature and extent of share-based payment arrangements that existed during the period:

(a) a description of each type of share-based payment arrangement that existed at any time during the period

(b) the number and weighted average exercise prices of share options:
  - (i) outstanding at the beginning of the period
  - (ii) granted during the period
  - (iii) forfeited during the period
  - (iv) exercised during the period
  - (v) expired during the period
  - (vi) outstanding at the end of the period
  - (vii) exercisable at the end of the period

(c) for share options exercised during the period, the weighted average share price at the date of exercise

(d) for share options outstanding at the end of the period, the range of exercise prices and weighted average remaining contractual life.

IFRS 2 also requires disclosure of information that enables users of the financial statements to understand how the fair value of the goods or services received, or the fair value of the equity instruments granted during the period was determined.

Entities should also disclose information that enables users of the financial statements to understand the effect of share-based payment transactions on the entity's profit or loss for the period and on its financial position:

(a) the total expense recognised for the period arising from share-based payment transactions;

(b) for liabilities arising from share-based payment transactions:
  - (i) the total carrying amount at the end of the period; and
  - (ii) the total intrinsic value at the end of the period of liabilities for which the counterparty's right to cash or other assets had vested by the end of the period.

### 4.7 The effect of IFRS 2

IFRS 2 has been controversial.

It is expected that many companies' earnings will be significantly reduced by the charge to the income statement. Companies involved in the new technology are likely to be particularly affected. 'E-businesses' often pay part of employees' remuneration in the form of options because they do not expect to be profitable for several years after they start to trade.

IFRS 2 represents a further instance in which fair values are used instead of historical cost.

Some investors have welcomed the standard on the grounds that directors' remuneration will be more transparent. Investors are often concerned at excessive directors' remuneration through share options.

However, many commentators have made serious objections.

- The most common objection has been to the principle that employees' share options are a cost borne by the company. The cost of issuing shares for less than their market value is not borne by the company, but by the investors as individuals. This is because the return on their investment is diluted by the new shares. Investors should be made aware that they bear this cost, but the best way of doing this would be by disclosing it in the notes to the accounts. The cost of issuing the shares does not belong in the income statement.
- Some commentators accept the principle that share-based payment should be recognised, but have pointed out other potential problems. For example, there are likely to be significant practical difficulties in measuring the fair value of options.
- Recognising the cost of employees' share options will have adverse economic consequences as employers will cease to introduce employee share plans. Employee share plans are believed to encourage good performance because they give employees a stake in the business.

## Summary

- There are two main types of pension plan: defined contribution plans and defined benefit plans.
- The expense of a defined contribution plan is equal to the contributions paid to the plan for the period.
- Where an entity has a defined benefit plan it must recognise a liability for the present value of its obligations under the plan less the fair value of any plan assets. Actuarial gains and losses are recognised in the income statement if they exceed the greater of 10% of the present value of the plan obligation and 10% of the fair value of plan assets.
- IFRS 2 requires an entity to reflect the effects of share-based payment transactions in its financial statements. When an entity receives goods or services as a result of a share-based payment transaction it recognises either an expense or an asset. If the goods or services were received in exchange for equity the entity recognises an increase in equity. If the goods or services were received or acquired in a cash-settled share-based payment transaction the entity recognises a liability.

Having completed your study of this chapter, you should have achieved the following learning outcome:

- discuss the recognition and valuation issues concerned with pension schemes and the treatment of actuarial deficits and surpluses.

## Self-test questions

**1** What are the two types of retirement benefit plans? (2.1)

**2** What is the difference between 'funding' and 'charging' in relation to retirement benefit plans? (2.3)

**3** What is the accounting objective in dealing with retirement benefit plans? (3.1)

**4** Why is it more difficult to account for a defined benefit retirement plan than for a defined contribution retirement plan? (3.3)

**5** What method of allocating benefit costs to accounting periods is required by IAS 19? (3.4)

**6** What are actuarial gains and losses? (3.6)

**7** What is the concept of the 'corridor' in accounting for actuarial gains and losses? (3.6)

**8** What is a cash settled share-based payment transaction? (4.3)

**9** How should an equity settled share-based payment transaction be measured? (4.4)

**10** What is the vesting period? (4.5)

## Objective test questions

### Question 1

Dreadnought issues share options to a number of its senior employees as part of their remuneration. According to IFRS 2 *Share-based Payment,* which of the following statements are correct in relation to the accounting treatment of this transaction?

I The cost to Dreadnought should be measured at the fair value of the options issued at the grant date.

II The cost of issuing the options should be recognised in the income statement in the period in which the shares are issued.

III The transaction should be recognised in Dreadnought's financial statements.

**A** I and II only

**B** I and III only

**C** III only

**D** All three statements

### Question 2

Cairns Inc operates a defined benefit pension plan.

The following information relates to the year ended 31 March 2004.

| | $m |
|---|---|
| Current service cost | 32 |
| Contributions paid | 40 |
| Expected return on scheme assets | 28 |
| Interest on pension scheme liabilities | 20 |
| Actuarial losses* | 36 |

* This amount is inside the corridor limit as defined by IAS 19.

Which of the following shows the correct amount charged in the company's income statement for the year to 31 March 20X4, based on the principles of IAS 19?

**A** $24m

**B** $32m

**C** $60m

**D** $68m

*For the answers to these questions, see the 'Answers' section at the end of the book.*

## Exam-type questions

### A

A, a public limited company, operates a defined benefit plan. A full actuarial valuation by an independent actuary revealed that the value of the liability at 31 May 20X0 was $1,500 million. This was updated to 31 May 20X1 by the actuary and the value of the liability at that date was $2,000 million. The scheme assets comprised mainly bonds and equities and the fair value of these assets was as follows:

| | *31 May 20X0* | *31 May 20X1* |
|---|---|---|
| | $m | $m |
| Fixed interest and index linked bonds | 380 | 600 |
| Equities | 1,300 | 1,900 |
| Other investments | 290 | 450 |
| | 1,970 | 2,950 |

The scheme had been altered during the year with improved benefits arising for the employees and this had been taken into account by the actuaries. The increase in the actuarial liability in respect of employee service in prior periods was $25 million (past service cost). The increase in the actuarial liability resulting from employee service in the current period was $70 million (current service cost). The company had not recognised any net actuarial gain or loss in the income statement to date.

The company had paid contributions of $60 million to the scheme during the period. The company expects its return on the scheme assets at 31 May 20X1 to be $295 million and the interest on pension liabilities to be $230 million.

The average expected remaining working lives of the employees is 10 years and the net cumulative unrecognized gains at 1 June 20X0 were $247 million.

**Required:**

Calculate the amount which will be shown as the net plan asset in the balance sheet of A as at 31 May 20X1, showing a reconciliation of the movement in the plan surplus during the year and a statement of those amounts which would be charged to operating profit. (Candidates should utilise IAS 19 *Employee Benefits* in answering the question.)

**(15 marks)**

**VIPER**

The directors of Viper, a public limited company, are reviewing the impact of IFRS 2 *Share-Based Payment* on the financial statements for the year ended 31 May 20X5.

The following share option schemes were in existence at 31 May 20X5:

| *Director's name* | *Grant date* | *Options granted* | *Fair value of options at grant date* | *Exercise price* | *Performance conditions* | *Vesting date* | *Exercise date* |
|---|---|---|---|---|---|---|---|
| | | | $ | $ | | | |
| J. Van Heflin | 1 June 20X3 | 20,000 | 5 | 4.50 | A | 6/20X5 | 6/20X6 |
| R. Ashworth | 1 June 20X4 | 50,000 | 6 | 6 | B | 6/20X7 | 6/20X8 |

The price of the company's shares at 31 May 20X5 is $12 per share and at 31 May 20X4 was $12.50 per share.

The performance conditions which apply to the exercise of executive share options are as follows:

**Performance Condition A**

The share options do not vest if the growth in the company's earnings per share (EPS) for the year is less than 4%. The rate of growth of EPS was 4.5% (20X3), 4.1% (20X4), 4.2% (20X5). The directors must still work for the company on the vesting date.

**Performance Condition B**

The share options do not vest until the share price has increased from its value of $12.50 at the grant date (1 June 20X4) to above S13.50. The director must still work for the company on the vesting date.

No directors have left the company since the issue of the share options and none are expected to leave before June 20X7. The shares vest and can be exercised on the first day of the due month.

**Required:**

Explain (with suitable calculations) how the directors' share options should be accounted for in the financial statements for the year ended 31 May 20X5 including the adjustment to opening balances.

**(10 marks)**

*For the answers to these questions, see the 'Answers' section at the end of the book.*

# Feedback to activity

## Activity 1

The net charge to the income statement is:

| | $m |
|---|---|
| Current service cost | 10 |
| Unwinding of discount | 4 |
| Less: expected return on assets | (8) |
| | 6 |

The net actuarial loss for the period is not recognised in the income statement. The fact that net cumulative unrecognised actuarial gains less losses from previous periods are immaterial suggests that the loss is within the 'corridor' limits.

# Chapter 13

# REPORTING THE SUBSTANCE OF TRANSACTIONS

## Syllabus content

- The principle of substance over form (IAS 1) and its influence in dealing with transactions such as sale and repurchase agreements, consignment stock, debt factoring, securitised assets, loan transfers and public and private sector financial collaboration.

## Chapter contents

## Introduction

The principle of 'substance over form' is one of the most important in modern financial reporting. It means that the financial statements recognise the economic and commercial substance of transactions and events, rather than their strict legal form, where these are different. If this principle is not followed, the financial statements can be very misleading.

Despite this, no international standard addresses the general principle of substance over form in any detail. This chapter examines the most common types of transaction affected and explains how to deal with them by applying the principles in the IASB *Framework.*

This chapter also looks at the related topic of revenue recognition, which is covered by IAS 18 *Revenue*. IAS 18 is also covered in Paper P7.

# 1 The principle of substance over form

### 1.1 Where substance and form are different

KEY POINT

Substance over form requires that transactions and other events should be accounted for and presented in accordance with their substance and financial reality and not merely with their legal form.

Substance over form requires that transactions and other events should be accounted for and presented in accordance with their substance and financial reality and not merely with their legal form.

In many cases, the substance of a transaction is the same as its legal form, particularly where the transaction is straightforward. Substance is more likely to be different from form where a transaction is complex.

***Example***

X sells goods on sale or return. At the balance sheet date goods costing $1,000 have been provisionally sold for $1,500, but the purchaser still has the right to return the goods without penalty. This right expires in one month's time.

How should these goods be shown in the financial statements at the balance sheet date?

***Solution***

The legal form is that the goods have been sold. In theory, X could recognise a sale of $1,500 and a profit of $500.

The economic substance is that no genuine sale has yet occurred, because the 'purchaser' can still return the goods. Therefore no sale should be recognised yet; the goods should be shown as inventory at their cost of $1,000.

If X sells most of its goods on sale or return, accounting for the legal form of the transactions could result in very misleading financial statements.

DEFINITIONS

**Creative accounting** is a form of accounting which, while complying with all regulations, nevertheless gives a biased impression (usually favourable) of the company's performance.

**Off balance sheet finance** is the organisation of transactions such that financial commitments are not included in the balance sheet of a company or a group.

### 1.2 Creative accounting and off balance sheet finance

**Creative accounting** is a form of accounting which, while complying with all regulations, nevertheless gives a biased impression (usually favourable) of the company's performance.

**Off balance sheet finance** is the organisation of transactions such that financial commitments are not included in the balance sheet of a company or a group.

The perceived benefits include the following:

- perceived lower level of gearing
- there may be a breach of loan agreements if further liabilities are recorded on balance sheet
- in most cases, off balance sheet finance schemes result in assets also being reduced. therefore a higher ROCE may result
- specialised activities, e.g. leasing and financial services (which have high gearing) can be removed from a group balance sheet.

KEY POINT

The principle of substance over form prevents off balance sheet finance because if the commercial reality is that the company has a financial commitment, that commitment should be included on the balance sheet.

The principle of substance over form prevents off balance sheet finance because if the commercial reality is that the company has a financial commitment, that commitment should be included on the balance sheet.

### 1.3 Common forms of off balance sheet finance

Ways in which companies have tried to keep items off the balance sheet in the past include the following.

- **Leasing of assets** – Before the issue of IAS 17 finance leases were not capitalised, i.e. the asset and its related financial commitment were not shown on the lessee's balance sheet.
- **Controlled non-subsidiaries** – Under previous defective definitions of a subsidiary, companies could control other companies but, as they were not technically subsidiaries, they were not consolidated in the group accounts. The effect of non-consolidation is that the assets and liabilities of the subsidiary were not included within the total assets and liabilities of the group.

  Since the issue of IAS 27, companies have had to be more ingenious in arranging their affairs so that off balance sheet arrangements continue to occur in entities which are not classified as subsidiaries under the definitions in the standard.
- **Innovations in the financial markets** – A number of (often complex) arrangements have been developed, often involving financial instruments, for which the accounting entries were not immediately obvious. The IASB has addressed such problems by issuing standards such as IAS 32 and IAS 39 (which are covered in a later chapter).

## 2 Reflecting the substance of transactions in financial statements

### 2.1 Introduction

The IASB's approach to reporting the substance of transactions involves several separate strands:

- The *Framework* document
- IAS 1 and IAS 8 to lay down the general principle
- Specific IASs for particular areas:
  - IAS 17 for accounting for leases
  - IAS 24 for related party disclosures

KEY POINT

The IASB *Framework for the Preparation and Presentation of Financial Statements* identifies substance over form as a necessary part of the reliability characteristic.

– IAS 31 for accounting for joint ventures

– IAS 32 for the disclosure and presentation of financial instruments.

## 2.2 The *Framework*

The IASB *Framework* for the preparation and presentation of financial statements identifies substance over form as a necessary part of the reliability characteristic.

'If information is to represent faithfully the transactions and other events that it purports to represent, it is necessary that they are accounted for and presented in accordance with their substance and economic reality and not merely their legal form.'

However the *Framework* is not an accounting standard, so it is necessary to repeat the substance over form principle in IAS 1.

## 2.3 IAS 1 and IAS 8

IAS 1 lays down the general principle:

'Financial statements shall present fairly the financial position, financial performance and cash flows of an entity. Fair presentation requires the faithful representation of the effects of transactions, other events and conditions in accordance with the definitions and recognition criteria for assets, liabilities, income and expenses set out in the *Framework*. The application of IFRSs, with additional disclosure when necessary, is presumed to result in financial statements that achieve a fair presentation.'

In the absence of a standard that specifically applies to a transaction, other event or condition, IAS 8 requires management to use its judgement to develop and apply an accounting policy that results in 'information that reflects the economic substance of transactions, other events and conditions, and not merely the legal form'.

## 2.4 Determining the substance of a transaction

Common features of transactions whose substance is not readily apparent are:

- the separation of the legal title to an item from the ability to enjoy the principal benefits and exposure to the principal risks associated with it
- the linking of a transaction with one or more others in such a way that the commercial effect cannot be understood without reference to the series as a whole
- the inclusion in a transaction of one or more options whose terms make it highly likely that the option will be exercised.

KEY POINT

A key step in determining the substance of a transaction is to identify its effect on the assets and liabilities of the entity.

Risk is important, as the party which has access to benefits (and hence an asset) will usually also be the one to suffer or gain if the benefits ultimately differ from those expected.

A key step in determining the substance of a transaction is to identify its effect on the assets and liabilities of the entity.

**Risk** is uncertainty as to the amount of benefits. It includes both potential for gain and exposure to loss. Risk often indicates which party has an asset. Risk is important, as the party which has access to benefits (and hence an asset) will usually also be the one to suffer or gain if the benefits ultimately differ from those expected.

KEY POINT

Assets and liabilities should be recognised if:

- it is probable that any future economic benefit associated with the item will flow to or from the entity;
- the asset or liability has a cost or value that can be measured with reliability.

KEY POINT

Disclosure of a transaction should be sufficiently detailed to enable the user of the financial statements to understand its commercial effect.

### 2.5 Inclusion of assets and liabilities in the balance sheet

Assets and liabilities should be recognised if:

- it is probable that any future economic benefit associated with the item will flow to or from the entity
- the asset or liability has a cost or value that can be measured with reliability.

### 2.6 Disclosure

Disclosure of a transaction should be sufficiently detailed to enable the user of the financial statements to understand its commercial effect.

A transaction may need to be disclosed whether or not it results in additional assets and liabilities being recognised. Where assets or liabilities are recognised but their nature differs from that of items usually found under the relevant balance sheet heading, the differences should be explained.

Where a transaction has not resulted in the recognition of assets or liabilities it is still necessary to consider whether disclosure of its nature and effect is required in order to achieve a fair presentation. For example the transaction may give rise to guarantees or other obligations.

### 2.7 'Vehicle' companies

Some off balance sheet financing arrangements include the use of another special purpose entity (a 'vehicle') to house certain assets and liabilities. Normally, the arrangement will be structured so that the vehicle does not meet the definition of a subsidiary. Where the commercial effect is no different from that which would result were the vehicle a subsidiary so that, in substance, the reporting entity controls the vehicle, the vehicle will meet the definition of a special purpose entity (or 'quasi subsidiary'). SIC 12 *Consolidation – Special Purpose Entities* requires such quasi subsidiaries to be included in consolidated accounts in the same way as if they were subsidiaries.

### 2.8 Offset

Offsetting of an asset and liability is generally not allowed by IAS 1, but there are special cases. Offset is allowed when the items do not constitute 'separate assets and liabilities'. Its main area of use would be certain types of bank balances and overdrafts.

## 3 Applying the substance over form principle

### 3.1 Introduction

We consider here the most common types of 'special purpose' transactions. There are other transactions which may require the application of substance over form as the business environment is now so complex that it is impossible to prescribe for every situation.

## 3.2 Consignment goods

DEFINITION

**Consignment goods** are inventory held by one party but legally owned by another, on terms which give the holder the right to sell the goods in the normal course of their business, or at their option to return it unsold to the legal owner.

Consignment goods are inventory held by one party but legally owned by another, on terms which give the holder the right to sell the goods in the normal course of their business, or at their option to return it unsold to the legal owner.

Legal title may pass when one of a number of events has occurred, for example, when the dealer has held the inventory for a specified period such as six months, or when the dealer has sold the goods. The sales price may be determined at the date of supply, or it may vary with the length of the period between supply and purchase, or it may be the manufacturer's factory price at sale.

Other terms of such arrangements include a requirement for the dealer to pay a deposit, and responsibility for insurance. The arrangement should be analysed to determine whether the dealer has in substance acquired the goods before the date of transfer of legal title.

KEY POINT

The key factor will be who bears the risk of slow-moving inventory.

The key factor will be who bears the risk of slow-moving inventory. The risk involved is the cost of financing the inventory for the period it is held. In a simple arrangement where inventory is supplied for a fixed price that will be charged whenever the title is transferred and there is no deposit, the manufacturer bears the slow-movement risk. If, however, the price to be paid increases by a factor that varies with interest rates and the time the inventory is held, then the dealer bears the risk. If the price charged to the dealer is the manufacturer's list price at the date of sale, then again the risks associated with the inventory fall on the manufacturer. Whoever bears the slow-movement risk should recognise the inventory on the balance sheet.

Consignment inventory arrangements are most common in the motor trade. A similar problem arises in the despatch of goods on sale or return. As above, the key question is determining who bears the risks and rewards over the period of time before the purchaser makes up their mind.

***Consignment inventory***

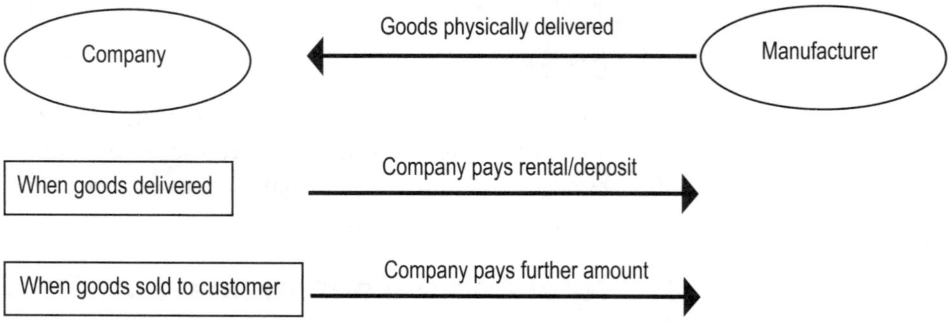


### *Example*

On 1 January 20X6 Gillingham, a manufacturer, entered into an agreement to provide Canterbury, a retailer, with machines for resale. Under the terms of the agreement, Canterbury pays a fixed rental per month for each machine that it holds and also pays the cost of insuring and maintaining the machines. The company can display the machines in its showrooms and use them as demonstration models.

When a machine is sold to a customer, Canterbury pays Gillingham the factory price at the time the machine was originally delivered. All machines remaining unsold six months after their original delivery must be purchased by Canterbury at the factory price at the time of delivery.

Gillingham can require Canterbury to return the machines at any time within the six-month period. In practice, this right has never been exercised. Canterbury can return unsold machines to Gillingham at any time during the six month period, without penalty. In practice, this has never happened.

At 31 December 20X6 the agreement is still in force and Canterbury holds several machines which were delivered less than six months earlier. How should these machines be treated in the accounts of Canterbury for the year ended 31 December 20X6?

***Solution***

The key issue is whether Canterbury has purchased the machines from Gillingham or whether they are merely on loan.

It is necessary to determine whether Canterbury has the benefits of holding the machines and is exposed to the risks inherent in those benefits.

Gillingham can demand the return of the machines and Canterbury is able to return them without paying a penalty. This suggests that Canterbury does not have the automatic right to retain or to use them.

Canterbury pays a rental charge for the machines, despite the fact that it may eventually purchase them outright. This suggests a financing arrangement, as the rental could be seen as loan interest on the purchase price. Canterbury also incurs the costs normally associated with holding inventory.

The purchase price is the price at the date the machines were first delivered. This suggests that the sale actually takes place at the delivery date. Canterbury

has to purchase any items still held six months after delivery. Therefore the company is exposed to slow payment and obsolescence risks. Because Canterbury can return the goods before that time, this exposure is limited.

It appears that both parties experience the risks and benefits. However, although the agreement provides for the return of the machines, in practice this has never happened.

**Conclusion:** The machines are assets of Canterbury and should be included in its balance sheet.

## 3.3 Sale and repurchase agreements

DEFINITION

**Sale and repurchase agreements** are arrangements under which assets are sold by one party to another on terms that provide for the seller to repurchase the assets in certain circumstances

Sale and repurchase agreements are arrangements under which assets are sold by one party to another on terms that provide for the seller to repurchase the assets in certain circumstances. The sale may be at market value or at some agreed percentage of market value. The repurchase arrangement may take a number of forms, for example, a commitment on the part of the seller, an option granted to the seller to require resale (a **call** option) or an option granted to the buyer to require repurchase (a **put** option). The arrangements often contain provisions to enable the seller to make use of the asset during its ownership by the buyer.

The repurchase price may be variable (depending on the original price and the period during which the asset has been held by the purchaser), agreed at the time of repurchase or subject to market price movements. The repurchase price may also be designed to permit the purchaser to recover incidental holding costs if these do not continue to be met by the seller.

The key question is whether the commercial effect is that of a sale or of a secured loan. A secured loan transaction will usually have the following features:

- the seller will secure access to all future benefits inherent in the asset, often through call options
- the buyer will secure adequate return on the purchase (interest on the loan, often through adjustment of the repurchase price) and appropriate protection against loss in value of the asset bought (often through put options).

The analysis should look at all features of the agreement that are likely to have a commercial effect in practice.

Sale and repurchase arrangements are common in property development and in maturing whisky inventories.

***Activity 1***

X has sold a building to Z, an investment company, for $1m when the current market value was $2m. X can repurchase the property at any time within the next three years for the original selling price ($1m) plus a sum, added quarterly, based on the bank base lending rate plus 2%. How should X account for this transaction?

*Feedback to this activity is at the end of the chapter.*

### 3.4 Sale and leaseback transactions

A sale and leaseback transaction takes place when an owner sells an asset and immediately reacquires the right to use the asset by entering into a lease with the purchaser. A common example is a company selling the freehold interest in its office/factory to a financial institution.

The first step is to determine whether the leaseback is an operating lease or a finance lease according to the rules in IAS 17.

***Finance lease***

KEY POINT

If the leaseback is a finance lease, the seller-lessee effectively re-acquires substantially all the risks and rewards of ownership of the asset. The leased asset remains on the seller's balance sheet and the amount received on the sale is treated as a lease obligation (a liability).

If the leaseback is a finance lease, the seller-lessee effectively re-acquires substantially all the risks and rewards of ownership of the asset. The leased asset remains on the seller's balance sheet and the amount received on the sale is treated as a lease obligation (a liability).

Sometimes a sale and leaseback resulting in a finance lease is arranged on terms reflecting a higher or lower capital value than the book value of the asset (i.e. so as to reflect an apparent profit or loss).

For example, an asset which has a carrying value of $70 may be sold at $120 and leased back on a finance lease. Therefore the lease payments are higher than if the sale and leaseback had been arranged at carrying value. IAS 17 requires that the $50 apparent profit should be deferred and amortised (i.e. credited to income) over the lease term.

As an alternative to calculating the apparent profit and deferring and amortising that amount, the same result can be achieved by leaving the previous carrying value unchanged, setting up the amount received on sale as an account payable and treating the lease payments partly as principal and partly as a finance charge. This treatment reflects the strict substance of the transaction, namely that it represents the raising of finance secured on an asset which is held and not disposed of.

***Operating lease***

If the leaseback is an operating lease, the seller-lessee has disposed of substantially all the risks and rewards of ownership of the asset and so has realised a profit or loss on the disposal. If the transaction is established at fair value, the profit or loss should be recognised immediately.

If the sale price is **below** fair value then the profit or loss should be recognised immediately.

If the sale price is **above** fair value, the excess is not genuine profit, but arises solely because the operating lease rentals payable in future years will also be at above fair value. Therefore the excess of sale price over fair value should not be recognised as profit in the year but should be credited to income, over the period for which the asset is expected to be used, so as to reduce the rentals payable to a level consistent with the fair value of the asset.

***Illustration***

The NBV of an asset is $70,000, the fair value is $100,000. Alternative sale prices and annual rentals (for five years) are:

| | *(a)* | *(b)* |
|---|---|---|
| | $ | $ |
| Sale price | 120,000 | 100,000 |
| Annual rental | 28,000 | 23,000 |
| The recognition of the profit will be as follows: | | |
| Recognise profit on sale (100,000 – 70,000) | 30,000 | 30,000 |
| Excess proceeds | 20,000 | |
| Credit excess proceeds to the income statement over five years | (4,000) | |
| Rentals | 28,000 | 23,000 |
| Net rental | 24,000 | 23,000 |

The net rentals charged to the income statement in (a) are higher than (b) reflecting the interest cost of the 'loan' of $20,000, (i.e. the artificially higher selling price).

***Alternative approach***

There is now an alternative approach to accounting for a sale and operating leaseback where the apparent sale price is above fair value.

Suppose that an asset with a fair value of $2 million is sold under an operating leaseback for $3 million. Lease rentals are $500,000 per annum compared with the normal annual rental of $300,000 for a similar asset.

The sale and leaseback is treated as two transactions:

(a) The asset is sold for $2 million.

(b) The lessee receives a loan of $1 million.

The sales proceeds of $2 million are recognised in the income statement and the remaining $1 million is recognised as a liability in the balance sheet.

The annual payments of $500,000 are split into:

(a) lease rentals of $300,000 (based on the normal market rate)

(b) loan repayments of $200,000.

### 3.5 Factoring of receivables

Factoring of receivables is a common method of obtaining finance. In most forms of factoring, an entity sells receivables to the factor, but the factor's degree of control over, and responsibility for those balances varies from one arrangement to another.

Typically, the seller receives cash earlier than would have been the case had the balances been unfactored. The key question is: has the seller sold the receivables or has it in fact received a loan secured on the receivables?

If the seller is essentially a borrower, and the factor a lender, then the seller normally pays the equivalent of interest to the factor on the timing difference between amounts received by him from the factor and those collected by the factor from the debtor. Such payment would be in addition to any other charges.

KEY POINT

It is necessary to identify who bears the risk (of slow payment) and the benefit (of early payment) from the receivables.

It is necessary to identify who bears the risk (of slow payment) and the benefit (of early payment) from the receivables. If the finance cost payable by the seller reflects events after the transfer of the receivables, then the seller is bearing the risks and rewards of the receivables and therefore has probably entered into a financing agreement. If the finance cost is determined when the transfer is made, with no other variable costs, then it is likely to be a straightforward sale.

***Factored receivables***

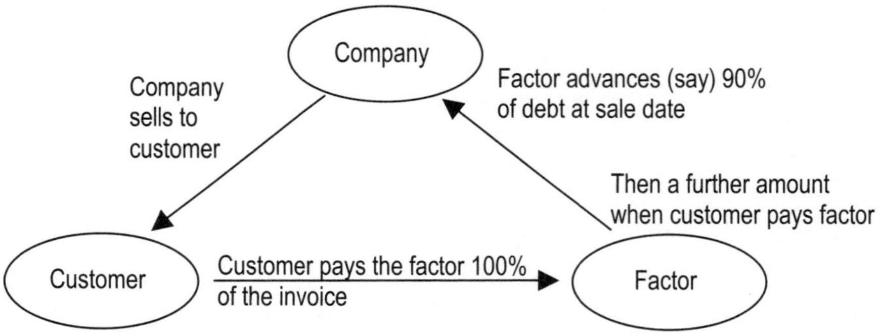


***Example***

On 1 January 20X6 Lewis entered into an agreement with Factoring whereby it transferred title to its receivables to Factoring subject to a reduction in bad debts based on past experience. Lewis received a payment of 90% of the total of net receivables. Under the terms of the agreement, the company had the right to a future sum the amount of which depended on whether and when the debtors paid. Factoring had the right of recourse against Lewis for any additional losses.

At 31 December 20X6, title had been transferred to receivables with an invoice value of $10m less a bad debt allowance of $300,000.

What is the appropriate accounting treatment for this transaction in the balance sheet of Lewis at 31 December 20X6?

***Solution***

The sum that Lewis ultimately receives depends on whether and when the receivables pay Factoring, and Factoring has recourse to Lewis for losses in excess of the bad debt allowance.

As Lewis retains the risk of slow payment and bad debts, the substance of the transaction is that of a financing arrangement and the company has not disposed of the receivables.

Therefore the balance sheet includes receivables of \$9.7 million (10 – 0.3) and current liabilities (recourse under factored receivables) for the same amount.

### 3.6 Securitised assets

KEY POINT

Securitisation involves the transfer of assets to a special purpose 'vehicle' which finances their purchase by the issue of debt, for example loan notes.

Securitisation involves the transfer of assets to a special purpose 'vehicle' which finances their purchase by the issue of debt, for example loan notes. The assets act as security for the loan notes, although the note holders are not exposed to any risks associated with the assets.

The assets transferred may be property, or inventory or receivables such as trade debts. However this type of arrangement is most common for property loans.

Suppose Company A issues property loans to home buyers. It is responsible for setting the loan rate and term and for credit control. A is known as the 'originator' as it originates the loans.

A packages together a group of loans and 'sells' them to Company B. B issues loan notes offering the property loans as security. Then B uses the proceeds from issuing the loan notes, to settle with A. B is known as the 'issuer'.

B usually has negligible equity, and the shares that it has are usually owned by a charitable trust or by a 'friend' of A. A does not control the friendly party and thus B is not a legal subsidiary of A.

A will usually continue to service the property loans and will extract profit from B by a servicing fee.

Where the originator retains significant benefits or risks then the property loans remain as an asset and the money it received is shown as a liability.

Derecognition of the asset is only appropriate where the originator has not retained any significant benefits.

### 3.7 Loan transfers

Loan transfers involve transferring the benefits and risks of a loan to a third party. Effectively the loan is 'sold' like a tangible asset.

The same principles apply here as for securitised assets.

### 3.8 Public/private sector financial collaboration

Under a typical collaboration contract, a private sector 'operator' constructs a capital asset (e.g. a hospital, a road, a school) and uses that asset to provide services to a public sector 'purchaser'. The key accounting issue is which party holds the asset, the purchaser or the operator?

The usual principles should be applied. If the purchaser has substantially all of the risks and rewards of ownership of the property, then the purchaser should show the asset and the corresponding liability on their balance sheet.

## 3.9 Special purpose entities

KEY POINT

Identifying special purpose entities is very similar to identifying assets. As for other types of 'special purpose' transaction, the key factors are risks and benefits.

Identifying special purpose entities is very similar to identifying assets. As for other types of 'special purpose' transaction, the key factors are risks and benefits.

The flow of benefits from the other entity is not normally the critical factor. Benefits obtained from subsidiaries (e.g. dividends) may not differ substantially from those obtained from other forms of investment.

Evidence of which party is exposed to benefits and risks is often given by determining which party stands to suffer or gain from the financial performance of an entity.

Control is also a key factor. Control is defined in IAS 27 as the ability to direct the financial and operating policies of an entity with a view to gaining economic benefit from its activities. The existence of control normally distinguishes a special purpose entity from other forms of investment.

If one party controls another, but does not obtain benefits from the other's net assets, it is effectively managing that party on behalf of another. There must be a flow of benefits in order to distinguish control from management.

Where the operating and financial policies of an entity have been determined in advance, then the company which obtains the benefits will be deemed to have control on those grounds alone.

It is important to look at the situation that arises in practice and not merely at the notional rights that may be held by various investors.

### *Example*

On 1 January 20X6 Sarton sold a factory that it owned to Bypass, a wholly owned subsidiary of the National Investment Bank. The sale proceeds were $15m. The factory had a book value of $12m. Bypass was financed by a loan of $15m from the National Investment Bank. Sarton was paid a fee by Bypass to continue to operate the factory. This fee represented the balance of profit remaining after Bypass had paid its parent company loan interest set at a level that represented current interest rates. If there was an operating loss, Sarton would be charged a fee that would cover the operating losses and interest payable.

How should these transactions be treated in the financial statements of Sarton for the year ended 31 December 20X6?

### *Solution*

Sarton manages the factory, which means that it controls its policies. Sarton also very clearly stands to suffer or gain from the financial performance of Bypass. The bank's return is limited to that of a secured lender. The commercial effect of the arrangement is exactly the same as if Bypass were a subsidiary of Sarton.

Bypass should be consolidated by Sarton. All transactions between the two companies should be eliminated from the accounts. The factory should be included in the consolidated balance sheet at its cost to the group ($12m) and the loan should also be included in the consolidated balance sheet. The loan interest should be included in the consolidated income statement.

### 3.10 Joint ventures

An entity may enter into joint ventures with other entities, in order to carry out specific projects. A joint venture may be a quasi-subsidiary of one of the venturers. Only if the venturers are genuine equals will a quasi-subsidiary relationship not exist.

Again, it is necessary to look at both control and benefits.

KEY POINT

The key factor that dictates the substance of a joint venture arrangement is normally the identity of the two investors and their objectives in entering into the arrangement.

The key factor that dictates the substance of a joint venture arrangement is normally the identity of the two investors and their objectives in entering into the arrangement. If one of the parties to the venture is a bank or other financial institution, seeking a lender's return on the venture, it is likely that the joint venture is a quasi-subsidiary of the other party.

If one of the parties stands to gain or lose more than the other from the financial performance of the venture, then the venture is probably a quasi-subsidiary of that party. Gains and losses do not only arise from actual profit sharing. They may arise through interest, management charges, guarantees or options to transfer assets. As usual, it is important to look at the situation which is likely to arise in practice.

## 4 IAS 18 *Revenue*

This standard is concerned with the question of when revenue and expenses should be recognised in the income statement.

### 4.1 Meaning of revenue

The term revenue could apply in any of the following situations:

- the supply of goods on cash or credit sale terms
- the provision of services on cash or credit terms
- rent received from equipment or property hired out, or
- interest or dividends received on a trade investment.

### 4.2 Measurement of revenue

Allowances for bad debts and returns are usually computed as a separate exercise and disclosed separately. If the anticipated collectable value on sales of $1,000 is $950, some accountants would argue that this should be shown as $950 revenue. Current practice, however, would show $1,000 as revenue and $50 as an expense in the income statement.

If the inflow of cash is deferred, the fair value of the consideration may be less than the nominal amount receivable. If the provision of interest free credit effectively constitutes a financing transaction, the fair value of the consideration is determined by discounting all future receipts. The difference between the fair value and the nominal amount of the consideration is recognised as interest revenue in the period or periods over which the credit is granted.

## 4.3 Revenue from the sale of goods

The following conditions must be satisfied before the revenue from the sale of goods can be recognised:

- the seller has transferred the significant risks and rewards of ownership to the buyer
- the seller does not retain continuing managerial involvement to the degree usually associated with ownership and does not have effective control over the goods sold
- the amount of revenue can be measured reliably
- it is probable that the economic benefits associated with the transaction will flow to the entity
- the costs incurred or to be incurred in respect of the transaction can be measured reliably.

KEY POINT

The following conditions must be satisfied before the revenue from the sale of goods can be recognised:

- the seller has transferred the significant risks and rewards of ownership to the buyer
- the amount of revenue can be measured reliably
- it is probable that the economic benefits associated with the transaction will flow to the entity.

## 4.4 Revenue from services

Revenue from services may be recognised, according to the stage of completion at the balance sheet date, when all the following conditions are met:

- the amount of revenue can be measured reliably
- it is probable that the economic benefits associated with the transaction will flow to the entity
- the stage of completion of the transaction at the balance sheet date can be measured reliably
- the costs incurred for the transaction and the costs to complete the transaction can be measured reliably.

If these conditions are not met, revenue should be recognised only to the extent of the expenses recognised that are recoverable.

## 4.5 Interest, royalties and dividends

Revenue from these sources may be recognised when it is probable that the benefits of the transaction will flow to the entity, and the amount of the revenue can be measured reliably.

Revenue should be recognised on the following bases:

- interest should be recognised on a time proportion basis that takes into account the effective yield on the asset
- royalties should be recognised on the accrual basis in accordance with the substance of the relevant agreement
- dividends should be recognised when the shareholder's right to receive payment is established.

## 4.6 Disclosure requirements

An entity should disclose:

(a) the accounting policies adopted for the recognition of revenue including the methods adopted to determine the stage of completion of transactions involving the rendering of services

(b) the amount of each significant category of revenue recognised during the period including revenue arising from:

(i) the sale of goods

(ii) the rendering of services

(iii) interest

(iv) royalties

(v) dividends

(c) the amount of revenue arising from exchanges of goods or services included in each significant category of revenue.

***Activity 2***

Briefly outline a suitable policy on revenue recognition for each of the following:

(a) the sale of cars on credit terms

(b) work-in-progress on a long-term contract.

*Feedback to this activity is at the end of the chapter.*

### 4.7 Aggressive earnings management

Since IAS 18 was originally issued, businesses and transactions have become much more complex. For example, computer companies frequently enter into barter transactions. Transactions may include options, for example to buy shares or to return goods within a specified time.

KEY POINT

Some entities have exploited the weaknesses in the standard in order to artificially enhance revenue (a practice sometimes called '**aggressive earnings management'**).

It is now generally recognised that IAS 18 only deals adequately with transactions in traditional businesses and that it becoming out of date. Some entities have exploited the weaknesses in the standard in order to artificially enhance revenue (a practice sometimes called **'aggressive earnings management'**). For example, some software companies recognise sales when orders are made, well before it is reasonably certain that cash will be received.

The main issue is one of timing. At what point in a transaction should an entity recognise revenue?

One possible solution would be to recognise revenue when the 'critical event' in an entity's operating cycle takes place. The 'critical event' is the point at which most or all of the uncertainty surrounding a transaction is removed. In most cases, this is when goods are delivered to the customer.

Another possibility is to focus on the idea of performance. Transactions that give rise to revenue are legally contractual arrangements, regardless of whether a formal contract exists. Revenue can only be recognised when an entity has performed its obligations under the contract. For example, an entity cannot recognise revenue at the time that it receives payment in advance. The basic principles of this approach are:

- At the time of performance of its contractual obligations a seller recognises a new asset, its right to be paid (normally in the form of a trade receivable or cash.) This asset is simultaneously reported as revenue.
- When a seller receives payment from a customer in advance of performance, it recognises a liability equal to the consideration received. This represents its obligation to provide goods or services to that value. When performance takes place, the liability is reduced and the amount of the reduction is simultaneously reported as revenue.
- Revenue should be measured at the fair value of the consideration receivable.

## 4.8 The balance sheet based approach to revenue recognition

The traditional approach to revenue recognition focuses on the **income statement**. The assets and liabilities in the balance sheet have arisen as a result of matching revenue and expenses with the accounting periods to which they relate. For example, inventories are a deferred expense.

KEY POINT

The *Framework* is **balance sheet orientated**. Gains and losses are defined in terms of changes in assets and liabilities, rather than in terms of matching transactions with accounting periods.

However, the alternative approach would be to follow the principles in the IASB *Framework*. The *Framework* is **balance sheet orientated**. Gains and losses are defined in terms of changes in assets and liabilities, rather than in terms of matching transactions with accounting periods.

The starting point for the revenue recognition process is always the effect that the transaction or other event involved has had on the reporting entity's assets and liabilities. Assuming that no contribution from owners (new capital) or transfer to owners (distribution) is involved:

- if net assets increase, a gain is recognised
- a loss is recognised if, and to the extent that, previously recognised assets are reduced or eliminated.

In most cases, this is simply a different view of established accounting practice and most transactions are dealt with in exactly the same way as before. For example, when an enterprise makes a sale its assets increase, because it has receivables (access to future economic benefits in the form of cash). Therefore it recognises a gain.

### *Activity 3*

On 1 October 20X1 a company received total subscriptions in advance of $288,000 for 12 monthly publications of a magazine. At the year end, the company had produced and despatched three of the 12 publications. The total cost of producing one issue of the magazine is estimated at $20,000.

According to the IASB *Framework*, how should the company treat the subscription revenue in the accounts for the year ended 31 December 20X1?

*Feedback to this activity is at the end of the chapter.*

The IASB has begun work on a revised standard, which is likely to be based on the principles in the *Framework*. This means that it will probably:

- define gains and losses in relation to changes in assets and liabilities (as these are clearly defined and recognition principles are set out in the *Framework*)
- require entities to report the substance of a transaction
- focus on the idea of performance: an entity should only recognise revenue when it has performed its obligations under a contract of sale or a contract for services.

This should not involve significant changes to current practice.

However, work on a new standard is at a very early stage.

## Summary

- IASs 1 and 8 and the *Framework* all require entities to report the substance of a transaction rather than its strict legal form. In order to determine the substance of a transaction, it is necessary to determine whether the assets or liabilities of the entity have changed as a result. The party to a transaction that suffers the risks and rewards attaching to an asset normally controls that asset and should recognise it in the balance sheet.
- IAS 18 covers revenue recognition. It sets out the conditions to be met before revenue can be recognised.

Having completed your study of this chapter, you should have achieved the following learning outcome:

- discuss the principle of substance over form applied to a range of transactions.

## Self-test questions

**1** What is off balance sheet finance? (1.2)

**2** What does the IASB Framework say about substance over form? (2.2)

**3** What are the common features of transactions whose substance is not readily apparent? (2.4)

**4** What is a 'vehicle' company? (2.7)

**5** What are consignment goods? (3.2)

**6** What is the key factor in identifying special purpose entities? (3.9)

**7** What conditions must be met before revenue from the sale of goods may be recognised? (4.3)

**8** What is aggressive earnings management? (4.7)

## Objective test questions

### Question 1

A company sells some of its goods on a sale or return basis. During the year ending 31 March 20X2 goods costing $54,000 had been sent to customers on this basis. At the year end 10% of these goods had yet to be accepted by customers. The company operates on a gross profit margin of 20%.

How much profit should appear in the income statement for these sales for the year ending 31 March 20X2 and what figure for inventory should appear in the balance sheet at that date?

### Question 2

A property company sells some land to a bank for $2 million on 1 January 20X2. The land originally cost $600,000 and has a book value of $1 million. The company has the right to repurchase the land at any time over the next year at a price of $2.2 million. The property company will require the use of the land within the next 12 months.

What figure will appear in the income statement for this transaction for the year ending 31 December 20X2?

*For the answers to these questions, see the 'Answers' section at the end of the book.*

## Exam-type question

### D

IAS 1 (Revised) **Presentation of Financial Statements** requires that a reporting entity's financial statements should report the substance of the transactions into which it has entered. In order to determine the substance of a transaction it is necessary to identify whether the transaction has given rise to new assets or liabilities for the reporting entity and whether it has changed the entity's existing assets or liabilities.

You are the management accountant of D which has three principal activities. These are the sale of motor vehicles (both new and second-hand), the provision of spare parts for motor vehicles, and the servicing of motor vehicles.

During the financial year ended 31 August 20X6, the company has entered into a type of business transaction not previously undertaken. With effect from 1 January 20X6, D entered into an agreement whereby it received motor vehicles on a consignment basis from E, a large manufacturer. The terms of the arrangement were as follows:

(a) On delivery, the vehicles remain the legal property of E.

(b) Legal title to a vehicle passes to D either when D enters into a binding arrangement to sell the vehicle to a third party or six months after the date of delivery by E to D.

(c) At the date legal title passes, E invoices D for the sale of the vehicles. The price payable by D is the normal selling price of E at the date of delivery, increased by 1% for every complete month the vehicles are held on consignment by D. Any change in E's normal selling price between the date of delivery and the date legal title to the goods passes to D does not change the amount payable by D to E.

(d) At any time between the date of delivery and the date legal title passes to D, the company (D) has the right to return the vehicles to E provided they are not damaged or obsolete. D does not have the right to return damaged or obsolete vehicles. If D exercises this right of return then a return penalty is payable by D as follows:

| *Time since date of delivery* | *Penalty as a percentage of invoiced price** |
|---|---|
| Three months or less | 50% |
| Three to four months | 75% |
| More than four months | 100% |

* i.e. the price that would otherwise be payable by D if legal title to the vehicles had passed at the date of return.

(e) E has no right to demand return of vehicles on consignment to D unless D becomes insolvent.

The managing director suggests that the vehicles should be shown as an asset of D only when title passes, and the purchase price becomes legally payable.

**You are required** to write a report to the managing director which:

(a) explains how an asset or liability is identified, and when an asset or liability should be recognised and should cease to be recognised, in the financial statements of a business **(12 marks)**

(b) evaluates, in the light of the principles you have explained in (a), the correctness, or otherwise of the managing director's suggested accounting treatment for the new transaction. **(8 marks)**

**(Total: 20 marks)**

*For the answer to this question, see the 'Answers' section at the end of the book.*

## Feedback to activities

### Activity 1

The substance of this deal is a secured loan from Z to X, with the expectation being that X will exercise its option to repurchase the building. No sale should therefore be recognised; the $1m is a loan received from Z.

### Activity 2

(a) The sale of a car on credit terms gives rise to two different types of revenue – trading profit and finance income. If the credit agreement is such that the user of the car becomes immediately or eventually the legal owner, then the trading profit can be regarded as being earned at the date the agreement is signed. The finance income will be spread over the duration of the agreement.

If the 'sale' is a lease whereby the user does not become the owner of the asset, it may be appropriate to spread the whole of the income over the lease period. There would, however, still be a strong argument for deeming the lease to comprise two types of profit.

(b) Work on a long-term contract may extend over several accounting periods. Thus revenue is earned over several periods as the services are being performed.

Cash is often received in part payments over the life of the contract, thus reinforcing the need to recognise before the contract is finished.

Accordingly some revenue should be recognised in each accounting period. However, the recognition of revenue then requires a matching of costs. IAS 11 does not allow any revenue to be recognised which exceeds costs charged to the income statement in the early stages of a contract, as it will not usually be clear that a profit will eventually be made.

## Activity 3

If we apply the accruals concept to this problem, \$72,000 ($3/12 \times 288,000$) is recognised in the income statement, with the balance of \$216,000 being taken to a deferred income account (an account payable) on the balance sheet.

According to the *Framework*, the starting point should be changes to assets and liabilities. As a result of receiving the subscriptions, the company now has a liability. It is obliged to produce and deliver the remaining nine issues of the magazine. However, this liability is not for the deferred income, but for the cost of producing the nine issues, \$180,000.

Therefore \$180,000 would be recognised as a liability in the balance sheet, while the remaining \$108,000 is recognised as revenue. This means that the profit on all twelve issues is recognised at the time the subscriptions are received.

Many commentators believe that this treatment is not prudent.

Chapter 14

# FINANCIAL INSTRUMENTS

## Syllabus content

- Financial instruments classified as liabilities or shareholders' funds and the allocation of finance costs over the term of the borrowing (IAS 32 & 39).
- The measurement and disclosure of financial instruments (IAS 39).

## Contents

# Introduction

This chapter is the final chapter on the measurement of income and capital and it focuses on financial instruments. Financial instruments include equity shares, debt and investments and these have become increasingly important in recent years because businesses have devised increasingly complex and sophisticated ways of financing their activities.

In most cases, complex financial instruments are used legitimately to raise finance and to manage risk. Unfortunately there have also been occasions when entities have used unusual and sophisticated instruments for creative accounting purposes: in order to hide the true level of debt and risk faced by the business.

Accounting for financial instruments is covered by three standards: IAS 32: *Financial Instruments: Presentation,* IAS 39 *Financial Instruments: Recognition and Measurement* and IFRS 7 *Financial Instruments: Disclosures.*

Accounting for financial instruments can be complicated, but remember that the Examiner will be looking for evidence that you understand the basic principles.

DEFINITIONS

A **financial instrument** is any contract that gives rise to both a financial asset of one entity and a financial liability or equity instrument of another entity.

A **financial asset** is any asset that is:

(i) cash

(ii) an equity instrument of another equity

(iii) a contractual right to receive cash or another financial asset from another entity, or

(iv) a contractual right to exchange financial instruments with another entity under conditions that are potentially favourable.

A **financial liability** is any liability that is a contractual obligation:

(i) to deliver cash or another financial asset to another entity, or

(ii) to exchange financial instruments with another entity under conditions that are potentially unfavourable

An **equity instrument** is any contract that evidences a residual interest in the assets of an entity after deducting all of its liabilities.

**Fair value** is the amount for which an asset could be exchanged, or a

# 1 Financial instruments

## 1.1 Definitions

IAS 32 and IAS 39 use the same definitions.

(a) A **financial instrument** is any contract that gives rise to both a financial asset of one entity and a financial liability or equity instrument of another entity.

(b) A **financial asset** is any asset that is:

  (i) cash

  (ii) an equity instrument of another entity

  (iii) a contractual right to receive cash or another financial asset from another entity, or

  (iv) a contractual right to exchange financial instruments with another entity under conditions that are potentially favourable.

(c) A **financial liability** is any liability that is a contractual obligation:

  (i) to deliver cash or another financial asset to another entity, or

  (ii) to exchange financial instruments with another entity under conditions that are potentially unfavourable.

(d) An **equity instrument** is any contract that evidences a residual interest in the assets of an entity after deducting all of its liabilities.

(e) **Fair value** is the amount for which an asset could be exchanged, or a liability settled, between knowledgeable, willing parties in an arm's length transaction.

(f) **Derivative**. A financial instrument or other contract with **all three** of the following characteristics:

  (i) its value changes in response to the change in a specified interest rate, financial instrument price, commodity price, foreign exchange rate, index of prices or rates, credit rating or credit index, or other variable (sometimes called the 'underlying') liability settled, between knowledgeable, willing parties in an arm's length transaction.

(ii) it requires no initial net investment or an initial net investment that is smaller than would be required for other types of contracts that would be expected to have a similar response to changes in market factors

(iii) it is settled at a future date.

***Activity 1***

Which of the following items are financial instruments?

(a) Inventory

(b) An investment in ordinary shares

(c) Prepayments for goods or services

(d) A liability for income taxes

(e) An entity's obligation to issue its own shares e.g. a share option

*Feedback to this activity is at the end of the chapter.*

## 1.2 Scope

Certain types of financial instrument are outside the scope of IAS 32 and IAS 39. These are:

(a) interests in subsidiaries, associates or joint ventures (see IAS 27, 28 and 31)

(b) employers' obligations under retirement benefit plans (covered by IAS 19)

(c) obligations under share based payment transactions (covered by IFRS 2)

(d) obligations under insurance contracts.

## 1.3 Derivatives

KEY POINT

A derivative is a financial instrument that derives its value from that of an underlying asset, price, rate or index.

In simple terms, a derivative is a financial instrument that derives its value from that of an underlying asset, price, rate or index.

Derivatives are designed to hedge against fluctuations in prices, exchange rates or interest rates. For example, suppose that a speculator pays a small deposit (say $100) now in order to buy a thousand units of wheat in three months time for $10,000. If in three months' time one thousand units of wheat costs $11,000, then the speculator has made an instant profit of $1,000. This is a 1,000% return on the original investment, which is one of the attractions of derivatives to speculators. But, if the price had dropped to $9,000, then the trader has made a $1,000 loss on a $100 investment.

Examples of derivatives include the following.

***Forward contracts***

The holder of a forward contract is obliged to buy or sell a defined amount of a specific underlying asset, at a specified price at a specified future date. For example, a forward contract for foreign currency might require £100,000 to be exchanged for $150,000 in three months' time. Both parties to the contract have both a financial asset and a financial liability. For example, one party has the right to receive $150,000 and the obligation to pay £100,000.

Forward currency contracts may be used to minimise the risk on amounts receivable or payable in foreign currencies.

***Example***

On 1 January 20X9 a dollar based company buys goods from an overseas company. This results in a liability for €8 million which must be settled on 31 March 20X9. The exchange rate on 1 January is €8 = $1. The company takes out a forward exchange contract to buy €8 million for $1 million on 31 March 20X9. This is at the exchange rate ruling at 1 January (i.e. €8 = $1).

At 31 March the exchange rate is actually €8.5 = $1. If the company had not taken out the forward exchange contract it would have made an exchange gain of $58,824 (1,000,000 – 941,176). By taking out the forward exchange contract it has given up the chance to make this gain, but has also protected itself against the possibility of making a loss. In other words, it has used the forward exchange contract to eliminate exchange rate risk.

***Forward rate agreements***

Forward rate agreements can be used to fix the interest charge on a floating rate loan. For example, a company has a $1m dollar floating rate loan, and the current rate of interest is 7%. The rates are reset to the market rate every six months, and the company cannot afford to pay more than 9% interest. The company enters into a six-month forward rate agreement (with, say, a bank) at 9% on $1m. If the market rates go up to 10%, then the bank will pay them $50,000 (1% of $1m for 6 months) which in effect reduces their finance cost to 9%. If the rates only go up to 8% then the company pays the bank $50,000.

***Futures contracts***

Futures contracts oblige the holder to buy or sell a standard quantity of a specific underlying item at a specified future date. Futures contracts are very similar to forward contracts. The difference is that futures contracts have standard terms and are traded on a financial exchange, whereas forward contracts are tailor-made and are not traded on a financial exchange.

***Swaps***

Two parties agree to exchange periodic payments at specified intervals over a specified time period. For example, in an interest rate swap, the parties may agree to exchange fixed and floating rate interest payments calculated by reference to a notional principal amount. This enables companies to keep a balance between their fixed and floating rate interest payments without having to change the underlying loans.

***Options***

These give the holder the right, but not the obligation, to buy or sell a specific underlying asset on or before a specified future date.

### 1.4 The need for an accounting standard

KEY POINT

Derivatives can be easily acquired, often for little or no cost, but their values can change very rapidly, exposing companies to the risk of large profits or losses.

Derivatives can be easily acquired, often for little or no cost, but their values can change very rapidly, exposing companies to the risk of large profits or losses. The example of the futures contract in wheat shows that losses on derivatives can be far greater than the carrying value of the related asset.

Because many derivatives have no cost, they may not appear in a traditional historical cost balance sheet, even if they represent substantial assets or liabilities of the entity. Gains and losses have traditionally not been recorded until cash is exchanged. If gains and losses are recognised on a cash basis, then management can choose when to report the gains and losses.

KEY POINT

If an entity uses derivatives, it is exposed to risk.

Because the value of derivatives depends on movements in underlying items, if an entity uses derivatives, it is exposed to risk.

Entities may use derivatives as a legitimate way of managing risk. However, in recent years there have been several cases in which companies have failed as a result of using derivatives, sometimes as a result of speculating on price, exchange or interest rate changes.

IAS 32 ensure and IFRS 7 that there is now adequate disclosure of these risks. IAS 39 has brought derivatives and other financial instrument items onto the balance sheet, and changes in the value of derivatives are now reported in the income statement.

# 2 IAS 32 *Financial Instruments: Presentation*

## 2.1 Liabilities and equity

KEY POINT

When an entity issues a financial instrument it should be classified as either equity or a liability. The classification should be based on the substance of the instrument, not its legal form.

When an entity issues a financial instrument it should be classified as either equity or a liability. The classification should be based on the substance of the instrument, not its legal form.

The instrument will be classified as a liability if the issuer has a contractual obligation:

- to deliver cash (or another financial asset) to the holder, or
- to exchange financial instruments on potentially unfavourable terms.

In many cases the classification is obvious, but problems may arise where an entity has complex instruments. The following points may be relevant:

- Where the issuer has to make fixed payments, the instrument is a liability.
- Where the issuer is required to redeem the instrument at a fixed or determinable future date, the instrument is a liability.
- Even if the issuer is unable to meet its obligations through lack of resources or legal restrictions, if an obligation exists there is still a liability.

### *Examples*

1 AB has one million $1 ordinary shares in issue. The amount of dividend paid each year depends on profits and is proposed by the directors.

2 AB has 100,000 8% $1 preference shares in issue. The shares are not redeemable.

3 AB has $200,000 of bonds in issue. No interest is payable, but the bonds are redeemable for $220,000 in five years' time.

4 AB has 2% $150,000 convertible bonds in issue. The holders have the option to convert their bonds into equity shares in five years' time at a rate of 1 equity share for every $5 of debt. The market price of AB's equity shares is $5.50 per share.

How should each of these instruments be classified?

### *Solutions*

1 The ordinary shares are an equity instrument and are shown at their par value of $1m in equity on the balance sheet. Although the holders of the shares are entitled to receive a share of any dividend or other distribution out of equity, AB does not have a contractual obligation to *make* such a distribution.

2 Although the preference shares are not redeemable, they qualify as financial liabilities because there is an obligation to pay a fixed amount of dividend each year. They are shown as non-current liabilities on the balance sheet.

3 Although there is no obligation to pay interest, the bonds are clearly financial liabilities, because there is an obligation to pay the principal at the redemption date (plus an additional amount which compensates the holders for the lack of interest and which is effectively a finance cost to AB). The bonds will be shown as non-current liabilities on the balance sheet.

4 Although AB intends to settle the obligation by issuing equity shares, rather than by paying cash, there is still an obligation to transfer economic benefit (the terms are unfavourable to AB) and the bonds must be treated as liabilities.

## 2.2 Classification of compound instruments

KEY POINT

A compound instrument must be shown on the balance sheet with the liability and equity elements separated.

A compound instrument is one which has both a liability and an equity component. For example, the value of a convertible bond consists of a liability component – the bond – and an equity component – the value of the right to convert in due course to equity.

The economic effect of issuing convertible bonds is substantially the same as the simultaneous issue of a debt instrument with an early settlement provision and warrants to purchase shares.

All such compound instruments must be shown in the balance sheet with the liability and equity elements separated.

### *Example*

An entity issues 2,000 convertible bonds at the start of Year 1. The bonds have a three year term, and are issued at par with a face value of $1,000 per bond, giving total proceeds of $2,000,000. Interest is payable annually in arrears at a nominal annual interest rate of 6%. Each bond is convertible at any time up to maturity into 250 common shares.

When the bonds are issued, the prevailing market interest rate for similar debt without conversion options is 9%.

### *Solution*

The liability component is valued first, and the difference between the proceeds of the bond issue and the fair value of the liability is assigned to the equity component. The reasoning behind this treatment is that equity is an entity's residual interest in its assets after deducting all liabilities. The sum of the liability component and the equity component are always equal to the carrying amount of the financial instrument as a whole.

The present value of the liability component is calculated using a discount rate of 9%, the market interest rate for similar bonds having no conversion rights, as shown.

| | | | $ |
|---|---|---|---|
| Present value of the principal $2,000,000 payable at the end of three years | | | 1,544,000 |
| Present value of the interest $120,000 payable annually in arrears for three years | | | 303,720 |
| Total liability component | | | 1,847,720 |
| Equity component (by deduction) | | | 152,280 |
| Proceeds of the bond issue | | | 2,000,000 |
| Discounting factors at 9%: | 1 year | 0.917 | |
| | 2 years | 0.842 | |
| | 3 years | 0.772 | |

### 2.3 Interest, dividends, losses and gains

KEY POINT

The accounting treatment of interest, dividends, losses and gains relating to a financial instrument follows the accounting treatment of the instrument itself.

The accounting treatment of interest, dividends, losses and gains relating to a financial instrument follows the accounting treatment of the instrument itself.

In other words, interest, dividends, losses and gains attributable to a financial instrument or part of a financial instrument classified as a financial liability must be reported in the income statement as expense or income, while distributions to holders of a financial instrument classified as equity must be debited direct to equity.

### 2.4 Offsetting of a financial asset and a financial liability

KEY POINT

A financial asset and a financial liability may only be offset in very limited circumstances.

In common with all IAS rules on offsetting, a financial asset and a financial liability may only be offset in very limited circumstances. The net amount may only be reported when the enterprise:

- has a legally enforceable right to set off the amounts
- intends either to settle on a net basis or to realise the asset and settle the liability simultaneously.

## 3 IAS 39 *Financial Instruments: Recognition and Measurement*

### 3.1 Initial recognition

KEY POINT

An entity should recognise a financial asset or a financial liability on its balance sheet when, and only when, it becomes a party to the contractual provisions of the instrument.

An entity should recognise a financial asset or a financial liability on its balance sheet when, and only when, it becomes a party to the contractual provisions of the instrument.

As examples of this principle:

- an unconditional receivable should be recognised as an asset when the entity becomes a party to the contract so that it has a legal right to receive cash
- a forward contract is recognised as an asset or liability on the commitment date, rather than waiting until the closing date when the exchange actually takes place.

Notice that this is different from the normal criteria for recognising assets and liabilities. An important consequence of this principle is that derivatives are recognised in the financial statements. They do not always meet the recognition criteria in most other standards (and the *Framework*):

- items should be recognised when there is a probable inflow or outflow of resources; and
- the item has a cost or value that can be measured reliably.

## 3.2 Derecognition

KEY POINT

An entity derecognises a financial asset when, and only when the contractual rights to the cash flows from the financial asset expire; or it transfers the financial asset.

An entity derecognises a financial asset when, and only when the contractual rights to the cash flows from the financial asset expire; or it transfers the financial asset.

An entity has transferred a financial asset if it has transferred the risks and rewards of ownership of the asset. In other words, the entity accounts for the substance of the transaction, rather than its legal form.

An entity removes a financial liability from its balance sheet when, and only when, it is extinguished, i.e. when the obligation specified in the contract is discharged or cancelled or expires.

On derecognition, the difference between the carrying amount of the asset or liability, and the amount received or paid for it, should be included in the net profit or loss for the period.

## 3.3 Measurement on initial recognition

KEY POINT

A financial asset or liability should initially be recognised at fair value.

A financial asset or liability should initially be recognised at fair value. This is the fair value of the consideration given or received (ie, its cost), plus directly attributable transaction costs (e.g. issue costs of shares or debt instruments).

Transaction costs are not included in fair value where a financial instrument is at fair value through profit or loss. This term is explained below.

## 3.4 Categories of financial instrument

KEY POINT

IAS 39 classifies financial assets into four categories:

- financial assets at fair value through profit or loss
- Held-to-maturity investments
- Loans and receivables
- Available for sale financial assets

For the purpose of measuring a financial asset subsequent to initial recognition, IAS 39 classifies financial assets into four categories.

***Financial assets at fair value through profit or loss***

A financial asset or liability at fair value through profit or loss meets one of the following conditions.

(a) It is classified as held for trading. A financial instrument is classified as held for trading if it is:

  (i) acquired principally for the purpose of selling or repurchasing it in the near term; or

  (ii) part of a portfolio of financial instruments that are managed together and for which there is evidence of a recent actual pattern of short-term profit-taking; or

  (ii) a derivative.

(b) Upon initial recognition it is designated by the entity as at fair value through profit or loss. An entity can only use this designation if:

(i) it eliminates or significantly reduces a measurement or recognition inconsistency (an 'accounting mismatch') that would otherwise arise from measuring assets or liabilities or recognising the gains and losses on them on different bases; or

(ii) a group of financial instruments is managed and its performance is evaluated on a fair value basis, in accordance with a documented risk management or investment strategy.

Investments in equity instruments that do not have a quoted market price in an active market and whose fair value cannot be reliably measured *cannot* be designated at fair value through profit or loss.

***Held-to-maturity investments***

Held-to-maturity investments are financial assets with fixed or determinable payments and fixed maturity that an entity has the positive intent and ability to hold to maturity other than those that fall into the other three categories.

***Loans and receivables***

Loans and receivables are financial assets with fixed or determinable payments that are not quoted in an active market, other than:

(a) those that the entity intends to sell immediately or in the near term, which should be classified as held for trading; or

(b) those designated as at fair value through profit or loss or as available-for-sale.

***Available for sale financial assets***

Available-for-sale financial assets are any remaining financial assets that do not fall into any of the three categories above.

***Examples***

At 31 December 20X5, Tewkesbury holds the following financial assets:

(a) A loan of $100,000 to Avon. Under the terms of the loan, Avon pays interest of 5% per annum and will repay $25,000 on 31 December each year, commencing on 31 December 20X6.

(b) 200,000 $1 shares in Barton. Tewkesbury purchased the shares on 1 December and it intends to sell them within the next two months.

(c) $150,000 5% bonds. The bonds mature on 31 December 20X8 and the company intends to hold them until that date.

(d) A forward exchange contract for E300,000 at a rate of E3 to $1 on 31 January 20X5. The current exchange rate is E2.5 to $1.

For each of these investments, state how it is classified and explain where it will be shown in the balance sheet at 31 December 20X5. Assume that none of these items will be designated as 'at fair value through profit or loss' or as 'available for sale' unless they obviously fall into these categories.

***Solutions***

(a) **Loan of $100,000 to Avon**. This is not quoted, and there are fixed repayments. This is classified under 'loans and receivables'.

(b) **Shares in Barton.** These are held for the very short term and so this investment appears to be 'held for trading'. It belongs in the category 'at fair value through profit or loss'.

(c) **5% bonds.** The bonds pay interest at a fixed rate and have a fixed maturity. The company intends to hold them to maturity; therefore they can be classified as 'held to maturity investments'.

(d) **Forward exchange contract**. This is a derivative and therefore it must be classified as 'at fair value through profit or loss'.

In the balance sheet, the bonds and the loan are recognised as non-current assets and are shown as a separate line item 'financial assets', which may be sub-classified.

The shares and the forward exchange contract are current assets and are also shown as 'financial assets'.

## 3.5 Subsequent measurement of financial assets

KEY POINT

After initial recognition, most financial assets (including derivatives that are assets) should be measured at **fair value.**

After initial recognition, financial assets (including derivatives that are assets) should be measured at **fair value**, except for:

- loans and receivables
- held-to-maturity investments
- any financial asset that does not have a quoted market price in an active market and where fair value cannot be reliably measured.

KEY POINT

Loans and receivables and held to maturity investments are measured at **amortised cost**.

Loans and receivables and held to maturity investments are measured at **amortised cost**.

Financial assets that do not have a quoted market price and whose fair value cannot be measured reliably are measured at **cost**.

KEY POINT

All financial assets should be reviewed for impairment at each balance sheet date.

All financial assets should be reviewed for impairment at each balance sheet date. If there is any objective evidence that a financial asset is impaired, it should be written down to its estimated recoverable amount.

## 3.6 Subsequent remeasurement of financial liabilities

After initial recognition, an entity should measure all financial liabilities at amortised cost, using the effective interest method.

The exception to this is financial liabilities at fair value through profit or loss (including derivatives). These are measured at fair value.

## 3.7 Amortised cost

The effective interest rate method calculates annual amortisation using the effective interest rate (i.e. the internal rate of return) of a financial asset or financial liability. Consider the example below.

***Example***

Loan notes are issued for \$1,000, redeemable in five years' time at \$1,250. Interest at 5.9% per year is payable.

The total finance cost is the interest plus the redemption premium ($5 \times \$59 + \$250 = \$545$) and this amount must be spread over the five-year life of the loan. The relevant percentage to show a constant rate of return on this figure can be calculated to be 10% per year.

The following table shows the allocation over the five years:

| *Year* | *Balance at beginning of year* | *Income statement: Finance cost for year (10%)* | *Cash paid during year* | *Balance at end of year* |
|---|---|---|---|---|
| | $ | $ | $ | $ |
| 1 | 1,000 | 100 | (59) | 1,041 |
| 2 | 1,041 | 104 | (59) | 1,086 |
| 3 | 1,086 | 109 | (59) | 1,136 |
| 4 | 1,136 | 113 | (59) | 1,190 |
| 5 | 1,190 | 119 | (1,250–59) | - |

The finance cost recognised in the income statement can be seen to be 10% of the balance outstanding at the beginning of each year. The balance outstanding increases each year to reflect the build-up of the $250 premium on redemption.

The balances carried forward at each year end represent the amortised cost valuation to be shown in the balance sheet.

***Activity 2***

An entity issues 2,000 convertible bonds at the start of Year 1. The bonds have a three-year term, and are issued at par with a face value of $1,000 per bond, giving total proceeds of $2,000,000. Interest is payable annually in arrears at a nominal annual interest rate of 6%. Each bond is convertible at any time up to maturity into 250 common shares.

When the bonds were issued, the prevailing market interest rate for similar debt without conversion options is 9%.

Immediately after the bonds were issued, they were recognised in the balance sheet at the following amounts:

| | $ |
|---|---|
| Equity component | 152,280 |
| Liability component | 1,847,720 |

How will the bonds be recognised in the financial statements for Year 1?

*Feedback to this activity is at the en*

KEY POINT

When financial instruments are carried at fair value they are remeasured at each balance sheet date. The way in which changes in fair value are recognised depends on the category of financial instrument.

## 3.8 Gains and losses

When financial instruments are carried at fair value they are remeasured at each balance sheet date. The way in which changes in fair value are recognised depends on the category of financial instrument.

Gains and losses on financial instruments at fair value through profit or loss are recognised in profit or loss (i.e. in the income statement).

Gains and losses on available for sale financial assets are recognised directly in equity and reported in the statement of changes in equity. When the asset is derecognised the cumulative gain or loss previously recognised in equity should be recognised in profit and loss (ie, recycled to the income statement).

Gains and losses on financial instruments carried at amortised cost are recognised in profit and loss as the asset or liability is amortised.

Special rules apply where financial assets and financial liabilities are hedged items. These are covered later in this chapter.

### 3.9 Classifying financial instruments

There are several things to note about the different categories of financial instrument.

(a) The general rule is that financial instruments are carried at fair value. All derivatives must remeasured to fair value at each balance sheet date and the resulting gains and losses must be recognised in the income statement. This ensures that users of the financial statements are made aware of the effect of derivatives upon an entity's financial performance and financial position.

(b) Even if a financial instrument could be measured at amortised cost an entity can choose to measure it at fair value through profit or loss. Note that this choice has to be made on initial recognition; once a financial instrument has been classified in this way it **cannot** be reclassified.

(c) In theory it is possible to carry a financial asset at amortised cost if it can be classified as 'held to maturity'. In practice, such an asset has to meet several conditions. The entity must have a **positive intent** and a **demonstrated ability** to hold the investment to maturity. These conditions are not met if:

   (i) the entity intends to hold the financial asset for an undefined period

   (ii) the entity stands ready to sell the financial asset in response to changes in interest rates or risks, liquidity needs and similar factors

   (iii) the issuer has the right to settle the financial asset at an amount significantly below its amortised cost (because this right will almost certainly be exercised)

   (iv) it does not have the financial resources available to continue to finance the investment until maturity

   (v) it is subject to an existing legal or other constraint that could frustrate its intention to hold the financial asset to maturity.

   **Equity** instruments cannot be classified as held to maturity.

(d) In addition, IAS 39 discourages entities from classifying instruments as 'held to maturity'. If an entity can no longer hold an investment to maturity, it must be re-measured to fair value. Unless this happens under certain very narrowly defined conditions, **all** remaining held-to-maturity investments must also be re-measured to fair value and classified as available-for-sale. No financial instrument can then be classified as 'held to maturity' during the current year or during the two years that follow.

### 3.10 Arguments for and against fair value

The arguments for using fair value for financial instruments rather than historical cost are as follows.

(a) Sometimes these items have no historical cost, and so they are ignored by conventional accounting.

(b) Fair valuation reports unrealised gains and losses as they arise, not just when they are realised. This gives a better and more objective indication of a company's performance.

(c) Fair valuation reports the way in which risks are being managed.

(d) Fair valuation promotes comparability. All financial instruments will be carried at their fair value at the balance sheet date, rather than at out of date historical costs. Different companies will also be using the same up-to-date fair values.

(e) Fair values have more predictive value.

(f) Management should already be using fair values in order to control their risks.

(g) It is practical, because many financial instruments are traded on active markets and are therefore easy to value.

However, fair value accounting is still controversial. Until recently, IAS 39 allowed any financial instrument to be treated as at fair value through profit or loss. Some supervisors of banks, insurers and other financial services objected to this because they were concerned that fair value could be used inappropriately.

(a) Entities could apply the fair value option to financial instruments whose fair value is not verifiable. Because the valuation would be subjective, entities might then have scope to manipulate profit or loss.

(b) Use of fair values might increase volatility in profit and loss.

(c) If an entity uses fair value to measure financial liabilities, it might recognise gains or losses as a result of changes in its own creditworthiness.

As a result of these objections, the IASB amended IAS 39 so that an entity can only use the 'fair value option' in specific circumstances (see section 3.4 above).

There are other arguments against measuring financial instruments at fair value:

(a) In practice, assets and liabilities are measured on different bases. Most assets are non-financial and so they are measured at historical cost, while most liabilities are financial and so they are measured at fair value.

(b) Many of the changes in fair value will never be realised. Therefore the income statement will show losses that never arise and profits that are never realised.

(c) It may not always be possible to value all financial instruments.

***Example***

During the year ended 31 December 20X4 Grasmere purchased the following financial instruments:

(1) $200,000 5% debentures in Rydal at 1 January 20X4 (their issue date). The term of the debentures was 5 years and on maturity Grasmere will receive $261,050. The effective rate of interest on the debentures is 10% and Grasmere intends to hold the debentures until their redemption.

(2) 150,000 $1 equity shares in Ullswater on 1 April 20X4 for $2.50 each as a short term investment. On 31 December 20X4 the fair value of these shares was $2.60 each.

(3) A futures contract costing $100 on 1 December 20X4 to purchase 100 tons of copper for $200,000 on 31 March 20X4. At 31 December 20X4 the fair value of the contract was $14,500.

The directors of Grasmere do not wish to designate financial instruments at fair value through profit or loss.

**Required:**

Explain how each of these financial instruments should be reported in the financial statements for the year ended 31 December 20X4.

***Solution***

**5% Debentures**

Grasmere intends to hold the debentures until their redemption and so they can be designated as a held-to-maturity investment. The debentures are measured at amortised cost.

On 1 January 20X4 the debentures are recorded at $200,000 (their cost).

At 31 December 20X4 they are included in the balance sheet as a financial asset at their amortised cost of $210,000.

| | $ |
|---|---|
| Initial cost | 200,000 |
| Interest at 10% | 20,000 |
| Cash at 5% | (10,000) |
| At 31 December 20X3 | 210,000 |

Finance income (interest) of $20,000 is recognised in the income statement.

**$1 equity shares**

Equity shares cannot be designated as held to maturity, nor are they loans or receivables. Grasmere can designate them either as at fair value through profit or loss (which the directors do not wish to do) or as available-for-sale.

Available for sale financial assets are remeasured to fair value at each balance sheet date and gains and loses are recognised in equity.

On 1 April 20X4 the shares are recorded at their cost of $375,000 (150,000 × 2.50).

At 31 December 20X4 they are remeasured to their fair value and reported in the balance sheet as a financial asset of $390,000 (150,000 × 2.60). The gain of $15,000 is recognised in equity (reserves) and reported in the statement of changes in equity.

**Futures contract**

This is a derivative. Therefore the directors **must** designate it as at fair value through profit or loss.

On 1 December 20X4 it is recorded at its cost of $100.

At 31 December 20X4 it is reported in the balance sheet as a financial asset at its fair value of $14,500. The gain of $14,400 is recognised in the income statement.

# 4 Hedging

## 4.1 Introduction

DEFINITION

**Hedging**, for accounting purposes, means designating one or more hedging instruments so that their change in fair value is an offset, in whole or in part, by the change in fair value or cash flows of a hedged item.

**Hedging**, for accounting purposes, means designating one or more hedging instruments so that their change in fair value is offset, in whole or in part, by the change in fair value or cash flows of a hedged item.

Hedging is a means of minimising risk. The simplest hedge is when an entity takes out a foreign currency loan to finance a foreign currency investment. If the foreign currency strengthens, then the value of the asset and the value of the liability will increase by the same amount. Any gains or losses will be cancelled out.

Hedge accounting recognises symmetrically the offsetting effects on net profit or loss of changes in the fair values of the hedging instrument and the related item being hedged. The hedging instrument is normally a derivative.

Under IAS 39 hedge accounting is **required** where there is a designated hedging relationship between a hedging instrument and a hedged item. It is prohibited otherwise.

IAS 39 identifies three types of hedge.

(1) **Fair value hedge** – This hedges against the risk of changes in the fair value of a recognised asset or liability. For example, the fair value of fixed rate debt will change as a result of changes in interest rates.

(2) **Cash flow hedge** – This hedges against the risk of changes in expected cash flows. For example, a UK entity may have an unrecognised contractual commitment to purchase a ship in a year's time for a fixed amount of US dollars.

(3) **Hedge of a net investment in a foreign operation** – This hedges against the risk of changes in exchange rates where an entity takes out a foreign currency loan to finance the acquisition of a foreign operation. We have already looked at this type of hedge in the chapter on foreign currency translation.

## 4.2 Conditions for hedge accounting

Hedge accounting can be used only if the hedging relationship meets all the following conditions.

(a) The hedging relationship must be designated as a hedge at its inception. There must be formal documentation, identifying the hedged item, the hedge instrument, the nature of the risk that is to be hedged and how the entity will assess the hedging instrument's effectiveness.

(b) The hedge is expected to be highly effective in achieving offsetting changes in fair value or cash flows attributable to the hedged risk.

(c) For cash flow hedges, the forecast transaction giving rise to the cash flow risk must be highly probable and could ultimately affect profit or loss.

(d) The effectiveness of the hedge can be measured reliably.

(e) The hedge is assessed on an ongoing basis (annually) and has been effective during the reporting period.

## 4.3 Accounting for a fair value hedge

KEY POINT

At each period end the hedging instrument is remeasured at fair value. All gains and losses are recognised in the income statement as part of the net profit or loss.

The hedged item is also re-measured to fair value and the change in the carrying amount of the hedged item is also recognised in profit or loss.

At each period end the hedging instrument is remeasured at fair value. All gains and losses are recognised in the income statement as part of the net profit or loss.

The hedged item is also re-measured to fair value and the change in the carrying amount of the hedged item is also recognised in profit or loss.

### *Example*

A company owns inventories of 100,000 tons of iron which cost $1,000,000 on 1 December 20X4.

If the price of iron falls, the company will make a loss when it eventually sells its inventories to a third party. Therefore it takes out a futures contract to deliver 100,000 tons of iron at $12 per ton on 31 January 20X5. This protects the company from a fall in the price of iron by fixing the amount for which the inventory will eventually be sold.

At 31 December 20X4 the market price of iron is $9 per ton and the futures price for delivery on 31 January 20X5 is $11 per ton.

What is the impact of the fair value hedge on the financial statements of the company at 31 December 20X4?

### *Solution*

Without hedge accounting, the inventory is reported in the balance sheet at its cost of $1,000,000. The futures contract is a derivative and therefore it is remeasured to fair value. Because prices have fallen, this results in a gain of $100,000 (100,000 × 12 – 11) which is recognised in the income statement. A financial asset of $100,000 is also recognised.

The overall effect on the income statement is a gain of $100,000.

With hedge accounting, the futures contract is remeasured to its fair value and a gain of $100,000 is recognised as before. The inventory is also remeasured to its fair value of $900,000 (100,000 × 9) and a loss of $100,000 (1,000,000 – 900,000) is recognised in the income statement.

The overall effect on the income statement is nil (gain of $100,000 less loss of $100,000).

## 4.4 Accounting for a cash flow hedge

KEY POINT

At each period end, the hedging instrument is remeasured at fair value. The gain (or loss) on the portion of the instrument that is deemed to be effective will be taken to equity and recognised in the statement of changes in equity.

The ineffective portion of the gain or loss on the hedging instrument is recognised immediately in the income statement.

(a) At each period end, the hedging instrument is remeasured at fair value. The gain (or loss) on the portion of the instrument that is deemed to be effective will be taken to equity and recognised in the statement of changes in equity.

(b) The ineffective portion of the gain or loss on the hedging instrument is recognised immediately in the income statement.

(c) When a hedging transaction results in the recognition of an asset or liability, changes in the value of the hedging instrument recognised in equity are either:

 (i) adjusted against the carrying value of the asset or liability; or

 (ii) affect the income statement at the same time as the hedged item (for example, through depreciation or sale).

***Example***

Brit plc, a UK entity, has contracted to buy one hundred tonnes of raw materials from a German entity. The materials will cost €500,000, and will be delivered and paid for in euros on 30 June 20X5. Shortly before its year-end of 30 April 20X5, Brit plc takes out a forward contract to buy €500,000 on 30 June 20X5.

***Solution***

This is an example of a cash flow hedge. The hedging instrument is the forward contract, taken out to hedge the risk of the overseas payment. The hedged item is the firm commitment to pay for the raw materials on 30 June 20X5.

At 30 April 20X5 the forward contract is included in the balance sheet at fair value, with the resulting gain or loss on revaluation being taken to equity and reported in the statement of changes in equity.

In the year to 30 April 20X6, the purchase of raw materials would be accounted for at the spot rate as normal. The gain or loss taken to equity in the previous year is removed from equity and recognised in the income statement. The advantage of the hedge accounting approach is that it matches the gain or loss on the hedging instrument with the transaction that it is hedging.

### 4.5 Hedges of a net investment in a foreign operation

This is the type of hedge that you are most likely to have to deal with in the exam.

As we have already seen, this normally arises where an entity making overseas investments raises the funds locally in an overseas currency.

***Accounting treatment***

A hedge of a net investment in a foreign operation is accounted for in a similar way to a cash flow hedge:

(a) the effective portion of the gain or loss on the hedging instrument (the loan) is recognised directly in equity through the statement of changes in equity

(b) the ineffective portion of the gain or loss is recognised in the income statement.

This means that neither any exchange difference arising on the investment nor on the matching loan are taken to the income statement before the ultimate disposal of the net investment. On disposal of the foreign operation, gains and losses on the loan that have been taken to equity are 'recycled' and recognised in the income statement.

## 5 IFRS 7 *Financial Instruments: Disclosures*

### 5.1 Introduction

KEY POINT

IFRS 7 requires entities to provide information that will enable them to evaluate:

(a) the significance of financial instruments; and

(b) the nature and extent of risks arising from financial instruments.

IFRS 7 requires entities to provide users of the financial statements with information that will enable them to evaluate:

(a) the significance of financial instruments for the entity's financial position and performance; and

(b) the nature and extent of risks arising from financial instruments to which the entity is exposed during the period and at the reporting date and how the entity manages those risks.

KEY POINT

**Risk** is uncertainty as to the amount of benefits. It includes both potential for gain and exposure to loss.

**Risk** is uncertainty as to the amount of benefits. It includes both potential for gain and exposure to loss. All businesses are exposed to various forms of financial risk. The balance sheet shows a variety of sources of finance (liabilities), along with financial investments (assets). But there will be many potential risks which are not obvious from the balance sheet, such as the likelihood of interest rates going up or down, or of currency fluctuations.

Also, the company may have taken steps to hedge against these risks, normally by issuing or buying other financial instruments. These in turn will have their own risks.

KEY POINT

IFRS 7 requires extensive disclosures.

The disclosures required are extensive and it is extremely unlikely that you will have to reproduce them in the exam. However, you do need a general awareness of the kind of information that should be disclosed in the financial statements.

IFRS 7 uses the same terminology as IAS 32 and IAS 39.

**Classes of financial instrument**

Some information is required to be disclosed for each class of financial instrument. An entity should group financial instruments into classes that are appropriate to the nature of the information disclosed and that take into account the characteristics of those financial instruments.

At a minimum, the entity should distinguish instruments measured at amortised cost from those measured at fair value.

An entity should provide sufficient information to permit reconciliation to the line items presented in the balance sheet.

## 5.2 Significance of financial instruments for financial position and performance

**Balance sheet**

IFRS 7 requires disclosure of the carrying amounts of each of the following:

(a) financial assets at fair value through profit or loss, showing separately assets designated as such upon initial recognition and assets held for trading

(b) held-to-maturity investments

(c) loans and receivables

(d) available-for-sale financial assets

(e) financial liabilities at fair value through profit or loss, showing separately liabilities designated as such upon initial recognition and liabilities held for trading; and

(f) financial liabilities measured at amortised cost.

Entities are also required to disclose further information about the following:

(a) financial assets or financial liabilities designated at fair value through profit or loss

(b) any financial assets reclassified from one category to another (e.g. from one measured at cost or amortised cost to one measured at fair value) including the reason for the reclassification; and

(c) any financial assets transferred in such a way that part or all do not qualify for derecognition.

### Income statement and equity

Entities should disclose net gains or net losses on:

(a) financial assets or financial liabilities at fair value through profit or loss, showing separately those on financial assets or financial liabilities designated as such, and those on financial assets or financial liabilities that are classified as held for trading

(b) available-for-sale financial assets, showing separately the amount of gain or loss recognised directly in equity during the period and the amount removed from equity and recognised in profit or loss for the period

(c) held-to-maturity investments

(d) loans and receivables; and

(e) financial liabilities measured at amortised cost.

Entities should also disclose:

(a) total interest income and total interest expense (calculated using the effective interest method) for financial assets or financial liabilities that are not at fair value through profit or loss

(b) fee income and expense arising from financial assets or financial liabilities that are not at fair value through profit or loss

(c) fee income and expense arising from trust and other fiduciary activities that result in the holding or investing of assets on behalf of individuals, trusts, retirement benefit plans, and other institutions; and

(d) the amount of any impairment loss for each class of financial asset.

### Other disclosures

IFRS 7 requires disclosure of:

(a) the measurement basis (or bases) and other accounting policies used; and

(b) information about hedge accounting, including descriptions of each type of hedge and the financial instruments used; and amounts recognised in the financial statements.

### Fair value

An entity should disclose the fair value of each class of financial asset and financial liability. The information should be disclosed in such a way that it can be compared with the corresponding carrying amount in the balance sheet.

For each class of financial instruments, the methods and assumptions applied in determining fair value should be disclosed.

Disclosures of fair value are not required:

(a) when the carrying amount is a reasonable approximation of fair value (e.g. for short-term trade receivables and payables); or

(b) for an investment in equity instruments that do not have a quoted market price in an active market, that is measured at cost in accordance with IAS 39 because its fair value cannot be measured reliably.

Where investments in equity instruments are measured at cost because their fair value cannot be measured reliably, that fact should be disclosed together with a description of the financial instruments: their carrying amount, an explanation of why fair value cannot be measured reliably, information about the market for the instruments; and information about whether and how the entity intends to dispose of the instruments.

### 5.3 Nature and extent of risks arising from financial instruments

IFRS 7 identifies several different types of risk to which an entity may be exposed:

(a) **Market risk** is the risk that the fair value or future cash flows of a financial instrument will fluctuate because of changes in market prices. Fluctuations can be caused by changes in foreign exchange rates (currency risk), changes in market interest rates (interest rate risk) or other factors.

(b) **Credit risk** is the risk that one party to a financial instrument will fail to discharge an obligation and cause the other party to incur a financial loss.

(c) **Liquidity risk** is the risk that an entity will encounter difficulty in raising funds to meet obligations associated with financial liabilities.

DEFINITION

**Market risk** is the risk that the fair value or future cash flows of a financial instrument will fluctuate because of changes in market prices.

**Credit risk** is the risk that one party to a financial instrument will fail to discharge an obligation and cause the other party to incur a financial loss.

**Liquidity risk** is the risk that an entity will encounter difficulty in raising funds to meet obligations associated with financial liabilities.

**Qualitative disclosures**

For each type of risk arising from financial instruments, an entity should disclose:

(a) the exposures to risk and how they arise

(b) its objectives, policies and processes for managing the risk and the methods used to measure the risk; and

(c) any changes in (a) or (b) from the previous period.

Many entities provide this information as part of a separate Operating and Financial Review (OFR) or Management Commentary, rather than in the notes to the financial statements. IFRS 7 allows this, provided the information is cross-referenced to the financial statements.

**Quantitative disclosures**

For each type of risk arising from financial instruments, an entity should disclose summary quantitative data about its exposure to that risk at the reporting date.

IFRS 7 also requires specific detailed information about credit risk, liquidity risk and market risk. This information includes:

(a) the amount that best represents the entity's maximum exposure to credit risk at the reporting date

(b) a maturity analysis for financial liabilities (i.e. an analysis of when liabilities fall due for payment) and a description of how the entity manages that risk

(c) a sensitivity analysis for each type of market risk to which the entity is exposed at the reporting date, showing how profit and loss and equity would have been affected by changes that were reasonably possible at that date.

If the data disclosed at the reporting date is unrepresentative of the entity's exposure to risk during the period, the entity should provide further information that is representative.

## Summary

- A financial instrument is any contract that gives rise to both a financial asset of one entity and a financial liability or equity instrument of another entity.
- IAS 32 deals with the presentation of financial instruments. Financial instruments must be classified as liabilities or equity according to their substance. The critical feature of a financial liability is an obligation to deliver cash or another financial instrument. Compound financial instruments (e.g. convertible bonds) are split into equity and liability components.

- IAS 39 deals with recognition and measurement issues. Financial assets and liabilities are initially measured at cost. Financial assets and liabilities are divided into four categories:
  - financial assets and liabilities at fair value through profit and loss (measured at fair value; changes taken to the income statement)
  - held to maturity investments (measured at amortised cost)
  - loans and receivables (measured at amortised cost)
  - available for sale financial assets (measured at fair value; changes taken to equity).
- IFRS 7 deals with the disclosure of financial instruments.

Having completed your study of this chapter, you should have achieved the following learning outcomes:

- discuss the possible treatments of financial instruments in the issuer's accounts (i.e. liabilities versus equity, and the implications for finance costs)
- identify circumstances in which amortised cost, fair value and hedge accounting are appropriate for financial instruments and explain the principles of these accounting methods.

## Self-test questions

**1** What is a financial instrument? (1.1)

**2** What is a financial liability? (1.1)

**3** What is an equity instrument? (1.1)

**4** What is a compound instrument? (2.2)

**5** How should interest, dividends, gains and losses derived from financial instruments be accounted for? (2.3)

**6** In what circumstances is it acceptable to offset a financial asset and a financial liability? (2.4)

**7** When should a financial asset be recognised on the balance sheet? (3.1)

**8** What is a held-to-maturity investment? (3.4)

**9** Should a held-to-maturity financial asset be shown on the balance sheet at fair value? (3.5)

**10** What is hedge accounting? (4.1)

## Objective test question

### Question 1

A company issues 4% bonds with a nominal value of $500,000 for $394,408 on 1 January 20X0. Redemption is at par in five years' time and the effective rate of interest of the bonds is 9.5%.

What figure would IAS 39 require to appear in the balance sheet at 31 December 20X2 for these bonds and in the income statement for the year ending 31 December 20X2?

| | *Balance sheet* | *Income statement* |
|---|---|---|
| | $ | $ |
| **A** | 451,951 | 20,000 |
| **B** | 451,951 | 40,946 |
| **C** | 500,000 | 20,000 |
| **D** | 500,000 | 47,500 |

*For the answer to this question, see the 'Answers' section at the end of the book.*

## Practice question

### Alpha Limited

Alpha Limited issued $1,000,000 of convertible bonds with a four year term at par on 1 January 20X7. The bonds carry interest at 8% pa and each $100 of bonds is convertible into ordinary shares from 31 December 20X7.

At the time of issue, the market rate of interest for such bonds was 10%.

**You are required** to calculate the initial division of the $1,000,000 into liability and equity elements.

Discounting factors at 10%:

| | |
|---|---|
| 1 year | 0.909 |
| 2 years | 0.826 |
| 3 years | 0.751 |
| 4 years | 0.683 |

**(5 marks)**

*For the answer to this question, see the 'Answers' section at the end of the book.*

## Exam-type question

### Financial instruments

Standard setters have been struggling for several years with the practical issues of the disclosure, recognition and measurement of financial instruments. The dynamic nature of international financial markets has resulted in the widespread use of a variety of financial instruments, and present accounting rules struggle to deal effectively with the impact and risks of such instruments.

**Required:**

(a) (i) Discuss the concerns about the accounting practices used for financial instruments which led to demands for an accounting standard. **(9 marks)**

(ii) Explain why regulations dealing with disclosure alone are unlikely to solve the problem of accounting for financial instruments in financial statements. **(4 marks)**

(b) The following draft disclosures were to be made in the financial statements of AX, a public limited company, for the year ended 30 November 1999.

| | *Carrying amount* | *Fair value* |
|---|---|---|
| | $m | $m |
| Non derivatives: | | |
| *Assets* | | |
| Equity securities and other financial assets held for trading | 5,000 | 6,000 |
| Fixed maturity investments to be 'held to maturity' | 4,000 | 5,500 |
| *Liabilities* | | |
| 7% Redeemable preference shares – redeemable at a premium of 8% in 2002 | 3,400 | 3,000 |
| Derivatives: | | |
| Assets | 2,960 | 3,460 |

Explain how the non derivative and derivative financial instruments should be accounted for in the financial statements of AX under IAS 39 *Financial Instruments: Recognition and Measurement.* **(7 marks)**

**(Total: 20 marks)**

*For the answer to this question see the 'Answers' section at the end of the book.*

## Feedback to activities

### Activity 1

(a) Inventory (or any other physical asset such as property, plant and equipment) is not a financial instrument since there is no present contractual right to receive cash or other financial assets.

(b) An investment in ordinary shares is a financial asset since it is an equity instrument of another entity.

(c) Prepayments for goods or services are not financial instruments since the future economic benefit will be the receipt of goods or services rather than a financial asset.

(d) A liability for income taxes is not a financial instrument since the obligation is statutory rather than contractual.

(e) A share option is a financial instrument since a contractual obligation does exist to deliver an equity instrument. Note however that an option to buy or sell an asset other than a financial asset (e.g. a commodity) would not qualify as a financial instrument.

### Activity 2

The equity component continues to be valued at $152,280 in the balance sheet.

The liability component is valued at amortised cost, as required by IAS 39:

| | $ |
|---|---|
| At beginning of year | 1,847,720 |
| Interest at 9% | 166,295 |
| Less: interest paid | (120,000) |
| | 1,894,015 |

A finance charge of $166,295 is reported in the income statement.

Chapter 15

# ANALYSING FINANCIAL STATEMENTS

## Syllabus content

- Ratios in the areas of performance, profitability, financial adaptability, liquidity, activity, shareholder investment and financing, and their interpretation.
- Interpretation of financial statements via the analysis of the accounts and corporate reports.
- Reporting the results of analysis.
- Limitations of ratio analysis (e.g. comparability of businesses and accounting policies).
- The identification of information required to assess financial performance and the extent to which financial statements fail to provide such information.
- Interpretation of financial obligations included in financial accounts (e.g. redeemable debt, earn-out arrangements, contingent liabilities).
- The effect of short-term debt on the measurement of gearing.
- The need to be aware of aggressive or unusual accounting policies ('creating accounting') (e.g. in the areas of cost capitalisation and revenue recognition).

## Contents

## Introduction

This chapter concentrates on ratio analysis. Some of this material should be familiar to you if you have already studied for Paper P7.

Analysis of financial statements and other financial information is a central topic in this paper and counts for 35% of the total marks. Although you will need to know how to calculate a range of ratios, you should not concentrate exclusively on the calculations. Most of the available marks in a question are awarded for comment and analysis, rather than the calculations themselves.

This chapter concentrates on analysing the financial statements themselves: the performance statements; the balance sheet (financial position); and the cash flow statement (financial adaptability). Later chapters will consider the other information that typically accompanies the financial statements.

Ratio analysis is a useful technique, but it has some serious limitations and the chapter concludes by looking at these limitations.

# 1 The interpretation of financial statements

### 1.1 Users and their information needs

A useful start in the interpretation of accounts is to establish which classes of people have an interest in the messages conveyed by accounts. In other words, we try to ascertain who are the users of accounts and what information they need.

**Shareholders and potential investors** are primarily concerned with receiving an adequate return on their investment, but it must at least provide security and liquidity.

**Creditors** are concerned with the security of their debt or loan and therefore evaluate the company's liquidity to determine the amount and period of credit they consider prudent.

**Management** are concerned with the trend and level of profits, since this is the main measure of their success. Salaries may be linked to profits.

KEY POINT

All users require information on liquidity and cash flow.

**Bank managers and financial institutions**, employees, professional advisors to investors, financial journalists and commentators are interested in liquidity, profit potential, or ownership of a company.

All users require information on liquidity and cash flow.

### 1.2 Types of ratio

Ratios can be classified into three main groups, these are summarised in the table below.

| **Type** | **Reflects** | **Examples** |
|---|---|---|
| Profitability | Performance of company and its managers including the efficiency of asset usage | ROCE<br>GP%<br>Inventory turnover<br>Receivables and payables days |
| Financial | Financial structure and stability of the company | Gearing<br>Current and liquidity ratios |

| | | |
|---|---|---|
| Investment | Relationship of the number of ordinary shares and their price to the profits, dividends and assets of the company | EPS<br>P/E ratio<br>Dividend yield<br>Dividend cover<br>Net assets per share |

The managers of the company are likely to be concerned about all aspects of the company and therefore may want to know about all of the key ratios in each category.

Shareholders or potential investors are concerned primarily with the investment ratios though certain financial stability and profitability measures are also likely to be of interest (for example gearing and ROCE).

Creditors are most likely to be concerned about financial stability, though a bank, acting as a major source of finance, will usually also look at profitability.

### 1.3 Commenting on the ratio

Most marks in exams are available for discussion and comment, not for calculating the ratios.

KEY POINT

Most marks in exams are available for discussion and comment, not for calculating the ratios.

Ratios are meaningless on their own. They are a starting point for interpretation and analysis. Questions to ask yourself might include:

- What does the ratio literally mean?
- What does a change in the ratio mean?
- What is the norm?
- What are the limitations of the ratio?

There is no such thing as an acceptable range of values for a ratio. Profitability rates will vary between industry sectors and within industries for many reasons. The financial structure of a business can also vary considerably and yet the business operates 'healthily'. An oft quoted norm for the current ratio is 2 and the quick ratio is 1 but a supermarket with no credit customers and strong influence on its suppliers will have ratios far lower than this. In general the most meaningful analysis of ratios in terms of their acceptability is how well a business does in relation to its competitors.

### 1.4 Illustration

Extracts from the financial statements of a company are shown below. These extracts will be used throughout the chapter to illustrate the calculation of the ratios.

**Summarised balance sheets at 30 June**

| | | *20X7* | | *20X6* |
|---|---|---|---|---|
| **Assets** | $000 | $000 | $000 | $000 |
| Property, plant and equipment | | 130 | | 139 |
| Current assets: | | | | |
| Inventories | 42 | | 37 | |
| Receivables | 29 | | 23 | |
| Bank | 3 | | 5 | |
| | | 74 | | 65 |
| | | 204 | | 204 |

| | | | | |
|---|---|---|---|---|
| **Equity & liabilties** | | | | |
| Equity | | | | |
| Ordinary shares of 50 cents | | 35 | | 35 |
| Share premium account | | 17 | | 17 |
| Revaluation reserve | | 10 | | – |
| Retained earnings | | 31 | | 22 |
| | | 93 | | 74 |
| Non-current liabilities | | | | |
| 5% secured loan stock | | 65 | | 65 |
| Current liabilities | | | | |
| Trade payables | 36 | | 55 | |
| Taxation | 10 | | 10 | |
| | | 46 | | 65 |
| | | 204 | | 204 |

**Summarised income statement for the year ended 30 June**

| | *20X7* | | *20X6* | |
|---|---|---|---|---|
| | $000 | $000 | $000 | $000 |
| Revenue | | 209 | | 196 |
| Opening inventory | 37 | | 29 | |
| Purchases | 162 | | 159 | |
| | 199 | | 188 | |
| Closing inventory | 42 | | 37 | |
| | | 157 | | 151 |
| Gross profit | | 52 | | 45 |
| Depreciation | | (9) | | (9) |
| Sundry expenses | | (14) | | (11) |
| Profit from operations | | 29 | | 25 |
| Finance costs | | (4) | | (4) |
| Profit before tax | | 25 | | 21 |
| Income tax expense | | 10 | | 10 |
| Profit for the year | | 15 | | 11 |
| | | | | |
| Equity dividends paid during the year | | 6 | | 5 |

# 2 Performance, profitability and activity

## 2.1 Return on capital employed (ROCE)

KEY POINT

ROCE is usually the most important measure of profitability. It shows how efficiently a business is using its resources.

The absolute figure of profit earned is not, in itself, significant since the size of the business earning that profit may vary enormously. It is significant to consider the size of the profit figure relative to the size of the business, size being expressed in terms of the quantity of capital employed by that business.

The return on capital employed is the ratio which measures this relationship. It is a key business objective, and is thus the key ratio in assessing financial achievement. It reflects the earning power of the business operations.

The ratio in simple form is:

$$\frac{\text{Profit}}{\text{Capital employed}} \times 100\%$$

***Example***

| *20X7* | *20X6* |
|---|---|
| 29/158 × 100 = 18.3% | 25/139 × 100 = 18.0% |

KEY POINT

ROCE is also known as the primary ratio because it is often the most important measure of profitability.

ROCE is also known as the primary ratio because it is often the most important measure of profitability.

The ratio shows how efficiently a business is using its resources.

Once calculated, ROCE should be compared with:

(a) **previous years' figures** – provided there have been no changes in accounting policies unless suitable adjustments have been made to facilitate comparison (note, however that the effect of not replacing non-current assets is that their value will decrease and ROCE will increase)

(b) **company's target ROCE** – where the company's management has determined a target return as part of its budget procedure, consistent failure by a part of the business to meet the target may make it a target for disposal

(c) **the cost of borrowings** – if the cost of borrowing is say 10% and ROCE 7%, then further borrowings will reduce EPS unless the extra money can be used in areas where the ROCE is higher than the cost of borrowings

(d) **other companies in same industry** – care is required in interpretation, since there may be:

  (i) different accounting policies, e.g. research and development expenditure, inventory valuation and depreciation

  (ii) different ages of plant – where assets are written down to low book values the ROCE will appear high

  (iii) leased assets which may not appear in the balance sheet at all. (IAS 17 requires assets held under finance leases to be on the balance sheet but not those held under operating leases).

## 2.2 Alternative ways of calculating ROCE

Return on capital employed can be calculated in a number of different ways.

One version is the return on shareholders' equity which is more relevant for existing or prospective shareholders than management.

$$\text{Return on equity} = \frac{\text{Profit after interest and tax}}{\text{Ordinary share capital + reserves}}$$

***Example***

**Return on equity**

| *20X7* | *20X6* |
|---|---|
| 15/93 × 100 = 16.1% | 11/74 × 100 = 14.9% |

## 2.3 Asset turnover

$$\frac{\text{Sales}}{\text{Operating assets}}$$

The resultant figure indicates how many $ of sales are being made for every $1 of operating assets or capital employed.

***Example***

$$20X6 = \frac{£196,000}{£139,000} = 1.41$$

$$20X7 = \frac{£209,000}{£158,000} = 1.32$$

This shows that, for every $1 invested in the business in 20X6, $1.41 of sales were being made whilst this has fallen to $1.32 of sales for every $1 invested in 20X7.

### 2.4 Net profit margin/operating profit margin

$$\frac{\text{Profit from operations}}{\text{Sales}}$$

***Example***

$$20X6 = \frac{£25,000}{£196,000} = 12.8\%$$

$$20X7 = \frac{£29,000}{£209,000} = 13.9\%$$

### 2.5 Factors affecting return on capital employed

There are two:

- profitability
- rate of asset utilisation.

Note that the product of these two gives the return on capital employed:

$$\frac{\text{Operating profit}}{\text{Sales}} \times \frac{\text{Sales}}{\text{Operating assets}} = \frac{\text{Operating profit}}{\text{Operating assets}} = \text{ROCE}$$

or: Operating Profit Margin × Asset Turnover = ROCE

In the example for 20X7 using total capital employed:

$$\text{ROCE} = \frac{£29,000}{£158,000} = 18.3\%$$

$$\text{Profit margin} = \frac{\text{Operating profit}}{\text{Sales}} = \frac{£29,000}{£209,000} = 13.9\%$$

$$\text{Asset turnover} = \frac{\text{Sales}}{\text{Operating assets}} = \frac{£209,000}{£158,000} = 1.32$$

13.9% × 1.32 × 100 = 18.3%

As ROCE is made up of the product of profit margin and asset turnover then any initial analysis of ROCE over a period will normally involve calculation of these two further ratios.

KEY POINT

Profit margin is often seen as an indication of the quality of products or services supplied (top-of-range products usually have higher margins). Asset turnover is often seen as a measure of how intensively the assets are worked.

Profit margin is often seen as an indication of the quality of products or services supplied (top-of-range products usually have higher margins). Asset turnover is often seen as a measure of how intensively the assets are worked.

A trade-off may exist between margin and asset turnover.

- Low-margin businesses (e.g. food retailers) usually have a high asset turnover.
- Capital-intensive manufacturing industries usually have relatively low asset turnover but higher margins (e.g. electrical equipment manufacturers).

***Activity 1***

Companies X and Y are both involved in retailing.

Relevant information for the year ended 30 September 20X5 was as follows:

| | *X* | *Y* |
|---|---|---|
| | $000 | $000 |
| Sales revenue | 50,000 | 200,000 |
| Profit before tax | 10,000 | 10,000 |
| Capital employed | 50,000 | 50,000 |

Prepare the following ratios for both companies and comment on the results:

(a) ROCE

(b) profit margin

(c) asset turnover.

*Feedback to this activity is at the end of the chapter.*

## 2.6 Gross profit percentage

KEY POINT

Gross profit percentage is the margin that the company makes on its sales.

$$\frac{\text{Gross profit}}{\text{Sales}} \times 100\%$$

***Example***

| *20X7* | *20X6* |
|---|---|
| $\frac{52}{209} \times 100 = 24.9\%$ | $\frac{45}{196} \times 100 = 23.0\%$ |

This is the margin that the company makes on its sales.

It is expected to remain reasonably constant. Since the ratio consists of a small number of components, a change may be traced to a change in:

- selling prices – normally deliberate though sometimes unavoidable for example, because of increased competition
- sales mix – often deliberate
- purchase cost – including carriage or discounts
- production cost – materials, labour or production overheads
- inventory – errors in counting, valuing or cut-off, inventory shortages.

Inter-company comparison of margins can be very useful but it is especially important to look at businesses within the same sector. For example food retailing is able to support low margins because of the high volume of sales. A manufacturing industry would usually have higher margins.

Low margins usually suggest poor performance but may be due to expansion costs (launching a new product) or trying to increase market share. Lower margins than usual suggest scope for improvement.

One of the many factors affecting the trading profit margin is depreciation, which is open to considerable subjective judgement. Inter-company comparisons should be made after suitable adjustments to align accounting policies.

## 2.7 Inventory turnover

$$\frac{\text{Inventory}}{\text{Cost of sales}} \times 365 \text{ days}$$

***Example***

| *20X7* | *20X6* |
|---|---|
| $\frac{42}{157} \times 365 = 98$ days | $\frac{37}{151} \times 365 = 89$ days |

An alternative way of calculating this is shown below:

$$\frac{\text{Cost of sales}}{\text{Inventory}}$$

This yields a multiple expressed as, say, 10 times pa.

***Example***

| *20X7* | *20X6* |
|---|---|
| $\frac{157}{42} = 3.7$ times pa | $\frac{151}{37} = 4.1$ times pa |

Sometimes an average (based on the average inventory) is calculated which has a smoothing effect but may dampen the effect of a major change in the period.

An increasing number of days (or a diminishing multiple) implies that inventory is turning over less quickly. This is usually regarded as a bad sign:

- it may reflect lack of demand for the goods
- it may reflect poor inventory control, with its associated costs such as storage and insurance
- it may ultimately lead to inventory obsolescence and related write offs.

However, it may not necessarily be bad where:

- management are buying inventory in larger quantities to take advantage of trade discounts
- management have increased inventory levels to reduce the risk of being unable to supply customers
- the increase is slight and due to distortion of the ratio caused by comparing a year end inventory figure with cost of sales for the year and that year has been one of increasing growth.

Inventory turnover ratios vary enormously with the nature of the business. For example, a fishmonger would have an inventory turnover period of one to two days, whereas a building contractor may have an inventory turnover period of 200 days. Manufacturing companies may have an inventory turnover ratio of 60–100 days; this period is likely to increase as the goods made become larger and more complex.

For large and complex items (for example railway wagons or aircraft) there may be sharp fluctuations in inventory turnover according to whether delivery took place just before or just after the year end.

A manufacturer should take into consideration:

- reliability of suppliers – if the supplier is unreliable it is prudent to hold more raw materials
- demand – if demand is erratic it is prudent to hold more finished goods.

## 2.8 Receivables turnover

$$\frac{\text{Trade receivables}}{\text{Credit sales}} \times 365 \text{ days}$$

This can be expressed as a number of days as above or as a percentage:

$$\frac{\text{Trade receivables}}{\text{Credit sales}} \times 100\%$$

***Example***

| *20X7* | *20X6* |
|---|---|
| $\frac{29}{209} \times 365 = 50.6$ days | $\frac{23}{196} \times 365 = 42.8$ days |

The trade receivables used may be a year end figure or the average for the year. Where an average is used to calculate a number of days the ratio is the average number of days' credit taken by customers.

For cash-based businesses like supermarkets, receivables days will be very low as there are few credit sales.

For other businesses the result should be compared with the stated credit policy. A period of 30 days or 'at the end of the month following delivery' are common credit terms.

KEY POINT

Increasing receivables days is usually a bad sign as it suggests lack of proper credit control.

Increasing receivables days is usually a bad sign as it suggests lack of proper credit control. However, it may be due to:

- a deliberate policy to extend the stated credit period to attract more trade
- one major new customer being allowed different terms.

Falling receivables days is usually a good sign, though it could indicate that the company is suffering a cash shortage.

The receivables days ratio can be distorted by:

- using year end figures which do not represent average receivables
- debt factoring which results in very low receivables
- other credit finance agreements such as hire purchase, where there is insufficient analysis of revenues (HP receivables should be shown separately) to calculate proper ratios.

### 2.9 Payables days

This is usually expressed as:

$$\frac{\text{Trade payables}}{\text{Purchases}} \times 365 \text{ days}$$

and represents the credit period taken by the company from its suppliers. An average of trade payables may also be used.

***Example***

| *20X7* | *20X6* |
|---|---|
| $\frac{36}{162} \times 365 = 81.1$ days | $\frac{55}{159} \times 365 = 126.3$ days |

Where purchases are not known, cost of sales is used, or failing that, sales.

The ratio is always compared to previous years. Once again there are two main contrasting points:

- a long credit period may be good as it represents a source of free finance; or
- a long credit period may indicate that the company is unable to pay more quickly because of liquidity problems.

Note that, if the credit period is long:

- the company may develop a poor reputation as a slow payer and may not be able to find new suppliers
- existing suppliers may decide to discontinue supplies
- the company may be losing out on worthwhile cash discounts.

## 3 Financial adaptability and liquidity

### 3.1 The cash cycle

The investment made in working capital is largely a function of sales and, therefore, it is useful to consider the problem in terms of a firm's (cash operating) cycle.

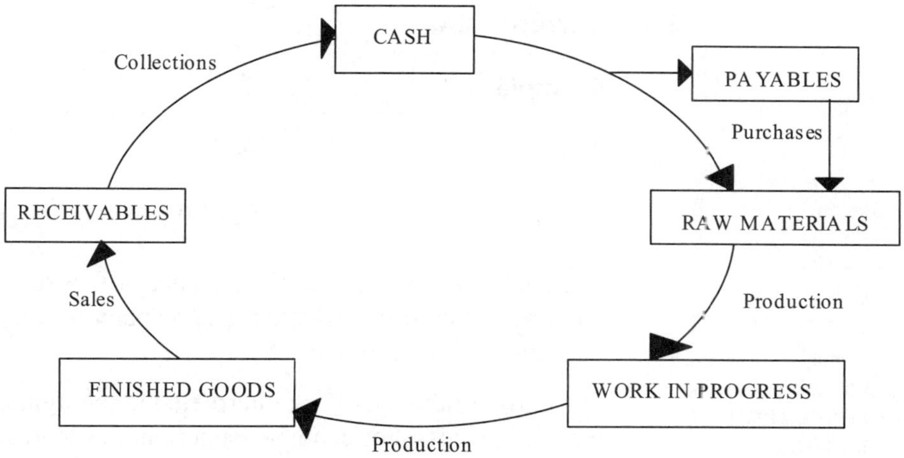


The cycle reflects a firm's investment in working capital as it moves through the production process towards sales. The investment in working capital gradually increases, firstly being only in raw materials, but then in labour and overhead as production progresses. This investment must be maintained throughout the production process, the finished goods holding period and up to the final collection of cash from customers. Note that the net investment can be reduced by taking trade credit from suppliers.

KEY POINT

The faster a firm can 'push' items around the operating cycle the lower its investment in working capital will be.

The faster a firm can 'push' items around the operating cycle the lower its investment in working capital will be. However, too little investment in working capital can lose sales since customers will generally prefer to buy from suppliers who are prepared to extend trade credit, and if items are not held in inventory when required by customers, sales may be lost.

With some fairly basic financial information it is possible to measure the length of the working capital cycle for a given firm.

***Activity 2***

Extracts from the income statement for the year and the balance sheet as at the end of the year for a company show:

| | $ |
|---|---|
| Sales | 250,000 |
| Cost of goods sold | 210,000 |
| Purchases | 140,000 |
| Receivables | 31,250 |
| Payables | 21,000 |
| Inventory | 92,500 |

How long is this company's working capital cycle?

*Feedback to this activity is at the end of the chapter.*

## 3.2 Ratios

Two ratios are used to measure a business's ability to meet its own short-term liabilities; these are:

- current or working capital ratio $\dfrac{\text{Current assets}}{\text{Current liabilities}}$
- liquidity, acid test or quick assets ratio $\dfrac{\text{Current assets} - \text{inventory}}{\text{Current liabilities}}$

## 3.3 Current ratio

***Example***

| *20X7* | *20X6* |
|---|---|
| $\frac{74}{46} = 1.61$ | $\frac{65}{65} = 1.0$ |

KEY POINT

The current ratio measures the adequacy of current assets to meet short-term liabilities.

KEY POINT

The current ratio should be interpreted in the light of what is normal for the type of business.

The current ratio measures the adequacy of current assets to meet short-term liabilities. It indicates whether the company is in a position to meet its liabilities as they fall due.

The current ratio should be interpreted in the light of what is normal for the type of business. For example, supermarkets tend to have low current ratios because:

- there are few receivables
- there is usually very tight cash control as there will be considerable investment in developing new sites and improving existing sites.

It is also worth considering:

(a) availability of further finance, for example – is the overdraft at the limit? – very often this information is highly relevant but not disclosed in the accounts

(b) seasonal nature of the business – one way of doing this is to compare the interest charges in the income statement with the overdraft and other loans in the balance sheet; if the interest rate appears abnormally high this is probably because the company has had higher levels of borrowings during the year

(c) long-term liabilities and when they fall due and how will they be financed

(d) nature of the inventory – as stated above where inventory is slow moving, the quick ratio probably provides a better indicator of short-term liquidity.

A very high current ratio is not necessarily a sign of good management. It may be due to:

- high levels of inventory and receivables (check working capital management ratios); or
- high cash levels which could be put to better use (for example by investing in non-current assets).

## 3.4 The quick ratio

***Example***

| *20X7* | *20X6* |
|---|---|
| $\frac{32}{46} = 0.7$ | $\frac{28}{65} = 0.43$ |

This is also known as the acid test ratio because by eliminating inventory from current assets it provides the acid test of whether the company has sufficient resources (receivables and cash) to settle its liabilities.

Like the current ratio it is relevant to consider the nature of the business (again supermarkets have very low quick ratios).

Sometimes the quick ratio is calculated on the basis of a six week time frame (i.e. the quick assets are those which will turn into cash in six weeks; quick liabilities are those which fall due for payment within six weeks). This basis would usually include the following in quick assets:

- bank, cash and short-term investments
- trade receivables

thus excluding prepayments and inventories.

Quick liabilities would usually include:

- bank overdraft which is usually repayable on demand
- trade payables, tax and social security.

Income tax may be excluded.

When interpreting the quick ratio, care should be taken over the status of the bank overdraft. A company with a low quick ratio may actually have no problem in paying its suppliers if sufficient overall overdraft facilities are available.

KEY POINT

Both the current and quick ratio may be distorted by window dressing.

Both the current and quick ratio may be distorted by window dressing; for example, if the current ratio is 1.4 and trade payables are paid just before the year end out of positive cash balances, the ratios improve as shown below:

| | *Before* | *Payment of $400 trade payables* | *After* |
|---|---|---|---|
| Current assets | $1,400 | –$400 | $1,000 |
| Current liabilities | $1,000 | –$400 | $600 |
| Current ratio | 1.4 | | 1.7 |

## 3.5 Overtrading

KEY POINT

Overtrading arises where expansion has been financed from short-term working capital rather than new sources of long-term capital.

A business must have a sufficient level of long-term capital to finance its long-term investment in non-current assets. A major addition to non-current assets such as the construction of a new factory or a major expansion of the business should normally be financed by raising long-term finance: for example, through a share issue or long-term borrowings.

Overtrading arises where a company expands its sales fairly rapidly without securing additional long-term capital adequate for its needs. The symptoms of overtrading are:

- inventory increasing, possibly more than proportionately to sales
- receivables increasing, possibly more than proportionately to sales
- cash and liquid assets declining at a fairly alarming rate
- payables increasing rapidly.

These symptoms imply that the company has expanded without giving proper thought to the necessity to expand its capital base. It has consequently continued to rely on its suppliers and probably its bank overdraft to provide the additional finance required. It will reach a stage where suppliers will withhold further supplies and bankers will refuse to honour further cheques until borrowings are reduced. The problem is that borrowings cannot be reduced until sales revenue is earned, which in turn cannot be achieved until production is completed, which in turn is dependent upon materials being available and wages paid. Overall result – deadlock and rapid financial collapse!

***Activity 3***

Calculate the liquidity and working capital ratios for P for the year ended 31 December 20X7.

| | *$m* |
|---|---|
| Sales revenue | 1,867.5 |
| Gross profit | 489.3 |
| Inventory | 147.9 |
| Trade receivables | 393.4 |
| Trade payables | 275.1 |
| Cash | 53.8 |
| Short-term investments | 6.2 |
| Other current liabilities | 284.3 |

*Feedback to this activity is at the end of the chapter.*

## 3.6 Interpreting financial obligations

KEY POINT

As well as calculating and interpreting liquidity ratios, it is important to be aware of other factors which may affect liquidity and cash flow.

As well as calculating and interpreting liquidity ratios, it is important to be aware of other factors which may affect liquidity and cash flow. These may not necessarily be recognised in current liabilities or even included in the balance sheet at all.

Examples of such financial obligations are given below.

***Earn out arrangements***

Where one company acquires another, part of the consideration may be deferred to a later date because it is dependent (contingent) on the performance of the acquired entity. If this is included in the latest financial statements it is likely to be based on an estimate. Alternatively, the acquirer's management may not have provided for the obligation because they believe that it is unlikely to become payable.

***Redeemable debt***

A company may have raised finance by issuing loan notes that it is committed to redeem or repurchase, probably at a premium.

***Contingent liabilities***

A **contingent liability** is:

(a) a possible obligation that arises from past events and whose existence will be confirmed only by the occurrence or non-occurrence of one or more uncertain future events not wholly within the control of the enterprise; or

(b) a present obligation that arises from past events but is not recognised because:

  (i) it is not probable that an outflow of resources embodying economic benefits will be required to settle the obligation; or

  (ii) the amount of the obligation cannot be measured with sufficient reliability.

For example, if company A sues Company B, it is likely to be some time before the case is settled and the outcome is clear. During that time Company B may have a contingent liability to pay damages.

Contingent liabilities are not recognised in the financial statements but must normally be disclosed in the notes.

***Interpretation***

In all cases such as these, the obligation may involve a material cash outflow in the near future.

Where there are either provisions based on estimates or contingent liabilities it is possible that the situation may have changed since the balance sheet date (for example, a contingent liability could have become an actual liability).

KEY POINT

If there is not enough information to make a realistic assessment, you should state this in your answer.

It is necessary to use whatever information that you are given (e.g. selected notes to the financial statements, details of events since the publication of the latest financial statements) to determine the likelihood of the cash outflow occurring, its timing and whether the entity is likely to be able to meet the obligation in practice. If there is not enough information to make a realistic assessment, you should state this in your answer.

# 4 Interpretation of cash flow data

## 4.1 Interpretation of a company's cash flow statement

Examination questions about liquidity may ask you to interpret a cash flow statement, as well as liquidity ratios. Points to watch for within the various headings in the cash flow statement include

(a) **Cash generated from operations** – The figure should be compared to the operating profit. The reconciliation of profit to net cash flow from operating activities is useful in this regard. Overtrading may be indicated by:

  (i) high profits and low cash generation

  (ii) large increases in inventory, receivables and payables.

  Profits are of high quality if they are matched by corresponding inflows of cash from operations.

KEY POINT

Profits are of high quality if they are matched by corresponding inflows of cash from operations.

(b) **Dividend and interest payouts** – These can be compared to cash generated from trading operations to see whether the normal operations can sustain such payments. In most years they should.

(c) **Investing activities** – The nature and scale of a company's investment in non-current assets is clearly shown. Remember however that a group may have increased significantly in size through 'paper' transactions (e.g. share for share issues) which will not be reflected on the statement.

(d) **Financing activities** – The changes in financing (in pure cash terms) are clearly shown. As with investing activities there may be significant non-cash flow changes in the capital structure of the business.

  Gearing can be considered at this point.

(e) **Cash flow** – The statement clearly shows the end result in cash terms of the company's activities in the year. Do not overstate the importance of this figure alone however. A decrease in cash in the year may be for very sound reasons (e.g. there was surplus cash last year) or may be mainly the result of timing (e.g. a new loan was raised just after the end of the accounting period).

### 4.2 The value of cash flow information

A cash flow statement can provide information which is not available from balance sheets and income statements.

KEY POINT

Cash flow statements should normally be used in conjunction with income statements and balance sheets when making an assessment of future cash flows.

However, a historical cash flow statement does not provide complete information for assessing future cash flows. Cash flow statements should normally be used in conjunction with income statements and balance sheets when making an assessment of future cash flows. The accruals accounting basis used in preparing income statements and balance sheets provides relevant information for projections.

Some cash flows result from transactions that took place in an earlier accounting period and some cash flows are expected to result in further cash flows in a future period.

To help in determining the future cash position other areas of the published accounts should be considered as illustrated below.

### 4.3 Cash requirements

There are four areas to consider when identifying whether or not the company has sufficient cash:

(a) repayment of existing loans

(b) increase in working capital – If the business is expanding (making more sales) working capital will also need to increase

(c) capital expenditure requirements – The notes to the financial statements should disclose capital expenditure contracted for. It is necessary to consider whether the company will have sufficient cash to meet this capital expenditure

(d) other commitments, e.g. contingent liabilities, leasing commitments.

## 5 Gearing

### 5.1 Introduction

DEFINITION

**'Gearing'** is the relationship between a company's equity capital and reserves and its debt.

'Gearing' is the relationship between a company's equity capital and reserves and its debt.

- A company is highly geared if it has a substantial proportion of its capital in the form of preference shares or loan notes.
- A company is said to have low gearing if only a small proportion of its capital is in the form of preference shares or loan notes.
- A company financed entirely by equity shares has no gearing.

Gearing affects:

- the creditworthiness of the company
- the potential return to ordinary shareholders.

### 5.2 The implications of high or low gearing

The importance of gearing can be illustrated by an example as follows.

### *Example*

Two companies, A and B, both have capital of $10,000. A has it all in the form of equity shares of $1 each, B has 5,000 $1 equity shares and $5,000 of 10% loan notes.

Both companies earn profits of $5,000 in year 1 and $2,000 in year 2. Tax is assumed at 35% and the dividend paid is 10c per share.

The position will be as follows.

| | *A* | *B* |
|---|---|---|
| | $ | $ |
| Shares | 10,000 | 5,000 |
| Loan notes | – | 5,000 |
| | 10,000 | 10,000 |

| | *A* | | *B* | |
|---|---|---|---|---|
| | *Year 1* | *Year 2* | *Year 1* | *Year 2* |
| | $ | $ | $ | $ |
| Profit before tax and loan interest | 5,000 | 2,000 | 5,000 | 2,000 |
| Loan interest | – | – | 500 | 500 |
| | | | 4,500 | 1,500 |
| Taxation (35%) | 1,750 | 700 | 1,575 | 525 |
| Earnings | 3,250 | 1,300 | 2,925 | 975 |
| Dividend (10%) | 1,000 | 1,000 | 500 | 500 |
| Retained profits | 2,250 | 300 | 2,425 | 475 |
| Earnings per share | 32.5c | 13.0c | 58.5c | 19.5c |

The effects of gearing can be seen to be as follows:

KEY POINT

Earnings of a highly geared company are more sensitive to profit changes.

- loan interest is an allowable deduction before taxation, whereas dividends are paid out of profits after taxation; company B has consistently higher retained profits than Company A
- earnings of a highly geared company are more sensitive to profit changes; this is shown by the following table.

| *Company* | *A* | *B* |
|---|---|---|
| Change in profit before interest and taxation | –60% | –60% |
| Change in earnings | –60% | $-66\frac{2}{3}$% |

The reason for the fluctuation is obviously the element of loan interest which must be paid regardless of profit level.

This more than proportionate change in earnings is important in relation to the share price of the companies. Many investors value their shares by applying a multiple (known as the P/E ratio) to the earnings per share. Applying a multiple of say 10 to the EPS disclosed above would indicate share valuations as follows.

| *Company* | *A* | | *B* | |
|---|---|---|---|---|
| Year | 1 | 2 | 1 | 2 |
| Share price | $3.25 | $1.30 | $5.85 | $1.95 |

KEY POINT

Gearing increases both the risk and potential returns of shareholders.

Thus the price of a highly geared company will often be more volatile than a company with only a small amount of gearing.

Not all companies are suitable for a highly geared structure. A company must have two fundamental characteristics if it is to use gearing successfully. These are as follows.

- **Relatively stable profits** – Loan interest must be paid whether or not profits are earned. A company with erratic profits may have insufficient funds in a bad year with which to pay loan interest. This would result in the appointment of a receiver and possibly the liquidation of the company.
- **Suitable assets for security** – Most issues of loan capital are secured on some or all of the company's assets which must be suitable for the purpose. A company with most of its capital invested in fast depreciating assets or inventory subject to rapid changes in demand and price would not be suitable for high gearing.

The classic examples of companies which are suited to high gearing are those in property investment and the hotel/leisure services industry. These companies generally enjoy relatively stable profits and have assets which are highly suitable for charging. Note that nonetheless these are industries that could be described as cyclical.

Companies not suited to high gearing would include those in the extractive industries and high-tech industries where constant changes occur. These companies could experience erratic profits and would generally have inadequate assets to pledge as security.

## 5.3 Methods of computation

There are two methods commonly used for expressing gearing:

(a) the debt/equity ratio, calculated by taking:

$$\frac{\text{Loans} + \text{preference share capital}}{\text{Ordinary share capital} + \text{reserves} + \text{minority interest}}$$

***Example***

| *20X7* | *20X6* |
|---|---|
| $\frac{65}{93} \times 100 = 69.9\%$ | $\frac{65}{74} \times 100 = 87.8\%$ |

(b) the percentage of capital employed represented by borrowings:

$$\frac{\text{Loans} + \text{preference share capital}}{\text{Total capital}}$$

***Example***

| *20X7* | *20X6* |
|---|---|
| $\frac{65}{158} \times 100 = 41.1\%$ | $\frac{65}{139} \times 100 = 46.8\%$ |

where total capital is loans, preference share capital, ordinary share capital, reserves and minority interests.

## 5.4 The effect of short-term debt

Debt is normally defined as long-term debt, which typically includes everything that is reported under long-term liabilities in the balance sheet: debenture loans; preferred shares; long-term borrowings; provisions; and the non-current portion of obligations under finance leases.

However, businesses may finance some of their activities through short-term debt such as a bank overdraft, or loans that are reported under current liabilities because they fall due for repayment within one year. The current portion of finance lease obligations may also be significant.

If there are indications that an entity is relying heavily on short-term finance, it is appropriate to take this into account when calculating the gearing ratio, for example:

$$\frac{\text{Loans} + \text{preference share capital} + \text{bank overdraft}}{\text{Ordinary share capital} + \text{reserves} + \text{minority interest}}$$

By doing this, it is possible (for example) to make a meaningful comparison between two entities, one of which has financed capital investment by raising long-term debt while the other has increased its bank overdraft.

### 5.5 Interest cover

This ratio emphasises the cover (or security) for interest payable. It is defined as follows:

$$\text{Interest cover} = \frac{\text{Profit before interest and tax}}{\text{Interest payable}}$$

***Example***

| *20X7* | *20X6* |
|---|---|
| $\frac{29}{4}$ i.e. 7.2 times | $\frac{25}{4}$ i.e. 6.2 times |

## 6 Investors' ratios

### 6.1 User focus

For equity investors, return on investment comprises a combination of dividend income and capital growth.

KEY POINT

Investors' ratios help to establish the characteristics of ordinary shares in different companies.

Investors' ratios help to establish the characteristics of ordinary shares in different companies.

Earnings per share is important to those looking for capital growth.

Dividend yield, dividend cover and dividends per share are useful to income seekers.

Ideally, investors should use forecast information when making investment decisions (e.g. forecast earnings, dividends and net asset values). This is because the value of investments depends primarily on *future* returns.

In practice, investors usually only have historical figures representing recent performance and need to draw conclusions on this basis.

### 6.2 Dividend yield

Dividend yield is calculated as follows.

$$\text{Dividend yield} = \frac{\text{Dividend per share}}{\text{Current market price per share}} \times 100\%$$

***Example***

Suppose that the company in the illustration is quoted on the Stock Exchange and that the market value of each ordinary share is 204 pence. This gives a dividend yield of

$$\frac{8.6c}{204c} \times 100 = 4.2\%$$

Dividend per share is calculated as:

$$\frac{\text{Total ordinary dividend}}{\text{Total number of ordinary shares}}$$

| *20X7* | *20X6* |
|---|---|
| $\frac{6,000}{70,000} = 8.6\ c$ | $\frac{5,000}{70,000} = 7.1\ c$ |

***Tutorial note:*** The ordinary share capital of the company is made up of \$35,000 of 50 cent shares. Therefore, there is a total of 70,000 shares.

The ratio measures dividend policy rather than performance.

Note that a high dividend yield based on the most recent dividends and current share price may arise because the share price has fallen in anticipation of a future dividend cut.

Rapidly growing companies may have low dividend yields based on historical dividends, especially if the current share price reflects anticipated future growth in earnings and dividends.

## 6.3 Earnings per share

The calculation of basic EPS is as follows.

$$EPS = \frac{\text{Profit available for ordinary dividends}}{\text{Number of ordinary shares in issue}}$$

***Example***

| *20X7* | *20X6* |
|---|---|
| $\frac{15,000}{70,000} = 21.4c$ | $\frac{11,000}{70,000} = 15.7c$ |

The calculation of EPS is looked at in more detail in a later chapter.

## 6.4 Dividend cover

Dividend cover is calculated as follows.

$$\text{Dividend cover} = \frac{\text{Earnings per share}}{\text{Dividend per share}}$$

***Example***

| *20X7* | *20X6* |
|---|---|
| $\frac{15,000}{6,000} = 2.5\text{ times}$ | $\frac{11,000}{5,000} = 2.2\text{ times}$ |

This ratio shows how many times a company could have paid its current dividend from available earnings, i.e. it indicates how secure dividends are. Dividend cover of less than 2 is usually considered inadequate.

Investors may be attracted to companies with relatively high dividend yield but if dividend cover is low, this indicates that dividends are at greater risk of being cut, and that the high yield is because the share price already reflects an anticipated cut in dividends.

### 6.5 Price-earnings ratio (P/E ratio)

The P/E ratio is calculated as follows.

$$\text{P/E ratio} = \frac{\text{Current market price per share}}{\text{Earnings per share}}$$

***Example***

For 20X7, the price earnings ratio is:

$$\frac{204\text{c}}{21.4\text{c}} = 9.5$$

The ratio is used to indicate whether shares appear expensive or cheap in terms of how many years of current earnings investors are prepared to pay for.

KEY POINT

A high P/E ratio usually indicates that investors expect significant future earnings growth and hence are prepared to pay a large multiple of historical earnings.

If calculated on historical earnings, a high P/E ratio usually indicates that investors expect significant future earnings growth and hence are prepared to pay a large multiple of historical earnings. Low P/E ratios usually indicate that investors consider growth prospects to be poor.

If a P/E ratio is based on forecast EPS, relatively expensive shares (ie with high P/E ratios) will not be attractive to shareholders.

## 7 Trend analysis

### 7.1 Published accounts

In order to appreciate the overall financial position or strength of a company or group it is important to review the trend of results. By including a summary of the results of the company for the last few years within the annual report, the reader is shown how the company has arrived at its present position, and is thereby enabled to view the year's results in the context of the disclosed trend.

Published accounts give comparative information in two main areas:

- the corresponding amounts for items shown in the balance sheet, income statement, cash flow statement, statement of changes in equity and notes. Such amounts are required by IAS 1 for virtually all items disclosed in the accounts
- any historical summary provided. Such summaries, which often take the form of four- or ten-year summaries, are not required by IASs, but have nevertheless become a common feature in the annual reports of quoted companies. Historical summaries are disclosed as information supplemental to the financial statements.

There are two important points to consider:

- Have there been any changes in accounting policies during the period and if so, have the summarised figures been restated?
- Have the summarised figures been adjusted for the effect of inflation and if not, what mental adjustments are necessary in order to draw any conclusions from the information?

### 7.2 Effect of inflation

A significant weakness of historic cost accounting is the misleading impression of the trend of a company's performance over a period of time as no account is taken of changes in the real value of money. Current cost valuations do not remedy this defect as the valuations reflect prices ruling at a balance sheet date and previous years' accounts only reflect valuations at previous years' prices.

### 7.3 Interpreting trends in accounting ratios

KEY POINT

Trends in accounting ratios may provide a more useful insight into an entity's financial performance and position than the latest financial statements taken on their own.

Despite the effect of inflation, trends in accounting ratios may provide a more useful insight into an entity's financial performance and position than the latest financial statements taken on their own.

Comparative figures for several years provide information about the way in which the performance and financial position of a business has changed over a period. For example, if a company has low liquidity ratios for a particular year this would normally indicate liquidity problems. However, if low liquidity ratios are viewed in the context of a steadily improving trend the picture is very different: the company is able to survive at this level, is overcoming its problems and is unlikely to go into receivership in the near future.

Trends in accounting ratios may provide information from which future performance can be predicted, particularly if the figures are very stable.

The extent to which amounts and ratios are stable or volatile can reveal a great deal. Ratios which are very volatile, or sudden changes in trends may indicate that the company will experience problems in the future, even if performance is apparently improving.

## 8 Limitations of ratio analysis

### 8.1 General limitations

KEY POINT

Accounting ratios are a useful means of identifying significant relationships between different figures. However, they cannot be considered in isolation.

Accounting ratios are a useful means of identifying significant relationships between different figures. However, they cannot be considered in isolation; they must always be interpreted in relation to other information, for example:

- budgeted figures
- industry averages
- 'ideal' figures
- figures for a similar business
- comparative figures for the same business.

The chief limitations of the usefulness of ratio analysis are as follows.

- Although there are general guidelines (for example, the quick ratio should not normally be less than 1), there is no such thing as an 'ideal' ratio. A quick ratio of less than 1 would be acceptable in some businesses, but would be dangerously low for many others.
- Unless ratios are calculated on a uniform basis, from uniform data, comparisons can be very misleading.
- The accounting periods covered by the financial statements may not reflect representative financial positions.
- Ratios based on historical cost accounts do not give a true picture of trends from year to year. An apparent increase in profit may not be a 'true' increase, because of the effects of inflation.
- Financial statements only reflect those activities which can be expressed in money terms. They do not give a complete picture of the activities of a business.
- Financial statements are based on historic information and may be several months out of date by the time they are published.

Some of these limitations are discussed in more detail below.

### 8.2 Interfirm comparisons

It can be useful to compare ratios for an individual company with those of other firms in the same industry. This is possible in several ways, according to the ratios under discussion.

- For Stock Exchange ratios, both dividend yield and P/E ratios are published in the financial press.
- Operating ratios are best compared via an interfirm comparison scheme. These have been set up in a number of industries. The general principle of such schemes is that participant firms supply data to an independent collator. In order to ensure comparability, data must be presented on a uniform basis. Data on other companies is collated and made available to participants in an anonymous form (as companies do not normally wish their competitors to be provided with detailed information about their operations). Individual companies may then compare their ratios with those typical of the industry.

Comparing the financial statements of similar businesses can be misleading because:

- the businesses may use different accounting policies (as discussed above)
- ratios may not be calculated according to the same formula. For example, there are several possible definitions of gearing and return on capital employed
- large organisations can achieve economies of scale (e.g. by negotiating extended credit periods, or discounts for bulk buying with suppliers). These measures may not be available to smaller businesses
- companies within the same industry can serve completely different markets and there may be differences in sales mix and product range. These can affect profitability and activity ratios such as profit margin and expenses to sales.

## 8.3 The impact that seasonal trading can have on calculated ratios

KEY POINT

The accounting periods covered by the financial statements may not reflect representative financial positions.

The accounting periods covered by the financial statements may not reflect representative financial positions.

Many businesses produce accounts to a date on which there is a relatively low amount of trading activity. In many countries retail organisations often have an end of February accounting date (after the peak pre-Christmas trading and the January sales). As a result the items on a balance sheet are not representative of the items throughout the accounting period.

Consider inventory levels in a retail organisation. They may vary as shown in the graph below.

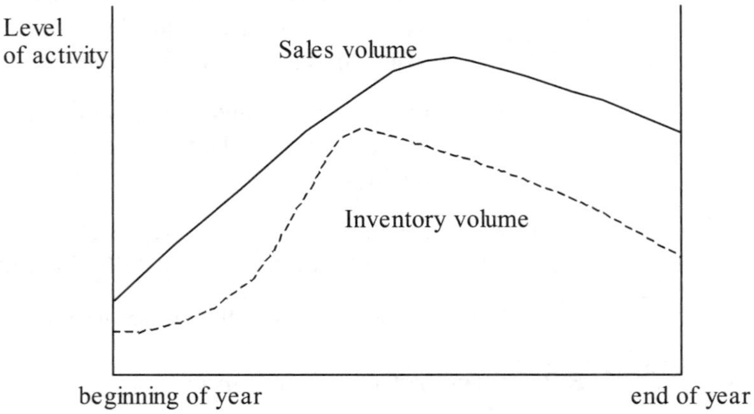


Adding opening and closing inventory and dividing by two, will not produce a fair average.

## 8.4 International comparisons

KEY POINT

Where the financial statements are prepared in accordance with the regulatory framework of different countries there may be particular problems in making direct comparisons between them.

As we have seen, there are several reasons why it can be misleading to compare the financial statements of similar businesses. Where the financial statements are prepared in accordance with the regulatory framework of different countries there may be particular problems in making direct comparisons between them.

(a) Despite international convergence, accounting standards can vary significantly between countries. This means that financial statements may have to be restated to comply with local practice. There is a general tendency for accounting standards to become more prescriptive with the result that particular accounting treatments which are required in some countries may not be allowed in others. For example, there are still some significant differences between IASs, UK GAAP and US GAAP.

(b) Accounting policies can also vary even where the requirements of accounting standards are broadly similar. For example, the last-in-first-out (LIFO) method of inventory valuation is permitted in many countries, including the US; it is not normally used in the UK. Similar considerations apply to items such as depreciation, bad and doubtful debts and valuation of non-current assets. Little or no information may be disclosed about the accounting policies adopted.

(c) The presentation of overseas accounts may be very different from that required by IASs. For example:

(i) it may be difficult to analyse liabilities between current and long-term (preventing calculation of meaningful gearing, current and quick ratios)

(ii) some countries require proposed dividends to be disclosed in the income statement and recognised as a liability in the balance sheet

(iii) accounts may use different terminology from that used by IASs.

(d) The business environment differs from country to country. For example:

(i) In some countries most finance is in the form of debt, rather than equity, meaning that very high gearing and low interest and dividend cover should not be interpreted as danger signs as they would be for a UK or US company.

(ii) Companies may be legally required to set aside a certain proportion of profits to a 'legal reserve'.

(iii) The use of short-term debt to finance long-term assets may be acceptable in some countries, meaning that current and quick ratios must be interpreted accordingly.

(iv) Tax legislation is likely to differ from country to country and this may affect the way in which the business operates.

(v) The priorities of shareholders affect the financial statements. If shareholders consist of the bank, customers and suppliers rather than institutional investors, they may prefer to concentrate on strengthening the business for the longer term rather than on short-term profits. This may mean that low profitability ratios are relatively acceptable. Likewise, if management feel secure in their employment and continuity is valued, short-term results will be less important to them.

(vi) Local customs may affect ratios such as inventory turnover and receivables turnover. Redundancies may be unacceptable, so that low inventory turnover indicates continuing production through slack times, rather than obsolete inventory or poor management.

International issues are covered in more detail in Chapter 18.

# 9 Analysing financial statements: practical issues

## 9.1 General interpretation technique

***Analysing the question requirement***

Interpretation questions normally contain a specific scenario, usually found in the opening lines of the question, where you will be told:

- what the company does
- why you are being asked to interpret the accounts.

Further information, such as accounting policies adopted or other important issues, is then usually provided in the notes following on from the numerical information.

The Examiner expects you to interpret the financial information in the light of the scenario and to use **all** the additional information. The general rule is that, if information is provided, it is almost certainly relevant.

A question may present you with a specific requirement (e.g. 'Comment on business factors affecting the company's performance'), or you may be made aware of the specific concerns of your audience (e.g. a shareholder suspects that the accounts have been manipulated). Alternatively, the requirement could be general ('Report to an individual investor commenting on the company's performance and financial position').

***Observation***

KEY POINT

Start by looking carefully at the financial statements. This can often tell you more, more quickly, than calculating ratios.

Start by looking carefully at the financial statements. This can often tell you more, more quickly, than calculating ratios (and does not depend on selecting the correct ratios).

The scenario will probably 'lead' you to particular areas of the financial statements. If this is the case, you should obviously concentrate on these areas.

If there are no clues in the scenario, consider the following issues in the balance sheet:

- Non-current assets: revaluations? significant additions – expansion, how financed?
- Working capital: in line with revenue, cost of sales?
- Loans: repaid – how? (shares issued?)
- Share capital: share issues – why? (repay debt, finance acquisition, expansion?)
- Reserves: anything interesting?

In the income statement and statement of changes in equity, consider the following issues:

- Sales growth v profit growth.
- Interest (relate to debt, economic factors).
- Dividends (trend, level, cover).

KEY POINT

You may need to indicate further information needed for fuller analysis.

Note that you may need to indicate further information needed for fuller analysis. Here are some ideas.

- additional information needed for specific ratios (e.g. share price for price/earnings ratio)
- segmental analysis
- industry averages
- changes in management policy (e.g. relating to inventories or credit terms given)
- reasons for specific changes not explained by information given.

***Calculation of ratios***

You may not have to do any calculations. Sometimes the Examiner provides you with ratios rather than financial statements. Alternatively, you may be asked for specific ratios.

However, if the requirement is silent as to which ratios to calculate, try to direct your answer at the reader (e.g. an investor: earnings per share, ROCE, profit margins, gearing), and/or the scenario (e.g. a sale and repurchase transaction: gearing, ROCE).

KEY POINT

Most users are concerned with return on capital employed, gearing, liquidity.

Note that most users of the financial statements are concerned with return on capital employed, profit margins, gearing and liquidity. Remember, though, that an audience can be interested in all of these, but sometimes attaches more weight to some factors and less to others.

For example, the directors of a company that wants to acquire another will be **most** interested in profitability and efficiency. Liquidity and gearing **may** be less relevant **if** the potential acquirer has surplus cash and can inject it

KEY POINT

Always remember that most marks in the exam are likely to be for specific, relevant comments rather than solely for computations.

into a new subsidiary. The scenario will probably give you clues as to the relative importance of the various factors in this kind of situation.

In the absence of guidance, go for variety. Try to cover all the main areas: profitability, liquidity, working capital management and gearing. Eight ratios is probably a reasonable number to aim at. More than ten ratios is probably too many.

Do not dwell on **calculating** ratios at the expense of interpretation. Always remember that most marks in the exam are likely to be for specific, relevant comments rather than solely for computations.

***Setting out your answer***

Most interpretation questions ask you for a report; some ask for a letter or a briefing note.

Whatever format is required, your answer should be headed up correctly, with the subject, the addressor, the addressee and the date.

Start with a **brief** introductory paragraph setting out your terms of reference (e.g. 'As requested, I have analysed the financial statements of X Ltd for the three years ended …')

Structure your answer with headings, for example:

- profitability, working capital management, liquidity, gearing; or
- specific issues highlighted in the scenario.

Remember to **interpret** the financial statements. It is not usually enough (for example) to say that gross profit margin has increased. You should explain **why** it has increased (if this is reasonably obvious) or try to offer possible explanations and/or say what further information you need. Try not to interpret the ratios in isolation; make connections between the different areas. Don't forget to use simple observation, too.

Unless the question asks you to do otherwise, present the ratios as an appendix, showing your calculations. This is especially important where there are different ways of calculating a ratio, e.g. the gearing ratio.

There should be a **conclusion**. This should summarise your findings and your recommendations (if you have been asked to make recommendations).

***Practice***

Interpreting financial statements is something you can only learn by actually doing. **Practise** on as many past exam and exam-standard questions as you can.

In the remainder of this section, we look at some of the issues that could feature as part of the scenario in a question.

## 9.2 Business factors

KEY POINT

Ratios may change over time or differ between companies because of the nature of the business or management actions.

The type of business affects the nature of assets employed and returns earned.

Ratios may change over time or differ between companies because of the nature of the business or management actions.

***The type of business***

This affects the nature of assets employed and returns earned.

- Manufacturing industries: capital intensive, therefore relatively low asset turnover.
- Service industries: principal resource is people, therefore asset turnover relatively high.

- Builder: inventories and work in progress high, therefore inventory turnover relatively low.
- Supermarket: perishable inventories, therefore inventory turnover high.

It can often be helpful to consider whether the income statements and balance sheets appear as they should for a particular type of business.

### *Activity 4*

Given below is information from the balance sheets of five companies expressed as percentages of total assets less current liabilities.

The respective areas of activity of the companies are:

A Manufacturing

B Insurance brokers

C Housebuilding

D Retail stores

E Investment in properties for rental

The assets and liabilities shown as a percentage of total assets less current liabilities are:

| | *1* | *2* | *3* | *4* | *5* |
|---|---|---|---|---|---|
| | % | % | % | % | % |
| Land and property | 16 | 32 | 83 | 96 | 72 |
| Other non-current assets | 7 | 42 | 14 | 1 | 23 |
| Inventory and work in progress | 148 | 47 | 13 | – | – |
| Trade receivables | 31 | 41 | 4 | 1 | 436 |
| Cash/short-term investments | 1 | 11 | 6 | 4 | 91 |
| | 203 | 173 | 120 | 102 | 622 |
| Trade payables | (36) | (60) | (11) | (2) | (509) |
| Bank overdraft | (67) | (13) | (9) | – | (13) |
| Total assets less current liabilities | 100 | 100 | 100 | 100 | 100 |

State which balance sheet belongs to each of the companies. Give your reasons.

*Feedback to this activity is at the end of the chapter.*

***Groups and individual companies***

Being part of a group can have quite a significant effect on the individual financial statements of a company.

This is because intra-group transactions often take place on terms that are different (usually more favourable) than between two independent companies trading at arms' length:

- Profit margins may be unusually high.
- Interest rates on intra-group loans may be unusually low.
- A group company may exist (for example) to supply essential goods or services to another, so that it has a guaranteed market for its output.
- Services (e.g. administration) may be supplied free of charge.

It may be difficult to compare the performance of a group company with that of a similar company that is not part of a group.

***Events taking place during the period***

These may include:

- acquisition or disposal of a subsidiary during the year
- management actions (e.g. price discounting to increase market share) or changes in nature of business (e.g. diversification or divestment)
- fund raising near the year-end
- significant asset sales or purchases near the year end.

Consider the following:

- What effect do these events have on performance (including cash flow) and key ratios for the current year?
- What effect might they be expected to have on performance and key ratios in the next period and in the longer term?
- What is the apparent or possible reason for the event? Has it taken place for a legitimate business reason, or is it a deliberate attempt to improve the appearance of the financial statements in the short term?

A significant event near the year end often distorts ratios for that year and makes it harder to predict future performance. For example, if long-term borrowings increase just before the year end, the income statement will not include a full year's interest charge on the new borrowings, earnings per share and interest cover will probably fall in the following period.

***Other business factors***

These may include:

- The nature of the business (e.g. highly seasonal, fashionable, high technology). Technology can be particularly vulnerable to sudden changes in fashion and in the market.
- Quality of management. Better managed businesses are likely to be more profitable and have better working capital management than businesses where management is weak.
- The state of the economy and market conditions. If the market or the economy in general is depressed, this is likely to affect companies adversely and make most or all of their ratios appear worse. The impact may differ between market sectors.

## 9.3 Impact of accounting policies

KEY POINT

Accounting policies can significantly affect the view presented by accounts, and ratios computed, without affecting a business's core ability to generate profits and cash.

Accounting policies can significantly affect the view presented by accounts, and ratios computed, without affecting a business's core ability to generate profits and cash.

Probably the most important example of this is the measurement of non-current assets at fair value rather than historical cost. This reduces earnings (profits decrease due to the additional depreciation) ROCE (capital employed increases while profits decrease) and gearing (capital employed increases, while debt remains the same). Another effect of fair value accounting is that profits and trends in ratios may become more volatile and therefore harder to interpret.

The potential impact of accounting policies is especially important where:

- accounting standards permit a choice (e.g. cost v fair value, capitalisation of borrowings v interest expense)

- judgement is needed in making accounting estimates (e.g. inventory valuation, depreciation, doubtful receivables, provisions)
- there is no accounting standard (e.g. some forms of revenue recognition).

Specific areas which may be important include:

***Leases***

Under IAS 17 finance leases must be capitalised and the related obligation included in long-term liabilities. This increases gearing and reduces ROCE. Operating leases do not have to be capitalised.

***Defined benefit pension plans***

IAS 19 allows a certain amount of flexibility in the treatment of actuarial gains and losses. An entity that chose to recognise these in the income statement immediately would have lower earnings than an entity applying the '10% corridor' rule.

***Joint ventures***

IAS 31 allows either proportional consolidation or equity accounting for jointly controlled entities. Where a jointly controlled entity has long-term debt, equity accounting results in lower gearing than proportional consolidation.

***Goodwill***

IFRS 3 has recently prohibited the amortisation of goodwill, which is now carried in the balance sheet indefinitely, subject to annual impairment reviews. This means that, for many entities, ROCE will decrease (net assets increase) but earnings will increase (no amortisation charge). Another possible effect is that earnings may become more volatile, because impairment losses will not necessarily occur in a predictable pattern.

***Capitalisation of borrowings***

IAS 23 allows a choice between capitalising borrowings relating to certain assets and recognising them as an expense in the period in which they are incurred. Capitalising borrowings will tend to decrease ROCE but increase earnings in the short-term.

***Share-based payment***

IFRS 2 has recently been issued. It requires entities to recognise the expense of share-based payment, which will significantly reduce earnings for many businesses.

***Financial instruments***

Some financial instruments are 'at fair value through profit and loss'. This may make profits very volatile.

## 9.4 Creative accounting

**Creative accounting** is a form of accounting which, while complying with all regulations, nevertheless gives a biased impression (usually favourable) of the company's performance.

An investor or another interested party may be openly suspicious that creative accounting has taken place. Alternatively, the scenario may highlight the fact that management has a strong motive for presenting the financial statements in the best possible light. For example:

- the directors want to sell the company in the near future
- the company is going through a difficult period (e.g. falling profits, lack of shareholder confidence, a possible takeover)
- directors' remuneration is strongly linked to performance (e.g. bonuses if earnings per share exceeds a certain amount)
- the company is in danger of breaching loan covenants (for example, if the current/quick ratio or the gearing ratio falls above or below a certain figure).

There are a number of ways in which creative accounting can take place.

***Unusual transactions***

IAS 1, IAS 8 and the *Framework* set out the general principle that an entity should report the substance of a transaction rather than its strict legal form. However, there is no accounting standard that specifically deals either with specific types of transaction (e.g. sale and repurchase agreements, debt factoring) or with substance in general.

It is still possible for a company to account for complex transactions so that significant assets and liabilities are not recognised on the balance sheet. This normally improves ROCE and gearing.

The issue of substance over form was covered in detail in an earlier chapter. Transactions most likely to feature in a question include sale and repurchase agreements and the use of special purpose entities (quasi-subsidiaries).

***Aggressive earnings management***

IAS 18 was covered in an earlier chapter. It does not cover certain specialised transactions and therefore some entities may seek to manipulate earnings by recognising revenue before it has been earned.

***Unusual assets***

A company may try to recognise an asset which strictly speaking is not an asset but an expense. Examples include marketing or advertising costs and recruitment costs (particularly where these have been incurred to recruit staff with essential skills or technical knowledge).

This kind of 'asset' should be tested against the principles set out in the *Framework*:

- An asset is a resource controlled by the entity as the result of past events and from which future economic benefits are expected to flow to the entity.
- An asset should only be recognised if:

  it is probable that any future economic benefit associated with the item will flow to the entity; and

  the item has a cost or value that can be measured with reliability.

If these conditions are not met then the item is not an asset. Remember that certain types of asset can never be recognised; these include internally generated goodwill and human resources.

***Changes to accounting policies or accounting estimates***

Changes to accounting policies are only justified if they are required by a new standard or if they result in more relevant information. However, revaluations can be partly motivated by a desire to improve the gearing ratio. It is also possible to review and lengthen the useful lives of non-current assets so that the depreciation charge is reduced and profit is increased.

***Profit smoothing***

Profit smoothing involves manipulating the profit figure by setting up assets or liabilities in the balance sheet and releasing these amounts to the income statement over time.

This is less common than it used to be. IAS 37 *Provisions, Contingent Liabilities and Contingent Assets* prohibits the recognition of provisions unless they are clearly liabilities at the balance sheet date.

### 9.5 Intangible assets and intellectual property

A traditional manufacturing business generates profits mainly from the use of property, plant and equipment. Its financial statements can be interpreted fairly easily because there is a clear relationship between the plant and equipment and working capital in the balance sheet and the profit or loss in the income statement.

Business practice has changed very significantly over the last 20 years. Many businesses now depend upon assets such as copyrights, patents, customer databases and the technical or interpersonal skills of their staff.

These assets are not normally recognised in the balance sheet, and there are important implications for analysis of the financial statements. Key ratios, such as ROCE and gearing may be virtually meaningless. Interpretations of performance have to be based on profit margins and sales growth. It can be much harder to predict future performance because this is more likely to be significantly affected by unpredictable events than in a business such as manufacturing or retailing. For example, in some situations it could be disastrous if several key members of staff left the company.

In an exam situation you will have to work with whatever information you are given, but it very important to be aware of what the financial statements do **not** tell you.

In a later chapter we will look at the limitations of traditional financial statements in more detail.

## Summary

- There are several techniques for interpreting financial information, of which the most frequently used is ratio analysis. Commonly used ratios include return on capital employed (ROCE), net profit margin, asset turnover, current ratio, quick (acid test) ratio, earnings per share and gearing. It is important to ask the following questions:
  - Who is the user of the accounts?
  - What decisions does he or she wish to make?
  - What information is relevant for this purpose?

- Although ratio analysis is a useful tool for interpreting financial statements, it has many limitations. Ratios should always be interpreted in the context of other information about the businesses involved, particularly the accounting policies adopted.

Having completed your study of this chapter, you should have achieved the following learning outcomes:

- calculate and interpret a full range of accounting ratios
- analyse financial statements (in the context of information provided in the accounts and corporate report) to comment on performance and position
- prepare a concise report on the results of an analysis of financial statements
- explain the limitations of accounting ratio analysis and analysis based on financial statements
- prepare and interpret interfirm and international comparisons.

## Self-test questions

**1** What information do all users require? (1.1)

**2** What is measured by ROCE? (2.1)

**3** Which two factors affect ROCE? (2.5)

**4** Define inventory turnover. (2.7)

**5** What are the symptoms of overtrading? (3.5)

**6** Which four things should be considered when deciding whether a company has sufficient cash? (4.3)

**7** What are the two main ways of calculating the gearing ratio? (5.3)

**8** What is measured by dividend cover? (6.4)

**9** What is a major problem in analysing trends over several years? (7.2)

**10** Give two examples of business factors that may affect ratios. (9.1)

## Objective test questions

### Question 1

Welwyn buys and sells a single product. The following is an extract from its balance sheet at 31 December 20X7.

| | *20X7* | *20X6* |
|---|---|---|
| | $000 | $000 |
| Inventories | 50 | 40 |
| Receivables | 16 | 24 |

Sales and purchases during 20X7 were $200,000 and $120,000 respectively. 20% of sales were for cash.

What were the average receivables' collection period and gross profit percentage for the year ended 31 December 20X7?

| | *Average receivables' collection period* | *Gross profit percentage* |
|---|---|---|
| **A** | 37 days | 35% |
| **B** | 37 days | 45% |
| **C** | 46 days | 35% |
| **D** | 46 days | 45% |

### Question 2

The asset turnover of Taplow is 110% of that of Stoke.

The return on capital employed by Taplow is 80% of that of Stoke.

Taplow's profit margin expressed as a percentage of that of Stoke is:

**A** 73%

**B** 88%

**C** 95%

**D** 138%

*For the answers to these questions, see the 'Answers' section at the end of the book.*

## Practice question

### SR

You are the management accountant of SR. PQ is a competitor in the same industry and it has been operating for 20 years.

Summaries of PQ's income statements and balance sheets for the previous three years are given below.

**Summarised income statements for year ended 31 December**

| | *20X7* | *20X8* | *20X9* |
|---|---|---|---|
| | $m | $m | $m |
| Sales revenue | 840 | 981 | 913 |
| Cost of sales | 554 | 645 | 590 |
| Gross profit | 286 | 336 | 323 |
| Selling, distribution and administration expenses | 186 | 214 | 219 |
| Profit before interest | 100 | 122 | 104 |
| Interest | 6 | 15 | 19 |
| Profit before tax | 94 | 107 | 85 |
| Tax | 45 | 52 | 45 |
| Profit for the year | 49 | 55 | 40 |

**Summarised balance sheets at 31 December**

| | *20X7* | *20X8* | *20X9* |
|---|---|---|---|
| Non-current assets: | $m | $m | $m |
| Intangible assets | 36 | 40 | 48 |
| Tangible assets at net book value | 176 | 206 | 216 |
| | 212 | 246 | 264 |
| Current assets: | | | |
| Inventory | 237 | 303 | 294 |
| Receivables | 105 | 141 | 160 |
| Bank | 52 | 58 | 52 |
| | 606 | 748 | 770 |

| | | | |
|---|---|---|---|
| Equity | | | |
| Share capital | 100 | 100 | 100 |
| Retained earnings | 299 | 330 | 346 |
| | 399 | 430 | 446 |
| Non-current liabilities: | | | |
| Long-term loans | 74 | 138 | 138 |
| Current liabilities: | | | |
| Trade payables | 53 | 75 | 75 |
| Other payables | 80 | 105 | 111 |
| | 606 | 748 | 770 |

You may assume that the index of retail prices has remained constant between 20X7 and 20X9.

**You are required** to write a report to the finance director of SR:

(a) analysing the performance of PQ and showing any calculations in an appendix to this report **(20 marks)**

(b) summarising five areas which require further investigation, including reference to other pieces of information which would complement your analysis of the performance of PQ. **(10 marks)**

**(Total: 30 marks)**

*For the answer to this question, see the 'Answers' section at the end of the book.*

## Exam-type questions

### F

You are employed in the small business section of a medium-sized bank. Some time ago the bank provided a local manufacturing company, F with an overdraft facility of $3,000,000. This limit was reached on 30 September 20X4 but was increased then to $5,000,000.

Your section head has just received the half-yearly financial statements of F for the period to 30 September 20X5. Having read these statements, your section head is extremely concerned as to the performance of the company over the last year and is considering recommending the termination of the overdraft facility. Before making any further decision, your section head wishes to have a second opinion. Accordingly, he leaves a file of information concerning F on your desk and requires a report recommending the best course of action.

Information contained in the file:

***Item 1:*** Income statements

| | *Six months to 30 September 20X5* | *Six months to 31 March 20X5* |
|---|---|---|
| | $000 | $000 |
| Sales | 10,000 | 11,000 |
| Cost of sales | (5,000) | (5,500) |
| Gross profit | 5,000 | 5,500 |
| Other operating expenses | (5,000) | (4,500) |

| | | |
|---|---|---|
| Operating profit | – | 1,000 |
| Interest payable | (1,000) | (900) |
| Profit/(loss) before tax | (1,000) | 100 |
| Tax estimate | – | – |
| Profit/(loss) after tax | (1,000) | 100 |

***Item 2:*** Balance sheets at 30 September

| | *20X5* | | *20X4* | |
|---|---|---|---|---|
| | $000 | $000 | $000 | $000 |
| Non-current assets: | | | | |
| Property | 5,000 | | 5,200 | |
| Plant | 3,500 | | 3,000 | |
| | | 8,500 | | 8,200 |
| Current assets: | | | | |
| Inventories | 3,000 | | 2,600 | |
| Receivables | 5,000 | | 4,600 | |
| Cash in hand | 80 | | 80 | |
| | 8,080 | | 7,280 | |
| Current liabilities: | | | | |
| Trade payables | 2,600 | | 2,600 | |
| Bank overdraft | 5,000 | | 3,000 | |
| | 7,600 | | 5,600 | |
| Net current assets | | 480 | | 1,680 |
| 12% loan notes | | | | |
| (secured against the property) | | (4,800) | | (4,800) |
| | | 4,180 | | 5,080 |
| Share capital ($1 shares) | | 4,000 | | 4,000 |
| Retained earnings | | 180 | | 1,080 |
| | | 4,180 | | 5,080 |

***Item 3:*** Estimated realisable values of the assets of F at 30 September 20X5, based on a 'forced sale' scenario

| | $000 |
|---|---|
| Property | 5,000 |
| Plant | 1,000 |
| Inventories | 800 |
| Receivables | 2,500 |
| | 9,300 |

**Required:**

(a) Using the items contained in the file, write a report to your section head which contains an appraisal of the performance and financial position of F and considers the implications for the bank of calling in the overdraft. **(11 marks)**

(b) Produce a short appendix to the report you have compiled in (a). This should summarise the limitations of the information available to you as a basis for making a recommendation as to the wisdom or otherwise of calling in the overdraft. **(4 marks)**

**(Total: 15 marks)**

### Webster

Webster is a diversified holding company that is looking to acquire a suitable engineering company. Two private limited engineering companies, Cole and Darwin, are available for sale. The summarised financial statements for the year to 31 March 2000 of both companies are as follows:

**Income statements:**

| | *Cole* | | *Darwin* | |
|---|---|---|---|---|
| | $000 | $000 | $000 | $000 |
| Sales revenues (note 1) | | 3,000 | | 4,400 |
| Opening inventory | 450 | | 720 | |
| Purchases (note 2) | 2,030 | | 3,080 | |
| | 2,480 | | 3,800 | |
| Closing inventory | (540) | (1,940) | (850) | (2,950) |
| Gross profit | | 1,060 | | 1,450 |
| Operating expenses | 480 | | 964 | |
| Debenture interest | 80 | | nil | |
| Overdraft interest (note 5) | nil | | 10 | |
| | | (560) | | (974) |
| Net profit | | 500 | | 476 |

**Balance sheets:**

| | *Cole* | | *Darwin* | |
|---|---|---|---|---|
| | $000 | $000 | $000 | $000 |
| Non-current assets | | | | |
| Property (note 3) | | 1,140 | | 1,900 |
| Plant (note 4) | | 1,200 | | 1,200 |
| | | 2,340 | | 3,100 |
| Current assets | | | | |
| Inventory | 540 | | 850 | |
| Accounts receivable | 522 | | 750 | |
| Bank | 20 | 1,082 | nil | 1,600 |
| Total assets | | 3,422 | | 4,700 |
| Equity and liabilities: | | | | |
| Equity shares of $1 each | | 1,000 | | 500 |
| Reserves: | | | | |
| Revaluation reserve | | nil | | 700 |
| Retained earnings 1 April 1999 | 684 | | 1,912 | |
| Profit for year to 31 March 2000 | 500 | 1,184 | 476 | 2,388 |
| | | 2,184 | | 3,588 |
| Non-current liabilities | | | | |
| 10% Debenture | | 800 | | nil |
| Current liabilities | | | | |
| Accounts payable | 438 | | 562 | |
| Overdraft | nil | 438 | 550 | 1,112 |
| Total equity and liabilities | | 3,422 | | 4,700 |

Webster bases its preliminary assessment of target companies on certain key ratios. These are listed below together with the relevant figures for Cole and Darwin calculated from the above financial statements:

| | Cole | | Darwin |
|---|---|---|---|
| Return on capital employed (500 + 80)/ (2,184 + 800) × 100 | 19.4% | (476/3,588) × 100 | 13.3% |
| Asset turnover (3,000/2,984) | 1.01 times | (4,400/3,588) | 1.23 times |
| Gross profit margin | 35.3% | | 33.0% |
| Net profit margin | 16.7% | | 10.8% |
| Accounts receivable collection period | 64 days | | 62 days |
| Accounts payable payment period | 79 days | | 67 days |

***Note:*** Capital employed is defined as shareholders' funds plus long-term debt at the year end; asset turnover is sales revenues divided by gross assets less current liabilities.

The following additional information has been obtained:

(1) Cole is part of the Velox Group. On 1 March 2000 it was permitted by its holding company to sell goods at a price of $500,000 to Brander, a fellow subsidiary. Cole's normal selling price for these goods would have been $375,000. In addition Brander was instructed to pay for the goods immediately. Cole normally allows a three-month payment period to customers.

(2) On 1 January 2000 Cole purchased $275,000 (cost price to Cole) of its materials from Advent, another member of the Velox Group. Advent was also instructed to depart from its normal trading terms that would have resulted in a charge of $300,000 to Cole for these goods. The Group's finance director also authorised a four-month payment period on this sale. Normal payment terms in this industry would be to receive two months' credit from suppliers. Cole had sold all of these goods at the year-end.

(3) Non-current assets:

Details relating to the two companies' non-current assets at 31 March 2000 are:

| | | *Cost/revaluation* | *Depreciation* | *Book value* |
|---|---|---|---|---|
| | | $000 | $000 | $000 |
| Cole | – property | 3,000 | 1,860 | 1,140 |
| | – plant | 6,000 | 4,800 | 1,200 |
| | | | | 2,340 |
| Darwin | – property | 2,000 | 100 | 1,900 |
| | – plant | 3,000 | 1,800 | 1,200 |
| | | | | 3,100 |

Both companies own very similar properties. Darwin's property was revalued to $2,000,000 at the beginning of the current year (i.e. 1 April 1999). On this date Cole's property, which is carried at cost less depreciation, had a book value of $1,200,000. Its current value (on the same basis as Darwin's property) was also $2,000,000. On this date (1 April 1999) both properties had the same remaining life of 20 years.

(4) Darwin purchased new plant costing $600,000 in February 2000. In line with company policy a full year's depreciation at 20% per annum has been charged on all plant owned at the year-end. The plant is still being tested and will not come on-stream until next year. The purchase of the plant was largely financed by an overdraft facility that resulted in the interest cost shown in the income statement. Both companies depreciate plant over a five-year life.

(5) The bank overdraft that would have been required but for the favourable treatment towards Cole in respect of the items in (i) and (ii) above, would have attracted interest of $15,000 in the year to 31 March 2000.

**Required:**

(a) Restate the financial statements of Cole and Darwin for the year to 31 March 2000 in order that they may be considered comparable for decision-making purposes. State any assumptions you make. **(10 marks)**

(b) Recalculate the key ratios used by Webster and, together with any other relevant points, comment on how the revised ratios may affect the relative assessment of the two companies. **(15 marks)**

**(Total: 25 marks)**

---

*For the answers to these questions, see the 'Answers' section at the end of the book.*

## Feedback to activities

### Activity 1

| | *X* | *Y* |
|---|---|---|
| ROCE | $\frac{10,000}{50,000} \times 100\%$ | $\frac{10,000}{50,000} \times 100\%$ |
| | = 20% | = 20% |
| Profit margin | $\frac{10,000}{50,000} \times 100\%$ | $\frac{10,000}{200,000} \times 100\%$ |
| | = 20% | = 5% |
| Asset turnover | $\frac{50,000}{50,000}$ | $\frac{200,000}{50,000}$ |
| | = 1 | = 4 |

The ROCE for both companies is the same. X has a higher profit margin, whilst Y shows a more efficient use of assets. This indicates that there may be a trade-off between profit margin and asset turnover.

### Activity 2

1 Payables
Average payment period

$= \left(365 \times \frac{\text{Payables}}{\text{Purchases}}\right)$ $\quad 365 \times \frac{21}{140} \quad = \quad$ (55 days)

2 Receivables:
Average collection period

$= \left(365 \times \frac{\text{Receivables}}{\text{Sales}}\right)$ $\quad 365 \times \frac{31.25}{250} \quad = \quad$ 46 days

3 Inventory turnover:

$= 365 \times \frac{\text{Inventory}}{\text{Cost of goods sold}}$ $\quad 365 \times \frac{92.5}{210} \quad = \quad$ 161 days

Length of working capital cycle 152 days

## Activity 3

| | | | |
|---|---|---|---|
| Current ratio | $\frac{147.9+393.4+53.8+6.2}{275.1+284.3}$ | = | $\frac{601.3}{559.4}$ |
| | | = | 1.07 |
| Quick ratio | $\frac{601.3-147.9}{559.4}$ | = | 0.81 |
| Receivables payment period | $\frac{393.4}{1{,}867.5}\times 365$ | = | 77 days |
| Inventory turnover period | $\frac{147.9}{1{,}867.5-489.3}\times 365$ | = | 39 days |
| Payables payment period | $\frac{275.1}{1{,}867.5-489.3}\times 365$ | = | 73 days |

Dividend yield $= \frac{3.5+5.5}{265}\times 100 = 3.4\%$

## Activity 4

**Company A (Manufacturing) – Balance sheet No 2**

Higher than average investment in other non-current assets (plant and equipment) together with relatively high inventories and work in progress and trade payables.

**Company B (Insurance) – Balance sheet No 5**

No inventories and work in progress and comparatively small investment in other non-current assets, but very high proportions of receivables and payables.

**Company C (Housebuilding) – Balance sheet No 1**

High investment in inventories and work in progress and relatively high payables.

**Company D (Retail stores) – Balance sheet No 3**

High investment in land and property (shops). Low trade receivables. High cash.

**Company E (Properties) – Balance sheet No 4**

High investment in land and property. Low other non-current assets and receivables. No inventories.

Chapter 16

# EARNINGS PER SHARE AND SEGMENT REPORTING

## Syllabus content

- Calculation of earnings per share under IAS 33, to include the effect of bonus issues, rights issues and convertible stock.
- Segment analysis: inter-firm and international comparison (IAS 14).

## Contents

## Introduction

This chapter begins by considering earnings per share in detail. Earnings per share is a widely used measure of a company's performance, particularly over a number of years and it is a component of the very important Stock Exchange yardstick – the price/earnings (P/E) ratio. Exam questions will almost certainly require calculations; they may also require you to explain the reasoning behind your calculations, to discuss the usefulness (or otherwise) of earnings per share as a performance measure or to use earnings per share to interpret financial information.

The other topic covered in this chapter is segment reporting. Many large companies carry out several different types of business or operate in several different geographical locations. Users of the financial statements need information about these different segments in order to be able to make a proper assessment of the company's financial performance and position. Exam questions may ask you to interpret segment information, with or without other extracts from the financial statements.

# 1 Earnings per share

### 1.1 The need for a standard for earnings per share

KEY POINT

Earnings per share is regarded as the key indicator of a company's performance.

Earnings per share is regarded as the key indicator of a company's performance. It is used widely by investors, potential investors and analysts.

In addition, the figure 'Earnings per share' (EPS) is used to compute the major stock market indicator of performance, the Price Earnings ratio (PE ratio). The calculation is:

$$\text{PE ratio} = \frac{\text{Market value of share}}{\text{EPS}}$$

KEY POINT

The stock market places great emphasis on a company's PE ratio and therefore a standard form of measurement of EPS is required.

Rightly or wrongly, the stock market places great emphasis on a company's PE ratio and therefore a standard form of measurement of EPS is required.

The EPS figure is also used to compute the dividend cover ratio.

### 1.2 The scope of IAS 33

KEY POINT

IAS 33 only applies to publicly quoted companies.

IAS 33 applies to entities whose ordinary shares are publicly traded.

Most entities whose shares are publicly traded present parent and consolidated financial statements. When this is the case, only EPS based on the consolidated figures is required.

### 1.3 Definitions

DEFINITION

An **ordinary share** is an equity instrument that is subordinate to all other classes of equity instruments.

A **potential ordinary share** is a financial instrument or other contract that may entitle its holder to ordinary shares.

The following terms are used in IAS 33 with the meanings specified.

- An **ordinary share** is an equity instrument that is subordinate to all other classes of equity instruments.
- A **potential ordinary share** is a financial instrument or other contract that may entitle its holder to ordinary shares.
- **Options, warrants** and their equivalents are financial instruments that give the holder the right to purchase ordinary shares.

Examples of potential ordinary shares are:

- debt or equity instruments, including preference shares, that are convertible into ordinary shares
- share warrants and options

shares which would be issued upon the satisfaction of certain conditions resulting from contractual arrangements, such as the purchase of a business or other assets.

## 1.4 Computation of basic earnings per share

IAS 33 states that an entity should calculate earnings per share for:

(a) profit or loss attributable to ordinary equity holders of the parent; and

(b) if presented, profit or loss from continuing operations attributable to those equity holders.

**KEY POINT**

The basic EPS is the earnings divided by the number of ordinary shares in issue. It must be disclosed on the face of the income statement.

$$\text{Earnings per share} = \frac{\text{Profit or loss attributable to ordinary shareholders}}{\text{Number of ordinary shares outstanding}}$$

(in cents or dollars and cents as appropriate)

However, the definition of both the numerator and the denominator can present difficulties of calculation in certain circumstances and these points are covered below.

## 1.5 Earnings

**KEY POINT**

The net profit or loss for the period attributable to ordinary shareholders should be the net profit or loss for the period attributable to the parent entity.

For the purpose of calculating basic earnings per share, the net profit or loss for the period attributable to ordinary shareholders should be the net profit or loss for the period attributable to the parent entity.

In other words, the earnings figure to be taken is the profit after:

- minority interests
- tax
- preference dividends.

A group's share of the income of an associate is included.

## 1.6 Shares in issue

**KEY POINT**

The number of ordinary shares to be included in the calculation is the weighted average number of ordinary shares outstanding during the period.

The number of ordinary shares to be included in the calculation is the weighted average number of ordinary shares outstanding during the period.

Where there has been an issue of shares during the period, shares are normally included in the weighted average number of shares from the date consideration is receivable, which is generally the date of their issue. For example:

- ordinary shares issued in exchange for cash are issued when cash is receivable
- ordinary shares issued as a result of the conversion of a debt instrument to ordinary shares are included as of the date that interest ceases accruing
- ordinary shares issued as part of the purchase consideration for an acquisition are included as of the date of the acquisition.

Ordinary shares that are issuable upon the satisfaction of certain conditions (contingently issuable shares) are not included in the computation until all the necessary conditions have been satisfied.

## 1.7 Issue of shares at full market price during the period

KEY POINT

Earnings should be apportioned over the weighted average equity share capital.

Earnings should be apportioned over the weighted average equity share capital (i.e. taking account of when shares are issued during the year).

***Example***

A company issued 200,000 shares at full market price ($3.00) on 1 July 20X8.

**Relevant information**

| | *20X8* | *20X7* |
|---|---|---|
| Ordinary profit attributable to the ordinary shareholders for the year ending 31 Dec | $550,000 | $460,000 |
| Number of ordinary shares in issue at 31 Dec | 1,000,000 | 800,000 |

**Calculation of earnings per share**

$$20X7 = \frac{\$460,000}{800,000} = 57.5c$$

$$20X8 = \frac{\$550,000}{800,000 + (\frac{1}{2} \times 200,000)} = 61.11c$$

Since the 200,000 shares have only contributed finance for half a year, the number of shares is adjusted accordingly. Note that the solution is to use the earnings figure for the period without adjustment, but divide by the average number of shares weighted on a time basis.

## 1.8 Bonus or scrip issues

Earnings should be apportioned over the shares in issue after the bonus issue.

KEY POINT

The number of shares as increased by the bonus issue is taken for the whole year, regardless of the date in the year when the bonus issue took place.

When an entity makes a bonus issue, the number of shares increases but no fresh capital comes in. To ensure that the EPS for the year of the bonus issue remains comparable with the EPS of previous years, the number of shares as increased by the bonus issue is taken for the whole year, regardless of the date in the year when the bonus issue took place, and comparative figures for earlier years are restated using the same increased figure.

***Example***

A company makes a bonus issue of one new share for every five existing shares held on 1 July 20X8.

**Relevant information**

| | 20X8 | 20X7 |
|---|---|---|
| Ordinary profit attributable to the ordinary shareholders for the year ending 31 Dec | $550,000 | $460,000 |
| Number of ordinary shares in issue at 31 Dec | 1,200,000 | 1,000,000 |

**Calculation of earnings per share in 20X8 accounts**

$$20X7 = \frac{\$460,000}{1,200,000} = 38.33c$$

$$20X8 \quad = \quad \frac{\$550{,}000}{1{,}200{,}000} \quad = \quad 45.83c$$

In the 20X7 accounts, the EPS for the year would have appeared as 46c (\$460,000 ÷ 1,000,000). In the example above, the computation has been reworked from scratch. However, to make the changes required it would be simpler to adjust directly the EPS figures themselves.

Since the old calculation was based on dividing by 1,000,000 while the new is determined by using 1,200,000, it would be necessary to multiply the EPS by the first and divide by the second. The fraction to apply is, therefore:

$$\frac{1{,}000{,}000}{1{,}200{,}000} \text{ or } \frac{5}{6}$$

Consequently, $46c \times \frac{5}{6} = 38.33c$.

Given that the scrip issue has not increased the assets in the company, similarly the market value of each share would be expected to be only 5/6 of the former price, since for every five shares previously held, the shareholder now has six.

Assuming a pre-issue market price of \$3.00, five shares would have a market value of \$15.00. After the issue six shares would, other things being equal, have the same value. Therefore, one share would have a theoretical post-issue price of \$15.00 ÷ 6 = \$2.50. The new EPS could in consequence equally well have been calculated by multiplying the old EPS by the theoretical new share price divided by the actual old price:

$$(\frac{\$2.50}{\$3.00} = \frac{5}{6})$$

Since there are now six shares in issue for every five previously held, the number of shares after the issue is similarly:

$$1{,}000{,}000 \times \frac{6}{5} = 1{,}200{,}000$$

or alternatively

$$1{,}000{,}000 \times \frac{3.00}{2.50} = 1{,}200{,}000$$

These interrelationships are important when considering a rights issue.

## 1.9 Rights issues

KEY POINT

Rights issues present special problems, because they are normally below full market price and therefore combine the characteristics of issues at full market price and bonus issues as above.

Rights issues present special problems, because they are normally below full market price and therefore combine the characteristics of issues at full market price and bonus issues as above. Determining the weighted average capital, therefore, involves two steps:

**Step 1**

Adjust for bonus element in rights issue, by multiplying capital in issue before the rights issue by:

$$\frac{\text{Actual cum rights price}}{\text{Theoretical ex rights price}}$$

**Step 2**

Calculate the weighted average capital in issue as above.

***Example***

A company issued one new share for every two existing shares held by way of rights at $1.50 per share on 1 July 20X8. Pre-issue market price was $3.00 per share.

**Relevant information**

| | 20X8 | 20X7 |
|---|---|---|
| Ordinary profit attributable to the ordinary shareholders for the year ending 31 Dec | $550,000 | $460,000 |
| Number of ordinary shares in issue at 31 Dec | 1,200,000 | 800,000 |

**Calculation of earnings per share**

20X7 Original per 20X7 accounts:

$$\frac{\$460{,}000}{800{,}000} = 57.5\text{c}$$

Adjusted for rights issue:

$$57.5\text{c} \times \frac{2.50}{3.00} = 47.92\text{c}$$

20X8 Based on weighted average number of shares:

1st half-year – actual in issue 800,000

– adjusted for bonus element $800{,}000 \times \frac{3.00}{2.50}$

= 960,000

2nd half-year – actual in issue, including bonus element, 1,200,000

Therefore, EPS $= \dfrac{\$550{,}000}{(960{,}000 + 1{,}200{,}000) \div 2}$

= 50.92c

**Notes on solution**

1 20X7

Pre-rights, two shares would be worth $6.00. Ex-rights, three shares would theoretically be worth $6.00 + $1.50 = $7.50, or $2.50 each. The appropriate fraction for the adjustment of comparatives is, therefore, $2.50 divided by $3.00.

The revised EPS figure could have been obtained by dividing the earnings figure of $460,000 by a share number adjusted for the bonus element, i.e.:

$$800{,}000 \times \frac{3.00}{2.50} = 960{,}000$$

$$\left(\frac{\$460{,}000}{960{,}000} = 47.92\text{c}\right)$$

2 20X8

The calculation must take account of the quasi-capitalisation. The share number used must, therefore, reflect the bonus element for the whole year and the increase in the fund of capital from the half year.

3 Relationship of rights issue to issue at full market price and capitalisation

Each of the examples used a pre-issue share price of $3.00. Both the rights issue and the issue at full market price raised $600,000 from shareholders. However, after the rights issue there were 1,200,000 shares in issue, whereas following the issue at full market value there were only 1,000,000.

If the latter had been followed immediately by a capitalisation to bring the number of shares issued up to 1,200,000, the EPS figures would have become:

20X7 $57.5c \times \frac{2.50}{3.00} = 47.92c$

20X8 $61.11c \times \frac{2.50}{3.00} = 50.9c$

These are, as would be expected, the same as those calculated for the rights issue.

***Activity 1***

On 31 December 20X1 the issued share capital consisted of 4,000,000 ordinary shares of 25c each, and the shares were quoted at $1. On 1 January 20X2 the company made a rights issue in the proportion of 1 for 4 at 50c per share. Its trading results for the last two years were as follows:

| | *Year ended 30 June* | |
|---|---|---|
| | *20X1* | *20X2* |
| | $ | $ |
| Net profit after tax | 400,000 | 425,000 |

Show the calculation of EPS to be presented in the final accounts in 20X2 (including the comparative figure).

*Feedback to this activity is at the end of the chapter.*

## 1.10 Diluted earnings per share

KEY POINT

Diluted earnings per share shows to what extent the amount available for ordinary dividends per share would have been affected if all the potential ordinary shares had been issued under the worst possible dilution.

Basic EPS figure could be misleading to users if at some future time the number of shares in issue will increase without a corresponding increase in resources. For example, an entity may have issued bonds convertible at a later date into ordinary shares. When the bonds are converted the number of ordinary shares will rise, but no fresh capital enters the entity. Earnings per share will fall. This effect is referred to as 'dilution'.

Diluted earnings per share shows to what extent the amount available for ordinary dividends per share would have been affected if all the potential ordinary shares had been issued under the worst possible dilution. It can be thought of as a 'warning signal'.

To calculate diluted earnings per share:

- the net profit or loss for the period attributable to ordinary shareholders is adjusted for:
  - dividends on potential shares (e.g. on convertible preference shares)
  - interest (e.g. on convertible loan stock)
  - any other changes in income and expense that would result from the conversion
- the weighted average number of ordinary shares that would be issued if all the potential ordinary shares were converted is added to the weighted number of ordinary shares. (Potential ordinary shares should be assumed to have been converted at the beginning of the period, or, if they were not in existence at the beginning of the period, the date of issue.)

Diluted EPS must be calculated and disclosed based on total profit attributable to ordinary shareholders **and** profit from continuing operations attributable to ordinary shareholders, if this is presented.

Examples of potential ordinary shares are:

- convertible bonds
- convertible preference shares
- options and warrants
- contingently issuable shares (these are shares that will only be issued in the future upon the satisfaction of certain conditions).

## 1.11 Convertibles

The principles of convertible bonds and convertible preference shares are similar and will be dealt with together.

***Example***

On 1 April 20X1, an entity issued by way of rights or otherwise \$1,250,000 8% convertible unsecured bonds for cash at par. Each \$100 nominal of the bonds will be convertible in 20X6/20X9 into the number of ordinary shares set out below:

| | |
|---|---|
| On 31 December 20X6 | 124 shares |
| On 31 December 20X7 | 120 shares |
| On 31 December 20X8 | 115 shares |
| On 31 December 20X9 | 110 shares |

**Relevant information**

Issued share capital:

- \$500,000 in 10% cumulative preference shares of \$1
- \$1,000,000 in ordinary shares of 25c = 4,000,000 shares.

Income tax rate is 45%.

**Trading results for the year ended 31 December**

| | *20X2* | *20X1* |
|---|---|---|
| | $ | $ |
| Profit before interest and tax | 1,100,000 | 991,818 |
| Interest on 8% convertible unsecured bonds | 100,000 | 75,000 |
| Profit before tax | 1,000,000 | 916,818 |
| Income tax | 450,000 | 412,568 |
| Profit after tax | 550,000 | 504,250 |

**Calculation of earnings per share**

1 **Basic earnings per share**

| | *20X2* | *20X1* |
|---|---|---|
| | $ | $ |
| Profit after tax | 550,000 | 504,250 |
| Less: Preference dividend | 50,000 | 50,000 |
| Earnings | 500,000 | 454,250 |
| Earnings per share based on 4,000,000 shares | 12.5c | 11.4c |

2 **Diluted earnings per share**

| | | *20X2* | | *20X1* |
|---|---|---|---|---|
| | | $ | | $ |
| Earnings as above | | 500,000 | | 454,250 |
| Add: Interest on the convertible unsecured bonds | 100,000 | | 75,000 | |
| Less: Tax | 45,000 | | 33,750 | |
| | | 55,000 | | 41,250 |
| Adjusted earnings | | 555,000 | | 495,500 |
| Diluted EPS based on 5,550,000 shares (20X1 – 5,162,500) | | 10c | | 9.6c |

***Notes:***

- Up to 20X5 the maximum number of shares issuable after the end of the financial year will be at the rate of 124 shares per $100, viz: 1,550,000 shares, making a total of 5,550,000.
- The weighted average number of shares issued and issuable for 20X1 would have been one-quarter of 4,000,000 plus three-quarters of 5,550,000, i.e. 5,162,500.

## 1.12 Options and warrants to subscribe for shares

An option may give the holder the right to buy shares at some time in the future at below the market price. In this case some cash does enter the entity at the time the option is exercised, and the diluted EPS calculation must allow for this.

IAS 33 has an ingenious solution to the problem. For the diluted EPS calculation, the number of shares in issue is not increased by the number of shares for which the option is exercised.

The number of shares for which the option is exercised is first reduced by the number of shares which could have been purchased at fair value by the consideration payable under the option. The remainder, the shares issued for no consideration, is added to the shares in issue.

***Example***

| | |
|---|---|
| Net profit for year 20X1 | $1,200,000 |
| Weighted average number of ordinary shares outstanding during year 20X1 | 500,000 shares |
| Average fair value of one ordinary share during year 20X1 | $20 |
| Weighted average number of shares under option during year 20X1 | 100,000 shares |
| Exercise price for shares under option during year 20X1 | $15 |

**Computation of earnings per share**

| | *Per share* | *Earnings* | *Shares* |
|---|---|---|---|
| Net profit for year 20X1 | | $1,200,000 | |
| Weighted average shares outstanding during year 20X1 | | | 500,000 |
| **Basic earnings per share** | $2.40 | | |
| Number of shares under option | | | 100,000 |
| Number of shares that would have been issued at fair value: (100,000 × 15)/20 | | * | (75,000) |
| **Diluted earnings per share** | $2.29 | $1,200,000 | 525,000 |

***Note:** It is not necessary to adjust the earnings figure because the total number of shares has been increased only by the 25,000 shares deemed to have been issued for no consideration.

## 1.13 Contingently issuable shares

Shares which will only be issued in the future if certain conditions are satisfied (e.g. if a particular division achieves a profit target) are called contingently issuable shares. Clearly they are not included in the calculation of the basic EPS until they have been issued.

IAS 33 requires contingently issuable shares to be included in the calculation for the diluted EPS with effect from the beginning of the period (or from the date of the contingent share agreement, if later), if the conditions have been met.

***Example***

In the year ended 31 December 20X7, PQ reported a net profit of $100,000. On 1 January 20X7 the company had $200,000 of issued share capital in the form of 50c ordinary shares.

PQ has agreed to issue 10,000 new shares for every new shop opened during 20X7. On 1 July 20X7 one new shop was opened.

Calculate the basic and diluted EPS for 20X7.

***Solution***

$$\text{Basic EPS} = \frac{\$100,000}{(\frac{6}{12}\times 400,000)+(\frac{6}{12}\times 410,000)} = 24.69c$$

(Note that 10,000 new shares were issued on 1 July 20X7).

$$\text{Diluted EPS} = \frac{\$100,000}{410,000} = 24.39c$$

(Note that the contingently issuable shares are included in the denominator with effect from the beginning of the accounting period.)

KEY POINT

Only potential ordinary shares that would dilute basic earnings per share should be taken into account when computing the diluted figure.

## 1.14 The effect on diluted EPS of the order in which dilutive factors are allowed for

Only potential ordinary shares that would dilute basic earnings per share should be taken into account when computing the diluted figure.

Where there is more than one issue of dilutive share the calculation is in two stages:

1 For each issue, calculate earnings per incremental share.

2 Adjust basic earnings per share for each issue from the most dilutive to the least dilutive.

***Example***

| | |
|---|---|
| Earnings – Net profit attributable to ordinary shareholders | $10,000,000 |
| Ordinary shares outstanding | 2,000,000 |
| Average fair value of one ordinary share during year | $75 |

**Potential ordinary shares**

| | |
|---|---|
| Options | 100,000 with exercise price of $60. |
| Convertible preference shares | 800,000 shares entitled to a cumulative dividend of $8 per share. Each preference share is convertible to 2 ordinary shares. |
| 5% convertible bond | nominal amount $100,000,000. Each $1,000 bond is convertible to 20 ordinary shares. |
| Tax rate | 40% |

**Step 1**

Calculate the increase in earnings attributable to ordinary shareholders on conversion of potential ordinary shares.

| | | *Increase in earnings* | *Increase in number of ordinary shares* | *Earnings per incremental share* |
|---|---|---|---|---|
| | | $ | | $ |
| **Options** | | | | |
| Increase in earnings | | nil | | |
| Incremental shares issued for no consideration | 100,000 × (75 – 60)/75 | | 20,000 | nil |

| | | | | |
|---|---|---|---|---|
| **Convertible preference shares** | | | | |
| Increase in net profit | 8 × $800,000 | 6,400,000 | | |
| Incremental shares | 2 × 800,000 | | 1,600,000 | 4.00 |
| **5% convertible bonds** | | | | |
| Increase in net profit | 100,000,000 × 5% × (1 – 0.4) | 3,000,000 | | |
| Incremental shares | 100,000 × 20 | | 2,000,000 | 1.50 |

The lower the incremental earnings per share, the higher the dilutive effect. This calculation shows that the most dilutive potential ordinary shares are the options, followed by the 5% convertible bonds and then the convertible preference shares. This is the order in which they should be considered in the earnings per share calculation.

**Step 2**

**Calculate diluted earnings per share.**

| | *Net profit attributable* | *Ordinary shares* | *Per share* | |
|---|---|---|---|---|
| | $ | | $ | |
| As reported | 10,000,000 | 2,000,000 | 5.00 | |
| Options | | 20,000 | | |
| | 10,000,000 | 2,020,000 | 4.95 | Dilutive |
| 5% convertible bonds | 3,000,000 | 2,000,000 | | |
| | 13,000,000 | 4,020,000 | 3.23 | Dilutive |
| Convertible preference shares | 6,400,000 | 1,600,000 | | |
| | 19,400,000 | 5,620,000 | 3.45 | Anti-Dilutive |

Since diluted earnings per share is increased when taking the convertible preference shares into account (from $3.23 to $3.45), the convertible preference shares are anti-dilutive and are ignored in the calculation of diluted earnings per share. Therefore, diluted earnings per share is $3.23.

### 1.15 Presentation

KEY POINT

Both basic and diluted EPS must be disclosed on the face of the income statement.

An entity should present basic and diluted earnings per share on the face of the income statement for each class of ordinary shares that has a different right to share in the net profit for the period.

An entity should present basic and diluted earnings per share with equal prominence for all periods presented.

Where profit from continuing operations is different from total profit, basic and diluted earnings per share should also be presented for profit from continuing operations.

If an entity reports a discontinuing operation it should disclose basic and diluted earnings per share for the discontinuing operation either on the face of the income statement or in the notes to the financial statements.

IAS 33 requires an entity to present basic and diluted earnings per share, even if the amounts disclosed are negative (a loss per share).

### 1.16 Disclosure

An entity should disclose the following:

- the amounts used as the numerators in calculating basic and diluted earnings per share, and a reconciliation of those amounts to the net profit or loss for the period
- the weighted average number of ordinary shares used as the denominator in calculating basic and diluted earnings per share, and a reconciliation of these denominators to each other.

In addition, an entity should disclose details of financial instruments that could potentially dilute basic earnings per share in future, but were not included in the calculation of diluted earnings per share because they were anti-dilutive.

### 1.17 Alternative measures of earnings per share

Provided the basic and diluted EPS are calculated and disclosed according to IAS 33, an entity may also present EPS figures using other measures of profit. For example, profit excluding large or unusual items could be taken.

In these alternatives, the number of shares must be calculated in accordance with IAS 33, and if the profit figure taken is not a line item in the income statement, a reconciliation must be provided between the figure used and a line item which does appear in the income statement.

Such information may help users to evaluate the detailed performance of the entity.

### 1.18 Limitations of EPS as a performance measure

KEY POINT

Although EPS is believed to have a real influence on the market price of shares, it has several important limitations as a performance measure.

Although EPS is believed to have a real influence on the market price of shares, it has several important limitations as a performance measure.

- An entity's earnings are affected by its choice of accounting policies. Therefore, it may not always be appropriate to compare the EPS of different companies.
- EPS does not take account of inflation. Apparent growth in earnings may not be true growth.
- EPS does not provide predictive value. High earnings and growth in earnings may be achieved at the expense of investment which may generate increased earnings in the future.
- EPS cannot be used as a basis of comparison between companies as the number of shares in issue in any particular company is not related to the amount of capital employed. For example, two companies may have the same amount of capital employed, but one company has 100,000 £1 shares in issue and reserves of £4,900,000. Another company may have 5 million 50p shares in issue and reserves of £2,500,000. The same level of earnings will produce different EPS.
- In theory, diluted EPS serves as a warning to equity shareholders that the return on their investment may fall in future periods. However, diluted EPS as currently required by IAS 33 is not intended to be forward looking but an additional past performance measure. For example, when calculating diluted EPS where there are warrants or options, fair value is based on the average price of an ordinary share for the period, rather than the market price at the period end. Therefore diluted EPS is only of limited use as a prediction of future EPS.

- EPS is a measure of profitability. Profitability is only one aspect of performance. Concentration on earnings per share and 'the bottom line' arguably detracts from other important aspects of an entity's affairs, for example, cash flow and stewardship of assets.

# 2 IAS 14 *Segment Reporting*

## 2.1 The need for a standard

Many entities carry on several classes of business or operate in several geographical areas, with different rates of profitability, different opportunities for growth and different degrees of risk. The purpose of segmental information is to provide information to assist the readers of financial statements:

- to appreciate more thoroughly the results and financial position of the entity by permitting a better understanding of the enterprise's past performance and thus a better assessment of its future prospects
- to be aware of the impact that changes in significant components of a business may have on the business as a whole
- to assess the risks and returns of the enterprise.

KEY POINT

The additional disclosures required by IAS 14 are designed to reveal significant information which might otherwise be hidden by the aggregation process.

The additional disclosures required by IAS 14 are designed to reveal significant information which might otherwise be hidden by the aggregation process of presenting a single income statement and balance sheet for a business.

Consider a business with three segments as follows:

| *Segment* | *A* | *B* | *C* | *Total* |
|---|---|---|---|---|
| | $000 | $000 | $000 | $000 |
| Operating profits | 100 | 200 | (250) | 50 |

Disclosing the three figures individually is obviously much more revealing than just disclosing an overall profit of £50,000.

## 2.2 Scope of IAS 14

IAS 14 applies only to entities whose equity or debt is publicly quoted or about to be publicly quoted.

IAS 14 encourages other entities to provide segmental information, and if they do they should comply with the provisions of IAS 14.

When consolidated financial statements are presented as well as those of the parent, the segmental analysis need only be disclosed on a group basis.

## 2.3 Key definitions relevant to segment reporting

***Business segment***

DEFINITION

A **business segment** is a distinguishable component of an entity that is engaged in providing an individual product or service or a group of related products or services and that is subject to risks and returns that are different from those of other business segments.

A **business segment** is a distinguishable component of an entity that is engaged in providing an individual product or service or a group of related products or services and that is subject to risks and returns that are different from those of other business segments.

Factors that should be considered in determining whether products and services are related include:

(i) the nature of the products or services

(ii) the nature of the production processes

(iii) the type or class of customer for the products or services

(iv) the methods used to distribute the products or provide the services

(v) if applicable, the nature of the regulatory environment, for example, banking, insurance, or public utilities.

### *Geographical segment*

DEFINITION

A **geographical segment** is a distinguishable component of an entity that is engaged in providing products or services within a particular economic environment and that is subject to risks and returns that are different from those of components operating in other economic environments.

A **geographical segment** is a distinguishable component of an entity that is engaged in providing products or services within a particular economic environment and that is subject to risks and returns that are different from those of components operating in other economic environments.

Factors that should be considered in identifying geographical segments include:

(i) similarity of economic and political conditions

(ii) relationships between operations in different geographical areas

(iii) proximity of operations

(iv) special risks associated with operations in a particular area

(v) exchange control regulations

(vi) the underlying currency risks.

### *Reportable segment*

DEFINITION

A **reportable segment** is a business segment or a geographical segment identified based on the foregoing definitions for which segment information is required to be disclosed by IAS 14.

A **reportable segment** is a business segment or a geographical segment identified based on the foregoing definitions for which segment information is required to be disclosed by IAS 14.

Evidence is offered in the standard in identifying whether a segment has to be separately reported – see later.

### *Segment revenue*

Segment revenue is revenue reported in the entity's income statement that is directly attributable to a segment and the relevant portion of enterprise revenue that can be allocated on a reasonable basis to a segment, whether from sales to external customers or from transactions with other segments of the same entity.

Segment revenue does not include:

(i) interest or dividend income

(ii) gains on sales of investments.

Segment revenue includes an entity share of profits or losses of associates, joint ventures, or other investments accounted for under the equity method only if those items are included in consolidated or total enterprise revenue.

Segment revenue includes a joint venturer's share of the revenue of a jointly controlled entity that is accounted for by proportionate consolidation in accordance with IAS 31 *Financial Reporting of Interests in Joint Ventures*.

***Segment expense***

Segment expense is expense resulting from the operating activities of a segment that is directly attributable to the segment and the relevant portion of an expense that can be allocated on a reasonable basis to the segment, including expenses relating to sales to external customers and expenses relating to transactions with other segments of the same enterprise.

Segment expense does not include:

(i) interest

(ii) losses on sales of investments

(iii) an entity's share of losses of associates, joint ventures, or other investments accounted for under the equity method (because included in segment revenue above)

(iv) income tax expense, or

(v) general administrative expenses, head-office expenses, and other expenses that arise at the entity level and relate to the entity as a whole. However, costs are sometimes incurred at the entity level on behalf of a segment. Such costs are segment expenses if they relate to the segment's operating activities and they can be directly attributed or allocated to the segment on a reasonable basis.

Segment expense includes a joint venturer's share of the expenses of a jointly controlled entity that is accounted for by proportionate consolidation in accordance with IAS 31.

## 2.4 Extent of segmental analysis

In view of these definitions, it may be seen that segmental analysis of the income statement is only required as far as operating profit, presumably because allocations of finance costs would be likely to be arbitrary. Even general administrative costs are excluded.

Segmental analysis of assets and liabilities must be consistent with that for revenue and expenses.

KEY POINT

Segmental analysis of assets and liabilities must be consistent with that for revenue and expenses.

## 2.5 Reportable segments

KEY POINT

In determining whether a segment is a reportable segment, a 10% rule is adopted.

In determining whether a segment is a reportable segment, a 10% rule is adopted. A segment is a reportable segment if most of its sales are to external customers and it has at least 10% of:

- total sales, including sales to other segments; or
- total profit of all profit-making segments, or total loss of all loss-making segments; or
- total assets of all segments.

A segment which is below these levels may still be designated as a reportable segment.

A segment below the 10% thresholds and not designated as a reportable segment may be combined with another similar segment. If this is not possible, it is included as an unallocated reconciling item.

The segmental analysis must cover at least 75% of the total consolidated or entity revenue. If the reportable segments total less than this, additional segments have to be identified, even if they do not meet the 10% tests, until at least 75% of the revenue is in fact included in the segmental analysis.

When a segment becomes reportable for the first time, comparative segmental figures have to be restated to include it, unless it is impracticable to do so.

If a segment which was previously reportable falls below the 10% thresholds, it may continue to be included as a reportable segment if the management considers it to be of continuing significance.

## 2.6 Identifying reportable segments

The main choice in identifying segments is between business segments and geographical segments. In fact, IAS 14 requires some segmental analysis for both of these, but the IAS 14 disclosure requirements are based on the idea of 'primary' and 'secondary' segment reporting formats. If classification by business is the primary format, a full segmental analysis is required on this basis, with limited disclosure in the secondary geographical format, and vice versa if the geographical format is chosen as primary.

Most businesses will probably choose analysis by business as their primary format. One could also envisage a single-product entity which produced geographical analysis only.

The geographical analysis may be done in two ways – by location of assets and by location of customers. There are thus three possible choices for the primary format:

- business (analysis by different products or services)
- geographical by location of assets
- geographical by location of customers.

### *Activity 2*

An airline operates services both within the United Kingdom and throughout the world. Its flights are sold to customers resident in the United Kingdom and throughout the world.

Its main asset is its aircraft fleet, the large part of which is registered in the United Kingdom.

How might it analyse turnover and net assets by geographical segment for the purpose of segmental reporting?

*Feedback to this activity is at the end of the chapter.*

## 2.7 The disclosure requirements in detail

The disclosure requirements of IAS 14 are extensive. The following chart summarises them.

| *Item* | *Primary analysis* | *Secondary analysis* | *Comments* |
|---|---|---|---|
| **Income statement items** | | | |
| Revenue – external | ✓ | ✓ | See note 1 |
| Revenue from other segments | ✓ | | |
| Basis of inter-segment pricing | ✓ | | |
| Profit or loss | ✓ | | |
| Depreciation or amortisation | ✓ | | |
| Significant non-cash expenses other than depreciation | ✓ | | |
| Income from associates or joint ventures | ✓ | | |
| Exceptional items | | | Disclosure for primary analysis encouraged but not required |
| **Balance sheet items** | | | |
| Total operating assets | ✓ | ✓ | } See note 2 |
| Cost of acquisition of non – current assets in period | ✓ | ✓ | } See note 2 |
| Total operating liabilities | ✓ | | |
| Investments in associates or joint ventures | ✓ | | |
| **Cash flow statement** | | | |
| Cash flows | | | Disclosure for primary analysis encouraged but not required by IAS 7 *Cash Flow Statements* |

***Notes:***

1 (a) If the primary analysis is by product or service, the secondary analysis should be by location of customers.

(b) If the primary analysis is geographical by location of assets, the secondary analysis should be by product or service, but with secondary details by location of customers also provided if different from the analysis by location of assets.

2 (a) If the primary analysis is by product or service, the secondary analysis of asset details should be by location of assets.

(b) If the primary analysis is geographical by location of assets, the secondary analysis should be by product or service, but again with secondary details by location of customers if different from the analysis by location of assets.

**Other disclosures**

(a) **Reconciliation** – The segmental figures for revenue, profit or loss, assets and liabilities must be reconciled to the totals in the financial statements.

(b) **Segment accounting policies** – Details of changes in segment accounting policies must be given.

(c) **Products and services provided** – The types of products or services in each segment must be disclosed.

(d) **Geographical segments** – The extent of each geographical segment must be disclosed.

Finally, IAS 14 encourages, but does not require, disclosure of all primary headings in the secondary format.

## 2.8 Segment accounting policies

The accounting policies used in compiling the segmental analysis must be the same as those for the main financial statements.

## 2.9 Illustration of segmental disclosure

The following table is reproduced from an appendix to IAS 14 and shows how segmental data could be presented. Some explanatory notes follow the primary analysis.

***Primary analysis***

**Information about business segments**

| | *Paper products* | | *Office products* | | *Publishing* | | *Other operations* | | *Eliminations* | | *Consolidated* | |
|---|---|---|---|---|---|---|---|---|---|---|---|---|
| | *20X2* | *20X1* | *20X2* | *20X1* | *20X2* | *20X1* | *20X2* | *20X1* | *20X2* | *20X1* | *20X2* | *20X1* |
| **Revenue** | *$000* | *$000* | *$000* | *$000* | *$000* | *$000* | *$000* | *$000* | *$000* | *$000* | *$000* | *$000* |
| External sales | 55 | 50 | 20 | 17 | 19 | 16 | 7 | 7 | | | | |
| Inter-segment sales | 15 | 10 | 10 | 14 | 2 | 4 | 2 | 2 | (29) | (30) | | |
| Total revenue | 70 | 60 | 30 | 31 | 21 | 20 | 9 | 9 | (29) | (30) | 101 | 90 |
| **Result** | | | | | | | | | | | | |
| Segment result | 20 | 17 | 9 | 7 | 2 | 1 | 0 | 0 | (1) | (1) | 30 | 24 |
| Unallocated expenses | | | | | | | | | | | (7) | (9) |
| Operating profit | | | | | | | | | | | 23 | 15 |
| Interest expense | | | | | | | | | | | (4) | (4) |
| Interest income | | | | | | | | | | | 2 | 3 |
| Share of net profits of associates | 6 | 5 | | | | | 2 | 2 | | | 8 | 7 |
| Income taxes | | | | | | | | | | | (7) | (4) |
| Profit | | | | | | | | | | | 22 | 17 |
| **Other information** | | | | | | | | | | | | |
| Segment assets | 54 | 50 | 34 | 30 | 10 | 10 | 10 | 9 | | | 108 | 99 |
| Investment in equity method associates | 20 | 16 | | | | | 12 | 10 | | | 32 | 26 |
| Unallocated corporate assets | | | | | | | | | | | 35 | 30 |

| | *Paper products* | | *Office products* | | *Publishing* | | *Other operations* | | *Eliminations* | | *Consolidated* | |
|---|---|---|---|---|---|---|---|---|---|---|---|---|
| | *20X2* | *20X1* | *20X2* | *20X1* | *20X2* | *20X1* | *20X2* | *20X1* | *20X2* | *20X1* | *20X2* | *20X1* |
| **Revenue** | *$000* | *$000* | *$000* | *$000* | *$000* | *$000* | *$000* | *$000* | *$000* | *$000* | *$000* | *$000* |
| Consolidated total assets | | | | | | | | | | | 175 | 155 |
| Segment liabilities | 25 | 15 | 8 | 11 | 8 | 8 | 1 | 1 | | | 42 | 35 |
| Unallocated corporate liabilities | | | | | | | | | | | 40 | 55 |
| Consolidated total liabilities | | | | | | | | | | | 82 | 90 |
| Capital expenditure | 12 | 10 | 3 | 5 | 5 | | 4 | 3 | | | | |
| Depreciation | 9 | 7 | 9 | 7 | 5 | 3 | 3 | 4 | | | | |
| Non-cash expenses other than depreciation | 8 | 2 | 7 | 3 | 2 | 2 | 2 | 1 | | | | |

**Explanatory notes:**

1 There are three segments here – the first three pairs of columns. The fourth pair of columns – other operations – takes in the remaining small part of the activities of the entity.

2 The fifth pair of columns – eliminations – is there to remove revenue from inter-segment sales and the segmental profit made on them. This is necessary because the segmental figures must include them but the consolidated total figures to which they are reconciled must exclude them.

3 Note how the total column at the right shows summarised income statement and balance sheet data for all headings, with segmental analysis only for those items for which IAS 14 requires it. Thus it would be wrong to give segmental analysis of interest received and paid or income taxes.

4 Capital expenditure, depreciation and non-cash expenses other than depreciation are shown at the end under 'Other information' because there is no specific heading in the summarised financial statements to which they can be related.

5 A narrative note would give the other information about the nature of products, the make-up of the geographical segments and inter-segment pricing policy.

***Secondary analysis***

Sales revenue by geographical market

| | *20X2* | *20X1* |
|---|---|---|
| | $000 | $000 |
| United Kingdom | 19 | 22 |
| Other European Union countries | 30 | 31 |
| Canada and the United States | 28 | 21 |
| Mexico and South America | 6 | 2 |
| Southeast Asia (principally Japan and Taiwan) | 18 | 14 |
| | 101 | 90 |

**Asset details by geographical location**

| | *Carrying amount of segment assets* | | *Additions to property, plant, equipment, and intangible assets* | |
|---|---|---|---|---|
| | *20X2* | *20X1* | *20X2* | *20X1* |
| | $000 | $000 | $000 | $000 |
| United Kingdom | 72 | 78 | 8 | 5 |
| Other European Union countries | 47 | 37 | 5 | 4 |
| Canada and the United States | 34 | 20 | 4 | 3 |
| Indonesia | 22 | 20 | 7 | 6 |
| | 175 | 155 | 24 | 18 |

Narrative notes would explain the geographical data presented. Check to see how the secondary figures agree with the consolidated totals alongside the primary segmental table.

## 2.10 Interpreting segmental information

It is possible to compute return on capital employed (ROCE), profit margin and asset turnover for each segment, based on the segmental information disclosed. This provides information on the profitability, efficiency and overall performance of each segment.

KEY POINT

Segmental information should be interpreted with caution. Although IAS 14 provides some guidance, in practice segments are determined by the directors.

However, segmental information should be interpreted with caution:

- Although IAS 14 provides some guidance, in practice segments are determined by the directors. Arguably, this provides too much flexibility. It also means that segmental information is only useful for comparing the performance of the same entity over time, not for comparing the performance of different entities.
- Common costs may be allocated to different segments on whatever basis the directors believe is reasonable. This can lead to arbitrary allocation of these costs.
- Interest costs are often based on the financial strategy of the organisation as a whole and therefore segmental results normally exclude interest charges. However, this can be misleading.
- A segment's operating results can be distorted by trading with other segments on non-commercial terms. However, IAS 14 requires segmental reports to include details of inter-segment trading and the disclosure of transfer pricing policies. This should help users of the financial statements to assess the effect of inter-segment trading on a segment's results.

# Summary

- Earnings per share (EPS) is calculated and disclosed for all companies whose ordinary shares are publicly traded. Complications arise if there has been a change in the amount of ordinary share capital in the period. As well as basic EPS, a diluted EPS must be disclosed whenever there are dilutive potential ordinary shares in issue.
- IAS 14 requires entities to report financial information for each significant business segment and geographical segment of the business.

Having completed your study of this chapter, you should have achieved the following learning outcomes:

- analyse financial statements (in the context of information provided in the accounts and corporate report) to comment on performance and position
- prepare and interpret segmental analysis.

## Self-test questions

1 What is the denominator of the EPS calculation? (1.4)

2 When is the weighted average method used to determine the number of shares to use in an EPS calculation?(1.7)

3 Does a bonus issue reduce or increase EPS? (1.8)

4 What is the ratio used in a rights issue to adjust for the bonus element of the rights? (1.9)

5 Give three examples of potential dilutions in an EPS calculation. (1.10)

6 To which entities do IAS 14 apply? (2.2)

7 What rules apply to determine whether a segment is a reportable segment? (2.5)

8 What are the primary and secondary disclosure headings required by IAS 14? (2.7)

## Objective test questions

### Question 1

A company has profits after tax for the year ending 30 June 20X2 of $77,540. At 1 July 20X1 the company had 600,000 shares in issue and on 30 September made a 1 for 6 rights issue at an issue price of $1.15. On that date the market value of the company's shares was $1.50. The published earnings per share for the year ending 30 June 20X1 was 10.8 cents.

What figures should appear in the income statement for the year ending 30 June 20X2 for earnings per share?

| | *30 June 20X2* | *30 June 20X1* |
|---|---|---|
| **A** | 11.4 cents | 10.8 cents |
| **B** | 11.5 cents | 10.4 cents |
| **C** | 11.6 cents | 11.2 cents |
| **D** | 11.4 cents | 10.4 cents |

### Question 2

At 30 June 20X2 Juniper has $800,000 of $0.50 ordinary shares in issue and $200,000 of 5% convertible debentures. The terms of the debentures are that they can be converted into$0.50 ordinary shares as follows:

| | | |
|---|---|---|
| 30 June 20X5 | 120 | $0.50 ordinary shares for £100 of debentures |
| 30 June 20X6 | 115 | $0.50 ordinary shares for £100 of debentures |
| 30 June 20X7 | 110 | $0.50 ordinary shares for £100 of debentures |

In the year ending 30 June 20X2 Juniper had a retained profit of $548,000 after paying an ordinary dividend of $102,000. Income tax is at the rate of 30%.

What is the basic earnings per share and diluted earnings per share?

### Question 3

Wimble has 1 million $1 ordinary shares in issue at the balance sheet date of 31 March 20X2. At that date there were options outstanding to purchase a further 200,000 ordinary shares at a price of $1.50. The average fair value of the ordinary shares during the year was $1.90. Wimble made a profit after tax of $208,000 during the year.

What is the basic earnings per share and the diluted earnings per share for the year?

*For the answers to these questions, see the 'Answers' section at the end of the book.*

## Exam-type question

### TAB

TAB, a UK company, has recently acquired four large overseas subsidiaries. These subsidiaries manufacture products which are totally different from those of the parent company. The parent company manufactures paper and related products whereas the subsidiaries manufacture the following:

| | *Product* | *Location* |
|---|---|---|
| Subsidiary 1 | Car products | Spain |
| Subsidiary 2 | Textiles | Korea |
| Subsidiary 3 | Kitchen utensils | France |
| Subsidiary 4 | Fashion garments | Thailand |

The directors have purchased these subsidiaries in order to diversify their product base but do not have any knowledge on the information which is required in the financial statements, regarding these subsidiaries, other than the statutory requirements. The directors of the company realise that there is a need to disclose segment information but do not understand what the term means or what the implications are for the published financial statements.

**Required:**

(a) Explain to the directors the purpose of segment reporting of financial information; **(4 marks)**

(b) Explain to the directors the criteria which should be used to identify the separate reportable segments (students should illustrate their answer by reference to the above information); **(6 marks)**

(c) Advise the directors on the information which should be disclosed in financial statements for each segment; **(7 marks)**

(d) Critically evaluate IAS 14 (revised) Segment reporting, setting out the major problems with the standard. **(8 marks)**

**(Total: 25 marks)**

---

*For the answer to this question, see the 'Answers' section at the end of the book.*

## Feedback to activities

### Activity 1

(a) **Past earnings per share (comparative figure)**

Because the rights issue contains a bonus element, the past earnings per share figures should be adjusted by the factor:

$$\frac{\text{Theoretical ex rights price}}{\text{Actual cum rights price}}$$

Consider a holder of 100 shares:

| | | | $ |
|---|---|---|---|
| Prior to rights issue | 100 shares | worth 100 × $1 = | 100.00 |
| Taking up rights | 25 shares | cost 25 × 50c = | 12.50 |
| | 125 | | 112.50 |

i.e. theoretical ex rights price of each share is $\frac{\$112.50}{125} = 90\text{c}$

Last year, reported earnings per share were $\frac{\$400{,}000}{4{,}000{,}000} = 10\text{c}$

Applying correction factor to calculate adjusted comparative figure of earnings per share:

$$10\text{c} \times \frac{\text{Theoretical ex rights price}}{\text{Actual cum rights price}} = 10\text{c} \times \frac{90\text{c}}{100\text{c}} = 9\text{c}$$

(b) **Current earnings per share**

Number of shares 1 July 20X1 to 31 December 20X1 (as adjusted):

$$4{,}000{,}000 \times \frac{\text{Actual cum rights price}}{\text{Theoretical ex rights price}} \times \frac{6\text{ months}}{12\text{ months}}$$

i.e. $4{,}000{,}000 \times \frac{100}{90} \times \frac{6}{12} = 2{,}222{,}222$ shares

Number of shares 1 January 20X2 to 30 June 20X2 (actual):

$\frac{6\text{ months}}{12\text{ months}} = \frac{6}{12} \times 5{,}000{,}000 =$ 2,500,000 shares

Total adjusted shares for year 4,722,222 shares

$\therefore$ Earnings per share $= \frac{\$425{,}000}{4{,}722{,}222} = 9\text{c}$ per share

***Tutorial note:*** Because the rights issue occurred during the current financial year, it is necessary to calculate the weighted average share capital during the year. However, since the rights issue is effectively a combination of an issue at full price and a bonus issue, it is necessary to adjust the number of shares for the six months prior to the rights issue for the bonus element.

For an issue at full price it would be necessary to calculate a weighted average number of shares as indicated by the 6/12 factor. The 100/90 factor in the first six months is used to adjust for the bonus element in the rights issue.

## Activity 2

A possible approach is illustrated by this extract from an accounting policy note.

**Turnover by destination**

Turnover from domestic services within the United Kingdom is attributed to the United Kingdom. Turnover from inbound and outbound services between the United Kingdom and overseas points is attributed to the geographical area in which the relevant overseas point lies.

**Turnover by origin**

Revenue is allocated to the area in which the sale is made.

**Geographical analysis of net assets**

The major revenue-earning asset of the company is its aircraft fleet, the large part of which is registered in the United Kingdom. Since the group's aircraft fleet is employed flexibly across its worldwide route network, there is no suitable basis of allocating such assets and related liabilities to geographical segments.

Chapter 17

# EXTENDING THE SCOPE OF EXTERNAL REPORTS

## Syllabus content

- Increasing stakeholder demands for information that goes beyond historical financial information and the model for an expanded Operating and Financial Review (OFR) proposed by the UK government.
- Environmental and social accounting issues, differentiating between environmental measures and environmental losses, capitalisation of environmental expenditure, and the recognition of future environmental costs by means of provisions.
- The Global Reporting Initiative: non-financial measures of environmental impact.
- Human resource accounting.
- Pressures for improved quality of financial reporting following large scale corporate collapses in the US and UK, and implications for corporate governance and external audit.

## Contents

## Introduction

This is the first of two chapters dealing with developments in financial reporting.

During the last few years, users of traditional financial statements have become increasingly aware of their limitations. Increasingly, many believe that traditional financial statements do not provide their users with enough information to judge a company's performance in its widest sense.

This chapter looks at ways in which the annual report (the financial statements and other information published with the financial statements) is evolving in order to meet the needs of users.

Arguably one of the most important ways in which additional information about a company is communicated is through environmental and social reporting. Public interest in protecting the natural environment has grown significantly during the last 10 to 15 years. This has led many large companies to disclose information about the effect of their activities on the environment, even though there is usually no specific legal requirement to do so. Environmental reporting is increasingly regarded as important both by the general public and by entities themselves.

Social and ethical reporting is the disclosure of information about the ways in which a business attempts to fulfil its responsibilities towards the wider community. It has developed partly as an extension of environmental reporting and partly as a result of factors such as increasing public concern about business ethics and changes in the political climate during the 1990s.

## 1 Background

### 1.1 The wider meaning of performance

KEY POINT

Large companies are increasingly accepting the idea that a business is not only responsible to its shareholders.

Large companies are increasingly accepting the idea that a business is not only responsible to its shareholders, but to several different stakeholders, which are usually taken to be:

- customers
- suppliers
- employees
- the government
- the local community
- society as a whole.

Investors and potential investors require dividends and capital growth and so a public enterprise's performance has traditionally been equated with the profits that it generates. If the needs of other stakeholders are taken into account, performance may encompass:

- providing fair remuneration and an acceptable working environment
- paying suppliers promptly
- minimising the damage to the environment caused by the enterprise's activities
- contributing to the community by providing employment or by other means.

Awareness of the needs of other stakeholders and the wider community is sometimes referred to as corporate social responsibility.

### 1.2 Pressure for change

In recent years there have been a number of major corporate collapses, both in the US and in Europe. In most cases, the financial statements were subsequently found to be fundamentally misleading. Probably the best-known of these cases was the collapse of Enron, a US conglomerate. Enron made use of a large number of special purpose entities which were set up in such a way that they did not have to be consolidated under US GAAP. This enabled the group to disguise the fact that it was making huge losses by keeping liabilities off the balance sheet. It also enabled the directors to disguise the true level of their 'fees'.

KEY POINT

Corporate collapses and accounting scandals can affect many thousands of people not directly connected with an entity.

Corporate collapses and accounting scandals can affect many thousands of people not directly connected with an entity. For example, in the UK, the collapse of financial services companies have resulted in a very large number of people losing their retirement benefits or their entire savings

There are a number of reasons why financial statements may be misleading, not least problems with individual accounting standards. However, users are becoming increasingly dissatisfied with financial statements and the published annual report in their current form.

## 2 The limitations of financial statements and how these might be overcome

### 2.1 Inherent limitations of financial statements

***A conventionalised representation***

Financial statements are a conventionalised representation of transactions and other events. They involve a substantial degree of classification and aggregation and the allocation of the effects of continuous operations to discrete reporting periods.

Presenting information in financial statements involves a loss of information, because if every single aspect of every relevant transaction and event were reported the overall picture would be obscured by the mass of detail.

Despite this, there is always a risk that information that is critical to understanding the financial performance and financial position of an entity will either not be given sufficient prominence or will be lost completely.

***Focus on the financial effects of transactions***

Financial statements focus on the financial effects of transactions and other events and do not focus to any significant extent on their non-financial effects or on non-financial information in general.

Most published annual reports include narrative discussion intended to put the numerical statements and disclosures in context (normally in the form of the Chairman's Statement and a Management Discussion and Analysis). However, the Management Discussion and Analysis is not mandatory. Although accompanying information is supposed to be consistent with the financial statements it may not be audited.

***Historical information***

Financial statements provide information that is largely historical. They do not reflect future events or transactions, nor do they anticipate the impact of potential changes in the economic environment.

It could be argued that some financial information may have predictive value in that past performance can provide a limited basis for predicting future performance. However, because there may be changes to the environment in which the business operates, this is not necessarily reliable and is not the same as forecast information.

Note also that, for practical reasons, there is often a time interval of several months between the year end and the publication of the financial statements. Most financial information is out of date by the time it is actually published.

## 2.2 More relevant information in financial statements

The income statement, balance sheet and notes have evolved in response to the needs of the managers and providers of capital to traditional manufacturing businesses. In many developed countries such as the UK, this type of business has been largely replaced by service based organisations. Human capital and intangible assets have become important for many businesses. In addition, the economic environment itself has become far more complex. Users now need more information and different information.

Suggestions have included:

- **Forecast information**, such as:
  - the entity's actual performance for the accounting period just past as compared with its previously published plan for that period.
  - management's explanations of any significant variances between the two
  - management's financial plan for the current and future accounting periods, together with explanations of the major assumptions used in preparing it.
- **Environmental and social reporting:** information about an entity and its effect on the physical environment; the human resources available to it and its use of those resources; and the way in which it affects the wider community to which it belongs.
- **More non-financial information**: for example:
  - accounting areas subject to uncertainty (e.g. the margin for error in accounting estimates)
  - innovation: the proportion of production that is new and self generated
  - effectiveness and lead time of research and development
  - the economic environment within which the entity operates: market share, market size, and the activities of competitors
  - staff resources
  - ownership, management and their responsibilities
  - comparative information about competitors or other entities in similar markets
  - information about the various risks (uncertainties) faced by the business and how these are managed.

## 2.3 Changing the financial reporting model

***The traditional accounting model***

KEY POINT

The business environment is now so sophisticated and complex that the traditional idea of performance may no longer be valid.

The traditional annual report reflects a particular view of what a business is and what it does or should do. But is this still correct? What exactly is performance and how should it be measured? The business environment is now so sophisticated and complex that the traditional idea of performance may no longer be valid. If the traditional model is no longer appropriate, what are the alternatives?

The traditional financial reporting model reflects the basic accounting equation: an entity's performance is the difference between the book value of its net assets at the start of the year and the book value of its net assets at the end of the year. The IASB *Framework* and the conceptual frameworks used by most other major standard setters (e.g. the UK ASB) all follow this model, except that certain assets and liabilities are remeasured to fair value. Current values or fair values provide more useful information to investors than historic costs. In addition, it is now accepted that an entity's performance includes holding gains and losses (e.g. gains and losses on revaluation) as well as realised profits.

***Shareholder value***

DEFINITION

**Shareholder value** is the total return to investors on their shares.

Some believe that this does not go far enough. The primary objective of a business should not simply be to generate profit in the short term, but to generate shareholder value. **Shareholder value** is the total return to investors on their shares. The idea behind the concept of shareholder value is that there are several 'drivers' within a business that can be managed to create value, e.g. growth in sales, increase in the operating profit margin, investment in human resources, safeguarding the reputation of the business.

If performance were measured and reported in terms of growth in shareholder value there would be two advantages: the annual report would reflect the economic reality of business operations; and users would be able to judge management on their ability to enhance the value of an entity in the long term, rather than on the profits that it generates in the short term. In theory there would be far fewer scandals and corporate collapses because it would no longer be in the interest of management to pursue short term growth at the expense of everything else.

To measure the growth in shareholder value, the financial statements would need to reflect all the drivers of value, including the workforce and internally generated intangibles. There are obvious practical problems at the moment, but some believe that eventually these will be overcome.

In the meantime, some entities include information about key 'drivers' of value in the annual report. Analysts have developed techniques that attempt to measure shareholder value, of which the best known is Economic Value Added (EVA).

***Sustainability accounting***

There are a number of other alternatives to the traditional financial reporting model. One of these is sustainability accounting. Sustainability accounting attempts to measure the performance of an entity as it relates to all stakeholders including the wider community, rather than just investors. There is a particular emphasis on the interaction of the business with the natural environment.

Sustainability accounting is still largely a theoretical concept. However, there is considerable interest in it, as it reflects the idea that business activities should have a positive effect on society as a whole. Environmental and social reporting is discussed later in this chapter.

## 2.4 The impact of the internet on financial reporting

The internet has several implications for financial reporting:

- online trading is relatively cheap and this means that the number of private investors is growing
- information about companies and other organisations is being accessed by an increasing number of people, many of whom are private investors
- the technology itself allows information to be presented in innovative ways.

It is likely that in the near future annual reports, interim reports and preliminary announcements will be published on the company's website as well as, or instead of being distributed to shareholders in printed form. Most large companies already place their annual report on their website.

***New possibilities***

At present, most companies simply post the printed annual report and accounts. There are other possibilities as follows.

- 'Hyperlinks' enable users to jump from one area of the financial statements to other areas where the same topic is discussed. This means that users can easily find the information that they need. Use of hyperlinks could help to overcome 'information overload' without removing detailed disclosures that are useful to analysts.
- Some companies already post financial statements on spreadsheets that can be downloaded and merged with those of other companies. This enables comparisons to be made. In future, companies may be able to place a database of audited financial information on the Internet from which users could prepare their own reports, presented in a way that best meets their particular needs.

Another possibility is that companies may report to shareholders at much more frequent intervals, so that much less emphasis is placed on the traditional annual report. Some commentators (although not all) believe that eventually companies will report in 'real time' so that annual financial statements will become obsolete.

## 2.5 Current developments

Radical changes to the way in which the financial statements themselves are prepared will almost certainly not happen in the near future.

However, the type of information disclosed in the annual report is evolving to meet users' expectations. In particular, there is an increased focus on non-financial information and on narrative disclosure. For example, IFRS 7 requires an entity to provide non-finanical information about the risks it faces as a result of holding financial instruments.

The rest of this chapter looks at the two main methods used to communicate this additional information: the operating and financial review; and environmental and social reports.

# 3 Operating and financial review

## 3.1 Purpose of the Operating and Financial Review

KEY POINT

An **Operating and Financial Review (OFR)**is a discussion of the main factors underlying a company's performance and financial position.

An **Operating and Financial Review (OFR)** is a discussion of the main factors underlying a company's performance and financial position. The OFR is sometimes known as the Management's Discussion and Analysis.

The purpose of the OFR is to assist the user's assessment of the future performance of the reporting entity by setting out the directors' analysis of the business.

Currently there is no requirement for entities reporting under IFRSs to prepare an OFR. The IASB intends to develop guidance on preparing a Management's Discussion and Analysis, but this is unlikely to be finalised within the next few years.

IAS 1 refers briefly to the OFR (called 'a financial review by management') and states that it describes and explains the main features of the entity's financial performance and financial position and the main uncertainties it faces'. It also states that the report may include:

(a) the main factors and influences determining financial performance, including changes in the environment in which the entity operates;

(b) the entity's policy for investment to maintain and enhance financial performance, including its dividend policy;

(c) the entity's sources of funding and its targeted ratio of liabilities to equity; and

(d) the entity's resources not recognised in the balance sheet (these might include internally generated intangible assets and human resources).

IAS 1 is clear that the OFR is outside the scope of IASs and IFRSs.

KEY POINT

In practice, most public companies now include some form of OFR in their annual report, even where this is not required by the listing authorities.

Until recently, the UK government intended to require quoted companies to prepare and publish an OFR. It is now unclear whether this will happen, but in practice most public companies include some form of OFR in their financial statements, even where they are not required to do so as this is now considered 'best practice'.

The EU Accounts Modernisation Directive (which applies from March 2006) will require large and medium-sized companies (including unquoted companies) to publish a review of the company's business in the Directors' Report accompanying the financial statements.

The UK government's draft regulations are summarised below to show the type of information that should be included in an OFR. The EU Directive requires similar information, but is not as detailed.

## 3.2 Content of the Operating and Financial Review

The UK government's draft regulations stated that an operating and financial review should be a balanced and comprehensive analysis of:

(a) the development and performance of the business of the company during the financial year

(b) the position of the company at the end of the year

(c) the main trends and factors underlying the development, performance and position of the business of the company during the financial year

(d) the main trends and factors which are likely to affect its future development, performance and position.

It should include the following core elements:

(a) a statement of the business, objectives and strategies of the company

(b) a description of the resources available to the company

(c) a description of the principal risks and uncertainties facing the company

(d) a description of the capital structure, treasury policies and objectives and liquidity of the company.

In addition, the OFR should contain certain other information where this is judged to be relevant to assessing the company's operations. This includes information about the company's policies in relation to its employees and on environmental, social and community issues; and information about related parties and transactions with them.

The OFR should also include analysis using key performance indicators, both financial and non-financial and, where appropriate, additional explanations of amounts included in the financial statements.

The draft requirements have been deliberately made very general. This is because the OFR is not intended to be a checklist of required disclosures, but a discussion of the matters which are genuinely relevant to shareholders and other users.

### 3.3 Potential problems

There are practical problems for those who prepare and review an OFR, normally the directors. Many company directors in the UK have argued that a statutory OFR will place an unacceptable burden on companies because of the time and cost of preparing it.

Preparers need to decide which matters are relevant to shareholders and this is necessarily subjective. Where matters are judged relevant, directors may be reluctant to disclose information, for example, because their credibility might be undermined if forecasts subsequently turn out to be incorrect or because competitors might be made aware of future plans. Directors are likely to resist disclosing any information that would show the company in a bad light, even if it is extremely relevant to understanding the company's business.

Any statutory OFR would probably be subject to audit. By its nature, some of the information in the OFR would be very difficult to verify. An auditor would also have to make judgements about narrative disclosures; this could include deciding whether the review deals even-handedly with good and bad aspects of performance and whether it highlights the matters that are most relevant to shareholders.

There is an argument that a company can avoid providing information that is genuinely useful, even if the OFR becomes compulsory. To prepare an OFR that is useful, the company must comply with the spirit of the regulation and not just the actual rules. The UK government avoided prescribing the content of the OFR in detail because it wanted to discourage companies from simply presenting a checklist of disclosures in very general terms that would not be helpful to users. Despite this, some companies may still try to present the OFR in such a way that it reveals as little as possible. In practice, some OFRs are little more than commentaries on the financial statements. Many do not include any analysis of the business itself or of its strengths and weaknesses and the risks that it faces.

# 4 Environmental reporting

## 4.1 Introduction

DEFINITION

**Environmental reporting** is the disclosure of information, in the published annual report or elsewhere, of the effect that the operations of the business have on the natural environment.

**Environmental reporting** is the disclosure of information, in the published annual report or elsewhere, of the effect that the operations of the business have on the natural environment.

During the late 1980s and early 1990s there were several well publicised environmental disasters, including the Exxon Valdez oil spill and the explosion at the Bhopal chemical factory. In addition, the Rio conference and the activities of organisations such as Greenpeace and Friends of the Earth drew the general public's attention to issues such as global warming.

There are now considerable incentives for businesses to take action to preserve the environment, such as controlling pollution, using recyclable materials, choosing renewable materials and developing environmentally friendly products. Public interest in safeguarding the environment affects businesses in two main ways.

- They may suffer direct losses as a result of their actions, for example, they may be legally or constructively obliged to incur the expense of rectifying environmental damage, or they may have to pay additional taxes or suffer financial penalties if they cause pollution.
- If a business is believed to cause damage to the environment or to otherwise act in an unethical way it may attract considerable adverse publicity. This leads to loss of customers. There is a positive side: a business can attract customers if it has a 'green' image. One obvious example of this in the UK is The Body Shop.

As a result of these factors, the number of companies disclosing information about the effect of their operations on the environment is steadily increasing.

## 4.2 Regulation of environmental reporting

KEY POINT

There is no UK or international accounting standard dealing specifically with environmental issues.

Different countries require different disclosures under their statutory framework. For example, at present there is very little direct regulation of environmental reporting in the UK. The law does not require entities to disclose the effect of their actions on the environment and there is no UK or international accounting standard dealing specifically with environmental issues.

This contrasts with the position in some other countries. For example, in the Netherlands, Sweden and Denmark large companies are required to present environmental information either in their annual report or in a separate environmental report. The Securities and Exchange Commission in the USA requires listed companies to disclose estimates of current and future environmental expenditure and the effects that compliance with environmental regulations may have on profits and the position of the business. Listed companies in the US are also required to disclose legal proceedings relating to environmental issues.

This lack of regulation leads to several potential problems.

(a) Because disclosure is largely voluntary, not all businesses disclose information. Those that do tend to do so either because they are under particular pressure to prove their 'green' credentials (for example, large public utility companies whose operations directly affect the environment) or because they have deliberately built their reputation on environmental friendliness or social responsibility.

(b) The information disclosed may not be complete or reliable. Many businesses see environmental reporting largely as a public relations exercise and therefore only provide information that shows them in a positive light. Environmental disclosures normally appear in the Chairman's Statement, in the Operating and Financial Review or in a 'stand alone' environmental report. Therefore they do not normally have to be audited and can be framed in very general terms.

(c) The information may not be disclosed consistently from year to year.

(d) Some businesses, particularly small and medium sized entities, may believe that the costs of preparing and circulating additional information outweigh the benefits of doing so.

### 4.3 The Global Reporting Initiative and other voluntary codes of practice

KEY POINT

Sustainability reporting integrates the environmental, social and economic aspects of performance.

There are a number of non-mandatory codes of practice and guidelines for preparing environmental reports. The most important of these are the *Sustainability Reporting Guidelines* published by the Global Reporting Initiative (GRI). Sustainability reporting integrates the environmental, social and economic aspects of performance (known as the three sustainability dimensions).

The *Guidelines* are intended to develop sustainability reporting practices worldwide so that they are comparable with financial reporting practices in terms of verification and comparability, and are intended to apply to all entities that prepare sustainability reports, including small and not-for-profit entities. They are intended to strengthen and complement traditional financial reporting by providing critical non-financial information that helps users assess the current and future performance of the reporting entity.

Compliance with the *Guidelines* is voluntary, but an increasing number of multinational companies now follow them in preparing environmental and social reports.

***Advantages of sustainability reporting***

The GRI points out that there are advantages for the reporting entity; sustainability reporting helps to:

(a) maintain and strengthen trust with community groups, investors, consumers and other stakeholders

(b) link various functions within an organisation into a more strategic vision and operation

(c) identify trouble spots and unanticipated opportunities, in supply chains, among customers, communities or regulators, or in the areas of reputation and brand management

(d) assess and measure the value of sustainability practices in the organisation in relation to its overall business strategy and competitiveness

(e) reduce share price volatility and uncertainty occasioned by surprise or incomplete disclosure.

***Basic requirements***

An entity beginning to report environmental information can use the *Guidelines* informally, by selecting certain principles, elements and indicators.

Alternatively, an entity can identify its report as prepared 'in accordance' with the *Guidelines*. This means that the report must meet certain minimum requirements:

(a) report on the organisational profile, governance and management systems

(b) include a GRI Content Index, linking GRI components to information actually contained in the report

(c) respond to each core indicator by either reporting on it, or explaining its omission

(d) ensure that the report is consistent with the GRI reporting principles

(e) include a statement signed by the Board or CEO indicating that the report was prepared in accordance with the 2002 GRI *Guidelines* and represents a balanced and reasonable presentation of the entity's sustainability performance.

***Reporting principles***

The *Guidelines* present a set of reporting principles. These are:

(a) Transparency: full disclosure of the processes, procedures and assumptions used.

(b) Inclusiveness: the reporting entity should engage its stakeholders in preparing and enhancing the quality of reports.

(c) Auditability: information should be recorded, compiled, analysed and disclosed in such a way as to make it auditable.

(d) Completeness: all material information should appear.

(e) Relevance: reporting entities should use the degree of importance that users assign to particular information to determine content.

(f) Sustainability context: reporting entities should seek to place their performance in the broader context of ecological, social or other issues where this adds significant meaning to the report.

(g) Accuracy: reports should achieve a degree of exactness and low margin of error to enable users to make decisions with a high degree of confidence.

(h) Neutrality: reports should avoid bias in selection and presentation of information and provide a balanced account of performance.

(i) Comparability: it should be possible for users to compare the report to earlier reports and reports of comparable organisations.

(j) Clarity: information should be understandable while still maintaining a suitable level of detail.

(k) Timeliness: reports should provide information on a regular schedule.

***Report content***

Five sections should appear in a sustainability report:

(a) Vision and strategy: a statement from the CEO and discussion of the reporting entity's sustainability strategy.

(b) Profile: an overview of the entity's organisation, operations, stakeholders and the scope of the report.

(c) Governance structure and management systems: a description of the entity's organisational structure, policies, management systems and stakeholder engagement efforts.

(d) GRI Content Index: a cross-referenced table that identifies the location of specified information to allow users to clearly understand the degree to which the entity has covered the content of the *Guidelines*.

(e) Performance indicators: measures of the performance of the reporting entity divided into economic, environmental and social performance indicators.

***Performance indicators***

KEY POINT

The GRI identifies performance indicators for each of the three sustainability dimensions: economic performance, environmental performance and social performance.

The GRI identifies performance indicators for each of the three sustainability dimensions: economic performance, environmental performance and social performance. It has said that the sustainability dimensions are the three 'bottom lines' of sustainability reporting – equivalent to the profit earned by an entity's financial performance.

There are core indicators, which are required for reporting in accordance with the *Guidelines,* and additional indicators, which can be used at the discretion of the entity.

**Economic indicators** include the reporting entity's wages, pensions and other benefits paid to employees; monies received from customers and paid to suppliers; and taxes paid and subsidies received.

**Environmental indicators** include the environmental impacts of products and services; energy, material and water use; greenhouse gas and other emissions; effluents and waste generation; impacts on biodiversity; use of hazardous materials; recycling, pollution, waste reduction and other environmental programmes; environmental expenditures; and fines and penalties for non-compliance.

**Social indicators** include labour practices (e.g. diversity, employee health and safety); human rights (e.g. child labour, compliance issues); and broader social issues affecting consumers, communities and other stakeholders (e.g. community relations). Many social indicators are not easily quantifiable, therefore GRI requests qualitative information where appropriate.

***Other voluntary codes of practice***

(a) The Federation des Experts Comptables Européens (FEE) has issued a Discussion Paper: *Towards a generally accepted framework for environmental reporting*. The object of the paper is to allow environmental reporting to gain the same degree of public acceptance as financial reporting. It discusses users' information needs and the qualitative characteristics of environmental reporting information, based on the IASB *Framework*. The Paper also includes the United Nations Environmental Program (UNEP)/SustainAbility 50 core reporting elements which entities may wish to consider when developing environmental reports.

(b) The Confederation of British Industry (CBI) has published a guideline entitled *Introducing Environmental Reporting*.

(c) ACCA has issued several guides to environmental reporting. It also publishes the criteria by which it judges the environmental reports submitted for its annual Awards scheme.

(d) The United Nations Conference on Trade and Development (UNCTAD) has published a report: *Environmental Financial Accounting and Reporting at the Corporate Level.*

In addition, a large number of academic and governmental bodies have published reports and guidelines that are available on the Internet.

Companies may register under the Eco-Management and Audit Scheme (EMAS). EMAS is an accredited environmental management system which certifies companies that meet its standard. To be certified, an enterprise must develop an environmental policy, environmental programme and environmental management system for each of its sites, carry out an annual audit and publish an independently verified report of its performance.

### 4.4 What information should be disclosed in the annual report?

Suggestions have included the following:

(a) **Environmental issues pertinent to the company and industry**

- (i) the entity's policy towards the environment and any improvements made since first adopting the policy
- (ii) whether the entity has a formal system for managing environmental risks
- (iii) the identity of the director(s) responsible for environmental issues
- (iv) the entity's perception of the risks to the environment from its operations
- (v) the extent to which the entity would be capable of responding to a major environmental disaster and an estimate of the full economic consequences of such a future major disaster
- (vi) the effects of, and the entity's response to, any government legislation on environmental matters
- (vii) details of any significant infringement of environmental legislation or regulations
- (viii) material environmental legal issues in which the entity is involved
- (ix) details of any significant initiatives taken, if possible linked to amounts in financial statements.

(b) **Financial information**

- (i) the entity's accounting policies relating to environmental costs, provisions and contingencies
- (ii) the amount charged to the income statement during the accounting period in respect of expenditure to prevent or rectify damage to the environment caused by the entity's operations. This could be analysed between expenditure that the entity was legally obliged to incur and other expenditure
- (iii) the amount charged to the income statement during the accounting period in respect of expenditure to protect employees and society in general from the consequences of damage to the environment caused by the entity's operations. Again, this could be analysed between compulsory and voluntary expenditure
- (iv) details (including amounts) of any provisions or contingent liabilities relating to environmental matters

(v) the amount of environmental expenditure capitalised during the year

(vi) details of fines, penalties and compensation paid during the accounting period in respect of non-compliance with environmental regulations.

KEY POINT

Entities may disclose information about the effect of their operations on the natural environment either in the published annual report or in a separate environmental report. Disclosure of such information is largely voluntary.

### 4.5 Environmental reporting in practice

There are two main vehicles that companies use to publish information about the ways in which they interact with the natural environment:

- the published annual report (which includes the financial statements)
- a separate environmental report.

A high proportion of larger quoted companies make some kind of environmental disclosure in the annual report. Information is normally disclosed in the Operating and Financial Review (OFR).

Most large public companies now publish environmental reports that are completely separate from the annual report and financial statements. The environmental report is often combined with information about other social and ethical issues. Notable UK examples of companies which produce such reports are The Body Shop, Thorn EMI plc, The Co-operative Bank, British Airways plc and BT plc. There are several awards for good environmental reports, for example, ACCA's 'UK Environmental Reporting Award'.

Because the environmental report is separate from the published annual report, companies can publish whatever they wish. Environmental reports do not have to be audited. However, many organisations do submit the information in their report to some kind of independent review or audit process.

Public and media interest has tended to focus on the environmental report rather than on the disclosures in the published annual report and financial statements. This separation reflects the fact that the two reports are aimed at different audiences. Shareholders are the main users of the annual report, while the environmental report is designed to be read by the general public.

### 4.6 The present situation

The first environmental reports were largely a public relations exercise and the aim was to demonstrate a company's commitment to the environment. Some entities continue to view them in this light. However, many others now view the environmental report as a vehicle for communicating an entity's performance in safeguarding the natural environment.

Some commentators believe that 'stand alone' environmental reports are not a substitute for clear disclosure of environmental costs in the financial statements. A business cannot be regarded as successful if it earns its profits by misusing natural resources and does not disclose the cost of these activities. There is an argument that a requirement to disclose environmental costs would encourage responsible behaviour.

There is also an argument that investors need information about environmental costs and potential liabilities, because environmental disasters can harm businesses, as well as society in general. For example, the Exxon Valdez oil spillage reduced the company's profits by almost 90% in one quarter alone.

# 5 Environmental accounting issues

## 5.1 Environmental costs

DEFINITION

**Environmental costs** include both environmental measures and environmental losses.

DEFINITION

**Environmental measures** are the costs of preventing, reducing or repairing damage to the environment and the costs of conserving resources. They can include:

- capital expenditure
- closure or decommissioning costs
- clean-up costs
- development expenditure
- costs of recycling or conserving energy.

DEFINITION

**Environmental losses** are costs which bring no benefi to the business, for example:

- fines, penalties and compensation
- impairment or disposal losses relating to assets which have to be scrapped or abandoned because they damage the environment.

KEY POINT

Environmental costs are accounted for in accordance with the requirements of current accounting standards.

**Environmental costs** include both environmental measures and environmental losses.

**Environmental measures** are the costs of preventing, reducing or repairing damage to the environment and the costs of conserving resources. They can include:

- capital expenditure
- closure or decommissioning costs
- clean-up costs
- development expenditure
- costs of recycling or conserving energy.

**Environmental losses** are costs which bring no benefit to the business, for example:

- fines, penalties and compensation
- impairment or disposal losses relating to assets which have to be scrapped or abandoned because they damage the environment.

The term 'environmental costs' can have a wide range of meanings, depending on the items included. There is no agreed definition, but those given here have been suggested.

This classification is not rigid. For example, closure costs could be classified as either environmental measures or environmental losses, depending on the way in which they arise.

There can be practical problems in deciding whether a particular cost is an environmental cost. For example, a company may replace its motor vehicles with others that use less fuel. These will pollute the environment less and use fewer natural resources, but the company will also make cost savings on fuel as a result. Is the cost of the vehicles an environmental cost or simply normal capital expenditure? Where environmental costs are disclosed in the annual report, there should be a clear explanation of which items are included.

## 5.2 Accounting for environmental costs

Environmental costs are treated in accordance with the requirements of current accounting standards:

- Most expenditure is charged in the income statement in the period in which it is incurred. Material items may need to be disclosed as unusual items in the notes to the accounts.
- Fines and penalties for non-compliance with regulations are charged to the income statement in the period in which they are incurred. This applies even if the activities that resulted in the penalties took place in an earlier accounting period, as they cannot be treated as prior period adjustments.
- Expenditure on non-current assets is capitalised and depreciated in the usual way (IAS 16 *Property, Plant and Equipment*).

- Non-current assets and goodwill may become impaired as a result of environmental legislation or new regulations. IAS 36 *Impairment of Assets* lists events that could trigger an impairment review; one of these is a significant adverse change in the statutory or regulatory environment in which the business operates.
- Research and development expenditure in respect of environmentally friendly products, processes or services is covered by IAS 38 *Intangible Assets*.

There are two areas which are potentially more complicated. These are provisions for future environmental costs and the capitalisation of environmental expenditure. These are dealt with below.

DEFINITION

A **provision** is a liability of uncertain timing or amount. (IAS 37)

DEFINITION

A **liability** is a present obligation of the entity arising from past events, the settlement of which is expected to result in an outflow from the entity of resources embodying economic benefits.

### 5.3 Provisions for future environmental costs

A **provision** is a liability of uncertain timing or amount. (IAS 37)

A **liability** is a present obligation of the entity arising from past events, the settlement of which is expected to result in an outflow from the entity of resources embodying economic benefits.

IAS 37 *Provisions, Contingent Liabilities and Contingent Assets* states that three conditions must be met before a provision may be recognised:

- the entity has a present obligation as a result of a past event
- it is probable that a transfer of resources embodying economic benefits will be required to settle the obligation
- a reliable estimate can be made of the amount of the obligation.

IAS 37 is relevant to provisions for environmental costs.

- The fact that the entity's activities have caused environmental contamination does not in itself give rise to an obligation to rectify the damage. However, even if there is no legal obligation there may be a constructive obligation. An entity almost certainly has a constructive obligation to rectify environmental damage if it has a policy of acting in an environmentally responsible way and this policy is well publicised.
- The obligation must arise from a past event. This means that a provision can only be set up to rectify environmental damage that has already happened. If an entity needs to incur expenditure to reduce pollution in the future it does not set up a provision. This is because in theory it can avoid the expenditure by its future actions, for example, it could discontinue the particular activity that causes the pollution.
- As some environmental liabilities only crystallise several years after the provision is set up, the amount provided may have to be discounted to its present value.
- If the entity cannot recognise a provision it may still need to disclose a contingent liability (apply the normal principles to determine whether this is the case).
- IAS 37 requires disclosure of the nature of the obligation or contingent liability for each separate class. This means that users of the financial statements will be made aware of the existence of any provisions or contingent liabilities relating to environmental matters. Provisions for environmental costs should be analysed separately from other provisions in the note showing movements during the year.

***Activity 1***

(a) An entity causes contamination but cleans up only when required to do so under the laws of the particular country in which it operates. One country in which it operates has had no legislation requiring cleaning up, and the entity has been contaminating land in that country for several years. At the balance sheet date it is virtually certain that a draft law requiring a clean-up of land already contaminated will be enacted shortly after the year end.

(b) An entity has constructed an oil rig. Under the terms of its licensing agreement it must remove the oil rig at the end of production and restore the seabed. Ninety per cent of the eventual costs of undertaking this work relate to the removal of the oil rig and restoration of the damage caused by building it, and 10% will arise through the extraction of oil. At the balance sheet date, no oil has yet been extracted.

(c) New legislation has been passed that requires an entity to fit smoke filters in its factories by 30 June 20X0. At 31 December 20X0 (the balance sheet date) the filters have not yet been fitted. According to the company's legal advisers, the new law is not yet being stringently enforced. In practice, provided that the filters are fitted within the next few months, there is a reasonable chance that the company will escape penalties for non-compliance.

State whether a provision should be recognised in each of these three cases.

*Feedback to this activity is at the end of the chapter.*

## 5.4 Capitalisation of environmental expenditure

The issue here is whether environmental expenditure provides access to future economic benefits. If it does, then it meets the IASB's definition of an asset. For example, the cost of the smoke filters in the Activity above would normally be capitalised and depreciated over the useful economic lives of the filters. The expenditure will enable the factory to generate profits without the risk of penalties in future periods.

An asset may also arise as the result of recognising a provision.

For example, suppose that a company has an obligation to recognise a provision for the costs of cleaning up a site. It cannot continue to generate income from the site without incurring the expenditure. Therefore the obligation gives the company access to future economic benefits and it has an asset.

***Activity 2***

Sphere has built a nuclear power station which is due to become operational on 1 January 20X1. It is estimated that the cost of decommissioning the power station will be $10 million and that decommissioning will take place in fifteen years' time. The risk free cost of capital for the company is 10%. The nuclear power station is depreciated on a straight line basis over its useful economic life of 15 years, starting from 1 January 20X1. Depreciation is based on the cost of the asset at 31 December each year. Sphere has recently won an award for the best environmental report published during the year.

State how the cost of decommissioning the power station should be treated in the financial statements for the years ended 31 December 20X0 and 31 December 20X1.

*Feedback to this activity is at the end of the chapter.*

# 6 Social and ethical reporting

## 6.1 Introduction

DEFINITION

**Social and ethical reporting** is the disclosure of information, in the published annual report or elsewhere, of the effect that the operations of the business have on society as a whole.

DEFINITION

**Socio-economic accounting** is the process of measuring, recording and disclosing the effect of exchanges between a business and its social environment.

**Social and ethical reporting** is the disclosure of information, in the published annual report or elsewhere, of the effect that the operations of the business have on society as a whole. It has evolved in part from the idea of socio-economic accounting.

**Socio-economic accounting** is the process of measuring, recording and disclosing the effect of exchanges between a business and its social environment.

Socio-economic accounting is based on the idea that a business interacts with several different environments, for example:

- the physical environment
- the biological environment
- the economic environment
- the sociological environment.

Traditional financial statements only report a business's interaction with the economic environment. They are an account of the business's transactions in goods and services expressed in money terms.

A business interacts with the physical and biological environments by using natural resources such as oil and fossil fuels and by converting them into goods and services. It may change the natural environment as a result of its activities, for example, by pollution. Environmental reporting is partly an attempt to measure and disclose these exchanges.

A business may interact with society in several ways:

(a) it employs human resources in the form of management and other employees

(b) its activities affect society as a whole, for example, it may:

  (i) be the reason for a particular community's existence

  (ii) produce goods that are helpful or harmful to particular members of society

  (iii) damage the environment in ways which harms society as a whole

  (iv) undertake charitable works in the community or promote particular values.

In theory, the social accounts of an entity would consist of a social income statement which measured and disclosed the benefits and costs of its activities to various sections of society and a social balance sheet which measured and disclosed the entity's human assets and its use of natural resources and public goods. In practice, any attempt to set a monetary value on these items can only be subjective. There would also be problems in establishing the boundary of the reporting entity: how far do its social responsibilities extend?

### 6.2 Reporting a business's effect on society

Ten years ago social and ethical reporting was almost non-existent, but many large public companies now publish information about their interaction with society. As with environmental reporting, there are two main vehicles for presenting information: the published annual report; and separate 'social reports'. Most of the attention of preparers and users of information is focused on the latter.

Although social reports are not yet as common as environmental reports, they tend to be published by the same kinds of organisations that publish environmental reports:

- businesses which have deliberately built their reputation on social responsibility (e.g. Body Shop, Traidcraft)
- large public companies which perceive themselves as being under particular pressure to prove that their activities do not exploit society as a whole or certain sections of it (e.g. Shell International plc and some other utility companies).

The social report may or may not be combined with the environmental report.

### 6.3 Social reporting in practice

KEY POINT

'Stand alone' social and ethical reports do not have to be audited and there are no regulations prescribing their content.

'Stand alone' social and ethical reports do not have to be audited and there are no regulations prescribing their content. However, there are some sets of non-mandatory guidelines and codes of best practice, for example, the standard AA1000, which has been issued by the Institute of Social and Ethical Accountability (ISEA). Some organisations have the data in their reports independently verified and include the 'auditor's report' in their published document.

The Co-operative Bank plc's annual *Partnership Report* is one of the best examples of good social reporting in the UK. The Bank has identified its stakeholders, or 'partners': shareholders; customers; staff; suppliers; society and the community; and future generations. It asks each group of stakeholders what matters to them most in their relationship with the bank and it sets specific targets based on the replies. It also sets targets relating to ethics and ecological sustainability. The report lists and explains all the targets and quantifies the extent to which they have been met (or have not been met).

## 7 Social accounting in the financial statements

### 7.1 What information must be disclosed?

Legal requirements vary from country to country. In the UK, companies legislation requires disclosure of the following information about the company and its relationship with the wider community:

(a) In the notes to the financial statements:

- (i) the average number of employees during the financial year; and the average number employed within particular categories to be determined by the directors
- (ii) staff costs analysed between wages and salaries; social security costs; and other pension costs
- (iii) detailed information about directors' emoluments.

(b) In the directors' report:

(i) information about directors and their share interests during the period

(ii) total of political and charitable donations

(iii) if the average number of UK employees exceeds 250, a statement of its policy relating to disabled employees

(iv) if the average number of UK employees exceeds 250, a statement of its policy relating to employee involvement

(v) a statement of its policy relating to the payment of its suppliers (public companies and some large private companies only).

In addition, listed companies must publish additional information about corporate governance and directors' remuneration.

In practice, most companies make the minimum necessary disclosure, with statements on disabled employees and employee involvement normally being framed in very general terms.

### 7.2 Statement of Human Resources

In 1994 CIMA published a Discussion Paper entitled *Corporate Reporting: The Management Interface*. This proposed that certain additional information normally only available to management should be disclosed in external financial reports. One of its recommendations was that financial statements include a Statement of Human Resources. This could disclose:

- days per year training for categories of staff
- expenditure on training, both in total and differentiated between categories of employees
- career and development policy, both vertically and horizontally
- a statement explaining the relevance of human resource policy to the future of the company
- information on staff turnover rates; average length of service; costs of recruitment; voluntary payments on termination of employment; and numbers of professionally qualified staff.

DEFINITION

**Human resource accounting** is the process of measuring and disclosing the value of an entity's human resources: its employees. It is one aspect of social accounting.

### 7.3 Human resource accounting

**Human resource accounting** is the process of measuring and disclosing the value of an entity's human resources: its employees. It is one aspect of social accounting.

Most businesses recognise that they could not operate without employees and the ability to recruit and retain the services of well qualified, motivated staff is essential to the survival of many organisations. One of the criticisms of conventional accounting is that the balance sheet does not represent the true value of a business because it fails to recognise assets such as internally created brand names – and human resources.

Normally, the cost of employing staff includes wages, salaries, social security costs, pensions and other benefits, training and other expenses and is charged to the income statement as it is incurred.

Under human resource accounting, the human resources of an entity are treated as an asset. They are capitalised as intangible non-current assets and amortised over the period from which the entity expects to derive benefit from their services.

***Activity 3***

What would be the advantages of human resource accounting?

*Feedback to this activity is at the end of the chapter.*

### 7.4 Are human resources assets?

An asset is a resource controlled by an entity as a result of past events from which future economic benefits are expected to flow to the entity (IASB *Framework*).

The employer has the ability to earn future profits and obtain future inflows of cash as a result of an employee's services to the entity. The asset is not the actual person, but this right to future economic benefit, which does not have to be certain.

KEY POINT

The main difficulty in treating human resources as assets is uncertainty as to whether the employer can control the benefits

The main difficulty in treating human resources as assets is uncertainty as to whether the employer can control the benefits. Control implies the ability to obtain any economic benefits that arise or to restrict the access of others to those benefits. Whether an employer can exercise control may depend on the terms of the employee's contract and on what happens in practice. For example, employees are normally required to work a minimum number of hours and there is usually an expectation that an employee will not provide services to anybody other than the employer.

KEY POINT

Human resources do not meet the IAS 38 definition of an asset. IAS 38 now specifically prohibits the recognition of either a team of skilled staff or specific management or technical talent as an intangible asset.

However, one of the main arguments against recognising human resources in the balance sheet is that employees are free to leave the employer if they wish to do so. This implies that the employer does not control the rights to future benefits from the employee's services and that human resources do not meet the IAS 38 definition of an asset. IAS 38 now specifically prohibits the recognition of either a team of skilled staff or specific management or technical talent as an intangible asset, unless it is protected by legal rights to use it and to obtain the future economic benefits expected from it.

### 7.5 Valuing human resources

Even if it could be argued that a human resource did meet the definition of an intangible asset, it can only be recognised in the financial statements if:

(a) it is probable that the expected future economic benefits that are attributable to the asset will flow to the entity; and

(b) the cost of the asset can be measured reliably.

The second of these two criteria is likely to cause problems in practice. In theory, a human resource asset could be valued at historic cost, at current value (value to the business) or at fair value.

- **Historical cost** – This is the actual cost of recruiting, employing and training an employee.
- **Value to the business** – This is the lower of replacement cost and recoverable amount. Replacement cost would be the cost of recruiting and developing another employee to the same level of competence as present staff. Recoverable amount would be value in use: the present value of the cash flows that the employee's services would generate in future periods. There is unlikely to be a net realisable value for an employee's services.

- **Fair value** – This is an employee's 'market value' (in practice, probably the cost of recruiting and developing another employee to the same level of competence).

In practice, human resources would almost certainly have to be valued at historical cost as it is doubtful whether any other basis would be sufficiently reliable. There would then remain the problem of deciding which costs to capitalise and of selecting an amortisation period.

***Deciding which costs to capitalise***

There is an argument for capitalising and amortising recruitment and training costs, because these are incurred specifically in order to obtain future economic benefits. Wages and salaries are the expense of obtaining an employee's services for a specific period and therefore it is logical to charge them to the income statement as they are incurred.

***Selecting an amortisation period***

This could be the average period of service of employees as a whole, or of the relevant category of employees.

### 7.6 Human resource accounting in practice

A form of human resource accounting has been used in a few published financial statements. Some football clubs have capitalised players' transfer fees and amortised them over the players' estimated period of service to the club.

However, apart from this, human resource accounting has not been an issue in the same way as, for example, recognition of brand names. Most commentators appear to believe that human resources cannot be recognised as assets because of the uncertainties involved. Increased disclosure of information about staff, either in the notes to the financial statements or in the management discussion and analysis, would be a practical alternative.

## Summary

- Financial statements have inherent limitations:
  - they are the result of classification and aggregation of information and the allocation of the effects of continuous operations to reporting periods
  - they only reflect the financial effects of transactions
  - they only provide historical information
  - In order to overcome these limitations, entities are disclosing an increasing amount of non-financial information, often in the form of a narrative Operating and Financial Review.
- Environmental and social reporting is the disclosure of information, either in the published annual report or in a separate report, about the effect of an entity's activities on the natural environment and on society and the community.
- In the financial statements, environmental costs should be treated in accordance with the requirements of existing accounting standards. IAS 37 covers the recognition of provisions for future environmental costs. Environmental expenditure that gives rise to future economic benefits can be capitalised.

- Human resource accounting involves capitalising the rights to future economic benefits arising from the employees' services to the entity. The main reason why this is not current practice is that the employer cannot control the benefits arising from the employee's services and therefore human resources do not meet the IAS 38 definition of an asset.

Having completed your study of this chapter, you should have achieved the following learning outcomes:

- discuss pressures for extending the scope and quality of external reports
- explain how financial information concerning the interaction of a business with the natural environment can be communicated in the published accounts
- identify those environmental issues which should be disclosed
- explain the process of measuring, recording and disclosing the effect of exchanges between a business and society – human resource accounting.

## Self-test questions

**1** What are the categories of stakeholders? (1.1)

**2** What are the shortcomings of traditional financial statements? (2.1)

**3** What is an Operating and Financial Review (OFR)? (3.1)

**4** What information about environmental expenditure might be disclosed in the financial statements? (4.4)

**5** Where in the financial statements do companies currently disclose information about the effects of their operations upon the environment? (4.5)

**6** What are environmental measures? (5.1)

**7** How should entities account for fines and penalties for non-compliance with regulations? (5.2)

**8** What kind of actions by an entity would normally give rise to a constructive obligation to rectify damage to the environment? (5.3)

**9** When should an entity capitalise environmental expenditure? (5.4)

**10** If a human resource is an asset, when should it be recognised in the financial statements? (7.4)

## Objective test question

### Question 1

A company has two foreign subsidiary companies, Ferndale and Fernbank.

The country in which Ferndale operates is about to pass a new law requiring environmentally sound adjustments to factory emissions. Ferndale has four such factories and the cost of the adjustments is estimated as $20,000 per factory.

Fernbank operates in a country where there is no environmental legislation, however the company has always, in the past, cleaned up any contamination that it has caused.

Fernbank is well known in this country for this policy. The estimated cost of cleaning up contamination caused to date by Fernbank Ltd is $100,000.

What provision should there be in the consolidated balance sheet for environmental costs?

**A** None

**B** $80,000

**C** $100,000

**D** $180,000

---

*For the answer to this question, see the 'Answers' section at the end of the book.*

## Exam-type question

### Redstart

You are the chief accountant of Redstart and you are currently finalising the financial statements for the year ended 31 December 20X1. Your assistant (who has prepared the draft accounts) is unsure about the treatment of two transactions which have taken place during the year. She has written you a memorandum which explains the key principles of each transaction and also the treatment adopted in the draft accounts.

**Transaction One**

One of the corporate objectives of the company is to ensure that its activities are conducted in such a way as to minimise any damage to the natural environment. It is committed in principle to spending extra money in pursuit of this objective but has not yet made any firm proposals. The directors believe that this objective will prove very popular with customers and are anxious to emphasise their environmentally friendly policies in the annual report.

Your assistant suggests that a sum should be set aside from profits each year to create a provision in the financial statements against the possible future costs of environmental protection. Accordingly, she has charged the income statement for the year ended 31 December 20X1 with a sum of $500,000 and proposes to disclose this fact in a note to the accounts.

**Transaction Two**

A new law has recently been enacted that will require Redstart to change one of its production processes in order to reduce the amount of carbon dioxide that is emitted. This will involve purchasing and installing some new plant that is more efficient than the equipment currently in use. To comply with the law the new plant must be operational by 31 December 20X2. The new plant has not yet been purchased.

In the draft financial statements for the year ended 31 December 20X1 your assistant has recognised a provision for $5m (the cost of the new plant). This has been disclosed as an exceptional item in the notes to the income statement.

The memorandum from your assistant also expresses concern about the fact that there was no reference to environmental matters anywhere in the published financial statements for the year ended 31 December 20X0. As a result, she believes that the financial statements do not comply with the requirements of International Accounting Standards and therefore must be wrong.

**Required:**

Draft a reply to your assistant which:

(a) reviews the treatment suggested by your assistant and recommends changes where relevant. In each case your reply should refer to the provisions of relevant International Accounting Standards **(12 marks)**

(b) replies to her suggestion that the financial statements for the year ended 31 December 20X0 are wrong because they make no reference to environmental matters. **(8 marks)**

**(Total: 20 marks)**

*For the answer to this question, see the 'Answers' section at the end of the book.*

## Feedback to activities

### Activity 1

As usual, for each of the items, ask two questions:

(a) Is there a present obligation as the result of a past event?

(b) Is a transfer of economic benefits probable as a result?

Recognise a provision if the answer to both questions is yes. In the absence of information to the contrary, it is assumed that any future costs can be estimated reliably.

(a) Present obligation? Yes. Because the new legislation is virtually certain to be enacted the contamination of the land is the past event that gives rise to a present obligation.

Transfer of economic benefits probable? Yes.

Conclusion: Recognise a provision.

(b) Present obligation? Yes. There is a legal obligation to remove the rig and restore the sea bed. However, there is no obligation to rectify any damage caused by extraction of the oil, because no oil has yet been extracted.

Transfer of economic benefits probable? Yes.

Conclusion: Recognise a provision for the best estimate of the eventual costs of decommissioning the oil rig. Do not recognise a provision for the cost of cleaning up damage caused by extraction of the oil.

(c) Present obligation? Yes. However, the obligation is not for the costs of fitting the smoke filters, because this has not yet happened. Even though avoiding penalties seems to be linked to the act of fitting the filters in the near future the company can avoid this expenditure (it can cease the activities that generate smoke, or it can continue to operate the factory without the filters at the risk of incurring penalties). The obligating event is the operation of the factory without the filters.

Transfer of economic benefits probable? On the basis of the facts above, fines or penalties are possible, rather than probable.

Conclusion: Do not recognise a provision, but disclose a contingent liability.

## Activity 2

Although there is no mention of laws requiring decommissioning it is clear that Sphere has a constructive obligation to do so. The obligating event (construction of the power station) has taken place and the transfer of economic benefits is certain. Commissioning the power station also gives rights to future economic benefits in the form of the ability to make profits from generating electricity. Therefore the decommissioning costs are part of the cost of constructing the power station and can be capitalised.

Year ended 31 December 20X0

Sphere should recognise a provision of $2.39 million ($10 \times 0.239$) for the decommissioning costs in its balance sheet at 31 December 20X0. It should also recognise an asset for the same amount. No depreciation is charged as the power station is not yet operating.

Year ended 31 December 20X1

At 31 December 20X1 the provision for decommissioning costs increases to $2.63 million ($10 \times 0.263$) and this results in a charge of $240,000 to the income statement, representing the unwinding of the discount.

Depreciation of $159,000 (£2.39m ÷ 15) is also charged to the income statement.

## Activity 3

In theory, there are several potential advantages of human resource accounting, particularly if it is coupled with greater disclosure of information about human resources in the notes to the financial statements:

- it would provide relevant information to investors and potential investors about the 'true' value of an entity
- it would demonstrate the contribution that an entity makes to a community, by providing employment
- it might provide useful information to employees and potential employees
- management would effectively be accountable to investors for effective use (stewardship) of the entity's human resources.

Chapter 18

# INTERNATIONAL ISSUES

## Syllabus content

- The influence of different cultures on financial reporting (not examinable).
- Major differences between IASs and US GAAP.

## Contents

# Introduction

This final chapter focuses on international convergence. International convergence means that generally accepted accounting practice (GAAP) in individual countries moves closer together, so that significant differences are eliminated. All the major standard setting bodies including the IASB, the US FASB and the UK ASB are now committed to convergence.

The chapter begins by briefly considering the advantages of international convergence before examining the reasons why accounting practice differs from country to country.

You need to be aware of the main differences between IASs and US GAAP. Exam questions may provide a reconciliation between IASs and US GAAP and ask you to comment on the reasons for the adjustments. Alternatively, you could be asked to prepare a reconciliation from information provided.

Finally, the text covers IFRS 1 *First-time Adoption of International Financial Reporting Standards.*

## 1 Advantages of international convergence

KEY POINT

The international convergence of accounting practices is in the best interests of both preparers and users of accounts.

### 1.1 Introduction

The international convergence of accounting practices is in the best interests of both preparers and users of accounts.

Increasingly businesses operate on a global scale and investors make investment decisions on a world-wide basis. There is thus a need for financial information to be presented on a consistent basis. In more detail, the advantages are as follows.

### 1.2 Multi-national companies

Multi-national companies benefit from closer harmonisation for the following reasons.

- Access to international finance is easier. The international financial markets understand the financial information presented to them more easily when it is provided on a consistent basis between companies irrespective of their country of origin.
- In a business which is operating in several countries, there tends to be improved management control as internal financial information can more easily be prepared on a consistent basis if externally required financial information is required on a uniform basis.
- There is greater efficiency in accounting departments.
- Consolidation of financial statements is easier.

### 1.3 Investors

If investors wish to make decisions based on the world-wide availability of investments then better comparisons between companies are required. At present most non-domestic investments are made by public investment companies and unit trusts which employ analysts skilled in the examination of financial statements from different countries.

An individual investor would have difficulty making an informed investment decision with the present differences in international financial reporting, although these are gradually becoming fewer.

### 1.4 International economic groupings

International economic groupings, e.g. the EU work more effectively if there is international harmonisation of accounting policies. Part of the function of international economic groupings is to make cross-border trade easier. Similar accounting regulations help this process.

## 2 Influences on financial reporting

KEY POINT

Financial reporting practice is influenced by a number of factors, the most important of which are:

- the nature of the legal system
- the main providers of capital to businesses.

### 2.1 Introduction

Several factors may influence the development of financial reporting practice within a country. Most experts agree that the most important of these are the legal system and the main providers of finance.

### 2.2 Legal systems

There are two basic forms of legal system:

- A 'common law' system: there is relatively little statute law, but this is interpreted by the courts which build up 'case law' to supplement the statutes. Therefore the law evolves over time in response to individual cases.
- A 'codified' system: statute sets out firm rules.

DEFINITIONS

A **'common law' system:** there is relatively little statute law, but this is interpreted by the courts which build up 'case law' to supplement the statutes. Therefore the law evolves over time in response to individual cases.

A **'codified' system:** statute sets out firm rules.

'Common law' systems are found in the UK, the USA, Canada, Australia and New Zealand. In these countries company law tends not to prescribe financial reporting practice in detail; this is left to the profession, which develops accounting standards to meet the needs of users and preparers of financial statements. Financial reporting practice evolves over time in response to changes in the business environment.

In contrast, most European countries and Japan have codified legal systems. Accounting practices and the content of financial statements are prescribed in detail by company law. In these countries companies often have to prepare their financial statements to comply with a 'chart of accounts' or uniform format. Accounting standards may be almost non-existent as there is very little scope for flexibility or for individual judgement.

### 2.3 Finance

KEY POINT

The main providers of finance are normally the most important users of financial statements.

The main providers of finance are normally the most important users of financial statements.

In some countries, such as the UK and the USA, many companies are publicly listed and rely on large numbers of equity shareholders who do not take any active part in the management of the company. Although there are also small family-owned companies, the regulatory framework is designed to ensure that external investors are provided with the information that they need in order to assess the performance of their investment and the stewardship of management. For example:

- There is an emphasis upon disclosure and upon presenting information 'fairly'. (The requirement to present 'a true and fair view' and the concept of 'substance over form' are important where external investors are the main users of accounts.)
- There is also a need for generally accepted principles such as accruals and consistency, because investors need to be able to compare one year with another and one company with another.

In other countries, such as France, Germany and Japan, most finance is provided by banks, rather than by equity investors. There are relatively few large public listed companies and even these tend to be controlled by large institutional investors. This means that there is normally one powerful provider of finance who is likely to have access to internal information. Therefore the main objective of financial reporting is to protect creditors. For example:

- It is common for companies to be required to transfer a proportion of their profits to a 'legal reserve'. This is non-distributable and ensures that there are extra funds available to repay creditors.
- Accounting estimates tend to be conservative, provisions or reserves for general risks may be set up, upward revaluations of non-current assets may be banned, companies may be required to use the depreciation method that produces the highest charge.

## 2.4 Taxation

In countries such as the UK, tax regulations have very little impact on financial reporting. Profit before tax in the accounts has to be adjusted for items such as disallowable expenses and capital allowances to arrive at profit chargeable to corporation tax.

KEY POINT

In some countries the financial statements must be drawn up in accordance with tax regulations.

In other countries, for example Germany, the financial statements must be drawn up in accordance with tax regulations, so that profit before tax in the accounts is the same as taxable profit. This is often the case where a country has a 'codified' legal system or where the government is one of the main users of the accounts.

## 2.5 Other influences

**Politics**

Where there is a strong central government and most or all business is nationalised, the main objective of financial statements is normally to provide the government with the information that it needs in order to control the economy. Accounts are used to assess the size of industries and resources, to measure the performance of various sectors, control prices and allocate funds. Until fairly recently this was the case in much of Eastern Europe and in China and may now apply in some developing countries.

**Inflation**

Where there is very high inflation, historical cost accounts are of very limited value and financial statements may be prepared using a form of current purchasing power accounting (CPP). This has been the case in many South American countries.

**History**

Former colonies tend to have accounting systems based on those of their mother countries. For example, Australia, New Zealand, India, Pakistan and Hong Kong all have accounting systems similar to that of the UK.

**Economic and trading links**

Economic and trading links or the desire to form them can also shape accounting practice. Examples include the way in which the EU countries have adopted similar accounts formats as a result of the EC Directives and the adoption of UK and US style accounting practices by some Eastern European countries and by China.

**Culture and local custom**

Financial reporting practice may be influenced by cultural factors in a number of ways.

- Religion may affect accounting practices, for example Islamic law forbids the charging or accepting of interest.
- Different nationalities have different attitudes to risk. For example in Japan high gearing is usual and is a sign of confidence in a company.

# 3 International convergence

## 3.1 Introduction

The International Accounting Standards Committee (IASC) was set up in 1973 and consists of representatives of accountancy bodies worldwide. It currently has about 140 member bodies from 104 separate countries.

The operating structure and processes of the IASB were explained in Chapter 1 of this text.

Countries whose accounting bodies are members of the IASC do not necessarily adopt the International Accounting Standards (IASs) issued by the IASC, because many countries have their own national standards. However, a number of countries have adopted IASs, and local standards issued in countries which have not adopted IASs are usually, as far as possible, consistent with IASs.

Although the IASB has no power to enforce its standards, it now has a great deal of influence on the major national standard setters, such as the UK Accounting Standards Board (ASB) and the US Financial Accounting Standards Board (FASB).

Two recent developments have significantly increased the pressure for international convergence with IAS.

## 3.2 The IASB and IOSCO

The International Organisation of Securities Commissions (IOSCO), is an influential organisation of the world's stock market regulators, in which the US Securities and Exchange Commission (SEC) is a key member.

In 1995 the IASC agreed with IOSCO that the IASC would develop a set of core accounting standards. If IOSCO believed these standards were of a sufficiently high quality, IOSCO would endorse them, so that accounts prepared for the purposes of cross-border capital raising and listings could be prepared in accordance with IASs.

KEY POINT

The IASC's status is enhanced now that IOSCO has endorsed IASs.

The IASC completed its core standards in December 1998 and submitted them to IOSCO. IOSCO's endorsement finally arrived in May 2000, so that IOSCO has now recommended that its members should permit multinational issuers to use IASs in their financial statements supporting capital offerings and listings.

KEY POINT

All EU **listed companies** will be required to prepare consolidated financial statements in compliance with **IASs**, rather than domestic standards, **from 2005 onwards**.

### 3.3 The IASB and the European Union (EU)

In June 2002 the EU adopted a Regulation which requires all EU listed companies to prepare their consolidated financial statements in compliance with IAS from 2005 onwards.

In addition, some EU countries, notably Germany, now allow certain companies to use IASs rather than domestic standards, subject to certain conditions. The UK government has recently announced that from 2005 all UK companies will be able to prepare both individual and consolidated financial statements using IAS as an alternative to UK standards.

### 3.4 How the IASB works with national standard setters

The IASB intends to develop a single set of understandable and enforceable high quality global accounting standards.

Almost certainly future international standards will be far more rigorous than previously and will no longer allow alternative treatments. The Chairman of the IASB, Sir David Tweedie has already stated that there will not be 'convergence for the sake of convergence by the issue of a set of 'lowest common denominator' accounting standards'.

KEY POINT

The IASB works in partnership with the major national standard-setting bodies.

Because the IASB on its own cannot enforce compliance with its standards, it needs the co-operation of national standard setters. Without their support, rigorous new international standards are unlikely to be adopted by everybody. Therefore, the IASB works in partnership with the major national standard setting bodies, including the UK ASB and the US FASB.

- All the major national standard setters are represented on the IASB and their views are taken into account so that a consensus can be reached. All national standard setters issue IASB Discussion Papers and Exposure Drafts for comment in their own countries, so that the views of all preparers and users of financial statements can be represented.
- Each major national standard setter 'leads' certain international standard setting projects. For example, the UK ASB is carrying out much of the work to develop a new international standard on leasing.

All the major national standard setters are now committed to international convergence and most of them are engaged in short-term convergence projects. For example:

- In principle, the UK ASB intends to replace its existing standards with IFRSs as they are issued or revised.
- The US FASB has entered into a joint project with the IASB (the Norwalk Agreement). This project aims to reduce differences between certain US accounting standards and certain IASs. IFRS 5 has been issued as a result of this project.
- The IASB has entered into convergence projects with both the Japanese and the Chinese standard-setting bosies.

### 3.5 Joint projects

For some years now, the major national standard setting bodies and the IASB have been working together to develop a common approach to specific financial reporting problems.

- Several recent UK standards (for example, FRS 11 *Impairment of Fixed Assets and Goodwill* and FRS 12 *Provisions, Contingent Liabilities and Contingent Assets*) were developed jointly with the then IASC and are virtually identical to IAS 36 and IAS 37. The IASB's current project on reporting financial performance has been heavily influenced by the work of the UK ASB.

- IFRS 2 *Share-Based Payment* was originally developed by a group of standard setters (the ASB, the FASB, the then IASC and the standard setting bodies of Australia, New Zealand and Canada).
- IAS 39 *Financial Instruments: Recognition and Measurement* was heavily influenced by the equivalent US standard.
- The IASB *Framework for the Preparation and Presentation of Financial Statements* is very similar to the framework documents used by other standard setters, notably by the UK ASB. Much of it was developed from work originally carried out by the US FASB.

KEY POINT

Differences in financial reporting practice have been steadily reducing over the last ten years.

Differences in financial reporting practice have been steadily reducing over the last ten years.

### 3.6 Potential obstacles to international convergence

- The IOSCO recommendation does not directly affect the situation in individual countries. In addition, it contains provisions for individual countries to demand additional disclosure and reconciliations where IASs do not comply with national standards. This means that individual countries are free to insist on their own variants of IASs. It can be argued that if this happens then in practice there may be less harmonisation, not more.
- The EC Regulation actually requires listed companies to adopt those IASs which it has formally endorsed. As a result, some people originally feared that there would be a European standard-setting body in all but name. So far, this has not happened. The EC Accounting Regulatory Committee has endorsed all standards to date. However, IAS 39 *Financial Instruments: Recognition and Measurement* was not fully endorsed until after it was amended to restrict the use of the 'fair value option' (see Chapter 14). This suggests that the EC may refuse to endorse new standards in the future if they are particularly controversial.
- IASs can never define a complete all-encompassing GAAP since they cannot cover many legal aspects of accounting, such as rules on issuing and redeeming share capital, the determination of distributable profits and rules on company insolvency. Such matters are dealt with by the company law of the country in which the company is based, so IASs can never cover all areas of accounting.
- Many interested parties, particularly in Europe, are becoming concerned at the increasing influence of the US Financial Accounting Standards Board (FASB) upon the IASB. This is discussed in more detail in the next section, but could lead to fewer unlisted companies adopting IFRS in preference to local GAAP.

In addition, there are some arguments for retaining domestic standards:

- They have been developed in response to the local economic environment and business practices.
- IASs have been developed largely to meet the information needs of investors in large public companies in the developed world. They may not always be suitable for small companies or companies in developing countries. Some countries, such as the UK, are developing a simplified financial reporting regime for smaller entities. The IASB now has a 'small entities' project, but this is at a very early stage. In the meantime, smaller entities may be better served by local GAAP.

However, most experts still believe that the advantages of international convergence far outweigh the problems.

# 4 IASs and US GAAP

## 4.1 Summary of the main differences

| | IAS | US GAAP |
|---|---|---|
| Departure from a standard where compliance would be misleading | Permitted in exceptional circumstances | Not directly addressed |
| Extraordinary items | Now prohibited | Permitted, but limited to a few events outside the control of the company |
| Development costs | Must capitalise and amortise if criteria met | Must be treated as expense |
| Tangible non-current assets | Carry at historic cost *or* valuation | Must carry at historic cost; revaluations not permitted. (N.B. this applies to *all assets* with the exception of some securities and derivatives) |
| Investment properties | Carry at fair value or historic cost | Treat as tangible non-current asset (must be at historical cost) |
| Capitalisation of borrowing costs | Optional (but policy must be applied consistently) | Compulsory for certain qualifying assets. Prohibited if assets do not qualify |
| Inventories | Carry at lower of cost and NRV. FIFO and weighted average methods both permitted. LIFO prohibited. | Carry at lower of cost and NRV. FIFO, LIFO and weighted average methods all permitted. LIFO most usual method |
| Segmental reporting | Segments based on main risks and returns faced by entity | Segments based on internal operating structure |
| Group accounts: | | |
| – definition of subsidiary | Based on control (dominant influence) | Based on majority ownership (with control) |
| – accounting for joint ventures | Proportional consolidation (preferred) *or* equity method | Equity method |

### 4.2 Differences in approach

Perhaps the most important difference between IASs/IFRSs and US GAAP is not about the content of individual standards, but about the general approach taken by each.

Both the IASB and the US FASB have developed conceptual frameworks, that is, sets of principles that underpin the requirements of individual accounting standards.

Most recent international standards are based on the main principles in the IASB *Framework*. One of the major advantages of this 'principles based' approach is that it encourages preparers to comply with the spirit of a standard rather than with its detailed content. It is harder to evade a principle than it is to evade a set of rules.

Although in theory US GAAP is principles based, in practice standards tend to be very complex and to be built on detailed rules. They also tend to be more conservative than IASs. Critics of US GAAP believe that this makes 'creative accounting' more likely, because preparers can devise transactions and arrangements that are not covered by the rules.

### 4.3 The influence of US GAAP

The USA is one of the few countries that still does not accept IFRS financial statements. When foreign companies seek a listing on a US stock exchange they must prepare a reconciliation of their results and financial position under IFRSs or domestic standards to their results and financial position under US GAAP. Given the dominance of the US economy, this remains a serious obstacle to true international convergence.

However, there are now some signs that this may eventually change. The US Securities and Exchange Commission (SEC) has stated that it may accept IFRS financial statements from 2009 onwards. This will only happen if it is satisfied that progress is being made in eliminating differences between IFRSs and US GAAP.

KEY POINT

As a result of the convergence project between the IASB and the FASB, IASs will almost certainly move much closer to US GAAP over the next few years.

As a result, convergence with US GAAP has become very important to the IASB. The IASB and the US Financial Accounting Standards Board (FASB) are currently working together on a short-term convergence project to eliminate differences in specific areas. In addition, there are also several joint projects in progress to develop new standards on business combinations, performance reporting and revenue recognition. Perhaps most significantly, the IASB and the FASB are now working together on a new conceptual framework that will eventually replace the IASB's *Framework for the Preparation and Presentation of Financial Statements* and its US GAAP equivalent.

Some preparers and users of financial statements fear that the FASB has effectively taken over the international standard-setting process and that IFRSs will become US GAAP in all but name. Even if this turns out to be an exaggeration, IFRSs will almost certainly move much closer to US GAAP over the next few years.

US GAAP is designed to meet the reporting needs of large multinationals. Standards based on it are unlikely to be suitable for most unlisted companies and companies that operate in developing economies. There would be practical problems in implementing them, because of the level of detail. This may discourage unlisted companies from adopting IFRS in future.

## 4.4 Reconciliation statements

KEY POINT

A company with a listing on more than one stock exchange may have to publish a reconciliation statement showing their results adjusted to accord with local GAAP.

A company with a large group of international investors and a listing on more than one stock exchange may need to produce financial information which is expressed in terms of the domestic accounting policies of the investors.

For example, UK companies with a listing on a US stock exchange are currently required to produce figures following US GAAP which consists of a reconciliation statement between UK and US GAAP. In addition a narrative statement summarising the differences in policies is required.

## 4.5 Restatement of overseas accounts

The Examiner may ask you to prepare a reconciliation statement similar to the one shown above, or to restate overseas accounts to comply with IASs. You should clearly state any assumptions that you make about accounting policies followed.

The two special problems you may have if the accounts presented in the examination question are not prepared in accordance with IASs are:

- The description and order of items in the financial statements may be different. Part of the mark allocation may be therefore for the reordering and change in narrative of the items.
- If the accounts are stated in a foreign currency (which is, of course, to be expected), the easiest approach is to perform your workings and reconciliation statement in that currency so that the accounts will balance and then translate all items using a suitable exchange rate.

Attempt the activity below before looking at the solution.

### *Activity 1*

The summarised financial statements of Genesis Inc., a company trading in Erewhon, are shown below.

| | ***20X3*** | *20X2* |
|---|---|---|
| | **$m** | $m |
| Revenue | **4,231.4** | 2,999.2 |
| Income after tax | **268.3** | 404.6 |
| **Assets** | | |
| Cash | **435.9** | 336.4 |
| Marketable securities | – | 51.8 |
| Accounts receivable | **719.1** | 427.4 |
| Inventories | **522.0** | 309.4 |
| Prepaid expenses | **38.0** | 16.3 |
| Income taxes | **44.7** | 25.9 |
| Other receivables | **77.3** | 17.4 |
| Total current assets | **1,837.0** | 1,184.6 |
| Property, plant & equipment | **1,071.0** | 291.8 |
| Investment in associated companies | **6.1** | 4.9 |
| Goodwill | **116.4** | 124.4 |
| Total assets | **3,030.5** | 1,605.7 |

| **Liabilities** | | |
|---|---|---|
| Bank loans & overdrafts | **113.3** | 89.1 |
| Short-term debt | **29.8** | 12.0 |
| Accounts payable | **600.9** | 276.8 |
| Other accounts payable & accrued expenses | **346.1** | 155.3 |
| Income taxes | **186.7** | 95.9 |
| Total current liabilities | **1,276.8** | 629.1 |
| Long-term debt | **103.6** | 62.1 |
| Deferred income taxes | **16.5** | 8.8 |
| Other liabilities | **258.9** | 79.6 |
| Total liabilities | **1,655.8** | 779.6 |
| Equity share capital | **87.4** | 22.1 |
| Retained earnings | **1,287.3** | 804.0 |
| Total equity | **1,374.7** | 826.1 |
| Total liabilities & equity | **3,030.5** | 1,605.7 |

The major accounting policies adopted and relevant figures are as follows.

(a) The goodwill relates to two acquisitions of subsidiaries. Goodwill is amortised over 20 years. The original amounts are $58m and $102m.

(b) Interest has been capitalised on certain properties which the group constructed for its own use. The total capitalised interest is $4.5m and $3.1m in 20X3 and 20X2 respectively. Interest capitalised in the period ended 20X3 was $900,000.

(c) The assets of the group are stated under the HC convention as required by local GAAP. Land is estimated to be worth $150m more than its book value at both balance sheet dates.

Produce a statement reconciling profit after tax per the above financial statements to profit after tax under IASs for 20X3 and a statement reconciling shareholders' equity per the above financial statements to shareholders' equity as at 31 December 20X3 under IASs. The ultimate parent of Genesis Inc prepares financial statements in accordance with IASs and has adopted accounting policies that maximise shareholders' equity wherever possible.

*Show the results in dollars.*

*Feedback to this activity is at the end of the chapter.*

# 5 IFRS 1 *First-time Adoption of International Financial Reporting Standards*

## 5.1 Background

IFRS 1 deals with issues that arise when an entity adopts international accounting standards for the first time. It became necessary to develop and issue a standard because listed entities in the EU will be required to prepare their financial statements in accordance with IFRSs from 2005 onwards.

KEY POINT

IFRS 1 sets out the procedures for making the transition from national accounting standards (previous GAAP) to international standards, and applies to all first time adopters for accounting periods beginning on or after 1 January 2004.

IFRS 1 sets out the procedures for making the transition from national accounting standards (previous GAAP) to international standards, and applies to all first time adopters for accounting periods beginning on or after 1 January 2004.

### 5.2 Date of transition: comparative figures

When IFRSs are adopted, they must be applied from the first day of the first accounting period, when there has to be an *opening IFRS balance sheet.* For example, for a EU quoted company with a year ending 31 December 2005, there must be an opening IFRS balance sheet as at 1 January 2005.

Because comparative statements must be published, the opening IFRS balance sheet for an entity adopting IFRSs for the year ending December 2005 will be 1 January 2004, which is the first day of the comparative period. Consequently, for many EU quoted companies and their subsidiaries, international standards will have to be applied from the beginning of 2004, and applied for the whole period from 1 January 2004.

### 5.3 Standards to adopt

KEY POINT

Accounting policies for first-time adopters must comply with IFRSs in force at the reporting date.

Accounting policies for first-time adopters must comply with IFRSs in force at the reporting date. This means that for EU quoted companies with a year ending 31 December, international standards in force at 31 December 2005 must be applied to the whole period commencing 1 January 2004.

### 5.4 Preparing the opening IFRS balance sheet

An entity should:

(a) recognise all assets and liabilities whose recognition is required by IFRSs

(b) not recognise items as assets or liabilities if IFRSs do not permit such recognition

(c) reclassify items that it recognised under previous GAAP as one type of asset, liability or component of equity, but are a different type of asset liability or component of equity under IFRSs

(d) apply IFRS in measuring all recognised assets and liabilities.

The accounting policies that an entity uses in its opening IFRS balance sheet may differ from those it used for the same date using its previous GAAP. The resulting adjustments arise from events and transactions before the date of transition to IFRS. Therefore, an entity should recognise those adjustments directly in retained earnings (equity) at the date of transition.

### 5.5 Exemptions

An entity may choose to apply any or all of a number of exemptions when preparing its opening IFRS balance sheet. The exemptions mean that the certain requirements of specific accounting standards are not applied retrospectively. They are intended to ensure that the cost of compliance with IFRSs does not outweigh the benefits to the user. For example:

- Previous business combinations do not have to be restated in accordance with IFRS 3. This means that combinations keep the same classification (e.g. uniting of interests, acquisition) as in the previous financial statements and the carrying amount of goodwill does not change (although goodwill must be tested for impairment at the date of transition).

- If it is not possible to establish the cost of an asset, then fair value at the date of transition can be used as deemed cost. (This exemption is unlikely to be used in a developed country where accurate accounting records have been kept.)
- Some actuarial gains and losses on pension schemes are left unrecognised under IAS 19. A first time adopter may elect to recognise all gains and losses at the date of transition.
- Past currency translation gains and losses included in revenue reserves need not be separated out into the currency translation reserve (ie, the cumulative translation differences for all foreign operations are deemed to be zero at the transition date; The gain or loss on a subsequent disposal of a foreign operation will exclude translation differences that arose before the transition date).
- IAS 32 requires compound financial instruments to be split at inception into separate liability and equity components. If the liability component is no longer outstanding at the date of the translation to IFRSs, the split is not required.
- If a subsidiary adopts IFRS later than its parent, then the subsidiary may value its assets and liabilities either at its own transition date or its parent's transition date (which would normally be easier).
- An entity need not apply IFRS 2 to share based payment transactions where equity instruments were granted and vested before the date of transition or liabilities arising from share based payment transactions were settled before the date of transition.

## 5.6 Situations where retrospective application is prohibited

There are also three situations where retrospective application of IFRS is prohibited. These relate to derecognition of financial assets and liabilities, hedging and estimates. The IASB thought that it would be impractical to obtain the information necessary to restate past financial statements, and that restating past fair values and estimates was open to manipulation.

KEY POINT

An entity's estimates under IFRSs at the date of transition must be consistent with estimates made for the same date under previous GAAP.

An entity's estimates under IFRSs at the date of transition must be consistent with estimates made for the same date under previous GAAP (after adjustments to reflect any difference in accounting policies) unless there is objective evidence that those estimates were in error.

## 5.7 Presentation and disclosure

KEY POINT

An entity's first IFRS financial statements must include at least one year of comparative information.

An entity's first IFRS financial statements must include at least one year of comparative information.

An entity should explain how the transition from previous GAAP to IFRSs has affected the entity's reported financial position, financial performance and cash flows by providing:

(a) a reconciliation of equity reported under previous GAAP to equity under IFRSs at the date of transition and at the balance sheet date

(b) a reconciliation of the profit or loss reported under previous GAAP to profit or loss reported under IFRSs for the period

(c) information about impairment losses recognised during the period

(d) information about any errors made under previous GAAP (which must be disclosed in the reconciliation)

(e) information about material adjustments to the cash flow statement (if applicable).

If an entity uses fair value as deemed cost, for each line item in the opening IFRS balance sheet it shall disclose: the aggregate of those fair values; and the aggregate adjustment to the carrying amounts reported under previous GAAP.

Comparative information need not comply with IAS 32 and IAS 39. The entity may apply its previous GAAP and disclose this fact together with information about the main adjustments that would be required to make the information comply with IAS 32 and IAS 39.

### 5.8 Other practical issues

Companies changing to IFRS should begin to plan for the change well in advance. They may also need to consider:

(a) Staff training – current staff may have little practical knowledge of IAS.

(b) Accounting systems and reporting timetables – can the existing accounting systems produce the information required to report under IAS?

(c) Investors – who may not fully understand the effect of the change. The directors may need to estimate the effect of IAS on results and key performance measures such as return on capital employed (ROCE) and gearing, so as to be able to reassure investors.

(d) Local law and regulation – some overseas subsidiaries may be required to prepare **two** sets of financial statements, one complying with domestic law and standards and one under IAS for the group accounts.

## Summary

- Financial reporting practice is influenced by a number of factors, the most important of which are:
  - the nature of the country's legal system
  - the main providers of capital to businesses.
- There are still several important differences between IASs and US GAAP, although these are decreasing. Arguably, the most important difference between the two is in their general approach: IASs are principles based, while US GAAP rely far more on detailed rules.
- IFRS 1 sets out the procedures for making the transition from national accounting standards (previous GAAP) to international standards, and applies to all first time adopters for accounting periods beginning on or after 1 January 2004.

Having completed your study of this chapter, you should have achieved the following learning outcomes:

- identify the influences on financial reporting of cultural differences across the world
- identify major differences between IASs and US GAAP.

## Self-test questions

**1** What four advantages are there for international companies of closer harmonisation? (1.2)

**2** How can inflation influence financial reporting practice? (2.6)

**3** Is IAS accounting for development costs similar to US GAAP? (4.1)

**4** What are the main differences between US GAAP and IASs relating to group accounts? (4.1)

**5** What disclosures must an entity make when it prepares IFRS financial statements for the first time? (5.7)

## Objective test question

### Question 1

Which of the following statements is correct?

**A** Under IASs and US GAAP capitalisation of borrowing costs when constructing one's own fixed assets is optional.

**B** Under IASs and US GAAP revaluation of property, plant and equipment is allowed.

**C** Under IASs the maximum useful life for goodwill is normally 20 years but under US GAAP goodwill may be retained indefinitely subject to an impairment test.

**D** Under IASs development costs must be capitalised but under US GAAP they must be expensed.

*For the answer to this question, see the 'Answers' section at the end of the book.*

## Exam-type question

### Home

Home, a limited liability company, is the wholly-owned subsidiary of a parent company which is incorporated in the US. Home prepares its financial statements in accordance with International Accounting Standards. However, in order to compile a set of financial statements which are suitable for use in the US consolidation, it is subsequently necessary to prepare a statement of adjustments to the accounts.

A summary of adjustments to the profit before taxation for the year ended 31 December 20X6 is given below:

| | $000 |
|---|---|
| Profit before taxation per International Accounting Standards | 12,000 |
| Adjustments to comply with US GAAP: | (900) |
| (a) Development costs incurred in the year written off (net of amortisation of development costs) | |
| (b) Revaluation adjustments written back: | |
| (i) excess depreciation | 1,000 |
| (ii) profit on sale | 500 |
| Profit before taxation per US GAAP | 12,600 |

The Managing Director of Home has read that the International Organisation of Securities Commissions (IOSCO) has recommended that its members accept financial statements that comply with International Accounting Standards. He does not understand why the reconciliation is still necessary.

**Requirements:**

(a) Explain why the reconciliation statement is still necessary, despite the recent agreement with IOSCO. **(5 marks)**

(b) Explain, for EACH of the adjustments in the table given for Home:

(i) the difference in accounting practice between International Accounting Standards and US GAAP

(ii) the International Accounting Standard followed by Home in accounting for the relevant item. **(5 marks)**

**(Total: 10 marks)**

*For the answer to this question, see the 'Answers' section at the end of the book.*

## Feedback to activity

### Activity 1

**Reconciliation of profit to IAS/IFRS**

| | *20X3* $m |
|---|---|
| Profit after tax as reported | 268.3 |
| Adjustment: | |
| Add back amortisation of goodwill (160/20) | 8.0 |
| Profit after tax under IAS/IFRS | 276.3 |

***Tutorial notes:*** IFRS 3 prohibits amortisation of goodwill, which is carried in the balance sheet and reviewed for impairment annually. IAS 23 permits capitalisation of interest. As this increases assets and therefore shareholders' funds, no adjustment has been made.

**Reconciliation of shareholders' equity as at 31 December 20X3**

| | $m |
|---|---|
| Shareholders' equity per accounts | 1,374.7 |
| Goodwill (160 – 116.4) | 43.6 |
| Revaluation of land | 150.0 |
| Shareholders' equity under IAS/IFRS | 1,568.3 |

# Chapter 19

# ANSWERS TO OBJECTIVE TEST, PRACTICE AND EXAM-TYPE QUESTIONS

## Chapter 1

### OBJECTIVE TEST QUESTIONS

#### Question 1

*The correct answer is B.*

(See Chapter 1 Section 1.)

#### Question 2

*The correct answer is C.*

(See Chapter 1 Section 1.)

### PRACTICE QUESTION

#### Conceptual framework

The advantages of an agreed 'framework of accounting principles' include the following:

(a) it assists the IASB in the development of new accounting standards and in the review of existing standards

(b) the IASB has a base when attempting to reduce the number of alternative accounting treatments permitted by an accounting standard

(c) preparers of financial statements have some guidance in dealing with topics and transactions that do not form the subject of an accounting standard

(d) assistance is given to auditors in forming an opinion on whether or not financial statements comply with accounting standards

(e) users of financial statements may find it easier to interpret the information contained in financial statements prepared in conformity with accounting standards

(f) it provides those who are interested in the work of the IASB with information about its approach to the formulation of accounting standards.

# Chapter 2

## OBJECTIVE TEST QUESTIONS

### Question 1

| **Consolidated reserves** | $000 |
|---|---|
| Vaynor | 90 |
| Weeton ((40 + 10) × 100%) | 50 |
| Yarlet ((70 – 30) × 80%) | 32 |
| | 172 |

### Question 2

*The correct answer is C.*

| **Goodwill** | $ | $ |
|---|---|---|
| Cost of investment | | 300,000 |
| Net assets acquired | | |
| Share capital | 200,000 | |
| Retained earnings | 36,000 | |
| Group share 75% × | 236,000 | (177,000) |
| | | 123,000 |

### Question 3

| | $000 |
|---|---|
| Cost of investment | |
| Cash | 1,000 |
| Shares at fair value (300 × 3) | 900 |
| Less share of fair value of net assets acquired (75% × 1,000) | (750) |
| Goodwill | 1,150 |

## PRACTICE QUESTION

### Oak and Chestnut

(a) **Consolidated balance sheet as at 30 September 20X8**

| | $ | $ |
|---|---|---|
| **ASSETS** | | |
| **Tangible non-current assets:** | | |
| Land and buildings (225,000 + 270,000 + 120,000) | | 615,000 |
| Plant (202,500 + 157,500) | | 360,000 |
| | | 975,000 |
| **Current assets:** | | |
| Inventory (255,000 + 180,000 less 10,500) | 424,500 | |
| Receivables (375,000 + 90,000 less 15,000) | 450,000 | |
| Bank (112,500 + 22,500) | 135,000 | |
| | | 1,009,500 |
| **Total assets** | | 1,984,500 |

| | |
|---|---|
| **EQUITY AND LIABILITIES** | |
| **Equity attributable to equity holders of the parent** | |
| Called up share capital | 1,125,000 |
| Reserves (W4) | 495,000 |
| | 1,620,000 |
| **Minority interest** (W5) | 154,500 |
| **Current liabilities** | |
| (157,500 + 67,500 less 15,000) | 210,000 |
| **Total equity and liabilities** | 1,984,500 |

***Workings***

(W1) **Group structure**

| | % |
|---|---|
| Oak (360,000/450,000) | 80 |
| Minority | 20 |
| | 100 |

(W2) **Net assets of subsidiary**

| | *At acquisition* | *At balance sheet date* |
|---|---|---|
| | $ | $ |
| Share capital | 450,000 | 450,000 |
| Reserves | 105,000 | 202,500 |
| Revaluation of land | 120,000 | 120,000 |
| | 675,000 | 772,500 |

(W3) **Goodwill**

| | |
|---|---|
| Cost of investment | 562,500 |
| Net assets acquired: | |
| Group share (80% × 675,000) | (540,000) |
| Goodwill | 22,500 |

(W4) **Group reserves**

| | $ |
|---|---|
| Oak (450,000 – 10,500) | 439,500 |
| Add: Group share of post acquisition reserves of Chestnut (80% of (772,500 less 675,000)) | 78,000 |
| Less: Goodwill previously written down (W3) | (22,500) |
| | 495,000 |

(W5) **Minority interest**

| | $ |
|---|---|
| Minority share (20% × 772,500) (W2) | 154,500 |

(b) When preparing the **consolidated accounts** of two companies, they are treated for accounting purposes as a single entity and therefore any trading transactions and balances must be adjusted for. In this example Oak has sold some goods to Chestnut during the year on which Oak has made a profit of $10,500.

This will affect the **consolidated income statement** and possibly the consolidated balance sheet.

The consolidated income statement should only show revenue and costs relating to transactions with third parties. Therefore the amount that Oak charged Chestnut for these goods must be excluded from both the consolidated revenue figure and consolidated cost of sales.

If the goods in question had already been sold by the year end then they would not be included in year end inventory in the balance sheet and no further adjustment would need to be made. However the goods are included in Chestnut 's inventory and they will have been valued at the amount that Chestnut paid for them. This is an over-valuation as far as the group is concerned and the group inventory figure must be reduced by the amount of the profit made by Oak, $10,500, in order to show the inventory at cost to the group.

This **unrealised profit** must also be removed from the consolidated income statement. Cost of sales is increased by $10,500 to reflect the reduction in the value of closing inventory.

The treatment of **inter-company balances** in the consolidated balance sheet follows the same principles. The only receivables and payables to be shown in the consolidated balance sheet are for amounts owing to or from third parties. In this instance, therefore, Oak's receivables will include $15,000 due from Chestnut, and Chestnut 's payables will include the same amount. Consolidated receivables and payables must both be reduced by $15,000, therefore the receivable and payable balances of $15,000 are effectively cancelled.

# Chapter 3

## OBJECTIVE TEST QUESTIONS

### Question 1

*The correct answer is D.*

All are assets or liabilities that existed on which a fair value must be placed.

### Question 2

In identifying whether an impairment of an asset may have occurred an entity should consider the following indications:

(i) there has been a significant decrease in the market value of the asset in excess of the normal process of depreciation

(ii) there has been a significant adverse change in either the business or the market in which the asset is involved. This will include changes in the technological, economic or legal environment in which the entity operates

(iii) there has been a significant adverse change in the manner in which the asset has been used

(iv) evidence is available that indicates that the economic performance of the asset will be worse than expected

(v) the asset has suffered considerable physical change, or obsolescence or physical damage

(vi) there has been an accumulation of costs significantly in excess of those originally expected in the acquisition or construction of an asset so that it may affect profitability

(vii) the management is committed to a significant reorganisation programme

(viii) where an asset is valued in terms of value in use and the actual cash flows are less than the estimated cash flows before discounting

(ix) market interest rates or other market rates of return on investments have increased during the period and those increases are likely to decrease materially the asset's recoverable amount.

***Note:*** Only three indications were required.

## EXAM-TYPE QUESTION

### Chrysanthemum

(a) **Goodwill in Daisy**

| | $000 | $000 |
|---|---|---|
| Cost (2,400 × $1.90) | | 4,560 |
| Less: fair value of net assets acquired: | | |
| Book values | 4,960 | |
| Increase in property, plant and equipment (6,700 – 6,300) | 400 | |
| Increase in inventories (1,700 – 1,600) | 100 | |
| | 5,460 | |
| Group share (80%) | | (4,368) |
| | | 192 |

***Explanation***

- The fair value of the shares in Daisy is their market value.
- The summary balance sheet shows the book values of Daisy's net assets and is the starting point for the fair value calculation. The fair value of receivables, payables and cash is normally their carrying value.
- The fair value of property, plant and equipment is its market value of $6,700,000.
- Inventories are stated at their fair value of $1,700,000.
- The fair value of the long-term loan is the present value of the amount expected to be paid. In this case, this is the same as its carrying value as interest of 10% per annum will be paid until the loan matures.

(b) **Consolidated balance sheet at 31 December 20X5**

| | $000 | $000 |
|---|---|---|
| *Non-current assets* | | |
| Property, plant and equipment (7,280 + 6,400 + 400 – 25) | | 14,055 |
| Intangible assets: goodwill | | 192 |
| | | 14,247 |
| *Current assets* | | |
| Inventories | 5,200 | |
| Receivables | 4,000 | |
| Cash and cash equivalents | 1,120 | |
| | | 10,320 |
| | | 24,567 |
| *Equity* | | |
| Share capital | | 4,000 |
| Retained earnings (W3) | | 2,732 |
| | | 6,732 |
| *Minority interests* (W4) | | 1,115 |
| | | 7,847 |
| *Non-current liabilities* | | |
| Long-term loan | | 8,000 |
| *Current liabilities* | | |
| Trade payables | 3,360 | |
| Taxation | 840 | |
| Bank overdraft | 4,520 | |
| | | 8,720 |
| | | 24,567 |

***Workings***

(W1) **Group structure**

Chrysanthemum

80% for 3 months

Daisy

(W2) **Net assets of subsidiary**

| | *At acquisition* | *At balance sheet date* |
|---|---|---|
| | $000 | $000 |
| Share capital | 3,000 | 3,000 |
| Retained earnings | 1,960 | 2,200 |
| Fair value adjustments: | | |
| Property, plant and equipment | 400 | 400 |
| Depreciation (400 × 25% × 3/12) | | (25) |
| Inventories | 100 | |
| | 5,460 | 5,575 |

(W3) **Consolidated retained earnings**

| | $000 |
|---|---|
| Chrysanthemum | 2,640 |
| Daisy: (80% × 5,575 – 5,460) (W2) | 92 |
| | 2,732 |

(W4) **Minority interests**

| | $000 |
|---|---|
| Net assets at 31 December 20X5 (20% × 5,575) (W2) | 1,115 |

# Chapter 4

## OBJECTIVE TEST QUESTIONS

### Question 1

*The correct answer is C.*

| | *Walcot* | *Ufton* | *Adjustment* | *Consolidated* |
|---|---|---|---|---|
| | $m | $m | $m | $m |
| Cost of sales | (11) | (10) | 3 | (19) |
| PURP | (1) | | | |

## PRACTICE QUESTIONS

### Question 1: N and S

**Consolidated income statement for the year ended 30 September 20X7**

| | $000 |
|---|---|
| Revenue | 5,350 |
| Cost of sales | 2,715 |
| Gross profit | 2,635 |
| Expenses | 1,620 |
| Profit before tax | 1,015 |
| Income tax expense | 280 |
| Profit for the year | 735 |

| | |
|---|---|
| Attributable to: | |
| Equity holders of the parent | 663 |
| Minority interests (40% × 180) | 72 |
| | 735 |

*Workings*

**Consolidation schedule**

| | *N* | *S* | *Adjusted* | *Consolidated* |
|---|---|---|---|---|
| | $000 | $000 | $000 | $000 |
| Sales | 4,500 | 1,100 | (250) | 5,350 |
| Cost of sales (W1) | 2,320 | 620 | (250)<br>25 | 2,715 |
| Gross profit (W1) | 2,180 | 480 | (25) | 2,635 |
| Expenses | 1,400 | 220 | | 1,620 |
| Income tax expense | 200 | 80 | | 280 |

(W1) **Unrealised profit in inventory**

$$\frac{25}{125} \times 250{,}000 \times \tfrac{1}{2} = \$25{,}000$$

***Tutorial note:*** The unrealised profit is eliminated in full against the group as it is the parent company which originally recorded the profit.

(W2) **Dividends received by N from S**

| | |
|---|---|
| | $000 |
| Ordinary 60% × 80 | 48 |
| All investment income is intra-group | |

## Question 2: R

**Consolidated income statement for the year ended 31 March 20X4**

| | |
|---|---|
| | $ |
| Gross profit | 1,310,500 |
| Less: Net operating expenses | (328,125) |
| Profit from operations | 982,375 |
| Less: Income tax expense | (265,750) |
| Profit for the year | 716,625 |
| Attributable to: | |
| Equity holders of the parent | 618,231 |
| Minority interests | 98,394 |
| | 716,625 |

**Consolidated statement of changes in equity for the year ended 31 March 20X4**

| | |
|---|---|
| | $ |
| Balance b/f | 673,000 |
| Profit for the year attributable to equity holders of the parent | 618,231 |
| Dividends paid | (200,000) |
| Balance c/f | 1,091,231 |

**Consolidation schedule**

| | *R* | *S* | *J* | *Consolidation adjustments* | *Group* |
|---|---|---|---|---|---|
| | $ | $ | $ | $ | $ |
| Gross profit | 728,000 | 74,500 (W1) | 510,000 | (2,000) (W2) | 1,310,500 |
| Net operating expenses | (182,000) | (18,625) (W3) | (127,500) | | (328,125) |
| Profit from operations | 546,000 | 55,875 | 382,500 | (2,000) | 982,375 |
| Investment income | 49,500 | | | (49,500) (W4) | |
| Profit before tax | 595,500 | 55,875 | 382,500 | (51,500) | 982,375 |
| Tax | (162,250) | (14,500) (W6) | (89,000) | | (265,750) |
| Profit after tax | 433,250 | 41,375 | 293,500 | (51,500) | 716,625 |
| Minority interests (W6) | | (10,344) | (88,050) | | (98,394) |
| Profit for the year | 433,250 | 31,031 | 205,450 | (51,500) | 618,231 |
| Equity b/f (W8) | 624,000 | - | 49,000 | | 673,000 |
| Profit for the year | 433,250 | 31,031 | 205,450 | (51,500) | 618,231 |
| Dividends (W7) | (200,000) | (7,500) | (42,000) | 49,500 | (200,000) |
| Equity c/f | 857,250 | 23,531 | 212,450 | (2,000) | 1,091,231 |

***Workings***

(W1) 6/12 × 149,000 = $74,500

(W2) 20% × 10,000 = $2,000

(W3) 6/12 × 37,250 = $18,625

(W4) Reconciliation of investment income

| | $ |
|---|---|
| Receivable from S: | |
| 75% × 10,000 | 7,500 |
| Receivable from J: 70% × 60,000 | 42,000 |
| | 49,500 |

(W5) 6/12 × 29,000 = $14,500

(W6) Minority interests are calculated as

| | $ |
|---|---|
| S 25% × 6/12 × 82,750 | 10,344 |
| J 30% × 293,500 | 88,050 |
| | 98,394 |

(W7) Cancellation of inter-company dividends

| | |
|---|---|
| S 75% × 10,000 | 7,500 |
| J 70% × 60,000 | 42,000 |
| | 49,500 |

(W8) Equity b/f at 1 April 20X3

| | |
|---|---|
| R | 624,000 |
| S Nil, since not acquired until October 'X3 | - |
| J 70% × (220,000 – 120,000 – 30,000) | 49,000 |
| | 673,000 |

# Chapter 5

## OBJECTIVE TEST QUESTIONS

### Question 1

| | | $ | $ |
|---|---|---|---|
| Goodwill on the acquisition | Cost | | 240,000 |
| | Share capital | 400,000 | |
| | Pre- acq profits | 200,000 | |
| | | 600,000 | |
| | | × 30% | 180,000 |
| | Goodwill | | 60,000 |
| Share of net assets (30% × $720,000) | | | 216,000 |
| Add goodwill | | | 60,000 |
| Equity value | | | 276,000 |

### Question 2

*The correct answer is A.*

(See Chapter 4 Section 3.)

## EXAM-TYPE QUESTION

### Bacup

**Consolidated balance sheet as at 31 March 20X7**

| | $000 | $000 |
|---|---|---|
| Non-current assets: | | |
| Tangible assets (3,820 + 4,425) | | 8,245 |
| Goodwill | | 460 |
| Investment in associate (W5) | | 420 |
| | | 9,125 |
| Current assets: | | |
| Inventory (2,740 + 1,280 – 40) | 3,980 | |
| Receivables (1,960 + 980 – 250) | 2,690 | |
| Bank (1,260 + 50 cash in transit) | 1,310 | |
| | | 7,980 |
| Total assets | | 17,105 |
| Equity attributable to equity holders of the parent: | | |
| Ordinary shares of 25 cents each | | 4,000 |
| Reserves: | | |
| Share premium | 800 | |
| Retained earnings (W3) | 4,272 | |
| | | 5,072 |
| | | 9,072 |
| Minority interest (W2) | | 233 |
| | | 9,305 |

| | | |
|---|---|---|
| Current liabilities: | | |
| Trade payables (2,120 + 3,070 – 200) | 4,990 | |
| Bank overdraft | 2,260 | |
| Taxation (400 + 150) | 550 | |
| | | 7,800 |
| Total equity and liabilities | | 17,105 |

***Workings***

(W1) **Group structure**

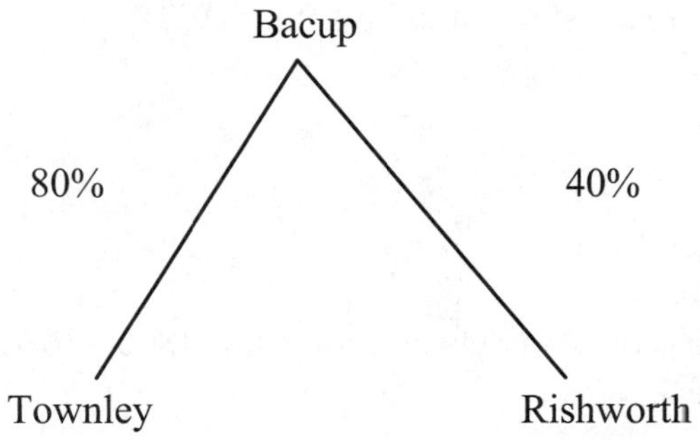


(W2) **Intra-group trading: provision for unrealised profit**

– Sold by Bacup to Rishworth, group share only as it is an associate, 40% of (125 × 25/125) = 10.
– Sold by Townley to Bacup, total profit as it is a subsidiary, 200 × 25/125 = 40.

(W3) **Net assets of subsidiary**

| | *At acquisition* | *At B/S date* |
|---|---|---|
| | $000 | $000 |
| Share capital | 500 | 500 |
| Share premium | 125 | 125 |
| Retained earnings | 380 | 780 |
| Development expenditure | (80) | (200) |
| Provision for unrealised profit (W2) | | (40) |
| | 925 | 1,165 |

(W4) **Goodwill**

| | $000 |
|---|---|
| Cost of investment | 1,200 |
| Group share of net assets acquired: (80% × 925) | (740) |
| | 460 |

(W5) **Associate – Rishworth**

| | $000 |
|---|---|
| Carrying value in the balance sheet at 31 March 20X7 | |
| Cost | 400 |
| Share of post acquisition profit (40% × 150 × 6/12) | 30 |
| Unrealised profit in inventory (W2) | (10) |
| | 420 |
| Alternative calculation: | |
| Share of net assets at balance sheet date (40% × 800) | 320 |
| Goodwill | 110 |
| Unrealised profit in inventory (W2) | (10) |
| | 420 |
| Goodwill: | |
| Cost | 400 |
| 40% of net assets on acquisition (800 – (6/12 × 150)) × 40% | (290) |
| Goodwill (premium) on acquisition | 110 |

(W6) **Minority interest**

| | $000 |
|---|---|
| Share of net assets at balance sheet date (20% × 1,165) | 233 |

(W7) **Group retained earnings**

| | $000 |
|---|---|
| Bacup | 4,060 |
| Unrealised profit on inventory (125 × 25/125 × 40%) | (10) |
| | 4,050 |
| Townley: (80% × 1,165 – 925) | 192 |
| Rishworth (40% × 150 × 6/12) | 30 |
| | 4,272 |

## Chapter 6

### OBJECTIVE TEST QUESTIONS

#### Question 1

| | | $ |
|---|---|---|
| Cost (50 + 350) | | 400,000 |
| Net assets acquired | (10% × (300 + 100) | (40,000) |
| | (60% × (400 + 100)) | (300,000) |
| | | 60,000 |

### Question 2

| | $ |
|---|---|
| Proceeds received | 460,000 |
| Less net assets sold (80% × $400,000) | 320,000 |
| Gain to group | 140,000 |
| Alternatively: | |
| Proceeds received | 460,000 |
| Less cost of investment | 330,000 |
| Gain to parent company | 130,000 |
| Less post acq profits sold | |
| (400 – 280 = 120 × 80%) | 96,000 |
| | 34,000 |
| Add goodwill written off | |
| (330 – 80% × 280) | 106,000 |
| | 140,000 |

## EXAM-TYPE QUESTION

### Harrods

**Consolidated balance sheet at 30 June 20X5**

| | $000 | $000 |
|---|---|---|
| **Assets** | | |
| Non-current assets: | | |
| Property, plant and equipment | | 47,700 |
| Goodwill | | 2,184 |
| | | 49,884 |
| Current assets: | | |
| Inventories (11,150 + 4,300 – 240) | 15,210 | |
| Receivables (5,200 – 1,200 + 1,100) | 5,100 | |
| Cash and cash equivalents | 1,500 | |
| | | 21,810 |
| | | 71,694 |
| **Equity and liabilities** | | |
| Equity attributable to equity holders of the parent: | | |
| Share capital | | 20,000 |
| Retained earnings | | 40,154 |
| | | 60,154 |
| Minority interests | | 1,940 |
| | | 62,094 |
| Non-current liabilities | | 4,000 |
| Current liabilities: | | |
| Trade and other payables | | |
| (2,100 + 2,200 – 1,200) | 3,100 | |
| Short-term borrowings | 2,500 | |
| | | 5,600 |
| | | 71,694 |

***Workings***

(W1) **Group structure**

Harrods

60% on 30/6/X1

30% on 1/11/X4

90%

Selfridges

(W2) **Net assets of subsidiary**

| | *30/6/X1* | *1/11/X4* | *Balance sheet date* |
|---|---|---|---|
| | $000 | $000 | $000 |
| Share capital | 10,000 | 10,000 | 10,000 |
| Retained earnings | 2,500 | 7,400 | 9,400 |
| | 12,500 | 17,400 | 19,400 |

(W3) **Goodwill**

| | |
|---|---|
| | $000 |
| Cost of investment | 15,450 |
| Less: net assets acquired (60% × 12,500) | (7,500) |
| (30% × 17,400) | (5,220) |
| | 2,730 |
| Impairment (20%) | (546) |
| | 2,184 |

(W4) **Minority interests**

| | |
|---|---|
| | $000 |
| Share of net assets at balance sheet date (10% × 19,400) | 1,940 |

(W5) **Consolidated retained earnings**

| | |
|---|---|
| | $000 |
| Harrods (36,200 – 240) (W6) | 35,960 |
| Selfridges (60% × 19,400 – 12,500) | 4,140 |
| (30% × 19,400 – 17,400) | 600 |
| | 40,700 |
| Impairment | (546) |
| | 40,154 |

(W6) **Provision for unrealised profit**

| | $000 |
|---|---|
| Profit in the accounts of Harrods: (25/125 × 1,200) | 240 |

## Apricot

(a)

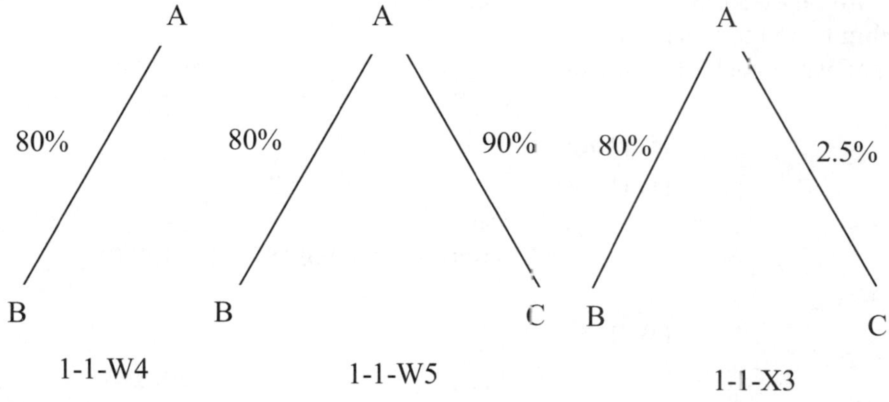


Sales of 350,000 shares leaves a holding of just 10,000 shares = 2.5%

From 1-1-X3, C is treated as a trade investment of A. The trade investment is valued at cost in the individual balance sheet of A. However, the group still owns 2.5% of the post-acquisition reserves of C and so the investment is 'frozen' at its carrying amount under the equity method at the date of disposal (i.e. 2.5% of its net assets at 1.1.X3).

**A**

**Consolidated income statement for the year ended 31 December 20X3**

| | $000 |
|---|---|
| Profit from operations (1,200 + 250) | 1,450 |
| Profit on sale of shares in C (W1) | 700 |
| Profit before tax | 2,150 |
| Tax (W2) | (629) |
| Profit for the year | 1,521 |
| Profit attributable to minority interests (20% × 190) | (38) |
| Profit attributable to the parent | 1,483 |

**A**

**Consolidated balance sheet as at 31 December 20X3**

| | $000 |
|---|---|
| Trade investment at cost (2.5% × 1,400) | 35 |
| Other net assets (W3) | 6,522 |
| | 6,557 |
| Share capital | 1,500 |
| Reserves (W4) | 4,767 |
| | 6,267 |
| Minority interests (20% × (1,260 + 190)) | 290 |
| | 6,557 |

(b) **A**

**Reconciliation of opening and closing consolidated reserves for 20X3**

| | *A* | *B* | *C* | *Adjustments* | *Consolidated reserves* |
|---|---|---|---|---|---|
| | $000 | $000 | $000 | $000 | $000 |
| Balance b/f | 3,300 | 272 (W5) | 612 (W6) | (900) (W7) | 3,284 |
| Retained profits for the year | 840 | 152 (W8) | – | – | 992 |
| Profit on disposal | 627(W9) | – | – | – | 627 |
| Elimination of C's reserves and write-back of goodwill | – | – | (595) (W6) | 459 (W7) | (136) |
| | 4,767 | 424 | 17 | (441) | 4,767 |

***Workings***

(W1)

| | $000 |
|---|---|
| Proceeds | 1,925 |
| Net assets disposed of (87.5% × 1,400) | (1,225) |
| | 700 |

(W2)

| | $000 | $000 |
|---|---|---|
| A's tax | | 360 |
| B's tax | | 60 |
| Tax on disposal | | |
| Proceeds | 1,925 | |
| Cost in A's books ($\frac{350}{360}$ × 1,120) | (1,089) | |
| Gain in A's books | 836 | |
| Taxed at 25% | | 209 |
| | | 629 |

(W3) Group net assets as at 31 December 20X3

| | | $000 |
|---|---|---|
| A as at 31.12.X2 | | 2,516 |
| Add: | Retained profits for year per draft income statement | 840 |
| | B as at 31.12.X2 | 1,260 |
| Add: | Retained profits for year per draft income statement | 190 |
| | Proceeds of sale of shares | 1,925 |
| Less: | Tax payable thereon (W3) | (209) |
| | | 6,522 |

(W4) In an exam it might be best to leave reserves as the balancing figure on the consolidated balance sheet, and prove it in part (b). However the figure of 4,767 can be proved as follows:

| **A** | $000 |
|---|---|
| Reserves at 1 Jan X3 | 3,300 |
| Retained profits for 20X3 | 840 |
| Net profit on disposal (see Working 9) | 627 |

| | |
|---|---|
| **B** | $000 |
| Reserves at 1 Jan X3 (see Working 5) | 272 |
| Retained profits for 20X3 (see Working 8) | 152 |
| Less: Elimination of goodwill when A bought B (see Working 8) | (428) |
| **C** | |
| Reserves retained after disposal (10/360 × 612) | 17 |
| Less: Elimination of goodwill remaining after disposal (10/360 × 472) | (13) |
| | 4,767 |

(W5) A's share of B's post-acquisition profits = 80% × (760 – 420) = $272,000.

(W6) A's share of C's post-acquisition profits = 90% × (1,000 – 320) = $612,000.

Elimination of reserves in C ($\frac{350}{360}$ × 612) = $595,000

(W7) Accumulated goodwill write-offs are as follows:

| | $000 |
|---|---|
| Investment in B (1,164 – (80% × (500 + 420))) | 428 |
| Investment in C (1,120 – (90% × (400 + 320))) | 472 |
| | 900 |
| Elimination of goodwill in C ($\frac{350}{360}$ × 472) | 459 |

(W8) 80% × 190 = $152,000

(W9)

| | $000 |
|---|---|
| Gain in A's books (W3) | 836 |
| Less: Tax at 25% | (209) |
| Net gain | 627 |

## Chapter 7

### OBJECTIVE TEST QUESTION

(1)

| | *Shrub* | | *Twig* |
|---|---|---|---|
| Group interest | 80% | (80% × 90%) | 72% |
| Minority interest | 20% | | 28% |
| | 100% | | 100% |

*Goodwill calculation*

| | | $ | | $ |
|---|---|---|---|---|
| Cost of investment | | **480,000** | | 320,000 |
| Less indirect holding adjustment (20%) | | | | (64,000) |
| | | | | 256,000 |
| Share capital | | 400,000 | | 200,000 |
| Pre acq reserves | | 160,000 | | 100,000 |
| | | 560,000 | | 300,000 |
| Group share | (80%) | **448,000** | (72%) | **216,000** |
| Goodwill | | **32,000** | | **40,000** |
| | | | **72,000** | |

(2)

| | | *Shrub* $ | | *Twig* $ |
|---|---|---|---|---|
| Share capital | | 400,000 | | 200,000 |
| Reserves | | 240,000 | | 120,000 |
| | | 640,000 | | 320,000 |
| Minority interest | (20%) | 128,000 | (28%) | 89,600 |
| Less indirect holding adjustment | | (64,000) | | |
| | | 64,000 | | |
| Total minority interest | | | 153,600 | |

## PRACTICE QUESTION

### H Ltd

Group structure

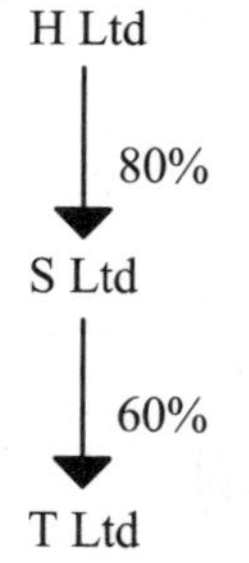


| *Shareholdings* | *S* | | *T* | |
|---|---|---|---|---|
| Group – direct | 80% | – indirect | 80% of 60% = | 48% |
| Minority | 20% | – direct | | 40% |
| | | – indirect | 20% of 60% | 12% |
| | | | | 52% |

(a) Net assets of subsidiaries

| | *S* | | *T* | |
|---|---|---|---|---|
| | *Acquisition* | *Balance sheet date* | *Acquisition* | *Balance sheet date* |
| | $ | $ | $ | $ |
| Share capital | 75,000 | 75,000 | 50,000 | 50,000 |
| Reserves | 10,000 | 60,000 | 8,000 | 40,000 |
| | 85,000 | 135,000 | 58,000 | 90,000 |

Goodwill

| | *S* | *T* |
|---|---|---|
| | $ | $ |
| Cost of investment: | | |
| S | 95,000 | |
| T (indirect) (80% × 48,000) | | 38,400 |
| Less: share of net assets acquired: | | |
| 80% × 85,000 | (68,000) | |
| 48% × 58,000 | | (27,840) |
| | 27,000 | 10,560 |

Minority interests

| | $ |
|---|---|
| S: (20% × 135,000 – 48,000) | 17,400 |
| T: (52% × 90,000) | 46,800 |
| | 64,200 |

Consolidated reserves

| | $ |
|---|---|
| H | 120,000 |
| S (80% × 135,000 – 85,000) | 40,000 |
| A (48% × 90,000 – 58,000) | 15,360 |
| | 175,360 |

(b) Net assets of subsidiaries

| | S | | T | |
|---|---|---|---|---|
| | *Acquisition* | *Balance sheet date* | *Acquisition* | *Balance sheet date* |
| | $ | $ | $ | $ |
| Share capital | 75,000 | 75,000 | 50,000 | 50,000 |
| Reserves | 12,000 | 60,000 | 18,000 | 40,000 |
| | 87,000 | 135,000 | 68,000 | 90,000 |

Goodwill

| | *S* | *T* |
|---|---|---|
| | $ | $ |
| Cost of investment: | | |
| S | 95,000 | |
| T (indirect) (80% × 48,000) | | 38,400 |
| Less: share of net assets acquired: | | |
| 80% × 87,000 | (69,600) | |
| 48% × 68,000 | | (32,640) |
| | 25,400 | 5,760 |

Minority interests

| | $ |
|---|---|
| S: (20% × 135,000 – 48,000) | 17,400 |
| T: (52% × 90,000) | 46,800 |
| | 64,200 |

Consolidated reserves

| | $ |
|---|---|
| H | 120,000 |
| S (80% × 135,000 – 87,000) | 38,400 |
| A (48% × 90,000 – 68,000) | 10,560 |
| | 168,960 |

(c)

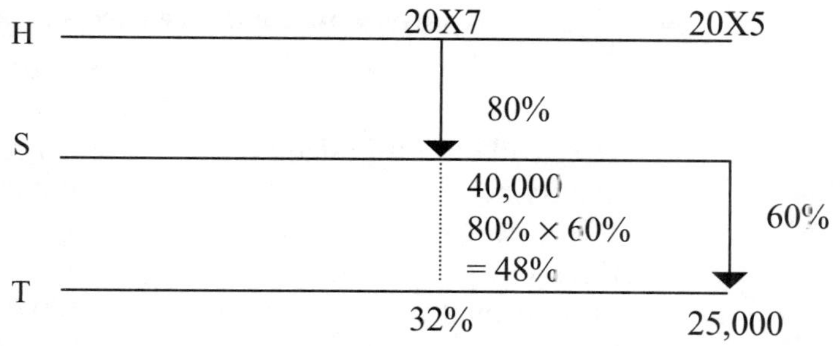


*Net assets of subsidiaries*

| | *S* Acquisition | *S* Balance sheet date | *T* Acquisition | *T* Balance sheet date |
|---|---|---|---|---|
| | $ | $ | $ | $ |
| Share capital | 75,000 | 75,000 | 50,000 | 50,000 |
| Reserves | 40,000 | 60,000 | 29,000 | 40,000 |
| | 115,000 | 135,000 | 79,000 | 90,000 |

Goodwill

| | *S* | *T* |
|---|---|---|
| | $ | $ |
| Cost of investment: | | |
| S | 95,000 | |
| T (indirect) (80% × 48,000) | | 38,400 |
| Less: share of net assets acquired: | | |
| 80% × 115,000 | (92,000) | |
| 48% × 79,000 | | (37,920) |
| | 3,000 | 480 |

Minority interests

| | $ |
|---|---|
| S: (20% × 135,000 – 48,000) | 17,400 |
| T: (52% × 90,000) | 46,800 |
| | 64,200 |

Consolidated reserves

| | $ |
|---|---|
| H | 120,000 |
| S (80% × 135,000 – 115,000) | 16,000 |
| A (48% × 90,000 – 79,000) | 5,280 |
| | 141,280 |

**Consolidated balance sheets as at 31 December 20X8**

| | (a) | (b) | (c) |
|---|---|---|---|
| | $ | $ | $ |
| Goodwill on consolidation | 37,560 | 31,160 | 3,480 |
| Sundry net assets | 302,000 | 302,000 | 302,000 |
| | 339,560 | 333,160 | 305,480 |
| Equity | | | |
| Share capital | 100,000 | 100,000 | 100,000 |
| Consolidated reserves | 175,360 | 168,960 | 141,280 |
| | 275,360 | 268,960 | 241,280 |
| Minority interests | 64,200 | 64,200 | 64,200 |
| | 339,560 | 333,160 | 305,480 |

## EXAM-TYPE QUESTION

### Exotic Group

(a) **Consolidated income statement of the Exotic Group for the year ended 31 December 1994**

| | $000 | $000 |
|---|---|---|
| Revenue | | 92,120 |
| Cost of sales | | (27,915) |
| Gross profit | | 64,205 |
| Distribution costs | | (7,362) |
| Administrative expenses | | (6,325) |
| Profit from operations | | 50,518 |
| Finance costs | | (325) |
| Profit before tax | | 50,193 |
| Taxation | | (17,931) |
| Profit for the year | | 32,262 |
| Attributable to: | | |
| Equity holders of the parent | | 28,548 |
| Minority interests | | 3,714 |
| | | 32,262 |
| Retained profits brought forward | | |
| Exotic | 20,013 | |
| Melon | 10,701 | |
| Kiwi | 6,846 | |
| | | 37,560 |
| Profit attributable to equity holders of the parent | | 28,548 |
| Dividends paid | | (9,500) |
| | | 56,608 |

(b) **Consolidated balance sheet for the Exotic Group as at 31 December 1994**

| | $000 | $000 |
|---|---|---|
| Non-current assets | | |
| Tangible (72,819 – 40 + 8) | 72,787 | |
| Goodwill (2,667 + 1,296) | 3,963 | |
| | | 76,750 |
| Current assets (19,476 – 30) | | 19,446 |
| | | 96,196 |
| Share capital | 8,000 | |
| Retained earnings | 56,608 | |
| | | 64,608 |
| Minority interest | | 8,454 |
| Current liabilities | | 23,134 |
| | | 96,196 |

Group structure

Exotic

90%

Melon 72%

80%

Kiwi

***Workings for consolidated income statement***

| | *Exotic* | *Melon* | *Kiwi* | | *(Dr)/Cr* | *Total* |
|---|---|---|---|---|---|---|
| | $000 | $000 | $000 | | $000 | $000 |
| Sales revenue | 45,600 | 24,700 | 22,800 | (a) | (740) | |
| | | | | (c) | (240) | 92,120 |
| Cost of sales | (18,050) | (5,463) | (5,320) | (a) | 740 | |
| | | | | (c) | 200 | (27,893) |
| Unrealised profit on inventory | | (15) | (15) | (b) | | (30) |
| Depreciation adjustment | | 8 | | (d) | | 8 |
| Gross profit | 27,550 | 19,230 | 17,465 | | | 64,205 |
| Distribution costs | 3,325 | 2,137 | 1,900 | | | (7,362) |
| Administrative expenses | 3,475 | 950 | 1,900 | | | (6,325) |
| Operating profit | 20,750 | 16,143 | 13,665 | | | 50,518 |
| Interest paid | 325 | | | | | (325) |
| Profit before tax | 20,425 | 16,143 | 13,665 | | | 50,192 |
| Tax | 8,300 | 5,390 | 4,241 | | | (17,931) |

| | | | | | | |
|---|---|---|---|---|---|---|
| Profit after tax | 12,125 | 10,753 | 9,424 | | | 32,262 |
| Minority interest | | | [10% + 28%] | (e) | 3,714 | (3,714) |
| Retained profit for year | | | | | | 28,548 |

(a) **Elimination of inter-company sales from revenue and cost of sales**

| | $000 |
|---|---|
| Kiwi | 480 |
| Melon | 260 |
| | 740 |

(b) **Elimination of unrealised profit on inventory**

| | $000 |
|---|---|
| Kiwi 20% of $75,000 | 15 |
| Melon 25% of $60,000 | 15 |
| | 30 |

(c) **Elimination of unrealised profit on non-current asset**

| | $000 |
|---|---|
| Sale price to Melon | 240 |
| Cost price to Exotic | (200) |
| Unrealised profit | 40 |

(d) **Adjust for depreciation on inter-company non-current asset sale**

| | $000 |
|---|---|
| 20% of sales price | 48 |
| 20% of cost price | (40) |
| Excess depreciation | 8 |

(e) **Minority interest**

| | $000 |
|---|---|
| Melon 10% of $10,753,000 | 1,075 |
| Kiwi 28% of $9,424,000 | 2,639 |
| | 3,714 |

(f) **Retained profit brought forward**

| | $000 |
|---|---|
| Exotic | 20,013 |
| Melon 90% of (13,315,000 – 1,425,000) | 10,701 |
| Kiwi 90% of 80% of (10,459,000 – 950,000) | 6,846 |
| | 37,560 |

(g) **Net assets of subsidiaries**

| | **Melon** | | **Kiwi** | |
|---|---|---|---|---|
| | *Acquisition* | *Balance sheet date* | *Acquisition* | *Balance sheet date* |
| | $000 | $000 | $000 | $000 |
| Share capital | 3,000 | 3,000 | 2,000 | 2,000 |
| Reserves | 1,425 | 24,075 | 950 | 19,898 |
| Provision for unrealised profit | | (15) | | (15) |
| Excess depreciation | | 8 | | |
| | 4,425 | 27,068 | 2,950 | 21,883 |

(h) **Goodwill**

| | *Melon* | *Kiwi* |
|---|---|---|
| | $ | $ |
| Cost of investment: | | |
| Melon | 6,650 | |
| Kiwi (indirect) (90% × 3,800) | | 3,420 |
| Less: share of net assets acquired: | | |
| 90% × 4,425 | (3,983) | |
| 72% × 2,950 | | (2,124) |
| | 2,667 | 1,296 |

(i) **Minority interests**

| | $ |
|---|---|
| Melon: (10% × 27,068 – 3,800) | 2,327 |
| Kiwi: (28% × 21,883) | 6,127 |
| | 8,454 |

(j) **Consolidated retained earnings**

| | $ |
|---|---|
| Exotic (22,638 – 40) | 22,598 |
| Melon (90% × 27,068 – 4,425) | 20,379 |
| Kiwi (72% × 21,883 – 2,950) | 13,631 |
| | 56,608 |

# Chapter 8

## OBJECTIVE TEST QUESTIONS

### Question 1

*The correct answer is D.*

(See Chapter 8 Section 4.)

### Question 2

| | $ |
|---|---|
| Write off debit balance on reserves | 900,000 |
| *Less* uplift in value of freehold | 200,000 |
| Reduction in capital | 700,000 |

## PRACTICE QUESTION
## P Group

**Consolidated balance sheet of the P group**

| | $m |
|---|---|
| Property, plant and equipment | 3,590 |
| Net current assets | 1,890 |
| | 5,480 |
| Share capital [P only] | 1,350 |
| Share premium [P only] | 1,550 |
| Reserves (W4) | 2,387 |
| Minority interest [40% × 145] | 58 |
| Non-current liabilities | 135 |
| | 5,480 |

**Consolidated balance sheet of E group**

| | $m |
|---|---|
| Property, plant and equipment | 610 |
| Net current assets | 470 |
| | 1,080 |
| Share capital [E only] | 300 |
| Other reserves (W5) | 600 |
| Retained earnings (W8) | 116 |
| Minority interest [20% × 120] | 24 |
| Non-current liabilities | 40 |
| | 1,080 |

***Workings***

(W1) **Group structure**

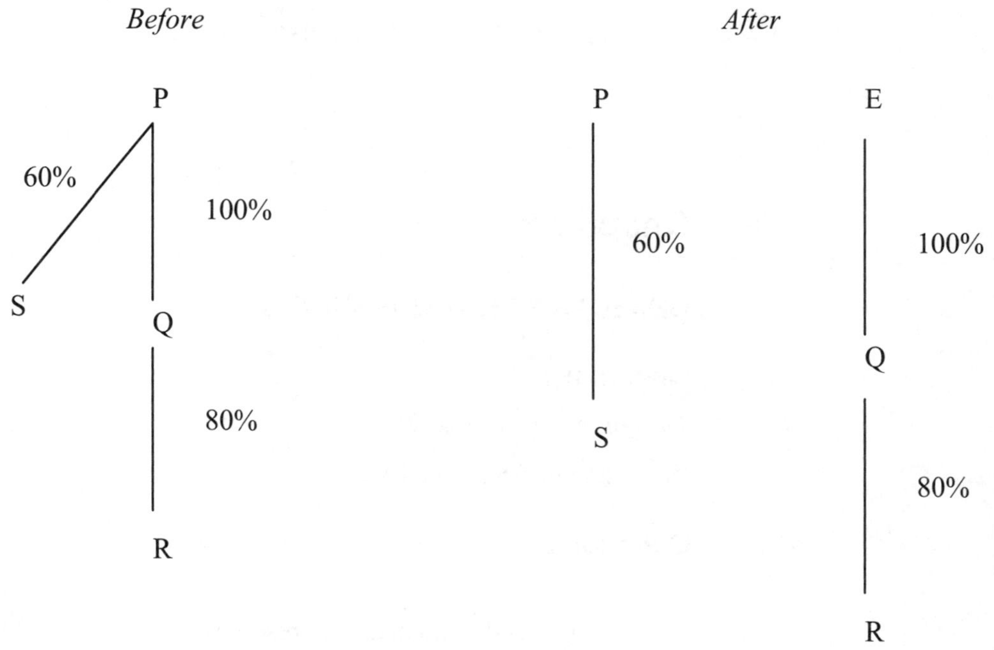

(W2) **Net assets of S**

| | *At acquisition* | *At B/S date* |
|---|---|---|
| | $m | $m |
| Share capital | 20 | 20 |
| Share premium | 20 | 20 |
| Retained earnings | 90 | 105 |
| | 130 | 145 |

(W3) **Goodwill**

| | $m |
|---|---|
| Cost of investment | 50 |
| Share of net assets (60% × 130) | (78) |
| | (28) |

(W4) **Consolidated reserves**

| | $m |
|---|---|
| P's reserves | 3,250 |
| Investment in Q distributed to shareholders | (900) |
| S's reserves [60% (145 – 130)] | 9 |
| Negative goodwill | 28 |
| | 2,387 |

(W5) **Other reserves**

E has issued 300 million shares of $1 to acquire an investment in Q that had a carrying value of $900m. In many jurisdictions, group reconstruction rules would allow the issue of shares to be recorded at par because the shares were issued to acquire an investment of 100% in Q. Given the fact that the reconstruction has no overall effect on the ultimate shareholders or on the minority interests there should be no effect on the amounts that are included in the consolidated balance sheet. The 'other reserve' is the difference between the nominal value of the shares issued and the original carrying value of the investment in Q that was previously in the balance sheet of P. Alternatively, the difference could be described as 'share premium'. Notice that the shares have been issued to the **shareholders** of P, not to P itself.

(W6) **Net assets of subsidiaries**

| | **Q** | | **R** | |
|---|---|---|---|---|
| | *At acq'n* | *At B/S date* | *At acq'n* | *At B/S date* |
| | $m | $m | $m | $m |
| Share capital | 100 | 100 | 30 | 30 |
| Share premium | 100 | 100 | 10 | 10 |
| Retained earnings | 250 | 810 | 60 | 80 |
| | 450 | 1,010 | 100 | 120 |

(W7) **Goodwill**

| | $m | $m |
|---|---|---|
| Cost of investment | 900 | 90 |
| Share of net assets (100% × 450)/(80% × 100) | (450) | (80) |
| | 450 | 10 |

(W8) **Reserves**

| | $m |
|---|---|
| Q (1,010 – 450) | 560 |
| R [80% (120 – 100)] | 16 |
| Goodwill written off: | |
| Q | (450) |
| R | (10) |
| | 116 |

# Chapter 9

## OBJECTIVE TEST QUESTIONS

### Question 1

*The correct answer is B.*

The question deals with the provisions of IAS 21 applied to direct business transactions.

The asset will not be subject to retranslation, so no gain or loss arises on this.

The receivable, being a monetary item, is restated at closing rate, the effect being as follows:

| | | $ |
|---|---|---|
| Original | €112,000/ 1.4 = | 80,000 |
| Closing rate | €112,000/ 1.6 = | 70,000 |
| Loss (charged in income statement) | | 10,000 |

### Question 2

*The correct answer is C.*

(See Chapter 9 Section 2.)

## EXAM-TYPE QUESTION

### FG

(a) **Balance sheet of JK at 31 December 20X8**

**Note:** Part (c) asks for a consolidated statement of changes in equity, so the best way to translate the balance sheet is to use the historic rate for share capital and pre-acquisition reserves.

| | C000 | *Rate* | $000 |
|---|---|---|---|
| Property, plant and equipment | 27,000 | 2 | 13,500 |
| Inventory | 16,200 | 2 | 8,100 |
| Trade receivables | 13,500 | 2 | 6,750 |
| Trade payables | (5,400) | 2 | (2,700) |
| Bank overdraft | (6,800) | 2 | (3,400) |
| Non-current liabilities | (18,000) | 2 | (9,000) |
| | 26,500 | | 13,250 |
| Share capital | 10,000 | 4.0 | 2,500 |
| Pre-acquisition reserves | 4,500 | 4.0 | 1,125 |
| Post-acquisition reserves | 12,000 | balancing figure | 9,625 |
| | 26,500 | | 13,250 |

**Consolidated balance sheet at 31 December 20X8**

| | $000 | $000 |
|---|---|---|
| ASSETS | | |
| Property, plant and equipment | | 31,500 |
| Intangible asset: Goodwill (W1) | | 3,000 |
| Current assets: | | |
| Inventories | 17,100 | |
| Trade receivables | 14,400 | |
| | | 31,500 |
| | | 66,000 |
| EQUITY AND LIABILITIES | | |
| Equity attributable to equity holders of the parent: | | |
| Share capital | | 10,000 |
| Reserves (W2) | | 20,160 |
| | | 30,160 |
| Minority interest (W3) | | 2,650 |
| | | 32,810 |
| Non-current liabilities: | | |
| Long-term borrowings | | 18,000 |
| Current liabilities | | |
| Trade payables | 6,300 | |
| Bank overdraft | 8,890 | |
| | | 15,190 |
| | | 66,000 |

(b) **Income statement of JK for the year ended 31 December 20X8**

| | C000 | *Rate* | $000 |
|---|---|---|---|
| Revenue | 54,000 | 2.4 | 22,500 |
| Cost of sales | (27,000) | 2.4 | (11,250) |
| Gross profit | 27,000 | | 11,250 |
| Operating expenses | (14,400) | 2.4 | (6,000) |
| Profit from operations | 12,600 | | 5,250 |
| Interest payable | (1,800) | 2.4 | (750) |
| Profit before tax | 10,800 | | 4,500 |
| Income tax expense | (3,800) | 2.4 | (1,583) |
| Profit for the year | 7,000 | | 2,917 |

**Consolidated income statement for the year ended 31 December 20X8**

| | $000 |
|---|---|
| Revenue | 67,500 |
| Cost of sales | (33,750) |
| Gross profit | 33,750 |
| Operating expenses | (19,500) |
| Profit from operations | 14,250 |
| Finance costs | (1,650) |
| Profit before tax | 12,600 |
| Income tax expense | (4,823) |
| Profit for the year | 7,777 |
| Attributable to: | |
| Equity holders of the parent | 7,194 |
| Minority interest (20% × 2,917) | 583 |
| | 7,777 |

(c) **Consolidated statement of changes in equity for the year ended 31 December 20X8**

| | $000 |
|---|---|
| At 1 January 20X8 (W5) | 23,520 |
| Profit for the year attributable to equity holders of the parent | 7,194 |
| Dividends paid | (3,500) |
| Exchange differences (W7) | 2,946 |
| At 31 December 20X8 | 30,160 |

*Workings*

(W1) **Group structure**

FG
|
80%
|
JH

(W2) **Goodwill**

| | C000 |
|---|---|
| Cost of investment (4,400 × 4) | 17,600 |
| Less: Share of net assets acquired: (80% × 14,500) | (11,600) |
| | 6,000 |

| Translated to dollars at each year end: | $000 |
|---|---|
| At acquisition (4) | 1,500 |
| At 1 January 20X8 (2.5) | 2,400 |
| At 31 January 20X8 (2) | 3,000 |

(W3) **Consolidated reserves**

| | $000 |
|---|---|
| FG: | 10,960 |
| JK: group share of post-acquisition profits (80% × 9,625) | 7,700 |
| Exchange gain on retranslation of goodwill (3,000 – 1,500) (W2) | 1,500 |
| | 20,160 |

(W4) **Minority interest**

| | $000 |
|---|---|
| Minority share of net assets at balance sheet date: (20% × 13,250) | 2,650 |

(W5) **Opening equity**

| | $000 |
|---|---|
| FG: | 18,000 |
| JK: group share of post-acquisition profits (80% × 5,775) (W6) | 4,620 |
| Exchange gain on retranslation of goodwill (2,400 – 1,500) (W2) | 900 |
| | 23,520 |

(W6) **Opening post-acquisition reserves in JK**

| | C000 | *Rate* | $000 |
|---|---|---|---|
| Share capital | 10,000 | 4.0 | 2,500 |
| Pre-acquisition reserves | 4,500 | 4.0 | 1,125 |
| Post-acquisition reserves | 9,000 | balancing figure | 5,775 |
| | 23,500 | 2.5 | 9,400 |

(W7) **Exchange differences (proof)**

| | $000 | $000 |
|---|---|---|
| Exchange differences on re-translation of opening net assets of JK: | | |
| At rate on 1 January 20X8 (23,500 ÷ 2.5) | 9,400 | |
| At rate on 31 December 20X8 (23,500 ÷ 2.0) | (11,750) | |
| Exchange gain | 2,350 | |
| Group share (80%) | | 1,880 |
| Exchange differences on re-translation of profit for the year: | | |
| At average rate | 2,917 | |
| At rate on 31 December 20X8 (7,000 ÷ 2.0) | (3,500) | |
| Exchange gain | 583 | |
| Group share (80%) | | 466 |
| Exchange difference on retranslation of goodwill (3,000 – 2,400) (W2) | | 600 |
| | | 2,946 |

## Chapter 10

### OBJECTIVE TEST QUESTIONS

#### Question 1

*The correct answer is B.*

**Minority interest**

| | $000 | | $000 |
|---|---|---|---|
| Cash paid (bal. fig.) | 40 | Balance b/d | 640 |
| Balance c/d | 700 | Income statement | 100 |
| | 740 | | 740 |

#### Question 2

*The correct answer is A.*

**Associate**

| | $000 | | $000 |
|---|---|---|---|
| Balance b/d | 360 | Cash receipt (bal fig) | 20 |
| Profits of associate | 60 | Balance c/d | 400 |
| | 420 | | 420 |

### Question 3

*The correct answer is A.*

**Tax paid**

| | $000 | | $000 |
|---|---|---|---|
| Cash paid (bal. fig.) | 50 | Balance b/d | 110 |
| Balance c/d | 120 | Income statement group tax | 60 |
| | 170 | | 170 |

## EXAM-TYPE QUESTIONS

### Abalone

**Cash flow statement for the year ended 31 March 20X7**

| | $m | $m |
|---|---|---|
| Operating activities | | |
| Profit before tax | 1,545 | |
| Depreciation and amortisation | 1,455 | |
| Interest expense | 375 | |
| Decrease in inventories (2,250 – 2,400 – 600) | 750 | |
| Increase in receivables (3,300 – 2,700 – 450) | (150) | |
| Decrease in payables (1,875 – 1,635 – 300) | (60) | |
| Cash generated from operations | 3,915 | |
| Interest paid | (375) | |
| Taxation (W2) | (480) | |
| Net cash from operating activities | | 3,060 |
| Investing activities | | |
| Purchase of non-current assets (W3) | (405) | |
| Purchase of subsidiary | (825) | |
| Bank overdraft acquired with subsidiary | (480) | |
| Net cash used in investing activities | | (1,710) |
| Financing activities | | |
| Capital element of finance lease payments (W4) | (675) | |
| Equity dividends paid to members of parent (2,850 + 870 – 3,300) | (420) | |
| Dividends paid to minority interests (W1) | (180) | |
| Net cash used in financing activities | | (1,275) |
| Increase in cash and cash equivalents for the year | | 75 |
| Cash and cash equivalents at beginning of the year | | (307) |
| Cash and cash equivalents at the end of the year | | (232) |

***Workings***

(W1) **Dividends paid to minority interests**

| | $m | | $m |
|---|---|---|---|
| Cash paid (bal. fig.) | 180 | Balance b/d | 930 |
| | | Income statement | 150 |
| Balance c/d | 1,125 | Acquisition (25% × 900) | 225 |
| | 1,305 | | 1,305 |

(W2) **Taxation**

| | $m | | $m |
|---|---|---|---|
| Cash paid (bal. fig.) | 480 | Balance b/d (CT) | 308 |
| | | Balance b/d (DT) | 345 |
| Balance c/d (CT) | 338 | Income statement | 525 |
| Balance c/d (DT) | 480 | Acquisition | 120 |
| | 1,298 | | 1,298 |

(W3) **Non-current assets**

| | $m | | $m |
|---|---|---|---|
| Balance b/d | 5,550 | Depreciation | 1,455 |
| Acquisition | 750 | | |
| Leased assets acquired | 900 | | |
| Cash purchases (bal. fig.) | 405 | Balance c/d | 6,150 |
| | 7,605 | | 7,605 |

(W4) **Finance leases**

| | $m | | $m |
|---|---|---|---|
| Cash paid (bal. fig.) | 675 | Balance b/d (< 1 year) | 675 |
| Balance c/d (< 1 year) | 750 | Balance b/d (> 1 year) | 1,800 |
| Balance c/d (> 1 year) | 1,950 | Acquisition | 900 |
| | 3,375 | | 3,375 |

## Wimborne

**Cash flow statement for the year ended 30 September 20X3**

| | $000 | $000 |
|---|---|---|
| **Operating activities** | | |
| Profit from operations | | 22,391 |
| Adjustments for: | | |
| Depreciation | | 3,197 |
| Operating profit before working capital changes | | 25,588 |
| Increase in inventories (19,773 – 205 – 17,702) | | (1,866) |
| Decrease in receivables (12,470 – 158 – 12,358) | | 46 |
| Decrease in trade and other payables (23,365 – 124 – 25,592) | | (2,351) |
| Cash generated from operations | | 21,417 |
| Interest paid | | (1,350) |
| Income tax paid (W1) | | (4,003) |
| Net cash from operating activities | | 16,064 |
| **Investing activities** | | |
| Investment income received | 175 | |
| Purchase of property, plant and equipment (W2) | (5,750) | |
| Proceeds from sale of non-current asset investment | 2,000 | |
| Purchase of non-current asset investment (W3) | (1,000) | |
| Purchase of current asset investments (7,500 – 5,000) | (2,500) | |
| Net cash used in investing activities | | (7,075) |
| **Financing activities** | | |
| Repayment of bank loans (11,850 + 476 – 7,500) | (4,826) | |
| Dividends paid to minority interest (W4) | (103) | |
| Equity dividends paid | (1,675) | |
| Net cash used in financing activities | | (6,604) |

| | |
|---|---|
| **Net increase in cash and cash equivalents** | 2,385 |
| Cash and cash equivalents at 1 October 20X2 | 100 |
| Effect of foreign exchange rate changes | 140 |
| Cash and cash equivalents at 30 September 20X3 | 2,625 |

***Workings***

(W1) **Income tax paid**

**Taxation**

| | $000 | | $000 |
|---|---|---|---|
| Cash paid (balancing figure) | 4,003 | Balance b/d: Current | 4,829 |
| Balance c/d: Current | 6,370 | Deferred | 3,094 |
| Deferred | 4,300 | Income statement | 6,750 |
| | 14,673 | | 14,673 |

(W2) **Property, plant and equipment**

**Property, plant and equipment**

| | $000 | | $000 |
|---|---|---|---|
| Balance b/d | 22,430 | Depreciation | 3,197 |
| Exchange gain | 2,117 | Revaluation | 1,400 |
| Additions (balancing figure) | 5,750 | Balance c/d | 25,700 |
| | 30,297 | | 30,297 |

(W3) **Non-current asset investments**

**Investments**

| | $000 | | $000 |
|---|---|---|---|
| Balance b/d | 6,900 | Disposals | 4,500 |
| Additions (balancing figure) | 1,000 | Balance c/d | 3,400 |
| | 7,900 | | 7,900 |

(W4) **Dividends paid to minority interests**

**Minority interests**

| | $000 | | $000 |
|---|---|---|---|
| Cash paid (balancing figure) | 103 | Balance b/d | 3,400 |
| Balance c/d: | 5,100 | Exchange loss | 258 |
| | | Income statement | 1,545 |
| | 5,203 | | 5,203 |

# Chapter 11

## OBJECTIVE TEST QUESTIONS

### Question 1

Deprival value can be summarised as:

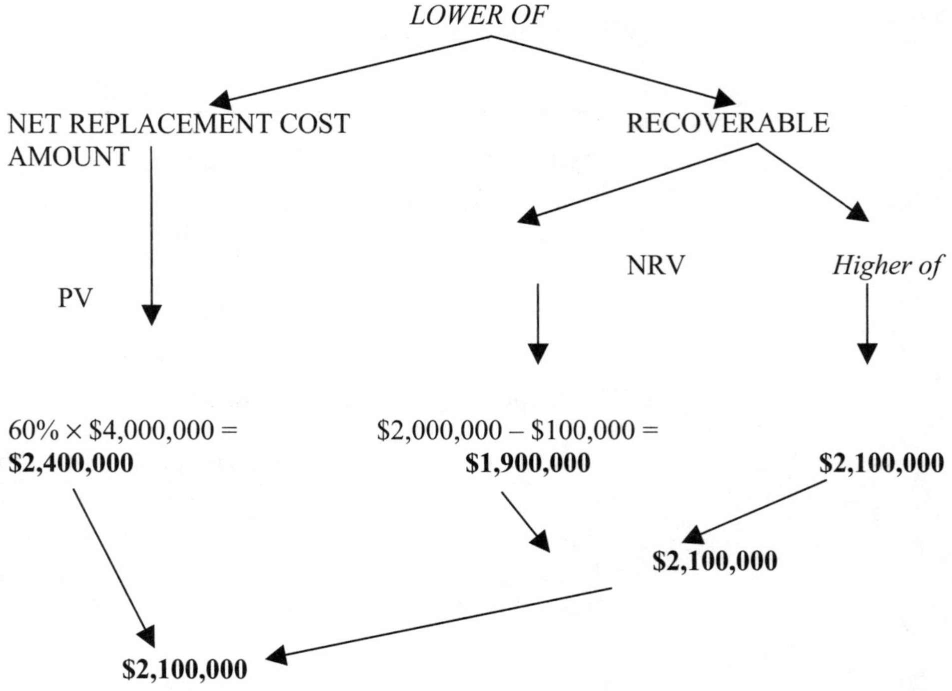


### Question 2

*The correct answer is C.*

(See Chapter 11, Sections 3 and 4.)

## EXAM-TYPE QUESTION

### Barty

(a) **The treatment of holding gains as a measure of business profit**

Holding gains are increases in the value of an asset while that asset is owned by a company. For example, a company might buy an item of inventory for $100 and then later sell it for $180 when its replacement cost had gone up to $150. The holding gain of $50 is realised at the date of sale; the 'real' profit, or operating gain, on the disposal is $30.

There are several alternative possible accounting treatments for holding gains, both realised and unrealised. Conventional historic cost accounting ignores unrealised holding gains, and includes realised holding gains in the income statement of the period in which the asset is disposed of. Current cost accounting, on the other hand, excludes realised holding gains on the disposals of inventory items by making an adjustment against reported profits so that only operating gains are reported as profits.

The significance of the treatment of holding gains is therefore the enormous effect that such treatment will have on reported profits. Although earnings per share is not the only important indicator of financial performance, it is still the most important, and the exclusion of holding gains from earnings will materially depress earnings per share and may thereby reduce the share price.

(b) **Arguments for the recognition of holding gains**

The accruals concept would suggest that gains and losses should be recognised in the period in which they occurred, rather than being deferred. So investments would be shown on the balance sheet at their market value. As a separate issue, prudence might dictate that gains should be credited to reserves rather than to the income statement, but the principle of revaluing investments in the balance sheet remains valid.

The objective of financial statements is set out in the Framework for the Preparation and Presentation of Financial Statements as being to provide useful information to a wide range of user groups. The current value of assets held is more relevant to the needs of users than the historic cost.

If holding gains are not recognised year-by-year, companies experiencing a bad year can flatter their reported profits by deciding to sell assets held for many years which have large unrealised holding gains. Often these assets may be immediately repurchased as a 'bed and breakfast' transaction. The profit generated on this deal does not reflect the genuine economic performance of the company in the period but under existing accounting practices may be all reported in the year of disposal.

In addition, asset-stripping hostile acquisitive companies will not be able to make money by breaking up target companies whose share prices do not reflect the real value of their underlying assets.

**Arguments against the recognition of holding gains**

The prudence concept seeks to prevent profits being included in the profit and loss account unless their realisation is reasonably certain.

Subjectivity and uncertainty exist in trying to determine the current value of an asset at the balance sheet date. An advantage of deferring holding gains until the date of disposal is the avoidance of this uncertainty.

If holding gains are included in reported profits and distributed out of the business, the company will not be able to finance the replacement of its assets without raising new funds externally. Operating capital will not be maintained if a policy of maximum distributions is carried on.

(c) **Comments on the adjusted earnings statement**

Barty is a company which invests in property. As such it is a value-based company which is attempting to maximise the return to shareholders primarily by long-term capital growth in the value of the investments.

The traditional income statement concentrates on current revenue and matches the immediate return of the shareholders (i.e. dividends) with the rental income.

The adjusted earnings statement recognises that the shareholders are interested in both revenue and capital gains. As can be seen, the unrealised gains exceed the revenue profit which is to be expected from such a company.

The shareholders are also interested in the protection from general inflation of their investment in the company. The inflation adjustment of $520,000 is the amount needed to maintain the purchasing power of the shareholders' investment during the year. Their equity investment at the beginning of the year was $13m, and applying 4% inflation gives $520,000. The unrealised gains are comfortably protecting the shareholders' investment.

# Chapter 12

## OBJECTIVE TEST QUESTIONS

### Question 1

*The correct answer is B.*

The cost of issuing the options should be recognised in the income statement over the period during which the employees must provide services in order for the options to vest.

### Question 2

*The correct answer is A.*

| | $m |
|---|---|
| Current service cost | 32 |
| Interest on scheme liabilities | 20 |
| | 52 |
| Less return on scheme assets | (28) |
| | 24 |

The actuarial losses are not recognised as they fall within the IAS 19 corridor.

## EXAM-TYPE QUESTIONS

### A

| | *31 May 20X1* $m |
|---|---|
| Present value of the obligation | 2,000 |
| Fair value of plan assets | (2,950) |
| Net surplus in plan | 950 |
| Unrecognised actuarial gains | (692) |
| Net plan asset | 258 |

***Workings***

(W1)

| | | $m |
|---|---|---|
| Unrecognised actuarial gains at 1 June 20X0 | | 247 |
| Actuarial gain/(loss) – obligation (2,000 – 1,500) | | (500) |
| Actuarial gain/(loss) – plan assets (2,950 – 1,970) | | 980 |
| Net contributions in year | | (30) |
| Actuarial gain recognised | | (5) |
| Unrecognised actuarial gain 31 May 20X1 | | 692 |
| Net contributions in year is Contributions | | 60 |
| | Net charge to income | (25) |
| | Actuarial gain | (5) |
| | | 30 |

(W2) The actuarial gain will be recognised as follows:

| | $m |
|---|---|
| Net unrecognised gain | 247 |
| Limits of 10% corridor (greater of 10% of 1,500 or 10% of 1,970) | (197) |
| Excess | 50 |
| Amortisation is therefore (50 ÷10 years) | 5 |

**Charge to income statement**

| | |
|---|---|
| Current service cost | 70 |
| Past service cost | 25 |
| Interest on liabilities | 230 |
| Actuarial gain recognised | (5) |
| Return on scheme assets | (295) |
| Net charge to income statement | 25 |

**Movement in plan surplus**

| | | | |
|---|---|---|---|
| Opening surplus | – asset | 1,970 | |
| | – liability | (1,500) | 470 |
| Unrecognised actuarial gain | | | (247) |
| Opening net surplus | | | 223 |
| Expense as above | | | (25) |
| Contributions | | | 60 |
| Closing net surplus in plan | | | 258 |

***Note:*** As the benefits are vested immediately following an alteration to the plan, the past service cost is recognised immediately.

## VIPER

**Accounting in the financial statements for the year ended 31 May 20X5**

IFRS2 requires an expense to be recognised for the share options granted to the directors with a corresponding amount shown in equity. Where options do not vest immediately but only after a period of service, then there is a presumption that the services will be rendered over the 'vesting period'. The fair value of the services rendered will be measured by reference to the fair value of the equity instruments at the date that the equity instruments were granted. Fair value should be based on market prices. The treatment of vesting conditions depends on whether or not the conditions relate to the market price of the instruments. Market conditions are effectively taken into account in determining the fair value of the instruments and therefore can be ignored for the purposes of estimating the number of equity instruments that will vest. For other conditions, such as remaining in the employment of the company, the calculations are carried out based on the best estimate of the number of instruments that will vest. The estimate is revised when subsequent information is available.

The options are valued as follows:

| | *Prior to 1 June 20X4* *Remuneration expense* $ | *Year ended 31 May 20X5* *Remuneration expense* $ |
|---|---|---|
| J. Van Heflin | | |
| 20,000 options × $5 × ½ | 50,000 | 50,000 |
| R. Ashworth | | |
| 50,000 options × $6 × 1/3 | | 100,000 |
| | 50,000 | 150,000 |

The conditions set out in performance condition A and the service condition by the director have been met. The expense is spread over two years up to the vesting date of 1 June 20X5.

The increase in the share price to above $13.50 in condition B has not been met but IFRS 2 says that the services received should be recognised irrespective of whether the market condition is satisfied. Additionally the director has to work for the company for three years for the options to vest and, therefore, the expense is spread over three years.

The opening balance of retained earnings at 1 June 20X4 would be reduced by $50,000 and equity (separate component) increased by $50,000.

The income statement for the year ended 31 May 20X5 would be charged with directors' remuneration relating to share options of $150,000 and equity (separate component) increased by the same amount.

# Chapter 13

## OBJECTIVE TEST QUESTIONS

### Question 1

| | | |
|---|---|---|
| Goods not yet accepted should appear as inventory at cost | = | $54,000 × 10% |
| | = | $5,400 |
| Remaining goods sold cost $48,600 ($54,000 × 90%) | | |
| Profit on these sales = $48,600 × 20/80 | = | $12,150 |

### Question 2

This transaction would be treated not as a sale of the land but as a loan secured on the land. The interest of $200,000, the difference between the sale value and the repurchase price, would be charged to the income statement for the year as an expense.

## EXAM-TYPE QUESTION

### D

**REPORT**

To: Managing Director of D

From: Management accountant

Date: XX XX XX

Subject: Comments on the treatment of assets and liabilities

(a) **Recognising assets and liabilities**

The central requirement of the substance over form concept is that entities should report the commercial substance of transactions in their financial statements, rather than their strict legal form. A key step in determining the substance of a transaction is to identify its effect on the assets and liabilities of the entity.

The IASB *Framework* defines an asset as 'a resource controlled by the entity as a result of past events and from which future economic benefits are expected to flow to the entity'. Control is the ability to obtain the future economic benefits relating to an asset and to restrict the access of others to those benefits. This means that it is more than the management of an asset. In practice, an entity which has access to benefits usually suffers or gains if those benefits turn out to be different from those expected. The ability to obtain benefits also implies exposure to risks. Evidence of whether an entity has benefits (and therefore has an asset) is given by whether it is exposed to the risks inherent in those benefits.

A liability is defined as an obligation to transfer economic benefits as a result of past transactions or events. If an entity cannot avoid an outflow of resources, it has a liability. The reason for the obligation may be legal or commercial (for example, an entity may have no realistic alternative to refunding the price of defective goods, even though there is no legal obligation to do so).

An asset or a liability should be recognised if there is sufficient evidence of its existence. Evidence of the existence of an asset or liability may include evidence that a future inflow or outflow of benefit will occur.

Assets and liabilities cannot be recognised unless they can be measured at a monetary amount with sufficient reliability. The fundamental concept of prudence is relevant here. A liability should be recognised where a reasonable estimate of the amount can be made. A greater level of reliability is necessary before an asset can be recognised.

Subsequent transactions may affect assets that have previously been recognised in the financial statements. For example, an asset may be financed by means of a sale and repurchase agreement.

Provided that this does not result in any significant changes to the entity's rights to benefits and exposure to risks inherent in those benefits, it should continue to recognise the asset in its financial statements. (The entity may also need to recognise a liability for the finance.)

Where a transaction transfers to others all significant rights to benefits associated with an asset and significant exposure to the risks inherent in those benefits, the entire asset should cease to be recognised.

(b) **Accounting treatment for the new transaction**

You have suggested that we only recognise the vehicles when title passes to us, which is to account for the strict legal form of the transaction. IAS 1 requires us to account for the commercial substance of the transaction, which may not be the same.

The key issue is whether D has the benefits and is exposed to the risks associated with the vehicles. If the company has the benefits and risks then it should recognise the vehicles in its financial statements.

The benefits normally associated with holding inventories are:

(i) the right to sell the goods and obtain future cash flows

(ii) insulation from increases in price charged by the manufacturer

(iii) the right to use the goods.

The risks normally associated with holding inventories are:

(i) the risk of making a loss on the sale

(ii) slow movement (possibly with increased holding and financing costs)

(iii) obsolescence.

D has the right to sell the vehicles, as E cannot normally demand their return (a benefit). The price at which it buys the vehicles depends on the date of delivery, not the date on which legal title passes (insulation from price rises – a benefit). D has the right to use the vehicles (a benefit).

E can demand the return of the vehicles if D becomes insolvent, but in practice, this is unlikely to happen.

D pays a penalty if it returns the vehicles to E. The size of the penalty means that D stands to lose a significant sum if it returns the vehicles (a risk). Although the transfer price rises by 1% for every complete month that the vehicles are held, this additional charge is effectively an interest charge (increased holding costs – a risk). D cannot return damaged or obsolete items (a risk).

In this case, it is fairly clear that D has the benefits and is exposed to the risks associated with holding the vehicles as inventory, even before legal title passes. In order to comply with the requirements of IAS 1, all vehicles held by the company at 31 August 20X6 must be included in the balance sheet as inventory. This also means that there will be a corresponding liability to E included in current liabilities, representing the amount that will be paid for the goods plus any accrued finance charges.

# Chapter 14

## OBJECTIVE TEST QUESTION

### Question 1

*The correct answer is B.*

| *Year* | *Amount b/f* | *Interest @ 9.5%* | *Interest paid* | *Amount c/f* |
|---|---|---|---|---|
| | *$* | *$* | *$* | *$* |
| 20X0 | 394,408 | 37,469 | (20,000) | 411,877 |
| 20X1 | 411,877 | 39,128 | (20,000) | 431,005 |
| 20X2 | 431,005 | 40,946 | (20,000) | 451,951 |

## PRACTICE QUESTION

### Alpha Limited

| | $ |
|---|---|
| Present value of $1,000,000 in four years | 683,000 |
| Present value of interest $80,000 payable annually in arrears for four years | 253,520 |
| Value of liability | 936,520 |
| Value of equity | 63,480 |
| Proceeds of bond issue | 1,000,000 |

***Workings***

| | | |
|---|---|---|
| Principal | | |
| $1,000,000 × 0.683 = | | 683,000 |
| Interest | | |
| $80,000 × 0.909 | 72,720 | |
| $80,000 × 0.826 | 66,080 | |
| $80,000 × 0.751 | 60,080 | |
| $80,000 × 0.683 | 54,640 | |
| | | 253,520 |

## EXAM-TYPE QUESTION

### Financial instruments

(a) (i) In recent years the growth and complexity of financial instruments has been quite significant. Companies use a range of instruments to transform and manage their financial risk. However, accounting standards have not developed at the same rate as the growth in the instruments. The main concern of standard setters is that many derivatives may not be recognised on the balance sheet. The main reason for this is the use of the historical cost concept in financial statements together with the fact that many derivatives have a nil cost. However, derivatives may be substantial assets and liabilities and may expose the entity to significant risk. Additionally many companies measure financial assets at amortised cost even though there are reliable quoted market prices that differ from amortised cost and the assets are readily saleable.

Until IAS 39 *Financial Instruments: Recognition and Measurement* unrealised gains and losses arising from changes in the value of many financial instruments were often ignored. Unrealised losses were recognised if the instrument was valued on the basis of the lower of cost or market value but ignored if the instrument was classed as a hedge. The danger is that such unrealised losses may be overlooked. Additionally companies could choose when they recognised profits on instruments in order that they could smooth profits. This applied both to derivatives and non-derivatives.

The use of hedge accounting caused significant problems. The practical problem with hedge accounting is translating business decisions into an accounting transaction that satisfies the hedging criteria. Hedge accounting relies on management intent and the result of this is that identical instruments can be accounted for differently depending upon the intentions of management in relation to them. Hedge accounting is often used for hedges of uncontracted future transactions and in these circumstances can be used to justify deferring almost any gain or loss on the derivative.

Circumstances can change quickly in the financial markets and the resultant effect on a company's derivatives can quickly transform the risk profile of a company. The accounting framework did not adequately make this movement in the position and risk apparent to users of financial statements.

(ii) Disclosure of the risk of an entity in relation to financial instruments is an important element of accounting for financial instruments and the IASC developed IAS 32 to deal with this issue. However disclosure requirements alone are not sufficient to deal with the problem. Recognition and measurement issues need to be dealt with. Many derivatives are kept off the balance sheet with unrealised gains and losses being ignored. Hedge accounting problems cannot be dealt with purely by requiring narrative disclosures of the hedging instrument or the amount of any deferred or unrecognised gain or loss. It is important that agreement is achieved over the possible measurement bases which can be used. The use of current values for financial instruments requires agreement as it is a critical measurement issue. For example, could current values be used for derivatives but not for non-derivatives? There are issues of impairment of financial instruments and the recognition of such instruments which need to be dealt with in a standard. Most issues in accounting are dealt with by standards focusing on measurement, recognition and disclosure issues. A financial instrument is no exception in this regard and it is such an important issue that disclosure alone could never effectively deal with the issues satisfactorily. The IASC issued IAS 39 *Financial Instruments: Recognition and Measurement* to deal with these issues.

(b) Under IAS 39, all financial assets and liabilities are recognised on the balance sheet and this includes all derivatives. They are originally measured at cost which is the fair value of whatever was paid or received to acquire the financial asset or liability. Subsequently, all financial assets are remeasured to fair value with the exception of certain specified items.

Of the financial assets specified in the question, two items will be measured at fair value ($6,000m and $3,460m respectively) and one at amortised cost. The equity securities and other financial assets held for trading and the derivative assets will be valued at fair value whereas the fixed maturity investments to be held to maturity are one of the categories of items to be carried at amortised cost.

Most financial liabilities are measured at original recorded amount less principal repayments and amortisation. Only derivatives and liabilities held for trading are remeasured to fair value. Thus the redeemable preference shares will remain at the carrying amount ($3,400m).

Both the derivatives and the non-derivative assets held for trading are categorised as financial assets at fair value through profit or loss. This means that in both cases the gain arising during the period should be recognised in the income statement.

# Chapter 15

## OBJECTIVE TEST QUESTIONS

### Question 1

*The correct answer is D.*

Credit sales $= \$200 \times 80\%$

$= \$160$

Average receivables $= \frac{(16+24)}{2}$

$= 20$

Receivables' turnover $= \frac{160}{20}$

$= 8$ times

Collection period $= \frac{365}{8}$

$= 46$ days

| | $000 | % |
|---|---|---|
| Sales | 200 | 100 |
| Cost of sales (40 + 120 – 50) | (110) | 55 |
| Gross profit | 90 | 45 |

## Question 2

*The correct answer is A.*

$$\frac{\text{Profit}}{\text{Capital employed}} = \frac{\text{Profit}}{\text{Revenue}} \times \frac{\text{Revenue}}{\text{Capital employed}}$$

(Return on capital employed) (Profit margin) (Asset turnover)

$$0.80 = \frac{\text{Profit}}{\text{Revenue}} \times 1.10$$

$$\frac{\text{Profit}}{\text{Revenue}} = \frac{0.80}{1.10}$$

$$= 0.73$$

## PRACTICE QUESTION

### SR

**REPORT**

To: Finance director

From: Management accountant

Date: 30 June 20XX

Subject: Performance of PQ and areas of further investigation.

This report deals with the performance of PQ over the three years from 20X7 to 20X9 and details areas where further investigation needs to be made. Calculations supporting figures used in this report can be found in the Appendix.

(a) Performance of PQ

(i) **Profitability** – The company has seen a dramatic reduction in return on capital employed in 20X9, whilst the gross profit percentage has remained almost static with a small increase in 20X9.

Hence an increase in capital employed in 20X8 and 20X9 has not resulted in a corresponding increase in sales revenue. Whilst the trading profit margin has not fallen significantly there has been an increase in interest expense arising from the increase in long-term loans.

Sales revenue has fallen by $68m in 20X9 compared to 20X8 – a fall of 7%.

(ii) **Working capital** – Both the inventory period and receivables days have increased over the period offset to some extent by payables turnover. This suggests that management of working capital might have deteriorated.

(iii) **Long-term finance** – Gearing has increased significantly over the period from 15.6% in 20X7 to 24.3% in 20X8 falling slightly to 23.6% in 20X9.

The debt/equity ratio has also increased from 18.5% in 20X7 to over 30% in both 20X8 and 20X9.

(b) Areas for further investigation

(i) **Sales revenue/profits** – The reason for the fall in sales in 20X9. Was this due to a loss of market share due to obsolescence of some product lines, or a change in product mix?

Are the increases in selling, distribution and administration expenses due to an increase in advertising costs in an attempt to increase sales in 20X10?

(ii) **Intangible assets** – What do these represent? Patents for new products or deferred development expenditure?

(iii) **Receivables** – Have PQ deliberately given customers (or certain classes of customers) longer credit periods?

(iv) **Interest** – Why has interest expense increased whilst long-term loans have remained the same in 20X8 and 20X9?

(v) **Other payables** – What does this figure consist of? As the company has a large cash balance it seems unlikely that other payables include bank overdrafts. Taxation and dividend levels have not changed, therefore they do not explain the increase.

**Appendix**

| | | *20X7* | *20X8* | *20X9* |
|---|---|---|---|---|
| | | $m | $m | $m |
| **Profitability ratios** | | | | |
| ROCE $\left(\frac{\text{Profit}}{\text{Capital employed}} \times 100\%\right)$ | | $\frac{100}{473}$ | $\frac{122}{568}$ | $\frac{104}{584}$ |
| | = | 21.1% | 21.5% | 17.8% |
| Gross profit percentage | | | | |
| $\frac{\text{Gross profit}}{\text{Sales revenue}} \times 100\%$ | | $\frac{286}{840}$ | $\frac{336}{981}$ | $\frac{323}{913}$ |
| | = | 34% | 34.3% | 35.4% |
| Trading profit margin | | | | |
| $\frac{\text{Trading profit}}{\text{Sales revenue}} \times 100\%$ | | $\frac{100}{840}$ | $\frac{122}{981}$ | $\frac{104}{913}$ |
| | = | 11.9% | 12.4% | 11.4% |
| Inventory period | | | | |
| $\frac{\text{Inventory}}{\text{Cost of sales}} \times 365 \text{ days}$ | | $\frac{237}{554}$ | $\frac{303}{645}$ | $\frac{294}{590}$ |
| | = | 156 days | 171 days | 182 days |
| Receivables days | | | | |
| $\frac{\text{Trade receivables}}{\text{Sales revenue}} \times 365 \text{ days}$ | | $\frac{105}{840}$ | $\frac{141}{981}$ | $\frac{160}{913}$ |
| | = | 46 days | 52 days | 64 days |
| Payables days | | | | |
| $\frac{\text{Trade payables}}{\text{Cost of sales}} \times 365 \text{ days}$ | | $\frac{53}{554}$ | $\frac{75}{645}$ | $\frac{75}{590}$ |
| | = | 35 days | 42 days | 46 days |

## EXAM-TYPE QUESTIONS

## F

**REPORT**

To: Section Head

From: Bank Accountant

Subject: F

Date: 22 November 20X5

(a) The performance of F appears to have deteriorated in the six months to 30 September 20X5. Sales and cost of sales have both fallen by 9%, so that the gross profit percentage of 50% has been maintained. However, operating expenses have increased, so that total operating costs equal operating income. There is no longer any cover for interest payments. The interest charge has also increased, following the increase in the overdraft facility.

Despite this deterioration in performance, non-current assets and working capital have increased. The additional $2 million provided by the bank (an increase in overdraft of 66%) appears to have been used to finance the purchase of plant at a cost of approximately $500,000 (the figure represents the change shown by the balance sheet and is net of depreciation). The additional depreciation has probably contributed to the increase in operating expenses.

The retained loss for the year is $900,000 but the actual cash outflow from operating activities is much greater than this. A rough calculation is given below:

| | $000 |
|---|---|
| Loss | 900 |
| Less depreciation (buildings only) | (200) |
| Increase in inventories | 400 |
| Increase in receivables | 400 |
| | 1,500 |

The company's financial position has deteriorated during the year. At 30 September 20X5 it had a current ratio of 1.06 :1 and a quick ratio of 0.67:1 (compared with 1.3:1 and 0.83:1 at 30 September 20X4). The company is likely to experience severe liquidity problems in the near future.

The company's gearing also gives cause for concern. The company is very dependent upon finance from outside the business. The most recent balance sheet shows a debt to equity ratio of 2.97:1 and gearing of 53%. Interest on the loan notes amounts to $576,000 annually. At current activity levels, this means that there is very little profit available for distribution or investment and very little interest cover. The loan notes are barely covered by the property on which they are secured.

The combination of adverse cash flow, increase in non-current assets and working capital and fall in profits seems to suggest bad management. However, it is impossible to reach a firm conclusion without further information.

The withdrawal of the overdraft facility would result in the liquidation of the company. It is estimated that the assets would realise $9,300,000. The loan note holders would be repaid their $4,800,000 in full, leaving a balance of $4,500,000 for the other creditors. This does not cover the $7,600,000 owed to the bank and the other creditors. Assuming that all unsecured creditors would rank equally, the bank would receive 59c in the dollar or $2,950,000. The bank would make a loss of $2,050,000.

These calculations show that the bank is facing considerable risk. If the overdraft facility is to be continued, the bank should consider re-negotiating the terms in order to take account of this risk.

(b) **Appendix**

Only limited information is available as a basis for making this decision.

One major shortcoming of conventional financial statements is that they are based on historical information. They give a good indication of the financial position at 30 September 20X5, but some time has already elapsed since that date. During that time the position could have changed dramatically. For example, the company could have won substantial new business, or receivables could have been realised, or inventory could have been sold. Financial statements are only of limited use in predicting the future of a company.

To make an informed decision, the bank would need information about several other factors which are not reflected in the financial statements. The velocity of circulation of working capital, the quality of the company's management and its ability to attract new business will all be crucial in determining whether or not F survives. For example, the decision to invest in additional plant and to increase inventory levels might have been taken as a result of several new orders. The bank would also need to assess the willingness of the loan note holders and other creditors to continue to support the company. For example, there is no information as to how soon the loan notes will become repayable or as to the means by which the company intends to repay the loan.

## Webster

(a) **Income statements to 31 March 2000**

| | *Cole* | | *Darwin* | |
|---|---|---|---|---|
| | $000 | $000 | $000 | $000 |
| Sales (3,000 – 125 W1) | | 2,875 | | 4,400 |
| Opening inventory | 450 | | 720 | |
| Purchases (W2) | 2,055 | | 3,080 | |
| | 2,505 | | 3,800 | |
| Closing inventory | (540) | (1,965) | (850) | (2,950) |
| Gross profit | | 910 | | 1,450 |
| Operating expenses | 480 | | 964 | |
| Depreciation adjustment | 40 | | (W3) (120) | |
| Debenture interest | 80 | | nil | |
| Overdraft interest | 15 | 615 | (W4) nil | (844) |
| Net profit | | 295 | | 606 |

**Balance sheets as at 31 March 2000**

| | Cole | | Darwin | |
|---|---|---|---|---|
| Non-current assets | | | | |
| Property (W3) | | 1,900 | | 1,900 |
| Plant | | 1,200 | | (W3) 720 |
| | | 3,100 | | 2,620 |
| Current assets | | | | |
| Inventory | 540 | | 850 | |
| Accounts receivable (522 + 375 (W1)) | 897 | | 750 | |
| Bank (W4) | nil | 1,437 | (W4) 60 | 1,660 |
| Total assets | | 4,537 | | 4,280 |
| Equity and liabilities | | | | |
| Equity shares of $1 each | | 1,000 | | 500 |
| Reserves: | | | | |
| Revaluation reserve (W3) | | 760 | | 700 |
| Retained earnings (684 + 295 + 40) | | 1,019 | (1,912 + 606) | 2,518 |
| | | 2,779 | | 3,718 |
| Non-current liabilities | | | | |
| 10% Debentures | | 800 | | nil |
| Current liabilities | | | | |
| Trade accounts payable (438 – 275 W2) | 163 | | 562 | |
| Overdraft (W4) | 795 | 958 | nil | 562 |
| Total equity and liabilities | | 4,537 | | 4,280 |

***Workings*:** all figures in $000

(W1) If the sale to Brander of $500 had been on normal commercial terms it would have been $375. Applying this would cause a reduction in sales of $125. The effect of applying normal credit arrangements would be that the revised sales figure of $375 would still be in accounts receivable and the original sale proceeds of $500 would not have been received and thus increase Cole's overdraft (see W4).

(W2) The purchase from Advent under normal trading terms would have resulted in an increase in cost of sales of $25. Applying a normal two-month credit period would mean that the goods would have been paid for by the year-end thus increasing the overdraft by a further $300, and accounts payable would be reduced by the original value of the transaction of $275.

(W3) Non-current assets/depreciation:

*Cole – property*

Depreciation for the year to 31 March 2000 based on the revalued amount would be the same as Darwin's, $100 (2,000/20 years), this would give Cole an additional depreciation charge of $40 (100 – 60). The revaluation of Cole's property would lead to a revaluation reserve of $800,000. An amount equal to the excess depreciation of $40 is normally transferred from the revaluation reserve to retained earnings.

*Darwin – plant*

As the plant acquired in February 2000 has not yet contributed to the operations of Darwin then, for comparability purposes, it would be logical to ignore its acquisition. The effects of this are:

- cost of plant would be reduced by $600. This would also affect the bank balance – see (iv) below
- depreciation of $120 (600 × 20%) would be reversed.

The overall effect of depreciation in the income statements would be:

| | *Cole* | *Darwin* |
|---|---|---|
| | $000 | $000 |
| Original depreciation on property (1,200 – 1,140) | (60) | |
| Depreciation on revalued amount | 100 | |
| Reversal of depreciation on new plant | | (120) |
| | debit 40 | credit (120) |

Summary of non-current assets:

| | *Cost/ revaluation* | | *Depreciation* | | *Carry valu* |
|---|---|---|---|---|---|
| | $000 | | $000 | | $00 |
| Cole – property | 2,000 | | 100 | | 1,90 |
| – plant (unchanged) | 6,000 | | 4,800 | | 1,20 |
| | | | | | 3,10 |
| Darwin – property (unchanged) | 2,000 | | 100 | | 1,90 |
| – plant | 2,400 | (3,000 – 600) | 1,680 | (1,800 – 120) | 72 |
| | | | | | 2,62 |

(W4) Bank balances

| | *Cole* | *Darwin* |
|---|---|---|
| | $000 | $000 |
| – balance b/f | 20 | (550) |
| – reversal of sale proceeds | (500) | |
| – payment for increased purchases | (300) | |
| – payment for plant reversed | | 600 |
| – payment/saving of overdraft interest | (15) | 10 |
| – balance c/f | (795) | 60 |

(b) **Ratios from question**

| | *Cole* | *Darwin* |
|---|---|---|
| Return on capital employed | 19.4% | 13.3% |
| Asset turnover | 1.01 times | 1.23 times |
| Gross profit margin | 35.3% | 33.0% |
| Net profit margin | 16.7% | 10.8% |
| Accounts receivable collection period | 64 days | 62 days |
| Accounts payable payment period | 79 days | 67 days |

**Ratios from restated financial statements:**

Return on capital employed

| | | | |
|---|---|---|---|
| $(295 + 80)/(2{,}779 + 800) \times 100$ | 10.5% | $(606/3{,}718) \times 100$ | 16.3% |
| Asset turnover (2875/3,579) | 0.80 times | (4,400/3,718) | 1.18 times |
| Gross profit margin $(910/2875) \times 100$ | 31.7% | | 33.0% |
| Net profit margin $(295/2{,}875) \times 100$ | 10.3% | $(606/4{,}400) \times 100$ | 13.8% |
| Accounts receivable collection period $(897/2875) \times 365$ | 114 days | | 62 days |
| Accounts payable payment period $(163/2055) \times 365$ | 29 days | | 67 days |

***Note:*** The figures without workings have not changed.

**Comments:**

An assessment of the performance of the two companies based on the unadjusted ratios would favour Cole as most of its 'key' ratios are better than Darwin's. Cole's overall profitability as measured by the ROCE is higher. This is due to higher profit margins as Darwin's asset turnover is in fact higher than Cole's. A point of note is that both companies have rather poor asset turnovers, implying inefficient use of assets.

The management of working capital of the two companies is rather similar with the exception that Cole is obtaining (or taking) a slightly longer credit period from its suppliers. Webster may be better advised to calculate liquidity ratios as well as working capital ratios. This would show that Cole's liquidity ratios are a healthy 2.5 (1,082/438) and 1.23 (542/438) for the current and quick ratios (acid test) respectively, whereas Darwin's figures are only 1.4 (1,600/1,112) and 0.7 (750/1,112) which are a cause for concern and further investigation.

When the above ratios are recalculated on the adjusted financial statements, the relative position is very much reversed. The favourable trading terms and conditions that have been orchestrated by Cole's parent company have favourably distorted its financial statements. Equally, due to the limitations of traditional ratio analysis, Darwin's ratios are unfavourably affected by its policy of revaluing property, and acquiring additional plant just before the year-end.

The revised ratios show Darwin is much more profitable than Cole with better margins and more efficient use of assets. Further Cole's 'true' liquidity position is not impressive; a current ratio of 1.5 (1,437/958) and a quick ratio of 0.93 (897/958). The management of working capital figures show poor credit control of accounts receivable (114 days) and, despite the question saying Cole normally takes two months' credit, there is very early payment of suppliers. This may be due to suppliers imposing strict terms as a result of past experiences, or Cole may have a poor credit rating. It can also be seen that Darwin's poor liquidity ratios are in the main due to financing the acquisition of the new plant from overdraft facilities. Darwin may be advised to re-finance this plant from medium-term borrowings (say a five-year debenture).

In coming to a decision about which company Webster should purchase there are many other factors that should be considered, for example:

(i) What is the asking price of the companies? If Cole is priced cheaply, reflecting its problems, and Darwin is expensive clearly this will be critical in any decision to purchase.

(ii) It must be remembered that Webster will be buying the future profits/cash flows of a company and past financial statements may be misleading in this respect. For example the new plant coming on stream will affect Darwin's future profits. Other aspects relating to this point is that other information (which may not be available to Webster) may be very useful e.g. profit and cash flow forecasts. Also non-financial information can be very important, for example, has either company got a full or an empty order book? Does either company have a history of good or poor labour relations?

(iii) It may be that neither company would be a good purchase and other potential acquisitions should be considered.

***Tutorial note***: Journal entries for the adjustments in part (a)

| | | $000 | $000 |
|---|---|---|---|
| **Cole** | | | |
| (i) | Dr Sales | 125 | |
| | Dr Accounts receivable | 375 | |
| | Cr Bank | | 500 |
| (ii) | Dr Purchases | 25 | |
| | Dr Trade accounts payable | 275 | |
| | Cr Bank | | 300 |
| (iii) | Dr Property (balance sheet carrying value) | 800 | |
| | Cr Revaluation reserve | | 800 |
| | Dr Depreciation (income statement) | 40 | |
| | Cr Property (balance sheet carrying value) | | 40 |
| (v) | Dr Overdraft interest | 15 | |
| | Cr Bank | | 15 |
| **Darwin** | | | |
| (iv) | Dr Bank | 600 | |
| | Cr Plant | | 600 |
| | Dr Plant | 120 | |
| | Cr Depreciation (income statement) | | 120 |
| | Dr Bank | 10 | |
| | Cr Overdraft interest | | 10 |

# Chapter 16

## OBJECTIVE TEST QUESTIONS

### Question 1

*The correct answer is D.*

Theoretical ex-rights price

| | | | | |
|---|---|---|---|---|
| | | | | $ |
| 6 shares | @ | $1.50 | = | 9.00 |
| 1 share | @ | $1.15 | = | 1.15 |
| 7 shares | @ | $1.45 | | 10.15 |

Current year EPS

| | | |
|---|---|---|
| Earnings | = | $77,540 |
| Shares | | |
| 600,000 × 3/12 × 1.50/1.45 | = | 155,172 |
| 700,000 × 9/12 | = | 525,000 |
| | | 680,172 |
| EPS 30 June 20X2 | = | $\frac{77,540}{680,172}$ |
| | = | 11.4 cents |

Comparative EPS

| | | |
|---|---|---|
| 10.8 cents × 1.45/1.50 | = | 10.4 cents |

### Question 2

Basic EPS $= \frac{548,000 + 102,000}{1,600,000}$

$=$ 40.6 cents

| | $ | $ |
|---|---|---|
| Diluted EPS | | |
| Basic earnings | | 650,000 |
| Add interest saved $200,000 × 5% | 10,000 | |
| Less tax | (3,000) | |
| | | 7,000 |
| | | 657,000 |

Number of shares = 1,600,000 + $200,000 × 120/$100

= 1,840,000

Diluted EPS $= \frac{657,000}{1,840,000}$

= 35.7 cents

## Question 3

**Basic EPS**

| | | $ |
|---|---|---|
| Basic EPS | = | $\frac{208,000}{1,000,000}$ |
| | = | 20.8 cents |
| **Diluted EPS – number of shares** | | |
| Options | = | 200,000 × $1.50 |
| | = | $300,000 |
| At fair value | = | $\frac{300,000}{1.90}$ |
| | = | 157,895 |
| Shares issued free | = | 200,000 – 157,895 |
| | = | 42,105 |
| Diluted EPS | = | $\frac{208,000}{1,042,105}$ |
| | = | 20.0 cents |

## EXAM-TYPE QUESTION

### TAB

(a) The purpose of segmental information is to provide users of financial statements with sufficient details for them to be able to appreciate the different rates of profitability, different opportunities for growth and different degrees of risk that apply to an entity's classes of business and various geographical locations. The segmental information should enable users to:

(i) appreciate more thoroughly the results and financial position of the entity by permitting a better understanding of the entity's past performance and thus a better assessment of its future prospects

(ii) be aware of the impact that changes in significant components of a business may have on the business as a whole.

(b) **IAS 14 requires that an entity should look to its internal organisational structure and internal reporting system for the purpose of identifying reportable segments.** In identifying separate reportable segments, the directors should have regard to the overall purpose of presenting segmental information and the need of the user of the financial statements to be informed where an entity carries on operations in different classes of business or in different geographical areas that:

- earn a return on investment that is out of line with the remainder of the business
- are subject to different degrees of risk
- have experienced different rates of growth
- have different potentials for future development.

A segment may be presumed significant where the sales revenue, profit or net assets exceed 10% of the business as a whole.

TAB could classify on a geographical basis under the headings 'Europe' and 'Asia'.

TAB has five types of products and more information is really required on the commonality of any of these five. A product split could thus be for five segments.

Likely candidates for grouping together are textiles and fashion garments, perhaps under the heading 'textiles' or 'textiles and clothing'. In addition it may be reasonable to group car products and kitchen utensils under the heading 'domestic products'.

(c) **IAS 14 requires that one basis of segmentation should be chosen as the primary basis, while the other is the secondary basis.** Disclosure is then required of:

Definition of each reported class of business and geographical segment.

For primary basis of segment reporting:

- sales or other operating revenues
- segment result
- segment assets employed
- basis of inter-segment pricing
- segment liabilities
- cost of non-current assets acquired during the period
- depreciation and amortisation expense
- non-cash expenses other than depreciation and amortisation
- share of net profits of associates and joint ventures.

For secondary basis of segment reporting:

- sales or other operating revenues
- segment assets employed
- basis of inter-segment pricing
- cost of non-current assets acquired during the period.

(d) Segmental disclosures appear to be presented by the affected companies quite easily. The case for increased disclosure had been argued for many years by users, particularly investment analysts, who required more information about the trading operations of large groups.

Perhaps the reason that companies have accepted segmental disclosures is that the standard is flexible as to the groupings shown and therefore the requirements are not seen as too demanding.

**Problems of segmental disclosure under IAS 14 are as follows.**

(i) Defining segments is not always easy. Differences will exist in segment identification making it difficult to make comparisons between organisations.

Directors have the responsibility for defining classes of business and geographical segments. Guidance is given in the standard but the decision of the basis is left with the directors. This could lead to bias in the selection of segments. Decisions may be influenced by a desire not to make any class or segment look unduly secure or at risk.

(ii) There are problems in the measurement of segmental performance if the segments trade with each other. Disclosure of details of inter-segment pricing policy may be considered to be detrimental to the good of a company.

There is little guidance on the policy for transfer pricing.

(iii) Common costs may be so significant that to ignore them would result in an incomplete picture, but to incorporate them would result in misleading data.

Common costs are to be treated in the way in which directors deem most appropriate. The result of this can be a lack of consistency of treatment.

(iv) Deciding on what segmental data is required is subjective. Various users require differing levels of disclosure and deciding on a level may be to the detriment of certain of these users.

# Chapter 17

## OBJECTIVE TEST QUESTION

### Question 1

*The correct answer is C.*

There is no legal or constructive obligation for Ferndale to incur the factory costs, therefore no provision is required.

Fernbank has a constructive obligation, due to its past actions, to clear up the contamination so a provision is required.

## EXAM-TYPE QUESTION

### Redstart

**MEMORANDUM**

To: Assistant Accountant

From: Chief Accountant

Date: 25 March 20X2

Subject: Accounting treatment of two transactions and disclosure of environmental matters in the financial statements

(a) Accounting treatment of two transactions

**Transaction One**

IAS 37 *Provisions, Contingent Liabilities and Contingent Assets* states that provisions should only be recognised in the financial statements if:

(i) there is a present obligation as a result of a past event

(ii) it is probable that a transfer of economic benefits will be required to settle the obligation

(iii) a reliable estimate can be made of the amount of the obligation.

In this case, there is no obligation to incur expenditure. There may be a constructive obligation to do so in future, if the Board creates a valid expectation that it will protect the environment, but a Board decision alone does not create an obligation. There is also some doubt as to whether the expenditure can be reliably quantified. An annual sum could be appropriated from profit and transferred to an environmental protection reserve, subject to formal approval by the Board. A note to the financial statements should explain the appropriation.

**Transaction Two**

Again, IAS 37 states that a provision cannot be recognised if there is no obligation to incur expenditure. At first sight it appears that there is an obligation to purchase the new equipment, because the new law has been enacted. However, the obligation must arise as the result of a past event. At 31 December 20X1, no such event had occurred as the new plant had not yet been purchased and the new law had not yet come into effect. In theory, the company does not have to purchase the new plant. It could completely discontinue the activities that cause pollution or it could continue to operate the old equipment and risk prosecution under the new law. Therefore no provision can be recognised for the cost of new equipment.

It is likely that the company will be disposing of the old plant before it would normally have expected to do so. IAS 36 *Impairment of Assets* requires that the old plant must be reviewed for impairment. If its carrying value is greater than its recoverable amount it must be written down and an impairment loss must be charged in the income statement. This should be disclosed as an exceptional item in the notes to the income statement if it is material.

(b) Reference to environmental matters in the financial statements

At present companies are not obliged to make any specific reference to environmental matters within their financial statements. Current financial reporting practice is primarily designed to meet the needs of investors and potential investors, rather than the general public. Some companies choose to disclose information about the ways in which they attempt to safeguard the environment, but this is almost invariably carried out as a public relations exercise. Disclosures are often framed in very general terms and appear outside the financial statements proper. This means that they do not have to be audited.

A few companies do publish fairly detailed 'environmental reports'. It could be argued that as Redstart's operations affect the wider community, it has a moral responsibility to disclose details of its activities and its environmental policies. However, at present it is not required to do so.

If a company has, or may have, an obligation to make good environmental damage that it has caused it is obliged to disclose information about this commitment in its financial statements (unless the likelihood of this is remote). If it is probable (more likely than not) that the company will have to incur expenditure to meet its obligation, then it is also required to set up a provision in the financial statements. In practice, these requirements are unlikely to apply unless a company is actually obliged by law to rectify environmental damage or unless it has made a firm commitment to the public to do so (for example, by promoting itself as an organisation that cares for the environment, as the directors propose that Redstart should do in future).

# Chapter 18

## OBJECTIVE TEST QUESTION

### Question 1

*The correct answer is D.*

## EXAM-TYPE QUESTION

### Home

(a) **Why the reconciliation statement is still necessary**

In May 2000 IOSCO recommended that its members, which include the US Securities and Exchange Commission (SEC), should allow the use of IAS for cross border listings.

However, this recommendation was qualified. Where multinationals file financial statements prepared under IASs, IOSCO members may require them to provide additional information. This may include reconciliations, for example net profit under IASs may need to be reconciled to net profit under US GAAP (generally accepted accounting principles). It is likely that the SEC will continue (at least in the short term) to require companies to provide additional information if they choose to file financial statements prepared under IASs.

Even if this were not the case, all companies must file financial statements drawn up according to generally accepted accounting principles in the countries in which they are incorporated. The US parent is required to prepare and file consolidated financial statements drawn up under US GAAP, regardless of whether IASs are accepted from foreign companies. While US GAAP and IASs are broadly similar in many respects, there are still many important differences in the detail. US accounting standards tend to be 'rule based' and very much more detailed than IASs. The differences are steadily reducing, but it is unlikely that the two sets of standards will ever be completely identical. Only when the US authorities are prepared to accept financial statements drawn up in IASs from all companies will the reconciliation no longer be needed.

(b) Adjustments

(i) Development costs

Home has followed IAS 38 *Intangible Assets*, which requires enterprises to defer development expenditure provided it meets a number of strict criteria (intended to ensure that expenditure is capitalised only if it is reasonably certain to generate income in future). Deferred development expenditure is amortised through the income statement on a systematic basis when production begins.

US GAAP does not permit development expenditure to be carried forward. It must be written off through the income statement in the period in which it was incurred.

(ii) Revaluations

IAS 16 *Property, Plant and Equipment* allows tangible non-current assets to be revalued upwards.

Revaluations are not permitted under US GAAP. All assets must be stated at historic cost. Therefore the excess depreciation on the revalued amount is written back to the income statement. An adjustment must also be made for the difference between profit on disposal of a revalued asset based on its historic cost and profit based on the revalued amount.

# APPENDIX

## Introduction

This Appendix covers the requirements of the standards that are examined in Paper P7 *Financial Accounting and Tax Principles.* If you have already studied for Paper P7 you should be familiar with this material.

These standards are not directly examinable in Paper P8. However, you may need to draw upon this knowledge when answering questions on other topics, particularly when analysing and interpreting financial statements.

## Contents

# 1 IAS 8 *Accounting Policies, Changes in Accounting Estimates and Errors*

## 1.1 Selecting accounting policies

**Accounting policies** are the specific principles, bases, conventions, rules and practices applied by an entity in preparing and presenting financial statements.

IAS 8 states that where an IAS, IFRS or IFRIC applies to a transaction, other event or condition, this determines the accounting policy.

Where there is no applicable standard or interpretation, management must use its judgement to develop and apply an accounting policy. The accounting policy selected must result in information that is:

(a) relevant to the economic decision-making needs of users; and

(b) reliable, in that the financial statements:

   (i) represent faithfully the financial position, financial performance and cash flows of the entity

   (ii) reflect the economic substance of transactions, other events and conditions, and not merely the legal form

   (iii) are neutral, i.e. free from bias

   (iv) are prudent, and

   (v) are complete in all material respects.

There are various sources of guidance available to management in this situation. IAS 8 states that management should use the following:

(a) First, the requirements and guidance in Standards and Interpretations dealing with similar and related issues; then

(b) the definitions, recognition criteria and measurement concepts for assets, liabilities, income and expenses in the *Framework*.

Management may also consider:

(a) the most recent pronouncements of other standard-setting bodies that use a similar conceptual framework to develop accounting standards. (These would include standards issued by the UK Accounting Standards Board and the US Financial Accounting Standards Board.)

(b) other accounting literature and accepted industry practices to the extent that these do not conflict with the sources above.

An entity must select and apply its accounting policies **consistently** for similar transactions, other events and conditions, unless a Standard or an Interpretation specifically requires or permits categorisation of items for which different policies may be appropriate.

If a Standard or an Interpretation requires or permits such categorisation, an appropriate accounting policy shall be selected and applied consistently to each category.

## 1.2 Changes in accounting policies

An entity can only change its accounting policy in two situations:

(a) the change is required by a Standard or an Interpretation; or

(b) it results in the financial statements providing reliable and more relevant information about the effects of transactions, other events or conditions on the entity's financial position, financial performance or cash flows.

## 1.3 Applying changes in accounting policies

IAS 8 states that, when an entity changes an accounting policy as a result of a new Standard or a new Interpretation, it should follow the transitional provisions, if any, in that Standard or Interpretation.

Where there are no transitional provisions, or where an entity changes an accounting policy voluntarily, it should apply the change **retrospectively**.

**Retrospective application** is applying a new accounting policy to transactions, other events and conditions as if that policy had always been applied.

This means that:

(a) the entity adjusts the opening balance of each affected component of equity (retained earnings and other reserves) in the statement of changes in equity; and

(b) comparative amounts are also adjusted.

However, a change in accounting policy does not have to be applied retrospectively where it is impracticable to determine either the period-specific effects or the cumulative effect of the change.

When it is impracticable to determine the cumulative effect of applying a new accounting policy to all prior periods, the entity shall adjust the comparative information to apply the new accounting policy **prospectively** from the earliest date practicable.

**Prospective application** of a change in accounting policy is:

(a) applying the new accounting policy to transactions, other events and conditions occurring after the date as at which the policy is changed; and

(b) recognising the effect of the change in the accounting estimate in the current and future periods affected by the change.

## 1.4 Changes in accounting estimates

A **change in accounting estimate** is an adjustment of the carrying amount of an asset or a liability, or the amount of the periodic consumption of an asset, that results from the assessment of the present status of, and expected future benefits and obligations associated with, assets and liabilities. Changes in accounting estimates result from new information or new developments and, accordingly, are not corrections of errors.

IAS 8 states that the effect of a change in an accounting estimate should be recognised **prospectively** by including it in profit or loss (the income statement) in:

(a) the period of the change, if the change affects that period only; or

(b) the period of the change and future periods, if the change affects both.

Where a change in an accounting estimate gives rise to changes in assets and liabilities, or relates to an item of equity, it is recognised by adjusting the carrying amount of the related asset, liability or equity item in the period of the change.

**Prospective recognition** of the effect of a change in an accounting estimate means that the change is applied to transactions, other events and conditions from the date of the change in estimate.

Because a change in accounting policy affects prior periods and a change in an accounting estimate does not, it is important to be able to distinguish the two. IAS 8 explains that:

(a) a change in the **measurement basis** applied is a change in an accounting policy

(b) when it is difficult to distinguish a change in an accounting policy from a change in an accounting estimate, the change is treated as a change in an accounting estimate.

An entity should disclose the nature and amount of a change in an accounting estimate.

## 1.5 Errors

**Prior period errors** are omissions from, and misstatements in, the entity's financial statements for one or more prior periods arising from a failure to use, or misuse of, reliable information that:

(a) was available when financial statements for those periods were authorised for issue; and

(b) could reasonably be expected to have been obtained and taken into account in the preparation and presentation of those financial statements.

Such errors include the effects of mathematical mistakes, mistakes in applying accounting policies, oversights or misinterpretations of facts, and fraud.

If these corrections are material in amount, their inclusion in the current financial statements without explanation could be misleading.

Omissions or misstatements of items are **material** if they could, individually or collectively, influence the economic decisions of users taken on the basis of the financial statements. Materiality depends on the size and nature of the omission or misstatement judged in the surrounding circumstances. The size or nature of the item, or a combination of both, could be the determining factor.

An entity should correct material prior period errors **retrospectively** in the first set of financial statements authorised for issue after their discovery by:

(a) restating the comparative amounts for the prior period(s) presented in which the error occurred; or

(b) if the error occurred before the earliest prior period presented, restating the opening balances of assets, liabilities and equity for the earliest prior period presented.

In other words, after correction, the financial statements should be stated as if the error had never occurred.

When it is impracticable to determine the cumulative effect, at the beginning of the current period, of an error on all prior periods, the entity shall restate the comparative information to correct the error **prospectively** from the earliest date practicable.

Corrections of errors must be distinguished from changes in accounting estimates. For example, the gain or loss recognised on the outcome of a contingency is not the correction of an error.

# 2 IAS 16 *Property, Plant and Equipment*

## 2.1 The provisions of IAS 16

Property, plant and equipment are tangible assets that:

(a) are held by an entity for use in the production or supply of goods or services, for rental to others, or for administrative purposes; and

(b) are expected to be used for more than one period.

**Depreciable amount** is the cost of an asset, or other amount substituted for cost in the financial statements, less its residual value.

**Depreciation** is the systematic allocation of the depreciable amount of an asset over its useful life.

## 2.2 Recognition

An item of property, plant and equipment should be recognised as an asset when:

(a) it is probable that future economic benefits associated with the asset will flow to the entity; and

(b) the cost of the asset can be measured reliably.

## 2.3 Initial recognition

A tangible non-current asset should initially be measured at its cost. The cost of an item of property, plant and equipment comprises:

(a) its purchase price

(b) any costs directly attributable to bringing the asset to the location and condition necessary for it to be capable of operating in the manner intended by management

(c) the initial estimate of the costs of dismantling and removing the item and restoring the site on which it is located.

Costs should be capitalised until the asset is physically ready for use. They include commissioning costs (e.g. sea trials for a ship, testing a computer system before it goes live).

The following costs are specifically excluded:

- administration and general overheads
- abnormal costs (repairs, wastage, idle time)
- costs incurred after the asset is physically ready for use
- costs incurred in the initial operating period (e.g. any further costs incurred before a machine is used at its full capacity).

## 2.4 Subsequent cost

An entity should apply the recognition principles to any costs incurred after the asset becomes operational. The costs of day-to-day servicing (repairs and maintenance) should not be capitalised. Instead, they should be included in the income statement as they are incurred. In contrast, the cost of replacing parts of items of property, plant and equipment is normally capitalised as it meets the recognition criteria. Examples:

- a furnace may require relining after a specified number of hours of use
- the interior walls of a building may need to be replaced.

## 2.5 Major inspection or overhaul costs

Assets like ships, power stations and so on often require major periodic inspections and overhauls. Failure to carry these out may result in the asset becoming unsafe.

In the past, companies built up provisions for these overhaul costs. When the costs were incurred they would be set against the provision. This complied with the prudence and accruals concepts, and reduced the volatility of profits. These provisions are no longer allowed by IAS 37 because they are avoidable and do not represent an obligation of the entity.

The cost of expected inspections and overhauls is treated as a separate component of the asset, provided it meets the recognition criteria.

## 2.6 Measurement subsequent to initial recognition

IAS 16 allows a choice between the cost model and the revaluation model.

***The cost model***

Property, plant and equipment should be valued at cost less accumulated depreciation.

***The revaluation model***

Property, plant and equipment may be carried at fair value less any subsequent accumulated depreciation.

If the revaluation model is adopted, two conditions must be complied with:

- revaluations must subsequently be made with sufficient regularity to ensure that the carrying amount does not differ materially from the fair value at each balance sheet date
- when an item of property, plant and equipment is revalued, the entire class of assets to which the item belongs must be revalued.

Fair value is normally market value. Where there is no appropriate market value (for example, because the asset is a specialised property of a type that is rarely sold on the open market) other methods such as depreciated replacement cost may be used.

On revaluation, the increase in carrying amount must be credited to equity under the heading of revaluation surplus unless, of course, the increase reverses a previous revaluation decrease of the same asset which was recognised as an expense in the income statement. In that case the increase is credited in the income statement.

Conversely, if the revaluation decreases the value of the asset, the decrease has to be recognised immediately as an expense in the income statement, unless there is a revaluation reserve representing a surplus on the same asset.

## 2.7 Depreciation

All assets with a finite useful life must be depreciated. Depreciation allocates the depreciable amount of an asset to the accounting periods expected to benefit from its use. It applies the accruals concept. The depreciable amount is the cost (or value) less its residual value.

***Example***

An asset costs $100,000 and has an expected useful life of ten years. The purchaser intends to use the asset for six years at which point the expected residual value will be $40,000 (at current prices). If inflation is taken into account the residual value will be $55,000.

The depreciable amount is $(100,000 – 40,000) $60,000 spread over six years. Which method of depreciation is used to allocate the charge is left for the purchaser to decide.

If an asset is held at historical cost, then the depreciation charge is also based on historic cost. If an asset is revalued then the depreciation charge in the income statement should also be based on the revalued amount.

### 2.8 Review of residual value, useful lives and depreciation method

The residual value and the useful life of an asset should be reviewed at least at each financial year-end and revised if necessary. Any adjustments are accounted for as a change in accounting estimate under IAS 8, rather than as a change in accounting policy. This means that they are reflected in the current and future income statements.

The depreciation method used must reflect the pattern in which the asset's future economic benefits are expected to be consumed by the entity.

Depreciation methods should be reviewed at least at each financial year end and changed as necessary. Again, the change is a change in accounting estimate, rather than a change in accounting policy. Therefore it affects the current and future income statement. It is not applied retrospectively.

### 2.9 Depreciation of separate components

Certain large assets are in fact a collection of smaller assets, each with a different cost and useful economic life. For example, an aeroplane consists of an airframe (which may last for 40 years or so) plus engines, radar equipment, seats, etc, all of which have a relatively short life. Instead of calculating depreciation on the aeroplane as a whole, depreciation will be charged on each component (airframe, engines, etc) instead.

***Example***

For example, a company buys a ship for $12m. The ship as a whole should last for 25 years. The engines, however, will need replacing after seven years. The cost price of $12m included about $1.4m in respect of the engines.

The annual depreciation charge will be $624,000 made up as follows:

- engines: $1.4m over seven years = $200,000 pa; plus
- the rest of the ship: $10.6m over 25 years = $424,000 pa.

### 2.10 Impairment losses

The provisions of IAS 36 *Impairment of Assets* must be applied to determine whether an impairment is to be recognised.

### 2.11 Derecognition

Assets are derecognised either on disposal; or when no future economic benefits are expected from their use or disposal.

The gain or loss on derecognition of an asset is the difference between the net disposal proceeds, if any, and the carrying amount of the item.

# 3 IAS 23 *Borrowing Costs*

## 3.1 Introduction

IAS 23 *Borrowing Costs* regulates the extent to which entities are allowed to capitalise borrowing costs incurred on money borrowed to finance the acquisition of certain assets.

## 3.2 The benchmark treatment

The benchmark treatment in IAS 23 is that no borrowing costs should be capitalised – all borrowing costs should be recognised as an expense in the period in which they are incurred.

## 3.3 The allowed alternative treatment

The allowed alternative treatment is that borrowing costs may be capitalised as part of the cost of an asset if that asset is one which necessarily takes a substantial time to get ready for its intended use or sale.

For example, a large building or a major construction contract could qualify if borrowing costs could be directly related to it.

An entity adopting the policy of capitalising borrowing costs must apply that policy to all qualifying borrowing costs.

## 3.4 The rate of interest to be taken

- **Borrowings specifically made to acquire a qualifying asset** – If the borrowings are specially made, the borrowing costs which may be capitalised are those actually incurred, less any investment income on the temporary investment of the borrowings.
- **Funds for the project taken from borrowings generally** – If the funds come from general borrowings, the weighted average cost of general borrowings is taken.

## 3.5 Commencement of capitalisation

Capitalisation of borrowing costs should commence when:

- expenditure for the asset is being incurred
- borrowing costs are being incurred
- activities that are necessary to prepare the asset for its intended use or sale are in progress.

## 3.6 Cessation of capitalisation

Capitalisation of borrowing costs should cease when substantially all the activities necessary to prepare the qualifying asset for its intended use or sale are complete.

## 3.7 Suspension of capitalisation

Capitalisation of borrowing costs should be suspended during extended periods in which active development is interrupted.

# 4 IAS 40 *Investment Property*

## 4.1 Introduction and definition

IAS 40 *Investment Property* prescribes the accounting treatment for investment property.

**Investment property** is property (land or a building – or part of a building – or both) held (by the owner or by the lessee under a finance lease) to earn rentals or for capital appreciation or both, rather than for:

(a) use in the production or supply of goods or services or for administrative purposes, or

(b) sale in the ordinary course of business.

Investment properties are not held for use within the business, but as investments. Therefore it is appropriate to use a different accounting treatment from that used for other types of land and buildings.

## 4.2 Recognition

IAS 40 requires recognition of investment properties as assets when they meet the normal requirements for the recognition of assets – future economic benefits will flow to the entity and the cost of the property can be measured reliably.

## 4.3 Initial measurement

An investment property should initially be measured at cost. Transaction costs (for example, legal fees) are included in cost.

## 4.4 Measurement subsequent to initial recognition

IAS 40 gives an entity the choice of adopting a cost model or a fair value model for its investment properties. The chosen policy must be applied to all the investment properties belonging to the entity.

## 4.5 The cost model

Under the cost model, investment properties are treated like other properties, using the cost model in IAS 16 *Property, Plant and Equipment* – that is, cost less accumulated depreciation and any accumulated impairment losses.

## 4.6 The fair value model

The fair value model requires the entity to revalue its investment properties at fair value each year, any gain or loss being included in the net profit or loss for the period.

Fair value is defined as the amount for which the property could be exchanged between knowledgeable, willing parties in an arm's length transaction.

Fair value will normally be obtainable by reference to current prices in an active market for similar properties in the same location and condition as the property under review. In the absence of such an active market, information from a variety of sources may have to be considered, including:

- current prices in an active market for properties of a different nature, condition or location, adjusted to reflect those differences
- recent prices in less active markets
- discounted cash flow projections based on reliable estimates of future cash flows.

If it becomes impossible to measure fair value reliably, the cost model above should be adopted and retained until the property is disposed of.

### 4.7 Operating leases

A property interest that is held by a lessee under an operating lease may be classified and accounted for as an investment property, if and only if, the property would otherwise meet the definition of an investment property. This classification is available on a property-by-property basis.

However, note that, where a property interest held under an operating lease is classified as an investment property, the fair value model **must** be used for **all** investment properties held by the entity.

### 4.8 Transfers

Transfers to or from investment property may be made only when there is a change of use.

There are four main possibilities:

- Transfer from investment property to owner-occupied property – **Use the fair value at the date of the change for subsequent accounting under IAS 16.**
- **Transfer from investment property to inventory** – Use the fair value at the date of the change for subsequent accounting under IAS 2 *Inventories*.
- **Transfer from owner-occupied property to investment property to be carried at fair value** – IAS 16 (cost less depreciation) will have been applied up to the date of the change. On adopting fair value, the normal treatment will be to recognise a revaluation gain in equity under the heading of revaluation surplus (in the same way as for a normal revaluation). A loss on revaluation is recognised in the income statement.

  The only exceptions to these treatments will arise if the property has previously been revalued upwards, when a decrease may be against the resultant revaluation surplus, or when an impairment loss has previously been recognised, when an increase may be recognised in the income statement.
- **Transfer from inventories to investment property to be carried at fair value** – Any difference between fair value at the date of the transfer and its previous carrying amount should be recognised in the income statement.

### 4.9 Disposals

Gains or losses on the disposal of investment properties should be determined as the difference between net disposal proceeds and the carrying amount of the asset. They will be recognised in the income statement unless IAS 17 *Leases* requires otherwise on a sale and leaseback.

# 5 IAS 38 *Intangible Assets*

## 5.1 Definitions

The more important definitions in IAS 38 are:

(a) **Asset** – an asset is a resource:

  (i) controlled by an entity as a result of past events

  (ii) from which future economic benefits are expected to flow to the entity.

(b) **Intangible asset** – an intangible asset is an identifiable non-monetary asset without physical substance.

(c) **Fair value** – fair value of an asset is the amount for which that asset could be exchanged between knowledgeable, willing parties in an arm's length transaction.

(d) **Active market** – an active market is a market where all the following conditions exist:

  (i) the items traded within the market are homogeneous

  (ii) willing buyers and sellers can normally be found at any time

  (iii) prices are available to the public.

(e) **Impairment loss** – an impairment loss is the amount by which the carrying amount of an asset exceeds its recoverable amount.

(f) **Carrying amount** – carrying amount is the amount at which an asset is recognised in the balance sheet after deducting any accumulated amortisation and accumulated impairment losses thereon.

## 5.2 Recognition of intangible assets

As implied in the definitions above, an intangible asset is recognised if, and only if:

- it is probable that the future economic benefits that are attributable to the asset will flow to the entity
- the cost of the asset can be measured reliably.

An asset meets the identifiability criterion in the definition of an intangible asset when it:

(a) is separable, i.e. is capable of being separated or divided from the entity and sold, transferred, licensed, rented or exchanged, either individually or together with a related contract, asset or liability; or

(b) arises from contractual or other legal rights, regardless of whether those rights are transferable or separable from the entity or from other rights and obligations.

An entity should assess the probability of expected future economic benefits using reasonable and supportable assumptions that represent management's best estimate of the economic conditions that will exist over the useful life of the asset.

The recognition of internally generated intangibles is not prohibited, but the following internally generated items may never be recognised:

- goodwill
- brands

- mastheads
- publishing titles
- customer lists.

Recognition is initially at cost. Cost includes purchase cost and any directly attributable cost of preparing the asset for its intended use. Any subsequent costs must meet the recognition criteria above, otherwise they are expensed when they are incurred.

If an intangible asset is acquired in a business combination, the fair value of that asset at the date of acquisition is taken.

Any intangible which cannot be measured reliably in an acquisition has to be included in goodwill.

## 5.3 Internally generated intangible assets

The main internally generated asset considered in IAS 38 is development costs.

The requirements are:

(a) **Research expenditure** – No intangible asset arising from research should be recognised. (This does not, of course, prevent the recognition of tangible assets used in research.)

(b) **Development expenditure** – An intangible asset arising from development (or from the development phase of an internal project) should be recognised if, and only if, an entity can demonstrate all of the following:

(i) the technical feasibility of completing the intangible asset so that it will be available for use or sale

(ii) its intention to complete the intangible asset and use or sell it

(iii) its ability to use or sell the intangible asset

(iv) how the intangible asset will generate probable future economic benefits. Among other things, the entity should demonstrate the existence of a market for the output of the intangible asset or the intangible asset itself or, if it is to be used internally, the usefulness of the intangible asset

(v) the availability of adequate technical, financial and other resources to complete the development and to use or sell the intangible asset

(vi) its ability to measure the expenditure attributable to the intangible asset during its development reliably.

The amount to be included is the cost of the development. Note that expenditure, once treated as an expense, cannot be reinstated as an asset.

## 5.4 Measurement after initial recognition

IAS 38 allows a choice between the cost model or the revaluation model. If an intangible asset is accounted for using the revaluation model, all the other assets in its class shall also be accounted for using the same model, unless there is no active market for those assets. A class of intangible assets is a grouping of assets of a similar nature and use in an entity's operations.

***Cost model***

An intangible asset is be carried at its cost less any accumulated amortisation and any accumulated impairment losses.

***Revaluation model***

Intangibles may be carried at a revalued amount, being fair value at the date of the revaluation less any accumulated amortisation and any subsequent accumulated impairment losses.

Fair value should be determined by reference to an active market. Revaluations should be made with sufficient regularity such that the carrying amount does not differ materially from that which would be determined using fair value at the balance sheet date.

The revaluation model does not allow:

- the revaluation of intangible assets that have not previously been recognised as assets, or
- the initial recognition of intangible assets at amounts other than their cost.

Note that an active market must exist if revaluation is to be permitted.

Revaluation gains and losses are accounted for in the same way as revaluation gains and losses of tangible assets under IAS 16.

## 5.5 Useful life

An entity should assess whether the useful life of an intangible asset is finite or indefinite. An intangible asset should be regarded as having an indefinite useful life when, based on an analysis of all of the relevant factors, there is no foreseeable limit to the period over which the asset is expected to generate net cash inflows for the entity.

Many factors are considered in determining the useful life of an intangible asset, including:

(a) the expected usage of the asset by the entity and whether the asset could be managed efficiently by another management team

(b) typical product life cycles for the asset and public information on estimates of useful lives of similar assets that are used in a similar way

(c) technical, technological, commercial or other types of obsolescence

(d) the stability of the industry in which the asset operates and changes in the market demand for the products or services output from the asset

(e) expected actions by competitors or potential competitors

(f) the level of maintenance expenditure required to obtain the expected future economic benefits from the asset and the entity's ability and intention to reach such a level

(g) the period of control over the asset and legal or similar limits on the use of the asset, such as the expiry dates of related leases

(h) whether the useful life of the asset is dependent on the useful life of other assets of the entity.

Computer software and many other intangible assets are susceptible to technological obsolescence. Therefore, it is likely that their useful life is short.

The useful life of an intangible asset may be very long or even indefinite. Uncertainty justifies estimating the useful life of an intangible asset on a prudent basis, but it does not justify choosing a life that is unrealistically short.

The useful life of an intangible asset that arises from contractual or other legal rights should not exceed the period of the contractual or other legal rights, but may be shorter depending on the period over which the entity expects to use the asset.

## 5.6 Amortisation

The depreciable amount of an intangible asset should be allocated on a systematic basis over its useful life. Amortisation should commence when the asset is available for use.

The amortisation method used should reflect the pattern in which the asset's economic benefits are consumed by the entity. If that pattern cannot be determined reliably, the straight-line method should be used.

The residual value of an intangible asset with a finite useful life is assumed to be zero unless:

(a) there is a commitment by a third party to purchase the asset at the end of its useful life; or

(b) there is an active market for the asset and residual value can be determined by reference to that market; and it is probable that such a market will exist at the end of the asset's useful life.

The amortisation period and the amortisation method should be reviewed at least each financial year end, and revised if necessary. Any adjustments are treated as changes in accounting estimates under IAS 8.

***Intangible assets with indefinite useful lives***

An intangible asset with an indefinite useful life should not be amortised.

The useful life of an intangible asset that is not being amortised shall be reviewed each period to determine whether events and circumstances continue to support an indefinite useful life assessment for that asset. If they do not, the change in the useful life assessment from indefinite to finite shall be accounted for as a change in an accounting estimate in accordance with IAS 8.

Reassessing the useful life of an intangible asset as finite rather than indefinite is an indicator that the asset may be impaired and therefore it should be tested for impairment as required by IAS 36.

## 5.7 Impairment losses

IAS 36 *Impairment of Assets* should be applied to determine whether the value of an intangible asset is impaired.

## 5.8 Retirements and disposals

An intangible asset is derecognised on disposal or when no future economic benefits are expected from its use or disposal.

The gain or loss arising from the derecognition of an intangible asset is the difference between the net disposal proceeds, if any, and the carrying amount of the asset.

# 6 IAS 2 *Inventories*

## 6.1 Lower of cost and net realisable value (NRV)

The basic principle of IAS 2 is that inventories should be valued at the lower of cost and NRV.

(a) **Cost**

(i) 'Cost' is the cost of bringing items of inventory to their present location and condition (cost of purchase and costs of conversion).

(ii) Cost of purchase comprises purchase price including import duties, transport and handling costs and any other directly attributable costs, less trade discounts, rebates and subsidies.

(iii) Cost of conversion comprises:

- costs which are specifically attributable to units of production, e.g. direct labour, direct expenses and sub-contracted work
- production overheads
- other overheads, if any, attributable in the particular circumstances of the business to bringing the product or service to its present location and condition.

(iv) Production overhead must be based on the normal level of activity.

The following costs should be excluded and charged as expenses of the period in which they are incurred:

(i) abnormal waste

(ii) storage costs

(iii) administrative overheads which do not contribute to bringing inventories to their present location and condition

(iv) selling costs.

(b) **NRV**

Estimated selling price less all costs to complete and all costs necessary to make the sale (i.e. all costs to be incurred in marketing, selling and distribution).

## 6.2 Valuation methods

Where items of inventory are not ordinarily interchangeable, IAS 2 requires such items to be shown at their actual individual costs.

Otherwise, the cost of inventories should be assigned by using either the first-in-first-out method (FIFO) or the weighted average cost method. The last-in-first-out method (LIFO) is no longer allowed.

The same method of arriving at cost should be used for all inventories having similar nature and use to the entity. For inventories with different nature or use, different cost methods may be justified.

# 7 IAS 11 *Construction Contracts*

## 7.1 Introduction

A construction contract is one for a substantial asset like a bridge, a building, a dam, a ship or a tunnel. Such contracts are likely to extend over more than one accounting period, and rules are needed to determine when the profit on them can be taken. One possibility would be to defer taking the profit until the contract was completed, but this could lead to very misleading income statements. The principle established in IAS 11 is that profit can be recognised once the outcome of the contract can be estimated reliably as profitable. The percentage of completion of the contract determines the profit that can be taken.

## 7.2 Recognition of contract revenue and expenses

Revenue and expenses may be recognised when the outcome of a contract can be estimated reliably.

If the expected outcome is a profit, revenue and expenses will be recognised according to the stage of completion of the contract.

If the expected outcome is a loss, the whole loss to completion should be recognised immediately.

IAS 11 establishes the conditions to be met before it can be taken that the outcome of a contract can be estimated reliably:

(a) **fixed price contracts**

- (i) total contract revenue can be measured reliably
- (ii) it is probable that the economic benefits associated with the contract will flow to the entity
- (iii) both the contract costs to complete the contract and the stage of contract completion at the balance sheet date can be measured reliably
- (iv) the contract costs attributable to the contract can be clearly identified and measured reliably so that actual contract costs incurred can be compared with prior estimates.

(b) **cost plus contracts**

- (i) it is probable that the economic benefits associated with the contract will flow to the entity
- (ii) the contract costs attributable to the contract, whether or not specifically reimbursable, can be clearly identified and measured reliably.

When the outcome of a construction contract cannot be estimated reliably:

- revenue should be recognised only to the extent of contract costs incurred that it is probable will be recoverable
- contract costs should be recognised as an expense in the period in which they are incurred.

An expected loss on the construction contract should be recognised as an expense immediately.

### 7.3 Determining the stage of completion of a contract

IAS 11 indicates several ways in which the percentage of completion of a contract may be arrived at:

(a) the proportion that contract costs incurred for work performed to date bear to the estimated total contract costs, or

(b) surveys of work performed, or

(c) completion of a physical proportion of the contract work.

It is important to remember that progress payments and advances received from customers often do not reflect the work performed.

In examination questions (a) is the most commonly found.

### 7.4 Presentation in financial statements

(a) **Income statement** – If no profit is being taken on the contract, but there is no reason to suppose that a loss will arise, the income statement will include revenue equal to recoverable costs incurred. The recoverable costs will also appear, so that no profit arises.

If the contract is at a stage when profit can be taken, revenue and expenses corresponding to the stage of completion reached will be taken. If profit has already been taken in one or more earlier periods, the revenue and costs recognised will obviously be the difference between their current levels and those recognised up to the previous income statement.

If a loss is expected on completion, the loss to date will be brought in by the inclusion of the revenue and costs to date. It is then necessary to include as an expense the remainder of the loss expected to arise between the current balance sheet date and completion of the contract.

(b) **Balance sheet** – The balance sheet should disclose:

(i) the gross amount due from customers for contract work as an asset

(ii) the gross amount due to customers for contract work as a liability.

The gross amount due from customers for contract work is the net amount of:

- costs incurred plus recognised profits, less
- the sum of recognised losses and progress billings

for all contracts in progress for which costs incurred plus recognised profits (less recognised losses) exceeds progress billings.

The gross amount due to customers for contract work is the net amount of:

- costs incurred plus recognised profits, less
- the sum of recognised losses and progress billings

for all contracts in progress for which progress billings exceed costs incurred plus recognised profits (less recognised losses).

The amount shown as an asset could thus include:

- progress billings not yet paid
- contract costs relating to future activity (e.g. an inventory of goods on site not yet billed to the customer).

# 8 IAS 17 *Leases*

## 8.1 Classification of leases

A **lease** is an agreement whereby the lessor conveys to the lessee in return for a payment or series of payments the right to use an asset for an agreed period of time.

IAS 17 recognises two types of lease – finance leases and operating leases.

A **finance lease** is a lease that transfers substantially all the risks and rewards incidental to ownership of an asset. Title may or may not eventually be transferred.

An **operating lease** is a lease other than a finance lease. In other words, an operating lease is one which runs for significantly less than the useful life of the asset concerned.

IAS 17 provides guidance as to the classification of leases as finance leases or operating leases. It gives the following list of situations in which a lease would normally be classified as a finance lease:

- the lease transfers ownership of the asset to the lessee by the end of the lease term (thus hire purchase transactions qualify)
- the lessee has the option to buy the asset at a price expected to be lower than fair value at that time
- the lease term is for the major part of the economic life of the asset even if title is not transferred
- at the beginning of the lease the present value of the minimum lease payments (see below) is approximately equal to the fair value of the asset (If the lease payments exceed 90% of the fair value, this is indicative of a finance lease.)
- the leased assets are of a specialised nature so that only the lessee can use them without major modification
- if the lease gives the lessee the right to cancel the lease, the lessor's losses associated with the cancellation are borne by the lessee
- gains or losses from fluctuations in fair value are borne by the lessee
- the lessee has the ability to continue the lease for a secondary period at a rent below the market rent.

***Accounting for operating leases***

Accounting for operating leases is simple. Hire charges due under the lease are debited to an expense account as they are incurred and appear in the lessee's income statement as an expense.

***Accounting for finance leases***

The IAS 17 treatment follows the definition of an asset in the IASB *Framework*: 'an asset is a resource controlled by the entity as a result of past events and from which future economic benefits are expected to flow to the entity'. Ownership is not necessary, control is the essential feature.

IAS 17 thus argues that an asset leased under a finance lease must be recorded as an asset and a corresponding liability in the lessee's accounting records.

## 8.2 Valuation of assets leased under finance leases

IAS 17 requires the asset and the associated liability to be recorded initially at its fair value or, if lower, at the present value of the minimum lease payments.

**Minimum lease payments** are the payments over the lease term that the lessee is, or can be required to make, together with:

(a) in the case of the lessee, any amounts guaranteed by the lessee, or

(b) in the case of the lessor, any residual value guaranteed to the lessor by the lessee.

In calculating the present value of the minimum lease payments the discount factor is determined by the interest rate implicit in the lease, if this is practicable to determine; if not, the lessee's incremental borrowing rate is used.

***Illustration – calculating the present value of the minimum lease payments (MLPs)***

An asset with a useful life of four years is to be leased for the four years at an annual cost of $2,000 payable annually in arrears. The cash price of the asset is $5,710.

The interest rate implicit in the lease is the rate at which the payments made under the lease must be discounted to make them equal to the initial cost. In this case the rate is 15%, as the following calculation shows:

| | | *Payment* | *Discount factor at 15%* | *Net present value* |
|---|---|---|---|---|
| | | $ | | $ |
| Year | 1 | 2,000 | 0.870 | 1,740 |
| | 2 | 2,000 | 0.756 | 1,512 |
| | 3 | 2,000 | 0.657 | 1,314 |
| | 4 | 2,000 | 0.572 | 1,144 |
| Present value of MLPs | | | | 5,710 |

In an examination question the interest rate implicit in the lease will normally be given.

## 8.3 Recording finance leases in the books of the lessee

***Initial entries***

At the start of the lease:

- the fair value of the asset (or the present value of the minimum lease payments if lower) should be included as a non-current asset, subject to depreciation
- the obligation to pay rentals should be included as a liability.

***Depreciation***

The related non-current asset should be depreciated over the shorter of:

(a) the economic useful life of the asset (as per IAS 16)

(b) the lease term.

The lease term is essentially the period over which the lessee has the use of the asset. It includes:

(i) the primary (non-cancellable) period, plus

(ii) any secondary periods during which the lessee has the contractual right to continue to use the asset, provided that it is reasonably certain at the outset that this right will be exercised.

***Allocation of finance charges***

(a) Over the period of the lease, the total finance charge is the amount by which the rentals paid to the lessor exceed the present value of the minimum lease payments.

(b) Each individual rental payment should be split between:

(i) finance charge (income statement item)

(ii) repayment of obligation to pay rentals (thus reducing the balance sheet liability).

(c) How should finance charges be allocated over the term of the lease? The basic aim is to allocate the charge in such a way as to produce a reasonably constant periodic rate of return on the remaining balance of liability. There are three main methods:

(i) actuarial method

(ii) sum of the digits (rule of 78) method

(iii) straight-line method.

Of the above methods the actuarial method gives the most accurate result.

### *Example of the actuarial method*

This example builds on the illustration earlier.

A company has two options. It can buy an asset for cash at a cost of $5,710 or it can lease it by way of a finance lease. The terms of the lease are as follows:

1 primary period is for four years from 1 January 20X2 with a rental of $2,000 pa payable on the 31 December each year

2 the lessee has the right to continue to lease the asset after the end of the primary period for an indefinite period, subject only to a nominal rent

3 the lessee is required to pay all repair, maintenance and insurance costs as they arise

4 the interest rate implicit in the lease is 15%.

The lessee estimates the useful economic life of the asset to be eight years. Depreciation is provided on a straight-line basis.

### *Solution*

**Step 1**

The asset is shown in the balance sheet at $5,710 (subject to depreciation).

Depreciation is over four years (presumably no residual value to the asset at the end of four years).

Annual depreciation charge = 1/4 × $5,710 = $1,428

**Step 2**

The liability is shown in the balance sheet at $5,710 but subsequently reduced by the capital portion of the leasing payments.

The total finance charge is \$(8,000 – 5,710) = \$2,290. The allocation of this to each rental payment and the consequent capital sum outstanding is calculated as follows:

| *1* Period (year ended 31 December) | *2* Capital sum at start of period | *3* Finance charge at 15% pa | *4* Sub-total | *5* Rental paid | *6* Capital sum at end of period |
|---|---|---|---|---|---|
| | \$ | \$ | \$ | \$ | \$ |
| 20X2 | 5,710 | 856 | 6,566 | (2,000) | 4,566 |
| 20X3 | 4,566 | 685 | 5,251 | (2,000) | 3,251 |
| 20X4 | 3,251 | 488 | 3,739 | (2,000) | 1,739 |
| 20X5 | 1,739 | 261 | 2,000 | (2,000) | – |
| | | 2,290 | | 8,000 | |

The finance charge each year is a constant periodic rate of return (15%) on the remaining balance of liability, e.g. \$856 is 15% of \$5,710, etc.

The format in step 2 is used whenever the payments under a lease are made in arrears. If the payments are due in advance, the rental paid is deducted from the capital sum at the start of the period before the interest is calculated. In other words, columns 3 and 5 would be reversed.

## 8.4 Recording operating leases in the books of the lessee

Rentals under operating leases should be charged to the income statement on a straight-line basis over the term of the lease unless another systematic and rational basis is more appropriate. Any difference between amounts charged and amounts paid should be adjusted to prepayments or accruals.

## 8.5 Leases of land and buildings

Land normally has an indefinite economic life and therefore the lessee normally does not receive substantially all of the risks and rewards incidental to ownership. Therefore a lease of land is normally an operating lease.

Where there is a lease of land and buildings, the land and buildings elements are considered separately for the purposes of lease classification. When the land has an indefinite economic life (which is normally the case), the land element is normally classified as an operating lease and the buildings element is classified as a finance or operating lease as appropriate.

Where a lease of land and buildings is treated as two separate leases, the minimum lease payments are allocated between the land and the buildings elements in proportion to the relative fair values of the leasehold interests in the land element and buildings element of the lease at the inception of the lease. If the lease payments cannot be allocated reliably between these two elements, the entire lease is classified as a finance lease, unless it is clear that both elements are operating leases, in which case the entire lease is classified as an operating lease.

# 9 IAS 37 *Provisions, Contingent Liabilities and Contingent Assets*

## 9.1 The problem

A **provision** is a liability of uncertain timing or amount.

A **liability** is a present obligation of the entity arising from past events, the settlement of which is expected to result in an outflow from the entity of resources embodying economic benefits.

Provisions may be made for items such as environmental liabilities, reorganisation costs, litigation and future losses. Before IAS 37 was issued there was no accounting standard covering the general topic of provisions.

This led to various problems:

- provisions were sometimes recognised as a result of an intention to make expenditure, rather than on an obligation to do so
- several items could be aggregated into one large provision that was reported as a single large item (the 'big bath')
- inadequate disclosure meant that in some cases it was difficult to ascertain the significance of the provisions and any movements in the year.

Therefore there was considerable scope for manipulation of earnings. In addition, the usefulness of the balance sheet as a statement of current financial position was considerably reduced. Inconsistencies in accounting practice reduced comparability of performance over time and between different companies.

## 9.2 Recognition

A provision should only be recognised when:

- the entity has a present obligation as a result of a past event
- it is probable that a transfer of resources embodying economic benefits will be required to settle the obligation
- a reliable estimate can be made of the amount of the obligation.

If a reasonable estimate of the amount required for a provision cannot be made, there should be disclosure of the nature of the obligation and the factors that are relevant in determining the amount and timing of the future expenditure.

A legal liability arises from the operation of law, e.g. contract or statutes. A constructive obligation arises from the facts in a particular situation where, although no legal entitlement exists, those outside the entity have other sanctions that leave the entity with no realistic alternative to certain expenditures. An example of a constructive obligation is a retail store that habitually refunds purchases by dissatisfied customers even though it is under no legal obligation to do so; a change to this policy would incur unacceptable damage to the entity's reputation.

## 9.3 Measurement

The amount recognised as a provision should be the best estimate of the expenditure required to settle the obligation that existed at the balance sheet date. The best estimate should be made on a prudent basis.

In determining a prudent estimate:

- regard should be had to the risks associated with the cash flows
- reasonably expected future events (e.g. changes in technology and new legislation) should be taken into account where there is sufficient objective evidence that they will occur
- the amount recognised should be discounted where this has a material effect.

Where the provision is discounted:

- the amount recognised should be calculated either by discounting cash flows measured at current prices using a real discount rate or by discounting cash flows measured at estimated future prices using a nominal discount rate
- the provision should be measured on a pre-tax basis, as the tax consequences of the provision are dealt with in accordance with IAS 12.

The amortisation of the discount should be included in interest, but separately disclosed from other interest on the face of the income statement.

## 9.4 Offset

Sometimes an entity is able to look to another party, such as an insurance company, to pay part or all of the expenditure required to settle an obligation. The question arises as to whether a provision should be recognised net of the amount to be reimbursed by the other party or whether the provision and the reimbursement should be recognised separately as a liability and an asset.

The IASB requires that generally the liability and the recovery should be treated as a separate liability and a separate asset. This is because, in most cases, the reporting entity remains liable for the full amount, regardless of whether it can recover expenditure from a third party.

Amounts should only be offset where the reporting entity no longer has an obligation for that part of the expenditure to be met by the third party.

## 9.5 Future operating losses

In the past, provisions have sometimes been recognised for future operating losses on the grounds of prudence.

No provisions should be recognised for future operating losses, although a net loss should be recognised when a contract becomes onerous.

An onerous contract is a contract entered into with another party under which the unavoidable costs of fulfilling the terms of the contract exceed any revenues expected to be received from the goods or services supplied and where the entity would have to compensate the other party if it did not fulfil the terms of the contract.

An example of an onerous contract is vacant leasehold property.

Where future operating losses are expected, the assets of the loss-making operation should be reviewed for impairment. Expected future losses are one of the indications that the value of assets may have become impaired.

## 9.6 Use of provisions

Provisions should be used only for expenditure that relates to the matter for which the provision was originally recognised.

## 9.7 Reorganisations and restructuring

A restructuring is a programme that is planned and controlled by management and has a material effect on:

(a) the scope of a business undertaken by the reporting entity in terms of the products or services it provides, or

(b) the manner in which a business undertaken by the reporting entity is conducted.

In the past, provisions have frequently been made for reorganisations and restructuring. Reorganisations may include terminating a line of business, the closure of locations where business is carried on, changes in management structure and cost reduction programmes.

The IASB requires that provisions for reorganisation/restructuring should be recognised only when an entity is demonstrably committed to the reorganisation, i.e. specific actions must have been taken so that others can be expected to act on the basis that the reorganisation will proceed and in so doing, leave the entity without realistic possibility of withdrawal.

A Board decision on its own is not a demonstrable commitment, unless the membership of the Board contains representatives of interests other than management, as is the case in some countries. Announcement of plans to the public or to employees might constitute commitment, depending on the level of detail communicated.

Provisions for reorganisations should include only those expenditures that are both:

(a) necessarily entailed by a reorganisation to which the entity is demonstrably committed

(b) not associated with ongoing or new activities of the entity.

## 9.8 Contingent liabilities and contingent assets

A contingent liability is:

(a) a possible obligation that arises from past events and whose existence will be confirmed only by the occurrence of one or more uncertain future events not wholly within the entity's control, or

(b) a present obligation that arises from past events but is not recognised because:

   (i) it is not probable that a transfer of economic benefits will be required to settle the obligation, or

   (ii) the amount of the obligation cannot be measured with sufficient reliability.

A contingent asset is a possible asset that arises from past events and whose existence will be confirmed only by the occurrence of one or more uncertain future events not wholly within the entity's control.

Contingent liabilities should not be recognised. They should be disclosed unless the possibility of a transfer of economic benefits is remote.

Contingent assets should not be recognised. (Recognition of contingent assets could result in the recognition of profit that may never be realised.) If the possibility of an inflow of economic benefits is probable, they should be disclosed.

Only if a gain is virtually certain should it be recognised (because it cannot then be a contingency).

# 10 Current tax

## 10.1 Income taxes

The income tax on the profits for the year is charged to the income statement. Any tax charged but not paid is shown as a liability in the balance sheet. In many countries the exact tax charge will not be known until after the financial statements have been published. In these cases the charge for the year will be the best estimate possible at the balance sheet date. Any difference between the actual and the estimated charge will be adjusted for in the following year.

## 10.2 Imputation and dividends paid

In some countries companies are required to make an early payment of income tax if and when they pay a dividend. This affects the timing of the tax payment, and not the amount. The tax charge in the income statement will not be affected by payments. The dividend charged to the Statement of Changes in Equity will be the dividend paid, excluding any tax payment. Any payment made will reduce the balance sheet liability for income tax.

## 10.3 Withholding taxes on dividends paid

In some countries companies are required to deduct tax from dividends paid to shareholders. This tax is then paid over to the tax authorities. This tax will be charged to equity as part of the dividend paid.

## 10.4 Tax on dividends received

In some countries dividends are received net of tax, with no further tax to pay. In the past these dividends were grossed-up with a notional amount of tax. Nowadays, the general rule is to recognise dividend income at the cash amount received.

# 11 Deferred tax

## 11.1 The need for deferred tax

Profit for tax purposes may differ from the profit shown by the financial statements. Such a difference may be caused by permanent or temporary factors. For example, if an expense in the income statement is not allowed for tax purposes, a permanent difference arises. Nothing can be done about that, and the increased tax charge just has to be accepted. A temporary difference arises when an expense is allowed for both tax and accounting purposes, but the timing of the allowance differs. For example, if relief for capital expenditure is given at a faster rate for tax purposes than the depreciation in the financial statements, the tax charge will be lower in the first year than it would have been if based on the accounting profit, but in subsequent years the tax charge will be higher.

***Example***

A company buys a non-current asset for $10,000. It has a useful life of five years and is to be depreciated on the straight-line basis.

For tax purposes, 50% of the cost is allowed in year 1 and the remainder spread equally over the remaining four years.

The relevant tax rate is 30% throughout.

At the end of each of the five years the values of the asset will be:

| | | *Tax value* | *Accounting value* | *Difference* |
|---|---|---|---|---|
| | | $ | $ | $ |
| On purchase | | 10,000 | 10,000 | |
| End year | 1 | 5,000 | 8,000 | 3,000 |
| | 2 | 3,750 | 6,000 | 2,250 |
| | 3 | 2,500 | 4,000 | 1,500 |
| | 4 | 1,250 | 2,000 | 750 |
| | 5 | nil | nil | nil |

At the end of year 1 the tax value is $3,000 less than the accounting value, and the taxable profit will also be $3,000 less than the accounting profit. As a result the tax payable will be $900 ($3,000 at 30%) less.

But, in the years 2 to 5, the difference gradually disappears. In each of these years, the taxable profit will be $750 more than the accounting profit, and thus the effect will be an increased tax charge of $225 in each year.

There are several possible courses of action to deal with this situation. One is to do nothing, and simply accept the reduced tax charge in year 1 and the increased tax charges in years 2 to 5. This is the so-called flow through method, in which differences between tax values and accounting values are ignored.

IAS 12 *Income Taxes* is based on the idea that the $900 reduction in tax in year 1 is only a temporary gain – a liability for it does arise in year 1 but it is deferred until the four later years in which the tax charge is increased.

## 11.2 Accounting entries and the effect on the income statement

Let us continue the example above to show the effect on the income statement. We will assume that the company's annual accounting profit before tax was $20,000 and that the only difference for tax purposes is the adjustment for the asset considered above.

**Income statements**

| Year 1 | *Flow through method* | | *With deferred tax* |
|---|---|---|---|
| | $ | $ | $ |
| Profit before tax | 20,000 | | 20,000 |
| Tax (30% × 17,000) | 5,100 | 5,100 | |
| Deferred tax | | 900 | 6,000 |
| | 14,900 | | 14,000 |
| Years 2 to 5 | | | |
| Profit before tax | 20,000 | | 20,000 |
| Tax (30% × 20,750) | 6,225 | 6,225 | |
| Less: Transfer from deferred tax | | (225) | 6,000 |
| | 13,775 | | 14,000 |

The result of introducing deferred tax is that the tax charge is based on the accounting profit in each year. This will seldom be the case in practice, of course, because there will be permanent differences which cannot be adjusted for.

## 11.3 Reasons for recognising deferred tax

It can be argued that failure to allow for deferred tax leads to distortion of the post-tax profit and failure to recognise a liability which will eventually arise.

**Reasons for recognising deferred tax**

(a) The accruals concept requires its recognition.

(b) The deferred tax will be a liability eventually.

(c) The overstatement of profit caused by failing to allow for deferred tax liabilities can lead to:

   (i) over-optimistic dividend payments based on inflated profits

   (ii) distortion of earnings per share and of the price/earnings ratio, both important indicators of a company's performance

   (iii) shareholders being misled.

## 11.4 Methods of accounting for deferred tax

There are two main methods of accounting for deferred tax – the deferral method and the liability method. The liability method may be subdivided into two – the income statement liability method and the balance sheet liability method.

***The deferral method***

Under the deferral method, the original amount set aside for deferred tax is retained without alteration for subsequent changes in tax rate.

***The liability method***

Using the liability method, the deferred tax balance is adjusted as tax rates change, thus maintaining the amount at the actual liability expected to arise.

***The income statement liability method and the balance sheet liability method***

The difference between these two methods is largely conceptual. The resultant deferred tax figure will be the same. The income statement liability method focuses on the differences between taxable profit and accounting profit, while under the balance sheet method the calculation is made by reference to balance sheet values and tax values of assets and liabilities.

IAS 12 requires the use of the balance sheet liability method.

## 11.5 The extent of the deferred tax provision

Whichever method of accounting for deferred tax is adopted, there is a choice as to the extent of the provision:

- **Nil provision** – This is the flow through method already referred to, in which no provision is made for deferred tax. Dissatisfaction with the results of this approach led to the development of methods of accounting for deferred tax.

- **Full provision** – Provision is automatically made for the tax effects of all temporary differences.

- **Partial provision** – Provision is only made to the extent that it is expected that a liability will actually arise.

IAS 12 requires full provision.

# 12 IAS 12 *Income Taxes*

## 12.1 Introduction

Although IAS 12 covers current tax, it is mainly concerned with the accounting treatment of deferred tax.

IAS 12 calls for the adoption of the balance sheet liability method, in which deferred tax is calculated by reference to the tax base of an asset or liability.

The tax base is the amount attributed to the asset or liability for tax purposes.

The tax base of an asset is therefore the amount that will be deductible for tax purposes against any future taxable benefits derived from the asset. If the benefits will not be taxable, the tax base of the asset is equal to its carrying amount.

The tax base of a liability is its carrying amount, less any amount that will be deductible for tax purposes in respect of that liability in future periods. In the case of revenue received in advance, the tax base of the resulting liability is its carrying amount, less any amount of the revenue that will not be taxable in future periods.

## 12.2 Temporary differences

The difference between the tax base of an asset or liability and its carrying value is described as a temporary difference.

If the carrying value of an asset exceeds the tax base, deferred tax must be provided for, and the temporary difference is said to be a taxable temporary difference.

If the tax base of an asset exceeds the carrying value, the temporary difference is a deductible temporary difference.

### *Example 1 – tax base of assets*

The ideas above are difficult to understand without some concrete examples, and IAS 12 provides them.

Here are five examples to illustrate deferred tax relating to assets. The tax rate is taken as 25% throughout both examples.

(a) A machine cost 100. For tax purposes, depreciation of 30 has already been deducted in the current and prior periods and the remaining cost will be deductible in future periods, either as depreciation or through a deduction on disposal. Revenue generated by using the machine is taxable, any gain on disposal of the machine will be taxable and any loss on disposal will be deductible for tax purposes.

The tax base of the asset is 70 (100 – 30), because 70 remains to be deducted in future periods.

If the carrying value in the accounting records is 90, there is a taxable temporary difference of 20, and a deferred tax liability of 5 would be recognised.

(b) Interest receivable has a carrying amount of 100. The related interest revenue will be taxed on a cash basis.

The fact that interest receivable exists as an asset means that the interest has already been recognised in the income statement. Tax will arise in the following accounting period in which the interest is actually received.

The tax base of the interest receivable is nil, because the accrual does not exist for tax purposes.

There is thus a taxable temporary difference of 100 (100 – 0), and a deferred tax liability of 25 must be recognised.

(c) Trade receivables have a carrying amount of 100. The related revenue has already been included in taxable profit.

This example differs from (b) because the 100 has been included in the income statement and in the taxable profit for the period just ended. There are no future taxable benefits, and therefore the tax base is equal to the carrying value. No deferred tax arises.

(d) Dividends receivable from a subsidiary have a carrying amount of 100. The dividends are not taxable.

Applying the same reasoning as in (b) above, the tax base is nil, leading to a taxable temporary difference of 100 but, as the dividend is not taxable, no deferred tax liability arises. Alternatively, we may say that, as the benefits will not be taxable, the tax base is equal to the carrying amount and no deferred tax arises.

(e) A loan receivable has a carrying amount of 100. The repayment of the loan will have no tax consequences.

The tax base of the loan is 100 and no deferred tax arises.

***Example 2 – tax base of liabilities***

(a) Current liabilities include accrued expenses with a carrying amount of 100. The related expense will be deducted for tax purposes on a cash basis.

The expense has been recognised but the tax effect has not. The tax base is therefore nil (100 – 100), and there is a deductible temporary difference of 100, leading to a deferred tax asset of 25.

(b) Current liabilities include interest revenue received in advance, with a carrying amount of 100. The related interest revenue was taxed on a cash basis.

As tax has already been charged, but credit has not yet been taken for the interest revenue, there is a deductible temporary difference of 100, and a deferred tax asset of 25 is recognised. (The tax base of the interest received is nil.)

(c) Current liabilities include accrued expenses with a carrying amount of 100. The related expense has already been deducted for tax purposes.

The expense and its tax expense have both been recognised. No deferred tax arises.

(d) Current liabilities include accrued fines and penalties with a carrying amount of 100. Fines and penalties are not deductible for tax purposes.

No amount will be deductible for tax purposes, and the tax base is accordingly 100. No deferred tax arises.

(e) A loan payable has a carrying amount of 100. The repayment of the loan will have no tax consequences.

Once again there will be no future tax effect. The tax base is the same as carrying value and there is no deferred tax.

## 12.3 Items which are neither assets nor liabilities

Some items have a tax base but are not recognised as assets and liabilities in the balance sheet. For example, research costs are recognised as an expense in determining accounting profit in the period in which they are incurred but may not be permitted as a deduction in determining taxable profit (tax loss) until a later period. The difference between the tax base of the research costs, being the amount the taxation authorities will permit as a deduction in future periods, and the carrying amount of nil is a deductible temporary difference that results in a deferred tax asset.

## 12.4 The fundamental principle of IAS 12

The fundamental principle of IAS 12 is that an entity should, with certain limited exceptions, recognise a deferred tax liability or asset whenever the recovery or settlement of the carrying amount of an asset or liability would make future tax payments larger or smaller than they would be if such recovery or settlement were to have no tax consequences.

It may be helpful to look again at the examples above with this principle in mind.

## 12.5 Recognition of deferred tax liabilities

IAS 12 requires a deferred tax liability to be recognised for all taxable temporary differences, with minor exceptions.

The main exception is that no deferred tax liability should be recognised if it arises from the initial recognition of goodwill.

IAS 12 thus requires full provision for deferred tax.

### *Examples of taxable temporary differences*

(a) Transactions affecting the income statement

- (i) Interest revenue received in arrears, included in the accounting profit on a time apportionment basis but taxable on a cash basis.
- (ii) Depreciation of an asset is accelerated for tax purposes.
- (iii) Development costs have been capitalised and will be amortised to the income statement but were deducted for tax purposes as incurred.
- (iv) Prepaid expenses have already been deducted on a cash basis for tax purposes but are to be charged in the income statement in a later period.

(b) Transactions affecting the balance sheet

(i) Current investments are carried at fair value which exceeds cost, but remain at cost for tax purposes.

(ii) Non-current assets are revalued upwards for accounting purposes with no adjustment for tax purposes.

## 12.6 Deferred tax and groups

***Fair value adjustments***

Fair value adjustments on consolidation give rise to temporary differences. The values at which the subsidiary's assets and liabilities are recognised in the consolidated financial statements changes, but there is no effect on the tax bases of the assets. This is because the tax charge is based on the profit made by the subsidiary, rather than by the group as a whole.

Deferred tax should therefore be provided.

***Intra-group adjustments***

An intra-group sale results in a provision for unrealised profit on any inventory that has not yet been sold outside the group. This provision for unrealised profit represents a temporary difference:

- When an intra-group sale is made, the profit is taxed both in the accounts of the individual group company making the sale **and** in the consolidated financial statements.
- However, from the point of view of the **group**, the profit does not arise until the following year, when the goods are sold outside the group and the provision for unrealised profit is released.

Therefore deferred tax must be provided.

## 12.7 Deferred tax assets

The basis for the recognition of deferred tax assets is not quite the same as that for deferred tax liabilities. The rule in IAS 12 is that deferred tax assets should be recognised for all deductible temporary differences 'to the extent that it is probable that taxable profit will be available against which the deductible temporary difference can be utilised'.

***Examples of deductible temporary differences***

- Accumulated depreciation of an asset in the financial statements is greater than the cumulative depreciation allowed up to the balance sheet date for tax purposes.
- The net realisable value of an item of inventory, or the recoverable amount of an item of property, plant or equipment, is less than the previous carrying amount and an entity therefore reduces the carrying amount of the asset, but that reduction is ignored for tax purposes until the asset is sold.
- Research costs (or organisation or other start up costs) are recognised as an expense in determining accounting profit but are not permitted as a deduction in determining taxable profit until a later period.
- Income is deferred in the balance sheet but has already been included in taxable profit in current or prior periods.

### 12.8 Tax losses

An important potential cause of a deferred tax asset is the existence of unrelieved trading losses being carried forward for relief against future profits. IAS 12 allows the recognition of a deferred tax asset only to the extent that it is probable that there will be sufficient future taxable profit to enable the loss relief to be used.

To ensure that there is a reasonable basis for the recognition of a deferred tax asset for unused loss relief, IAS 12 requires the disclosure of the evidence supporting its recognition.

The following points should be considered in deciding whether sufficient future taxable profit will be available:

- whether it is probable that there will be sufficient taxable profits before the unused tax losses expire
- whether the unused tax losses result from identifiable causes which are unlikely to recur
- whether tax planning opportunities exist to enable the entity to create taxable profit within the period of availability of the unused loss relief
- whether the entity has sufficient taxable temporary differences which will result in taxable amounts against which the unused tax losses can be utilised before they expire.

### 12.9 Deferred tax relating to revaluations

Most deferred tax items relate to income statement items, and the deferred tax balance is increased or reduced by transfers as part of the period's tax charge in the income statement.

Another cause of deferred tax, revaluation, requires an entry direct to equity. On revaluation, the appropriate percentage of the revaluation surplus should be credited to deferred tax, so that only the net amount remains to the credit of revaluation surplus.

## 13 IFRS 5 *Non-Current Assets Held for Sale and Discontinued Operations*

### 13.1 Background

IFRS 5 specifies the accounting treatment for assets held for sale and the presentation of discontinued operations. It replaces IAS 35 *Discontinuing Operations.*

The additional disclosures are intended to provide users of the financial statements with useful information:

(a) Information about assets held for sale provides information about the amount and timing of future cash flows (which could have a material effect on liquidity).

(b) Users are more interested in future profits than past profits. They will be able to make a better assessment of future profits if they are informed about planned closures to a business, so that they can exclude these profits (or losses) from their forecasts.

(c) Information about discontinued operations may encourage users to look more closely at the various elements of an entity's performance, rather than using the earnings per share figure in a simplistic way.

## 13.2 Assets 'held for sale'

***Classification***

A non-current asset or disposal group should be classified as held for sale if its carrying amount will be recovered principally through a sale transaction rather than through continuing use.

A **disposal group** is a group of assets to be disposed of, by sale or otherwise, together as a group in a single transaction, and liabilities associated with those assets that will be transferred in the transaction.

For an asset (or disposal group) to be classified as held for sale:

(a) it must be available for immediate sale in its present condition subject only to terms that are usual and customary for sales of such assets; and

(b) its sale must be highly probable.

For the sale to be highly probable:

(a) management must be committed to a plan to sell the asset

(b) an active programme to locate a buyer and complete the plan must have been initiated

(c) the asset must be actively marketed for sale at a price that is reasonable in relation to its current fair value

(d) the sale should be expected to take place within one year from the date of classification; and

(e) it is unlikely that significant changes to the plan will be made or that the plan will be withdrawn.

If the sale does not take place within one year, an asset (or disposal group) can still be classified as held for sale, provided that the delay has been caused by events or circumstances beyond the entity's control and there is sufficient evidence that the entity remains committed to its plan to sell.

An asset that is to be abandoned cannot be classified as held for sale. This is because its carrying amount will be recovered principally through continuing use. However, the disposal group to be abandoned may meet the definition of a discontinued operation.

***Measurement***

An asset (or disposal group) that is held for sale should be measured at the lower of its carrying amount and fair value less costs to sell (this is effectively net realisable value).

An impairment loss is recognised if fair value less costs to sell is lower than the asset's carrying amount. This is an exception to the normal rule in IAS 36 *Impairment of Assets*. Under IAS 36 assets are normally measured at their recoverable amount, which is the higher of net realisable value and value in use. Assets held for sale do not come within the scope of IAS 36.

An asset held for sale should not be depreciated, even if it is still being used by the entity.

## 13.3 Discontinued operations

***Definition***

A **discontinued operation** is a component of an entity that either has been disposed of, or is classified as held for sale, and

(a) represents a separate major line of business or geographical area of operations

(b) is part of a single co-ordinated plan to dispose of a separate major line of business or geographical area of operations; or

(c) is a subsidiary acquired exclusively with a view to resale.

A **component** of an entity comprises operations and cash flows that can be clearly distinguished, operationally and for financial reporting purposes, from the rest of the entity.

***Presentation***

An entity should disclose:

(a) a single amount on the face of the income statement comprising the total of:

  (i) the post-tax profit or loss of discontinued operations; and

  (ii) the post-tax gain or loss recognised on the measurement to fair value less costs to sell or on the disposal of the assets or disposal group(s) constituting the discontinued operation.

(b) an analysis of the single amount in (a) into:

  (i) the revenue, expenses and pre-tax profit or loss of discontinued operations

  (ii) the related income tax expense

  (iii) the gain or loss recognised on the measurement to fair value less costs to sell or on the disposal of the assets or the discontinued operation, and

  (iv) the related income tax expense.

The analysis in (b) may be presented in the notes or on the face of the income statement. If it is presented on the face of the income statement it must be presented in a section identified as relating to discontinued operations, i.e. separately from continuing operations.

In addition, an entity should disclose the net cash flows attributable to the operating, investing and financing activities of discontinued operations. These disclosures may be presented either in the notes or on the face of the financial statements.

These analyses are not required for disposal groups that are newly acquired subsidiaries that meet the criteria to be classified as held for sale on acquisition.

***Gains or losses relating to continuing operations***

Any gain or loss on the remeasurement of a non-current asset (or disposal group) classified as held for sale that does not meet the definition of a discontinued operation should be included in profit or loss from continuing operations.

## 13.4 Presentation of a non-current asset or disposal group classified as held for sale

IFRS 5 states that:

(a) A non-current asset classified as held for sale and the assets of a disposal group classified as held for sale should be presented separately from other assets in the balance sheet.

(b) The liabilities of a disposal group classified as held for sale should be presented separately from other liabilities in the balance sheet.

(c) Assets and liabilities held for sale should not be offset and presented as a single amount.

(d) The major classes of assets and liabilities classified as held for sale must be separately disclosed either on the face of the balance sheet or in the notes.

## 13.5 Additional disclosures

The following disclosures are required in the notes in the period in which a non-current asset (or disposal group) has been either classified as held for sale or sold:

(a) a description of the non-current asset (or disposal group)

(b) a description of the facts and circumstances of the sale or the disposal and the expected manner and timing of that disposal

(c) details of any impairment losses recognised when the item was classified as held for sale and, if not separately presented on the face of the income statement, the caption in the income statement that includes that gain or loss

(d) if applicable, the segment in which the non-current asset (or disposal group) is presented in accordance with IAS 14 *Segment Reporting*.

Where an asset or disposal group is classified as held for sale after the balance sheet date but before the issue of the financial statements, details should be disclosed in the notes. (However, note that this is a non-adjusting event; the asset should not be accounted for as held for sale unless it meets the criteria during the current accounting period.)

## 13.6 Example

IFRS 5 contains the following example of an income statement showing the required disclosures.

**XYZ Group – Income statement for the year ended 31 December 20X2**

| | 20X2 | 20X1 |
|---|---|---|
| **Continuing operations** | $m | $m |
| Revenue | X | X |
| Cost of sales | (X) | (X) |
| Gross profit | X | X |
| Other income | X | X |
| Distribution costs | (X) | (X) |
| Administrative expenses | (X) | (X) |
| Other expenses | (X) | (X) |
| Finance costs | (X) | (X) |
| Share of profit of associates | X | X |

| | | |
|---|---|---|
| Profit before tax | X | X |
| Income tax expense | (X) | (X) |
| Profit for the period from continuing operations | X | X |
| **Discontinued operations** | | |
| Profit for the period from discontinued operations | X | X |
| Profit for the period | X | X |
| Attributable to: | | |
| Equity holders of the parent | X | X |
| Minority interest | X | X |
| | X | X |

This example shows the minimum possible disclosure on the face of the income statement. Profit for the period from discontinued operations would be analysed in the notes. Alternatively the analysis could be shown on the face of the income statement.

# 14 Related party disclosures

## 14.1 The distortion that related party transactions can cause to financial statements

A related party relationship can affect the financial position and operating results of an entity in a number of ways.

- Transactions may be entered into with a related party which may not have occurred if the relationship did not exist, e.g. a company may sell a large proportion of its production to its parent company, where it might not have found an alternative customer if the parent company had not purchased the goods.
- Transactions may be entered into with a related party on terms different from those with an unrelated party, e.g. the terms under which a subsidiary leases equipment to another subsidiary of a common parent may be imposed by the common parent and might vary significantly from one lease to another because of circumstances entirely unrelated to market prices for similar leases; indeed, the terms may be such that no financial consideration passes between the parties.
- Transactions with third parties may be affected by the existence of the relationship, e.g. two entities in the same line of business may be controlled by a common party that has the ability to increase the volume of business done by each.

## 14.2 Requirements of IAS 24 *Related Party Disclosures*

IAS 24 requires the disclosure of information about certain related party relationships and transactions.

***Definition***

A party is **related** to an entity if:

(a) directly, or indirectly through one or more intermediaries, the party:

(i) it controls, is controlled by, or is under common control with, the entity (this includes parents, subsidiaries and fellow subsidiaries)

(ii) it has an interest in the entity that gives it significant influence over the entity; or

(iii) it has joint control over the entity

(b) the party is an associate of the entity

(c) the party is a joint venture in which the entity is a venturer

(d) the party is a member of the key management personnel of the entity or its parent

(e) the party is a close member of the family of any individual referred to in (a) or (d)

(f) the party is an entity that is controlled, jointly controlled or significantly influenced by, or for which significant voting power in such entity resides with, directly or indirectly, any individual referred to in (d) or (e); or

(g) the party is a post-employment benefit plan for the benefit of employees of the entity, or of any entity that is a related party of the entity.

**Key management personnel** are those persons having authority and responsibility for planning, directing and controlling the activities of the entity, directly or indirectly, including any director (whether executive or otherwise) of that entity.

**Close members of the family** of an individual are those family members who may be expected to influence, or be influenced by, that individual in their dealings with the entity. They may include:

(a) the individual's domestic partner and children

(b) children of the individual's domestic partner

(c) dependants of the individual or the individual's domestic partner.

***Interpreting the definition***

This is a long and complex definition.

IAS 24 states that attention should be paid to the substance of the relationship and not merely the legal form. It also states that the following are not necessarily related parties:

(a) two entities simply because they have a director or other member of key management personnel in common

(b) two venturers simply because they share joint control over a joint venture

(c) providers of finance, trade unions, public utilities, and government departments and agencies, simply by virtue of their normal dealings with an entity (even though they may affect the freedom of action of an entity or participate in its decision-making process)

(d) a customer, supplier, franchisor, distributor or general agent with whom an entity transacts a significant volume of business, merely by virtue of the resulting economic dependence.

The main thing to remember is that, in a related party relationship, one party **controls** or has **significant influence** over the other. Control and significant influence have the same meanings as in IASs 27, 28 and 31.

### 14.3 Identifying related parties

In order to identify related parties it is necessary to apply the definition in IAS 24. There are many situations in which it is obvious that a related party relationship exists. For example, a subsidiary is clearly a related party of a parent.

In more complicated situations it may be necessary to consider whether the parties are included in the list above and to consider the basic principle of control and influence. What actually happens within a relationship in practice is often important.

### 14.4 Types of transactions

Transactions between related parties are a normal feature of business. IAS 24 gives some examples:

- purchases or sales of goods (finished or unfinished)
- purchases or sales of property and other assets
- rendering or receiving of services, e.g. accounting, management, engineering or legal services
- agency arrangements
- leasing arrangements, e.g. allowing the use of an asset, whether for a rental or not
- transfer of research and development
- licence agreements
- finance (including loans and equity contributions in cash or in kind)
- guarantees or collaterals
- management contracts.

### 14.5 Disclosures required

***Disclosure of control***

Where the reporting entity is controlled by another party, there should be disclosure of the related party relationship and, if different, that of the ultimate controlling party. If neither the entity's parent nor the ultimate controlling party produces financial statements available for public use, the name of the next most senior parent that does so is disclosed.

These disclosures must be made whether or not any transactions have taken place between the controlling parties and the reporting entity. They are intended to enable users of financial statements to form a view about the effects of related party relationships on an entity.

***Disclosure of transactions and balances***

If there have been transactions between related parties, the reporting entity should disclose the nature of the related party relationships, as well as the information about the transactions and the details necessary for an understanding of the financial statements. Disclosure should be made irrespective of whether a price is charged. The disclosure should include:

(a) the amount of the transactions

(b) the amount of outstanding balances, and:

(i) their terms and conditions, including whether they are secured, and the nature of the consideration to be provided in settlement; and

(ii) details of any guarantees

(c) provisions for doubtful debts

(d) the expense recognised during the period in respect of bad or doubtful debts due from related parties.

These disclosures should be made separately for each of the following categories: the parent; entities with joint control or significant influence; subsidiaries; associates; joint ventures in which the entity is a venturer; key management personnel of the entity or its parent; and other related parties.

Items of a similar nature may be disclosed in aggregate except when separate disclosure is necessary for an understanding of the effects of related party transactions.

***Compensation***

The reporting entity should disclose compensation paid to key management personnel in total and for each of the following categories:

(a) short-term employee benefits

(b) post-employment benefits

(c) other long-term benefits

(d) termination benefits

(e) equity compensation benefits.

### 14.6 Exemptions

Intra-group items that have been eliminated on consolidation do not have to be disclosed. This covers eliminations:

- in the consolidated financial statements
- in the parent's own financial statements, where these are presented with the consolidated financial statements.

Note that the existence of the relationship would still have to be disclosed.

In addition, related party transactions in the separate financial statements of a parent, venturer or investor must still be disclosed.

## 15 IAS 10 *Events After the Balance Sheet Date*

### 15.1 Introduction

**Events after the balance sheet date** are those events, both favourable and unfavourable, that occur between the balance sheet date and the date on which the financial statements are authorised for issue.

### 15.2 Definitions

The date on which the financial statements are authorised for issue is the date the board of directors formally approves a set of documents as the financial statements. In respect of unincorporated entities, the date of approval is the corresponding date. In respect of consolidated accounts, the date of approval is the date when the consolidated accounts are formally approved by the board of directors of the parent company.

Suppose the year end of a company is 31 December 20X7 and the directors approve the financial statements at a board meeting held on 22 March 20X8. Certain events occurring during the intervening period provide information which will help in preparing the financial statements.

There are two types of events after the balance sheet date:

(a) those that provide further evidence of conditions that existed at the balance sheet date (**adjusting events after the balance sheet date**)

(b) those that are indicative of conditions that arose subsequent to the balance sheet date (**non-adjusting events after the balance sheet date**).

If an event after the balance sheet date indicates that the going concern assumption is inappropriate for the entity then the balance sheet should be adjusted onto a break-up basis.

An entity must disclose the date when the financial statements were authorised for issue and who gave that authorisation.

## 15.3 Dividends

Dividends proposed after the balance sheet date may not be included in the balance sheet as liabilities. They are non-adjusting events after the balance sheet date and must be disclosed by note.

## 15.4 Examples of events requiring adjustment

These events provide additional evidence of conditions existing at the balance sheet date. For example, bad debts arising one or two months after the balance sheet date may help to quantify the bad debt allowance as at the balance sheet date. Such events may, therefore, affect the amount at which items are stated in the balance sheet.

Examples include:

- allowances for inventories and bad debts
- amounts received or receivable in respect of insurance claims which were being negotiated at the balance sheet date
- the discovery of fraud or errors.

The entity adjusts the amounts recognised in the financial statements to reflect these events.

## 15.5 Examples of events requiring disclosure by note

These are events arising after the balance sheet date but which, unlike those events above, do not concern conditions existing at the balance sheet date. Such events will not, therefore, have any effect on items in the balance sheet or income statement. However, where non-adjusting events after the balance sheet date are of such importance that non-disclosure would affect the ability of the users of the financial statements to make proper evaluations and decisions, an entity should disclose the following information for each non-adjusting event after the balance sheet date:

- the nature of the event
- an estimate of its financial effect, or a statement that such an estimate cannot be made.

The following are examples of non-adjusting events after the balance sheet date that may be of such importance that non-disclosure would affect the ability of the users of the financial statements to make proper evaluations and decisions:

- a major business combination after the balance sheet date
- the destruction of a major production plant by a fire after the balance sheet date
- abnormally large changes after the balance sheet date in asset prices or foreign exchange rates.

# Index

KAPLAN PUBLISHING FOULKS LYNCH

# STUDY TEXT REVIEW FORM
## Paper P8

Thank you for choosing a Kaplan Publishing Foulks Lynch CIMA Study Text. As we are constantly striving to improve our products, we would be grateful if you could provide us with feedback about how useful you found this Study Text.

Name: ....................................................................................................................................

Address: ................................................................................................................................

..............................................................................................................................................

Email: .....................................................................................................................................

**Why did you decide to purchase this Study Text?**

Have used them in the past ☐
Recommended by lecturer ☐
Recommended by friend ☐
Saw advertising ☐
Other (please specify) ☐

**Which other Kaplan Publishing Foulks Lynch products have you used?**

Exam Kit ☐
Distance Learning Course ☐
Pocket Notes ☐

**How do you study?**

At a college ☐
On a distance learning course ☐
Home study ☐
Other ☐

Please specify..........................................................................................................................

**Overall opinion of this Study Text**

| | *Excellent* | *Adequate* | *Poor* |
|---|---|---|---|
| Introductory pages | ☐ | ☐ | ☐ |
| Syllabus coverage | ☐ | ☐ | ☐ |
| Clarity of explanations | ☐ | ☐ | ☐ |
| Clarity of definitions and key points | ☐ | ☐ | ☐ |
| Diagrams | ☐ | ☐ | ☐ |
| Practice/exam-type questions | ☐ | ☐ | ☐ |
| Self-test questions | ☐ | ☐ | ☐ |
| Layout | ☐ | ☐ | ☐ |
| Index | ☐ | ☐ | ☐ |

If you have further comments/suggestions or have spotted any errors, please write them on the next page.

Please return this form to: Mirjana Jeremic, Editor, Freepost RRAT-HLYC-5KXA, FTC Foulks Lynch, Unit 2 The Business Centre, Molly Millars Lane, Wokingham, RG41 2QZ

**Other comments/suggestions and errors**

KAPLAN PUBLISHING

FOULKS LYNCH

# CIMA Publications

# Student Order Form

Please send your completed order form by post to:
Leeds NDL, West Gate, 6 Grace Street, Leeds LS1 2RP
Tel (UK): 0845 678 0022
Tel (International): + 44 (0) 113 200 6360
Fax: +44 (0) 113 243 0133
Order online: www.kaplanfoulkslynch.com
Email: cimaflexiblelearning@ftckaplan.com

| Examination date: Nov 06 ☐ | | Study Text £28.00 each | Exam Kits £15.00 each | Pocket Notes £10.00 each | Practice 4 Success CDs 100Qs £10.00 300Qs £25.00 | | Course in a Box (Text, Kit, P/Notes, Tests, CD, Folder) £150.00 each | Total Value |
|---|---|---|---|---|---|---|---|---|
| | | Quantity | Quantity | Quantity | 100Q | 300Q | Quantity | |
| **Professional level** | | | | | | | | |
| Paper P1 | Management Accounting Performance Evaluation | ☐ | ☐ | ☐ | ☐ | ☐ | ☐ | |
| Paper P2 | Management Accounting Decision Making | ☐ | ☐ | ☐ | ☐ | ☐ | ☐ | |
| Paper P3 | Management Accounting Risk and Control Strategy | ☐ | ☐ | ☐ | - | - | ☐ | |
| Paper P4 | Organisational Management & Information Systems | ☐ | ☐ | ☐ | ☐ | ☐ | ☐ | |
| Paper P5 | Integrated Management | ☐ | ☐ | ☐ | ☐ | ☐ | ☐ | |
| Paper P6 | Management Accounting Business Strategy | ☐ | ☐ | ☐ | - | - | ☐ | |
| Paper P7 | Financial Accounting and Tax Principles | ☐ | ☐ | ☐ | ☐ | ☐ | ☐ | |
| Paper P8 | Financial Analysis | ☐ | ☐ | ☐ | ☐ | ☐ | ☐ | |
| Paper P9 | Management Accounting Financial Strategy | ☐ | ☐ | ☐ | - | - | ☐ | |
| | | | | | | | | |
| **TOPCIMA** | | | | | | | | |
| Test of Professional Competence in Management Accounting Study Text | | £28.00 ☐ | | The Knowledge | | | £28.00 ☐ | |

| | |
|---|---|
| **SUB TOTAL** | £ |
| **PLUS DELIVERY CHARGE (see chart below)** | £ |
| **TOTAL** | £ |

**Cardholder Details**

Name on card: ...............................................................................

Address:

...............................................................................

...............................................................................

...............................................................................

Telephone:

...............................................................................

**Delivery address (if different from above – a signature will be required)**

Name:

...............................................................................

Address:

...............................................................................

...............................................................................

...............................................................................

Telephone: ...............................................................................

**Payment**

1 I enclose Cheque/Postal Order/Bankers Draft for £ ....................................

Please make cheques payable to '**Kaplan Publishing Foulks Lynch**'.

2 Charge MasterCard/Visa/Switch/Delta no:

Valid from:

Expiry date:

Issue no:
(Switch only)

Security Code:

Signature: ........................................ Date: ..........................

| POSTAGE | Text Books | Pocket Notes | Course in a Box |
|---|---|---|---|
| UK | £5 for one book + £2 for each extra | £2 for one book + £1 for each extra | £6 for one package + £4 for each extra |
| Europe | £7 for one book + £4 for each extra | £3 for one book + £2 for each extra | £12 for one package + £8 for each extra |
| Rest of World | £22 for one book + £8 for each extra | £8 for one book + £5 for each extra | £30 for one package + £20 for each extra |

Please note that all prices on this form are subject to change.

**KAPLAN PUBLISHING**
FOULKS LYNCH

# CIMA Publications

## College & Bookshop Order Form

Please send your completed order form by post to:
Kaplan Publishing Foulks Lynch,
Unit 2 The Business Centre,
Molly Millars Lane, Wokingham RG41 2QZ
or by fax to 0118 979 7455

**For all queries relating to this order please call 0118 912 3000 or e-mail info@kaplanfoulkslynch.com**

**ACCOUNT:** ____________

**Examination Date: Nov 06** ☐

| | | Study Text £28.00 each | Exam Kits £15.00 each | Pocket Notes £10.00 each | Practice 4 Success CDs 100Qs £10.00 300Qs £25.00 | | Course in a Box (Text, Kit, P/Notes, Study Notes, Tests, CD, Folder) £150.00 each | Total Value |
|---|---|---|---|---|---|---|---|---|
| **Certificate (Current syllabus only)** | | Quantity | Quantity | Quantity | 100Q | 300Q | Quantity | |
| Paper C1 | Management Accounting Fundamentals | ☐ | ☐ | ☐ | ☐ | ☐ | ☐ | |
| Paper C2 | Financial Accounting Fundamentals | ☐ | ☐ | ☐ | ☐ | ☐ | ☐ | |
| Paper C3 | Business Mathematics | ☐ | ☐ | ☐ | ☐ | ☐ | ☐ | |
| Paper C4 | Economics for Business | ☐ | ☐ | ☐ | ☐ | ☐ | ☐ | |
| Paper C5 | Business Law | ☐ | ☐ | ☐ | ☐ | ☐ | ☐ | |
| **Professional** | | | | | | | | |
| Paper P1 | Management Accounting Performance Evaluation | ☐ | ☐ | ☐ | ☐ | ☐ | ☐ | |
| Paper P2 | Management Accounting Decision Making | ☐ | ☐ | ☐ | ☐ | ☐ | ☐ | |
| Paper P3 | Management Accounting Risk and Control Strategy | ☐ | ☐ | ☐ | - | - | ☐ | |
| Paper P4 | Organisational Management & Information Systems | ☐ | ☐ | ☐ | ☐ | ☐ | ☐ | |
| Paper P5 | Integrated Management | ☐ | ☐ | ☐ | ☐ | ☐ | ☐ | |
| Paper P6 | Management Accounting Business Strategy | ☐ | ☐ | ☐ | - | - | ☐ | |
| Paper P7 | Financial Accounting and Tax Principles | ☐ | ☐ | ☐ | ☐ | ☐ | ☐ | |
| Paper P8 | Financial Analysis | ☐ | ☐ | ☐ | ☐ | ☐ | ☐ | |
| Paper P9 | Management Accounting Financial Strategy | ☐ | ☐ | ☐ | - | - | ☐ | |

**TOPCIMA**

| | | | | |
|---|---|---|---|---|
| Test of Professional Competence in Management Accounting Study Text | £28.00 ☐ | The Knowledge | £28.00 ☐ | |

| | |
|---|---|
| **SUB TOTAL** | £ |
| **LESS ________% DISCOUNT** | £ |
| **TOTAL** | £ |

**Account details**

Contact name: ..........

Address: ..........

..........

..........

Telephone: ..........

**Delivery address (if different to above)**

Name: ..........

Address: ..........

..........

..........

..........

Telephone: ..........

**Payment**

1 Please invoice account ..........

under Purchase Order Reference ..........

2 I enclose Cheque/Postal Order/Bankers Draft for £..........

(Please make cheques payable to '**Kaplan Publishing Foulks Lynch**')

3 Charge MasterCard/Visa/Switch/Delta no:

Valid from:   Expiry date:

Issue no: (Switch only)   Security Code:

Signature: .......... Date: ..........

Please note that all prices on this order form are subject to change